The Aristocracy
in England
1660–1914

For Christine

The Aristocracy in England
1660–1914

J. V. BECKETT

Basil Blackwell

© J. V. Beckett 1986

First published 1986

First published in paperback 1988

Basil Blackwell Ltd
108 Cowley Road, Oxford OX4 1JF, UK

Basil Blackwell Inc.
432 Park Avenue South, Suite 1503,
New York, NY 10016, USA

British Library Cataloguing in Publication Data

Beckett, J.V.
The aristocracy in England 1660–1914.
1. England—Nobility—History
I. Title
305.5'2'0942   HT653.G7
ISBN 0-6311-13391-7
ISBN 0-631-16072-8 Pbk

Library of Congress Cataloging in Publication Data

Beckett, J.V.
The aristocracy in England, 1660–1914.
Includes index.
1. Aristocracy.   2. England—Nobility—History.
3. England—Gentry—History.   I. Title.
HT653.G7B43   1986   305.5'223'0942   86-11779
ISBN 0-631-13391-7
ISBN 0-631-16072-8 Pbk

Typeset by Alan Sutton Publishing Limited, Gloucester
Printed in Great Britain by Billing & Sons Ltd

Contents

Preface

English aristocrats have fascinated historians for many generations; but only with the growth of economic and social history, and with the increasing accessibility of family estate papers as County Record Offices have opened since 1945, has an opportunity been provided for detailed studies of individual families and groups of families. For the post-Restoration period historians have been greatly indebted to two books which appeared in 1963, G. E. Mingay's *English Landed Society in the Eighteenth Century*, and F. M. L. Thompson's *English Landed Society in the Nineteenth Century*. Both books were based on primary source materials, and the few secondary studies available at the time, but both were described by their authors as preliminary accounts. Since they appeared an array of books, articles and theses have examined individual families and areas, as a result of which new conclusions and ideas have been developed about the English aristocracy. However, no comparable surveys have appeared, with the exception of D. W. Howell's *Land and People in Nineteenth-Century Wales* (1977). Consequently the time seemed right to try to bring together the various strands of thinking about the aristocracy which have emerged over the past twenty years, and at the same time to offer some sort of answer to the question which has increasingly fascinated historians as more and more evidence has become available – how did the aristocracy maintain their position in English society and politics despite industrialization and urbanization?

No study of this kind would have been possible but for the research output of the past twenty years. I am very grateful to the authors whose work I have been able to call upon as a result of this effort, and I hope that I have neither misinterpreted nor misused their findings. I should like to thank the archivists of the various repositories in which I have worked over the past few years, and the Huntington Library, California, for granting me a visiting fellowship in the summer of

1983, during which time I was able to carry out research for this book. The Twenty-Seven Foundation and the University of Nottingham made generous contributions towards the cost of travel. I should also like to take this opportunity of expressing my thanks to a number of people who have helped me in various ways. Alan Cameron, Eveline Cruikshanks, David Hayton, Geoffrey Holmes, Helen Meller, Angela Muncaster, Martin Pugh, Michael Watts and David Young were kind enough to supply me with information, or to read various chapters in draft. Rita Holt provided invaluable assistance in preparing the figures for the appendix; Clyve Jones supplied me with various references, provided occasional hospitality in London, and read two chapters; and my former colleague William Doyle willingly read the whole manuscript at short notice despite other pressing commitments. Finally, my wife Christine has been a constant source of encouragement even though her historical interests lie in the more distant past. The faults that remain – and I am aware that they are many – are my own.

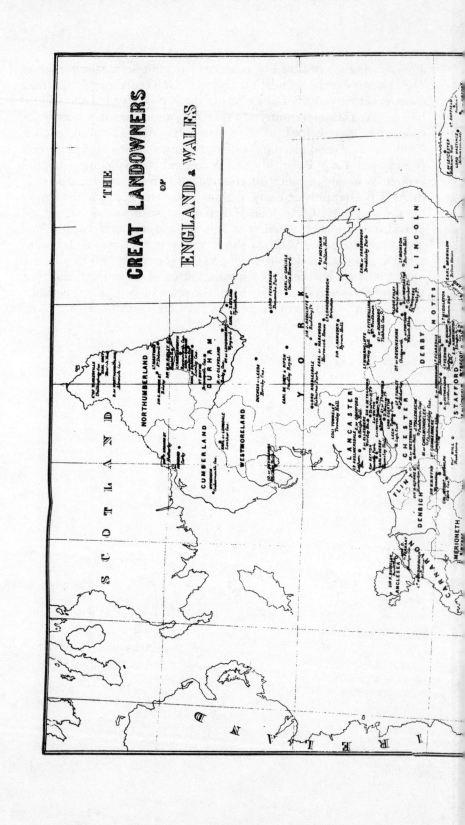

THE
CREAT LANDOWNERS
OF
ENGLAND & WALES

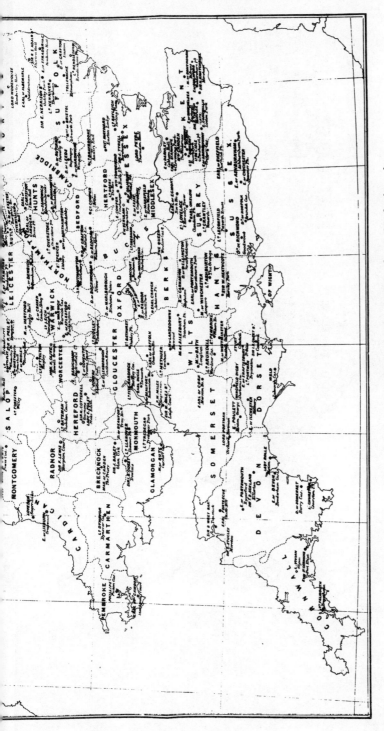

Map 1   The Great Landowners of England & Wales (from Sanford and Townshend, *Great Governing Families*, Edinburgh, 1865)

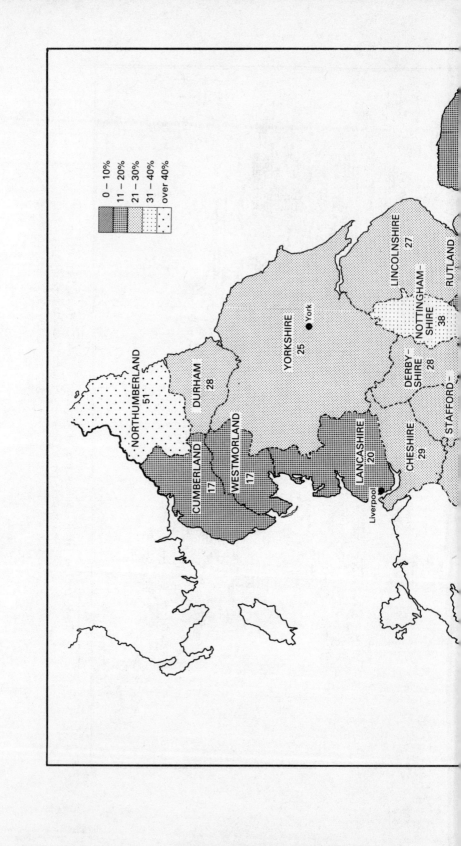

0 – 10%
11 – 20%
21 – 30%
31 – 40%
over 40%

NORTHUMBERLAND
51

DURHAM
28

CUMBERLAND
17

WESTMORLAND
17

YORKSHIRE
25

● York

LANCASHIRE
20

Liverpool ●

CHESHIRE
29

DERBY-
SHIRE
28

NOTTINGHAM-
SHIRE
38

LINCOLNSHIRE
27

RUTLAND

STAFFORD-

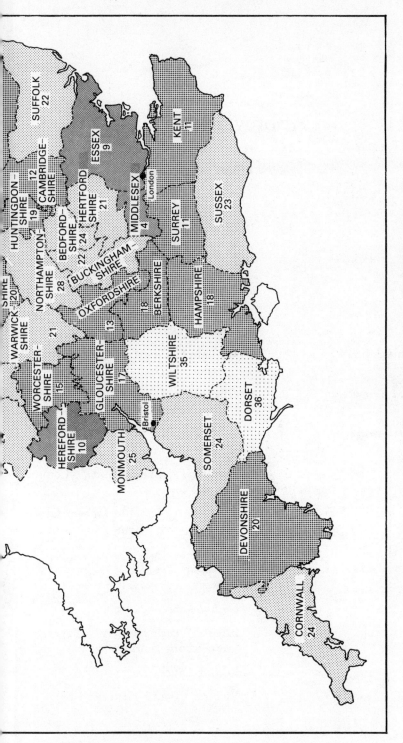

Map 2   Proportion of each county held in estates of 10,000 acres or more (c. 1870)

Abbreviations

Beckett, thesis — J. V. Beckett, 'Landownership in Cumbria, 1680–1750' (University of Lancaster, Ph.D. thesis, 1975)

CJ — *Commons Journal*

Clements Library — William L. Clements Library, Ann Arbor, Michigan, USA

Complete Baronetage — GEC[okayne], *Complete Baronetage* (5 volumes, 1900–6)

Complete Peerage — GEC[okayne], *The Complete Peerage* (13 volumes, 1910–59)

HMC — Historical Manuscripts Commission

Huntington Library — The Henry E. Huntington Library, San Marino, California, USA

JRASE — *Journal of the Royal Agricultural Society of England*

LJ — *Lords Journal*

Parl. Papers — British Parliamentary Papers, nineteenth century

RO — Record Office

VCH — Victoria County History

Introduction

In the years since 1914, English government and society have undergone a profound change. At the outbreak of the First World War the social and political conventions remained those of an aristocracy; as late as 1879, when England was already fully industrialized, T. H. S. Escott commented on how 'the influence and power of the great families of England are ubiquitous. There is no escaping from them; they are shown alike in city and country, in town and suburb.'[1] The emergent middle class and even, to a lesser extent, the working class had tolerated the status quo, but since 1914 the situation has changed. The aristocracy has declined, unable to maintain its traditional landed estates. Country houses have been pulled down or sold off, and the political control which was already beginning to slide by 1914 has now virtually disappeared. All is not lost. The House of Lords remains capable of playing an obstructive role in politics, while interest in the activities of the aristocracy is still apparent in television series,[2] in country-house visiting[3] and in the gossip columns of the tabloid press.[4] Even an element of deference remains, since aristocrats are favoured as patrons, presidents and chairmen of charities and similar

---

[1] T. H. S. Escott, *England: its people, polity and pursuits* (1879), vol. I, p. 53.

[2] These have included Robert Lacey's series *Aristocrats*, and *Brideshead Revisited*, in recent years.

[3] Adrian Tinniswood, 'Such Lofty Magnificence! Popular perceptions of the country house', *Bulletin of Local History: East Midlands Region*, 19 (1984), pp. 15–22.

[4] One popular newspaper recently reviewed Adeline Hartcup's *Love and Marriage in the Great Country Houses* (1985) under the headline 'Sexy secrets of the stately home set': *Daily Mail*, 19 January 1985. In fairness, fascination with the tittle tattle of the aristocracy is by no means new. Sir Bernard Burke broke from his genealogical research to produce *Anecdotes of the Aristocracy* 2 vols. (1849) in order to investigate legend and romance attached to aristocratic houses.

institutions. When Viscount Norwich, one of the completely landless twentieth-century peers, tried to suggest friends with greater interest and knowledge of the charities he was asked to head, his suggestions were ignored because the people he proposed were untitled.[5] Hardly surprisingly, the rapid decline of aristocratic influence is relatively easy to document, but a much greater problem is posed by the question of how it was maintained for so long in the changing economic and social conditions of post-Restoration England. J. H. Hexter asked over twenty years ago, 'how did they do it?', and more recently Norman Gash has commented:

what was remarkable was not that British society, growing more urbanized and industrialized with each decade, was slowly slipping beyond their control, but that by a process of astute adaptation they had maintained that control so long and with so little resentment on the part of the rest of the community.[6]

Some explanation is clearly needed, if only to fulfil the historian's purpose of examining the past to 'remind us how different the present has turned out to be from what past generations expected'.[7]

The aristocracy which led England down to 1914 was a small, but immensely powerful and confident group. Theoretically it was an open elite, subject to penetration by all and sundry, but in practice this was a well-rehearsed myth. Although a certain vagueness existed in regard to its lower limits – which helped to sustain the myth – peerages and baronetcies, the ranks that really mattered since they were inheritable, were closely confined. Entrance was available only to those who accepted the vital principles of aristocratic life. Of these, the first and most critical was property ownership. Property, in particular land, was the key to status and position in English society, underlying the subleties of the graded hierarchy. As late as 1894 the editors of Burke's *Landed Gentry* could claim that landownership was the principal 'test of rank and

---

[5] Roy Perrott, *The Aristocrats* (1968), p. 37.

[6] J. H. Hexter, *Reappraisals in History* (1961), p. 19; Norman Gash, *Aristocracy and People: Britain 1815–1865* (1979), p. 350.

[7] Alan Bullock, 'Breaking the tyranny of the present', *Times Higher Education Supplement*, 24 May 1985.

position'.[8] Sometimes its role was overt: property qualifications existed for a whole series of positions, from the right to vote, through places in local and central government, and even the shooting of game. At other times it was covert, such as the careful gradations within the peerage, or the right to wear the red coat on the hunting field. Always it was there, and virtually no one rose through the ranks without the requisite property holding. However, to maintain the sanctity of the group it was crucial that the property remained firmly in the family. To avoid the loss of prestige suffered by Continental nobilities with large numbers of poverty-stricken brethren, the English answer was a set of land laws which made disposing of the property extremely difficult. Over the period from 1660, when the new rules were adopted, this had the effect of monopolizing land into fewer hands, thereby increasing the exclusiveness of the aristocracy, and making penetration through size of estate wellnigh impossible. While it became acceptable for potential entrants to buy a smaller estate, very few families penetrated the higher reaches of the peerage before 1914 unless they owned a substantial acreage.

Unfortunately for aspirants, land alone was not enough. Considerable stress was laid upon pedigree, the need for a family to spend time soaking up the manners and methods of the lifestyle. Since this usually disbarred first-generation wealth, the second generation had to be prepared for entrance by means of an acceptable education and marriage into the elite. If these ground-rules were followed, acceptance could be anticipated, initially at the local level, but in time by promotion through the ranks depending upon a variety of considerations including landownership, state service and general acceptability. Since it was possible for individuals to drop out at any stage, the sifting procedure meant that few reached the top, and that those who progressed in the hierarchy did so along a well-grooved track to ensure their suitability.

The dominance of these values reflected the aristocracy's confidence in its role as an elite, and also the readiness of other groups to accept the rules. The middle class, in the form in which it emerged in the early nineteenth century, showed relatively little desire to displace the entrenched aristocracy; indeed, after achieving political representation in 1832 the group turned out to be a remarkably conservative force. Richard Cobden, the veteran radical,

[8] The point is noted by D. C. Moore, 'The gentry', in *The Victorian Countryside*, ed. G. E. Mingay (1981), p. 385.

wrote despairingly in 1857 that 'the higher classes never stood so high in relative social and political ranks, as compared with the other classes, as at present. The middle class has been content with the very crumbs from their table.'[9] He was still complaining a few years later: 'manufacturers and merchants as a rule seem only to desire riches that they may be enabled to prostrate themselves at the feet of feudalism.'[10] Foreign observers were constantly impressed by this phenomenon. Walter Bagehot pointed to the acceptance of hierarchy in England, and attributed the survival of Cabinet government to 'the readiness of the business community to tolerate, at least in peace time, a high degree of incompetence in the highest places'. Aristocratic government, he argued, actually preserved the state from the rule of wealth:

There is no country where 'a poor devil of a millionaire is so ill off as in England'. The experiment is tried every day, and every day it is proved that money alone − money *pur et simple* − will not buy 'London Society'. Money is kept down, and so to say, cowed by the predominant authority of a different power.[11]

Hippolyte Taine claimed to have been told during the 1860s by a leading industrialist that the middle class was not aiming to overthrow the aristocracy; rather, it was ready to leave government and high office in their hands because they had been born and bred to the work for generations.[12] Two decades later the American commentator Adam Badeau observed that 'hereditary, permanent rank, is what most Englishmen prize above all earthly honours. It is permanency, especially that they value.'[13] Badeau's fellow countryman Grant Allen put it in similar vein at the turn of the century: the ambition of the middle class was 'to hang on the skirts of the aristocracy if it can, to ape them in everything, and if possible to rise at least as far to their level as the attainment of a knighthood.'[14]

The acceptance of the aristocratic ethos by the middle classes partly reflected the lack of prestige attached to making money in

[9] Quoted by Norman McCord, 'Cobden and Bright in politics 1846–1857', in *Ideas and Institutions in Victorian Britain*, ed. R. Robson (1967), p. 113.

[10] Quoted by O. F. Christie, *The Transition from Aristocracy 1832–67* (1927), p. 112.

[11] Walter Bagehot, *The English Constitution* (1963 edn), p. 122.

[12] Hippolyte Taine, *Notes on England* (1872), p. 155.

[13] Adam Badeau, *Aristocracy in England* (1886), p. 39.

[14] Quoted by W. L. Arnstein, 'The myth of the triumphant Victorian middle class', *The Historian*, 37 (1975), p. 219.

nineteenth-century England. Far from adjusting to middle-class morality, as Marx and others have argued, the aristocracy seems successfully to have persuaded the middle class to accept its cultural values. With a gradual loss of confidence in the entrepreneur and in technological progress after the mid-Victorian highpoint of the 1851 Great Exhibition, the public schools – where the middle classes sent their sons to establish social connections with the existing elite – helped to mould an elite which disliked city life, and which regarded the industrial spirit as in some sense not English. The consequences for the middle class were considerable. They developed no platform from which to challenge the aristocracy; indeed, as Escott noted in the 1890s, they had assimilated 'the tastes and prejudices of their new connections'.[15] Perhaps as a result, one of the most poignant images of late Victorian England was the desire for state honours, in the form of knighthoods and other orders, which suggested a concern with establishment recognition rather than with bourgeois values.

The aristocracy governed and dictated the social norms because they regarded it as their birthright, but the acceptance of this situation has to be sought in terms of their contribution to the economic, social and political leadership of the state. Land was the basis of their credibility, and estates were regarded as possessions held in trust from generation to generation. Selling land devalued the family's standing, while buying more, whatever its economic return, could be seen as increasing status. The symbol of aristocratic confidence was the country house. Building or renovating a house said a good deal about a family's future expectations, while the eighteenth-century fashion for parks reflected a further expression of confidence in the future. Moreover, because landowners had a stake in the country it was widely accepted that they had the best qualification to govern, and part of the aristocratic ethos lay in service. There was an assumption of aristocratic superiority or, in A. P. Thornton's phrase, a 'habit of authority'.[16] It grew out of *duty*, a word which was seldom far from the lips of a state servant like the Duke of Wellington during the Napoleonic wars. Wellington in England went to church each week to fulfil his public duty in the country, whereas he rarely attended when in London.[17] An independent income gave the aristocracy freedom to exercise

[15] Ibid.; A. J. Mayer, *The Persistence of the Old Regime* (1981), pp. 79, 87.
[16] A. P. Thornton, *The Habit of Authority* (1966).
[17] Brian Masters, *The Dukes: the origins, ennoblement and history of twenty-six families* 2nd edn (1980), p. 247.

impartial judgement, thus providing their credentials for government. Although on occasion their willingness to rule was not all
it might have been, and a tension always existed between the
preference for London life and the need to spend time on their
estates, the majority of aristocrats accepted that their inheritance
included an ethos of service in the community.

Since estates were a trust from generation to generation, the ethos
demanded that they be preserved, and preferably improved. Not all
heirs could be relied upon to accept this responsibility, although the
land laws usually prevented them from wreaking irredeemable
havoc. For the majority, however, duty to the family – and, by
extension, to the state – meant looking to develop the economic
potential of the estate, whether by improving the farming, or
exploiting the natural resources (timber and minerals), or by
improving the value by urban development. Most chose to be
rentiers, in whichever of these roles they were playing, largely
because the wealthier members of the elite expected to spend a
considerable proportion of their time away from their estates. But
being a *rentier* was not the same as opting out; indeed, the role that
they played resembled that of director, and most played it with
considerable acumen, despite the absence of any formal training.
First, they had to appoint and oversee the management team.
Without good stewards and agents they could never expect their
concerns to flourish, but their long absences increased the premium
on finding honest and able men to fill these positions. Loyalty did
not come cheaply, and many landowners went to considerable
lengths to cultivate it. Second, they had to accept that dissatisfied
tenants would appeal over the head of the management team in the
expectation of a more favourable opinion from the owner. This gave
them a crucial role in assessing grievances, and smoothing over
relationships on the estate. Finally, they had to take policy
decisions, such as rent levels in vital parliamentary constituencies.

When it came to developing as opposed to merely conserving the
estate, the role became even more crucial. Decisions with regard to
farming practice required the owner's approval, since they could
often involve him in venturing risk capital for enclosure, drainage
and farm-building schemes. Over time the level of financial
commitment increased, to reach an all-time record in the agri-
culturally depressed years of the late nineteenth century. Similar
decisions were needed in regard to mineral exploitation. Letting to
tenants presupposed the existence of resources, and the discovery
and proving of these required landlord investment. Technological
breakthroughs in the coal industry largely depended on landlord

initiative, especially in regard to the expensive and inefficient Newcomen engine. Consequently landowners played a vital role in the early stages of developing their resources, only letting them when the scale of enterprise suggested a capital investment requirement beyond their immediate capacity. Even then the responsibility did not end. Landlords had to take decisions about the terms of leases, sometimes they had to make capital available, and on occasion, when a tenant could not be found, direct management had to be resumed. Those with urban land usually undertook a similar role. Selling to developers reduced the family holding, but long leases represented a more socially conscious attitude, since these enabled them to try to ensure the orderly development of the site. They took responsibility for laying out the roads and providing drainage and other facilities, before leaving developers to provide the housing. As with minerals, the landowner was responsible for initiating the enterprise before leaving risk-sharing partnerships to take it further. In addition, improving the estate often involved them in promoting better ancillary services. A moral imperative (their role as justices) lay behind support for road improvements, but this did not operate with private promotions for private ends, such as canals and, later, railways. Consequently most aristocrats were primarily concerned with schemes which had a bearing on their own interests, usually branch lines feeding into the main system. Since good communications raised land values, it was in their interest to promote or subscribe to improvements, while many spread their portfolios when the financial returns became apparent during the nineteenth century. On occasion, individuals had to take the major responsibility for a project, particularly when harbour development for coal transportation was involved.

In general, the aristocracy played a positive role in developing the economic potential of their estates, but they have seldom received a good press for their overall contribution. Usually they are accused of not going far enough: their home farms were dilettante interests rather than proper experimental farms; they were too willing to lease their minerals, and insufficiently concerned with promoting other business concerns; they obstructed communications improvements by impossible demands for route changes and compensation; and they consumed vast amounts of capital (much of it borrowed) in non-productive concerns such as housebuilding and racehorses. Some of these accusations undoubtedly contained a grain or more of truth. Few aristocratic home farms provided examples which could be followed, so that the spread of new ideas was largely left to lesser landowners and tenant farmers. Canal and railway routes did have to be carefully planned to avoid opposition from landowners. On the other hand the principle of public utility was always in the minds of aristocrats, and when this could be shown their support was almost guaranteed. To this end they promoted agricultural shows, and acted as patrons to farming and engineering societies; once public benefit could be shown for a canal or railway, they asked only for reasonable compensation (although some lesser landowners and freeholders may have held out for extortionate sums); and, far from acting as moguls and pharaohs in urban development, they used their lease controls to ensure well-maintained streets and houses. Above all, the key to their attitude lay in Parliament. Although they are best known for their public roles, including defending the landed interest via the Corn Laws and similarly reactionary legislation, the majority played a vital role – in both houses – steering through locally significant legislation. Enclosure, turnpike, canal and railway improvements all required legislation, which could only be obtained by careful guidance through Parliament: hence the importance of aristocratic approval in advance of proposed communications improvements. Even if aristocrats were not leading industrialists – and this was largely because the limits of their enterprise usually stopped at the boundary of their estates – they played a vital role on behalf of business interests in Parliament, partly because entrepreneurs failed to penetrate Westminster in any numbers before the mid-nineteenth century.

Finally, even the much-vaunted indebtedness of the aristocracy was not necessarily detrimental to the economy. The extent of debt is easily exaggerated; after all, few aristocrats went to the wall, even if the majority had adopted a form of professional pessimism on the subject. Some debt undoubtedly came about in order to invest in profitable enterprise, while it is arguable that even housebuilding was a more productive use of the money involved then the original saver had contemplated. Above all, however, their notion of duty was such that aristocrats were ready to carry on investing beyond the point at which a hardnosed businessman might well have called it a day. This is clear in relation to the capital invested in drainage schemes in the later nineteenth century, at a time when it was apparent that the economic return was negligible; and also for more extensive undertakings. Some of the largest debts were run up by the Duke of Bridgewater when building his famous canal, by the marquesses of Bute and Londonderry in their promotions at Cardiff and Seaham respectively, and by the dukes of Devonshire, who continued to pump vast sums into nineteenth-century Barrow and Eastbourne, despite the scale of their indebtedness. For all the criticisms levelled by historians, aristocratic spending does not seem to have deprived the economy of capital, and contemporaries do not appear to have considered their contribution inadequate; indeed, it is arguable that their expensive lifestyle was *expected*, and that any cutback in spending to facilitate economic development would merely have harmed their prestige.

The responsibility exercised by the aristocracy in economic development was matched by a similar concept of duty and service in regard to the leadership of both the locality and the nation. The aristocratic power base lay in rural England, symbolized by the country house and its attendant park on which they lavished vast sums of money to maintain the family's prestige. Despite a preference for London living, and a variety of reasons that provided good cause for spending many months of the year in an urban environment, most aristocrats recognized that time in the country made sound economic sense and fulfilled their duty to stand at the head of the community. Their houses were not merely homes; they were also centres of consumption and employment, of entertainment and community cohesion. Events in the 'big house' were shared locally in a manner reminiscent of the way twentieth-century royalty shares its weddings and funerals nationally through the medium of television. Dinners and other festivities reflected the sense of duty involved in looking after the welfare of people living on or around the estate. Most local activities were designed to enforce the social hierarchy. Game could only be shot by property owners – a provision which was socially divisive, but which could be mollified by allowing occasional shoots to unqualified freeholders and farmers, and by discriminate enforcement of the game laws. During the summer, cricket matches brought landlord and community together in a mutually convivial atmosphere, while in the winter foxhunting constituted the most obvious example of how aristocratic values pervaded the whole community. Farmers were invited to join the hunt, and, if this was largely to prevent their objecting to having the hounds run amok in their fields, it also reflected landlords' willingness to consider their interests. Other members of the community could, and frequently did, follow the hunt on foot, to be in at the kill. Middle-class acceptance of aristocratic values was nowhere better illustrated than in the way they propped up the older hunts in the difficult economic conditions of the later nineteenth century.

The aristocratic role was essentially a paternalistic one designed to cement the ties of social deference. To this end their duties included both the formal and the informal channels of local control. The formal positions in local government were protected by property qualifications, but fell predominantly on the lesser members of the group who were most likely to be resident for the greater part of the year. It was their role to sit on the bench at Quarter Sessions, or to administer justice at petty sessions, and in their own home. Their wealthier neighbours might participate in these activities during a summer visit, and often leading members of county society made themselves available for grand jury service. Informal control was exercised in a variety of ways, from undertaking Poor Law chores to building churches, schools and cottages, letting allotments, and providing all manner of local facilities. In addition, money might be dispensed at the park gates, or food and clothing could be provided during harsh winters. Community deference could be encouraged by providing prizes for agricultural shows, and cups for horseracing, as well as attendance at hunt balls and race meetings.

Finally, the concept of service was carried into the government of the state. With their large stake in the land, the aristocracy expected to govern, and they often did so at great personal cost, since London life was expensive and neither MPs nor peers were paid. In the wake of the revolution of 1688, the aristocracy came to control every aspect of government, both executive and legislative. They dominated the Cabinet, the highest ranks of the armed forces, the civil service and, to a lesser extent, the judiciary. The House of Lords was the debating chamber of the peerage, and, after stiff resistance from the independent country gentlemen during the 1690s, the Commons also fell under their spell. Seats were purloined in order to return members, and sons and other retainers were inserted into them. This situation remained virtually unchanged until towards the end of the nineteenth century, despite gloomy prognostications at the time of the 1832 Reform Act, and when change did come it was largely on terms laid down by the aristocracy. Three reasons can be suggested as to why this was the case. First, the deferential nature of the electorate, not in the sense that they were dragged complainingly to the polls, but that they willingly accepted aristocratic leadership. As Walter Bagehot expressed it:

Aristocracy is a power in the constituencies. A man who is an honourable, or a baronet, or better yet, perhaps, a real earl, though Irish, is coveted by half the electing bodies; and *caerteris paribus*, a manufacturer's son has no chance with him. The reality of the deferential feeling in the community is tested by the actual election of the class deferred to, where there is a large free choice betwixt it and others.[18]

Joseph Chamberlain was expressing the same sentiment in his

[18] Bagehot, *The English Constitution* pp. 176–7.

celebrated remark, 'every Englishman dearly loves a lord.'[19] It followed that the aristocracy expected to govern, and were accepted as the governors, since, in Edmund Burke's terminology, they represented the collective wisdom of the ages. A sense of security existed in the state when power was in landed hands, so that subordination to a landowning aristocracy provided the only firm and effective basis for national government. Even Disraeli was prepared to defend the power enjoyed by the aristocracy on the grounds of their talents and services.[20]

Secondly, popular deference was maintained by the relative openness of the political system. Only the rottenest boroughs were closed, and they had relatively few electors, so that the great majority of the enfranchised regularly had an opportunity to exercise their preferences. Patrons and MPs recognized the need to nurture constituencies between and during elections. Browbeating was unacceptable, although a little treating was widely practised. Even so, electors were only expected to commit one of their two votes to the landlord's candidate, and efforts to influence the second were more likely to bring opprobrium on the landowner than to achieve the desired end. Thirdly, middle class acceptance of the status quo retarded any breakthrough into political power. The veteran radical MP, J. A. Roebuck, told the young Lord Stanley in 1859 that a businessman might set himself the goal of achieving office, whereas a young man of the aristocracy could 'step right into the business of government'.[21] Richard Cobden, who can be seen as the prime middle-class representative of his age, never held Cabinet office, although he was offered the presidency of the Board of Trade in 1859, while Queen Victoria objected to the offer of a Privy Councillorship to John Bright and was not amused when Disraeli promoted W. H. Smith to the post of First Lord of the Admiralty in 1877. She complained that 'it may not please the Navy in which so many of the highest rank serve . . . if a man of the middle classes is placed above them in that very high post'.[22]

Since the aristocracy never lost confidence, the erosion of its position has to be explained in other terms. Unlike so many of their European counterparts in the years after 1789, English aristocrats did not have to survive in a society ripe for revolution; they never

[19] Quoted in Arnstein, 'The myth of the triumphant Victorian middle class', p. 246.
[20] W. L. Guttsman, *The British Political Elite* (1963), pp. 62–9.
[21] Quoted in ibid., p. 55.
[22] Arnstein, ibid., pp. 209–15.

became isolated from the community in which they lived; privilege did not appear as an outstanding social evil; and they did not allow government to become top heavy with bureaucracy. Economic leadership, through commercial farming and industrialization, gave the aristocracy a popularity in society which negated any underlying dissension that might have been stirred up in less prosperous conditions. Moreover, as the middle class took shape during the nineteenth century it did so in union with the aristocracy, not in opposition to it, thereby perpetuating the consensual acceptance of aristocratic values and leadership.[23]

None of this should be taken to suggest that the aristocracy was without fault, nor that the group was able to remain above criticism. Attacks were spasmodic, but they became increasingly vocal through time. Although the aristocracy strengthened its position in the state after 1688, the form of government it devised was put under severe strain by the radical movement during the years after 1789. Tom Paine led a vigorous anti-aristocratic campaign during the 1790s, and although dissent was crushed at the time it was not killed off. Much of it was channelled into the Parliamentary reform movement, although the subsequent legislation of 1832 was conceived of by Earl Grey and leading Whigs as a means of preserving the best of legitimate aristocratic influence. Even so, the concerted opposition in the Lords to reform brought upon it a brief but vitriolic campaign of abuse in the 1830s, which only evaporated after the 1835 Municipal Corporations Act. Aristocratic government survived, and Lords reform disappeared from the radical agenda to the point where it was not even among the demands of the Chartists.

Survival beyond the 1840s is surprising in view of the aristocracy's failure to carry out its governing functions with tact and diplomacy. During the eighteenth century, landed concern with local government declined. Many JPs failed to act, leaving the bench to clergymen and creating a fusion between church and state which was not in the best interests of either. Harsh enforcement of the game laws, and the new Poor Law of 1834, resulted in discontent focusing on the magistracy, while neglect of the Anglican Church may have encouraged dissent, 'closed' villages suggested a reluctance to accept the wider problems of society, and charity was hardly disinterested when landlords were far more likely

[23] M. L. Bush, *The English Aristocracy* (Manchester, 1984), pp. 11–13, 159–60; A. S. Turberville, 'Aristocracy and revolution: the British peerage 1789–1832', *History*, 26 (1942), pp. 240–63.

to put money into towns where they expected to influence elections than elsewhere. Such partiality inevitably attracted criticism, but the fact that it did not provoke positive action reflected the ability of the group to deflect attacks on its performance. Thus Parliament attempted to tackle some of the more obvious problems. The scandal of closed villages was addressed in the 1834 Poor Law Act, and again in the 1865 Union Chargeability Act. The reform of the municipal corporations in the 1830s took place when it was clear that aristocratic control in the towns could not be maintained, while changes to rural local government were resisted down to the 1880s since this was where the group's power base continued to lie.

By the second half of the nineteenth century it was clear that the grip was beginning to slip, although this was insidious rather than overt. Criticism was voiced over aristocratic handling of the Crimean War in the 1850s, while Parliamentary reform in 1867 further reduced the ability of patrons to control individual seats. The secret ballot of 1872, and the more fundamental electoral reforms of the 1880s undermined their position, while the growing strength of the land reform movement from the 1840s clearly rattled the aristocracy. The Lords request in 1872 that claims of a land monopoly based on figures in the 1861 census should be countered by a nationwide survey, and the government decision to satisfy the sectional demands of the aristocracy by financing such a survey, bear the hallmarks not just of sensitivity to criticism but of distinct fears about what might happen if no attempt was made to counteract such accusations. The 1870s and 1880s saw those aristocrats who had retained a significant urban interest coming under severe pressure, while the peers' attitude to Irish Home Rule brought calls for Lords reform in 1873.

Financial difficulties from the 1870s and with them the turnover of landed estates – aristocracies have not been able to survive the loss of their land[24] – helped to weaken the traditional position. In the countryside landlords clashed with their tenants in 1862 over proposals in the Game Preservation Act; 1869 saw the first sustained attack on foxhunting; and in the agricultural depression after 1873 farmers increasingly questioned the right of the hunt to cross their land. Other clashes occurred over the Game Preservation Act of 1862, legislation in favour of tenant right in 1875, and the Settled Estates Act of 1877, which was designed to strengthen the position of tenants for life. Farmers began to lose faith in landlord leadership as agricultural

[24] Robert Lacey, *Aristocrats* (1983), pp. 157, 219.

imports surged into the country. Gradually disputes were settled in favour of the tenants. The Ground Game Act of 1880 allowed occupiers to destroy hares and rabbits on their land, while in 1883 adequate rights of compensation were granted to tenants on departure from an estate.

By the closing years of the nineteenth century few areas of society and government were unaffected by change. The admission of industrialists into the peerage weakened some of the traditional ethos, and continuing radical activity, both in the land reform movement and the activities of the Independent Labour Party, suggested that the old society was passing away. The middle class invaded the Commons and the Cabinet, and finally, after a series of clashes between the Liberal government and the Lords during the early years of the twentieth century the upper house was partially neutered by the Parliament Act of 1911. Even so, contemporaries were far from writing off the aristocracy, and in social terms their leadership remained unchallenged.[25] But by 1918 the world was a different place, and since that time the aristocracy has gracefully declined into a position of decorative splendour.

[25] Arthur Ponsonby, *The Decline of Aristocracy* (1912), p. 16.

Part I

The English Aristocracy

Chapter One

Who Were the Aristocracy?

Miss BONCASSEN: Here you think so much of rank. You are – a duke.

Duke of OMNIUM: But a Prime Minister can make a Duke; and if a man can raise himself by his own intellect to that position, no one will think of his father or his grandfather. . . . Our peerage is being continually recruited from the ranks of the people, and hence it gets its strength.

Anthony Trollope, *The Duke's Children*
(1880; Oxford, 1983 edn), p. 390

Anthony Trollope's fictional exchange between the granddaughter of a New York dockside labourer and a duke who was the epitome of social respectability sums up two abiding concerns in English society: the obsession with rank, and the belief that upward mobility was possible for anyone. The Duke's boast reflected a cherished view in his own generation, which has come down almost unimpaired into the twentieth century, that no one need feel themselves prevented from making upward progress, because society was open and mobile. Alexis de Tocqueville argued that England was the only country in which the caste system had been totally abolished, permitting nobility and commoners to join forces in business, the professions and – even – marriage.[1] In the later 1870s W. E. H. Lecky wrote of how

in England the interests of the nobles as a class, have been carefully and indissolubly interwoven with those of the people. They have never claimed for themselves any immunity from taxation. Their sons, except the eldest, have descended after one or two generations, into the ranks of the

---

[1] A. de Tocqueville, *The Old Regime and the French Revolution* (1856), tr. Stuart Gilbert (New York, 1955), pp. 8–9.

commoners. In the public school system the peers and the lower gentry are united in the closest ties. The intermarriage of peers and commoners has always been legal and common.[2]

Among twentieth-century historians Sir Lewis Namier has written of the openness of eighteenth-century society, and G. M. Young of a similar situation in Victorian England. Most recently Harold Perkin has referred to an 'open aristocracy', which underpinned pre-industrialized society.[3] Furthermore, this openness has been regarded as a vital intermediary in the relatively painless merger of the upper social ranks during the closing decades of the nineteenth century.[4]

Despite the persuasiveness of these arguments, closer study suggests that the Duke of Omnium's dictum may have been fine in theory, but that it bore little relationship to practice. Ploughboy to duke in a single generation was a romantic idea but hardly a practical proposition. Entrance into the aristocracy was far from easy, and penetrating the uppermost reaches took careful planning, considerable good fortune and, above all, patience. The Duke might boast of the openness of society, but Trollope noted his fervent belief in group solidarity to prevent intrusion: he had a feeling, 'as part of his birthright', that his family ought to maintain the sanctity of aristocracy by marrying within the group.[5] It was this 'feeling' which inspired flesh-and-blood aristocrats to maintain their estates against the possible depradations of spendthrift heirs; to build houses and lay out parks which emphasized their family's solidity; and to take a lead in the economic, social and political affairs of the state. In short, it was the underlying ethos of aristocratic society that the purity of blue blood should be maintained against the danger of its being watered down through too much intrusion from below. And yet, ironically, this had to be achieved by voluntary rather than legal means. None the

[2] W. E. H. Lecky, *A History of England in the Eighteenth Century* (1878; 1904 edn), vol. I, p. 214.

[3] Sir Lewis Namier, *England in the Age of the American Revolution*, 2nd edn (1961), pp. 6–13; G. M. Young, *Victorian England: portrait of an age*, 2nd edn (1953), p. 85; Harold Perkin, *The Origins of Modern English Society, 1780–1880* (1969), pp. 56–62

[4] A. Meija, 'The upper classes in late Victorian and Edwardian England: a study of the formation and perpetuation of class bias' (Stanford University, California, Ph.D. thesis, 1968), pp. 240–4; F. M. L. Thompson, 'English landed society in the nineteenth century', in *The Power of the Past*, ed. Pat Thane *et al.* (Cambridge, 1984), pp. 195–7.

[5] Anthony Trollope, *The Duke's Children* (1880; Oxford, 1963 edn), pp. 390–1.

less, recent studies suggest that despite the lack of formal constraints mobility was effectively limited.[6]

THE EVOLUTION OF THE ARISTOCRACY

If in theory the English aristocracy was not a closed caste, entry and promotion were an extraordinarily complicated process which makes it extremely difficult to decide who belonged to the group at a given point in time. In fact, any attempt to decide on the constitution of the aristocracy must begin by examining the group's evolution. In the early fourteenth century the governing elite was the *nobility*, the 3000 or so landowners with incomes of £20 a year or more. Earls were predominant by reason of their rank, but the rest were all lords, whether they were barons, bannerets, knights or esquires. With the establishment of the House of Lords a clearer distinction arose between the hereditary nobility (the peerage) and the other ranks, although all remained technically noble. The distinguishing marks of the group were coat armour and the concept of gentility.[7] Prior to 1500 gentle (*gentil*) meant noble, rendering all gentlemen noble by means of their birth. This distinction remained even after the word 'gentleman' began to take on a separate group identity in the fifteenth century. In the words of Sir Thomas Smith, the noted Elizabethan social commentator:

Of gentlemen, the first and chief are the king, the prince, the duke, marquesses, earls, viscounts, barons, and these are called the nobility, and all these are called lords and noblemen: next to these be knights, esquires and simple gentlemen.[8]

In his view the major distinction lay between the titled peerage, the *nobilitas major*, and the untitled gentry, the *nobilitas minor*.[9] Sir Henry Spelman summed up the situation in 1626:

[6] Lawrence Stone and Jeanne C. Fawtier Stone, *An Open Elite? England, 1540–1880* (Oxford, 1984); John Cannon, *Aristocratic Century: the peerage of eighteenth-century England* (Cambridge, 1984).

[7] K. B. McFarlane, *The Nobility of Later Medieval England* (Oxford, 1973), pp. 6–7; T. B. Pugh, 'The magnates, knights and gentry', in *Fifteenth-Century England, 1399–1509*, ed. S. B. Chrimes, C. D. Ross and R. A. Griffiths (Manchester, 1972), p. 96; J. A. F. Thomson, *The Transformation of Medieval England, 1370–1529* (1983), p. 104; W. T. MacCaffrey, 'England: the crown and the new aristocracy', *Past and Present*, 30 (1965), p. 52.

[8] Sir Thomas Smith, *De Republica Anglorum: a discourse on the Commonwealth of England*, ed. L. Alston (Cambridge, 1906), p. 31.

[9] Ibid., pp. 31, 32.

Gentleman is the lowest class of the lesser nobility in England. The appellation, however, is fitting even for the greatest; but it applies to the former generically as being the threshold of nobility, to the latter specifically as the highest degree of the name. For we call those 'gentlemen' simply, who have no more illustrious title such as Esquire, Knight etc.[10]

The dissolution of the seamless noble robe, and its replacement by a distinctive nobility, in the sense of hereditary peerage and gentry, took place gradually, until early nineteenth-century writers were able to emphasize the loss of position. Sixteenth- and seventeenth-century commentators emphasized the *nobility* of the gentry. In 1600 Thomas Wilson retained Smith's distinction of major and minor, only adding to the latter 'lawyers, professors and ministers, archdeacons, prebends and vicars'.[11] By 1691 Guy Miégé noted a clearer distinction. For him the English nobility was the hereditary peerage:

Next to the Nobility, which is looked upon as the flower of the kingdom, let us take a view of the English *gentry*, called by some the lesser (or lower) Nobility, and keeping a middle rank betwixt the nobles and the common people.[12]

As time passed, the position became ever clearer: Dr Johnson defined a gentleman as 'not noble', and in 1830 another commentator was able to write that, 'in the Empire of Great Britain, the term *nobility* has always been confined to the *peerage*; in France it comprehends all those to whom we should formerly, in strictness, have applied the term *gentry*.'[13]

The growing division between the two parts of the nobility was exacerbated by the widespread, unauthorized adoption of the titles 'esquire' and 'gentleman' to a point where it was feared that not all members of the peerage would be willing to own to being gentlemen.[14] James Lawrence put the case most forcibly in 1824 when he argued that the term 'gentleman' had been so widely adopted and abused that it had become separated from nobility: 'every plebian in England who lives above the vulgar has of late years presumed to style himself a gentleman.' From this premise he drew the obvious conclusion:

[10] Quoted in A. Smythe-Palmer, *The Ideal of a Gentleman* (1908), p. 14.

[11] Thomas Wilson, *The State of England, Anno Dom. 1600*, ed. F. J. Fisher, Camden Miscellany, 3rd ser., XVI (1936), p. 23.

[12] G. Miégé, *The New State of England under their Majesties King William and Queen Mary* (1691), p. 223.

[13] *Monthly Review*, 42 (1830), p. 281.

[14] *Gentleman's Magazine*, 81 (1811), pt I, p. 124.

It is only since the gentry permitted the plebians to encroach on them that the peers began to disdain the title of gentleman, a title which the first peers, nay, the princes of the blood, would have not disdained.[15]

Similar reasoning was advanced by the Rev. John Hamilton Gray in an introductory essay to the fourth edition of Sir Bernard Burke's *Landed Gentry* in 1862. He attempted to remind the untitled gentry of their historical social parity with the peerage, within the nobility, since 'the well-born Englishman was in fact a nobleman'. In his view, the English gentry were entitled to the appellation of noble 'in the real and original sense of the word'. The 'country squire of good old blood' was just as noble as a German baron, a French count or an Italian *marchese*. Such sentiments lay behind what seems in the twentieth century to have been the almost inexplicable Victorian concern with the concept of a gentleman.[16]

This confusion over the concept of nobility encouraged use of the broader term, *aristocracy*. An anonymous pamphlet of 1830 placed within the umbrella term 'aristocracy' the peerage, the unpaid magistracy and 'the country gentlemen of small properties'.[17] Isaac Tomkins wrote that

the nobility of England, though it forms the basis and the bulk, forms not the whole of our Aristocratic body. To all practical purposes we must include under that name all their immediate connections, and even all who live in the same circles, have the same objects, and from time to time attain the same privileges.

Thus the aristocracy ought to include 'all persons who, from their fortune and education, live with the noble families habitually'.[18] John Hampden wrote in 1846 that

[15] J. Lawrence, *On the Nobility of the British Gentry* (1824), pp. 26, 41.

[16] J. Hamilton Gray, 'An essay on the position of the British gentry', in *A Genealogical and Heraldic Dictionary of the Landed Gentry of Great Britain and Ireland*, ed. Sir Bernard Burke, 4th edn (1862), vol. I, pp. i–xviii. It is not possible to pursue this particular topic further, nor to develop the nineteenth-century interconnections with chivalry and the cult of medieval England: Mark Girouard, *The Return to Camelot: chivalry and the English gentleman* (New Haven, Conn., 1981); D. T. Andrew, 'The code of honour and its critics: the opposition to duelling in England, 1700–1850', *Social History*, 5 (1980), pp. 409–34. This cult was partly responsible for the proliferation of marks of distinction during the nineteenth century: see Jonathan Powis, *Aristocracy* (Oxford, 1984), pp. 8–14.

[17] Anon., *The Aristocracy and the People* (Manchester, 1830), p. 8.

[18] Isaac Tomkins, *Thoughts upon the Aristocracy of England*, 11th edn (1835), pp. 3, 6.

there are specimens of a certain amphibious sort of animal called knights or baronets, who, though not acknowledged by the constitution as more than commoners, are, by property, by degree or rank, and often still more by association, birth, education, or interests, mixed up regularly with the aristocracy of the upper house.[19]

Writing at the beginning of the twentieth century, Arthur Ponsonby referred to the aristocracy as 'the nobility and the leisured gentlefolk', preferring the term to more amorphous phrases such as 'upper class', 'society' and 'the rich'.[20] These difficulties have not lessened with time. Evelyn Waugh commented in 1956 that 'the relationship between aristocracy and nobility in England is certainly baffling. I do not suppose you could find any two people in complete agreement about it.'[21] Sir Anthony Wagner, Garter King of Arms, who of all people ought to know, was sufficiently unsure of the current situation to write an article in 1963 under the title 'Have we a nobility?'[22] Finally, the 1965 edition of *Debrett's Peerage* suggested that the custom had arisen of using the word 'nobleman' for members of the peerage and baronetage, together with those who by courtesy bear titles by virtue of their immediate connection with noble houses. At the same time it was accepted that everyone bearing duly authorized arms was equally entitled to be styled noble, whether he was a peer, a baronet, a knight or a gentleman.[23]

In sum, the English aristocracy was a governing class, a social estate or rulers and leaders. As such it stretched from the peerage assembled in the House of Lords, through the titled non-peers, to the gentry landowners acting as justices of the peace. Within this range social distinctions were recognized, but all were part of a single indivisible whole. The fourteenth Earl of Derby told the House of Lords in 1846 that by aristocracy he meant 'the great body of the landed proprietors in this country', many of whom were 'unennobled by rank', and 'undistinguished by great wealth', but whose families had been at the centre of their localities for generations, and who had conducted business in their counties, influenced opinion in their neighbourhoods, exercised decent hospitality, and presided over 'a tenantry who have hereditary claims upon their considerations and affections'.[24]

---

[19] John Hampden, *The Aristocracy of England* (1846), p. 322.

[20] Arthur Ponsonby, *The Decline of Aristocracy* (1912), pp. 6, 24.

[21] Evelyn Waugh, 'An open letter', in *Noblesse Oblige*, ed. Nancy Mitford (1956), p. 68.

[22] Sir Anthony Wagner, 'Have we a nobility?', in Sir Bernard Burke's *Peerage, Baronetage and Knightage*, 103rd edn (1963), pp. xxi–xxiv.

[23] Roy Perrott, *The Aristocrats* (1968), p. 19.

[24] Quoted in J. J. Bagley, *The Earls of Derby 1485–1985* (1985), pp. 172–3.

Originally this group had been characterized as 'nobility', but as the term became corrupted, 'aristocracy' supplanted it in use. Although strictly speaking it refers to a form of government rather than to a social group, 'aristocracy' can usefully be employed in an English context because it implies membership of an elite of *governors*. The term came into widespread use only in the eighteenth century, and refers to 'government by the best in birth and fortune'. The *Oxford English Dictionary* includes under the umbrella term all those 'who by birth or fortune occupy a position distinctly above the rest of the community'. As such it aptly describes the very amorphous nature of the post-1688 governing elite. L. G. Pine put it succinctly when he wrote that 'the English aristocracy has never known a dividing line between those with title and those without', so that it could include 'the untitled country families as well as the peers and baronets'.[25] Such a loose definition is not inadequate, since the English aristocracy incorporated all those families that at one level or another played a role in the organization and direction of the state.[26] This and the next two chapters discuss the size of the aristocracy, and the qualifications for entrance, on the assumption that it was predominantly a landed elite, which, despite differences of wealth and social position, encompassed at one and the same time peers in the House of Lords and locally significant gentry families, all of them bound together by the knowledge of their common role as the governing class.

THE ENGLISH ARISTOCRACY AND THE CONTINENTAL NOBILITY

The changing nature of the English aristocracy needs to be set in context. European nobilities were by no means homogeneous, and recent studies have tended to lay stress on the similarities between the English aristocracy and their Continental counterparts.[27] Entrance into the group, for example, may have been no easier in England than

[25] The need to distinguish between 'nobility' in its Continental and English uses is noted by M.L. Bush, *Noble Privilege*, (Manchester, 1983) p. viii; L. G. Pine, *The Story of the Peerage* (1956) pp. 181–2.

[26] For fuller discussions of the concept of aristocracy, in both its English and its European contexts, see Powis, *Aristocracy*, and Bush, *The English Aristocracy* and *Noble Privilege*, as well as the older texts, A. Goodwin (ed.), *The European Nobility in the Eighteenth Century* (1953), and David Spring (ed.), *European Landed Elites in the Nineteenth Century* (1977).

[27] Powis, *Aristocracy*; M. L. Bush, *The English Aristocracy* (Manchester, 1984). Cannon, *Aristocratic Century*, pp. 8–9, draws specific attention to recent writing which has emphasized the similarities of England and the Continent.

in some parts of Europe, belying the traditional view of a uniquely open society. In the 1740s the Duke of Newcastle cited the openness of the French nobility as grounds for the award of a peerage in England. Although creations were by royal grant, entry into the highest ranks has always been extremely difficult. It was the uncontrolled admission into the lower echelons of the gentry – which afforded would-be newcomers a toehold on the ladder of preferment, without formal entry requirements – that gave England its reputation for openness, although the situation may not have been substantially different in France.[28] Even the belief that the English aristocracy showed greater readiness to pay taxes than their counterparts elsewhere is now debated.[29]

Possibly the English group's most distinctive feature was ease of exit, since younger sons automatically descended into the gentry. On the Continent a nobleman's children all enjoyed noble status, although they could forfeit the position by marrying out of the group or by pursuing ignoble employment. In the hereditary ranks of the English aristocracy, title descended only in the eldest male line. Younger sons of dukes and marquesses were permitted the courtesy title 'lord', but only for themselves, not for their children. For the rest the only status was that of a gentleman, and there was no guarantee that they would be able to maintain even that position. Alternative means of admission, such as buying the land of a noble, were also unavailable. In any case, such a course of action implied wealth, which many of them lacked. In Cumbria, between 1680 and 1750, only one younger son of the gentry was able to purchase land and climb back into the group.[30] Nor did younger sons have automatic claims to particular offices, such as the armed forces. What this meant in practice, especially with the full development of the strict family settlement after 1660, was that younger sons received a cash payment to set themselves up as best they could. Fortunately opportunities in the professions were increasing, and for many the church, the law and the armed forces served as a convenient escape, for much of the eighteenth and

---

[28] Duke of Newcastle to Sir Benjamin Keene, 26 July 1752, in *The Private Correspondence of Sir Benjamin Keene*, ed. Sir Richard Lodge (Cambridge, 1933), pp. 28–9; Guy Chaussinand-Nogaret, *The French Nobility in the Eighteenth Century*, tr. William Doyle (Cambridge, 1984), p. 4.

[29] P. Mathias and P. O'Brien, 'Taxation in Britain and France, 1715–1810', *Journal of European Economic History*, 6 (1976), pp. 601–50.

[30] Bush, *Noble Privilege*; J. P. Cooper, 'General introduction', in *New Cambridge Modern History*, vol. IV: *The Decline of Spain and the Thirty Years War, 1609–48/59* (Cambridge, 1970), pp. 15–30; Beckett, thesis, p. 105.

nineteenth centuries. Respectable alternatives were few in number. Trade was permitted, although some families discouraged their sons from pursuing such openings, and the interaction of land and commerce through younger sons seems to have been limited. A few are known to have turned to business, but the majority simply disappeared from historical view, with the added result that the English aristocracy neatly overcame the problem familiar on the Continent of noble poverty.[31]

A second difference between England and the Continent was in the matter of noble privilege. English aristocrats did not lack privileges but they enjoyed a rather different − and much more limited − range than their counterparts abroad. Moreover, the privileges were limited to peers, and only to the male holder of the title, not his family. English peers had seigneurial rights imparted by landownership, and privileges of noble rank, although neither was closely confined. Land was an exchangeable commodity, while several so-called privileges were also available to men who did not need to be noble, including the freedom from arrest of Members of Parliament in civil causes during parliamentary sessions. Other peerage privileges included representation in a separate House of Parliament, the use of proxy voting in that house, the right to enter protests in the *Lords Journal*, and the right to trial by fellow peers in the upper house for all but offences occurring in the armed forces. Between 1499 and its abolition in 1948 this latter privilege was used on thirty-four occasions, but it did not necessarily work in favour of the peer. Peers enjoyed neither fiscal privileges nor rights of hereditary military office-holding. If nothing else, the absence of privilege in the advanced form found elsewhere ensured that there was no excuse for an English revolution in the Continental manner, which would single out juridical privilege as the real cause of the trouble.[32]

The key to an understanding of the differences between England and the Continent lies in the social assessment of status used in the former, as opposed to the objective legal tests applied in the latter. In England it was the gradual failure of legal tests which led to the development of

[31] Joan Thirsk, 'Younger sons in the seventeenth century', in *The Rural Economy of England* (1984), pp. 335–57; Stone and Stone, *An Open Elite?*, pp. 228–39; F. Crouzet, *The First Industrialists* (Cambridge, 1985), p. 74; G. Holmes, *Augustan England: professions, state and society, 1680–1730* (1982). On younger sons and the church, see D. McClatchey, *Oxfordshire Clergy, 1777–1869* (Oxford, 1960), and A. D. Gilbert, *Religion and Society in Industrial England, 1740–1914* (1976), p. 133.

[32] C. R. Lovell, 'The trial of peers in Great Britain', *American Historical Review*, 55 (1949–50), pp. 69–81; Bush, *Noble Privilege*; Bush, *The English Aristocracy*, ch. 2.

social assessment in defining aristocratic status. This did not happen with the peerage, baronetage or knighthood, which remained in the gift of the Crown – although the appellation 'knight' acquired a rather different significance through time – but it became critical in regard to the lowest gentry titles of esquire and gentleman. As with the term 'knight', 'esquire' originally had connotations with the battlefield, and as early as 1390 it had inherited some of the chivalric aura which surrounded the more prestigious title. At that stage it was a rank which could be conferred by the monarch, while during the sixteenth century it acquired its own Office of Arms definition. For official purposes it was limited to the younger sons of peers, the heirs of knights, and men who 'by long prescription . . . can show that their lineal ancestors were so styled'. In addition, sheriffs, justices of the peace and certain officers of the Crown were entitled to the style. 'Gentleman' emerged as a separate title in connection with the Statute of Additions (1413), which required that in original suits and indictments every defendant should give his 'estate, degree and mystery'.[33] As with esquire, its earliest use appears to have been for certain categories of men, such as younger sons and brothers of esquires, male heirs of esquires, and a number of honorary members from the learned professions. The connection with gentry was estab-lished by the fact that the lowest social position recognized as armigerous was that of gentleman.

While the Office or Arms could lay down definitions, it lacked the teeth to enforce its authority. Heraldic visitations began in 1530 to ensure that anyone claiming gentry status could prove their right. Anyone failing to satisfy the heralds was to disclaim the title, and a list of those who had assumed a style without being able to prove arms was posted in the shire town of the county involved. But visitations were rare, the turnover of families rapidly outdated the findings, and the heralds had great difficulty enforcing their decisions, especially after the abolition of the Earl Marshal's court in 1641. Attempts to establish heraldic authority on a statutory basis after 1660 failed, and visitations came to an end in 1686. The old distinctions still held in the later seventeenth century. No one below the rank of esquire was permitted to be a justice of the peace or, under the 1671 Game Act, to appoint a gamekeeper. Esquires, and even gentlemen, were still expected to pay for their status in poll taxes levied at the end of the century, but this

---

[33] N. Saul, *Knights and Esquires: the Gloucestershire gentry in the fourteenth century* (Oxford, 1981), pp. 18, 26–9.

could not prevent a commoner invasion of gentry privileges which divested them of aristocratic significance.[34]

Since the lower regions of the gentry could not be controlled, a different yardstick was required for assessing a man's entitlement to be part of the aristocracy. This took the form of property qualifications for positions in central and local government, which were introduced in the wake of the 1688 revolution. Peers, notably, were excluded from the need to provide proof of their financial worth, since their nobility was not doubted, but everyone else was expected to jump certain hurdles in order to be classed as a member of the governing elite. It was no longer sufficient simply to be a gentleman, and the knock-on effect was that wealth became the determining factor in assessing social position. Being a gentleman might still qualify a man for membership of the nobility, but not necessarily for what came to be recognized as the aristocracy.

NUMBERS OF THE ARISTOCRACY

The absence of legal distinctions similar to those found on the Continent lends an air of vagueness to any definition of the English aristocracy. This situation is not improved by approaching the problem from the opposite direction and attempting to assess the group by counting numbers, because the exercise merely reveals that if Englishmen knew well enough how to recognize an aristocrat they had few ideas about how many of them there were. Since titles from duke to knight were in the Crown's gift, records survive from which some quantification is possible. More difficulty is encountered when an attempt is made to number esquires and gentlemen, and to try to establish the parameters of the group both nationally and locally.

Titles were granted in a variety of different ways. Peerages and baronetcies could be of English, Scottish or Irish descent, although the recipient did not necessarily have to be a native of the country involved. English peerages to 1707, peerages of Great Britain from the union with Scotland until 1801, and of the United Kingdom from the Act of Union with Ireland that year, were the most prestigious. They carried seats in the House of Lords, whereas the Scottish and Irish peers elected sixteen and twenty-eight of their number to the Lords for each parliamentary session. As a result, many creations within the English,

[34] M. J. Sayer, *English Nobility: the gentry, the heralds and the Continental context* (Norwich, 1979), pp. 8–9; *L.J.*, vols 11–14 (index references under 'Nobility'); Bush, *The English Aristocracy*, p. 27.

British or United Kingdom peerages went to men who already had a title in one of the other orders. Baronetcies were similarly awarded, Scottish titles ceasing in 1707 and Irish in 1801. Knighthoods were awarded rather differently, either as unadorned bachelors, or within the *orders*. The highest orders were the Garter (1348), the Thistle (1687) and St Patrick (1783), which were invariably filled by peers. From 1725 knighthoods were also awarded within the Order of the Bath, which was originally limited to thirty-five members. During the nineteenth century the number of orders, and the number of members of each, increased steadily to provide many new entrance points.[35]

In 1658 the English peerage was estimated to number 119; by 1900 this figure had grown to over 520, an increase of nearly 350 per cent. This had taken place as a result of sporadic leaps rather than along a generally upward curve. Particularly important were the immediate post-Restoration years, the period from 1780 to 1830 and the later Victorian decades. It has long been known that Tudor frugality in the matter of peerage creation was succeeded by lavish dispensation under the first two Stuarts. Less appreciated has been the remorseless round of creations after 1660, as a result of which the peerage roughly trebled in the seventeenth century. Charles II had granted forty-three new peerages by 1684, at which point the peerage was one-third greater than on the eve of his accession.[36] The most spectacular change was among the dukes. Except for the controversial dukedom awarded to Buckingham in 1623, the title had been reserved mainly for a small

---

[35] The statistical basis of the following paragraphs is developed in greater detail in the Appendix.

[36] Huntington Library, Hastings MSS, Misc. Box 1, 'List of peerages created to 1684'. The available figures are often inconsistent. Lawrence Stone, *The Crisis of the Aristocracy* (Oxford, 1965), has produced the most widely accepted for the early seventeenth century. He suggests that between 1603 and 1641 the peerage was increased by 94 new, resumed, recognized or restored titles, but 22 extinctions left a net gain of 72 (p. 757). However, his figures can also be taken to suggest an increase in the peerage from 55 to 121 over the years 1603–41, i.e. only 66 (p. 758). According to J. P. Cooper, 'The counting of manors', *Economic History Review*, 2nd ser., 8 (1956), pp. 378, 389, the net increase was 60 over the years 1603–40, but 87 if the years to 1646 are included. For Charles II's reign, an anonymous *A List of the Peers* (1719) gives 64 creations and 53 extinctions (the latter presumably counting from 1649–85), a net increase of 11, and for James II 8 creations and 8 extinctions. These figures do not do justice to the turnover within the peerage, since on this basis between 1603 and 1688 the Stuarts created 193 peers while extinctions ran at 99 (51 per cent). From the *L.J.* index it is apparent that 89 peers were introduced into the upper house during Charles II and James II's reigns. See also John Cannon, 'The isthmus repaired: the resurgence of the English aristocracy, 1660–1760', *Proceedings of the British Academy*, 48 (1982), p. 436.

number of families with close ties to the Crown. Charles II, however, awarded them to his mistresses and six bastard children, with the result that there were fourteen creations and revivals of dukedoms during his reign.[37] From no more than two between 1500 and 1658, numbers soared to over twenty by the beginning of the eighteenth century, at which level they remained into the twentieth.

At the revolution in 1688 there were around 160 English peers, an overall increase of 100 since the accession of James I. William III created twenty-seven new titles,[38] including seven dukedoms, and he called six sons of existing peers to the Lords in their fathers' lifetimes. He also promoted sixteen men to higher ranks in the peerage. Many of these honours were distributed in two groups, during the spring of 1689 and the spring of 1694.[39] As a result, by 1702 thirty-six of the 162 lay peers owed their current titles to William. Queen Anne created forty-five titles, fifteen by promotion within the peerage and thirty by elevating commoners into the group. At her death in 1714 the peerage numbered 170. The Stuarts' willingness to create peers was not shared by their successors. For sixty years after 1714 admission was tightly controlled. Sir Robert Walpole found George II more set against making peers than against any other measure he could propose: Lord Hervey told Henry Fox in 1734 that 'there are no new peers to be made; and if I can guess at the way of thinking of those where the power of creation lies, it is one that will be long dormant and very sparingly used'; and the Duke of Bedford thought creations so unlikely in 1746 that he did not even bother to mention the subject.[40] George III was equally set against expanding the peerage. He informed the Marquess of Rockingham in 1766 that 'as to the peerages I thought I had yesterday as well as on many former occasions expressed an intention of not at least for the present increasing the peerage; and remain entirely now of that opinion.' Three months later he wrote to the Earl of Chatham to tell him that he objected to raising the ambitious Earl of Northumberland to a dukedom for 'fear it should be

[37] R. A. Kelch, 'The dukes: a study of the English nobility in the eighteenth century' (Ohio State University, Ph.D. thesis, 1955), p. 43.

[38] The term 'new titles' is more accurate than 'new peers' because only a small number of grants were to men not already in the peerage, particularly during the period 1714–84.

[39] H. Horwitz, *Parliament, Policy and Politics in the Reign of William III* (Manchester, 1977), p. 311.

[40] Cannon, *Aristocratic Century*, p. 14; *Lord Hervey and his Friends*, ed. Earl of Ilchester (1950), p. 200; *Correspondence of John, Fourth Duke of Bedford*, ed. Lord John Russell (1842), vol. I. p. 126.

opening the door for more applications', although he did eventually go ahead.[41]

Given these views, it is hardly surprising that down to the 1780s entry into the peerage was more than usually restricted, and that many of the new titles went to existing members of the group. George I created twenty-eight new peers, many of them in the first two years of his reign. They included four dukedoms, a marquessate, nine earldoms, three viscountcies and twelve baronies. He also called up two eldest sons in their father's barony. All the upper titles went to existing peers who were simply promoted, including James Brydges, who was created Earl of Caernarvon three days after his father's death.[42] One of the viscountcies and four of the baronies went to members of the Irish peerage, and only eight new creations were made, one to the second son of an earl, four to baronets, one to a knight and just two to men lacking a title. In the whole reign just three viscountcies and five baronies went to men who were not either sons of peers, Irish peers, or baronets and knights.[43] George II followed this precedent. His only dukedom was granted to the existing Duke of Newcastle; the marquessate went to an earl, and of the twenty-six new earldoms all but three of the men involved were already peers, and one of the others was the eldest son of a Scottish peer. The two viscountcies went to an Irish peer and a baronet; and of the thirty-five baronies four went to eldest sons called up in their fathers' lifetimes, four to Irish peers, three to the second sons of peers, four to Knights of the Bath, three to baronets, three to knights and fourteen to men without previous title. Sir Thomas Watson Wentworth made perhaps the most remarkable progress, receiving a barony in 1728, an earldom in 1734 and a marquessate in 1746.[44] From 1760 until the early 1780s George III

[41] *Correspondence of King George III*, ed. Sir John Fortescue (1927), vol. I, pp. 354–5, 398–9; Brian Masters, *The Dukes*, 2nd edn (1980), pp. 254–6.

[42] C. H. C. and M. I. Baker, *The life and circumstances of James Brydges, first Duke of Chandos* (Oxford, 1949), p. 96, maintain that the title was bestowed on Brydges's father, Lord Chandos, the day before he died, but this was not so: *Complete Peerage*, vol. III, p. 129.

[43] A. S. Turberville, *The House of Lords in the XVIII Century* (Oxford, 1927), pp. 501–13.

[44] Not content with this progress, he applied for a dukedom in 1756: BL Add. MSS, 32,996, fol. 397. Successive promotion turned out to be an expensive business, illustrating why it was necessary for a peer to have a substantial income. At the time of his elevation to the earldom in 1734, the former Baron Malton had to pay fees of £679. 17s. to the Crown Office, and additional fees to various other offices which brought the total to £967. 6s. 4d. In addition, when he entered the House of Lords under his new title, additional fees totalled £18. 10s. When he was raised to the

pursued a similarly parsimonious policy, creating two dukedoms for existing earls; eleven earldoms for ten peers and William Pitt the elder; nine viscountcies for six peers, one Irish peer, one second son of a peer and one commoner; and forty baronies for six Irish peers, seven sons of peers, four Knights of the Bath, six baronets, two knights, one Lord Chief Justice, one right honourable, one son called up in his father's barony and twelve commoners.

Hanoverian policy ensured that numbers remained almost stationary from 1720 until 1780 at around 190, and but for a reduction of extinction rates they might have been expected to fall. Of James I's peerages 54 per cent were extinct within a century, and the level ran at 59 per cent for Charles II's creations. This figure fell to only 33 per cent for peerages created between 1720 and 1739, and between 1760 and 1779, not because of changes in fertility but owing to the increasing use of special remainders to prevent a title from disappearing in the event of main-line failure. This practice was seldom used in the seventeenth century, but nearly half of George I's peerages included special remainders to younger sons and brothers.[45] As a result, numbers remained steady, and fewer than forty families gained admission to the peerage between 1714 and 1783 who did not already have strong connections with the titled elite.

From the 1780s the policy changed, and over the years to 1830 the peerage increased considerably in size. Numbers in the peerage of Great Britain rose from 189 in 1780 to 220 in 1790, and to 267 in 1800, an overall increase of 41 per cent over the two decades, while numbers in the Irish peerage rose by more than 50 per cent. Overall, between 1780 and 1832 the peerage of Great Britain and the United Kingdom increased by 166, and at Victoria's accession the upper house was approximately double the size it had been in 1783.[46] Much scorn was poured upon William Pitt the younger as the instigator of these changes; indeed, as late as the 1840s the ease with which a peerage could be obtained from him was still thought worthy of comment.[47]

---

marquessate twelve years later, the fees totalled £580. In addition, he was made a Knight of the Bath in 1725, for which the fees totalled £524, and there must have been additional outgoings when he was made a baron: Sheffield City Library, Wentworth-Woodhouse MSS, M13/5–22. I should like to thank Clyve Jones for drawing my attention to this information.

[45] Cannon, 'The isthmus repaired', pp. 436–8.

[46] A. S. Turberville, *The House of Lords in the Age of Reform 1784–1837* (1958), pp. 42–3.

[47] A. S. Turberville, 'The younger Pitt and the House of Lords', *History*, 21 (1936–7), pp. 350–8; Clements Library, Lacaita–Shelburne MSS, Mr Panizzi to ?, 7 October 1841.

In practice, the situation needs to be kept in perspective. In 1800, 113 of the 257 titles dated from 1780, but twenty-five were promotions of men already in the peerage, twenty-four were from the Scottish[48] and Irish peerages, two were raised in their fathers' baronies, and fifty-five of the other sixty-two had some links with peerage families. Pitt was merely continuing an eighteenth-century trend whereby peerages went almost exclusively to men already closely connected with families already in the group.[49]

The most serious accusation which can legitimately be levelled against Pitt was that he undammed the floodtide, and the breach was never repaired. Numbers of peers passed 300 by 1830, 400 by the 1860s, and 500 by the end of the century. Between 1837 and 1911 a total of 463 individuals received 497 new titles, and by 1900 the peerage was virtually double what it was a century earlier. Creations ran at 4.3 per annum between 1837 and 1851, 4.1 per annum over the years 1852–66, and 7 per annum between 1867 and 1881. They increased to 8.3 per annum between 1882 and 1896, and to 9.5 per annum during 1896–1911. Despite this increase, three out of every ten recipients in mid-Victorian England were existing peers receiving promotion, two-fifths were gentry – sometimes ennobled after intermarrying with the peerage, and sometimes in distant succession to titles – and only one-quarter were from backgrounds not normally bringing close social relations with the peerage.[50]

At the Restoration Charles II regarded baronetcies and knighthoods as particularly useful for rewarding faithful friends, and he created almost as many baronetcies as his father and grandfather between them, and more knighthoods than his father. By 1665 he had distributed 304 English and 51 Scottish and Irish baronetcies, together with 471 knighthoods. The limit for baronetcies had originally been set at 200 by James I, but this was ignored and in 1681 the entrance fee was abolished.[51] After 1665 Charles slowed down the

[48] On the position of the Scottish peers, see M. W. McCahill, 'The Scottish peerage and the House of Lords in the late eighteenth century', *Scottish Historical Review*, 51 (1972), pp. 172–96. From 1782 Scottish peers increasingly demanded peerages of Great Britain, and a number were successful (see table A2, p. 488). Among those requesting preferment was the Earl of Buchan: Clements Library, Lacaita–Shelburne MSS, Earl of Buchan to William Pitt, 24 July 1782.

[49] Cannon, *Aristocratic Century*, p. 24, and pp. 28–9 on the low calibre of some Irish peers.

[50] R. E. Pumphrey, 'The introduction of industrialists into the British peerage: a study of the adaptation of a social institution', *American Historical Review*, 65 (1959), pp. 4, 7–8.

[51] A. Briton, *The Baronetage under Twenty-Seven Sovereigns, 1308–1910* (1910), p. 28.

grants, and during the final two decades of his reign he distributed 125 English baronetcies, 89 Scottish and Irish baronetcies and 509 knighthoods. Overall, he created more baronetcies than any other monarch before the twentieth century, and only Victoria topped him for knighthoods, albeit in very different circumstances. No other monarch was so profligate. Taking baronetcies and knighthoods together, Charles averaged sixty-three creations a year; by contrast, numbers fell to thirty-eight under James II, eighteen under William III, fifteen under Queen Anne, thirteen under George I, and slightly fewer than six in George II's reign. The tightening up in distribution occurred not only in the peerage but also in the baronetage and knighthood.

George III averaged thirteen creations over the first two decades of his reign, but from the 1780s he eased the restrictions. By 1800 he had created 244 British and 77 Irish baronetcies (nearly three-quarters of them since 1780) and 362 knights bachelor. A further 131 baronetcies (including United Kingdom titles from 1801) were created during the first decade of the nineteenth century. George IV made 171 grants as regent (from 1812) and king (1820–30), and William IV another fifty-five. Between her accession in 1837 and 1884 Victoria's creations averaged around five a year and totalled 246, but from 1885 numbers spiralled upwards, with 194 creations over the following fifteen years (averaging twelve a year). This increased pace was maintained into the twentieth century, with a further 271 creations between 1900 and 1915.

The knighthood was expanded rather more spectacularly. Between 1720 and 1760, 194 knights bachelor were dubbed, but this was the low point, and the next two forty-year periods witnessed 349 and 885 dubbings respectively. The opportunities increased dramatically under the pressure of demand for honours in the course of George III's reign. George III dubbed about nine knights bachelor a year, and filled vacancies in the thirty-five-man Order of the Bath. In 1814 the Order of the Bath was reconstituted as three separate groups, and the honour became predominantly for military service. The same year the regent founded the Royal Hanoverian Guelphic Order, ostensibly to reward civil and military service among Hanoverian subjects, although both he and his brother William IV showered it profusely upon British people. Members were not expected to be titled 'Sir', so that anyone the monarch wished to carry this title had also to be dubbed bachelor. The Order was discontinued in an English context in 1837 when the Hanoverian crown was separated from the English throne. However, in 1818 the Order of St Michael and St George was founded for natives of the Ionian Islands and Malta, membership being limited to natural and naturalized subjects holding high office in dominions beyond seas, and for loyal service in relation to the foreign affairs of the Empire. Gradually numbers in the Orders were increased: the Bath reached 1300 members by 1900 and the Order of St Michael and St George around 1000. In addition, the Star of India was introduced in 1861 – of which numbers reached nearly 300 by 1897 – the Order of the Indian Empire in 1878, and the Royal Victorian Order for the sovereign's private use in 1896.[52] These developments had significant consequences. In 1843 there were 451 knights bachelor, and 787 members of the Orders, although only about 200 of the latter carried the title 'Sir'.[53] Between 1840 and 1880 Victoria dubbed 576 bachelors, but between 1881 and 1900 the number was 699. Membership of the Orders reached 2410 in 1890, 2827 in 1900 and over 4000 by 1915. Three-quarters of these were Companions, leaving about 1000 eligible to carry the title 'Sir' in 1915 if they had no more exalted rank. Bachelors totalled nearly 500 in 1900 and over 1000 by 1915.[54]

Any attempt to count esquires and gentlemen, and to assess the overall size of the group, is fraught with considerable problems. In 1600 Thomas Wilson estimated that England had around 16,000 gentleman, while more recently G. E. Aylmer has suggested that in the 1630s esquires totalled between 7000 and 9000, and gentlemen between 10,000 and 14,000.[55] His estimates may have been too high for esquires, since both R. Blome and Gregory King thought in terms of 3000 for the later seventeenth century. The real problem lay with the gentlemen. In his county-by-county listing, Blome recorded just 1685 gentlemen in 1673. This was obviously too low; he found none at all in Cambridgeshire, and only thirty-one in Cumberland, whereas a local list for 1680 named sixty-six.[56] Gregory King was all at sea, toying with figures for gentlemen ranging up to 39,000, and finally settling for 12,000. Nor were other contemporaries better informed: in a parliamentary debate during the 1690s Paul Foley suggested a figure of 100,000 gentlemen, which Edward Seymour promptly

---

[52] A full account of these new orders is given in the introduction to W. A. Shaw, *The Knights of England* (1906), vol. I. See also E. Halevy, *England in 1815* (1961 edn), p. 197.

[53] *Royal Kalendar* (1843).

[54] Twentieth-century figures are given in H. J. Hanham, 'The sale of honours in late Victorian England', *Victorian Studies*, 3 (1960), pp. 278–9.

[55] Wilson, *The State of England*, p. 23; G. E. Aylmer, *The King's Servants* (1961), pp. 330–1.

[56] R. Blome, *Britannia* (1673), repr. as *An Alphabetical Account of the Nobility and Gentry* (1892). Carlisle RO, D/Lons/W, Sir John Lowther's Commonplace Book, fols 201–3.

doubled. One firmer indicator that King underestimated is the fact
that the 1702 Land Tax Act named roughly 32,000 commissioners,
few of them below the rank of gentleman.[57] On the other hand, when
Patrick Colquhoun attempted a King-style survey at the beginning of
the nineteenth century he counted 6000 esquires in 1806 and 11,000
in 1814 (although in the latter case he numbered them with the
knights). Gentlemen, together with ladies living on incomes, he numbered at 20,000 in 1806 and 35,000 in 1814.[58] Although the terms
meant something at the end of the seventeenth century, by Colquhoun's
time the exercise was increasingly futile; as one contemporary put it in
1828, the titles of esquire and gentleman were 'so confounded in
modern use and applicaion as to be no longer distinguishable'.[59]

The impossibility of counting esquires and gentlemen compounds
the difficulties of assessing the overall size of the aristocratic group.
One means of attempting this is to examine how many families were
armigerous. It was the Heralds' intention that a coat of arms should be
vital to holding gentle status in society, hence the visitations to
exclude those who could not prove the right. Alan Everitt and J. T.
Cliffe have used possession of arms as a yardstick for measuring the
gentry of early seventeenth-century Kent and Yorkshire, but similar
studies of Lancashire and Cheshire found that this qualification was too
narrow to include all the gentry.[60] After 1660 the failure of visitations
and the inability of the heralds to enforce their decisions further
weakened arms as a line of social demarcation; indeed, the period
1670–1770 saw a trough in the granting of arms. Although arms
remained a criterion for membership of the aristocracy, social historians have found the heraldic records to be more or less unusable as a
guide to gentry status.[61] Consequently, evidence about coats of arms

[57] H. Horwitz (ed.), *The Parliamentary Diary of Narcissus Luttrell, 1691–1693*
(Oxford, 1972), pp. 144, 160; G. S. Holmes, 'Gregory King and the social structure
of pre-industrial England', *Transactions of the Royal Historical Society*, 5th ser., 27
(1977), pp. 57–8.

[58] Patrick Colquhoun, *A Treatise on Indigence* (1806), p. 23, and *A Treatise on the
Wealth, Power and Resources of the British Empire* (1814), p. 124. In 1806 he was
assessing England and Wales, but in 1814 the whole of Britain.

[59] *The Manual of Rank and Nobility* (1828), pp. 189–95.

[60] Alan Everitt, *Change in the Provinces: the seventeenth century* (Leicester, 1969), p.
56: J. T. Cliffe, *The Yorkshire Gentry* (1969), p. 3; J. S. Morrill, *Cheshire, 1630–1660:
county government and society during the English revolution* (Oxford, 1974), pp. 13–15,
J. P. Cooper, .The social distribution of land and men in England, 1436–1700',
Economic History Review, 2nd ser., 20 (1967), p. 426.

[61] L. Stone and J. C. F. Stone, 'Country houses and their owners in Hertfordshire,
1540–1879', in *The Dimensions of Quantitative Research in History*, ed, W. O. Aydelotte
et al. (1972), p. 100.

can do no more than offer an indication of the aristocracy's parameters. In 1798, 9458 families were armigerous,[62] but numbers grew considerably during the nineteenth century as a result of Victorian concern with rank and the revival of chivalric ideals. New grants of arms averaged nearly seventy a year during the 1850s,[63] while other evidence tells a similar tale. The number of carriages in Britain licensed to carry arms grew from under 14,000 in 1812 to over 20,000 by 1830 and to a peak of 24,000 in 1841. When the assessment basis was altered in 1853, numbers fell from around 22,000 to only 12,000, rising again to nearly 16,000 by 1868. In 1870 the number was over 21,000, but it declined gradually as private coaches gave way to rail travel.[64] These figures overestimate the number of families, since they record individual carriages rather than the individuals paying the tax. Even greater numbers were paying for the privilege of displaying quarterings on writing paper and on family silver and cutlery. Numbers rose from around 7000 in 1830 to 43,000 in 1868, a peak above the plateau on which they rested during the closing decades of the century. Such figures are not easy to interpret, but they suggest a core group of families in the region of 12,000 to 15,000 strong.[65]

A second way of attempting to count the aristocracy is to use material supplied in a variety of county lists. Contemporaries knew who belonged to local society and occasionally drew up lists to this effect. A surviving Derbyshire list for 1662 named forty-four men who represented the core of local society, and among similar compilations is one for Cumberland dating from 1680. More formal local lists include commissions of the peace, and of the land tax, although since many families were excluded from these for one reason or another they are not particularly accurate guides.[66] By the nineteenth century such compilations tended to appear in directories, while the most easily handled source of information is *Walford's County Families of the United*

[62] Lawrence, *On the Nobility of the British Gentry*, p. 5.

[63] Parl. Papers, *Return of a Number of Applications for Grants of Arms* . . . (1863), 157, vol. XLVIII, pp. 281–5. Between 1850 and 1862, 869 grants were made.

[64] Parl. Papers, *13th Report of the Commissioners of Inland Revenue: assessed taxes – schedule K, armorial bearings* (1870), vol. XX, p. 179; Parl. Papers, *24th Report . . . : armorial bearings licences* (1881), vol. XXIX, p. 367.

[65] F. M. L. Thompson, 'Britain', in *European Landed Elites in the Nineteenth Century*, ed. D. Spring (1977), pp. 31–2. The College of Arms was unable to supply any realistic means of counting the number of armigerous families between 1660 and 1914 from their records (private communication from Chester Herald, March 1985).

[66] S. C Newton, 'The gentry of Derbyshire in the seventeenth century', *Derbyshire Archaeological Journal*, 76 (1976), pp. 1–30; Carlisle RO, D/Lons/W, Sir John Lowther's Commonplace Book, fols 201–3.

Kingdom. By counting the number of families in the latter it ought to be possible to assess the size of the governing class. The results from this exercise for 1895 are given in table 1.1. Clearly there are problems of interpretation here, since landowners with scattered estates tend to appear in more than one list. Thus the Duke of Bedford appears four times, and the Duke of Westminster three.

Table 1.1   County families of the United Kingdom, 1895

County	Families
England	
Bedfordshire	77
Berkshire	187
Buckinghamshire	133
Cambridgeshire	76
Cheshire	257
Cornwall	157
Cumberland	140
Derbyshire	183
Devon	405
Dorset	156
Durham	132
Essex	221
Gloucestershire	245
Hampshire	305
Herefordshire	169
Hertfordshire	183
Huntingdonshire	44
Isle of Wight	34
Kent	331
Lancashire	425
Leicestershire	143
Lincolnshire	181
Middlesex	79
Norfolk	299
Northamptonshire	145
Northumberland	165
Nottinghamshire	117

County	Families
Oxfordshire	128
Rutland	41
Shropshire	200
Somerset	287
Staffordshire	245
Suffolk	231
Surrey	273
Sussex	293
Warwickshire	179
Westmorland	86
Wiltshire	188
Worcestershire	165
Yorkshire	673
England	7978
Wales	
Anglesey	51
Breconshire	58
Caernarvonshire	60
Cardiganshire	72
Carmarthenshire	91
Denbighshire	88
Flintshire	49
Glamorgan	139
Merionethshire	56
Monmouthshire	95
Montgomeryshire	70
Pembrokeshire	95
Radnorshire	43
Wales	967
Total (England and Wales)	8945

Source: Walford's County Families of the United Kingdom (1895)

The accuracy of this exercise is further called into doubt when findings from the *Walford's* survey are compared with local directory evidence. In the case of Nottinghamshire, for example, *Walford's* recorded 117 families in 1895, but *Kelly's Directory* for 1895 and *White Directory* for 1894 named, respectively, 157 and 152 principal seats. Only 79 of Walford's families also appeared in the two directories, and the figures suggest that this survey underestimated the total by 20 per cent or more.[67] Multiplied across the country, this would suggest an overall figure of nearer 10,000. The results show the difficulties of drawing up a definitive list for a single county, and Nottinghamshire does not appear to have been an isolated example. Three lists of South Lindsey gentry were compiled in the early 1870s, in Burke's *Landed Gentry, Walford's County Families,* and *White's Directory.* Of the 115 names only 22 appeared in all three lists (19 per cent).[68]

Such is the disparate and inconclusive nature of the surviving evidence that any attempt to assess the size of the aristocracy through time cannot hope to offer more than trend guidelines. Figures for the titled elite given in table 1.2 indicate a significant post-Restoration increase in numbers, largely as a result of Charles II's profligacy with titles. Hanoverian parsimony brought decline during the first half of the eighteenth century, and in spite of William Pitt's efforts overall numbers in 1800 were slightly below those of a century earlier. Numbers gradually increased over the first half of the nineteenth century prior to the post-1850 honours explosion largely associated with the expansion of the orders of knighthood. Table 1.2 indiscriminately lumps the orders together, and, since it does not distinguish those with foreign-service connections, numbers are inevitably on the high side. On the other hand, they serve to emphasize the later Victorian obsession with honours. Arthur Ponsonby, writing in 1912, noted that within the previous thirty years six new orders, two new decorations and several new medals (not war medals) had been instituted as part of this passion.[69]

Projecting from these figures to calculate the overall size of the aristocracy is hazardous in the extreme. The uniqueness of the English honours system was that many of the governing elite did not have a formal honour to which they could point. Despite status abuse, Lord Macaulay still regarded an esquire as 'in some most important points a gentleman. He was a member of a proud and powerful aristocracy, and

---

[67] *Walford's County Families of the United Kingdom* (1895), p. 1160; *Kelly's Nottinghamshire* (1895), pp. viii–ix; *White's Nottinghamshire* (1894), pp. x–xii.
[68] J. Obelkevich, *Religion and Rural Society: South Lindsey, 1825–1875* (Oxford, 1976), p. 28n.
[69] Ponsonby, *The Decline of Aristocracy*, pp. 124–5. Michael De-la-Noy, *The Honours System* (1985), chronicles the growth of the different orders.

was distinguished by many both of the good and the bad qualities which belong to aristocrats.[70] John Hamilton Gray made the same link in 1862: 'every man born a gentleman, who happens not to be the heir to a hereditary title, which is the case with nine-tenths of the British aristocracy, possesses a certain status in society.'[71] After all, the sons of peers' younger sons and the sons of baronets were no more than esquires. Consequently, the essential flexibility of English society ensured that those members with inheritable titles were not exclusively the elite. Primogeniture may have prevented younger children from inheriting titles, but it did not exclude them from the elite; hence James Lawrence's argument that families bearing arms were all members of the 'nobility', and that the minor or gentry part of the group held a similar position to the Continental *noblesse*.[72]

Recognizing that many members of the elite were untitled is easier than attempting to count them. On the basis of armorial figures F. M. L. Thompson has suggested a mid-nineteenth-century core of perhaps 12,000 to 15,000 families, while material derived from *Walford's County Families* also indicates a figure of up to 10,000. In the 1870s Adam Bisset Thom published *The Upper Ten Thousand*, a biographical handbook of the titled and official classes. His list included peers and baronets, people with a recognized title conferred by the sovereign, MPs, judges, admirals, generals, higher clergy and colonial governors.[73] During the following decade John Bateman found 14,000 owners of 300 acres or more, which tends to support these rough calculations. Possibly the size of the group had grown through time; Cumberland and Westmorland, for example, had 108 gentry families in 1700, but 215 in 1895.[74] Further study of Burke's *Landed Gentry*, *Walford's County Families*, and local directories would undoubtedly improve upon these rather crude estimates. The obvious danger in attempting to refine the statistics is that the social factors which

---

[70] Lord Macaulay, *History of England* (1913 edn), vol. I, p. 311.

[71] Hamilton Gray, 'An essay on the position of the British gentry', p. xviii.

[72] Lawrence, *On the Nobility of the British Gentry*, pp. 5–6.

[73] Adam Bisset Thom (ed.), *The Upper Ten Thousand for 1876: a biographical handbook of all the titled and official classes of the kingdom*, 2nd annual edn (1876). In the later nineteenth century *The Queen* ran a regular column called 'the upper 10,000 at home and abroad', which listed society events and their personnel: Leonore Davidoff, *The Best Circles: society, etiquette and the season* (1973), p. 62.

[74] Thompson, 'Britain', p. 31; John Bateman, *The Great Landowners of Great Britain and Ireland* (1883; Leicester, 1971); Beckett, thesis, p. 97; *Walford's County Families of the United Kingdom* (1895), pp. 1141, 1169–70. The 1895 figure excludes peers, but taking into account overlap between the two counties is complicated because they are attributed a different seat in each place.

defined aristocracy were inevitably vague. By its very nature the English aristocracy was amorphous; while individuals could be assessed as belonging, the absence of legal restraints ensured that it was never a closely defined group. Peer-group acceptance was the only real test of belonging, and that makes accurate counting almost impossible. However, there is little doubt that it was a small elite, both relatively and absolutely. The titled elite numbered 1546 in 1700 out of a population of around 5.5 million, or one to every 3500 people. By 1900, even allowing for the orders, the proportion had shrunk to one to every 6500. The comparison with the Continent is stark. In the eighteenth century, Russia had half a million nobles, Hungary 416,000, Poland 700,000–850,000, Spain 722,000 and France around 350,000. Numbers decreased after 1789, but European nobles still represented more than one to every 100 or the population throughout the Continent by 1820.[75] Even if the wider figure of 10,000 members of the aristocracy is accepted for England, the proportion was still one aristocrat to every 3200 members of the population in 1900. These figures emphasize the crucial difference between England and her Continental neighbours in the matter of exit from the aristocracy. Since in the hereditary ranks succession was only in the male line, and in the other ranks acceptance was purely conditional on the situation of the current generation, numbers inevitably remained small.

REQUIREMENTS FOR ADMISSION

If the limits were so vague the question arises of how an individual could tell when he had gained admission? Anyone who received a peerage or a baronetcy could regard themselves as having qualified. Beyond this the process of admission and promotion (which in effect was what the grant of a peerage or baronetcy implied) was complex, and no one could guarantee that, once a certain level had been reached, further progress would be possible. Those who believed with the Duke of Omnium in the essential openness of the elite might argue that no theoretical barriers existed. In practice, entrance required the negotiation of a series of hurdles in a competition with rules heavily biased against newcomers. The chief requirement was the ownership of land, and down to the later nineteenth century a man without an estate

---

[75] Jean Meyer, *Noblesses et pouvoirs dans l'Europe d'Ancien Régime* (Paris, 1973), pp. 30–4.

Table 1.2 The size of the titled elite, 1660–1900

		Peers		Baronets	Knights	
Date	England	Scotland	Ireland		Bachelors	Orders
1660	119	107	96	678	270[a]	
1700	173	135	88	860	290	
1760	181	82	118	638	70	
1800	267	68	169	765	160	
1850	388	43	129	886	451	787 (200)[b]
1900	524	38[c]	91[c]	954	488	2827 (1000)[b]

[a] Only 23 per cent of the knights created 1660–1700 survived in 1700. The 1660 figure is arrived at by taking a similar proportion for the previous forty years, although this may overestimate numbers, since knights were not dubbed during the 1650s.

[b] Figures in brackets are the approximate number carrying the title 'Sir' if they did not already hold a higher title.

[c] The Scotland and Ireland figures are for 1890.

Sources; see appendix 1

could not expect to make much progress. Moreover, quantity mattered, since the more a man owned the greater his chances of rising through the ranks. Since legal restrictions ensured that substantial estates were not easily acquired, the chances of a newcomer making rapid progress in this part of the race were impeded.

Virtually all the other hurdles presupposed clearing this first one, the ownership of land. The range of alternative and additional channels varied, but probably the most important admission requirement after land was longevity. Magical transitions from ploughboy to duke simply could not take place within a single generation, but the longer a family was established – and that meant established on the land – the greater its chances of preferment. It might take longer to jump this particular hurdle from a commercial than from a professional background, in one time period than another, and in one area than another. But it had to be jumped at some point, and the run-up could usefully be employed in toning up the muscles: building a country house, extending the property, marrying into the existing elite, and ensuring a sound education for the next generation. Each of these alternatives raised its own particular difficulties, such as the preference of members of the elite for marrying within the group to keep incomers at bay. Alternatively it might be possible to use an inside bend for overtaking purposes. Party loyalty could often speed up promotion, as could service in the state. Naturally, however, such channels were only open to those who already owned land or were closely connected with the elite, since – for example – membership of Parliament carried a property qualification, and a commission in the armed forces had to be purchased.

Finally, how could a man tell when the race was won? Unfortunately even the finishing tape was not clearly visible. The obvious signs of having broken it were acceptance within county society, signified perhaps through admission to the commission of the peace. This did not automatically translate into other benefits such as knight of the shire, a baronetcy or a peerage. Each might involve a separate race, and admission was guaranteed to no one; indeed, one-third of the greatest landowners in the 1870s had failed to gain either a baronetcy or a peerage. The vagaries of demography and the excesses of an heir soon put paid to the pretensions of many up-and-coming families. Consequently terms such as 'open' or 'closed' imply a straightforwardness that never existed in practice. No one was denied admission, but equally it was offered only on condition that a potential newcomer entered the race on the terms laid down. At each hurdle he might fall, and there was never any guarantee of how far a family might progress. What made it worth entering the competition was the gold medal of social, economic and political power offered to the winners. Chapters two and three look in greater detail at these problems of admission.

Chapter Two

The Making of the Aristocracy: Land

Almost down to the First World War land was the most important single passport to social and political consideration, and the more a family owned the greater its chance of preferment. Land represented not merely wealth, but stability and continuity, a fixed interest in the state which conferred the right to govern. Rolling acres guaranteed admission, sooner or later, into the inner sanctums of power, both social and political. In William Marshall's words, 'landed property is the basis on which every other species of material property rests; on it alone, mankind can be said to live, to move, and to have their being.'[1] Or, as S. G. Finney argued in 1860, 'you cannot, from the nature of things, look upon land as a mere commercial article . . . having purchased the land you have obtained all that can possibly be obtained by money; that being the case land cannot and never will rank as any other article of trade.' Essentially it offered 'position in society',[2] so that, as the *Economist* put it in 1870, 'it would pay a millionaire in England to sink half his fortune in buying 10,000 acres of land to return a shilling per cent, and live upon the remainder . . . he would be a greater person in the eyes of more people.' In sum, according to J. A. Froude, 'land is sought after for the social consequences and for the political influence which the possession of a large estate in such a country as ours confers.'[3]

---

[1] William Marshall, *On the Landed Property of England* (1804), p. 1.
[2] S. G. Finney, *Hints to Landlords, Tenants and Labourers* (1860), p. 3. A similar comment was made by a correspondent of the *Gentleman's Magazine*, 32 (1762), pp. 67–8, to the effect that land was valued 'upon account of power, stability &c'.
[3] *The Economist*, 16 July 1870, quoted in F. M. L. Thompson, 'Britain', in *European Landed Elites in the Nineteenth Century*, ed. D. Spring (1977), p. 29; J. A. Froude, 'On the uses of a landed gentry', *Fraser's Magazine*, new ser., 14 (December 1876), p. 679.

LAND AND STATUS

The link between landownership and social standing is clear from the gradations of the hierarchy. In 1883 the four largest English estates were all owned by dukes, and the ten estates of 60,000 acres or more all belonged to peers. Among the 331 owners of 10,000 or more English acres were twenty of the twenty-one dukes, seventeen of the nineteenth marquesses, seventy-four of the 115 earls, ten of the twenty-five viscounts and fifty of the 248 barons, a neatly sliding scale of 95 per cent, 89 per cent, 64 per cent, 40 per cent and 20 per cent. This elite also included forty-six baronets but only two knights, which reflected a gradual divorce of this rank from landownership. On the other hand, a large estate was no guarantee of promotion – 104 of the 331 were untitled.[4]

Land had long been the necessary credential, if not the guarantee of rank. Peers, for example, were expected to have an income commensurate with their dignity. Viscount Longueville suggested in 1701 that £4000 ought to be the minimum for a new viscount and £3000 for a baron. The second Earl of Warrington claimed that his father's decision to accept an earldom in 1690 when he had an income of only £2000 a year was taken against family advice that he could not afford the title.[5] Marlborough's wife was reluctant to see him accept a dukedom in 1702 because of his financial position, and she was only mollified by the grant of a £5000 state pension. Stratfield Saye was bought for Wellington at a cost of £263,000 to give him an estate suitable to his dukedom; £120,000 of state money was spent on an estate near Salisbury which was renamed Trafalgar Park and annexed to the title Earl Nelson; and as late as 1919, when Field Marshal Haig

---

[4] John Bateman, *The Great Landowners of Great Britain and Ireland* (1883; Leicester, 1971). The group was completed with six peeresses, one maharajah and one younger son. The number of owners within what might be termed this super-elite has been disputed. F. M. L. Thompson, *English Landed Society in the Nineteenth Century* (1963), pp. 28–9, puts the figure at 363 'owners of estates over 10,000 acres', while David Spring, 'Land and politics in Edwardian England', *Agricultural History*, 58 (1984), p. 21, has suggested 326. Like these writers, the present author has used Bateman's calculations, and the figure of 331 agrees with H. A. Clemenson, *English Country Houses and Landed Estates* (1982), p. 20.

[5] Geoffrey Holmes, *British Politics in the Age of Anne* (1967), p. 394n.; J. V. Beckett and Clyve Jones, 'Financial improvidence and political independence in the early Eighteenth century: George Booth, 2nd Earl of Warrington', *Bulletin of the John Rylands Library*, 65 (1982), p. 17. Compare also Lady Lechmere to (Lord Carlisle), 19 August 1721, 'My Lord Warwick is gone off very young; I hear he made no will and there is but £300 a year goes with the title, which will make a very poor earl'; HMC, *Carlisle MSS*, p. 35.

made it clear that he could accept a peerage only if it came with an adequate grant, both were forthcoming.[6] Applicants for peerages pointed to their landed estates. In January 1712 Richard Norton told the Earl of Oxford: 'I would be most glad to serve you in the upper house. I never made less of my estate than £4,000 yearly, and can always do so.' Peers seeking advancement pointed out that their estate could support a more exalted title, and even in the early nineteenth century ministers took the trouble to ensure that applicants could sustain promotion. But no one was guaranteed elevation. In 1641, according to Lawrence Stone's calculations, the peerage represented only about two-thirds of the greater landowners, and the situation had not changed greatly by 1883.[7]

Much more difficult to control was the loss of wealth experienced by some peers, as land and title occasionally parted company. The thirteenth Lord Willoughby of Parham unexpected succeeded to the title in 1680 at a time when he was a small-scale farmer in Lancashire with lands reputedly worth no more than £100 a year, while in 1713 Lord Colepeper was described as having 'not in the world above £200 a year', and Lord Haversham was 'perfectly honest, and very poor'. Government pensions were awarded to improverished peers, partly as a means of facilitating their attendance at the House of Lords, and partly because it was accepted that those in distress ought to be supported by the Crown regardless of their politics. Between 1754 and 1762 the Duke of Newcastle distributed £50,000 'dole' to sixteen peers. By the 1880s John Bateman was able to identify sixty-odd peers who had less than 2000 acres or £2000 landed income, eleven of whom owned 50 acres or less. Even so, a critical point in the retention of respect for the English aristocracy must have been the general absence of poverty, a situation facilitated by the practice of primogeniture. As a result, the Continental problem of noble poverty was never an issue in England.[8]

[6] Edward Gregg and Clyve Jones, 'Hanover, pensions and the "poor lords", 1712–13', *Parliamentary History*, 1 (1982), p. 175; *Gentleman's Magazine*, 84 (1814), pt II, p. 284; Brian Masters, *The Dukes*, 2nd edn (1980), p. 232; Thompson, *English Landed Society*, p. 51.

[7] HMC, *Portland MSS*, vol. V, p. 136; M. W. McCahill, 'Peerage creations and the changing character of the British nobility, 1750–1830', *English Historical Review*, 96 (1981), pp. 275–8; Lawrence Stone, *The Crisis of the Aristocracy, 1558–1641* (Oxford, 1965), pp. 57, 59.

[8] Gregg and Jones, 'Hanover, pensions and the "poor lords"', pp. 173–80; John Cannon, *Aristocratic Century* (Cambridge, 1984), pp. 11–12; Sir Lewis Namier, *The Structure of Politics at the Accession of George III*, 2nd edn (1957), pp. 221–5; Thompson, *English Landed Society*, p. 51; Bateman, *The Great Landowners*, pp. 499–500; M. L. Bush, *Noble Privilege* (Manchester, 1983), pp. 206–7.

Although few men made the peerage without a substantial estate, William Pitt was accused of awarding titles to men with insufficient land,[9] and he undoubtedly took a more liberal view of who should receive them than some of his contemporaries. During the Quebec Government Bill debate of May 1790, Charles James Fox elaborated the conventional view that the House of Lords ought to be composed of 'noble families of ancient origin, or . . . peers newly created on account of their extended landed property'. By contrast, Pitt argued that the peerage was 'not merely respectable on account of its property . . . it was essentially respectable for its hereditary distinctions flowing from the Crown as the fountain of honour.'[10] Despite such differences of opinion, most of those ennobled during Pitt's premiership were men from the older and more established landed families. Only Robert Smith, the banker who became Lord Carrington, in any way fitted the epithet of a City peer, and even he was remarkably well connected.[11] Nor did the situation change greatly in the nineteenth century. One-third of those ennobled between 1802 and 1830 possessed little or no land at the time of their elevation,[12] but to an extent this was exceptional, since a mere one-fifth of creations between 1833 and 1885 possessed less than 3000 acres when the *Return of Owners of Land* was drawn up in the 1870s. Alfred Lord Tennyson was the only new peer to be virtually landless and without close connections. Even the much-heralded so-called business peerages awarded after 1885 generally went to men with between 2000 and 10,000 acres. This continued stress on the land qualification may help to explain the demand for land among the newly enriched even after 1883.[13]

[9] *Gentleman's Magazine*, 54 (1784), pt II, pp. 576–8.

[10] *Cobbett's Parliamentary History*, vol. XXIX (1791–2), pp. 410, 415. In his speech on the state of the nation as a result of George III's illness in 1789, Pitt made similar comments, stressing 'the propriety of occasionally raising monied men to the peerage, in order to give the landed interest its fair balance and share of the honours in the power of the Crown to bestow': ibid., vol. XXVII (1788–9), pp. 942–3.

[11] Cannon, *Aristocratic Century*, p. 23. Whether Pitt would have convinced George III of the need to promote non-landed men is more debatable: A. S. Turberville, *The House of Lords in the Age of Reform, 1784–1837* (1958), pp. 41–51; 'The Younger Pitt and the House of Lords', *History*, 21 (1936–7), pp. 350–8.

[12] McCahill, 'Peerage creations', p. 274, points out that the early nineteenth century was a period when the number of men supporting their dignity with public funds was at an unprecedentedly high level. It may have reflected the weakness of the Crown, given George III's aversion to raising even a national hero such as Nelson to a peerage because he lacked a landed estate.

[13] Thompson, *English Landed Society*, pp. 60, 62; W. D. Rubinstein, 'New men of wealth and the purchase of land in nineteenth-century Britain', *Past and Present*, 92 (1981), pp. 133, 146. See chapter three for the business peerage.

According to the rules drawn up in 1611, the baronetcy was limited to families owning land in possession or reversion worth £1000 a year.[14] Although this qualification was occasionally abused, the link remained. When the Earl of Carlisle proposed James Graham of Netherby for a baronetcy in 1782 he did so on the grounds that

> by the death of his elder brother he has lately come into the possession of estates to the amount as I am informed of nine thousand pounds per annum. . . . He has been led to think that in consideration of his fortune, his family, and his consequence in the county where he resides, that an humble application to his Majesty to confer upon him the dignity of Baronet would not be deemed too assuming on his part.[15]

The solicited title duly arrived the following year. As with peerages, Pitt was accused of bending the rules. It was suggested in 1798 that of his seventy-one new creations 'not more than twenty can be considered in the character of country gentlemen, even in the widest sense of the term'.[16] His successors in the ministry were also indicted; one commentator in 1814 referred to baronetcies having been conferred upon 'small country gentlemen or new families of sudden fortune', who had 'taken the place of the Old Country Gentlemen in almost every County in England, and shoved them into insignificance'.[17] Burke suggested in 1861 that a landed income of £500 a year might be enforced for a baronetcy, and throughout the nineteenth century the title was granted primarily to men of landed fortune, even if political and other considerations dictated which such men should be honoured.[18]

The knighthood also had a landed connection, at least in the seventeenth century. Apart from those granted on the battlefield, it was traditional to award knighthoods to armigerous families which could afford the necessary accoutrements. According to Sir Thomas Smith, writing in the later sixteenth century, the practice was to choose them 'according to the yearly revenue of their lands being able

[14] Stone, *The Crisis of the Aristocracy*, pp. 84–5.

[15] Clements Library, Lacaita–Shelburne MSS, Earl of Carlisle to Earl of Shelburne, 8 November 1782.

[16] Samuel Egerton Brydges, *Reflections on the Late Augmentations of the English Peerage* (1798), p. 44.

[17] *Gentleman's Magazine* 84 (1814), pt I, p. 32.

[18] Thompson, 'Britain', pp. 39–41, and *English Landed Society*, p. 111; H. J. Hanham, 'The sale of honours in late Victorian England', *Victorian Studies*, 3 (1960), p. 278.

to maintain that estate'.[19] James I expected all gentry worth £40 to present themselves for knighthood, and Charles I raised over £170,000 from those who failed to comply.[20] The connection never entirely disappeared. At Queen Victoria's coronation in 1838 James Peart was recommended by Lord John Russell for a knighthood partly because he had recently married a lady of landed estate, while William Coleman of Poulton-le-Fylde wrote to stress his qualifications: 'I have estates in Surrey, Kent, Monmouthshire, Middlesex and Lancashire, I have lately made a small purchase of some land in Surrey of Mr Waltham, as agent for the Duke of Norfolk, and enfranchised some copyhold property.' For good measure he wrote again the following day to add that he was 'the freehold lay proprietor of a great portion of the tithes of Dorking which produce me about £500 a year'.[21] The father's status or occupation can be traced for nearly 70 per cent of the knights in 1882. Of this group 82 per cent came from traditional backgrounds, with fathers who were peers, baronets, knights, landowners, military and naval officers, civil servants and Anglican clergy.[22]

The connection with land stretched right down the social hierarchy. When heraldic visitations commenced in the sixteenth century, Garter King of Arms ordered that to qualify for the right to bear arms a freehold income of £10 a year had to be proved.[23] Even in the 1690s Thomas Barlow based his petition for a grant of arms on the fact that he 'hath a sufficient estate to support the condition of a gentleman'. However, by the time the definitive edition of Burke's *General Armory* was published in 1884, most of the 60,000 families noticed possessed little or no land.[24] F. M. L. Thompson has suggested that merely to support the status of a landed gentleman required an income of approximately £1000 a year in the nineteenth century, and that the figure was only slightly less in the eighteenth.[25]

Not surprisingly, land was a sought-after commodity. No legal restrictions existed with regard to who might buy and sell, and price

---

[19] Sir Thomas Smith, *De Republica Anglorum: a discourse on the Commonwealth of England*, ed. L. Alston (Cambridge, 1906), pp. 33–4.

[20] Stone, *The Crisis of the Aristocracy*, pp. 74–7, 81–2, 95.

[21] Clements Library, Lord John Russell MSS, K. Holland to Lord John Russell, 22 June 1838, W. Coleman to Lord John Russell, 21 and 22 June 1838.

[22] Thompson, 'Britain', pp. 40–1.

[23] T. B. Pugh, 'The magnates, knights and gentry, in *Fifteenth-Century England, 1399–1509*, ed. S. B. Chrimes, C. D. Ross and R. A. Griffiths (Manchester, 1972), p. 97.

[24] BL Stowe MSS, 591, 'Creations of nobility'; John Scott, *The Upper Classes: property and privilege in Britain* (1982), p. 91.

[25] Thompson, *English Landed Society*, pp. 111–12.

evidence suggests that it was seldom in short supply. Turnover was considerable: the wealthiest families in late seventeenth-century Myddle had only an evens chance of retaining their estate over two or three generations, and the local chronicler Richard Gough found one farm had been sold five times in little more than the space of a century.[26] However, the market was subject to artificial constraints. Landowning families had every incentive to preserve what they already possessed, and to try to purchase additional acres as a means of climbing the social ladder. Here the emphasis was on the family, since the benefits of ownership belonged to the individual only as a trust: in Edmund Burke's words, landownership was 'a partnership not only between those who are living, but between those who are living, those who are dead, and those who are to be born'.[27] J. A. Froude made the same point when he argued that land was sought after 'from an ambition to leave our names behind us, rooted into the soil to which the national life is attached'.[28] To facilitate preservation the landowners sought legal safeguards: primogeniture, which ensured that in the event of an owner dying intestate the property would pass intact through a single male heir; and the strict family settlement, a legal means of holding the estate together while providing for younger children. However, if successful, this policy of preservation and extension had serious implications for the working of the market. Contemporaries believed that men of wealth invariably sought to buy land in order to achieve status. If existing estates were successfully preserved and extended, while increasing numbers of wealthy men were entering the market, the expected result would have been a shortage of land and high prices. Furthermore, since power and position followed property, the anticipated result of a restricted market would have been social friction. The absence of a painful collision suggests that preservation did not work — which flies in the face of the nineteenth-century belief in a land monopoly — or that contemporary perceptions were incorrect, or even that newcomers were content with something less than a major landholding. Since the general trend of land prices implies that there was never a severe shortage of property on the market, the answer must lie somewhere between these extremes.

[26] Richard Gough, *History of Myddle*, ed. D. Hey (Harmondsworth, 1981), pp. 21, 216. This is not the place to discuss in detail the almost intractable problems of tabulating the overall distribution of landownership at any given date. I have discussed the problem at greater length elsewhere: J. V. Beckett, 'The pattern of landownership in England and Wales, 1660–1880', *Economic History Review*, 2nd ser., 37 (1984), pp. 1–22.

[27] Quoted in D. Sutherland, *The Landowners* (1968), p. 4.

[28] Froude, 'On the uses of a landed gentry', p. 679.

THE DISTRIBUTION OF LAND AND THE CONSOLIDATION OF ESTATES

Landownership can best be approached from the great survey of the 1870s, and the reworked figures produced by John Bateman a decade later. No other set of such comprehensive data was ever compiled (table 2.1). Bateman's figures are distorted by the omission of London

Table 2.1   The distribution of landownership in the 1870s

Class or size	No. of owners	Acreage	cultivated acreage (%)
Peers and peeresses	400	5,728,979	17.4
Commoners with 3000 acres or more, or £3000 rental	1,288	8,497,699	25.8
1000–3000 acres, or up to £3000 rent	2,529	4,319,271	13.1
300–1000 acres	9,585	4,782,627	14.5
1–300 acres	241,461	8,076,078	24.5
Public bodies	14,459	1,443,548	4.4
Cottagers	703,289	151,148	0.5
All	973,011	32,999,350[a]	100.0

[a]   Modern figures give a total acreage for England and Wales of 37 million, but Bateman's calculations omitted London, and land of unascertainable value such as roads, rivers and wastes.

Source: John Bateman, *The Great Landowners of Great Britain and Ireland* (1883: Leicester, 1971 edn), p. 515

from the survey, and the use of acreage rather than valuation figures. When capital values are substituted for acreage distribution, only about 30 per cent of the property value was owned by the elite, as opposed to the 56 per cent of land which apparently fell to 0.43 per cent of proprietors.[29]

[29] Avner Offer, *Property and Politics, 1870–1914* (Cambridge, 1981), p. 130.

Bateman's figures reveal a pyramid structure of landownership. At the apex was a tiny elite of 1688 owners of substantial estates exceeding 3000 acres. Collectively they owned 43 per cent of the acreage.[30] Far and away the most extensive estate was the Duke of Northumberland's 186,000 acres, the great majority of it in the barren reaches of Northumberland. Next came the Duke of Devonshire with 139,000 acres, the Duke of Cleveland with 104,000 acres and the Duke of Bedford with 86,335. Just ten owners had 60,000 or more acres, and forty-nine exceeded 30,000. Generally the greater owners had their estates scattered across the country. Of those with 10,000 acres or more 76 per cent had land in more than one county, and nearly half had land in three or more. Bedford, Cleveland, Devonshire and Earl Cowper had property scattered through eleven counties, while two others – Earl Howe and Lord Overstone – could muster property in ten. With estates went houses. Devonshire owned a total of nine: Chatsworth House and Hardwick Hall in Derbyshire, Holker Hall in North Lancashire, Bolton Abbey in Yorkshire, Compton Place in Sussex, Devonshire House and Chiswick House in London, Beaufort House in Newmarket, and Lismore Castle on the Irish estates.

Below the elite in Bateman's pyramid came the squirearchy, with 1000–3000 acres, and the greater yeomen, who owned 300–1000 acres. In effect, these were the gentry, men substantial enough to be living from their landed income, but in a rather different league from the greater owners of land. Nearly one-quarter of the land was in the hands of owners with between one and 300 acres. Probably not more than 10 per cent of this was owner-occupied, while much of the rest was in the hands of families combining small-scale farming with other wealth-getting activities.[31] Contemporaries argued that the main conclusion to be drawn from these figures was that the land had been monopolized by a relatively small group of owners. Four-fifths of the soil, it was argued, was in the hands of a mere 7000 proprietors, and this narrowing of the ownership profile had come about partly because owner-occupiers had been displaced at the expense of great landed estates.[32]

---

[30] For Wales, see D. W. Howell, *Land and People in Nineteenth-Century Wales* (1977), ch. 2, and B. L. James, 'The great landowners of Wales in 1873', *National Library of Wales Journal*, 14 (1966), pp. 301–20.

[31] For a discussion of this particular group of landowners, see J. V. Beckett, 'The decline of the small landowner in England and Wales, 1660–1900' (forthcoming).

[32] Arthur Arnold, *Free Land* (1880), p. 287. The figures were used by the land reform movement to press their case for a change in the law, to permit the free movement of land and thus encourage a wider distribution of property: David Martin, 'Land reform', in *Pressure from Without in Early Victorian England*, ed. Patricia Hollis (1974), pp. 131–58.

Apart from the great estates with their considerable scatter of property and houses, the ideal family holding was a consolidated block of territory centred on a chief seat. Of the 331 greater owners in Bateman's survey, 79 had all their land in one county, and several others had only a small acreage outside. Most of these were close to the 10,000-acre minimum, but some were considerable, including the Hon. Mark Rolle's 56,000 acres in Devon, the Earl of Leicester's 44,000 acres in Norfolk, and two Yorkshire estates, Lord Londesborough's 52,000 acres and the Earl of Feversham's 39,000 acres. Since chief seats were not equably scattered, larger estates tended to be concentrated in certain areas. During the eighteenth century the East Midlands magnates concentrated their attentions on the triangle between Grantham, Stamford and Leicester, and the middle Trent valley between Stone and Newark. John Holles, Duke of Newcastle (1662–1711), bought extensively between 1688 and 1714, concentrating on the forty miles around Welbeck and other estates on his route to London. Beyond the confines of Nottinghamshire and Derbyshire his primary concern was with large estates in the hands of impoverished owners. By 1708 virtually the entire East Midlands knew of his search for land, and offers flooded in to his agents. In neighbouring Lincolnshire, Kesteven witnessed the consolidation of larger estates, the open market in Lindsey provided scope for rising gentry, and the break-up of estates belonging to absentee owners in Holland increased the number of small owner-occupied farms.[33]

Concentration is also clear from the 1873 figures. Four of the 331 greater owners had 9000 acres or more in Rutland and between them owned half the county. Two had their chief seats within the county borders, and the other two at Stamford, just outside. Further north, twenty-eight of the group owned at least 7000 acres in Northumberland. Twenty-four had chief seats in the county, and collectively they owned 46 per cent of the non-waste acreage. One-fifth of Northamptonshire was owned by nine of the group, eight having a

---

[33] B. A. Holderness, 'The land market in the East Midlands, 1670–1820', in *Land and Power in the Regions*, ed. M. D. G. Wanklyn (Wolverhampton, 1979), pp. 29–30; O. R. F. Davies, 'The Dukes of Devonshire, Newcastle, and Rutland, 1688–1714' (University of Oxford, D.Phil. thesis, 1971), pp. 171–9; B. A. Holderness, 'The English land market in the eighteenth century: the case of Lincolnshire', *Economic History Review*, 2nd Ser., 27 (1974), p. 573; R. J. Olney, *Rural Society and County Government in Nineteenth-Century Lincolnshire* (Lincoln, 1979), p. 26. Distinct local differences were also apparent in Hertfordshire: A. M. Carpenter, 'The value of the tithe surveys to the study of landownership and occupancy in the mid-nineteenth century', *Hertfordshire Past and Present*, 7 (1967), pp. 48–52.

chief or major seat in the county. At the other end of the scale, only eleven possessed more than 3000 acres in Essex, and the five who had their chief seats in the county owned a mere 5.3 per cent of the acreage. Similarly in Herefordshire only six of the 331 had more than 3000 acres in the county, and the three with chief seats owned 5.4 per cent of the acreage; while in Kent twelve had 3000 acres or more and the eight with chief seats controlled 7.6 per cent of the acreage.[34]

What had emerged was a pattern of mutual exclusivity between greater and lesser estates. Generally the larger estates were accumulated at a distance from London, and there may have been a correlation with counties remaining unenclosed down to the end of the eighteenth century. It seems possible that in counties of old enclosure small and medium estates survived better because the scope did not exist for building a large estate.[35] Thus in Devon the majority of manors were in the hands of 350 gentle families in 1650, and little change had taken place by 1800.[36] Other areas apparently offered no interest to greater owners. Between 1680 and 1750 in Cumbria, for example, peers sold proportionately more land than they purchased.[37] Collectively these various forces produced a situation in 1873 whereby larger and smaller estates existed apart from each other. When the thirty-nine English counties (not including Monmouth) are ranked by proportions of estates of 300 acres or less and 3000 acres or more, small and great estates appear to have been mutually exclusive, with only Bedfordshire, Lancashire and Cornwall departing noticeably from this norm.[38]

How were these large estates put together, and then kept together? The simple answer – land purchase – was by no means the whole story. The fact that most of the great estates in the 1870s were already

[34] The counties cited here were among the most and the least dominated by large estates, using Bateman's calculations. Rutland and Northumberland were the only two counties with more than half their acreage in the hands of owners of 10,000 acres or more (52 and 51 per cent respectively), Nottinghamshire was third, (38 per cent), Northamptonshire eighth (28 per cent), Essex thirty-ninth (9 per cent), Herefordshire thirty-eighth (10 per cent) and Kent thirty-sixth (11 per cent). Middlesex and Surrey – fortieth with 4 per cent and equal thirty-sixth with 11 per cent – were both affected by London. See also Clemenson, *English Country Houses*, pp. 21–6.

[35] Alan Everitt, 'Past and present in the Victorian countryside', *Agricultural History Review*, 31 (1983), pp. 160–1.

[36] W. G. Hoskins, 'The ownership and occupation of the land in Devonshire, 1650–1800' (University of London, Ph.D. thesis, 1938).

[37] Beckett, thesis, ch. 3.

[38] D. R. Mills, *Lord and Peasant in Nineteenth-Century Britain* (1980), p. 137.

substantial before 1700 is indicative of the importance of careful long-term planning. Most established families expected to purchase additional property within the spatial limits of their major concerns. The dukes of Northumberland owned 134,000 acres in their native county in 1807, but between 1817 and 1847 the third duke spent £375,000 on land, and by 1850 they owned about 161,000 acres. His successor spent a further £94,000 by 1865, and three years later the total had reached 166,000 acres. Between 1814 and 1848 the second Marquess of Bute laid out £150,000 on land purchases as part of a planned reorganization of his Glamorgan estate, and in 1839 the fourth Duke of Newcastle laid out £375,000 on Worksop Manor, to consolidate his Nottinghamshire properties.[39] If ready capital was unavailable, money was often borrowed to secure a purchase. Between 1773 and 1790 the Duke of Devonshire borrowed £170,000 to spend on land, while Newcastle financed the acquisition of Worksop Manor through the good services of his bankers. Since the widely accepted Ricardian view held that rents would rise in line with population, thereby increasing the value of land, borrowing made economic sense. A similar viewpoint lay behind James Loch's insistence that the Sutherlands should divert their fortunes into land for the longer-term benefit of the family.[40] However, extending the holding also meant purchasing smaller parcels of land. The minerals entrepreneur Sir James Lowther of Whitehaven was prepared to acquire even the smallest parcels that lay intermingled with his West Cumberland properties, to facilitate his eighteenth-century coalmining activities. His successors followed a similar policy as well as extending their interests to take in virtually every property coming on to the Cumbrian market.[41] In Glamorgan, the Mansells of Margam bought throughout the period 1660–1760 in order to fill out their estate. A similar policy was followed on the Tollemache estate in Cheshire between 1750 and 1850, while between 1780 and 1816 Thomas William Coke laid out

[39] W. L. Burn, *The Age of Equipoise* (1964), pp. 306–7: J. H. Davies, *Cardiff and the Marquesses of Bute* (Cardiff, 1981), pp. 60–1; K. Brand, 'The Park Estate, Nottingham: the development of a nineteenth century fashionable suburb', *Transactions of the Thoroton Society*, 88 (1984), pp. 61–3.

[40] David Cannadine, 'The landowner as millionaire: the finances of the Dukes of Devonshire, *c*. 1800–*c*. 1926', *Agricultural History Review*, 25 (1977), pp. 77–80; Eric Richards, *The Leviathan of Wealth* (1973), pp. 31, 288.

[41] J. V. Beckett, *Coal and Tobacco: the Lowthers and the economic development of West Cumberland, 1660–1760* (Cambridge, 1981), pp. 223–4; C. E. Searle, '"The odd corner of England": a study of a rural social formation in transition, Cumbria, *c*. 1700–*c*. 1914' (University of Essex, Ph.D. thesis, 1983), pp. 195–7.

more than £50,000 in Norfolk on internal rounding-off of property, sometimes to acquire holdings of no more than an acre.[42]

Apart from outright purchase, landowners also contemplated property exchanges and the sale of detached properties to realize capital for acquisitions nearer home. Except for the greatest estates, most families recognized the advantages for political influence of a consolidated property. Since this took priority over mere quantity of acres, it was possible to swap the holdings around. Lord Morpeth sought private legislation in 1715 to permit him to sell Nottinghamshire property remote from his main Huntingdonshire estates, and to lay out the money on a London town house and further acreage near his main seat.[43] Edward Gibbon, father of the historian, wrote to George Grenville in 1765 to sound him out on an exchange:

I am informed you are desirous of purchasing what lands you can in Buckinghamshire. I have a pretty considerable estate and manor that lies in the parish of Buckingham, now if I could sell that, to my mind I could lay it out in Hampshire for the same reason that you might choose to purchase in your own county.[44]

The Earl of Egremont, concentrating his attentions on West Sussex, bought 14,000 acres outright, and between 1800 and 1830 acquired another 1200 by exchange.[45]

If these were the most obvious ways of increasing the size of an estate, they were not necessarily the most successful. The majority of the largest estates in 1873 represented a coalescence which at some point had included inheritance. This could take place either as a result of marriage, or when property was left to a distant male relative in the absence of a more direct descent. Demographic conditions[46] artificially inflated the number of heiresses during the eighteenth century. Nationally, one-third of all peerage marriages between 1700 and 1719 were with heiresses, and the total fell below one-fifth only in the

---

[42] Joanna O. Martin, 'The landed estate in Glamorgan, 1660–1760' (University of Cambridge, Ph.D. thesis, 1978), p. 252; C. S. Davies, *The Agricultural History of Cheshire, 1750–1850* (Manchester, 1960), p. 13; R. A. C. Parker, *Coke of Norfolk* (Oxford, 1975), pp. 84–90.

[43] 3 Geo. II, c. 14, copy in House of Lords RO. Many other private Acts were for the same purpose: B. English and J. Saville, *Strict Settlement: a guide for historians* (Hull, 1983), pp. 49–52.

[44] Huntington Library, STG Box 365/42, Edward Gibbon to George Grenville, 22 April 1765.

[45] H. A. Wyndham, *A Family History, 1688–1837* (1950), p. 300.

[46] See chapter three for a full discussion of demographic conditions.

second half of the century. Of the forty Glamorgan families that failed
in the male line between 1700 and 1760 for which details have
survived, eighteen passed their property through a daughter and eight
through two or more daughters. [47] Where a single heiress was involved,
she became an outstanding marriage catch, and some families did
extraordinarily well out of fashioning such alliances. Richard
Grenville, a substantial gentleman at the end of the seventeenth
century, married the heiress of Viscount Cobham, and acquired a
country house – Stowe – lands in Buckinghamshire and Warwickshire,
and a peerage. Richard's grandson married the daughter and co-heiress
of Lord Nugent, thereby acquiring property in Ireland, Cornwall and
Essex, and paving the way to a marquisate. Finally, the first marquess's
son married the third Duke of Chandos's heiress, inherited property in
Hampshire, Middlesex and Somerset, and acquired a dukedom. [48]
Heiress marriages also benefited the Leveson-Gowers and the
Grosvenors. The latter's massive London estates originated with an
alliance of 1677. [49] On a less dramatic scale, because the heiresses of
Welsh squires tended to marry English peers, the result was a
concentration of land in South Wales. [50]

Marriage to an heiress was not always the success story that these
illustrations imply. Usually an heiress in possession was a relatively
trouble-free acquisition, but she could prove a liability. The land
might well be settled in such a way that if she failed to produce
children it would revert to another designated heir rather than pass to
her husband's family. Alternatively, the property might be settled on a
younger son of the marriage to preserve a separate family identity.
Marrying on heiress in reversion could be inadvisable. All the
problems of an heiress in possession were compounded by the
possibility of her father marrying again and having a further family, or
even making a change in the settlement. [51] For these reasons the

[47] D. M. Thomas, 'The social origins of marriage partners of the British peerage
in the eighteenth and nineteenth centuries', *Population Studies*, 26 (1972), p. 105;
Martin, 'The landed estate in Glamorgan', p. 224.

[48] The family history can be pieced together from the Stowe MSS in the
Huntington Library. I hope to write a longer account of their fortunes on another
occasion.

[49] J. R. Wordie, *Estate Management in Eighteenth-Century England* (1982); F. H. W.
Sheppard, 'The Grosvenor estates, 1677–1977', *History Today* (November 1977), pp.
726–33. Other examples include Joan Wake, *The Brudenells of Deene* (1953), p. 182,
and – for the dukes of Buccleuch – Masters, *The Dukes*, pp. 101–2.

[50] Philip Jenkins, *The making of a ruling class* (Cambridge, 1983), p. 43.

[51] C. Clay, 'Marriage, inheritance and the rise of large estates in England,
1660–1815', *Economic History Review*, 2nd ser., 21 (1968), pp. 505–6n. All sorts of

popularity of heiresses may have declined during the eighteenth century. Evidence from Ireland suggests that such alliances made little difference to estate accumulation, since landowners decided that a large portion – paid in hand – represented a better bargain.[52] Large portions laid out in land could have just the same effect, although by no means all portions were used to this end.[53]

Inheritance as a result of male line failure also proved extremely lucrative to a number of families. Robert Lowther of Maulds Meaburn in Westmorland inherited a small and indebted estate from his father at the beginning of the eighteenth century. To ease his financial worries he married a rich, elderly widow, and, as a result, by the time he died in 1745 he owned a substantial gentry estate. His son James (by his second wife) inherited during the 1750s the Lowther Hall estates of the third Viscount Lonsdale, the Whitehaven-centred property of Sir James Lowther, and the Marske (Yorkshire) estates of Sir William Lowther of Holker. He also acquired a baronetcy and became one of the wealthiest commoners in the country. An earldom followed in 1784, but he left no children and at his death in 1802 the property descended to yet a further branch of the family, the Lowthers of Swillington in Yorkshire. Collectively, four branches of the Cumbrian Lowthers produced only a single heir during the eighteenth century, so that in 1802 the estates

---

restrictions were imposed, including name changes to preserve continuity: Wake, *The Brudenells*, pp. 261–4; Martin, 'The landed estate in Glamorgan', p. 225. Dr Martin also cites the case of Jocelyn Sidney (1692–1743) who, to ensure that he would not miss inheriting his wife's estates through her death in childbed, refused to sleep with her for the first three years of their marriage. Her response was to refuse connubial rights thereafter: pp. 223–4.

[52] A. P. W. Malcomson, *The Pursuit of the Heiress: aristocratic marriage in Ireland, 1750–1820* (Belfast, 1982), pp. 16–18, 33, 47–8; Clay, 'Marriage, inheritance and the rise of large estates', p. 507.

[53] Until recently it was believed that the majority of portions were laid out in further land purchases: H. J. Habakkuk, 'Marriage settlement in the eighteenth century', *Transactions of the Royal Historical Society*, 4th ser., 23 (1950), p. 28. However, plenty of contrary examples were already known when Habakkuk wrote, as, for example, in the case of the Earl of Sunderland, who married his son to the Duke of Newcastle's daughter in 1694 on the understanding that the young lady's portion (£24,000) would be applied to the payment of his debts: HMC, *Portland MSS*, vol. II, pp. 169–70. Recent research has confirmed that the older view was misplaced: Clay, 'Marriage, inheritance and the rise of large estates', pp. 508–9; 'Property settlements, financial provision for the family, and the sale of land by the greater landowners', *Journal of British Studies*, 21 (1981), pp. 18–38; L. Bonfield, 'Marriage settlements, 1601–1740: the development and adoption of the strict settlement' (University of Cambridge, Ph.D. thesis, 1978), pp. 13–14; R. Trumbach, *The Rise of the Egalitarian Family* (1978), p. 82; Joan Thirsk, (ed.), *The Agrarian History of England and Wales*, vol. V, pt II: *1640–1750: Agrarian Change* (Cambridge, 1985), pp. 193–6.

passed to a distant cousin connected through a great-great-grandfather
who died in 1637. Such cases were not common, and on occasion an
inheritance of this type could prove a burden. The property might be
detached from the new owner's chief seat, causing administrative
problems and burdening him with an extra country house. Consequently he might consider selling the property, either for financial
reasons, or to buy closer to home.[54]

THE IMPORTANCE OF ESTATE SETTLEMENT

What gave inheritance a particular significance in this period was the
evolution of primogeniture and the strict family settlement, and in
particular of a system of entails which paralleled developments
elsewhere in Europe. Throughout most of western Europe during the
sixteenth and seventeenth centuries legal devices were introduced to
prevent estate fragmentation. These were seldom legally confined to
nobility, except in Bohemia and Austria, where the *fideicommissum*
(landownership rights reserved for the nobility) was exclusive to men of
noble status until 1848. The strength of entails also varied. In France
they were weak, and after the Revolution – except for a brief
experiment – they disappeared completely.[55] By contrast, in England
they held firm almost into the twentieth century. The English estate
system was rooted in the desire of landowners to order their estates in
order to establish a dynasty. For this purpose a system of perpetual
entails was devised in the medieval period, but the evils of the system
soon became apparent, and a means of breaking entails was found in
1472. During the following 200 years the courts and Parliament
resisted attempts to invent restrictions on alienation and succession
which would ensure the future of an estate beyond the current owner's
lifetime. However, amidst the confusion of the 1640s and 1650s the
courts accepted the landowners' plea that the protection of property
was paramount, and they received encouragement in this direction
from the abolition of the Court of Wards in 1660. As a result, the strict
family settlement emerged, which provided landowners with two

[54] Lawrence Stone and Jeanne C. Fawtier Stone, *An Open Elite? England,
1540–1880* (Oxford, 1984), p. 134, found that in the counties of Northumberland,
Northamptonshire and Hertfordshire one-quarter of inheritor-sellers were disposing
of superfluous houses. For other examples, see Thirsk (ed.), *The Agrarian History of
England and Wales*, vol. V; pt II, pp. 166–70.

[55] Bush, *Noble Privilege*, p. 193. I should like to thank Professor William Doyle for
drawing my attention to some of the European parallels.

important benefits. First, estates could now be settled on unborn children. Coupled with primogeniture, whereby the courts accepted that an estate should pass intact to the eldest surviving male heir, this ensured that, at least in theory, estates would be held together from generation to generation. Second, the strict family settlement made full provision for the family, determining not merely the wife's jointure – as settlements always had done – but also the provision for younger sons and daughters. It also meant that daughters could be barred from the succession in favour of distant male relatives. When, as was inevitably the case, successions were disputed, and the case went to Chancery, the judges' first priority was the interests of the family. In practice they were upholding the landowners' argument that the stability of landed society was vital for the stability of the state, a view stoutly defended by Edmund Burke in the light of events in revolutionary France.[56]

The strict settlement was widely adopted by landowning families. Soon after 1660 it was in use by all classes of landowner in Kent and Northamptonshire, and by 1764 Sir John Dalrymple estimated that nearly half of all English land was settled.[57] Estimates for the nineteenth century range between one-quarter and three-quarters of all land. In the 1880s it was assumed that all estates of 6000 acres and more would be settled, and as late as 1901 an experienced conveyancing lawyer suggested that nearly all the greater estates remained settled. Possibly settled estates embraced one-quarter of all tenure in the early 1880s.[58] On the other hand, settlements were no guarantee against an estate falling into the hands of a life tenant with full powers of disposal. To work, a new settlement had to be agreed in each generation, ideally between the tenant for life and his adult son (the tenant-in-tail). Generally this took place at the marriage of the heir, or when he attained majority. In early eighteenth-century Kent and Northamptonshire, however, only 33 per cent of fathers survived

---

[56] Lloyd Bonfield, *Marriage Settlements, 1601–1740* (Cambridge, 1983); English and Saville, *Strict Settlement*; J. P. Cooper, 'Patterns of inheritance and settlement by great landowners from the fifteenth to the eighteenth centuries', in *Family and Inheritance*, ed. J. Goody *et al.* (1976), pp. 192–305; Peter Roebuck, 'Post-Restoration landownership: the impact of the abolition of wardship', *Journal of British Studies*, 18 (1978), pp. 67–85; Edmund Burke, *Reflections on the Revolution in France*, Everyman edn (1967), p. 49.

[57] Bonfield, *Marriage Settlements*, p. 92; J. Dalrymple, *Considerations upon the Policy of Entail in Great Britain* (1764), p. 57.

[58] Thompson, *English Landed Society*, pp. 66–9; Norton, Trist and Gilbert, 'A century of land values', *Journal of the Royal Statistical Society*, 54 (1891), p. 128; English and Saville, *Strict Settlement*, pp. 30–1; Offer, *Property and Politics*, p. 130.

to celebrate their eldest son's twenty-first birthday, which meant either that a high proportion of estates were often out of settlement, or that more land was being passed by will, to which similar provisions applied as for deeds of strict settlement.[59] Many families clearly failed in the longer-term hope of achieving successive resettlement. Only three of the ninety-three Yorkshire baronet families managed to do so throughout the seventeenth and eighteenth centuries, and the proportion of direct inheritances slid markedly in post-1700 Northamptonshire.[60] When demographic conditions changed after mid-century, families must have been more successful in maintaining their estates, and there is evidence that this was the case in Kent, Essex and Lincolnshire.[61]

More to the point, however, the strict settlement was believed not merely to have enabled families to hold together the property they owned but also to have encouraged accumulation. In the words of George Brodrick, writing in 1881:

a land system founded on the law of primogeniture and guarded by strict family settlements has a direct tendency to prevent the dispersion of land . . . it must have the further effect of promoting the aggregation of land in a small and constantly decreasing number of hands.[62]

Settlement was held to have been 'a deliberate invention of the aristocracy to preserve the land in the hands of the few, at the expense . . . of the community at large', and as such it was condemned by a string of commentators beginning with Adam Smith.[63] Female and

[59] A. W. B. Simpson, *An Introduction to the History of Land Laws* (1961), p. 221; Trumbach, *The Rise of the Egalitarian Family*, p. 70; P. M. Laurence, *The Law and Custom of Primogeniture* (1878), p. 63. The question of how much land was settled at marriage and how much by will has been debated. The case for marriage has been made by Bonfield, *Marriage Settlements*, and in two articles: 'Marriage settlements and the "rise of great estates": the demographic aspect', *Economic History Review*, 2nd ser., 32 (1979), pp. 483–93; 'Marriage settlements, 1660–1740: the adoption of the strict settlement in Kent and Northamptonshire', in *Marriage and Society*, ed. R. B. Outhwaite (1981), pp. 101–16. The alternative argument is associated with English and Saville, *Strict Settlement*, where the advantages and uses of wills are discussed, with examples.

[60] Peter Roebuck, *Yorkshire Baronets, 1640–1760* (Oxford, 1980), p. 287; Stone and Stone, *An Open Elite?*, pp. 106–8.

[61] See below, pp. 64–5, 96–8.

[62] George Brodrick, *English Land and English Landlords* (1881), pp. 91, 152.

[63] Adam Badeau, *Aristocracy in England* (1886), p. 239. For opposition to strict settlement, see Adam Smith, *Wealth of Nations*, Everyman edn (1904), vol. I, pp. 429–30; Tom Paine, *Rights of Man*, Everyman edn (1969), pp. 259, 264–5; James

indirect inheritance, planned according to the strict settlement, ensured that despite the demographic troubles the number of estates passing by some form of inheritance showed little or no change over time, and although this did not prevent property from coming on to the market after inheritance it hardly explains the much-vaunted aggregation.[64] A few suggestions can be made as to why settlement should have facilitated accumulation of property. First, the demographic crisis may have aided estate growth. With fewer children to provide for, landowners would have had a reduced burden of settled charges to tolerate, and more money to spend. Second, minorities were frequent between 1660 and 1760, and offered opportunities for retrenchment and reorganization which were in the long-term interest of the estate.[65] Third, smaller properties were particularly abundant on the market between the mid-eighteenth and mid-nineteenth centuries.[66] Fourth, although the burden of landed indebtedness was already considerable by 1770, many owners were still in a position where they could borrow the purchase money to acquire property.

Above and beyond these reasons, however, the prospect of holding the estate intact in the family was sufficient to induce a psychological willingness among existing owners to acquire further land wherever possible in order to build up the family holding. As Coke of Norfolk's biographer has written, 'the extent of Coke's buying of land was determined by the amount of land (in particular parts of north-western Norfolk) that came up for sale . . . and not by causes directly affecting

---

Caird, *The Landed Interest and the Supply of Food* (1878), p. 40; Brodrick, *English Land and English Landlords*, p. 338. Even in the late nineteenth century it was possible to mount a defence: C. S. Kenny, *The History of the Law of Primogeniture in England* (Cambridge, 1878). For a modern account of the whole nineteenth-century debate over the law of settlement, see E. Spring, 'Landowners, lawyers and land law reform in nineteenth-century England', *American Journal of Legal History*, 21 (1977), pp. 40–59. Various changes were made in the law during the nineteenth century, but the first substantive – and effective – alteration was the Settled Land Act of 1882, which permitted life tenants to sell land of their own volition.

[64] Stone and Stone, *An Open Elite?*, p. 190; Clay, 'Marriage, inheritance and the rise of large estates'.

[65] Roebuck, 'Post-Restoration landownership'; Parker, *Coke of Norfolk*, pp. 1–11; J. V. Beckett, 'The Lowthers at Holker: marriage, inheritance and debt in the fortunes of an eighteenth-century landowning family', *Transactions of the Historic Society of Lancashire and Cheshire*, 127 (1978), pp. 47–64. On minorities, see chapter three below.

[66] This was a consequence of enclosure and the post-Napoleonic war years, a point developed by Sir John Habakkuk in his Ford Lecture at the University of Oxford, 22 February 1985.

his willingness or ability to buy.'[67] Brodrick believed that owners expanded their strictly settled estates primarily at the expense of smaller owners and freeholders, but they may also have been the only people in a position to acquire some of the larger properties that came on to the market. Although established landowners who made substantial acquisitions were seldom able to do so merely on the basis of a steady agricultural rental income, they had usually benefited from marriage or inheritance, or from industrial and urban developments. Typical in the nineteenth century were the Grosvenors, dukes of Westminster. From their vast London-based fortune they spent £780,000 between 1805 and 1855 on estates in Cheshire, Hampshire, Dorset and Hertfordshire.[68] The real suspicion must be that the impact of the strict settlement was exaggerated by those who wished to see an end to the existing estate system. By arguing that it was designed to exclude newcomers – for which there was little hard evidence – the reformers turned settlement into a scapegoat. Closer investigation reveals that most of the greater landowners were already in place by 1700, and that the really significant trend thereafter was the ability of the group to retain its overall landholding through marital and inheritance patterns.

Finally, evidence of land sales reveals the inability of many families to hold their estates together despite the strict settlement. A number of peers sold out of their Cumbrian properties between 1680 and 1750, and several of their counterparts in the East Midlands disposed of all or part of their property between 1670 and 1820. Among them was the Duke of Kingston. Initially after coming of age in 1733 he made a number of small consolidatory purchases in Nottinghamshire, partly financed by sales in Yorkshire. Other sales were simply to relieve his financial position; hence the disposal of property in Wiltshire and Hampshire for £43,000 in 1737, and of other Wiltshire estates in 1742 and 1748.[69] Of the eighty-three resident or semi-resident Glamorgan gentry in the later seventeenth century, 15 per cent had sold all or a large part of their property by 1775.[70] Not even the largest estates

---

[67] Parker, *Coke of Norfolk*, p. 93.

[68] Thirsk (ed.), *The Agrarian History of England and Wales*, vol. V, pt II, p. 188; M. J. Hazelton-Swales, 'Urban aristocrats: the Grosvenors and the development of Belgravia and Pimlico in the nineteenth century' (University of London, Ph.D. thesis, 1981), pp. 132, 162; T. J. Raybould, *The Economic Emergence of the Black Country* (Newton Abbot, 1973), pp. 115–22.

[69] Beckett, thesis, pp. 63–5; Holderness, 'The land market in the East Midlands', pp. 29–30; G. E. Mingay, 'The Duke of Kingston and his estates' (University of Nottingham, BA thesis, 1952), pp. 129–40.

[70] Martin, 'The landed estate in Glamorgan', pp. 29–30.

were immune. The dukes of Ancasters' estate was divided in 1779 on the death of the fourth duke, and, although reunited when the fifth duke died in 1809, it was in the female line and the title became extinct. A variety of alliances eventually led to the creation of an earldom of Ancaster in 1892, when the family owned 40,000 acres in Lincolnshire.[71] The steady stream of Estate Acts passing through Parliament also suggest that land was coming on to the market, although many of these were to permit the sale of distant estates and capital investment nearer to home. However, sales certainly took place for less laudable family reasons. The third Viscount Lonsdale sold outlying properties in Yorkshire and Durham following the South Sea Bubble in 1720, to fund his debts without breaking up the family estates around Lowther Hall in Westmorland. The fifth Earl of Cardigan sold estates in Lincolnshire for £60,000 in 1791, partly to fund a portion of £25,000.[72]

Turnover among lesser families also suggests a volatility which belies the effectiveness of the strict settlement.[73] Older landed families frequently had to part with their estates, and often they were replaced by newcomers of a similar status. Only rarely were their lands swallowed up by a neighbouring greater owner, and even if turnover slowed down by the nineteenth century it remained considerable. In Shropshire only forty-two of the county's 193 gentry in 1715 survived in 1896, while only a handful of gentry established in Essex prior to 1700 remained in the 1770s. Comparison of tithe survey material for the 1840s and the *Return of Owners of Land* reveals the rate of turnover in just three decades. In Essex there were twenty greater owners at both dates, but four families in the 1840s owned no land in 1873, and three of those listed in 1873 were not owners in 1840. Of those with 300–1000 acres, 23 per cent were newcomers between the 1840s and 1873, and 38 per cent of those with 100–300 acres arrived between the two dates. A similar picture is true of Kent. Only 54 per cent of those with 100–300 acres in 1840 still owned land in 1873, and 27 per cent of these had smaller holdings.[74]

The evidence of land sales and family turnover suggests that the role

---

[71] Olney, *Rural Society and County Government*, p. 23.

[72] English and Saville, *Strict Settlement*, pp. 49–52; Beckett, thesis, pp. 173–4, 203; Wake, *The Brudenells*, p. 335.

[73] The extent to which lesser owners employed settlements has been debated. Although they probably employed the device less frequently than their greater neighbours, the difference is unlikely to have been considerable. Even yeomen employed forms of settlement in eighteenth-century Cumbria: Beckett, thesis, ch. 5.

[74] S. Leighton, 'Changes in land ownership in Shropshire', *Transactions of the Shropshire Archaeological Society*, 8 (1896), pp. 13–14; Thompson, *English Landed*

played by the strict family settlement in estate accumulation may have
been exaggerated by nineteenth-century commentators anxious to see
its abolition. This is not to suggest that the tendency for estates to
grow through time was a complete figment of the imagination.
Between 1690 and 1740 just under half the land changing hands in
Northamptonshire came to families settled in the county for sixty years
or so. Most already had substantial territorial empires in 1660,
including the Duke of Grafton, the earls of Rockingham, Halifax,
Sunderland and Bridgewater, Viscount Strafford and Lord Fitzwilliam.
A further two-fifths went to newcomers building large territorial
aggregations, including the Duke of Marlborough, Lord Trevor and
Lord Bathurst. The drift was towards the stable and conservative
elements in society. The picture seems to have repeated itself in other
counties with a high proportion of chief seats, including
Buckinghamshire, Hertfordshire and Nottinghamshire.[75] By contrast,
landed magnates showed little tendency to strengthen their interests
during the century or so after 1660 in areas as far apart as Cumbria,
Yorkshire, Lincolnshire, Devon, Cornwall and Glamorgan.[76] Some
areas saw consolidation in the later eighteenth and nineteenth
centuries, including parts of Sussex and Essex.[77] Witnesses before
government commissions noted the absorption of smaller properties
into larger estates in 1833 in Cheshire, Cumberland and the North
Riding of Yorkshire, and in 1846 in Essex.[78] The proportion of estates

---

Society, pp. 126–7; R. J. P. Kain, 'Tithe surveys and landownership', *Journal of
Historical Geography*, 1 (1975), pp. 39–48.

[75] H. J. Habakkuk, 'English landownership, 1690–1740', *Economic History
Review*, 10 (1939–40), p. 5; Thirsk (ed.), *The Agrarian History of England and Wales*
vol. V, pt I, p. 332; vol. V, pt II, p. 164.

[76] Beckett, thesis; Roebuck, *Yorkshire Baronets*, p. 328; Holderness, 'The English
land market', p. 573; Hoskins, 'The ownership and occupation of the land in
Devonshire', pp. 79–98; Martin, 'The landed estate in Glamorgan', pp. 31–2, 298.

[77] S. Farrant, 'The changing structure of land ownership in the lower Ouse
Valley, 1780–1840', *Sussex Archaeological Collections*, 116 (1978), pp. 261–8; E. J. T.
Collins, *A History of the Orsett Estate* (Thurrock, 1978), pp. 10–11. The fact that
estates in Essex were held together more successfully after about 1770 may reflect the
increasing awareness among landowners of the value of urban land. A further example
comes from Ealing, west of London, where estates were breaking up and being
re-formed from fragments in the second half of the eighteenth century, but the major
property was stabilized by the Beaufoy family towards the end of the century. By the
time of the tithe award in the 1840s, an extensive core holding had been built up,
which was to become the base for a new residential area within reach of the City: J. R.
Ravensdale, *History on Your Doorstep* (1982), pp. 39–47.

[78] Parl. Papers, *Report of the Select Committee on Agriculture* (1833), vol. V, pp. 109,
281, 309; *Report of the Select Committee of the House of Lords on the Burdens of Real Property*
(1846), vol. VI, pt 1, p. 55.

over 1000 acres increased slightly in both Essex and Kent between the 1840s and 1873, and the quantity occupied by estates in excess of this figure rose in Kent from 42 to 50 per cent. Survival was also more likely among those with larger properties: of those owning 1000–3000 acres, 70 per cent held their own between the two dates, while the rate was even higher – although numbers were fewer – for those with 3000–5000 acres.[79] Finally, the whole movement towards consolidation was slower in Wales, and over a longer time-span, than was the case in England.[80]

This general tendency in the direction of estate consolidation is confirmed by the problems encountered by the handful of men who looked to acquire a considerable holding. Samuel Whitbread I bought land in eight counties between 1760 and 1785, and leased further property in two others. Altogether this gave him 5600 acres. Accumulation and rationalization of this scattered territory only became possible when he was able to buy out the fourth Viscount Torrington in 1795. As a result, by the end of that year 10,500 of his 12,300 acres were in Bedfordshire, and his son Samuel Whitbread II further consolidated the estate by selling off a number of outliers.[81] Lord Overstone's massive spending in the nineteenth century bought him one of the most scattered of the greater estates. His 31,000 acres lay in a total of eleven English and Welsh counties in 1883. In addition to 15,000 acres and a chief seat in Northamptonshire, he also bought between 280 and 5000 acres in Warwickshire, Buckinghamshire, Cambridgeshire, Huntingdonshire, Leicestershire, Oxfordshire and Berkshire, as well as smaller parcels elsewhere.[82] It was simply becoming more difficult to find a large estate for sale. In Lincolnshire, estates in existence in 1800 were generally held together down to 1875, while in Kent between 1840 and 1873 only one of the estates of more than 10,000 acres decreased in size, and all the owners with between 5000 and 10,000 acres retained part or all of their property.[83]

[79] Thompson, *English Landed Society*, pp. 122–7; Kain, 'Tithe surveys and landownership', pp. 39–48.

[80] Martin, 'The landed estate in Glamorgan', pp. 31–2, 298.

[81] Dean Rapp, 'Social mobility in the eighteenth century: the Whitbreads of Bedfordshire, 1720–1815', *Economic History Review*, 2nd ser., 27 (1974), pp. 382–3.

[82] Bateman, *The Great Landowners*, p. 348; Overstone's landed estates are examined by R. C. Michie, 'Income, expenditure and investment of a Victorian millionaire: Lord Overstone, 1823–33', *Bulletin of the Institute of Historical Research*, 58 (1985), pp. 59–77.

[83] Olney, *Rural Society and County Government*, p. 26; R. J. P. Kain and Hugh Prince, *The Tithe Surveys of England and Wales* (Cambridge, 1984), p. 244; G. Shaw Lefevre, *Agrarian Tenures* (1893), pp. 11–12.

NEWCOMERS TO THE LANDED ELITE

Nineteenth-century commentators were not averse to highlighting
what they considered to be the problems faced by would-be landowners, including the intricacies of the land transfer procedures, and
the dire results of the strict family settlement. According to Adam
Badeau, strict settlement actually prevented rich men from turning
themselves into landed gentry: 'the wealthiest tradesmen, bankers,
brewers, merchants, find their consequence incomplete until they can
purchase estates and rank with the county families. To keep these new
people out is one of the objects of the system of entail.'[84] In practice,
the gloomy prognostications of the jeremiads were obviously exaggerated, since newcomers seem to have been satisfied without prices rising
to intolerable levels. They came from all sorts of backgrounds, and
included owner-occupiers building a larger property, and tenant
farmers, estate agents and country attorneys, all of whom had a
particular knowledge of the market. Many were businessmen, ranging
from small-scale country tradesmen, to the merchant princes of
London. As Adam Smith noted in the 1770s, 'merchants are
commonly ambitious of becoming country gentlemen', and a century
later George Brodrick was still able to maintain that they aspired to
purchase property 'which for them is the sure passport to social
consideration'.[85] However, the crucial question concerns how much
they bought.

In the seventeenth and eighteenth centuries, relatively few men
apart from prosperous merchants were in a position to invest heavily in
the land market. Sir Josiah Child maintained in 1693 that, 'if a
merchant in England arrives at any considerable estate, he commonly
withdraws his estate from trade before he comes to the confines of old
age.'[86] Some of the greatest fortunes of the age took this course,
including those of Sir Stephen Fox and Sir John Banks. Fox, for
example, invested well over £100,000 in land between 1672 and

---

[84] Badeau, *Aristocracy in England*, p. 239. Badeau was in England for most of the
period 1870–81, and later wrote a commentary based on his perceptions: *Dictionary of
American Biography*, vol. I (1928), p. 485.

[85] Smith, *Wealth of Nations*, vol. I, p. 454; Brodrick, *English Land and English
Landlords*, p. 153. Similar sentiments abound in other sources – for example, Henry
Mackenzie's novel *The Man of Feeling* (1771). Harley, the fictional hero, is depicted as
one of the few remaining gentlemen of antiquity in his district, 'great part of the
property of the neighbourhood being in the hands of merchants' (p. 7). See also
Harold Perkin, *The Origins of Modern English Society, 1780–1880* (1969), p. 87.

[86] Quoted in Stone and Stone, *An Open Elite?*, p. 18.

1686, predominantly in his native Wiltshire.[87] Other London merchants who established dynasties in the later seventeenth century included Sir Francis Chaplin, Lord Mayor in 1678, and Thomas Vyner, great-nephew of another holder of this office, both of whom established their families in Lincolnshire.[88] Planters from the East and West Indies also bought heavily in England in an attempt to find a secure home for their newly gotten gains. Edward Stephenson returned from Bengal with the intention of investing his fortune in his native Cumbria. He bought property at Abbey Holme for £11,000 in the 1730s, and reportedly had £150,000 to spend in the county. In 1744 he bought out the Forsters of Stonegarthside Hall, and in 1750 the Gilpins of Scaleby. The latter family had first put their estate on the market ten years earlier when interest was shown by 'Holmes' brother who has got a great deal in the East Indies', and 'Mr Smith from Barbadoes'.[89] Eighteenth century nabobs who laid out their gains in land included Thomas Pitt and Robert Clive. The latter spent considerably over £200,000 in Shropshire during the 1760s and 1770s, and both he and Pitt laid the foundations for earldoms.[90] Traditionally lawyers were large-scale purchasers of land, although only prominent London lawyers and Lord Chancellors appear to have been able to progress to the landed elite in a single generation.[91] However, lawyers constituted one-third of all new buyers of country houses in early eighteenth-century Northamptonshire, Northumberland and Hertfordshire, and they remained prominent in

[87] Christopher Clay, *Public Finance and Private Wealth* (Oxford, 1978), pp. 164–91; Sir John Habakkuk, 'The rise and fall of English landed families, 1600–1800: did the gentry rise?', *Transactions of the Royal Historical Society*, 5th ser., 31 (1981), pp. 214–15.

[88] J. W. F. Hill (ed.), *Letters and Papers of the Banks Family of Revesby Abbey, 1704–1760* (Lincoln, 1952), p. v.

[89] J. W. Kaye, 'Governor's House, Keswick', *Transactions of the Cumberland and Westmorland Antiquarian and Archaeological Society*, new ser., 66 (1966), pp. 339–46; C. R. Hudleston, 'The Forsters of Stonegarthside Hall', *Transactions of the Cumberland and Westmorland Antiquarian and Archaeological Society*, 61 (1961), pp. 186–7. Carlisle RO, D/Lons/W, Sir James Lowther to John Spedding, 27 May 1732, 24 October 1744, 14 March 1747, 27 December 1748; Spedding to Lowther, 22 October 1740; D/Lec/170, Mr Webb to the Duke of Somerset, 10 June 1738; William Hutchinson, *History of Cumberland* (1794), vol. II, p. 573.

[90] G. E. Mingay, *English Landed Society in the Eighteenth Century* (1963), p. 73; Philip Lawson and Jim Phillips, '"Our execrable banditti": perceptions of nabobs in mid-eighteenth century Britain', *Albion*, 16 (1984), pp. 225–41. A fuller account of nabob land purchasing is given in J. M. Holzman, *The Nabobs in England* (New York, 1926), pp. 70–3, 123–30.

[91] David Duman, *The Judicial Bench in England, 1727–1815* (1982), pp. 127–8.

Lincolnshire, where 'the number of properties under mortgage to lawyers at a particular time which later ended up as their fee simple was not purely fortuitous.' At least two dozen estates of 500 acres or more were assembled by lawyers, including Sir Joseph Banks of Sheffield, who spent about £40,000 on property between 1705 and 1727. Among Cumbrian purchasers were the Carletons of Hillbeck, who ran a successful practice in Appleby and spent £18,000 on property over the period 1687–1749.[92]

The majority of incomers, in this and later periods, already had an interest in the rural community. Owner-occupiers and tenant farmers were the most mobile, adding acre to acre over time until they emerged as landed gentry. The smaller gentry of pre-1640 Glamorgan gradually became the backbone of post-1760 county society when demographic problems carried off the older families. In Lincolnshire, the Dixon family progressed from graziers to tenant farmers, and then to landed gentry, all by way of piecemeal acquisitions from small landowners over the period 1760–1870.[93] Surveyors, land agents and estate stewards also used their specialist knowledge to acquire small estates, including the Fillinghams of Syerston in Nottinghamshire.[94] Of families infiltrating in these various ways it has been estimated for Lincolnshire that about twenty put together 1000 acres or more in the eighteenth century, with half a dozen exceeding 2000, although agricultural profits were seldom sufficient on their own to permit such transformation.[95]

The clearest reason for the pattern described here is that insufficient wealth existed to permit great numbers of newcomers to acquire large estates. Alternative income sources seldom provided spectacular windfalls in the seventeenth and eighteenth centuries. Government office offered rich pickings for only a few, including James Brydges,

[92] Stone and Stone, *An Open Elite?*, pp. 200–1; Holderness, 'The English land market', pp. 566–7; Hill (ed.), *Letters and Papers of the Banks Family*; Beckett, thesis, p. 105.

[93] K. Wrightson, *English Society, 1580–1680* (1982), pp. 26–7; Philip Jenkins, 'The creation of an "ancient gentry": Glamorgan, 1760–1840', *Welsh History Review*, 12 (1984), pp. 29–49; H. A. Fuller, 'Landownership in Lindsey, *c.* 1800–1860' (University of Hull, MA thesis, 1974), pp. 76–80. Other examples include Cumbria and Lancashire: Beckett, thesis, ch. 4; B. G. Blackwood, *The Lancashire Gentry and the Great Rebellion, 1640–1660* (Manchester, 1978).

[94] Holderness, 'The land market in the East Midlands', p. 38.

[95] Holderness, 'The English land market', pp. 571–2. A good example of a nineteenth-century family building up a gentry estate in this manner is provided by the Greenes of Whittington on the Lancashire–Cumbria border: B. M. Copeland, *Whittington: the story of a country estate* (Guiseley, 1981), pp. 14–23.

paymaster of the forces in 1705–12. He siphoned off sufficient profit to rebuild Cannons, accumulate landed property worth upwards of £10,000 annually, and also to lose vast sums on the stock exchange. In the process he also contrived to acquire first an earldom and then a dukedom. Neither industrial profits nor urban ground rentals were yielding incomes sufficient for a newcomer to establish himself with a considerable estate, although both the Lowthers in Cumberland and the Tempest family in the north-east used industrial profits to extend their already considerable landholdings.[96] Sources such as these only began to yield lucrative profits as industrialization proceeded, and, had all the wealthy men who appeared in post-1750 England chosen to invest their newly gotten gains in landownership, business interests could have been starved of capital, and land prices would have risen to astronomical levels. Neither of these possibilities occurred, largely because of an important change of emphasis in the land market.

With a few exceptions, the days when a man of fortune converted his wealth into landed acreage were already numbered by the end of the seventeenth century, and the practice had more or less disappeared by the mid-eighteenth century. A few businessmen still made the top rank in a single throw, including the banking Hoare family in the south-west, the Whitbreads in Bedfordshire and the nineteenth-century banker Lord Overstone. The latter valued his estate at £3,044,000 in 1876.[97] Increasingly, however, heavy expenditure on land seemed to be illogical. Laying out £100,000 on property which would bring a net return probably not exceeding $2\frac{1}{2}$ per cent per annum made little economic sense to successful businessmen, particularly when social acceptance was not guaranteed to the first generation. With plenty of lucrative alternative investment opportunities, it seemed more sensible to buy a small estate with a country seat (or space to build one), while maintaining the balance of resources in alternative pursuits. Since existing landed gentry were increasingly experienced in business enterprise, either through the stockmarket, or through the commercial exploitation of mineral resources, they were hardly anti-capitalist, or indeed in a position to criticize this judicious division of

[96] C. H. C. and M. I. Baker, *The Life and Circumstances of James Brydges, First Duke of Chandos* (Oxford, 1949); Thirsk (ed.), *The Agrarian History of England and Wales*, vol. V, pt II, pp. 188–93.

[97] C. G. A. Clay, 'Henry Hoare, banker, and the building of the Stourhead estate' (forthcoming); Rapp, 'Social mobility in the eighteenth century', pp. 380–94; W. D. Rubinstein, 'New men of wealth and the purchase of land in nineteenth-century England', *Past and Present*, 92 (1981), pp. 127–8; Michie, 'Income, expenditure and investment', p. 74.

resources. The change of emphasis also made social sense. When they first purchased land, newcomers were not always in a position to make a heavy investment, without seriously weakening their alternative business interests. They may not initially have had ideas of founding a dynasty; many, for example, used the trust form of settlement to divide their land among their children, rather than passing it all to the eldest son. Land was viewed as a convenient means of transmitting wealth to a future generation, while offering current social status. Moreover, they could leave the decisions about founding a family to the second and third generations, who in any case were more likely to be admitted to the social elite,[98] or at a later stage in their life they could pull out more wealth into land. In the meantime an estate offered security for wealth, and a pleasant retreat from business matters. Such purchasers did not attempt to acquire the landed means to run a large country house, because their commitment to land was less than total.[99]

THE CHANGING PATTERN OF LAND INVESTMENT

The change of emphasis in land buying meant that for many incomers land became the conspicuous social investment section of a wider financial holding. Local men continued to emerge from farming and local business to set up as gentlemen through piecemeal land acquisition, and a few men continued to transfer the bulk of their business fortunes into property. For the majority, however, the pattern was changing. The ideal became a smallholding, often of no more than a few hundred acres, with a suitable house, preferably within easy reach of existing business interests. This left open the option of buying a family estate, either by piecemeal acquisition or by selling the original holding in order to move further afield. The effects of this change of emphasis can be seen in two ways: first, through the pattern of purchasing close to expanding towns; and, second, through the evidence of land prices.

London and the Home Counties provide the clearest evidence of

[98] Thompson, *English Landed Society*, p. 21, and 'Britain', p. 30. Examples of business incomers are given in chapter three below. However, Stone and Stone, *An Open Elite?*, pp. 213–14, note the case of William Medhurst, who bought Kippax Hall in 1741 after a successful career in the Leeds cloth trade. His sons took over the firm in 1745, but they were more interested in rural pleasures, and the firm failed in 1780.

[99] M. Culme-Seymour, 'The house and the estate', in *The Destruction of the Country House*, ed. R. Strong, *et al.* (1974), p. 140.

ge of practice really meant. As early as 1667 it was
commanded higher prices in the vicinity of the capital,
ınd market and other towns further afield.[100] Since
successful merchants had bought their way into land on
the city.[101] The diarist John Evelyn went to visit Sir
state in Epping Forest in 1683, and found the area full
ınd suddenly monied men'. Child had bought property
decade earlier, and achieved a baronetcy in 1678, but
impressed by the rapid progress of a man who began as
ɔprentice, made a fortune from East India stock, and
is daughter to the eldest son of the Duke of Beaufort,
of £30,000.[102] A few years later Daniel Defoe was
the trend. He claimed during the 1720s to be able to
name '500 great estates, within a hundred miles of London, which
within eighty years past, were the possession of the ancient English
gentry, which are now bought up, and in the possession of citizens and
tradesmen, purchased fairly by money raised in trade.' In another book
he commented on their profusion in Essex and Surrey, and in yet
another on the fact that 'in the two counties of Kent and Essex only,
there was not one-fifth part of the ancient gentry remaining . . . near
200 houses of merchants and tradesmen settled in those counties with
immense wealth and estates, having purchased the estates of the
ancient gentry.'[103] A century later William Cobbett was still
bemoaning the influence of the Great Wen. Passing through Surrey, he
noted that gentry estates were still being acquired by 'new men' better
able to afford the lifestyle.[104]

Despite these claims, by no means all the wealthy Londoners who
had transferred assets into land did so at the expense of existing gentry.
From the early seventeenth century, newcomers from the city often
looked for little more than a few hundred acres and a convenient seat

---

[100] H. J. Habakkuk, 'The price of land in England, 1500–1700', in *Wirtschaft, Geschichte und Wirtschaftsgeschichte* ed. W. Abel *et al.* (Stuttgart, 1966), pp. 119–28.

[101] Sylvia Thrupp, *The Merchant Class of Medieval London* (Chicago, 1948), pp. 25–9, 378–85.

[102] E. S. de Beer (ed.), *The Diary of John Evelyn* (Oxford, 1955), vol. IV, pp. 305–6. Child's daughter, Rebecca, married Charles Somerset (1660–98) in 1682. He was the eldest surviving son of the Duke of Beaufort (created duke in 1682). After her husband's death she remarried, in 1703, John Granville, who was created Baron Granville the same year.

[103] Daniel Defoe, *Plan of the English Commerce* (1728), pp. 83–4; *Tour Through the Whole Island of Great Britain* (Harmondsworth, 1971 edn), pp. 57, 167–8, 177; *Complete English Gentleman* (1890), p. 263.

[104] William Cobbett, *Rural Rides* (Harmondsworth, 1967 edn), p. 33.

within easy reach of London, so that they could continue to enjoy the trappings of gentility and also participate in urban, genteel culture.[105] Country estates that came on to the market in south-western Essex were sometimes divided to attract Londoners for whom the ideal holding was a villa and no more than 300–400 acres.[106] Moreover, as London grew and communications improved, potential owners were able to look further afield for their weekend, holiday and eventual retirement home. Hertfordshire and Bedfordshire became popular retreats. Between 10 and 15 per cent of Hertfordshire's country house owners were newcomers from business until about 1760, and 20 per cent thereafter. Middle-aged London businessmen were buying in the county 'merely because of its rural charms and its closeness to London'.[107] Purchasers between 1760 and 1819 included eleven East India Company members (six of them directors). Arthur Young described what had happened in the county when he reported to the Board of Agriculture in 1813 that land had been divided 'by great numbers of wealthy persons, to purchase land for building villas'.[108] In Bedfordshire, according to the board's reporters, 'the great influx of wealth has of late years been the means of making . . . property more general.' Incomers had included Sir Samuel Ongley, a linen draper and director of the East India Company; Nathaniel Polhill, a city banker and tobacco merchant; and Charles Higgins, Sir Hugh Inglis and Godfrey Thornton, all of them London merchants, the last two being directors of the East India Company.[109] Contemporary sale catalogues emphasized the type of property available. One in 1817 for

[105] R. G. Lang, 'Social origins and social aspirations of Jacobean London merchants', *Economic History Review*, 2nd ser., 27 (1974), pp. 28–47; Henry Horwitz, 'London merchants in the later seventeenth century' (unpublished paper read at the University of Oxford, May 1978); Nicholas Rogers, 'Money, land and lineage: the big bourgeoisie of Hanoverian London', *Social History*, 4 (1979), pp. 448–9. Professor Rogers traces the movement towards small-scale purchasing among eighteenth-century London aldermen.

[106] Colin Shrimpton, 'The landed society and the farming community of Essex in the late eighteenth and early nineteenth centuries' (University of Cambridge, Ph.D. thesis, 1965), pp. 100–1; Lucy Sutherland, *A London Merchant, 1695–1774* (1933), p. 5.

[107] Stone and Stone, *An Open Elite?*, pp. 161–80, 202–3.

[108] William Marshall, *Review and Abstract of the County Reports to the Board of Agriculture* (York, 1818), vol. V, p. 24; Shrimpton, 'The landed society and the farming community of Essex', pp. 93–152.

[109] W. James and J. Malcolm, *General View of the Agriculture of the County of Buckingham* (1794), p. 10; Rapp, 'Social mobility in the eighteenth century', pp. 386–7.

Toddington, Bedfordshire, described 'a new brick-built and sashed house, neatly fitted up, and fit for the residence of a genteel family'.[110] As a result of these trends, by 1873 Middlesex, Surrey and Essex were among the five counties with the smallest number of large estates, while in Hertfordshire 35 per cent of the non-waste acreage was divided into properties of between 300 and 3000 acres, 7 per cent above the national average.

What happened around London was repeated on a smaller scale in the vicinity of newly expanding commercial and industrial centres elsewhere. The expansion of trade was reflected in the interest of overseas merchants in land. Hull merchants looked to acquire a seat in the East Riding of Yorkshire, and Whitehaven's merchants started buying land near to the town in the later seventeenth century. The more substantial of them acquired sizeable holdings by the mid-eighteenth century.[111] A similar trend occurred around industrial towns. The gentlemen merchants of Leeds returned much of their fortune into land, since the norm of achievement was to adopt the landowners' way of life. From his wool-trade profits William Milner spent £17,000 on a 2385-acre estate, and by 1740 the family connection with Leeds and its trade was largely severed. Six of the town's thirteen great merchant dynasties between 1700 and 1780 moved out into a major country seat.[112] Birmingham and Black Country industrialists looked for land throughout the West Midlands, many moving into Warwickshire and Shropshire. The Board of Agriculture reporter for Shropshire noted that

manufacture and commerce, the profession of arms and of the law, raise men of small fortunes to affluence, and their riches enable them to concentrate the estates of others . . . men of hereditary fortune become forced to alienate their domains, and these, perhaps, are parcelled out among purchasers of inferior wealth.[113]

Wedgwood, famed for his pottery, built Etruria and Barlaston halls, while the Peels bought Drayton Manor and Tamworth estates; and Cobbett could write scathingly of how Lord Somers had sold an estate in Worcestershire to 'a Brummingeham banker of the name of

---

[110] E. O. Payne, *Property in Land in South Bedfordshire, 1760–1832* (Bedfordshire Historical Record Society, 1946), p. 51. On movement into Kent and Sussex, see Thirsk (ed.), *The Agrarian History of England and Wales*, vol. V, pt I, p. 295.

[111] G. Jackson, *Hull in the Eighteenth Century* (Oxford, 1972), p. 112; Beckett, *Coal and Tobacco*, p. 114.

[112] R. G. Wilson, *Gentlemen Merchants* (Manchester, 1971), pp. 220–30.

[113] Marshall, *Review and Abstract*, vol. II, p. 227.

Taylor, for, it is said, seventy thousand pounds'.[114] Manufacturers moving into land were dividing up Lancashire property by the end of the eighteenth century; while seventy-three of the 250 Cheshire families recorded in *Walford's County Families* for 1879 had made their money in manufacturing or trade.[115] Affluent businessmen from Nottingham, Leicester and South Yorkshire were buying land throughout the East Midlands over the period 1670–1820, with a number of self-made men establishing secure dynasties of several generations' standing. A witness from Loughborough told the 1833 Select Committee on Agriculture that smaller estates in his area were often sold to manufacturers.[116] The Walkers, Rotherham ironmasters, began purchasing in the 1790s, and by 1806 were able to set themselves up as landed gentry proper, while other newcomers included the Foleys, Hardys, Guests, Wilkinsons and Thomas Williams, from among the metals entrepreneurs, and Arkwright and Strutt from among the textile giants.[117]

These were the well-known names, but many lesser-known businessmen also bought property. Salisbury tradesmen started purchasing land in the Avon Valley south of the town from about 1660. The Cornish tin industry offered a variety of opportunities for local entrepreneurs, and a number rapidly established themselves as country gentlemen, including the Carlyons, who had benefited from mining both tin and copper.[118] Eighteenth-century Lincolnshire newcomers included substantial tradesmen from market towns, mercers, tanners, butchers, innkeepers and bankers. A similar variety sought land in Essex in the later eighteenth and early nineteenth centuries. John Strutt of Terling, a prosperous miller, acquired sufficient land in the county to be regarded as one of its principal landowners within his own lifetime.[119] In 1833 it was

---

[114] Perkin, *The Origins of Modern English Society*, p. 87; Cobbett, *Rural Rides*, p. 388.

[115] Marshall, *Review and Abstract*, vol. IV, p. 292; vol. II, p. 227; vol. I, pp. 270–1; J. M. Lee, *Social Leaders and Public Persons* (Oxford, 1963), p. 23.

[116] Holderness, 'The land market in the East Midlands', pp. 35–6; Parl. Papers, *Report of the Select Committee on Agriculture* (1833), vol. V, p. 399.

[117] Holderness, 'The land market in the East Midlands', pp. 34–7; Perkin, *The Origins of Modern English Society*, p. 87; Thompson, *English Landed Society*, p. 120.

[118] M. O. Hernaman, 'Land use and settlement before 1850 in the Avon Valley, south of Salisbury' (University of London, Ph.D. thesis, 1980), p. 556; V. M. Chesher, 'Some Cornish landowners, 1690–1760: a social and economic study' (University of Oxford, B. Litt. thesis, 1956), pp. 16–19.

[119] Holderness, 'The English land market', pp. 565 ff.; Shrimpton, 'The landed society and the farming community of Essex', pp. 73–91.

noted that many of the ancient freeholders of North Yorkshire were selling out to prosperous purchasers from Stockton and Whitby, and from Norfolk in 1897 it was reported that yeomen were selling chiefly to people successful in trade, including butchers, dealers and horse breeders. [120]

The trend towards buying villas also reached the provinces. Leeds was ringed by small, well-kept merchant estates, with two dozen or more families acquiring only 100–300 acres. Among the 207 Lancashire textile masters known to have owned land in 1873, only thirteen held more than 3000 acres, while of those with 10 or more acres nearly 30 per cent had acquired between 100 and 500 acres. The preference was for suburban mansions within easy reach of the mill. [121] Property with even smaller acreages was increasingly built for such incomers, hence the ornamental villas which began to appear on the outskirts of towns early in the nineteenth century. These were substantial, detached residences for the business and professional classes, with an approach road, and a walled kitchen garden of perhaps 2–10 acres. In effect, they were country residences in miniature, aimed at people who in earlier times might have expected to acquire a landed estate, but who now sought merely to ape the lifestyle of the gentry. Some even had a small agricultural property attached, to satisfy the instincts of the would-be gentleman farmer. [122]

Land purchase did not bring the division of property in the provinces that was noted around London, possibly because of the small acreages often involved. When estates of 300–3000 acres are ranked by county, Surrey comes out top with 40 per cent, followed by Essex (35 per cent) and Hertfordshire (34 per cent). Kent also comes in the top seven, but while Lancashire and Shropshire were above average, Warwickshire and Staffordshire were well below. Clearly market pressures were not such as to swamp the elite through property division, and it may have been that there was a greater tendency to buy ready-made estates in the provinces. More substantial buyers may have looked to acquire a gentry estate, while those at the bottom of the scale were happy to buy the property of

---

[120] Parl. Papers, *Report of the Select Committee on Agriculture* (1833), vol. V, p. 120; Royal Commission on Agriculture Depression, *Final Report*, C. 8540 (1897), vol. XV, pt 1, p. 131, Q. 16,010.

[121] Wilson, *Gentlemen Merchants*, p. 229; A. Howe, *The Cotton Masters, 1830–1860* (Oxford, 1984), pp. 29–30, 252.

[122] T. R. Slater, 'Family, society and the ornamental villa on the fringes of English country towns', *Journal of Historical Geography*, 4 (1978), pp. 129–44.

an owner-occupier. Such men were often content to continue with their business, or to combine it with farming the new property.[123]

The expense and complication of buying a sizeable estate close to London or one of the emerging towns persuaded some families to look further afield, particularly those wanting to make a substantial landed investment. Londoners continued to play 'a surprisingly important role' in the eighteenth-century Lincolnshire land market, their numbers including such giants of the city as Sir Gilbert Heathcote and Sir Samson Gideon. In addition, Hull merchants, West Riding manufacturers, and bankers from Nottingham, Leicester and Lancashire, all made homes in the county.[124] Hampshire was also popular with Londoners. The largest purchasers in the Avon Valley south of Salisbury after 1660 tended to be from the metropolis, and Cobbett listed a series of estates in the vicinity of Whitchurch which had fallen prey to outside wealth.[125] Others looked further afield, possibly to their native counties, including the case reported from Cumbria in 1724 of 'one Mr Grisedale, a brewer in London, this countryman, who has an estate adjoining to Hewthwaite'.[126] London merchants returning 'home' to buy an estate included William Beckford who built Fonthill in Wiltshire.[127] During the nineteenth century, northern businessmen looked to the Lake District. Newcomers to the area included John Marshall, the Leeds millowner, who spent nearly £90,000 between 1810 and 1826 on property at Loweswater, Buttermere and Ullswater, and Sir John Bolton, a Liverpool merchant and slave trader. Bolton bought Storrs Hall at the turn of the century, and proceeded to build up an estate of 1000 acres. Another incomer was George Moore, who bought Whitehall in Cumberland on the profits of lace, while the Ecroyds channelled Lancashire worsted profits into 3685 acres

---

[123] Mingay, *English Landed Society*, p. 73; Thompson, *English Landed Society*, p. 21; Beckett, 'The decline of the small landowner'. Since it has been recognized for over twenty years that business purchasers usually acquired only gentry estates at most, it is somewhat surprising to find Stone and Stone arguing *against* 'the alleged fact of the ease of upward mobility by successful men of business into the higher levels of landed society', only to find that 'the numbers of purchasers and purchase-entrants were never large enough to swamp the older elite families': *An Open Elite?*, pp. 5, 279.

[124] Hill (ed.), *Letters and Papers of the Banks Family*, p. v; Holderness, 'The English land market', p. 563.

[125] Hernaman, 'Land use and settlement . . . in the Avon Valley', pp. 556–66; Cobbett, *Rural Rides*, pp. 269–71.

[126] Carlisle RO, D/Lec/170, J. Christian to the Duke of Somerset, 16 January 1724.

[127] Rogers, 'Money, land and lineage', p. 448.

around Penrith.[128] By 1886 it was reported from the Lakes that 'a new class of competitors for the ownership of the soil has arisen in the merchant princes of the manufacturing districts, who eagerly buy up any nook where they may escape from their own smoke, and enjoy pure air and bracing breezes, with shooting and fishing.'[129]

Finally, some of those who initially purchased only a small property later made a second move further afield into the countryside which signified either their retirement or their decision to turn themselves into landed gentry. This was particularly true around London, where estates changed hands rapidly, and other growing towns. Writing in 1876, J. A. Froude suggested:

watch the land tenure in any busy county in England and you will be surprised to see how rapidly a similar process is going on. I was standing a few years ago on a hill about fifteen miles from London . . . I asked my companion how long on average an estate remained about there in the same family. He answered, perhaps twenty years.[130]

Eighteenth-century Essex purchasers often bought from ex-merchants anxious to move further from the capital,[131] and the Webster family provides a good example of this transitional process. Godfrey Webster, a citizen and clothworker of London, converted part of his business fortune into Essex real estate at the end of the seventeenth century. Both he and his son extended the family interest in and around Hornchurch and Ongar, but from the 1720s the focus of attention switched to Sussex. Sir Thomas Webster, the son, inherited a commercial fortune through his wife, and in the 1720s he bought the Battle Abbey estate and the manor of Robertsbridge. He immediately turned his attention in the direction of becoming a country gentleman and an iron manufacturer, and during the 1730s and 1740s he parted with some of his Essex interests.[132] The double movement also became popular in other parts of the country. Hull merchants moved into the

[128] W. G. Rimmer, *Marshalls of Leeds, Flax Spinners, 1788–1886* (Cambridge, 1960), pp. 99–102; Searle, '"The odd corner of England"', pp. 224, 333–4.

[129] C. Webster, 'On the farming of Westmorland', *JRASE*, 2nd ser., 4 (1868), p. 8.

[130] Froude, 'On the uses of a landed gentry', p. 677.

[131] Shrimpton, 'The landed society and the farming community of Essex', pp. 101–2. This was exactly the route taken by the fictional Sir Andrew Freeport: *The Spectator*, 549, 29 November 1712.

[132] J. A. Brent, *A Catalogue of the Battle Abbey Estate Archives* (East Sussex RO, 1973), pp. 3–16.

popular Wolds villages west of the town, but on retirement uprooted themselves further afield,[133] and northern industrialists followed a similar practice. Merchants and industrialists from Liverpool, Manchester and the other developing towns were reported in the mid-nineteenth century to be leaving Lancashire 'when they seek a permanent investment for their property in land', in search of 'a more genial climate, a more fertile soil, a higher class of farmers and farming, and a more tempting investment than Lancashire can offer'. Usually they went south.[134]

Summarizing the net result of these trends among newcomers is not easy. Despite the turnover of land, the end result is usually considered to have been a state of near balance between different groups,[135] but some areas were obviously more prone to newcomer penetration than others. Office, law and brewing wealth were prominent in Hertfordshire, but virtually nonexistent in Northumberland. Manufacturers bought their way into Lancashire, but the only one to penetrate Northamptonshire was an ironmaster in 1800. Five shipping, mining and metallurgy entrepreneurs bought their way into Northumberland after 1835, whereas in Hertfordshire – apart from brewers – a local paper manufacturer and a couple of northcountry textile manufacturers were the only businessmen to make much headway in the county's land market.[136] Evidence drawn from Shropshire, Oxfordshire and Essex indicates that infiltration was more likely in the eighteenth than in the nineteenth century,[137] while the activities of individual groups tends to confirm this trend. The majority of judges called to the bench after 1820 did not invest extensively in property; only thirty (29 per cent) owned land with gross rents exceeding £1000, reflecting a preference for public funds and other securities. Most of the forty-six men who held government war supply contracts between 1775 and 1783 were leading members of the London merchant community, and at least eight bought country estates. They included Sir George Wombwell, who re-acquired ancestral property at Beckenham in Kent alienated in less prosperous times. However, none appears to have purchased on a large scale, and some of the wealthiest still had their residence in London when they

[133] K. J. Allison, *'Hull Gent. Seeks Country Residence', 1750–1850* (York, 1981).
[134] W. J. Garnett, 'Farming of Lancashire', *JRASE* 10 (1849), p. 6
[135] G. E. Mingay, *The Gentry* (1976), p. 59.
[136] Stone and Stone, *An Open Elite?*, pp. 204–8.
[137] Thompson, *English Landed Society*, pp. 122–7.

died. On the other hand, the three that received baronetcies were among the land purchasers.[138]

The trend towards purchasing less land can also be seen from John Bateman's analysis of 1883. Of the 700 or so largest estates in the United Kingdom no more than 7 per cent had been constructed from business fortunes, and less than 10 per cent were the product of business and professional wealth created since 1780. Many newcomers had simply not acquired sufficient land to appear in his analysis of those with 2000 acres or £2000 gross income per annum. Fourteen out of 43 brewing families holding landed estates in the 1870s (33 per cent) owned less than 2000 acres. The territorial stakes necessary for admission into the aristocracy were beginning to slip in such a way as to permit the entrance of men with a home but not necessarily a large landed estate in the country; indeed, the coming of the railway was gradually permitting the 'house in the country' to vie with, and possibly even to succeed, the country house.[139] Up to two-fifths of the new millionaires of nineteenth-century England who were in a position to buy land prior to the 1870s may have taken this course of action, although the extent of opting out of landownership by the new middle classes remains in dispute.[140]

Land prices offer further evidence of the change in emphasis among purchasers. For most of the period down to 1700 the

---

[138] Duman, *The Judicial Bench*, pp. 127–40; Norman Baker, *Government and Contractors* (1971), ch. 9. Wombwell's case appears to be a rare example of a family revitalizing its declining fortunes through commercial enterprise.

[139] A fictional but illustrative example of this trend to a villa, or a house in the country within commuting distance of London, is provided by John Galsworthy's *Forsyte Saga* (1922). Central to this tale of intrigue and feuding in a rising bourgeois family is a typical villa-type property with 20 acres at Robin Hill (p. 380). It is described as within sight of the Epsom grandstand on a clear day (p. 390), and close enough to London to travel up daily, first by carriage, and later by car.

[140] D. W. Gutzke, 'The social status of landed brewers in Britain since 1840', *Histoire sociale – Social History*, 17 (1984), pp. 110–13; Rubinstein, 'New men of wealth', pp. 144–5; F. M. L. Thompson, 'English Landed Society in the nineteenth-century', in *The Power of the Past* ed. P. Thane, *et al.* (Cambridge, 1984), p. 211. By using Bateman's threshold Rubinstein seems to have set an artificially high qualification on what constituted a significant foray into landownership: Michie, 'Income, expenditure and investment', pp. 67–8. However, a minimum possession of 2,000 acres was required for inclusion in Burke's *Landed Gentry* down to 1914, which suggests some contemporary justification for the figure: Scott, *The Upper Classes*, p. 91. A powerful critique of Rubinstein's view is contained in F. M. L. Thompson's as yet unpublished paper, 'The landed aristocracy and business elites in Victorian Britain'.

formula for calculating the capital value of freehold land was twenty years' purchase at the full annual value at which it could be let to a tenant (rack rent). Other formulas applied when a house and park were involved, and when other forms of tenure were included. Copyhold and three-life leaseholds, for example, were valued at fourteen years' purchase.[141] These rules seem to have applied nationwide, with any variations commencing from the principle of twenty years' purchase. A real land market emerged only in the course of the seventeenth century, but for much of the immediate post-1660 period prices were depressed at between sixteen and eighteen years' purchase. They rose in the 1690s, fell back from around 1707, but began to rise at such a rate from about 1713 that the old adage of twenty years' purchase was finally and irreparably breached. Prices gradually climbed to stand at between twenty-five and thirty years' purchase for much of the second half of the eighteenth century.[142]

The old calculations about the amount of income a given piece of land would produce in the foreseeable future had been replaced by new considerations about the scale of property on the market and the number of potential purchasers, as well as the size of resources they would be willing to invest. Just how complicated the calculations became is apparent from the suggestions made by Lord Newark's steward in regard to the sale of an 83-acre farm in 1798:

in my opinion [Mr Launder] ought to pay for convenience, as your estate lies intermixed with his, and by purchasing yours, it will make his own become of greater value. Consequently you have a right to expect more of him than a market price, and particularly more so, as you would not sell it, was it not for the sake of accommodating him; and you therefore have a right to set £3,000 upon it instead of £2,500. If he will give you that there is no great harm in parting with the farm.[143]

These complicated considerations in turn reflected the opening up of new investment opportunities. The old joint-stock trading companies had always offered investment openings, and a number of aristocrats had taken up the offers. The Duke of Portland held £10,000 stock in the New East India Company in 1698, and

[141] Giles Jacob, *The Country Gentleman's Vade Mecum* (1717).

[142] Christopher Clay, 'The price of freehold land in the later seventeenth and eighteenth centuries', *Economic History Review*, 2nd ser., 27 (1974), pp. 173–89.

[143] BL Egerton MSS, 3516 fol. 178, William Sanday to Lord Newark, 22 January 1798.

between 1689 and 1707 a total of twenty-nine members of the upper house had investments in the company, mostly in excess of £1000. During the 1690s this type of opportunity increased considerably as a result of government efforts to fund the expensive French wars. As the Treasury borrowed increasing amounts, investment in government became a highly profitable enterprise. Nine peers and thirty MPs were among the proprietors of bank stock when the Bank of England was founded in 1694. Peers who supported the 1688 revolution and the subsequent war effort inevitably felt a moral obligation to continue subscribing, and among those with bank holdings in 1709 was an array of revolution families, including Godolphin, Halifax, Marlborough, Newcastle, Somers and Sunderland.[144]

Although the link between the rate of interest and the price of land was forged during the post-revolution years, possibly the most significant event was the South Sea Bubble crisis of 1720. The South Sea Company was founded in 1711 as a Tory rival to the Whig-dominated Bank of England, and it was essentially a finance corporation designed to consolidate £9 million of public debt which was not secured against taxation. As a result of this scheme, and the absence of proper controls on the company, speculation was rife in the opening months of 1720, with the price of stock rising from 128 (par 100) in January, to a peak of 1050 on 24 June. In August the Bubble burst, and the price plummeted to 290 on 1 October. Around 30,000 creditors were affected, and although a few had been sufficiently clear-headed to dispose of their holdings before the Bubble burst – including Lord Gower, who disposed of most of his £20,000 stock in time – the majority were not so lucky. In July 1720 the Duke of Chandos reckoned himself a net gainer by £855,000, but by September he owed £70,000 and could not raise £10,000 by any means. Thomas Coke paid £48,000 for stock, and his losses totalled £38,000. Lord Lonsdale borrowed £20,000 to speculate. For many the crash was a disaster. The Duke of Portland took a colonial governorship and spent the rest of his life in Jamaica, a course of action considered also by Lonsdale, quite apart from his reputed efforts to stab one of the company's directors. Joseph Pennington of Muncaster in Cumberland was said to be going 'from church to church praying for better times', while confident reports were abroad about his fellow countrymen: Sir Wilfrid Lawson's 'head

---

[144] P. G. M. Dickson, *The Financial Revolution in England, 1688–1756* (1967). Information on peerage holdings courtesy of Clyve Jones.

is turned', Lord Carlisle was 'undone', and Robert Lowther of Maulds Meaburn had lost £30,000. The Duke of Chandos wrote that 'the distress mankind was in was inconceivable and a general bankruptcy was apprehended.'[145]

The repercussions of the crash were considerable, not merely for individual families, but also for the price of land. Those who had made a windfall profit, or had escaped without damage from the débâcle, looked to land purchase as a secure haven for their money. In eighteen months after the Bubble burst Lord Cowper invested £13,000 in land, which was as much as during the previous thirteen years.[146] With so much money around, purchase prices soared, albeit briefly, only falling as impoverished owners put property on the market, and the estates of the company's directors were put up for sale.[147] Although 1720 was unique, the link between the two sets of prices was firmly established. Those with an eye to purchasing property took careful note of the prevailing rate of interest. Rather than pay £7000 for an estate in reversion in 1726, the Duke of Chandos preferred to keep the capital where it would yield £400–500 for certain. Moreover whereas in 1725 he sold Herefordshire property for twenty-four years' purchase, by 1729 he was looking for higher prices because

the interest of money in the public funds being then one per cent higher than it is at present, lands were then in proportion less valuable, and it is very well known that since interest of money came to be so low the

---

[145] Wordie, *Estate Management in Eighteenth-Century England*, p. 138; Baker and Baker, *The Life and Circumstances of James Brydges*, pp. 80–1; Parker, *Coke of Norfolk*, pp. 13–20; J. V. Beckett, 'Cumbrians and the South Sea Bubble', *Transactions of the Cumberland and Westmorland Antiquarian and Archaeological Society*, new ser., 82 (1982), pp. 141–50; G. Davies, 'Letters from James Brydges, created Duke of Chandos, to Henry St John, created Viscount Bolingbroke', *Huntington Library Bulletin* (April 1936), p. 155. There were many other examples, among them Wake, *The Brudenells*, pp. 240–1, and, for a contemporary account of destitution, *The Gentleman's Journal and Tradesman's Companion*, 5 (29 April 1721). Rumours spread like wildfire, hence Dr William Stratford's comment to Edward Harley, 4 November 1720, that 'we are now told here positively that Lord Sunderland himself has been deeply engaged in South Sea, some say he has sold out, others that he is still in': HMC *Portland* MSS, vol. VII, p. 282.

[146] C. G. A. Clay, 'Two families and their estates: the Grimstons and Cowpers, 1650–1815' (University of Cambridge, Ph.D. thesis, 1966), p. 215.

[147] Cambridge University Library, C(H) 88/43, provides an account of the real (£693,173) and personal (£1,396,923) estates of the company's directors sold by the end of 1726.

monied people have endeavoured to vest it in land and thereby raised the price of estates over the whole kingdom.[148]

Money was retained in the funds until such time as a suitable land purchase became available. Thus, when Earl Temple was negotiating for property in Buckinghamshire in 1753, he wanted the matter resolving quickly

to enable me to pay the money, as I have a great part of it ready in India Bonds. Those may be deposited in the custody of any eminent banker and assigned to you at the price they shall bear on any fixed day, you to receive the interest and the rents of the estate till such time as the purchase can be completed.[149]

War came to be a vital consideration. In periods of conflict the price of government stock was low and its yield high. Consequently mortgages were hard to come by, and land prices were depressed. The type of considerations involved were stated in 1753 in a letter to George Grenville:

The value of the land rises daily and the high premium on the public funds shew clearly the value of money. I know what my estate produces and have calculated what I should recover from £8,800 vested in 3 per cent annuities, and cannot make an abatement in my price set upon the estate without doing myself injustice. If peace continues two or three years longer I am persuaded I shall make more of the estate than I asked of you for it, and if a war, which God avert, should break out the price of [land] will fall in Norfolk as well as in Oxfordshire, and my only reason for selling in the one is to purchase in the other.[150]

Lord Temple was advised in 1771 that, in view of 'the uncertainty of the continuance of the pacific reverie', it would be better to lend money on good security 'than to suffer it to continue in the Funds in these times of uncertainty'.[151]

Prospective purchasers were no longer timing their acquisition in relation to the potential return on an estate. Once land reached thirty years' purchase, the net return of $2\frac{1}{2}$ per cent was rather less

---

[148] Huntington Library, ST57/27, fol. 224, Duke of Chandos to Mr Brydges, 22 January 1726; ST57/33, fol. 120, Chandos to Mr Jones, 27 May 1729.

[149] Huntington Library, STG/425, Earl Temple to E. Bacon, 18 September 1753.

[150] Huntington Library, STG/365, E. Bacon to George Grenville, 18 August 1753.

[151] Huntington Library, STG/418, Thomas Astle to Earl Temple, 7 August 1771.

than the 4 per cent which most money would make when invested.
Potential purchasers began to time their move into land according
to the investment alternatives available, and it is hardly surprising
that they bought only as much as was necessary to produce the social
status they sought. William Marshall noted in the 1790s that 'the
interest of the funds will always have more or less influence on the
price of land. Hence, those who wish to secure lands at a moderate
price, should purchase when the funds are advantageous.' A
correspondent told the Earl of Sheffield in 1807 that 'faith in funded
property is tottering daily and the value of land rising in
proportion', and an anonymous author considering the likely effects
of peace in 1815 reflected that, as after the American war, the
retreat of government from the market would permit 'loans and
discounts on fair terms'.[152] Landowners responded by switching
their interests around according to the rate of interest. Sir John
Griffin Griffin held £12,000 stock in 1765, and over the next
three decades his varied holdings included bank stock, 1756 3½ per
cents, East India bonds, and both 4 per cent and 3 per cent
consolidated annuities (i.e. consolidated government securities). At
his death the total holding was valued at £14,000, but it had varied
considerably since 1765.[153] Not surprisingly, however, as land
became a social commodity even the link with interest rates
weakened. As prices rose to as much as forty years' purchase in the
1860s and 1870s, variations in interest rates were no longer regarded
as an explanatory factor.[154] Clearly such a situation could never have
come about if wealthy businessmen and entrepreneurs had expected
to invest considerable sums in land. Although rent remained the
major determinant of capital value, it was only when land had
become an item of conspicuous social consumption that it was
possible for newcomers to take so little interest in the expected rate of
return.

[152] William Marshall, *The Rural Economy of the Midland Counties* (2 vols, 1790), vol.
I, p. 16; Clements Library, Sheffield Papers, R. Way to the Earl of Sheffield, 6
December 1807; anon., *Thoughts on the Effects of Peace on Landed Property* (1815), p. 14.

[153] J. D. Williams, 'The finances of an eighteenth-century Essex nobleman', *Essex
Archaeology and History*, 9 (for 1977, 1979), p. 118.

[154] Norton, Trist and Gilbert, 'A century of land values'; G. H. Peters *et al.*, 'A
century of land values, 1781–1880', *Oxford Agrarian Studies*, II (1982), pp. 93–107.

ALTERNATIVE INVESTMENTS

As a key for unlocking the door to social and political status and power, land .retained its significance down to the 1880s, if not beyond. At that point a combination of agricultural depression, the partially successful conclusion to the long campaign to reform the estate settlement legislation, and the shifting balance of political power in the state finally began to deflate the mystique of land; indeed, almost before the ink was dry on the multifarious calculations of John Bateman, the greater landowners began to offload property. Land started to come on to the market during the 1880s and 1890s, but although sellers were ready to accept lower prices than had been current in the middle decades of the century much of the property available failed to find a purchaser. The real tidal change arrived in the years 1910–14, as prices recovered and owners took the opportunity to sell. In one week during June 1910 over 72,000 acres in thirty-six counties were offered for sale in England, and during the corresponding week a year later the total rose to 98,000 acres. In 1912 no fewer than nineteen peers were believed to have property for sale, and by the outbreak of the First World War it was calculated that perhaps 800,000 acres had changed hands over the previous five years.[155] Yet, even as the estate system began to break up, peerages were still going predominantly to men with property – even if they were first-generation purchasers. The real collapse was postponed until after the 1914–18 war had shattered much of what remained of the old society.

By 1914 even defenders of the traditional order could hardly deny that the position of landowners was radically different from that of their forebears in 1660. At the Restoration most landowners were just that; men who lived on the rents of their estates, with few if any other investments. By 1914 the owner who maintained such a singleminded concern was increasingly difficult to find.[156] The estates which survived most successfully tended to be those where land alone was not necessarily the principal source of income. In both Bedfordshire and Hertfordshire the estates which best maintained their size during the half-century after 1873 were the ones on

---

[155] Thompson, *English Landed Society*, pp. 318–20, 322; H. Durant, 'The development of landownership with special reference to Bedfordshire, 1773–1925', *Sociological Review* (1936), pp. 85–98.

[156] He generally turned up most often in novels, in the form, for example, of Roger Carbery in Anthony Trollope's *The Way We Live Now* (1875).

which rents had been allied with trade or industry.[157] Mineral incomes and urban ground rents were invaluable to those lucky enough to enjoy them during the 1880s and 1890s, while many trod a path into the City. The experiences of these years changed the attitudes displayed towards alternative investments, particularly as it became clear that confidence in the security of land was misplaced. Many families had abandoned the stockmarket after the experiences of 1720. Between 1720 and 1842 the Cokes of Holkham did not purchase securities to more than a negligible amount, and the Leveson-Gowers also turned their backs on the City.[158] Some were undeterred. Even in 1724 the Duke of Chandos was complaining that landed profits were so low that he often 'repent[ed] that I have laid out so much in land and wish I have kept my money in the Funds'.[159] Lord Dudley inherited South Sea stock, bank stock and other paper securities in 1725 with a face value of £21,110, while the inveterate speculator Lord Lonsdale had 'above £11,000' in the funds at his death in 1751. Thomas Thornhill of Fixby in Yorkshire had holdings in the 1740s amounting to £96,350, while Sir James Lowther of Whitehaven probably had the largest aristocratic holding of his generation. Often, however, it was women whose names were prominent in the City, and stock was used in marriage settlements and to support widows and spinster sisters of genteel families. In 1751 twenty-nine aristocrats or their wives and widows appeared among the voting proprietors of the Bank of England, but despite this the City was dominated by London-based mercantile groups, and landowners did not make a significant contribution at any level.[160]

In the course of the nineteenth century, and particularly towards the end of the century, aristocrats again sought out the City. After seventy years of self-imposed exile from the City, the Leveson-Gowers began to acquire consols in the 1790s, and by 1816 the second Marquess of Stafford held stocks totalling £411,534. This had doubled to £1.1 million by 1833, at which point the annual

---

[157] Durant, 'The development of landownership . . . Bedfordshire', p. 94.

[158] Parker, *Coke of Norfolk*, p. 20; Wordie, *Estate Management in Eighteenth-Century England*, pp. 138, 152.

[159] Huntington Library, ST57/24, fol. 28, Duke of Chandos to Captain Oakley, 16 April 1724. In 1741 Chandos was still buying lottery tickets, 'it being the only method I have I think now of putting myself in fortune's way': ibid., STB/22/64, Chandos to John Farquarson, 19 January 1741.

[160] Raybould, *The Economic Emergence of the Black Country*, p. 29; Beckett, 'Cumbrians and the South Sea Bubble', and *Coal and Tobacco*, pp. 211–19; Sir John Clapham, *The Bank of England* (Cambridge, 1944), vol. I, p. 285.

dividend of £34,000 was producing a net income probably greater than all the family's landed estates combined. At Holkham the second Lord Leicester began investing in the stockmarket during the 1840s and 1850s. By the 1880s his investments included railways in England and America, government bonds, mortgages and breweries.[161] The Portlands were also heavily involved. In 1844 capital invested in the funds yielded £13,000 a year, and by the 1870s fines for renewal of Marylebone leases were immediately invested in consols. In 1872 the face value of consols holdings totalled over £232,000 before sales raised £70,000 to finance a loan. This left the consols total at £177,000, but further investments had increased it to over £280,000 by 1877. Together with other loans, this contributed to a dividend income of £11,000 in 1872, and over £14,000 in 1877. The family were just one of many who were protecting themselves against agricultural difficulties in the 1880s by acquiring a liquid equities portfolio. Others kept themselves afloat by selling books and works of art. In 1892, for example, the fifth Earl Spencer sold his private library for £210,000, with which he paid off a mortgage debt of £54,000 and built up his equities portfolio.[162]

STABILITY OF LANDOWNERSHIP

For all the tribulations of the 1880s and 1890s, most of the great estates at the end of the century had been in place in 1700; indeed, nine-tenths of the richest owners in Bateman's survey lived on an accumulation of wealth which predated the industrial revolution. A few of these territorial empires had changed relatively little through time, although the majority had grown in size, and through the period aggregation was more frequent than division. The capacity of owners to hold their estates together through time, and to add to them both by purchase, and more particularly via inheritance, may

---

[161] Wordie, *Estate Management in Eighteenth-Century England*, p. 152; E. Richards, 'An anatomy of the Sutherland fortune: income, consumption, investments and returns, 1780–1880', *Business History*, 21 (1979), p. 50; Spring, 'Land and politics in Edwardian England', pp. 22–3.

[162] Nottingham University Library, Pwk 503a, Duke of Portland to Marquess of Titchfield, 19 May 1844; Nottinghamshire RO, DD4P/57/30, 31, St Marylebone estate; Spring, 'Land and politics in Edwardian England', pp. 22–7, points out that exactly how much was transferred in this way is unknown. The City could, however, prove more hazardous than land: S. D. Chapman, 'Sudely and the City: the financial problems of the fourth Lord Sudely' (forthcoming).

even have narrowed the apex of the pyramid. Gregory King and Patrick Colquhoun recognized social gradations, but no amount of juggling with their income figures suggests that they recognized the kind of super-elite Bateman identified. Even Sanford and Townsend, writing only a decade prior to 1873, underestimated the number of great estates by more than 30 per cent.[163]

Contemporaries looked upon what they regarded as the monopoly of land as a consequence of the strict settlement, and restrictions in the land market. According to Adam Badeau:

The importance of keeping consequence and power in the hands of a few, is so much considered that even if an estate is not entailed by will or settlement, the law steps in to enforce the sacred principle of pri-mogeniture, and whenever a man dies without a will the eldest son inherits all the land. More even than this, in order to limit the ownership of the soil every impediment is placed by the State in the way of transfer . . . one of the most difficult things to do in all England is to purchase landed property . . . The tendency therefore is steadily to the disap-pearance of small estates, and the accretion of larger ones . . . And this system is not only the result of circumstances . . . it is the object and aim of present legislation and politics.[164]

Some commentators went further, to argue that accumulation was primarily an eighteenth-century phenomenon. In retrospect, however, these views seem too simple. Families certainly regarded their property as a trust to be passed from generation to generation, but the development of the strict settlement could not of itself have created a monopoly. Land still came on to the market with some frequency, and many families did not stay the course. Generally the greater owners appear to have survived more successfully than their lesser neighbours, but much of the time this was only possible via the contortions of special remainders, and enforced name changings in order to give a fictional appearance of continuity.[165] Holding the estate together, particularly the central block surrounding the chief mansion house, was a critical consideration, a work almost of piety,

[163] J. L. Sanford and M. Townsend, *The Great Governing Families of England* (2 vols, Edinburgh, 1865), gave pen-portraits of thirty-one greater families, and mapped what they took to be the 207 great houses.

[164] Badeau, *Aristocracy in England*, pp. 243–4.

[165] Stone and Stone, *An Open Elite?*, pp. 126–42. Evidence from Nottinghamshire suggests families at all social levels survived through these methods: Sheila Aley, 'The Nottinghamshire landowners and their estates, *c.* 1660–*c.* 1840' (University of Nottingham Ph.D. thesis, 1985), pp. 105 ff.

to which end most of the more substantial families planned and plotted with more or less success.

Below the greater landowners Bateman's squires and greater yeomen (to distinguish them from the essentially social rather than economic category of gentry) were probably less successful in the longer run at maintaining their holdings. Here, however, the difficulty of interpreting contemporary evidence is at its most acute. The declining lesser gentry seem to have been almost as constant a historical phenomenon as their rising counterparts, if the anguished tone of contemporary writing is to be believed. In 1669 Samuel Pepys wrote of 'the old rule . . . that a family might remain 50 miles from London 100 years, 100 miles off from London 200 years, and so, farther or nearer London, more or less years'. Even in his day such maxims no longer applied. He pointed to 'the decay of gentlemen's families in the country', and such sentiments were echoed time and again in the eighteenth century.[166] Various studies have depicted the decline of gentry estates,[167] and comparisons of material from tithe surveys and the *Return of Owners of Land* confirm the volatility of the smaller owners. Despite the fact that it was still possible to argue in the 1870s that 'the first step for a wealthy *parvenu* is to buy up land right and left',[168] it seems likely that most newcomers were buying only relatively small properties, hence the modern conclusion that the overall gentry holding did not diminish through time; in other words, whatever happened to individual families, the total land owned by the group was not diminished.

The trend away from large-scale land purchase was long term and may have been barely perceptible to contemporaries. London, even in the early eighteenth century, already had a mercantile plutocracy, many members of which happily remained within the confines of the city despite their enormous wealth. A knighthood became their hoped-for reward, and thoughts of founding a dynasty seem not to have troubled them. Provincial towns began to acquire

---

[166] R. C. Latham and W. Matthews (eds), *The Diary of Samuel Pepys*, vol. IX: *1668–1669* (1976), p. 550; J. P. Cooper, 'The social distribution of land and men in England, 1436–1700', *Economic History Review*, 2nd ser., 20 (1967), p. 434; W. Allen, *Ways and Means of Raising the Value of Land* (1736); anon. *A Letter to a Freeholder on the Late Reduction of the Land Tax* (1732), pp. 33–4; Lord Nugent, *Considerations on a Reduction of the Land Tax* (1749), pp. 22–3; *A Letter to Sir T. Bunbury Bt . . . on the Poor Rate . . .*, by a *Suffolk Gentleman* (1795), pp. 4–5.

[167] Two recent studies are R. J. Colyer, 'Nanteos: a landed estate in decline, 1800–1930', *Ceredigion*, 9 (1980), pp. 58–77, and C. Towse, *A Garton Estate History, 1537–1800* (Cardiff, 1980).

[168] Howard Evans, *Our Old Nobility* (1879), vol. II, p. 226.

similar groups over time, as part of the development of an urban
culture in which towndwelling became increasingly respectable.[169]
For this reason many men tried to have the best of both worlds – a
villa on the outskirts of a town, permitting them the benefits of
land without losing the advantages of urban life. Some still
deliberately set out to found a family, as was the case with the Leeds
flax merchant John Marshall,[170] but the logic of large-scale land
purchase was increasingly tenuous. It took perhaps two or three
generations in some areas to penetrate county society, let alone
London, while the coveted title all too often proved elusive. After a
century of active creations, one-third of the greatest owners in the
land in 1883 did not have so much as a baronetcy. Nineteenth-
century Lincolnshire has even been described by its historian as
notable for its untitled aristocracy.

Ultimately much depended on where a family resided. After
comparing Hertfordshire and Northumberland, Lawrence Stone
concluded that they were 'utterly different societies'.[171] In the
forsaken wastes of pre-Romantic Cumbria no one challenged the
gradual property accumulation of the Lonsdales, and both small
owning and small farming prospered. Across the Pennines in
Northumberland the established greater owners were hardly
challenged in the land market. Elsewhere the situation was rather
different. Around London newcomers from law and business fanned
out into the countryside, breaking up the existing land pattern and
leavening the traditional lump of landed society. On a lesser scale,
newcomers also penetrated the countryside around the new
industrial and commercial centres, but they paid relatively little
attention to counties distant from such centres, unless they were
looking to found a family rather than to acquire amenity land. But
it still took courage to opt out altogether. As later chapters will
show, the all-pervasive importance of property ownership turned it
into the prime symbol of achievement, of having taken a responsible
stake in the nation. A man purchased the perquisites of a lifestyle.
To purchase beyond the minimum was to buy for the family, to
acquire a trust for generations to come: to cultivate the trappings of
the aristocratic family.

---

[169] P. Borsay, 'The English urban renaissance: the development of provincial urban
culture, *c.* 1680–*c.* 1760', *Social History*, 2 (1977), pp. 581–603; E. P. Thompson,
'Eighteenth-century English society: class struggle without class', *Social History*, 3
(1978), pp. 142–3.

[170] Rimmer, *Marshalls of Leeds*, p. 101.

[171] Stone and Stone, *An Open Elite?*, p. 209.

Chapter Three

The Making of the Aristocracy: The Channels of Admission

Landownership, although an essential qualification, was no guarantee that a man would be able to penetrate the aristocracy himself, or prepare an entrance for his family. Adam Badeau noted in 1886 that, although wealth was an essential qualification for the peerage, other attributes played an important part. Politics and marriage were significant openings, while some occupations were more likely to produce the desired result than others. Physicians, for example, never succeeded, while 'the great brewers nearly all attain to the aristocratic degree.'[1] Disentangling the maze of paths into the aristocracy is an exercise fraught with difficulty, but there is no doubt about the desire to succeed. Alexis de Tocqueville explained the absence of middle-class hostility towards the aristocracy on the grounds that they were concerned not to destroy but to enter the group: 'the result was that everyone who hovered on its outskirts nursed the agreeable illusion that he belonged to it and joined forces with it in the hope of acquiring

---

[1] Adam Badeau, *Aristocracy in England* (1886), pp. 260–1. Brewers seem to have been relatively favoured entrants into society. Samuel Whitbread had no difficulty penetrating Bedfordshire society in the second half of the eighteenth century, although his family had owned land in the county prior to amassing the brewing fortune: Dean Rapp, 'Social mobility in the eighteenth century: the Whitbreads of Bedfordshire, 1720–1815', *Economic History Review*, 2nd ser., 27 (1974), pp. 380–9. Brewers also penetrated Hertfordshire society: Lawrence Stone and Jeanne C. Fawtier Stone, *An Open Elite? England, 1540–1880* (Oxford, 1984), pp. 204–8. Charles Dickens made Herbert Pocket remind readers of *Great Expectations* (1860; Harmondsworth, 1965), p. 203, that 'I don't know why it should be a crack thing to be a brewer; but it is indisputable that while you cannot possibly be genteel and bake, you may be as genteel as never was and brew.' D. W. Gutzke, 'The social status of landed brewers in Britain since 1840', *Histoire Sociale – Social History*, 17 (1984), p. 106, suggests reasons for this easy assimilation including the traditional nature of the trade and its approximation with the gentry lifestyle.

prestige or some practical advantage under its aegis.'[2] Both Walter
Bagehot and Henry James commented on the willing acceptance of
hierarchy in England, and according to Adam Badeau 'hereditary
permanent rank is what most Englishmen prize above all earthly
honours. It is the permanency, especially, that they value.'[3] Nor were
aspirants slow in coming forward. Applications for peerages and for
promotions survive in many collections of papers, particularly those of
prime ministers.[4] Among the supplicants in the mid-eighteenth
century was the fourth Earl of Cardigan, who badgered monarchs and
ministers alike to revive the dukedom of Montagu on his behalf, and
who finally succeeded on the coat-tails of the equally ambitious Earl of
Northumberland.[5]

No one course of action existed which was guaranteed to project a
man and his family into the aristocracy. Acceptance varied according
to the type of family background and the area of the country, as well as
changing through time, but a number of guiding principles existed to
which most aspirants adhered. The first simply involved waiting, since
longevity and patience were vital attributes for making progress. As a
result, the family founder seldom progressed very far, but time spent
in this aristocratic purgatory could usefully be employed pursuing
some more active principles, such as building a manor house,
extending the property, acquiring a coat of arms, intermarrying with
the local elite, and ensuring a proper education for the next generation.
Careful pursuit of these practical goals normally led in time to an offer
of the hand of fellowship, even if it did take the form of an invitation
to hold the expensive and unpopular post of high sheriff. The sure sign

[2] Alexis de Tocqueville, *The Old Regime and the French Revolution* (1856; New
York, 1955), pp. 88–9.

[3] Geoffrey Best, *Mid-Victorian Britain, 1851–70* (1979 edn), p. 260; Badeau,
Aristocracy in England, p. 39.

[4] For Sir Robert Walpole, Cambridge University Library, C(H) P80/323, undated
memorial of Sir John Meres for the title Viscount Lanesborough, and 324/1–2,
undated petition of Viscount Micklethwait for promotion (he held an Irish viscountcy
in 1727–33). Among the Duke of Newcastle's papers are a series of requests for
peerages, lists of men to be promoted, and even an account of extinctions and
creations in George II's reign: BL Add. MSS, 32,995 fols 52, 258, 260; 32,996, fol.
397; 32,997, fols 193–4; 32,998, fol. 413; 32,999, fols 142–3. Requests to the Earl
of Shelburne (prime minister, 1782–3) survive in Clements Library, Lacaita–
Shelburne MSS (letters for those years), and for William Pitt the Younger among his
family papers in the Public RO (PRO 30/8/101–363). In addition, see Duke of
Argyle, *Intimate Society Letters of the Eighteenth Century* (1910), vol. I, p. 326, for a
letter of Pitt to the Earl of Galloway, 9 May 1789, delicately deflating his pretensions
to a British peerage.

[5] Joan Wake, *The Brudenells of Deene* (1953), pp. 267–76.

of local acceptance was to be admitted to the commission of the peace. Progress thereafter could be made in a number of ways. Representing the locality in Parliament was a good bet, and service to a particular party or the state could prove to be a profitable channel of promotion. However, the problem here was that getting into Parliament required a substantial landed estate and an aristocratic patron (for much of the period), and state service was largely determined by restrictive practices in civil and military promotion. Each stage of the process had to be tackled separately, and there was no guarantee that a particular family would even make the next grade. The English aristocracy may have been open to all comers, but the path lay through a maze and not along a motorway.

FAMILY PEDIGREE

To be considered for membership of the aristocracy, a family had first to be able to show its pedigree. Daniel Defoe's view was that only the third generation of a new family could be accepted into county society,[6] and even in the later nineteenth century Hippolyte Taine believed that it took a generation or two for a family to become deeply embedded in county society.[7] Establishing a pedigree became a matter of great concern, hence the tedious lists which filled the early county histories produced in the later seventeenth and eighteenth centuries.[8] In the nineteenth century this effort was channelled into that indispensable guide to the upper class, Burke's *Landed Gentry*, which was first published in 1833 with the intention of recording the pedigrees of commoners who possessed considerable estates but did not

---

[6] Daniel Defoe, *Complete English Gentleman* (1890 edn), p. 14, lamented what he saw as the declining interest in pedigree in his own day, recounting a mythical conversation between two gentlemen:

'I am Aubrey de Vere, Earl of Oxford,' says the earl; 'my father was Aubrey de Vere, Earl of Oxford; my grandfather was Earl of Oxford; my great-grandfather was Francis de Vere, lieutenant-general to Queen Elizabeth; his father Horatio de Vere, colonel of Horse, and so back to a long race.' 'I am William, Lord ____, my father was the Lord Mayor of London, and my grandfather was the Lord knows who, and so I am of as good a race as any of you.'

[7] Hippolyte Taine, *Notes on England* (1872), p. 173.

[8] William Dugdale's *Antiquities of Warwickshire* (1656), the prototype of these great compilations, was dedicated to 'the gentry of Warwickshire'. Pedigrees, heraldry and engravings of country seats proved a successful formula for raising the money to publish such works.

claim hereditary honours. It began with about 400 families, but broadened its scope over time to include those who had made their fortune in industry and trade, but had also acquired land; indeed, substantial ownership remained a necessary condition of entry until 1914.[9] Unfortunately the need for a pedigree produced some spurious connections. Falsifying pedigrees was nothing new – Joseph Addison commented scathingly on the practice in 1714 – but Burke's publications offered apparent legitimacy to some highly dubious claims.[10] Despite Burke's claims as a rigorous revisionist, in 1877 E. A. Freeman, Regius Professor of History at Oxford, launched a stinging attack on his works. He argued that many of the pedigrees which purported to stretch back into the Middle Ages were either mythical or, in many cases, 'the work of deliberate invention'. In turning the pages of Burke's work, he concluded, 'we light on much wild nonsense.'[11]

The importance of pedigree is clear from the attacks launched on new peers and baronets who apparently lacked this qualification. In 1830 the *Quarterly Review* looked back to Charles II as the first offender in this repect:

he began to depart in a more marked manner, from the classes from whom the peerage had been taken in former centuries. They were, for the most part, of honourable, and sometimes of noble descent; but they were not equally the representatives of old feudal property, being rather men who had been enriched by themselves, or within a generation or two, by offices, places, professions, or marriage.[12]

Such an accusation could hardly be levelled at George II, as is clear from the Duke of Newcastle's efforts to obtain a red ribbon for Sir Benjamin Keene, as a reward for diplomatic service. Keene was of humble birth, and, according to Newcastle, 'his Majesty made the objection which you know or at least guess, and much blamed us in England for not laying a proper stress upon those things.'[13] When Nathaniel Curzon applied to Lord Bute in November 1760 to raise

---

[9] Not until well into the twentieth century were families recorded who had not owned land but qualified by way of an interesting pedigree or a coat of arms: W. L. Guttsman, *The British Political Elite* (1963), p. 132.

[10] Joseph Addison, *The Spectator*, 612, 27 October 1714.

[11] E. A. Freeman, 'Pedigrees and pedigree-makers', *Contemporary Review*, 30 (1877), p. 12, 39.

[12] *Quarterly Review*, 84 (1830), p. 302.

[13] Richard Lodge (ed.), *The Private Correspondence of Sir Benjamin Keene* (Cambridge, 1933), pp. 28–9.

with George III an ancient claim to a dormant peerage, he took the precaution of sending a pedigree drawn by the Somerset herald.[14] One of the accusations levelled against Pitt was that he took insufficient notice of pedigree:

> it becomes a matter of very alarming concern indeed, how profusely this bauble of a coronet is showered down on the heads of improper and undeserving men. . . . I am sure that, in general, the odious elevation to a new peerage can alone be rendered palatable to a nation by dignity of descent, and long acknowledged superiority . . . of the seventy eight names which had been added by Mr Pitt to the Baronage, candour must allow, that there were many not only totally unknown to the general historian, but which it would be difficult to find surrounded with much lustre, or traced with much clearness, even in our provincial memoirs, or the dull records of the genealogist.[15]

Similar comments were made about the baronetcy. Originally, applicants had to show that they had been armigerous for at least three generations. By the 1780s the title had been abused to the extent that in 1782 an Order in Council decreed that in future baronets were to enter their arms and pedigree in the College of Arms before their patent could be completed. Until the right to the title had been proved to the satisfaction of the college, it was not to be used in any official documents.[16] None the less, for the majority of Pitt's baronets, according to one commentator, 'all pretence to birth is totally out of the question.'[17]

The desire to show a pedigree, and the accusations levelled at ministers for failing to vet newcomers, reflected a deeper problem – the fact that there were simply not enough families suitably qualified for promotion if longevity was the sole criterion. Primogeniture in the male line had the long-term effect of depriving families of a succession. Since younger sons did not inherit nobility, families failed to spawn the distant lines so familiar among their European counterparts. Of

[14] Sir John Fortescue (ed.), *Correspondence of King George III* (1927), vol. I, pp. 5, 12. He was created Baron Scarsdale in 1761.

[15] Samuel Egerton Brydges, *Reflections on the Late Augmentations of the English Peerage* (1798), pp. 9, 15, 34.

[16] Lawrence Stone, *The Crisis of the Aristocracy* (Oxford, 1965), pp. 84–5; A. Briton, *The Baronetage under Twenty-Seven Sovereigns, 1307–1910* (1910), p. 37; Foster's *Peerage Baronetage, Knightage*, vol. I (1880), preface; *Gentleman's Magazine*, 53 (1783), p. 1060. The position of baronets was much debated during the 1830s and 1840s. See, for example, the comments in Benjamin Disraeli's *Sybil* (1845; Oxford, 1981 edn), pp. 49, 238–9, 358.

[17] Brydges, *Reflections*, p. 44.

course an inheritance could pass through the family in the event of the eldest son's death. The order of progression, according to the rules of primogeniture, was to a younger brother, nephew, great-nephew or uncle, and finally a cousin. Even so, the demographic problems of the English upper classes between the mid-seventeenth and mid-eighteenth centuries had significant repercussions for family continuity. Among the peerage the mortality rate rose during the seventeenth century, reaching a peak in 1675, after which it declined gently until the mid-1740s. In addition, an increase in the age of marriage effectively reduced fertility. The replacement rate fell below 1.0 for cohorts born 1650–1724, at which rate the peerage was failing to reproduce itself. Coupled with a tight Hanoverian creation policy, the effect was of a peerage heading towards extinction by 1750 and saved only by the use of special remainders (allowing the title to pass not merely in the direct male line, but also to brothers, uncles, and other relations). The situation changed after about 1750, with three periods of mortality decline between 1745 and 1764, 1800 and 1819, and 1860 and 1874. Consequently, from the mid-eighteenth to the mid-nineteenth century the replacement rate remained above unity, and mortality gradually declined over the period 1740–1895.[18]

In practical terms these trends produced a relatively short-lived peerage. A contemporary estimate drawn up in 1838 revealed that only 22 per cent of the 359 peers held a title at the revolution of 1688, while 55 per cent dated from the time that Pitt began to open up the group. Eighty-five peers, one-quarter of the House of Lords, had been ennobled during the previous seventeen years. Only seventeen peers, a mere 5 per cent of the total, had been ennobled before the accession of the House of Tudor. Small wonder that Arthur Ponsonby could claim in 1912 that only thirty-seven peers were descended from families known to have been founded before the seventeenth century, and that many lacked a long-established background.[19]

The material is not as comprehensive for the gentry, but there is enough to enable conclusions to be drawn. Of 1226 baronets created within the English and British ranks between 1611 and 1800, only

[18] T. H. Hollingsworth, 'The demography of the British peerage', *Population Studies*, supplement, 18 (1964), pp. 33, 51, 70; 'Mortality in the British peerage families since 1600', *Population*, 32 (September 1977), pp. 337–8.

[19] Clements Library, Lord John Russell Papers, vol. 2, MS list of peers created 1264–1828; Arthur Ponsonby, *The Decline of Aristocracy* (1912), p. 156. In 1979 only three English, eleven Scottish and two Irish earldoms survived which predated 1500: M. Bence-Jones and H. Montgomery-Massingberd, *The British Aristocracy* (1979), p. 74.

295 (24 per cent) survived in 1928, while nearly 22 per cent of all baronetcies failed in the first generation.[20] In Yorkshire, of 93 first grants made in 1611–1800, 51 (55 per cent) were extinct at the latter date, and of these only 11 had lasted more than a century, and half had failed in fifty years or less. Nationally the demographic crisis brought a decline in numbers of baronets from 860 to 621 between 1700 and 1770, which would have been even more dramatic but for the creation of more than 200 new titles over the same period. Allowing for some baronetcies that disappeared through promotion into the peerage, this still suggests a decline of 50 per cent.[21] Nor was it merely the baronets who were suffering. Among Yorkshire gentry families, the tendency towards extinction was particularly sharp between 1670 and 1740, and more than half of the established Roman Catholic families in the West Riding failed in the male line between 1700 and 1770. The ancient Roman Catholic gentry of the north-east were almost eliminated in the early eighteenth century, while on the other side of the Pennines in Cumbria the story was much the same. Just twenty-five of the sixty-two esquire families of 1700 survived in 1747, and only one of the thirty-two gentlemen of 1700 turned up in the same group at the later date.[22] Further south, in Cambridgeshire the established gentry faded away in the first half of the eighteenth century. In 1674 the county elite consisted of twenty-one squires, but only three appeared in the list of forty leading families in 1753, and just ten of the forty prominent squires at the latter date had ancestors in the male line predating 1680. In Essex only a handful of the landowners in 1770 had been established in the county before the century began. In the middle of the century complaints were frequently voiced concerning the speed with which seats were changing hands.[23] Finally, in Wales the county

[20] R. J. Beevor, 'Distinction and extinction', *The Genealogists' Magazine*, 4 (1928), pp. 60–2.

[21] P. Roebuck, *Yorkshire Baronets, 1640–1760* (Oxford, 1981), p. 276; J. Cannon, *Aristocratic Century* (Cambridge, 1984), p. 32. Brydges, *Reflections*, counted 946 baronetcies created 1611–1700, of which 667 were extinct by 1798. The origin of the figure is mysterious, since *Complete Baronetage* lists 838 English and 375 Scottish and Irish titles. However, Brydges's calculations were used by J. P. Cooper, 'The counting of manors', *Economic History Review*, 2nd ser., 8 (1955–6), p. 378.

[22] J. P. Jenkins, 'The demographic decline of the landed gentry in the eighteenth century: a South Wales study', *Welsh History Review*, 11 (1982), pp. 31–3; Edward Hughes, *North Country Life in the Eighteenth Century: the north east, 1700–1750* (Oxford, 1952), p. 79; Beckett, thesis, pp. 96–7.

[23] J. P. Jenkins, 'Cambridgeshire and the gentry: the origins of a myth', *Journal of Regional and Local Studies*, 4 (1984), pp. 1–17; Colin Shrimpton, 'The landed society and the farming community of Essex in the late eighteenth and early nineteenth centuries' (University of Cambridge, Ph.D. thesis, 1965), pp. 49–50.

families of Caernarvonshire dwindled away after 1688, and a similar decline took place in both Glamorgan and Monmouthshire.[24]

By the mid-eighteenth century the demographic crisis had taken its toll at all levels of the governing elite. Collectively the peerage, baronetage and knighthood totalled only 1075 by 1760, a fall of 30 per cent since the beginning of the century, and among the lesser gentry in the counties the position appears to have been much the same. Thereafter the demographic position changed, and what amounted to a new elite emerged after the mid-century low point. In Glamorgan, for example, the gentry that owned much of the county during the nineteenth and twentieth centuries can be dated with some precision between 1760 and 1810. It is perhaps not surprising, given their relatively short pedigrees, that the newcomers sought to build up an image of themselves as long rooted in the county, via an interest in antiquity and antiquarianism.[25]

The old values were still supposed to exist in the nineteenth century. In his novel *Sybil* Benjamin Disraeli parodied the situation by including a passage in which it was claimed that when considering potential peers the Tories would not take any notice of a baronet whose lineage extended back to a Lord Mayor of London in James I's reign. This was 'not the sort of old family' which qualified, when they could look to others who had been living on the land for centuries before that time.[26] Such views, however, were more mythical than real. Undoubtedly a few families slipped through the net. Even today a dozen or more gentry families survive in descent from a medieval ancestor who took his name from lands they still own. But such cases are exceptional, and it seems unlikely that many substantial families of ancient pedigree survived down to the end of the eighteenth century without gaining promotion. Samuel Egerton Brydges calculated in 1798 that 714 knights bachelor were dubbed during Elizabeth I's reign. Of their families, 210 had become peers, 84 baronets and 45 members of the Scottish and Irish peerages; in other words, nearly half had entered the elite. Given what is known of demographic trends, it is hardly surprising that the supply of old families available for promotion had dwindled to a trickle even in Disraeli's day.[27]

[24] Philip Jenkins, *The Making of a Ruling Class: the Glamorgan gentry, 1640–1790* (Cambridge, 1983), pp. 35–9.

[25] Cannon, *Aristocratic Century*, p. 32; J. P. Jenkins, 'The creation of an "ancient gentry": Glamorgan, 1760–1840', *Welsh History Review*, 12 (1984), pp. 29–49.

[26] Disraeli, *Sybil*, p. 241.

[27] Bence-Jones and Montgomery-Massingberd, *The British Aristocracy*, pp. 137–9; Brydges, *Reflections*, pp. 113–36.

ADMISSION VIA EDUCATION

Once a newcomer accepted that his own chances of progress through the aristocracy were slim, he had the choice of settling in the country for his own pleasure – as was the case with many businessmen – or of laying the foundations for his family's absorption. For those choosing the latter course the obvious entry points were education and marriage. If an heir was educated as a gentleman, he would be prepared for a place among the landed gentry. Defoe stressed the significance of a correct education for elite acceptance, and one of the great arrivistes of the seventeenth century, Sir Stephen Fox, projected the two sons of his second marriage into dazzling social careers via education at Eton, Christ Church (Oxford) and the Grand Tour. In similar vein the eighteenth-century brewer Samuel Whitbread put his son through Eton and Oxford.[28] Since this was the course followed by the aristocracy, it is hardly surprising that it was increasingly aped by newcomers in an effort to qualify their sons. An education alongside boys already being trained as part of the governing elite was expected to fit them for such responsibilities, to ensure that they possessed attitudes in common with the sons of the aristocracy, and to provide a network of acquaintances which would be useful later in life.

The first stage was for a boy to be educated as a gentleman. Although it has been argued that the quality of teaching in eighteenth-century public schools was declining, and that as a result aristocrats favoured private education at home, the weight of evidence does not support this contention. Many schools were operating, from local institutions catering for the children of county gentry, to the great public schools, and a considerable proportion of the governing classes passed through the latter. Of peers born before 1680, only 16 per cent attended the major public schools of Eton, Westminster, Winchester and Harrow, but the proportion increased to 35 per cent for those born in 1681–1710, to 59 per cent for those born in 1711–40, and to 72 per cent for those born after that date. Among ministers of state holding office between 1775 and 1800, 87 per cent attended a classical boarding school, and in 83 per cent of cases it was one of the more prestigious English endowed foundations. The number of MPs receiving a public school educa-

---

[28] Christopher Clay, *Public Finance and Private Wealth: the career of Sir Stephen Fox, 1627–1716* (Oxford, 1978), p. 329; Rapp, 'Social mobility in the eighteenth century', p. 387.

tion in the course of the eighteenth century rose in proportion, while the sons of gentry and peers were by far the most numerous attenders in the first half of the nineteenth century.[29]

The simple matter of aping the aristocracy took on a new dimension in the mid-nineteenth century with the reform of public schools under the influence of Thomas Arnold's Rugby. A public school education began to encourage an attitude of public service, which grew out of the historic connection between land and power. This partly reflected the significance of landowners' sons among the clientele of public schools, although even *nouveaux riches* from South Wales sent their sons to Westminster school;[30] but it also had something to do with the way in which public service came over time to be held up as a moral status symbol, so that education was geared to government service and a military life rather than to trade or business. Community leadership rather than private enterprise became the order of the day, but, far from discouraging the middle class from sending their sons to the schools, these changes led to their being sent in ever-increasing numbers. Suggestions have been made to the effect that Arnold and his followers set out to adapt the public schools to the needs of the new middle class, and instilled entrepreneurial ideals into the sons of the aristocracy.[31] However, more persuasive is the view that the later nineteenth-century public schools captured middle-class talent in promoting gentry-class power.[32] Sons of aristocrats and bankers, and a smaller number of businessmen, rubbed shoulders in acquiring the same form of education, and it was accepted that in itself this made them gentlemen. Instead of their having to earn gentility through acquiring landed acreage, it was possible for them to obtain it via the public schools. As a result, the public schools helped to maintain the quasi-hereditary elite, and at the same time to fulfil the status hopes of professional and some business families. A public

[29] Cannon, *Aristocratic Century*, pp. 40–4: M. V. Wallbank, 'Eighteenth-century public schools and the education of the governing elite', *History of Education*, 8 (1979), pp. 1–2; T. W. Bamford, 'Public schools and social class, 1801–1850', *British Journal of Sociology*, 12 (1961), pp. 224–35, may have overemphasised the preponderance of landed sons.

[30] Jenkins, *The Making of a Ruling Class*, p. 221.

[31] Harold Perkin, *The Origins of Modern English Society, 1780–1880* (1969), pp. 297–8. A similar defence was offered by T. H. S. Escott, *Social Transformations of the Victorian Age* (1897), ch. 13.

[32] Rupert Wilkinson, *The Prefects: British leadership and the public school tradition* (1964), pp. ix, 8–25. The establishment attitude towards business is discussed at greater length below, pp. 117–21.

school education now made a gentleman. Moreover, since admission to the civil service, commissions in the armed forces and many of the posts associated with the growth of the Empire were largely determined by competitive examinations geared to the type of education offered in the public schools, movement into the elite was best achieved through such a channel. The result was a welding of landed and middle classes, but on terms laid down by the old establishment.[33]

Similar attitudes were to be found in the ancient universities. Against a background of declining attendance during the eighteenth century, the number of peers attending Oxford or Cambridge was on the increase, rising from 36 per cent of those born before 1680, to 57 per cent for those born after 1741. As a proportion of the student body, the peerage more than doubled during the eighteenth century, and continued to grow during the first two decades of the nineteenth. Peers tended to congregate in certain colleges, particularly Christ Church, Oxford, and Trinity and St John's at Cambridge. The effect of example was considerable. Sir William Blackstone encouraged potential lawyers to attend the ancient universities, and his views influenced the Inns of Court to decide in 1762 that graduates might be called to the bar in three rather than the statutory five years. Blackstone's point was that a liberal and classical education was essential for a barrister, since he had to be a gentleman as well as a legal practitioner. The universities thus became important stepping stones to the bar, and attendance became a regular part of the educational careers of future English judges. Over 60 per cent of them went to Oxford or Cambridge between 1727 and 1875.[34]

[33] M. J. Wiener, *English Culture and the Decline of the Industrial Spirit, 1850–1980* (Cambridge, 1981), ch. 2, goes further to argue that the business world was positively disparaged in the public schools, but this seems to be a rather extreme viewpoint, considering the multifarious business concerns of a great many aristocrats: F. M. L. Thompson, 'English landed society in the nineteenth century', in *The Power of the Past*, ed. P. Thane *et al.* (Cambridge, 1984), pp. 208–9. The whole question of businessmen using public schools to project themselves across the social divide is also examined in D. C. Coleman, 'Gentlemen and players', *Economic History Review*, 2nd ser., 26 (1973), pp. 95–115, while in an as yet unpublished paper delivered in the University of London in January 1986 W. D. Rubinstein has questioned how many *industrialists* sent their sons to public schools. Y. Cassis, 'Bankers in English society in the late nineteenth century', *Economic History Review*, 2nd ser., 38 (1985), pp. 212–15, examines bankers' educational backgrounds.

[34] Cannon, *Aristocratic Century*, pp. 48–52; David Duman, *The Judicial Bench in England, 1727–1875* (1982), pp. 41–4. For Anglican bishops, see D. H. J. Morgan, 'The social and educational background of Anglican bishops – continuities and changes', *British Journal of Sociology*, 20 (1969), p. 298.

Nineteenth-century Oxbridge still offered a predominantly gentry culture, and together with the public schools it provided an education deriving from landed and establishment origins, and paying relatively little attention to industrial and commercial pursuits.[35] Ironically the arriviste faced the possibility that in order to infiltrate his son into the governing class he might need to provide him with an education which, while fitting him for public service, might also influence him against business. As Arthur Ponsonby expressed it rather acidly, 'after a generation or two the boast of noble blood will be made and habits of idleness and indolence will be fully developed. All the grit and force of character, which made the first peer successful, will have disappeared.'[36]

School and university apart, the education of a young gentleman was fashioned at the Inns of Court and on the Grand Tour. The Inns flourished as a finishing school for wealthy gentlemen in the seventeenth century, but this role declined in the eighteenth as they reverted to their original purpose as professional training grounds. The fall-off in aristocratic attendance was particularly marked between 1680 and 1740, and although something of a revival took place from the 1760s the Inns never recaptured their earlier importance. This was partly because aristocratic attenders learned insufficient law to make the exercise worthwhile, and partly because new educational opportunities opened up in the form of the Grand Tour.[37] Increasingly from the second half of the seventeenth century those who could afford the exercise sent their sons abroad with a private tutor to imbibe culture (and perhaps life experience as well) in foreign climes. It was, however, an expensive business; it cost the Earl of Bedford £5000 to send his two eldest sons across

---

[35] The significance of university education has been disputed. The view preferred here is that of Cannon, *Aristocratic Century*, mainly because of his scholarly demolition of the alternative scenario suggested by Lawrence Stone, and because Stone's most recent findings tend to support the view of a rise in landowning attendance at Oxbridge during the eighteenth century: Stone and Stone, *An Open Elite?*, p. 264. At the same time Dr Jenkins has noted that the number of Glamorgan men matriculating at Oxford, and from the greater gentry families, fell sharply between the seventeenth and eighteenth centuries: *The Making of a Ruling Class*, p. 223.

[36] Wiener, *English Culture*, pp. 22–4; Ponsonby, *The Decline of Aristocracy*, p. 156.

[37] P. Lucas, 'A collective biography of students and barristers of Lincoln's Inn, 1680–1804: a study in the "aristocratic resurgence" in the eighteenth century', *Journal of Modern History*, 46 (1974), pp. 227–61; Stone and Stone, *An Open Elite?*, p. 265; Jenkins, *The Making of a Ruling Class*, pp. 225–8.

Europe for six years between 1660 and 1666.[38] Furthermore, the amount of knowledge absorbed was often questioned, as critics pointed to the much-vaunted disorderly behaviour of young gentlemen abroad, and the ignorance of foreign languages which made learning difficult.

ADMISSION VIA MARRIAGE

The problems associated with marriage as a channel of admission into the aristocracy were rather different. Marriage was a social duty, because it obliged the family and helped to widen social contacts;[39] indeed, so important was the interest of the family that Parliament took pains to prevent runaway mismatches. For eighty years down to the 1750s, the House of Lords made it a particular concern to introduce effective marital regulations, and it finally succeeded in overcoming the scruples of the Commons with Hardwicke's Marriage Act of 1753. Almost certainly the measure was intended to strengthen patriarchal authority, which was considered to be in the best interests of the family and the group.[40] The social standing of the family was endangered by marriage outside the group. As Sir William Robinson told his wife in the early eighteenth century:

Lord Harry Pawlett is married to one Mrs Parry of little fortune, probably his children may be Dukes of Bolton. The young men are in a strong vein of wedding, Sir William St Quinton and I were reckoning up at least six that lately has undone themselves and their families in that manner.[41]

In view of these considerations it is hardly surprising that marriage partners were generally sought within a narrow social elite which severely restricted the opportunities for incomers. Like Trollope's Duke of Omnium, most aristocrats regarded marital equality as part

[38] G. Scott Thomson, *Life in a Noble Household, 1641–1700* (1937), pp. 95–110; Elizabeth Hamilton, *The Mordaunts: an eighteenth-century family* (1965), pp. 159–83.
[39] Miriam Slater, 'The weightiest business: marriage in an upper gentry family in seventeenth-century England', *Past and Present*, 72 (1976), p. 31.
[40] Cannon, *Aristocratic Century*, p. 74.
[41] Leeds Archives Office, Vyner MSS, letter 13,898, Sir William Robinson to his wife, 6 April (?). I should like to thank Clyve Jones for bringing this reference to my attention. Lord Harry (1691–1759) married Catherine, daughter of Charles Parry of Oakfield, Berkshire, sometime envoy to Portugal. He succeeded his brother Charles as fourth duke in 1754; *Complete Peerage*, vol. II, p. 214.

of the natural order of events, and potential brides and grooms moved in circles where they were more than likely to meet partners of the same rank. Consequently, while marriage might be seen as an important financial transaction, especially where a large portion or even an inheritance could be used for the payment of debts, or the extension of family property, it was even more crucial as a means of cementing the social fabric of the group.

To protect and possibly increase the family standing, fathers were primarily interested in ensuring that their sons, and especially their eldest sons, married within a socially acceptable field. In the eighteenth century 84 per cent of heirs, and in the nineteenth 82 per cent, married, while the proportion of younger sons was 63 and 70 per cent respectively. Only eight of the eighty-one eighteenth-century dukes died unmarried, and three of these were minors. Moreover, the pressure to marry within the group was also considerable. During the eighteenth century the eighty-one dukes contracted 102 marriages, of which 53 were with the daughters of peers (including 12 with the daughters of other dukes) and 49 with commoners. Of the latter only five lacked a gentle background. Overall, 49 per cent of dukes and marquesses, 28 per cent of earls and 19 per cent of viscounts and barons married within the peerage, while the respective nineteenth-century figures were 32, 29 and 17 per cent. During the two centuries 40 per cent of all heirs to titles married within the group, as did nearly half as many younger sons.[42] Such was the prevailing ethos that anxious fathers looked to marry their daughters as advantageously as possible, and some did particularly well. The second Earl of Nottingham, for example, found ducal partners for three of his five daughters who married.[43] On the other hand, heirs who succeeded before marriage were not bound by family constraints, while others eloped when it became clear that social and fiscal considerations were likely to make a proposed alliance unsatisfactory. During the eighteenth century, cases are known of peers marrying the daughters of a butcher, a boatman, a barber and a printer, while in the nineteenth century love matches included alliances with daughters of a labourer, a

[42] D. M. Thomas, 'The social origins of marriage partners of the British peerage in the eighteenth and nineteenth centuries', *Population Studies*, 26 (1972), p. 101; R. A. Kelch, 'The dukes: a study of the English nobility in the eighteenth century' (Ohio State University, Ph.D. thesis, 1955), pp. 247–53.

[43] H. J. Habakkuk, 'Daniel Finch, 2nd Earl of Nottingham: his house and estate', in *Studies in Social History*, ed. J. H. Plumb (1955), pp. 139–78.

blacksmith and a college servant. A steady stream of peers married singers and actresses, although the extent of socially inferior marriages has sometimes been exaggerated.[44]

Financial considerations often determined a family's marital priorities. Heiresses were regarded as particularly good catches for relieving financial troubles, and over the period 1700–60 never less than 20 per cent of in-marriages among the peerage were to heiresses. But there were never enough heiresses within the group, particularly when they became less common in the second half of the century. Often, therefore, it was necessary to look elsewhere, and eldest sons marrying outside the group compensated for social difference by seeking financial wealth. As a result, down to 1780, between 22 and 46 per cent married commoner heiresses.[45] Possibly the most frequent image is of an impoverished aristocrat going, coronet in hand, in search of a wealthy City bride to relieve financial plight. The second Earl of Warrington made no bones about the matter: 'my encumbrances being greater than I could struggle with,' he told his younger brother in 1715, 'to make money (to ease me of some part) the chief view in marriage'. When various overtures to wealthy brides drew a blank, he turned to the City. In 1702 he commissioned two agents to the tune of 1000 guineas to find him a suitable spouse, and as a result he married Mary Oldbury, eldest daughter of a rich London merchant. Her portion, reputedly of £40,000, was earmarked to relieve his desperate financial condition by paying off his debts.[46] However, Warrington was a rarity; only 3

---

[44] Thomas, 'The social origins of marriage partners', p. 108; J. M. Bulloch, 'Peers who have married players', *Notes and Queries*, 169 (August 1935), pp. 92–4; Cannon, *Aristocratic Century*, pp. 76–7. Misalliances were a common consideration in novels, including Samuel Richardson's *Pamela* (1740) and *Clarissa* (1747–8). Lovelace, the villain of the latter novel, had what was termed 'a youthful frolic' with a Miss Betterton. She was 'but a tradesman's daughter. The family indeed was grown rich, and aimed at a new line of gentry; and were unreasonable enough to expect a man of my family would marry her': Everyman edn (1976), vol. II, p. 147. The extent to which it was the family and not just the individual that suffered from a mismatch is clear from Jane Austen's *Pride and Prejudice* (1813), in which Elizabeth Bennet expected her putative relationship with Mr Darcy to be dashed by her younger sister's elopement (Harmondsworth, 1972 edn), pp. 295–6.

[45] Thomas, 'The social origins of marriage partners', p. 105.

[46] J. V. Beckett and Clyve Jones, 'Financial improvidence and political independence in the early eighteenth century: George Booth, 2nd Earl of Warrington', *Bulletin of the John Rylands Library*, 65 (1982), pp. 21–2. Another example was the first Duke of Chandos' third wife, a middle-class widow with a fortune of £40,000, while the third duke's first wife was a middle-class heiress with a fortune of £150,000: C. H. C. and M. I. Baker, *The Life and Circumstances of James Brydges, First Duke of Chandos* (1949), p. 234; Kelch, 'The dukes', p. 252.

per cent of aristocratic men married the daughters of wealthy merchants in the eighteenth century, and the prejudices against such alliances remained overwhelming in the nineteenth century. When the attitude towards marriages within the group began to soften in the late nineteenth century, replacement partners included American and banking brides. Some of the transatlantic alliances were undoubtedly contracted for financial reasons, but the trend also reflected a merging of high societies. Only in the twentieth century did the proportion of marriages within the business category exceed 10 per cent of all commoner marriages, and even then the preference was for the daughters of merchants and bankers rather than those of the new industrial bourgeoisie.[47]

In any case, there is no reason to assume that City financiers were begging landed gentlemen to marry their daughters. Wealthy men who were still in business when their daughters became eligible for marriage might not be in a position to offer a large portion, and it may be significant that the Earl of Warrington finally lighted on a City girl whose father was already dead. Furthermore, while in the seventeenth century City men automatically considered land purchase, by the eighteenth they were increasingly content to stay within London bourgeois society. If they had no intention of founding a landed family, they had little reason to prepare the ground by marrying their daughter into the landed elite. Intermarriage between City families and the peerage 'probably decreased' in the eighteenth century, although it is possible that this marked a greater incidence of alliances with gentry families.[48] In the three counties of Northamptonshire, Northumberland and Hertfordshire, marriages with daughters of businessmen peaked at 11 per cent in the early eighteenth century, but fell below 3 per cent after 1800, with a sharply accelerating divergence between land and money after 1750. Heirs of purchasers from the monied interest had more difficulty finding elite brides than inheritors. In the three counties only 29 out of 174 (17 per cent) managed the transition, although the partner's origin is unknown in 20 per cent of cases, and many marriages were with men from the law and

[47] R. Trumbach, *The Rise of the Egalitarian Family* (1978), p. 84; Thomas, 'The social origins of marriage partners', p. 106; Cassis, 'Bankers in English society', pp. 217 ff.; A. Howe, *The Cotton Masters, 1830–1860* (Oxford, 1984), pp. 77–8. Several brewers cemented their social success with advantageous marriages: Gutzke, 'Social status of landed brewers', p. 106.

[48] N. Rogers, 'Money, land and lineage: the big bourgeoisie of Hanoverian London', *Social History*, 4 (1977), pp. 444–5.

office-holding.[49] By contrast, City evidence suggests that a rising proportion of businessmen were marrying daughters of the gentry.[50]

Under the circumstances, marriage into the elite was by no means easy for either the first or the second generation.[51] None the less it had to be done. Newcomers during the eighteenth century had almost invariably intermarried with the group before ennoblement. Between 1600 and 1799, 59 per cent of peerage newcomers had married within the higher reaches of the English aristocracy, while a list compiled in 1820 suggested that 8 per cent of peers and 2 per cent of baronets had been promoted as a result of marital alliances.[52] The situation remained much the same at the end of the nineteenth century. Even in the lower reaches of the group, social climbing required careful marriage planning. Thomas Coltman, who died in 1826, was only the third generation of his family to reside in Lincolnshire, and his estate was under 2000 acres. His place in Spilsbyshire society was secured by a favourable marriage into the Burtons of Somersby, which provided links with other notable families.[53] Commonly, however, the most reliable means of entry was by an adjustment of the financial terms. The preference for endogamous marriage ensured that, if two young people of the same group could be brought to agree upon an alliance, the social and pecuniary considerations were adjustable accordingly.[54] The same adjustment was also acceptable for marriages outside the group. By the end of the seventeenth century the relationship between the portion provided for a daughter at her

[49] Stone and Stone, *An Open Elite?*, pp. 247–9.

[50] Rogers, 'Money, land and lineage', p. 445, suggests that 40 per cent of aldermanic marriages may have been with gentry, which goes against the impression that this type of union was frowned upon: W. A. Speck, 'Conflict in society', in *Britain after the Glorious Revolution*, ed. G. S. Holmes (1969), p. 146.

[51] Daniel Defoe, *Complete English Tradesman* (1726), p. 374, was shocked to find the sons of two City merchants marrying into the families of the dukes of Bedford and Marlborough, merely because they had ancestors with trading connections.

[52] Cannon, *Aristocratic Century*, p. 92; *Peerage Chart* (1820).

[53] R. J. Olney, *Rural Society and County Government* (Lincoln, 1979), p. 29.

[54] I am not concerned here with the complicated question of changing attitudes towards marriage whereby 'arrangements' for the good of the family were increasingly subservient to the needs of the children in the course of the eighteenth century. This view can be found most clearly expressed in Lawrence Stone's *The Family, Sex and Marriage* (1977) and Trumbach, *The Rise of the Egalitarian Family*. It has been debated by Lloyd Bonfield, 'Marriage, property and the "affective family"', *Law and History Review*, 1 (1983), pp. 297–312, and Eileen Spring, 'Law and the theory of the affective family', *Albion*, 16 (1984), pp. 1–20.

marriage, and the jointure promised by the spouse as an annual payment in the event of the husband dying first, had settled into a ratio of £1000:£100. Usually the portion was determined by the father's own settlement, but during the course of the eighteenth century 15–25 per cent of his estate was usually jointured (net of all outgoings except parliamentary taxes). By going over the odds it was possible for a family to hope to attract a good match. For a daughter this meant raising the size of the portion relative to the jointure, while for a son it involved increasing the jointure and also the size of the allowance to younger children. In 1726 the banker Henry Hoare attracted the daughter of a minor peer by offering a jointure of £1200 a year when receiving a portion of only £10,000.[55] When Alexander Baring's daughter married a younger son of the Marquess of Bath in 1830, the maximum jointure was fixed at only 5 per cent of the young lady's fortune. Large portions also helped. Samuel Whitbread I gave his daughter Emma £12,000 when she married the twelfth Lord St John, while in the nineteenth century the daughter of a banker or of a new landed family marrying into the older elite – or even of the lesser peerage marrying into the higher – might have a portion of £50,000 to £60,000.[56] Entry into society through the marriage market was achieved only at a cost, and according to rules laid down by those already inside the group.

ADMISSION VIA POLITICAL AND STATE SERVICE

Once a family had staked its claim to the aristocracy via the traditional channels of land, birth, education and marriage, the means of rising higher were not straightforward. The most obvious fast channels to a peerage, a baronetcy, or to promotion within the ranks, involved party or state service. In the post-revolution decades, powers of patronage passed from the monarch to his or her ministers, and party loyalty became a vital consideration. Robert Harley, Earl of Oxford, set the trend when he persuaded Queen Anne to create twelve new peers in 1711–12, in order to save his ministry from defeat in the Lords. From then onwards the die was cast, and applications for promotion were often couched in party

[55] Roebuck, *Yorkshire Baronets*, p. 329; Christopher Clay, 'Henry Hoare, banker, and the building of the Stourhead estate' (forthcoming).

[56] Rapp, 'Social mobility in the Eighteenth Century', p. 387; F. M. L. Thompson, *English Landed Society in the Nineteenth Century* (1963), pp. 100–1.

terminology. In 1748 William Perry asked the Duke of Newcastle to consider his wife's claim to the barony of L'Isle. He requested the title of Baron Sidney, 'of some place in Ireland', and reminded the duke of his allegiance to the Pelham ministry: 'these circumstances I trouble your Grace with to evidence that I have in all cases and at all places been a steady follower, and a firm adherent to your Grace's House.'[57] Lord Scarsdale addressed his request for promotion direct to George III in 1764, resting his hopes on 'your Majesty's graciousness rather than ministerial favour'.[58] Pitt was frequently accused of allowing political considerations to sway his judgement on promotions, and the fact that twenty of his creations between 1784 and 1801 between them controlled forty-one seats in the lower house adds substance to the suggestion. In an undated list probably from the 1780s, Lord Belmore was said to have solicited promotion to an Irish viscountcy, and has 'supported government on receiving strong hopes of this mark of favour. His lordship has recently increased his Parliamentary weight by the purchase of the borough of Newcastle.' The list was annotated, 'to be viscount on the first promotion', and he was elevated in 1789.[59]

Party considerations became critical in the processing of applications, but, whereas a political promotion to the Lords had usually been viewed as a reward for distinguished service, after 1800 it was no longer necessary for vigorous politicians to jeopardize their careers.[60] The stronger an administration, the less likely it was to create new peerages, while those with a minority in the upper house usually sought to correct the imbalance. Political loyalties were carefully scrutinized. As leader of the House of Commons, Lord John Russell was involved in processing applications for promotion at Queen Victoria's accession. He was against the offer of peerages to men recently defeated in county elections, and he opposed Ridley Colborne, 'as he is not altogether with us'. Among proposals for baronetcies he considered that 'Mr Elton has claims as being descended from a baronet, and being a country gentleman who supports the party', but that others had better qualifications.

---

[57] BL Add. MSS, 32,715, fols 52–3. Perry's application was unsuccessful.

[58] Fortescue (ed.), *Correspondence of King George III*, vol. I, p. 66. Scarsdale was unsuccessful.

[59] I. R. Christie, *Wars and Revolutions* (1982), p. 26; Huntington Library, ST74, vol. 1, fol. 52.

[60] However, relatively few opted to stay in the House of Commons: M. W. McCahill, 'Peerage creations and the changing character of the British nobility, 1750–1830', *English Historical Review*, 96 (1981), pp. 269–72.

Writing to Lord Melbourne three years later, Russell accepted that a Mr Easthope could be made a baronet because 'he is a rich man, of fair character, who has done a great deal to support us.'[61] In the 1830s it was argued that 'if Whig administrations had prevailed from 1784 in the same proportion that the Tories have Lord Melbourne would now be supported by a considerable majority of the House of Lords', and over the course of the century the two parties had identical creation records. Baronetcies were seen increasingly as a reward for backbench politicians with ample private means and a recognized status in the Commons or the constituencies.[62]

State service took a number of forms. Between 1660 and 1720 peerages were awarded to men who had aided their royal masters in securing the throne. Charles II elevated several supporters in the 1660s, and after 1688 William III ennobled five of his foreign servants and a number of prominent revolution activists. George I also distributed a number of titles as rewards for supporting his claim to the throne in 1714. These, however, were isolated examples, and more common were awards to men who had served the state in the ministry, the foreign and diplomatic services, the armed forces and local government. Eighteen new peerages were attributed to service in the Irish Union controversy of 1799–1800, although the accusation was often levelled at the government that Irish peerages were used as a means of compensating men thought unworthy of the Westminster House of Lords. Be that as it may, no one with a rent roll of less than £5000 could expect promotion, and a knighthood was the best hope of those with less.[63] Over time, the knighthood became an honour predominantly used to reward political service, or other types of distinguished activity which did not fall into the existing categories.

Ministerial favours had a long history. In the eighteenth century George II's only dukedom went to the existing Duke of Newcastle, while two other leading politicians – Sir Robert Walpole and William Pulteney – both received earldoms. Generally George II

---

[61] Clements Library, Lord John Russell papers, vol. 1, Russell to Viscount Melbourne, 24 July 1841; vol. 4, 'Peerages'.

[62] Ibid., vol. 2, MS list showing the strength of the Houses of Lords and Commons in respect of Lord Melbourne's ministry; R. E. Pumphrey, 'The introduction of industrialists into the British peerage: a study in the adaptation of a social institution', *American Historical Review*, 65 (1959), pp. 6–7.

[63] G. C. Bolton, *The Passing of the Irish Act of Union* (Oxford, 1966), pp. 100–1, 153, 197, 205.

was reluctant to make grants on the grounds of service, and even a brilliant lawyer like William Murray had difficulty achieving a peerage on his appointment as Lord Chief Justice in 1756. When Lord Hardwicke suggested the following year that Henry Bilson Legge should be made a peer and first Lord of the Admiralty, George II is reputed to have retorted that he would not do two great things for one man at the same time.[64] Exactly what rewards were offered to state servants was a matter of some delicacy, as is clear from William Pitt's letter to Viscount Sydney in 1784 regarding the elevation of the Master of the Rolls:

It was in contemplation to make him a knight first, that there might not be a precedent of annexing the rank of baronet to the office, but as so much time has elapsed since, it cannot now have that effect; and if the King agrees to [it], Mr Kenyon will I know like it much better to be a baronet at once.[65]

This delicate balancing led by the mid-nineteenth century to the possibility of strengthening the legal talent of the upper house by grants of life peerages. Such a policy was widely supported by, among others, Walter Bagehot, who recognized that as the debating chamber of the landed interest the Lords was moving out of step with the nation. In his view 'an aristocracy is necessarily inferior in business to the classes nearer business; and it is not therefore a suitable class, if we had our choice of classes, out of which to frame a chamber for revising matters of business.'[66] The issue was tested by Palmerston's Cabinet, which in 1856 elevated Sir James Parke to a life peerage as Lord Wensleydale. The Lords objected, with much loose talk about opening the floodgates to all and sundry, and Parke was given an ordinary hereditary peerage (although he was seventy-four and had no surviving sons). It was only in 1876 that Disraeli finally carried legislation authorizing the grant of life baronies to a maximum of four judges eligible to sit in the Lords. Despite considerable debate from 1869 onwards, non-judicial life peerages were not introduced until the 1950s.[67]
Diplomatic service could also bring promotion, but again it was

---

[64] H. Horwitz, *Parliament, Policy and Politics in the Reign of William III* (Manchester, 1977), p. 311; J. B. Owen, 'George II reconsidered', in *Statesmen, Scholars and Merchants*, ed. A. Whiteman *et al.* (Oxford, 1973), p. 121.

[65] Clements Library, Pitt Papers, vol. 3, William Pitt to Viscount Sydney, 1784.

[66] W. Bagehot, *The English Constitution* (1867; 1963 edn), p. 143.

[67] P. G. Richards, *Patronage in British Government* (1963), pp. 222–30.

not granted lightly. Newcastle pressed the claims of Sir Benjamin Keene in 1752 on the grounds of his service at the Spanish court, and in 1746 the Duke of Bedford sought a similar distinction for Thomas Villiers. The absence of acknowledgement from his own government of the role played by Villiers in drawing up the Treaty of Dresden appeared to give the impression that 'you was not so well, either with his Majesty and those in the administration, as you deserved to be.' Bedford put this point to the Secretary of State, Lord Harrington, who 'threw out that a riband, or some such mark of distinction, was the usual and proper method taken by our Court to distinguish such ministers in foreign courts who had merited the King's favour by any signal service.' After service in the missions at Dresden, Vienna and Berlin, Villiers was eventually created Earl of Clarendon, although not until 1776. The need for patience was also demonstrated in the case of Lord Macartney. Despite diplomatic service in Russia and the chief secretaryship of Ireland, his request for a peerage in 1769 was undoubtedly premature. In 1775 he became Governor of Grenada, which proved to be the basis of an Irish peerage. After spending the years 1781–5 as president of Fort St George, Madras, he looked for a British peerage, but again he was unsuccessful, and it was only in 1792 that he was raised to a viscountcy. After spending the following two years as ambassador in China, he received an earldom in March 1794, but it was yet another two years – and after an unofficial mission to Louis XVIII at Verona – before he finally achieved a barony in the British peerage, twenty-seven years after his first application.[68] Military service was a surer means of speedy promotion. Marlborough was awarded a dukedom for his part in the War of the Spanish Succession, while titles and land were showered on Wellington and Nelson for their contribution to the wars with revolutionary and Napoleonic France. Wellington's promotion was unprecedented as he moved rapidly from viscount (1802) to earl (1812), marquess (1812) and finally duke (1814).

Finally, a few men were advanced as a result of, or in expectation of, performing significant roles in local government. The lord-lieutenancy of a county usually called for a man at the head of the peerage. When Lord Malton was given this post for the West Riding

[68] Lodge (ed.), *The Private Correspondence of Sir Benjamin Keene*, pp. 28–9; Lord John Russell, *Correspondence of John, Fourth Duke of Bedford* (1842), vol. I, pp. 125–34; P. Roebuck (ed.), *Macartney of Lisanoure, 1737–1806* (Belfast, 1983), pp. 23, 74–5, 81, 90, 210, 212, 218, 265. Macartney was also a landowner, although the gross rental from his Irish estates was only £1119 in 1789 (p. 147).

of Yorkshire in 1733, he wrote to the Duke of Newcastle, asking him to solicit a further promotion within the peerage:

Though I am most heartily sorry for the vacancy I must return my most humble thanks to your Grace for thinking of me at this distance for the lieutenancy of this Riding etc. I know the disadvantage of succeeding a very popular man, and it will be impossible for me to be of much use unless my family be made of equal weight with those who have enjoyed that post before, who of late have always been earls. I desire your Grace will be so good as to represent this in the most favourable manner to his Majesty, and I humbly hope he will consider the pretensions I have to lay such a claim before him.[69]

The earldom was forthcoming in November 1734. In 1766 Lord Maynard was created viscount after succeeding to the lieutenancy of Suffolk. By contrast, those who could only offer service did not always succeed. This was Lord Scarsdale's experience when he requested promotion in 1764 because it 'might increase my consideration in the Eye of the World, and particularly might enlarge my abilities of serving your Majesty in the County of Derby.'[70]

The proportion of newcomers elevated through these various service channels was never entirely clear, although contemporaries speculated endlessly on the subject. In the later years of the eighteenth century two correspondents supplied the *Gentleman's Magazine* with lists of such creations during the previous fifty years. The first named nine navy and four army peers, fourteen from the law and four from trade; while the second listed twelve navy and eight army peers, seven diplomatic peerages, four for service in India, nineteen from the law and ten from commerce. In practice, the Pitt peerages went almost entirely to men who fell within the approved categories, including those who had served the state, politicians, soldiers, sailors and lawyers, with the great majority coming from the more substantial landed families.[71] The exercise was repeated in 1820 when it was argued that out of 291 peers 116 were created 'chiefly on account of their property

---

[69] BL Add. MSS, 32,688, fol. 265.

[70] Clements Library, Lacaita–Shelburne MSS, Duke of Grafton to (Shelburne), 27 September 1766; Fortescue (ed.), *Correspondence of King George III*, vol. I, p. 66.

[71] *Gentleman's Magazine*, 68 (1798), pt II, p. 1035; 69 (1799), pt I, p. 36; Cannon, *Aristocratic Century*, p. 23. According to Derek Jarrett, *Pitt the Younger* (1974), p. 132, a reading of the Chatham papers preserved in the Public RO does not suggest that he gave away honours indiscriminately.

and Parliamentary influence', 24 through marriage, 27 via legal service, 7 through diplomatic service, 33 by military service, 22 because they were statesmen and 13 who were younger sons. Promotions within the baronetage were also carefully documented, as is clear from table 3.1.[72] At the end of the decade another calculation suggested that, of 235 creations since 1760, 25 came via the law, 25 through state service and 23 from military service. Of the rest, 80 were Irish and Scottish peers, 46 were landed commoners, 17 were younger sons and 5 were peeresses. The total was completed by 14 renewals and confirmations.[73]

Despite these claims, men elevated to the peerage and baronetage usually had solid claims to a landed background. Where this was lacking, the tendency was to avoid offering a hereditary title as a reward for achievement in favour of conferring a knighthood. Once the baronetcy offered some permanency to landowners at the head of the gentry this practice became increasingly common. In the first year of his reign Charles II knighted two merchants and most of the London aldermen, and the following year he honoured a brewer, a shipbuilder, several lawyers, and a merchant 'on board his own ship at Blackwall'. Some knights were even rewarded for specified achievements, including William Phipps, 'captain, governor of Massachusetts Bay; for good services in a late expedition, bringing considerable treasure home that had lain in the sea forty-four years' (1687), and the solicitor who managed the Sacheverell trial (1710).[74]

The significance of this trend became increasingly apparent as the number of creations declined. A sprinkling of merchants was less obvious during Charles II's reign than in the more parsimonious days of the later Stuarts and early Hanoverians. In 1702 the fourteen knights included the mayors of Oxford and Bristol, the Attorney-General and the Solicitor-General, a captain in the Royal Navy, a linen draper in Cheapside, an alderman of London, and an Essex silk merchant. Although under the Hanoverians a few non-landed men crept into the baronetage, the majority were rewarded with knighthoods. In 1714 George I dubbed John Vanbrugh, 'Clarenceux King of Arms, and comptroller of works and surveyor of gardens', seven London aldermen, a brewer, two directors of the East India Company, a director of the Merchant Adventurers Company, a director of the Royal Africa Company, two serjeants-at-law and a doctor of medicine.

---

[72] *Peerage Chart* (1820).

[73] *Quarterly Review*, 42 (1830), p. 321.

[74] Information in this and the following paragraphs is from W. A. Shaw, *The Knights of England* (2 vols, 1906).

Men with similar backgrounds often accounted for all the knighthoods granted in a particular year; in 1729, for example, the five knights were a Dutch merchant, two serjeants-at-law, the Sheriff of London and the deputy governor of the Merchant Adventurers; while in 1736 those honoured were the Lord Chief Justice in the Court of Common Pleas, the late Governor of Bombay, and the Lord Mayor of Dublin. George III's grants were to country sheriffs, judges, military officers, diplomats and a selection of physicians, brewers and miscellaneous worthies including the President of the Royal Academy (1769).

The knighthood became a means of rewarding talent, reminiscent perhaps of its earlier military connotations. As one defender of its new role wrote in 1787, it had become 'a mark of Royal favour conferred by the Sovereign upon a subject for some particular personal desert, whether the person who received it was a soldier, a statesman, a scholar, a lawyer, a merchant, or eminent in any of the learned professions, arts or sciences'. Although it had customarily been offered 'to any one who carried up an address to the Crown, when perhaps it was sometimes improperly bestowed', generally the merit appraisal had ensured that new knights included 'many of our eminent statesmen, lawyers, soldiers, seamen, antiquaries, mathematicians, physicians, merchants, and learned writers'.[75] The new orders of knighthood in the nineteenth century were specifically reserved as rewards for service and merit.

These changes in the channels of admission were normally greeted with wails of protest to the effect that the aristocracy was being devalued. In Disraeli's *Sybil* one of the female characters argues that 'a baronetcy has become the distinction of the middle classes; a physician, our physician for example, is a baronet, and I dare say some of our tradesmen; brewers, or people of that class.'[76] As late as 1922, W. R. Inge could argue that during the previous century 'lavish new creations of peers turned the House of Lords into the predominantly middle class body which it is now.'[77] Few contemporaries were ready to accept that the group should evolve to reflect social change. William Pitt was a lone voice in the 1790s, as was an anonymous author writing in 1832. The latter argued that in practice the peerage had adapted to changing circumstances. Originally land was the sole qualification, but medieval monarchs called members to the House of Lords by writ, and the

---

[75] *Gentleman's Magazine*, 57 (1787), pt II, pp. 677–8. In Jane Austen's *Pride and Prejudice*, p. 65, Sir William Lucas is said to have been a knight because he had presented an address to the king. Until his elevation he had been in trade.

[76] Disraeli, *Sybil*, p. 104.

[77] W. R. Inge, *The Victorian Age* (Cambridge, 1922), p. 52.

grounds for admission had been further widened with the sixteen elected Scottish representatives from 1707 and the twenty-eight Irish from 1801. Consequently it could be argued that the admission of state servants, and lawyers and judges whose skills were required in the House of Lords, was merely an extension of the evolutionary principle.[78] More typical, however, were reactionary views, including the *Gentleman's Magazine* correspondent of 1784 who was 'sorry to see the dignity of peerage made so cheap by such a multitude of new creations'. Others criticized what they saw as the devaluation of the knighthood,[79] while the *Quarterly Review* argued in 1830 that 'the genius of the British constitution cannot be satisfied but by the interposition of a strong aristocracy, and that such an aristocracy cannot exist unless it be mainly formed of the ancient and historic families.'[80]

In practice, the complaints were greatly exaggerated. Baronetcies went to hard-working country gentlemen, a few manufacturers with a notable record of local service, and a miscellany of worthies including the Lord Mayor of London, court physicians, sailors and soldiers, judges, colonial governors and ambassadors not quite worth a peerage, and community leaders. Almost invariably the recipients had a substantial landed income.[81] Even among the knights, the military men, lawyers, doctors and diplomats receiving the honour more often than not had strong links with the old elite. Of those surviving in 1882, 84 per cent had gained their honour as a result of public or official service, and thirty years later the proportion was roughly the same. In 1882 only nine came from the commercial sector of agriculture, industry, trade or transport, just 1.4 per cent, and this figure and risen to only 3.6 per cent by 1912. The father's status or occupation can be traced for nearly 70 per cent of the 1882 knights, and only eighteen individuals stated that their fathers had been in business or trade.[82]

---

[78] Anon., *The Prerogative of Creating Peers* (1832), pp. 81–4.

[79] *Gentleman's Magazine*, 54 (1784), pt II, pp. 576–8.

[80] *Quarterly Review*, 42 (1830), p. 328.

[81] F. M. L. Thompson, 'Britain', in *European Landed Elites in the Nineteenth Century*, ed. D. Spring (1977), pp. 39–41; H. J. Hanham, 'The sale of honours in late Victorian England', *Victorian Studies*, 3 (1960), p. 278.

[82] Thompson, 'Britain', pp. 40–1; Howe, *The Cotton Masters*, pp. 262–6, shows that few Lancashire industrialists were honoured. It might be argued that the change in the concept of knighthood renders the rank scarcely applicable as part of the aristocracy. However, in the nineteenth century it still offered an opening into society, and even in 1985 a correspondent of a national newspaper could include the position within the aristocracy: *The Guardian*, 25 April 1985.

Table 3.1   Baronetcies granted to 1821

	Number	Percentage
Chiefly on account of wealth	392	62.8
Diplomatic service	11	1.8
Naval service	52	8.3
Military service	56	9.0
Civil service	20	3.2
Legal service	27	4.3
Medical service	14	2.2
Civic service	20	3.2
Courtiers	10	1.6
By marriage	12	1.9
Unknown	10	1.6
Total	624	100.0

Source: *Peerage Chart* (1821)

ADMISSION VIA COMMERCE AND INDUSTRY

The complaints raised about newcomers arose from a latent paranoia in regard to the infusion of commercial wealth into the traditional aristocracy. Attacks on newcomers were essentially directed at men with business rather than professional backgrounds, and the prejudice was longstanding. Social climbing was relatively easy in the heady days of James I and Charles I when peerages, baronetcies and knighthoods were distributed as if there was no tomorrow. The display of largesse continued in the immediate aftermath of the Restoration, and the peak period for mobility between land and trade may have been reached in the years 1650–90.[83] In the aftermath of the 1688 revolution the situation changed. The new monied men thrown up by the financial revolution were regarded as a threat to the established government of the landed interest. Property qualifications were introduced in an

[83] R. Grassby, 'Social mobility and business enterprise in seventeenth-century England', in *Puritans and Revolutionaries*, ed. D. Pennington and K. Thomas (Oxford, 1978), p. 357.

attempt to prevent such men from assuming positions within the state without acquiring land, and many years ago Habakkuk noted that after 1690 'there was less interlocking of the two classes [land and commerce] than there had been under Elizabeth and the early Stuarts.'[84] The issue was complicated by John Locke's pronouncement that trade was 'wholly inconsistent with a gentleman's calling'. By no means everyone agreed, but Daniel Defoe, for example, was among those who argued that a man who had made his fortune by working could never be a gentleman. He was only prepared to 'open the door to the politer son, and the next age quite alters the case'.[85] By the nineteenth century such views posed considerable problems for a generation of Victorians brought up on a diet of self-help and the new Poor Law. If bettering oneself was such a crucial aspect of good in the community, defining a gentleman as a man of leisure seemed somewhat incongruous. On the other hand, if a man could work his way to become a gentleman – an issue debated since Sir Thomas Smith wrote in the sixteenth century – this seemed to offer free passage to businessmen and merchants, and even, some radicals argued, to anyone who worked. The question was vital, since in Victorian England being a gentleman made the difference between belonging to, or being excluded from, the social elite. It troubled novelists from Thackeray through Dickens to Trollope, and other thinkers including Samuel Smiles, John Ruskin and Cardinal Newman. Yet, as the anonymous contributor to *Chambers' Journal* concluded in 1856, while a gentleman was real enough he was 'not to be defined'.[86]

None of these views was clearly thought through. It was hard, after all, to reconcile contempt for business with the considerable aristocratic involvement in industrial and other commercial concerns.[87] Much of it was sheer prejudice, and even as accomplished a historian as G. M. Young found it difficult to understand why 'in a money-making age, opinion was, on the whole, more deferential to birth than to money . . . in a mobile and progressive society, most regard was had to the element which represented immobility, tradition and the past.' Young's tentative answer was that the rich Englishman

---

[84] H. J. Habakkuk, 'English landownership, 1680–1740', *Economic History Review*, 10 (1939–40), p. 17.

[85] Daniel Defoe, *Complete English Gentleman* (1890 edn), pp. 257–8.

[86] *Chambers' Journal*, 5 (1856), p. 399, quoted in A. Smythe-Palmer, *The Ideal of a Gentleman* (1908), p. 62.

[87] Wiener, *English Culture*, has tried to explain this contradiction in terms of the *rentier* nature of much aristocratic involvement. As later chapters will show, this view overstresses the extent of aristocratic withdrawal from business.

still needed to escape from the source of his wealth into 'the life, beyond wealth, of power and consideration on the land'.[88] Whatever the validity of this view, there seems little doubt that at least after about 1850 entrepreneurs were particularly concerned to imitate the aristocratic lifestyle, and the most important medium in this transition lay in the education of their sons at the public schools. England thus became an industrial nation without developing a straightforward bourgeois or industrial elite.[89]

In the meantime promotions into the peerage and baronetage of men with business backgrounds were usually met with scorn. In 1798 it was argued that over the previous fifty years peerages had been conferred upon individuals 'possessing large properties acquired by commerce', many of whom had moderate and even obscure backgrounds. Samuel Egerton Brydges was even more vehement, arguing that from the early seventeenth century until Pitt's day no one had entered the peerage who had actually engaged in trade. He expatiated on the baronetcies awarded to seven or eight East India men, seven citizens and many other courtiers.[90] For another contemporary, Pitt was 'a god of the City, and the City and Stock Exchange were his gods in return. He considered a Coronet a feather, which was light payment for any favour, without caring on whose head it fell.' Furthermore, when 'a coronet thus becomes cheap, a baronetage sunk into perfect insignificance. Then it fell in profusion on citizens, East Indians, placemen' and others similarly lacking the conventional social roots.[91]

Such prejudices affected marriage patterns and social attitudes, despite the clear evidence that the majority of men receiving a title of one sort or another had established links with the existing elite. In fact it was only in the closing decades of the nineteenth century that the prejudice against first-generation wealth finally broke down, and long

---

[88] G. M. Young, *Portrait of an Age: Victorian England*, 2nd edn (Oxford, 1953), p. 85. In John Galsworthy's *Forsyte Saga* (1922), p. 740, Soames Forsyte informs his second wife, a young Frenchwoman, that 'our professional and leisured classes still think themselves a cut above our business classes, except of course the very rich. It may be stupid, but there it is, you see. It isn't advisable in England to let people know you ran a restaurant or kept a shop or were in any kind of trade. It may have been extremely creditable, but it puts a sort of label on you, you don't have such a good time or meet such nice people — that's all.'

[89] Wiener, *English Culture*, pp. 8–14. The prejudice against retail trade was by no means confined to England. See, for example, G. Chaussinand-Nogaret, *The French Nobility in the Eighteenth Century*, tr. William Doyle (Oxford, 1985), p. 92.

[90] *Gentleman's Magazine*, 68 (1798), pt II, p. 1035; Brydges, *Reflections*, p. 44.

[91] *Gentleman's Magazine*, 84 (1814), pt I, p. 32.

establishment became less important as a criterion for admission to the aristocracy. Prior to the 1880s a few peers retained banking and commercial links alongside a landed status acquired over the previous generation or two, but most were from established landed and professional families closely related to the peerage by blood or marriage. From Victoria's accession until 1885 only seven new peers had a commercial or industrial background, and with the exception of Edward Strutt (Lord Belper) they all had public service connections. The situation began to change with the ennoblement of men whose background lay firmly in industry or commerce. W. E. Gladstone attempted to create non-landed peers, but he ran into opposition from the queen, and his efforts were scuppered when his nominees, Samuel Whitbread and Samuel Morley, refused to accept the offer. However, in 1886 three industrialists without aristocratic connections were elevated: Sir Henry Allsopp, Sir Michael Bass – both of them, significantly, brewers – and Sir Thomas Brassey. Thereafter men from industry and commerce made up one-third of all new creations (table 3.2), although the extent of the upheaval needs to be kept in perspective. Between 1885 and 1911 fewer than fifty unlanded families were added to the body, and the true 'self-made men' represented at most a quarter of the new peers. Within the body they represented a tiny minority, despite scaremongering talk of the English peerage becoming a middle-class institution. If anything, the main impact of their admission was that many peers with land felt less obliged to refrain from business connections, and by 1896 167 peers were company directors.[92]

Possibly the most damaging feature of these creations was the fact that some were undoubtedly purchased. The expansion of honours in the later nineteenth century reflected the indifference of the ministers, and, since many were handed out in return for political service, nominations began to originate with the Chief Whip in the Commons. This led to horse-trading. By the 1890s Liberal Party finances were in dire straits, hence Gladstone's decision to sell peerages to a banker and a manufacturer in 1891 in return for

---

[92] Hanham, 'The sale of honours', pp. 277–8; Sir Anthony Wagner, *English Genealogy* (Oxford, 1960), p. 101; Pumphrey, 'The introduction of industrialists', pp. 8–16; Thompson, *English Landed Society*, pp. 293–4. The proportion of peers, baronets and knights among steel manufacturers rose from one in seven in 1865 to one in five in 1875–95. The group also showed signs of looking for socially acceptable marriages, and increasingly they had attended public schools and the older universities. By contrast, few hosiers followed their example: C. Erickson, *British Industrialists: steel and hosiery, 1850–1950* (Cambridge, 1959).

substantial contributions to party-political coffers. Although he regarded this as a temporary expedient, it actually set a precedent for what became common practice in the early years of the twentieth century.[93]

Table 3.2   Family background of new peers, 1837–1911

		Peerage		Gentry		Other	
Period	Total	Number	%	Number	%	Number	%
1837–51	60	27	45	27	45	6	10
1852–66	58	23	40	25	43	10	17
1867–81	103	42	41	45	45	15	14
1882–96	118	26	22	51	43	41	35
1897–1911	124	16	13	55	44	53	43
1837–1911	463	134	29	204	44	125	27

Source: R. E. Pumphrey, 'The introduction of industrialists into the British peerage: a study in the adaptation of a social institution', *American Historical Review*, 65 (1959), p. 7

ADMISSION VIA LOCAL OFFICE

To what extent were these prejudices reflected in admission to the aristocracy? Any measurement is fairly crude, but some indication can be gained from examining office holders, particularly in local government positions. What might be expected is that few families would gain immediate acceptance, and that they might need to be established for a generation or two before receiving the hand of fellowship from the established elite. The exact timing was likely to vary regionally. It might also be anticipated that men who had originated in the professions would be accepted more speedily than those with a background in business and trade. If so, this would suggest that local prejudice was as strong as national bias.

[93] Hanham, 'Sale of honours', pp. 277–89. For an account of twentieth-century sales, see Michael De-la-Noy, *The Honours System* (1985), pp. 89 ff.

The available evidence suggests that entrance was not as restrictive as might have been anticipated. Traditionally the first step was to accept the post of sheriff, a prestigious but expensive and time-consuming position that the local gentry preferred to avoid. Newcomers could use the post as a means of intimating their social ambitions. In Hertfordshire, Londoners and nabobs were more likely to allow themselves to be pricked for this position than established families. During the eighteenth century in Shropshire the position was held by an assortment of men, including Job Walker, an iron master, in 1730, the son of a Shrewsbury draper in 1755, and a rich Liverpool merchant without a coat of arms in 1800.[94] According to Sir James Lowther, Cumbrian country gentlemen believed the Whitehaven tobacco merchants were better placed than themselves to hold the position; the wealth of the merchants 'puts the gentlemen on trying to get the great traders into the list given the judges at the Assizes'. Merchants are known to have held the post in 1725, in 1736 when William Hicks was the man pricked, and in 1747, although Lowther used his influence on more than one occasion to have another of Whitehaven's wealthy traders excused.[95]

Attaining a position on the county bench was possibly the most clear-cut evidence of social acceptance. In Hertfordshire, Londoners and nabobs were both more willing and more anxious to serve on the bench, although their hopes were thwarted by the willingness of the old elite to pack the bench at the expense of newcomers. This was not so in Northamptonshire, where newcomers were just as likely to be accepted, at least prior to the nineteenth century.[96] In the south-west, clothiers sat on the Wiltshire bench during the eighteenth century, while in Gloucestershire by the 1780s a core of established landowning families were supplemented by a dozen or so clothiers from Stroud, ten Bristol merchants, two doctors, three barristers, a brewer, a mercer and a banker. The Bristol merchants included a number of men who had bought estates without severing their commercial interests.[97] Peter How, although twice excused

---

[94] Stone and Stone, *An Open Elite?*, p. 165. Information on Shropshire courtesy of Dr M. D. G. Wanklyn.

[95] Carlisle RO, D/Lons/W, Sir James Lowther to John Spedding, 17 February, 17 November 1737, 17 November 1747; J. Nicolson and R. Burn, *History and Antiquities of the Counties of Cumberland and Westmorland* (1777), vol. II, pp. 575–6.

[96] Stone and Stone, *An Open Elite?*, pp. 165, 247

[97] VCH, *Wiltshire*, vol. V, p. 176; Esther Moir, *The Justice of the Peace* (Harmondsworth, 1969), p. 84.

the post of sheriff, joined the Cumberland commission in 1737 at a time when he was heavily involved in promoting the tobacco trade, while Joseph Burrow, collector of customs in the port of Whitehaven, was a JP by 1750, although his first known land purchase was not until 1754.[98] Newcomers appear to have stood their best chance of inclusion on the bench where the local gentry were weak. Cumberland had relatively few gentry, and a shortage of numbers in South Wales permitted iron and coal masters an entrance on to the bench. The scarcity of resident gentry in Middlesex produced a more notorious situation. According to Edmund Burke, in 1780, the county's justices

were generally the scum of the earth – carpenters, bricklayers and shoemakers – some of whom were notoriously men of such infamous character that they were unworthy of any employ whatever, and others so ignorant that they could scarcely write their name.[99]

During the nineteenth century it proved increasingly difficult to keep non-landed men off the bench. Potential newcomers were not slow to stake a claim. Edward Sugden put his case to Lord Sheffield in 1817:

About four years ago I bought a part of Tilgate Forest, Sussex, upon which I have laid out some thousands of pounds in planting and building, and which I intend to make my country residence during the rest of my life. I am therefore desirous to be in the commission of the peace and I take the liberty respectfully to request your Lordship to place me there. I practiced under the bar four years, and have been upwards of nine years at the Bar, and am now a practicing barrister in the Court of Chancery.[100]

The older values were still respected, although it was particularly difficult to keep out newcomers in counties affected by commercial

[98] Carlisle RO, Quarter Sessions Records; J. R. E. Borren, 'The Burroughs of Carlton Hall', *Transactions of the Cumberland and Westmorland Antiquarian and Archaeological Society*, 69 (1969), p. 195.

[99] A. H. John, *The Industrial Development of South Wales, 1750–1850* (Cardiff, 1950), p. 68. Burke is quoted by S. and B. Webb, *English Local Government: statutory provisions for special purposes* (1922), pp. 387–8. More will be said about the bench in chapter eleven, but it is perhaps worth pointing out that Norma Landau, *The Justices of the Peace, 1679–1760* (1984), p. 318, argues that, even among the landed community, membership of the commission of the peace became less exclusive between 1679 and 1760.

[100] Clements Library, Sheffield Papers, E. B. Sugden to Sheffield, 25 January 1817.

and industrial development. Lord Melbourne argued that manufacturers should be excluded from the county magistracy on the
grounds that country gentlemen usually had better characters, while
the Duke of Wellington commented in 1838 that JPs ought to be
'gentlemen of wealth, worth, consideration, and education: that
they should have been educated for the bar, if possible; and that,
above all, they should be associated with, and be respected by the
gentry of the country.' In practice such attitudes gave the existing
magistrates what amounted to a veto on unacceptable newcomers.
In Merioneth during the 1830s, for example, the magistrates
refused to act, in protest at the appointment of a man who, within
living memory, had operated a retail shop, and was a Methodist. [101]
A similar case occurred in Buckinghamshire during the same
decade. The first Duke of Buckingham, the lord-lieutenant, acting
on a request for information from the Lord Chancellor, dispatched
one of his agents to ascertain the qualifications of two men who had
been proposed for the bench. Both were found to reside in the
county, but one turned out to be living in a paper mill, 'where he
carried on the business of a paper manufacturer'. Soundings at petty
sessions revealed that the paper manufacturer was unacceptable to
the bench; indeed, there were dark murmurings that two JPs
intended to resign if he was selected. Neither candidate had
property in the county, but Colonel Crewe, the second man vetted,
was a gentleman, and therefore acceptable to the bench.
Buckingham was not slow to pick up this hint in his reply to the
Lord Chancellor:

the county of Bucks not being a manufacturing county, and there
being no want of resident gentry, I have ever strictly drawn the rule
of maintaining the respectability and independence of the magistracy by carefully withholding from the commission all persons
actually engaged in trade, and I should more especially draw that
line in the present instance, inasmuch as the trade of papermaking
in the vicinity of High Wycombe would necessarily were I to
recommend a paper maker to be a magistrate, bring him in constant
contact with the lower orders upon points unconnected with his
duty as a magistrate, and thereby place him in an invidious and
unbefitting situation. [102]

---

[101] Carl Zangerl, 'The social composition of the county magistracy in England and
Wales, 1831–37', *Journal of British Studies*, 40 (1971), pp. 117, 120.

[102] Huntington Library, STG Box 377/83, Thomas Tindal to the Duke of
Buckingham, 2 December 1836, Buckingham to the Lord Chancellor, 7 December
1836.

Hardly surprisingly, the paper manufacturer was not recommended. A similar attitude was taken by Lord Brownlow in Lincolnshire during the 1820s and 1830s. He believed that the post of justice ought to be limited to members of the traditional landed elite, men with a clear yearly landed income of around £2000, connections with old county families and the right educational background. The figure of £2000 could be bent if necessary, rather than accept men with a professional or commercial background. Finally, when in 1831 the rural area around Keswick in the Lake District required a magistrate, one of the Cumberland gentry, Humphrey Senhouse, informed Lord Lonsdale that he thought none of the men residing in the vicinity of the town was properly qualified, mainly because they were small freeholders working their own land, or because the money with which they had acquired their land had recently been derived from business.[103]

Such entrenched attitudes were hard to sustain over time. The predominantly rural counties appear to have retained their landed benches almost intact, possibly accepting the occasional brewer. Sometimes this was achieved only by understaffing or through considerable use of clergymen. By 1831 Lincolnshire had 52 clerical justices in a total magistracy of 111. Given the size of the county this was a relatively small bench, and the situation had not altered significantly by 1876 when 57 of the 183 magistrates were clergymen. Other counties to use a high number of clergy during the nineteenth century were Sussex, Herefordshire, Essex and Yorkshire, while only Derbyshire totally refused to make use of them.[104]

Elsewhere businessmen could not long be denied. Newly landed men with business connections had little difficulty attaining the East Riding bench during the nineteenth century, and ironmasters were admitted in the Black Country.[105] In the heartland of the industrial revolution – Lancashire – wealthy cotton manufacturers could meet the legal requirement for the magistracy shortly after

---

[103] Olney, *Rural Society and County Government*, pp. 98–100; Thompson, *English Landed Society*, pp. 110–11.

[104] Gutzke, 'Social status of landed brewers', pp. 108–9; Zangerl, 'The social composition of the county magistracy', pp. 118–20; B. Keith-Lucas, *The Unreformed Local Government System* (1980), p. 50; Moir, *The Justice of the Peace*, pp. 107, 162, 161. More will be said regarding clerical magistrates in chapter eleven.

[105] J. T. Ward, *East Riding Landed Estates in the Nineteenth Century* (York, 1967), p. 6; D. Phillips, 'The Black Country magistracy, 1835–1860', *Midland History*, 3 (1976), pp. 161–90.

1800, but they were excluded from the bench down to the 1830s by blatant social prejudice. Existing JPs found them unacceptable on account of their lack of true gentility, their supposed inability to be impartial in cases involving workers and masters, and of course their involvement in trade. The policy came unstuck as a result of the growth of population and industry in the Manchester area. Business on the Salford Hundred bench increased rapidly as a result, leaving the few resident local gentry severely overstretched. By 1831 the Hundred had only one active magistrate for every 14,852 of the population, whereas none of the county's other five Hundreds had a ratio in excess of 1:7307. To ease the situation, a few manufacturers were admitted to the bench, but normally only if they had retired from business and owned non-industrial property. In 1832, however, G. W. Wood, a leading Manchester cotton merchant and a member of the town's chamber of commerce, was elected MP for South Lancashire, and he immediately became a consultant on nominations to the bench. This helped to break the log-jam; by 1837 fourteen cotton manufacturers had been appointed, and by 1841 21 per cent of the acting bench was associated with the industry. All the barriers were effectively broken down by 1851, at which point it was normal for textile masters to act in the county.[106]

If the middle class were admitted to county benches later than in Lancashire, infiltration was none the less inevitable. In general terms, before mid-century it would have been unthinkable for an individual to remain active in commerce or manufacturing – with the possible exception of brewing – but this was increasingly the case towards 1900. Such people represented nearly 11 per cent of all justices in Caernarvonshire, Derbyshire, Westmorland, Hertfordshire and Somerset by 1867, over 16 per cent of those appointed during the following decade, and 30 per cent of those added between 1877 and 1887. Business magistrates penetrated the Cheshire bench in such numbers by the 1880s that 'government by Quarter Sessions in the 1880s was in fact rule by a class of successful business people presided over by the great landowners or county political patrons.'[107] However, such men could not automatically penetrate

[106] D. Foster, 'Class and county government in early-nineteenth century Lancashire', *Northern History*, 9 (1974), pp. 48–61; Howe, *The Cotton Masters*, pp. 254–7.

[107] Zangerl, 'The social composition of the county magistracy', p. 124; J. M. Lee, *Social Leaders and Public Persons* (Oxford, 1963), pp. 22–3. Zangerl's figures may be too high. According to Gutzke business JPs represented little more than 10 per cent of the total as late a ʼ887: 'Social status of landed brewers', pp. 98–9.

the benches. In late nineteenth-century Cumbria, no more than one-fifth of the magistrates had direct industrial or commercial connections, despite the fact that the county was now widely industralized.[108] In non-industrial counties numbers were even more restricted. Over the period 1868–89, when the third Duke of Buckingham was Lord Lieutenant of Buckinghamshire, the old values were enforced wherever possible, and active business interests were regarded as an automatic disqualification. By 1887 9 per cent of the eighty-eight justices nominated by the duke had direct connections with the business world, and five out of the eight men involved were landed gentry. Only fourteen of the eighty-eight were professional or businessmen lacking any landed connection, and many of these had been educated at a public school or ancient university.[109]

A final test of local acceptance was to stand as an MP, but here the obstables were formidable. Existing landowners controlled the Commons through the return of their own family connections, and by borough patronage. Incomer penetration was consequently difficult, and in Northamptonshire, Northumberland and Hertfordshire the problems may have increased after 1700.[110] Sir Charles Holt was chosen and mandated by Birmingham industrialists in 1774 when he stood for one of the two Warwickshire seats, and thereafter the town returned a candidate until 1832. By the later eighteenth century a fair sprinkling of men who had bought landed estates moved into Parliament without abandoning their business interests. A number of bankers and merchants held seats, and, although the majority of the latter were in business in London, prominent outports which sent such a member to Westminster included Bristol, Liverpool and Newcastle. No identifiable industrialists made the Commons before 1790, but, according to one estimate, by 1812 representatives of big business, commerce and banking constituted about one-quarter of the membership.[111] However, in 1837 only ninety-seven MPs from banking, manufacturing and trade could be identified, and as late as

[108] J. D. Marshall and J. K. Walton, *The Lake Counties from 1830 to the Mid-Twentieth Century* (Manchester, 1981), p. 120.

[109] W. C. Lubenow, 'Social recruitment and social attitudes: the Buckinghamshire magistrates, 1868–1888', *Huntington Library Quarterly*, 40 (1976–7), pp. 247–68.

[110] Stone and Stone, *An Open Elite?*, p. 246. On social climbers in Parliament in the 1760s, see Sir Lewis Namier, *The Structure of Politics at the Accession of George III*, 2nd edn (1957), pp. 111–14.

[111] J. Brooke, *The House of Commons, 1754–1790* (Oxford, 1964), pp. 193–203; Christie, *Wars and Revolutions*, p. 28.

1865 just 122 members were identifiably from trade.[112] Even an anti-aristocratic observer could believe that because the group was accustomed and educated to perform the duties of government it was more likely to produce men suited for such work than any other social group[113]. Hippolyte Taine regarded the group as socially exclusive. Even when accepted in the rural community, a newcomer 'will not succeed in being returned to represent them in Parliament . . . the public will say "He is too little known, he does not belong to the county yet"'.[114] It was only in 1880 that a Parliament was elected in which business and industry had a majority. Over the period 1868–1910, MPs whose livelihood was based on industry and trade increased from 31 to 53 per cent of Conservative MPs, and from 50 to 66 per cent among Liberals.[115]

PATTERNS OF UPWARD MOBILITY

From the late seventeenth century the established pattern was for a family to buy land, but thereafter progress over the social hurdles followed no set pattern. The price of land and the problems of moving further into society ensured that only a handful of newcomers turned themselves into substantial landowners within a short time-span. During the demographically difficult decades from the mid-seventeenth to the mid-eighteenth centuries, interpenetration of land with office, law and business was intense in Northamptonshire, Northumberland and Hertfordshire, with few gentry families on the move unless they had assistance from other income sources. Non-landed incomes penetrated the land market

---

[112] E. J. Evans, *The Forging of the Modern State, 1783–1870* (1983), p. 216; W. L. Guttsman (ed.), *The English Ruling Class* (1969), pp. 149–58. For the particular case of the Lancashire cotton masters after 1832, see Howe, *The Cotton Masters*, pp. 95–132.

[113] Ponsonby, *The Decline of Aristocracy*, p. 15. The sentiment can be found in contemporary novels. In Disraeli's *Coningsby* (1844; Harmondsworth, 1983), pp. 434–5, Lord Monmouth instructs the young Coningsby to stand for Darlford; while in Trollope's *The Duke's Children* (1880; Oxford, 1983), pp. 104–5, the Duke of Omnium simply informs Silverbridge – his eldest son – that he will sit for the family borough, whatever his political persuasion. Among flesh-and-blood examples, Lord John Manners was not untypical, finding himself in Parliament at the age of twenty-three under the tutelage of his father the Duke of Rutland: Guttsman (ed.), *The English Ruling Class*, pp. 160–1.

[114] Hippolyte Taine, *Notes on England* (1872), p. 173.

[115] Thompson, 'Britain', pp. 24–5; Guttsman, *The British Political Elite*, p. 104.

only to reach the lowest rung of the social ladder.[116] What happened thereafter? Some survived and established a family, while others merely acquired a country house or a villa which they could use for their own lifetime. Those who left it to future generations to establish the family are not easy to trace, although a few examples help to illustrate the process. Godfrey Webster (d. 1720), a 'citizen and clothworker of London', sent his son Thomas to the Middle Temple in 1697, and cemented the family fortune made in the City by acquiring property in Essex and London. Thomas (1677–1751) gradually obtained the trappings of gentility: a baronetcy in 1703; Sheriff of Essex, also in 1703; and a seat in Parliament for Colchester in 1705. The family fortunes were relocated in Sussex during the 1720s, although some of the Essex property was retained for a younger son, and for a trust to provide an income for his wife. In 1721 Sir Thomas Webster married his daughter into the landed gentry, and he began to live the life of a country gentleman. By the later nineteenth century the family holding was approximately 6000 acres yielding £5000 annually.[117]

John Spedding, estate steward to Sir James Lowther of Whitehaven in the first half of the eighteenth century, originally trained his own son James to follow him in the post. In the 1740s James Spedding made a rapid fortune when the Whitehaven tobacco trade boomed, and by the later 1740s he was turning himself into a local landowner. His eldest son became a country gentleman with no attachment to the town.[118] Richard Arkwright may have been a pioneer of the industrial revolution, but his son and grandsons gradually moved into county society, and by the 1840s the only obvious reminder of the origin of their wealth 'was merely the hank of cotton, argent, on the crest of each of the landed brothers'.[119] Thomas Greene (d. 1810), a London solicitor, married his son Thomas (1794–1872) to the daughter of a baronet and paved the way for social climbing. Thomas the son bought a 600-acre estate in 1821, described as 'well adapted to the residence of a genteel

---

[116] Stone and Stone, *An Open Elite?*, pp. 209–10.

[117] Judith A. Brent, *A Catalogue of the Battle Abbey Estate Archives* (East Sussex RO, 1973), pp. 3–16. The family sold Battle Abbey in 1857 to the future fourth Duke of Cleveland, but repurchased it in 1901: *Complete Baronetage*, vol. IV, pp. 188–9.

[118] J. V. Beckett, *Coal and Tobacco: the Lowthers and the economic development of West Cumberland, 1660–1760* (Cambridge, 1981), p. 114.

[119] E. L. Jones, 'Industrial capital and landed investment: the Arkwrights in Herefordshire, 1809–1843', in *Agriculture and the Industrial Revolution* (1974), pp. 175–6.

family'. Three years later he was returned to Parliament for Lancaster, and his local duties included chairing Quarter Sessions. During the 1830s he built a new manor house at Whittington, and began to buy additional property to consolidate the estate. His son Dawson (1822–97) continued this policy, to leave an estate of between 900 and 1100 acres. Only death duties brought this progress to a halt, and the estate was sold in 1924.[120] Finally, Francis Hall (1717–1801) was a Nottingham hosier in the mid-eighteenth century, but his son Thomas (1742–1835) bought his way into shares and consols, lent money on mortgages, and from 1781 began to buy land. By 1826 he had amassed 1939 acres in eleven separate parcels through Nottinghamshire and Leicestershire. However, he managed to consolidate much of the property by the time of his death in order to establish his son Thomas Dickinson Hall as the new squire. T. D. Hall graduated from the Inner Temple in 1837, obtained a coat of arms the following year, married into the local gentry in 1840, and served as high sheriff for the county in 1843. He built himself a manor house at Whatton, became a magistrate in both Nottinghamshire and Leicestershire, and a deputy-lieutenant in Nottinghamshire. At his death in 1879 he bequeathed to his widow 2664 acres in Nottinghamshire, 556 acres in Leicestershire, 20 acres in Lincolnshire, with a gross annual value of £6197. The family now figured among John Bateman's greater owners, whereas a century earlier they had been hosiers.[121]

Few incentives existed for a family to attempt entrance into the landed elite within a single generation, and it seems clear that by the nineteenth century the majority of newcomers bought on a smaller scale than their predecessors. The option of developing a family dynasty was left to later generations.[122] Existing families did what they could to maintain their estates intact, through the strict settlement or, in the case of line failure, via indirect inheritance. Increasingly in the later eighteenth and nineteenth centuries this practice was accompanied by demands that the heir should

[120] B. M. Copeland, *Whittington: the story of a country estate* (Guiseley, 1981), pp. 14–33, 144.

[121] A. Henstock, 'The Halls of Whatton: the faltering rise of a Victorian landed family', *Transactions of the Thoroton Society*, 86 (1982), pp. 197–205.

[122] W. D. Rubinstein, 'New men of wealth and the purchase of land in nineteenth-century England', *Past and Present*, 92 (1981), pp. 138–42; Stone and Stone, *An Open Elite?*, pp. 206–7.

substitute the family surname in place of his own.[123] As a result, newcomers generally had to create an estate piecemeal, and even that did not guarantee their acceptance into local society, which varied across the country and through time; indeed, local differences were such that, while it still took a couple of generations to join county society in parts of rural Lincolnshire during the nineteenth century, newcomers to South Lindsey did not find their commercial and urban origins a stumbling block to local acceptance.[124] Similarly, individuals also found that conditions varied. Richard Arkwright's son, also Richard, encountered suspicion among his Derbyshire neighbours, the dukes of Rutland and Devonshire, but like other industrialists he had little difficulty penetrating Herefordshire society. Although one landowner could still refer to the family as tradesmen, the Duke of Norfolk pointedly invited the younger Arkwright to dine at his seat of Holme Lacy.[125] Disparities are also clear from the pre-1888 county magistracy. By absorbing and utilizing new men, especially in the counties where industry and trade were becoming preponderant, the magistracy ensured its own survival in local government, and benches gradually came to reflect the social make-up of the counties that they served. Even on the eve of reform, the traditional landed hegemony was far from broken in areas such as Buckinghamshire and Lincolnshire, although it had been impossible to deny entrance to new men in the expanding commercial and industrial regions. If a single generalization is warranted, it is that rising gentry, office holders and lawyers were always more generally acceptable to county society than men with a business background, thus reflecting a long-held bias against 'trade'.

The implications of these trends will become apparent in later chapters. In part III the social and political hold of the established elite is examined in greater detail, to show why their values were accepted and everyone else conformed. However, a major reason for this acceptance is that the aristocracy never became anachronistic, and a primary explanation for this was their positive economic contribution, which is examined next.

---

[123] A full explanation of this process is offered in Stone and Stone, *An Open Elite?*, pp. 126–42.

[124] Olney, *Rural Society and County Government*, p. 29; J. Obelkevich, *Religion and Rural Society: South Lindsey, 1825–1875* (Oxford, 1976), pp. 28–9.

[125] Jones, 'Industrial capital and landed investment', pp. 170–1.

Part II

The Aristocracy and the Economy

Chapter Four

————◦❀◦————

The Aristocratic Estates

The landowners are the capitalists to whom the land belongs. Their property comprises the soil and all that is beneath it, and the buildings and other permanent works upon it, required for the accommodation of the people, and of the working stock employed in its cultivation. In nearly all permanent improvements arising from the progress of agriculture he is also expected to share the cost. And he is necessarily concerned in the general prosperity and good management of his estate. The property of the landowners, independent of minerals, yields an annual rent of sixty-seven millions sterling, and is worth a capital value of two thousand millions. There is no other body of men in the country who administer so large a capital on their own account, or whose influence is so widely extended and universally present.

James Caird, *The Landed Interest and the Supply of Food* (1878), 5th edn (1967), pp. 57–9

Despite their social and, to a lesser extent, political leadership throughout the period 1660–1914, the aristocracy have not generally received a good press for their contribution to economic development. They are accused of opting out, by retreating from farming into *rentier* status, by leaving risk-taking to tenants, and by acting negatively in terms of entrepreneurialism. According to Harold Perkin, their role was 'not direct industrial enterprise'; rather, they provided the land and fixed capital, thereby creating the preconditions for enterprise undertaken by others. Even this, he argues, arose from 'pure self-interest' rather than from any spirit of public duty or desire to promote economic development. While conceding that the aristocracy played a significant role in agriculture and mining, urban development and communications, Perkin none the less concluded that it was 'not their function' to be the makers of the industrial revolution. Their role was to seek profits, and to create 'the climate and conditions in which a spontaneous industrial revolution could take place'.[1] M. L. Bush has taken a similar view: in commercial matters:

the aristocracy shunned direct involvement. . . . The bulk of aristocratic revenues went in current rather than capital expenditure, and the aristocrat's capital spending and credit resources were mostly devoted to the payment of annuities, doweries, portions, the building and rebuilding of family seats, landscaping, estate accumulation, imparking, and other non-productive ventures.

In the process of industrialization 'they neither directly promoted new techniques of production nor provided fixed or working capital for the manufacturing process', although Bush does concede that, as a result of the aristocracy's political power, capital resources and landownership, it was natural that the group should play a role in industrialization. Overall, however, his view is that 'for the most part the English aristocracy remained aloof from industrial production, seeking rigorously to maintain the role of rentier and determined to receive its income in the form of rents, royalties and dividends, rather than of a directly earned profit or salary.'[2] Money was to be made in order to withdraw from the business side of estate management, and to improve the family by means of a larger house and greater ostentation. Moreover, M. J. Wiener has argued that, by inculcating this view into the newly rising business classes, in the longer term the aristocracy had an inhibiting effect on the national economy. In Wiener's view the aristocracy succeeded in the second half of the nineteenth century in 'reshaping the industrial bourgeoisie in its own image'. New wealth was absorbed into old, as entrepreneurs turned themselves into the image of the class they were supposedly usurping. As a result, Britain industrialized without developing a straightforward bourgeois or industrial elite. He indicts the aristocracy not only for failing to take a lead themselves, but also for producing an unfavourable climate for economic endeavour, although his assumption of a tacit acceptance of this ethos by businessmen may not be justified in view of what is known, for example, of their land-purchasing activities.[3]

The most serious objection to this negative viewpoint is that it may downgrade the significance of the aristocratic contribution to economic development, and in the following chapters an attempt will be made to

[1] Harold Perkin, *The Origins of Modern English Society, 1780–1880* (1969), pp. 74–9.

[2] M. L. Bush, *The English Aristocracy* (Manchester, 1984), pp. 173, 187–8, 196.

[3] Martin J. Wiener, *English Culture and the Decline of the Industrial Spirit, 1850–1950* (Cambridge, 1981), pp. 8, 10, 14, 173–4.

redress the balance. Although there is little doubt that some aristocrats took a reactionary attitude towards economic change – outlawing industry from their closed villages, refusing to work iron ore deposits if the result would be a scarred landscape, and vigorously defending property rights in Parliament – the overall picture is much more optimistic, even if it cannot always be measured in quantitative terms. An estate was an inheritance, and consequently the current owner could not escape responsibility for its improvement, development and conservation. What this actually involved changed through time almost out of recognition. Already by the end of the seventeenth century demesne farming had effectively disappeared in England, although most landlords retained a home farm with which to supply family needs. Consequently the majority of aristocrats let at least part of their resources to tenants. In this sense capitalist relations had arrived in the English countryside, but it is quite a different matter to argue that responsibility had therefore passed from the landowners. In the two and a half centuries after 1660 the task of managing a landed estate became infinitely more complex. Agricultural developments, particularly the revolution in techniques, demanded a much higher level of skill and greater capital investment. The exploitation of mineral deposits – vital to industrialization – demanded investment and efficient organization, while, for the lucky few, urban development offered yet more opportunities for lucrative enterprise.

None of this was possible without leadership from the top, and the fact that the English aristocracy let their property to tenants did not necessarily imply either a desire or even an ability to opt out of running the estate. Increasingly from 1660 the London season and, from the 1690s, annual parliaments drew the most substantial property owners to the capital, and possibly also to one of the spas, for several months of each year. The landowner as farmer could no longer survive, and demesne farming on a large scale gave way to farm leasing by paid managers. However, efficient stewardship depended on the ability of the owner to appoint a suitable agent, on his willingness to make regular visits to oversee the activities of his servant, make policy decisions and ensure that the tenants were working harmoniously with the manager; and on his capacity to develop a rapport with his tenants. To this end it was necessary to make decisions about farm sizes, rents and investments. Only by overseeing the management team could the owner hope to extract the best from his estate, and effective oversight demanded that he be well informed. Furthermore, this element of knowledge and active personal control was most apparent in relation to agricultural practice. With a few notable exceptions, home farms were usually not centres of experimentation and innovation, but this did not prevent owners from playing a significant role in agricultural societies and shows, and in promoting favourable parliamentary legislation. Leasing did not absolve a landlord from responsibility, and the improvement of farming was certainly not in spite of landlord influence.

In terms of contribution to economic development, it is all too easy to look at a few notable aristocratic examples, and to ignore the wider, overall role of the group. Essentially the aristocracy played a consistent role. They were happy to exploit or to promote the exploitation of their resources, especially coal and other minerals, to take responsibility for the roads, and to lay down ground plans for urban development. By contrast, manufacturing industry, artificial communications such as canals and railways, and urban building, they left to business and merchant entrepreneurs. The fact that they had a set of values associated with their estate resources is not an indication that they took no interest in development elsewhere, but a recognition that like all good entrepreneurs their prime responsibility lay with their wholly owned resources. Possibly the most important industrial contribution came in the early stages of economic development. Some vital technological breakthroughs were pioneered by aristocrats, including the Newcomen engine, which they adopted in its formative stages in order to overcome the problem of flooding which prevented deep mining. Even if they opted out as industrial development became more complex, and risk-sharing more attractive, they still had to take responsibility for granting reasonable leases, undertaking trial borings, promoting necessary legislation and protecting colliery landscapes – none of which suggests a particularly passive role. Moreover, those who stayed the course – and there were a number of them – reaped the financial reward.

In promoting communications improvements, the aristocratic role was undeniably important. A few were risk-taking pioneers, notably, of course, the Duke of Bridgewater with his canal, and also the marquesses of Bute and Londonderry in port development. Aristocrats also played a vital parliamentary role in promoting legislation to establish turnpike trusts and canal and railway companies. Although it is true that they sometimes took a shortsighted attitude to improvements which was only cured with time, they played a critical role in financing road improvement, and many took an active part, particularly in railway development. As landowners, the aristocracy were in a position to promote, delay or even to prevent urban development. For family reasons they showed a distinct preference for ground-rent leasing, since this gave them a long-term interest in the value of the land. Where they owned part of a site, their preference was usually for middle-class housing, although market forces tended to dictate whether their hopes could be realized. Overall, they were most influential in setting development in motion, and in long-term site planning. By contrast, they were not often involved in the actual building process.

Did all this amount to helping or hindering economic development? There are no simple answers to this question, but it is clear that as a unit of business the potential profitability of an estate depended on the level of investment. If anything was destined to test an aristocrat's commitment, it was his financial involvement, and here opting out was almost impossible. The owner's capital consisted of the land, the farm buildings, fences, hedges, gates, access roads and drainage works, all of which required annual maintenance. In addition, a large country house tended to be an expensive annual burden. Taxation apart, a proportion of each owner's gross income was always spoken for in advance, but estates also benefited from capital outlay, and here each owner was confronted with a variety of choices. Replacing or extending the country house, together with laying out the grounds in contemporary fashion, often enhanced a man's prestige within the community, but at the expense of reducing the capital available for longer-term productive investment. More pertinently, the demands on an owner's capital increased through time as a result of the benefits accruing from agricultural and industrial developments. Admittedly he was usually responsible only for the fixed and not for the working capital, which was provided by the tenant, and this arrangement was basically equitable. The tenant was not required to use valuable capital for durable improvements affecting farm buildings, which were likely to prove beneficial beyond his time, but since he took the greater risk he also reaped the larger share of the profits. Despite this, the owner had to take decisions about the use of his own capital. He had to decide between agricultural and industrial demands, conspicuous outlay on building works, and calls on his finance away from the estate.

In this sense it has to be remembered that an estate was expected to produce a level of profit sufficient to support the lifestyle expected of an aristocrat. He had to finance portions and jointures, a London household, electoral expenditure, and other outgoings depending on his personal predilections. Through time, many estates seem not to have produced sufficient income for their owners, resulting in an increasing level of debt. Capital starvation could have severe repercussions. An owner lacking capital for investment in infrastructural improvements, such as building, fencing and drainage, was unlikely to be able to provide an environment in which he could attract tenants capable and willing to adopt advanced techniques.

Consequently the question arose whether landed indebtedness retarded progress by reducing the level of landlord capital. Whether this was the case is difficult to determine. Cheap capital was readily available in nineteenth-century England, and it may be that the use to which aristocrats put it helped to promote consumption and stimulate the economy. In this sense, the fact that they might have to borrow, to finance drainage improvements and rebuild farms, did not necessarily ensure that their debts were detrimental to the economy. On balance, their contribution was a positive one, even if their decision-making did not always follow strictly business lines.

RESPONSIBILITIES OF ESTATE MANAGEMENT

For the majority of their wealth English aristocrats depended on the produce of their estates, either in the form of rents, or via the profits of agricultural and industrial enterprise. Since an estate was merely in trust to the life tenant – on the understanding that he would preserve and develop it for future generations – most owners accepted that they had a management responsibility. Financial need and family interest together produced generations of conscientious owners ready to take their duties seriously. Naturally a few were not so keen. On unexpectedly succeeding to Wroxton Abbey in 1817 Frederic North expressed uncompromising sentiments:

like every other person who succeeds to an estate I am in all probability straightened in circumstances for the remainder of my life, and all my schemes of comfort completely overset by new concerns and relations, freedom from which made me always bless my lot in being born a younger brother.

Having inherited 'this detestable estate', he found it necessary to return to England from Italy in order to establish his claim, but he soon returned to southern Europe expressing his determination to avoid future business.[4] The Marquess of Titchfield clearly experienced similar sentiments in the 1840s when his father, the fourth Duke of Portland, proposed 'that we should change places, that you should make me an allowance to allow me to live in a corner of this house [Welbeck], and that you should take upon yourself the whole management and possession of everything else.' Portland, in his mid-seventies, had clearly had enough, but his appeal fell on deaf ears.

[4] Clements Library, Sheffield MSS, F. North to Lord Sheffield, 4 February 1817.

'Upon the general scheme,' Titchfield replied, 'the more I think the greater the horror I have of it altogether. I cannot reconcile myself to the thoughts of it at all.' Despite a further appeal, Portland found his son adamant, which is perhaps not surprising in view of the fact that when he finally became the fifth duke a decade later Titchfield lived the life of a recluse at Welbeck.[5] Successive nineteenth-century dukes of Bedford were also known to dislike the responsibility thrust upon them by having to run the extensive family estates. The seventh duke considered himself a well-paid agent with an income of £12,000 annually.[6]

For the majority of those who succeeded to an estate, any such qualms were firmly suppressed in the interests of the family. The knowledge they possessed for the task confronting them must have varied considerably. Some had undoubtedly trained on the job, under their father's tutelage, although many others must have inherited without such experience, particularly in the demographically difficult decades around the turn of the eighteenth century. Sir James Lowther, who inherited his father's West Cumberland estates in 1706, had received tutelage on estate matters from his father while resident in London during the 1690s. His only known visit to the area was for a month in the summer of 1703.[7] Joshua Trimmer, writing in the 1840s, noted that landowners were 'generally ignorant of everything relating to the management of landed property, except that which ministers to the amusements of the turf, the sports of the field, and the political influence connected with the land'. A decade later James Caird claimed that there was no proper training for landowners, who frequently inherited when still ignorant of the duties involved and conscious of their inability to perform them. Later he noted that the profession of landowner was the only one for which neither training nor aptitude was considered necessary.[8] Plenty of literature was available, offering advice on every aspect of the task in hand, but how many owners were ready to engage in a course of intensive study is unknown.[9]

[5] Nottingham University Library, Portland MSS, Pwk 502a, Duke of Portland to the Marquess of Titchfield, 17 and 22 May 1844; Pwk 370d, Titchfield to Portland, 20 May 1844; A. S. Turberville, *Welbeck Abbey and its Owners* (1939), vol. II, pp. 444–6.

[6] Brian Masters, *The Dukes*, 2nd edn (1980), p. 155.

[7] Carlisle RO, D/Lons/W, James Lowther to Sir John Lowther, 8 June 1703.

[8] Joshua Trimmer, *On the Improvement of Land as an Investment for Capital* (1847), p. 30; James Caird, *English Agriculture in 1850–51* (1852), p. 493, and *The Landed Interest and the Supply of Food* (1878), 5th edn (1967), pp. 102–3.

[9] Owners were offered an increasingly large body of literature. An early text was Giles Jacob's *The Country Gentleman's Vade Mecum* (1717), a pocket-book obviously

What is clear is that the job varied with the size of the estate and the extent of interests. Since the greater owners almost invariably had estates and houses scattered over a wide area, personal control was impossible. Regular visits were useful if tedious when many properties were involved, and it was not unknown for distant properties – particularly in Ireland – to be entirely neglected; the sixth Duke of Somerset even found his English estates a burden, failing to visit his Cumberland property between 1688 and his death in 1748.[10] Consequently the multiplicity of functions – household, estate or industrial – which characterized great estates ensured that owners had to divide responsibilities with managers. Just who did what within the partnership varied. On smaller estates owners were better placed to take a day-to-day interest in affairs, but even here there were complications. Some owners were away from their estates for long periods, particularly with regular meetings of Parliament and the increasing attraction of urban living.

---

designed as an everyday companion for the landowner as he made his way around the estate, and including information on husbandry, parks, gardens, timber, and the type and number of employees required as well as their wages. Similar, although more extensive in scope, was *The Country Gentleman's Companion* (1753), reputedly written by 'a country gentleman, from his own experience'. Later works in the same mould included Nathaniel Kent's *Hints to Gentlemen of Landed Property* (1775), Walter Robinson's *The Landlord's Pocket Lawyer* (1780), Thomas Stone's *Essay on Agriculture with a View to Inform Gentlemen of Landed Property whether their Estates are Managed to the Greatest Advantage* (1785) and Charles Ley, *The Nobleman, Gentleman, Land Steward and Surveyor's Compleat Guide* (1787). As the last of these titles implies, much of the information on offer came in books which were at least ostensibly addressed to stewards. Ley's subtitle made it clear that the information provided was 'for the use and information of noblemen, as well as stewards'. The classic eighteenth-century text aimed at the steward, Edward Laurence's *The Duty of a Steward to his Lord* (1727), was dedicated to the Duchess of Buckinghamshire, and included an introduction basically addressed to the problems associated with choosing a steward. As the tasks became more complex, the books became longer. Laurence's work was updated by John Mordaunt, *The Complete Steward* (1761), but, whereas Laurence had contained his comments within 212 pages, Mordaunt's work ran into two volumes and to over 900 pages. These two works were themselves updated by *The Modern Land Steward* (1801), which showed its modern outlook by including information on letting urban building land – 'one of the surest methods of raising a great estate' (p. 70) – as well as the need to consider the possibility of establishing manufactories. Among a vast nineteenth-century outpouring of a similar nature was David Low's *On Landed Property and the Economy of Estates* (1844) and J. L. Morton's *The Resources of Estates* (1858). The *Journal of the Royal Agricultural Society of England* also provided a ready stream of information available to owners and agents alike.

[10] Carlisle RO, D/Lons/W, Sir James Lowther to Thomas Tickell, 19 May 1688, Sir James Lowther to John Spedding, 13 September 1743, 15 December 1747.

If the size of estates affected the structure of management, the variety of interests also played a part. In the world of 1660 the chief management tasks involved collecting the rent and overseeing established farming methods. Over time a variety of new interests complicated the job. The revolution in agricultural techniques raised the level of competence required in controlling an estate, while the industrial interests which many owners developed required a level of knowledge and efficiency beyond the reach of essentially amateur landlords. Alterations in the road network, the building of canals and the exploitation of urban land added extra interest to the landowner's role, but also increased the required level of specialist knowledge. Each of these developments raised the level of management expertise needed to run an estate. Not surprisingly, sophisticated organizational structures were developed to cater for such changes, but because these spread haphazardly a reincarnated owner of 1660 would have found much he could recognize even at the end of the nineteenth century.

PROFESSIONALIZATION OF ESTATE MANAGEMENT

In the later seventeenth century there were almost as many forms of management as estates, but increasing standardization took place through time, especially on the larger estates. Landowners were faced with a variety of possibilities. They could employ one or more full-time managers to look after the estate, perhaps with an over-manager when scattered properties were involved. Alternatively, on a smaller estate they might prefer to employ someone on a part-time basis, perhaps combining the work with a farm tenancy or a legal practice. The major alternative was personal involvement in management, although few aristocrats were sufficiently competent to control a large estate. However, personal involvement went further than playing the part of manager. Even when the landlord opted out of direct control, it was still necessary to play a vital part both in choosing and overseeing his paid employees, and also in dealing with a variety of matters for which responsibility invariably fell on the owner. If an owner chose neither to visit his estate, nor to correspond with his steward, the results could be extremely damaging for the conduct of estate affairs.[11]

---

[11] Peter Roebuck, 'Absentee landownership in the late seventeenth and early eighteenth centuries: a neglected factor in English agrarian history', *Agricultural History Review*, 21 (1973), pp. 1–21.

To manage a landed estate was to run a business; indeed, for all the impact of the industrial revolution, the great landed estate was one of the largest enterprises in the Victorian economy, with turnover on rental income exceeding £200,000 a year on some estates.[12] Consequently it is hardly surprising that owners went to great lengths to ensure good stewardship. The manager's responsibilities lay with the home farm, the house and park, the woodlands and mineral resources, and the tenants. It was not merely a matter of collecting the rents; the job involved letting farms and surveying boundaries, enforcing covenants on recalcitrant tenants, sifting requests for landlord expenditure, and taking responsibility for the estate accounts. In addition, the manager might be expected to take a role in running electoral contests, excluding paupers from the parish, promoting turnpike roads, and controlling the activities of lesser servants, including bailiffs, under-stewards and gardeners.[13] John Hardy (1745–1805), land steward to Walter Spencer-Stanhope in the West Riding of Yorkshire between 1773 and 1803, provides a good example. Hardy's tasks included buying and selling land, fixing agreements, advising on tax and investments, suggesting mineral resources for exploitation, and estimating what interest ought to be taken in canal and iron companies. He offered advice on the reorganization and improvement of the estate – in which he advocated the enclosure of both open field and waste land – and on mineral workings. He was also responsible for maintaining soil quality, and the drains, fences and buildings. He suggested the alteration of farmhouses to accommodate looms and thereby encourage domestic textile production, and the conversion of corn mills into spinning mills for the woollen industry. Perhaps his most vital role, however, was to act as intermediary between an upper-class squire and the more doughty of the tenant farmers. As such he was the pulse the owner could feel in order to discover the health of his estates and tenants, and he did all this for £80 a year and the favourable lease of Barnby Hall with extensive farmlands.[14]

---

[12] Eric Richards, 'The land agent', in *The Victorian Countryside,* ed. G. E. Mingay (1981), p. 439.

[13] Edward Hughes 'The eighteenth-century estate agent', in *Essays in British and Irish History,* ed. H. A. Cronne, T. W. Moody and D. B. Quinn (1949), pp. 185–99; G. E. Mingay, 'The eighteenth-century land steward', in *Land, Labour and Population,* ed. E. L. Jones and G. E. Mingay (1967), pp. 3–27.

[14] Gary Firth, 'The roles of a West Riding land steward, 1773–1803', *Yorkshire Archaeological Journal,* 51 (1979), pp. 105–16.

The largest estates, particularly where they were scattered across several counties, were normally in full-time management, which developed an increasingly standardized format through time. In the early eighteenth century, methods varied considerably. The Northamptonshire estates of the dukes of Grafton were managed during the 1720s by a five-man committee which met as required in London or Northamptonshire, to decide the terms of leases, which buildings to repair, and other matters. The duke attended on occasion, to take the final decision on difficult or controversial measures. Meantime the dukes of Devonshire and Rutland were still relying on bailiffs to undertake most of their work.[15] By around 1750 estates were increasingly organized along lines which were recognizably familiar across the country in one form or another, and which had been emerging over several decades. The need for a proper structure became apparent, as estate business grew in complexity, and owners were absent for longer periods. The result was growing professionalization symbolized in the early nineteenth century by the emergence of the land agent to replace the old position of steward. Training continued to be by experience on estates, at least prior to the opening in 1845 of the Royal Agricultural College at Cirencester. By 1882 most of the students trained there became land agents, although a professional association was formed only in 1902, and formal examinations were not instituted until the 1920s.[16] The shortage of good men was reflected in the high salaries paid to the elite. Francis Blaikie, steward at Thomas William Coke's Holkham in the early nineteenth century, had a salary of £650 (until it was cut by £100 in 1822 to help relieve Coke's financial difficulties), while Earl Fitzwilliam's agent received £1200 a year in 1811, and in 1861 Christopher Haedy was paid £1800 by the Duke of Bedford.[17]

[15] Michael Reed, *The Georgian Triumph, 1700–1830* (1984 edn), p. 87; O. R. F. Davies, 'The Dukes of Devonshire, Newcastle and Rutland, 1688–1714: a study in wealth and political influence' (University of Oxford, D.Phil. thesis, 1971), ch. 5.

[16] David Spring, *The English Landed Estate in the Nineteenth Century: its administration* (Baltimore, Md, 1963), pp. 4, 58, 101; Richards, 'The land agent', p. 445; F. M. L. Thompson, *English Landed Society in the Nineteenth Century* (1963), pp. 158–9, 165–6. Professor Spring's book examines management on some of the greater nineteenth-century estates in more detail than can be attempted here. For administration on the properties of the dukes of Westminster, Northumberland, Cleveland and Devonshire, see also T. H. S. Escott, *England: its people, polity and pursuits*, (1879), vol. I, pp. 42–71. Morton, *The Resources of Estates*, p. 32, argued that standards of management would have benefited from the establishment of university chairs of agriculture.

[17] Richards, 'The land agent', p. 441. Blaikie's role is examined in detail by R. A. C. Parker, *Coke of Norfolk* (Oxford, 1975).

Usually the steward, or, as he became, the agent, operated from London, or from the aristocrat's main country seat. The Duke of Newcastle (d. 1711) had a 'man of substance' to run each of his estates, with a chief manager in London to oversee the whole. His successor, the famous politician, retained a similar structure. The central office was at his house in Lincoln's Inn Fields, from where a man known as the supervisor of the whole, or sometimes just as the secretary, operated.[18] Some of the men of business in London became powerful figures as the eighteenth century progressed. Peter Walter, for example, landowner, MP and attorney, acted in this role for a number of aristocrats in the second and third decades of the century. He only occasionally left London, although in 1724 he spent three months on a tour of inspection of thirty different estates.[19]

London was not necessarily a convenient location, and professional agents preferred to be on the land rather than in an office, with the result that many chief managers made their residence on the owner's main estate. On the Leveson-Gower estates in the West Midlands early in the eighteenth century, George Plaxton revitalized the existing management system by introducing underagents to oversee tenant bailiffs who had been full-time tenants collecting rents only in a part-time capacity.[20] Full-time administration became an increasingly popular trend, as the case of Longleat illustrates. Between 1779 and 1807 the Longleat estate of the Marquess of Bath was run part-time by Thomas Davis, who was answerable to the London-based receiver-general who overlooked the scattered estates. Locally, Davis was recognized as highly competent. He was succeeded in the post by his son Thomas, who in turn trained his own son for the position. However, when Thomas II died in 1839 the post went to Robert Robertson, as part of a management shake-up. Robertson, the first man to enjoy the title of agent rather than steward, had ultimate control of all the marquess's estates, and combined managing Longleat with supervising the accounts of the Herefordshire, Shropshire and Gloucestershire estates. More power and responsibility was matched by more money. Thomas Davis I had received £160 a year, but Robertson's salary was £800.[21]

[18] Davies, 'The Dukes of Devonshire, Newcastle and Rutland', p. 153; R. A. Kelch, *Newcastle: a duke without money* (1974), pp. 20–2.

[19] Howard Erskine-Hill, *The Social Milieu of Alexander Pope* (1975), ch. 4.

[20] J. R. Wordie, *Estate Management in Eighteenth-Century England* (1982), pp. 26–7.

[21] D. P. Gunstone, 'Stewardship and landed society: a study of the stewards of the Longleat estate, 1779–1895' (University of Exeter, MA thesis, 1972).

Over time, a small number of land agents became increasingly influential, so that by 1877 about sixty individuals controlled two-thirds of England.[22] However, only the larger estates could justify full-time management, and below this level two alternatives were most popular. The first of these was to employ a part-time steward who combined the job with other activities. Some might be small landowners themselves, as was the case with John Dicken, who acted for the Rev. Richard Hill in Shropshire.[23] More often than not, however, part-timers were attorneys. It was logical enough to employ a lawyer in this role, since, after rent-collecting, work of a legal nature loomed large in management. Apart from drawing up marriage and estate settlements, lawyers were needed in conjunction with land transactions and leases, and to hold manor courts.[24] However, agricultural experts were almost unanimous in condemning the employment of lawyers as stewards. A country attorney attempting to run a number of estates as well as his normal practice certainly conjures up a picture of inadequacy, and lawyers were frequently accused of neglect; but the real complaint – which became more pertinent as the agricultural revolution proceeded – concerned their ignorance of farming practice. Among reporters to the Board of Agriculture at the end of the eighteenth century, complaints were voiced from as far afield as Devon and Cornwall, Surrey and Middlesex, Derbyshire, Leicestershire and Staffordshire, and the North Riding of Yorkshire. From Derbyshire came the news that attornies were increasingly replacing stewards because salaries were too low to support full-time managers.[25] Even so, the number of lawyer-stewards did not begin to fall until the 1870s, and it was only in the 1890s that their position was finally undermined, as landowners increasingly needed practical men who could look after farms that came in hand.[26]

[22] Richards, 'The land agent', p. 445. For a detailed account of nineteenth-century agency, see Spring, *The English Landed Estate*, ch. 1.

[23] E. M. Jancey, 'An eighteenth-century steward and his work', *Transactions of the Shropshire Archaeological Society*, 56 (1957–8), pp. 34–48.

[24] R. Robson, *The Attorney in Eighteenth-Century England* (Cambridge, 1959), ch. 7. Lawyers were acceptable when management involved little more than enforcing the legal relationship between owners and their tenants, but much less satisfactory as estate management became increasingly complex. As farming became more sophisticated, expert agriculturalists were required: Spring, *The English Landed Estate*, p. 114.

[25] William Marshall, *The Review and Abstract of the County Reports to the Board of Agriculture* (York, 1818), vol. I, p. 465; vol. IV, pp. 29, 130, 187; vol. V, pp. 125, 376, 535, 571.

[26] Richards, 'The land agent', pp. 445. The decline came even later in Wales than in England: D. W. Howell, *Land and People in Nineteenth-Century Wales* (1977), p. 44.

The second alternative on smaller estates was to employ a land agency firm. These organizations only began to operate during the eighteenth century, but they became increasingly popular through time. In their earliest form the agencies were essentially advisers called in to supervise reorganization, and to suggest means of improvement. In essence, this was the role of Thomas Browne, a herald and land surveyor, who inspected the Earl of Egremont's Yorkshire and Cumberland estates during the 1750s and recommended that six bailiffs be replaced by a single steward, that farms should be revalued, and that customary tenants ought to be enfranchised. It was also the role played by Nathaniel Kent, who by the 1790s had established a major land agency business, with two partners, and with offices in Charing Cross.[27] Increasingly such individuals or firms took over the management of estates, sometimes in combination with an advisory role. James Loch, for example, nationally renowned as principal agent to the Sutherland estates, also acted in the management of property for Lord Francis Egerton, the Earl of Carlisle, the Bridgewater Trust, and the trust estates of the earls of Dudley and Viscount Keith. Lord Wharncliffe was told that even a few minutes' conversation with Loch 'would be worth guineas of manuscripts'.[28]

In the course of the nineteenth century, land agency firms played an increasingly important role in management. Christopher Comyns Parker and his son John Oxley Parker administered at least twenty different estates during the seventy years of a land agency practice in Essex, and in 1836 they were reckoned to be supervising 20,000 acres in the county. On a national level, Messrs Rawlence and Squarey were supervising about one-quarter of a million acres in twenty-four counties by the 1890s, and a number of firms operated at both national and local level.[29] While it is clear that they may have been primarily concerned with institutional estates, this was not always the case. Some greater owners used an agency to supervise distant properties rather than hiring a full-time manager, while the extent of their involvement with private landlords is clear from the East Riding of Yorkshire. Of eleven estates exceeding 10,000 acres in the Riding in the 1870s, only six had a resident agent. Although the greater and

[27] H. A. Wyndham, *A Family History, 1688–1837* (1950), pp. 134–6; Pamela Horn, 'An eighteenth-century land agent: the career of Nathaniel Kent (1737–1810)', *Agricultural History Review*, 30 (1982), pp. 1–16.

[28] E. Richards, *The Leviathan of Wealth* (1973), p. 29.

[29] J. Oxley Parker (ed.), *The Oxley-Parker Papers* (Colchester, 1964), p. 166; Richard, 'The land agent', p. 442.

lesser owners together accounted for 60 per cent of the land, just 25 per cent of it was administered by resident stewards and agents.[30]

Rather than employ agents, some landowners preferred to undertake the task of management themselves. The first Baron Ashburnham ran his family's Sussex property with some success in the later seventeenth century, and the second Baron Gower made a competent job of looking after his family's West Midlands estates during the 1720s and 1730s. Sir John Griffin Griffin of Audley End in Essex was also successful, inheriting 3257 acres in 1762, and leaving at his death in 1797 an improved, modernized and enlarged estate. In the early nineteenth century the second Marquess of Bute, with six widely scattered estates, came as near as was possible in such circumstances to personal management. Only his barrister-agent O. T. Bruce was privy to matters relating to all the properties, and Bute proved temperamentally suited to the role of professional landowner.[31] Personal control was easiest on small estates. When old Essex families were replaced by newcomers with lesser properties, resident stewards tended to be replaced by owner-managers.[32]

Increasingly, personal control became a burden and an imposition, and it may have been symbolic that following Lord Gower's personal management an official hierarchy was established on his estates in 1742. Management was simply becoming too complicated for what were often the hamfisted efforts of the owners, although misguided enthusiasts like the first Marquess of Bute were still capable of convincing themselves that they were making a good job of the task.[33]

[30] Barbara English, 'Patterns of estate management in East Yorkshire, *c.* 1840– *c.* 1880', *Agricultural History Review*, 32 (1984), pp. 29–48. Dr English's findings raise doubts about Professor Spring's argument that the 'distinctive mark' of greater estates was their resident agent. In his view, owners with estates of 9000 acres or more 'almost invariably employed a resident land agent': *The English Landed Estate*, pp. 3–4, 7.

[31] G. E. Mingay, *English Landed Estates in the Eighteenth Century* (1963), pp. 59–67; Wordie, *Estate Management*, pp. 35–40; J. D. Williams, 'The landowner as manager', *Essex Journal*, 15 (1980), pp. 74–82; John Davies, *Cardiff and the Marquesses of Bute* (Cardiff, 1981), pp. 42–8. Arthur Young, *General View of the Agriculture of Lincolnshire*, 2nd edn (1813), pp. 22–3, wrote approvingly of the management of Sir Joseph Banks's estate at Revesby largely because of the careful layout of his estate office.

[32] Colin Shrimpton, 'The landed society and the farming community of Essex in the late eighteenth and early nineteenth centuries' (University of Cambridge, Ph.D. thesis, 1965), p. 206.

[33] Davies, *Cardiff and the Marquesses of Bute*, pp. 34–5.

The advantages of professional control became clearer through time, as, for example, in the case of accounting. A steward was expected to keep proper accounts, whereas a landowner acting on his own behalf did not always bother. Sir Daniel Fleming of Rydal in Westmorland kept his own accounts in the second half of the seventeenth century, although his third son Daniel was effectively estate steward until his death in 1698. The accounts were entered in two fat ledgers, but rents were not included and they were never balanced. Similarly, Humphrey Senhouse of Netherhall on the West Cumberland coast also maintained unbalanced running accounts.[34] Over time, such practices became a liability. According to one Cardiganshire landowner in the 1830s, an owner's rental was likely to be regarded as insufficiently professional to act as supporting evidence in disputes with tenants.[35] In the mid-nineteenth century, James Caird claimed that landlords were doubly guilty if they not only were ignorant of good practice themselves, but also failed to appoint qualified agents in their places. In view of what is known of the role played by stewards and agents in agricultural improvement, there would seem to have been good grounds for such comments.[36]

ABSENTEE LANDLORDS AND ESTATE MANAGEMENT

Employing a good manager did not mean that the owner divested himself of responsibility for the estate. Writing in about 1670 on the decay of rents, Sir William Coventry found one of the chief causes to be a shortage of tenants caused 'by the nobility and gentry's living so much in London'. Since they no longer farmed, landowners had more land to lease, which gave potential tenants a greater bargaining power, and incomers preferred to farm on the estates of non-resident owners, since these were likely to be mismanaged.[37] Edward Laurence's viewpoint was much the same when he addressed country stewards in 1726:

every temptation should be encouraged which tends to invite noblemen and others to visit their estates in person every summer; for, without such a presence, whatever others may think who have not a sense of it, I who know

---

[34] Beckett, thesis, p. 121.

[35] Howell, *Land and People in Nineteenth-Century Wales*, p. 42.

[36] Richards, 'The land agent', pp. 442–3; Caird, *English Agriculture*, pp. 493–5.

[37] Joan Thirsk and J. P. Cooper (eds.), *Seventeenth-Century Economic Documents* (Oxford, 1972), pp. 81–2.

the misfortunes and losses that have happened by continued absence must *aver*, that nothing has tended more to the abuses and ruin of brave estates, than the lord's neglect of looking *himself* sometimes into his own affairs.[38]

In similar vein the Board of Agriculture reporter for the North Riding of Yorkshire commented at the end of the century that

those [estates] which are never visited by their owner, but abandoned to the care of a steward, perhaps a law agent, or other person still less acquainted with the management of land, and resident in London, are, as may naturally be expected, specimens of waste, neglect, barbarism, and poverty.

Fortunately such examples were 'not numerous'.[39]

Essentially two accusations were levelled at owners who failed to pay regular visits to their estates: they were not accepting the responsibilities of ownership, and they were opening the door to mismanagement. Regular visits were regarded as vital for the decision-making process, and conscientious stewards welcomed them. The Earl of Cardigan's Yorkshire steward implored his employer not to allow ill health to prevent his visits during the 1720s, and John Spedding urged Sir James Lowther not to miss his visit to West Cumberland for the second successive year in 1744 because it would be 'a great hindrance to your affairs here which it is impossible to carry on with the same success as if you were here'.[40]

Physical presence was important for all sorts of reasons, from taking decisions on capital investment, to ensuring that rents were paid on time. Timothy Banks, chief steward on Colonel James Grahme's Westmorland estates during the 1690s, complained in 1692 that rents stopped coming in after his employer returned to London, and Alan Wilson – Banks's successor – wrote in similar vein in 1711 that 'Christopher Wilson's rent does not come in whilst your Honour stays at London.'[41] Innovations and alterations in estate policy were always more acceptable to tenants if approved by the owner during a visit to the estate, rather than merely being conveyed through the manager. Furthermore, agents were paid to be efficient, but many owners

[38] Edward Laurence, *The Duty of a Steward to his Lord* (1727), p. 57.

[39] Marshall, *The Review and Abstract*, vol. I, p. 456.

[40] Joan Wake, *The Brudenells of Deene* (1953), pp. 241–2; Carlisle RO, D/Lons/W, John Spedding to Sir James Lowther, 6 May 1744.

[41] J. V. Beckett, 'The finances of a former Jacobite: James Grahme of Levens Hall', *Transactions of the Cumberland and Westmorland Antiquarian and Archaeological Society*, new ser., 85 (1985), p. 135.

preferred to temper their employee's enthusiasm. They might decide to maintain *in situ* a long-established tenant who could not afford a rack rent, rather than following the steward's advice to find new but untried men who would promise the full rate. To this end the dukes of Bedford did not always operate their estate 'on strictly commercial lines'; indeed, the chief object of administration was 'to realise among the agricultural population such a standard of moral and physical well-being as would have been unattainable by strict adherence to commercial lines of administration'.[42] Finally, presence could be used to ensure loyalty among the tenants. Owners did not generally quiz potential tenants on the state of their allegiances, but feasts and balls during a visit could help to keep them loyal. Visits were often calculated according to when they were likely to have the most electoral effect.

Failure to pay regular visits permitted stewards and agents a degree of latitude which could prove highly embarrassing to landlords. It was always possible to correspond, and Sir James Lowther wrote long letters every post day to his Whitehaven steward, who was expected to reply at similar length. If an owner was unable to visit his estates, the steward might be expected to present the accounts in person. However, the cost and problems of transport combined to ensure that few stewards could hope to send, or to present in person, more than abstracts of accounts, and this could lead to much being hidden. Since travel was slow, owners could not easily make surprise visits, and they could seldom hope to see distant estates for more than a short annual visit. On such a trip major decisions might be needed with relatively little information available, while it could be difficult to spot irregularities in the accounts. The double-entry bookkeeping system may have been invented to protect owners from the machinations of venal stewards, and one who admitted to having been deceived was Corbyn Morris. After inheriting a distant estate, he had determined to pay regular visits to the property, but for one reason or another these did not always take place, and over time he could not even understand the accounts submitted to him in London. He published a set of accounting procedures that could be used by landowners to try to prevent such occurrences.[43] Not surprisingly, in view of these problems, employees and employers usually kept a wary distance between each other. Lord Lansdowne wrote to Thomas Coutts in August 1798 in a manner many other owners would doubtless have echoed:

[42] Duke of Bedford, *A Great Agricultural Estate*, 3rd edn (1897), p. 79.
[43] Sidney Pollard, *The Genesis of Modern Management* (1965), pp. 209–10; Corbyn Morris, *A Plan for Arranging and Balancing the Accounts of Landed Estates* (1759).

from your knowledge of business, Agents &c cannot be kept at too great a distance. Their natural tendency is to intrigue and undermine each other, that where things have been long under consideration it is dangerous to adopt new principles of any kind however plausible.[44]

The distrust which existed between owners and managers inevitably affected the structure of decision-making. Much depended on the energy of the owner, his knowledge of the property, the competence of the steward, and the level of trust between the two men. Some owners sent detailed memoranda on how the estate was to be organized. In 1735 the third Earl of Carlisle instructed his Cumberland steward on the policy to be pursued in collecting rent arrears, the discharge of a bailiff, spending on repairs, and the enquiries he wanted making in regard to a possible purchase. The sixth Earl of Thanet sent similarly detailed memoranda to his Westmorland steward Thomas Carleton. They ran to nine pages in 1720 and to thirteen pages two years later, but sadly Thanet found his manager less than willing to comply with instructions, and when in 1724 he inspected the 1722 list he found that 'Carleton has performed few or none of them as he ought to have done.'[45] The level of detail on which a steward was expected to solicit an owner's opinion varied considerably. In 1702 William Clerke consulted John Mordaunt about hedge cutting and minor repair works, while in the 1770s Lord Temple expected his Somerset steward Richard Codrington to consult him over the details of farm lettings. Codrington was unable to let three farms previously valued at £154 a year, and he asked Temple for permission to accept local opinion that the farms were not worth above 100 guineas because of the soil conditions.[46] Other landowners used more sinister means of keeping a check on their servants. At Levens, Colonel Grahme corresponded separately with his stewards and under-stewards, although often on the same subject, and when at home kept separate accounts, possibly as a check on those presented by his stewards.[47]

The key to successful management was to find an able, loyal man who could be relied upon for his honesty. Careful selection was the first priority. Lord Sheffield was told by a fellow landowner in 1815 that 'I do not think it would answer for me to have Mr Wakefield for a

[44] Clements Library, Marquess of Lansdowne (Shelburne) Papers, letter to Thomas Coutts, 8 August 1798.

[45] Beckett, thesis, pp. 80–1.

[46] Elizabeth Hamilton, *The Mordaunts: an eighteenth-century family* (1965), pp. 112–13; Huntington Library, STG Box 419, fol. 7, Richard Codrington to Lord Temple, 16 May 1770.

[47] Beckett, 'The finances of a former Jacobite', p. 134.

steward, one main objection is, his politics which would be too much relished in this county.' Edward Wakefield, a London-based agent, worked on a number of estates including Sheffield's, and was well known for his ability.[48] Once selected, owners sought means of securing loyalty. An obvious course was to pay a high salary, to make dipping into the proverbial till less of an enticement, but stewards were also encouraged by small concessions. The Earl of Cardigan franked Daniel Eaton's letters to his sister, to relieve her of the burden of paying the postage, and provided a rent-free cottage for his widowed mother.[49] Stewards were also encouraged to pursue their own interests. Walter Stanhope-Spencer allowed his long-serving steward John Hardy the favourable lease of a farm in the 1770s, while the Marquess of Bath permitted Thomas Davis not only the lease of a farm, but also time to pursue a variety of additional interests. These included writing the county report on Wiltshire agriculture, and acting as an enclosure commissioner on a number of occasions.[50] Davis also illustrates another landlord ploy – dangling the carrot of the succession to his son. Both Davis's son and grandson followed in his footsteps, and the family held the Longleat stewardship continuously from 1779 until 1839. The relationship between the Lowthers and the Spedding family provides a similar example. John Spedding was originally employed in 1700 as a domestic servant and, like Daniel Eaton, provided with an education by his employer. He worked his way through the estate hierarchy to the stewardship, while his brother Carlisle became colliery steward. Carlisle's son James combined both posts from 1758 until 1779. In addition to the encouragement of the succession, the Lowthers obtained sinecure customs positions for their stewards, backed their separate business enterprises, and acted as godfathers to their children.[51] Finally, taking an interest in the steward's work helped to encourage loyalty. While visiting her north-eastern estates in 1775, Elizabeth Montagu wrote of her steward Edward Brown:

I did not in the least degree doubt that I should find all these things answer the abstracts which we settled every year, but it is a satisfaction to every

---

[48] Clements Library, Sheffield Papers, (?) to Lord Sheffield, 15 June 1815; Spring, *The English Landed Estate*, pp. 6–7.

[49] Wake, *The Brudenells of Deene*, p. 213.

[50] Firth, 'The roles of a West Riding land steward', pp. 108–9; Gunstone, 'Stewardship and landed society', pp. 26 ff.

[51] J. V. Beckett, *Coal and Tobacco: the Lowthers and the economic development of West Cumberland, 1660–1760* (Cambridge, 1981), pp. 27–9.

honest agent to have these things examined, and to every prudent employer of an agent to do it.[52]

Despite such success stories, there were any number of counter-balancing failures as a result of the enormous frustrations landowners encountered in trying to run an estate at a distance. Peculation was rife, and the stories of corrupt stewards were legion. Many owners found it almost impossible to keep their steward in order, but before contemplating dismissal they had to weigh up the possibilities of finding an adequate replacement. This seems to have been Sir Jacob Bouverie's problem. In letters between 1716 and 1722 he frequently admonished his steward, Henry Barton of Folkestone, but ultimately drew back from the logical conclusion of his complaints. In 1716 the Earl of Thanet blamed the low rents on his property around Appleby in Westmorland on his steward Thomas Carleton's 'carelessness, which plainly appears by this account'. Further complaints followed, but it was not until 1723 – and then on the pretext of Carleton's duplicity in a by-election that year – that Thanet summoned up the courage to order his dismissal.[53] In the 1750s Philip Williams of Duffryn in Glamorgan was alleged to have increased his small estate of £40–£50 a year to one of £400–£500 at the expense of his absentee employer, partly by raising the rents and keeping the excess for himself, while the manager of the Glynllech estate, Brecknockshire, was described during the 1840s as 'a drunken vagabond'.[54]

It would be misleading to blame the problems which occurred solely on the managers. Many owners were inattentive to business, and however conscientious the agent there was little he could do if his employer refused to answer letters.[55] Some landowners simply employed the wrong man for the job, and James Caird pointed out that this often happened as a result of their own ignorance.[56] Some were their own worst enemies, including Sir Thomas Lowther of Holker in

---

[52] Huntington Library, Montagu Box 80, Mo 5978, Elizabeth Montagu to Sarah Scott, 28 July 1775.

[53] G. E. Mingay, 'Estate management in eighteenth-century Kent', *Agricultural History Review*, 4 (1956), pp. 108–13.

[54] Joanna Martin, 'Estate stewards and their work in Glamorgan, 1660–1760: a regional study of estate management', *Morgannwg*, 23 (1979), p. 18; Howell, *Land and People in Nineteenth-Century Wales*, p. 45.

[55] Roebuck, 'Absentee landownership'.

[56] Richards, 'The land agent', pp. 443–4; Caird, *English Agriculture*, pp. 27–8, 417. The Board of Agriculture reporters complained about ignorant stewards in Lincolnshire and Leicestershire: Marshall, *The Review and Abstract*, vol. III, p. 41; vol. IV, p. 187.

North Lancashire. Lowther wrote weekly to his steward, expected replies as frequently, and insisted on properly drawn accounts, but his ability to discipline the steward was weakened by his using him as a source of credit. The debt began to accumulate during the 1720s and reached over £1000 by 1734, at which point Lowther agreed to redeem part of it through timber sales. This proved to be only a temporary reprieve, and the sum outstanding had reached £1145 at the time of his death in 1745.[57] Ralph Sneyd, a Tory country gentleman with land in Staffordshire, relied on the honesty of his steward, only to find himself in financial difficulties by the 1840s which were at least partly a consequence of inattention to business. He then had to employ the noted Victorian land agent Andrew Thompson to advise on a way out of his problems. Sir Clifford Constable of Burton Constable in the East Riding never even listened to business, and when faced with financial difficulties in the years before he died in 1870 did not understand enough of his affairs to bring his agents to order. Almost invariably it was the failure to attend to business which was the root cause of trouble, and, incredible though it may seem, even in the nineteenth century some owners still did not insist on regular audits, while those who suffered at the hands of an unscrupulous agent often refused to prosecute for fear of the publicity.[58]

Between the best and the least well-managed estates a great gulf yawned. The highly efficient organizational structure found on an estate such as that of the dukes of Bedford was worlds away from the motley collection of bailiffs, tenant farmers, part-time agents, and others – often with family connections – who continued to feature in the management of landed estates throughout the period. Landowners had to look after their estates whether they liked it or not, and it is hardly surprising that the level of competence varied enormously. Employing a competent steward or agent might relieve some of the pressure, but it was never sufficient on its own; indeed, if anything the demands on landlords' decision-making increased through time. From about 1820 they needed to be well versed in agricultural practice if they were to be able to overcome the problems thrown up by the agricultural depression. As a result, by the middle of the century

[57] J. V. Beckett, 'The Lowthers at Holker: marriage, inheritance and debt in the fortunes of an eighteenth-century landowning family', *Transactions of the Historic Society of Lancashire and Cheshire*, 127 (1978), pp. 50–1, 57.

[58] David Spring, 'Ralph Sneyd: Tory country gentleman', *Bulletin of the John Rylands Library*, 28 (1956), pp. 535–55: English, 'Patterns of estate management', pp. 41, 47.

administration was taking up at least as much, and probably more of the owner's time than in the past. The coming of the railway improved the situation, since owners were able to pay more frequent visits to their estates, and David Spring's conclusion after examining the administration of nineteenth-century estates was that landowners were essentially businesslike and maximized their income wherever possible.[59] If they did not wish to run their estates in person, landowners could employ full- or part-time agents, and this option became increasingly popular as the London season and urban life grew in attraction. This could never relieve them of the fundamental responsibilities which necessitated frequent visits to their estates, and careful supervision of their employees.

The variety and extent of the decision-making and other functions that an owner had to make in the interests of his estate will become apparent in the chapters that follow, but it needs to be clear from the outset that English aristocrats were vitally involved in the running of their estates. For the most part they may have rented out their land, but this did not mean that they were passive rent receivers.

[59] Spring, *The English Landed Estate*, pp. 178–82; Thompson, *English Landed Society*, p. 177.

Chapter Five

The Aristocracy and the Agricultural Revolution

Between 1660 and 1914 agricultural conditions changed out of all recognition. Inflation during the period 1500–1650 stimulated productivity, but price stability over the following hundred years encouraged cost-cutting innovations. Convertible husbandry, the spread of new crops, improved stockbreeding and implements, regional specialization, enclosure and drainage were the critical factors in what was in effect an ongoing revolution on the estates of the English aristocracy.[1] But what role did the landowners themselves play in these events? Landowners had long accepted that their estates were units of production and not merely instruments of feudal and social prestige, and clearly it was in their commercial interests to take a positive lead in promoting change. Just as leasing did not absolve an owner from responsibility for his estate, neither did it allow him to expect improved agriculture to take place without his intervention. He had a number of possible options. First, he could point the way by farming unlet land in a progressive manner. Second, he could encourage his tenants, either passively by promoting new cultivation methods, or more actively by capital investment, adjustments to the size of farms and careful wording of tenancy agreements. Both roles required positive decision-making and capital investment. Moreover, the rising income coveted by any landowner could be achieved only by careful planning. An owner lacking investment capital, or unwilling to finance infrastructural improvements such as building, fencing and draining, was unlikely to be able to provide the environment into which he could attract tenants capable and willing to adopt new techniques, and to pay high rents. Hardly surprisingly, landlord commitment varied considerably, but it is arguable that English

[1] J. D. Chambers and G. E. Mingay, *The Agricultural Revolution, 1750–1880* (1966).

agriculture developed in a landlord-conceived framework which permitted an adequate response to market demand as population grew. Much of the credit for this must lie with the aristocracy.

ARISTOCRATS AS FARMERS: THE HOME FARM AND INNOVATION

Aristocratic farming on a large scale came to an end in the fourteenth and fifteenth centuries, leaving only smaller owners and freeholders with a direct interest in agricultural production. However, in two significant ways large landowners continued to play an influential role in farming. First, most substantial owners had land 'in hand' from time to time, either deliberately in the form of a home farm, or sometimes by accident when a suitable tenant could not be found for land which was normally let. The example that they set in the use of such land could be important for local practice. Second, aristocratic owners were in a position to promote agricultural improvement on a wider scale, through their membership of local and national organizations which were established to help disseminate new ideas to landlords and tenant farmers alike.

After the retreat from demesne farming, most large landowners maintained home farms to supply food for consumption in the country house, and fodder for farm stock as well as for the stables and kennels. These varied considerably, depending on the size of the household and the frequency of visits. Sir John Lowther, an irregular visitor to his West Cumberland estates in the 1680s and 1690s, opened up a home farm there when he retired in 1698, but some of the activities were curtailed in 1709 when it became clear that the heir intended to spend little time in the north. By contrast, in 1759 the Marquess of Rockingham's home farm at Wentworth Woodhouse supplied the house with wheat and barley to the value of £195, the stables with hay, straw and oats worth £1229, and quantities of meat and dairy produce.[2]

Although home farms were maintained primarily to supply the house, they came to be regarded as having a much more important role as experimental concerns. Writing in 1726, John Laurence informed his readers that

I should think myself extremely happy if I could be instrumental in reviving among gentlemen, whose affairs do not oblige them to spend a great part of

---

[2] J. V. Beckett, *Coal and Tobacco: the Lowthers and the economic development of West Cumberland, 1660–1760* (Cambridge, 1981), p. 34; G. E. Mingay, *English Landed Society in the Eighteenth Century* (1963), p. 169.

their year in London, a spirit of improving their estates and employing their time in making experiments, which cannot be expected from the farmer. He, whose thoughts must be fixed on making up his rent and maintaining his family by early and constant labour, cannot venture the expense of a trial, which, if it should not succeed, must deeply injure his fortune, and half starve his children. But the very pleasure and amusement, which a gentleman will find in such exercise of his body and mind, will be cheaply purchased by the loss he may sometimes meet with.[3]

In 1804 William Marshall summed up what was by then the fashionable view – that the home farm was the proper place to introduce the tenants to valuable practices not yet known on the estate, and also to test doubtful ideas which might have gained some local credence. In addition, it ought to be regarded as a proper place for public shows of stock and samples of produce, which would help to raise the spirit of emulation.[4] Much the same argument was still being put forward in the 1860s, when Thomas Bowick suggested that the home farm could prove extremely valuable to the owner: 'he gets a greater insight into rural affairs, he is better able to judge of all that pertains thereto, and he can more readily sympathise with the losses which his tenants at any time experience.' Furthermore, according to Bowick, the home farm could be more than just an example:

a much more tangible influence is exerted where a thoroughbred bull or stallion is kept not only for the use of the home farm, but for the benefit of the tenantry as well. If pure-bred bull-calves are also disposed of to those on the property, at reasonable prices, material improvement in the stock may be expected. In like manner, select varieties of seed-corn, clean and true, may be disseminated with much advantage.[5]

This was the theory, but in practice by no means all home farms were run along the ideal lines suggested by contemporary authorities. Some aristocrats showed an active concern with promoting farming progress. The first Duke of Chandos told his steward in 1735 that, if one of his Berkshire farms could not be tenanted, 'I intend to try one more experiment with them which I have learnt in Hampshire.'[6] Lord

---

[3] John Laurence, *A New System of Agriculture* (1726), preface.
[4] William Marshall, *On the Landed Property of England* (1804), pp. 417–18.
[5] T. Bowick, 'On the management of a home farm', *JRASE*, 23 (1862), pp. 266, 267.
[6] Huntington Library, STB Correspondence, box 19/7, Duke of Chandos to J. Farquharson, 13 November 1735.

Lansdowne, after many years as a politician which carried him briefly to the post of prime minister in 1782–3 (as Earl of Shelburne), retired to conduct experiments on his home farm at Bowood, and hoped his son would follow a similar interest:

I have nothing so much at heart as to give Henry a taste for agricultural improvement. The last thing I told him was that he would find not only more profit but more happiness and consideration from cultivating the Irish property settled upon him, than from all the secretaryships, ministerships, or favouriteships in the power of all the princes in the world to bestow.[7]

Some of those who translated such piety into practice were held to have created havens of successful experimentation and innovation. The seventh Duke of Bedford extolled the virtues of his ancestor the fifth duke, claiming that in the later eighteenth century he was 'among the first to initiate an agricultural system which was designed, some years later, to make the agricultural industry of Great Britain a model for the whole civilized world.'[8] Lord Ernle wrote in glowing terms of a number of landowners, none more so than Thomas William Coke, 'the most celebrated champion' of the new system of large farms and large capital; and other names mentioned in the same breath included Viscount 'Turnip' Townshend, the third Earl of Egremont, the Marquess of Rockingham and, most famously of all, 'Farmer' George III himself.[9] To this list could be added the third Earl Spencer, recognized by contemporaries as 'the great patron of English agriculture', and responsible for the promotion and instigation of the most important schemes during the 1830s and 1840s; Sir James Graham, with his major farm at Netherby in Cumberland; and Prince Albert, who remodelled the Flemish farm at Windsor and turned it into a masterpiece incorporating the most approved principles of the day, as well as supervising the construction of a new royal dairy at Frogmore.[10] A Staffordshire reporter suggested in 1869 that 'perhaps

[7] Clements Library, Marquess of Lansdowne (Shelburne) Papers, letter to Thomas Coutts, 7 November 1796.

[8] Duke of Bedford, *A Great Agricultural Estate*, 3rd edn (1897), pp. 26–7.

[9] Lord Ernle, *English Farming Past and Present*, 6th edn (1961), pp. 213, 221; Pamela Horn, 'The contribution of the propagandist to eighteenth-century agricultural improvement', *Historical Journal*, 25 (1982), p. 314.

[10] E. A. Wasson, 'The third Earl Spencer and agriculture, 1818–1845', *Agricultural History Review*, 26 (1978), p. 89; David Spring, 'A great agricultural estate: Netherby under Sir James Graham, 1820–45', *Agricultural History*, 29 (1955), pp. 73–81; Stuart Macdonald, 'Model farms', in *The Victorian Countryside*, ed. G. E. Mingay (1981), pp. 214–26.

nowhere in England have the example and patronage of the great proprietors had a greater and more beneficial influence on agriculture than in the case of the great Staffordshire landowners.' He was presumably referring to – among others – the estates of Viscount Dudley and the Leveson-Gowers, on both of which landlord influence was considerable.[11] Finally, Nottinghamshire's larger owners had particularly progressive farms, most of them situated in the so-called Dukeries area. The Dukes of Portland and Newcastle, Earl Manvers and the Mellish and Savile families all maintained farms which were recognized as examples of first-class husbandry.[12]

While such laurels were justified for a number of aristocrats, it is not clear how many were really so deserving. There is little doubt, for example, that Ernle's eulogy on Coke of Norfolk was greatly exaggerated. According to Ernle, from 1778 until 1842 Coke 'stood at the head of the new agricultural movement', and turned a landscape without wheat, and yielding only scanty rye, into a thriving and progressive estate. However, this view actually originated from Coke himself, and modern research has demonstrated that, far from leading by example, Coke depended on the willing co-operation of tenants whose progress impressed visitors as much as the home farm.[13] Perhaps more significantly, contemporaries recognized that by no means all landowners were fascinated by agriculture. In the later eighteenth century the West Somerset reporter to the Board of Agriculture noted that 'very few gentlemen of landed property in this county have shown that attention to the advancement of rural economy, or to the improvement of agriculture, which a science of such importance merits'; while in the 1850s James Caird was disappointed by the Oxfordshire landowners: 'as a general rule the landlords of this county interest themselves very little in agriculture. Few of them are practically acquainted with, or engaged in farming.'[14] Thomas Bowick noted that for every Holkham and Woburn there were a great number of home farms which, far from setting an example of

[11] H. Evershed, 'The agriculture of Staffordshire', *JRASE*, 2nd ser., 5 (1869), p. 287.

[12] A. C. Pickersgill, 'The agricultural revolution in Bassetlaw, Nottinghamshire, 1750–1873' (University of Nottingham, Ph.D. thesis, 1979), ch. 3.

[13] Ernle, *English Farming Past and Present*, pp. 217–19; Edward Rigby, *Holkham, its Agriculture &c.*, 2nd edn (Norwich, 1817), pp. iii–iv; Earl Spencer, 'On the improvements which have taken place in West Norfolk', *JRASE*, 3 (1842), pp. 1–9; R. A. C. Parker, *Coke of Norfolk* (Oxford, 1975), pp. 71–82.

[14] William Marshall, *The Review and Abstract of the County Reports to the Board of Agriculture* (York, 1818), vol. V, p. 605; James Caird, *English Agriculture in 1850–51* (1852), p. 27.

good farming practice, had 'proved a by-word and an example to be avoided'.[15] Such appears to have been the case in South Lincolnshire, where many of the home farms were as badly managed as those of the humblest tenants.[16]

Many home farms seem never to have taken on an experimental role, and often did not divert from their primary functions as household producers. In eighteenth-century Essex Sir John Griffin Griffin's Audley End home farm was essentially a self-sufficient productive unit geared to household needs, with no real innovation in a purely agricultural sense.[17] Most Cumbrian landowners maintained home farms purely for rearing stock and fattening cattle *en route* from Scotland to the south of England. Evidence of innovation is fragmentary, although the Earl of Carlisle had a progressive farm on which turnips and grasses were extensively used. Disappointingly, landowners with innovative farms elsewhere in the country made little attempt to give Cumbria the benefit of their experience. The sixth Duke of Somerset was an improver in Sussex, but ignored his northern estate; Sir James Lowther was impressed by the husbandry practised on the Middlesex estate he acquired in the 1740s but failed to imitate it in Cumberland; and the Pennington family of Muncaster had a progressive farm in the East Riding, but made little attempt to introduce new ideas into Cumberland.[18] Similarly, in Glamorgan the eighteenth-century home farms do not appear to have been designed as leaders in agricultural innovation.[19]

Even when home farms were models of agricultural experimentation, they did not necessarily set a good example. John Laurence in the 1720s saw them as venues for trial and error, where the landowner could underwrite possible failure, but this lack of cost-effectiveness increasingly worked against aristocratic leadership. It was all well and good for Lord William Bentinck to return from India in 1807 with £20,000 to invest in improving Norfolk marshlands and find the experiment going wrong, but it was quite another matter for a

[15] Bowick, 'On the management of a home farm', p. 247.

[16] D. B. Grigg, *The Agricultural Revolution in South Lincolnshire* (Cambridge, 1965), p. 82. Welsh home farms were also uneconomic: D. W. Howell, *Land and People in Nineteenth-Century Wales* (1977), p. 35.

[17] J. D. Williams, 'The management of an eighteenth-century home farm', *Essex Journal*, 16 (1981), pp. 19–23.

[18] J. V. Beckett, 'Absentee landownership in the late seventeenth and early eighteenth centuries: the case of Cumbria', *Northern History*, 19 (1983), pp. 99–100.

[19] J. O. Martin, 'The landed estate in Glamorgan, *c.* 1660–*c.* 1760' (University of Cambridge, Ph.D thesis, 1978), pp. 126 ff.

tenant farmer to take risks.[20] Tenants argued that owners did not have to live with the ever-present reality of the annual rent charge, while improvements emanating from a loss-making home farm provided little positive inducement to hard-headed farmers.

The trouble was that all too many of these farms were unprofitable. The Earl of Carlisle's progressive Cumberland farm was loss-making in the early eighteenth century, and even Coke's famous enterprise could not always make a profit. In the difficult years after the end of the Napoleonic wars a loss of £11,760 was recorded between 1817 and 1826. Earl Grey's home farm at Howick in Northumberland made a loss in only two of the years for which accounts survive between 1803 and 1833. In some years profits topped £2000, and for the whole period they averaged £1015 annually. However, the farm was not providing any single family with a way of living, since it was to a certain extent regarded merely as hobby farming.[21] When the seventh Duke of Bedford inherited his estates in 1839, he made it clear that he had no intention that the Woburn home farm should be an extravagant pastime. Other owners could make a profit, and he was aware of the drawbacks of a loss-making concern as far as tenants were concerned, but he was still unable to place it on a firm financial footing. In Wales, the Picton Castle home farm was so expensive in the 1860s that the family solicitors recommended buying the articles produced from other sources to cut costs. Some model farms were even set up without regard to cost or feasibility, including those of Lord Bateman at Uphampton in Herefordshire (1861), and the Earl of Lonsdale's in Cumbria, while when Hippolyte Taine was shown a profitable farm in the 1860s he sought to explain what he called 'this miracle' by the farmer's attitude.[22]

As a result of these question marks over the real significance of home farms for agricultural innovation, it may well have been that smaller landowners, estate stewards and tenant farmers played the most significant role in the dissemination of new agricultural ideas. In Cumberland, innovation was a combined effort between some of the

[20] J. Rosselli, 'An Indian governor in the Norfolk marshland: Lord William Bentinck as improver, 1809–27', *Agricultural History Review*, 19 (1971), pp. 42–64.

[21] Parker, *Coke of Norfolk*, p. 170; W. M. Hughes, 'Lead, land and coal as sources of landlord's income in Northumberland between 1700 and 1850' (University of Newcastle, Ph.D. thesis, 1963), vol. I, pp. 127–70; vol. II, p. 58.

[22] David Spring, *The English Landed Estate in the Nineteenth Century: its administration* (1963), pp. 46–7; Howell, *Land and People in Nineteenth-Century Wales*, p. 35; Macdonald, 'Model farms', pp. 219–21; Chambers and Mingay, *The Agricultural Revolution*, pp. 173–4.

lesser gentry and one of the stewards of a non-resident peer. Further south, in Cheshire, gentlemen were the most important contributors to the agricultural revolution, while in Leicestershire the major improvements were found on large farms, many of which were occupied by their owners. In the East Riding early in the nineteenth century Sir Christopher Sykes of Sledmere led a group of wealthy country gentlemen who set about improving the Wolds:

> by assuidity and perseverance in building and planting and enclosing the Yorkshire wolds in the short space of thirty years [he] set such an example to other owners of land, as has caused what was once a bleak and barren tract of country to become now one of the most productive and best cultivated districts in the county of York.[23]

At about the same time Philip Pusey's estate was a well-known trial ground in Buckinghamshire, and there are plenty more similar examples of less prominent country gentlemen taking a positive lead. Some of the more active owners were those who had recently acquired land with the profits of industrial enterprise, since they tended to bring to the land the same business mentality which had marked their earlier success. This was the case in Cheshire, although elsewhere Richard Arkwright – of all people – seems to have lacked the enthusiasm for investment and improvement which might have been expected from a newcomer.[24]

ARISTOCRATS AS FARMERS: AGRICULTURAL SHOWS AND SOCIETIES

If the role of the home farm in spreading agricultural innovation was limited, this did not mean that aristocrats failed to make a substantial contribution in other ways. What they may have lacked in practical effort they made up for in paternalist endeavour, lending their support, and their name, to improvement efforts. This could be achieved either through individual effort or via group conduct. Agricultural shows and sheep-shearings were organized by a number of

[23] Quoted in Olga Wilkinson, *The Agricultural Revolution in the East Riding of Yorkshire* (York, 1956), pp. 13–14; Beckett, 'Absentee landownership', pp. 98, 101; Marshall, *The Review and Abstract*, vol. IV, p. 188; C. S. Davies, *The Agricultural History of Cheshire, 1750–1850* (Manchester, 1960), p. 129.

[24] G. E. Mingay, *The Gentry* (1976), pp. 96–7; Marshall, *The Review and Abstract*, vol. II, p. 24; E. L. Jones, 'Industrial capital and landed investment: the Arkwrights in Herefordshire, 1809–43', in *Agriculture and the Industrial Revolution* (1974), p. 177.

landowners to publicize the new ideas. Coke's annual sheep-shearing became an important date on the farmers' calendar. It probably began shortly after he inherited the estate in 1776, although it was the early years of the nineteenth century before the event received wide publicity. Although the emphasis was on sheep, the gatherings were in effect agricultural shows providing opportunities for implements to be displayed, for the Park Farm to be inspected, and for participants to share their experiences. Annual sheep-shearings began at Woburn in 1797, and attracted landowners and farmers from Europe and North America as well as all over England. Also during the 1790s the Earl of Egremont established a cattle show at Petworth. These were the premier events, but other aristocrats took their own initiatives. The Duke of Portland, for example, patronized agricultural shows at Newark and ploughing competitions at Southwell.[25]

These were the great individual events, but landowners lent their collective weight to spreading the new farming gospel through improvement, and later specifically agricultural societies. The Royal Society of Arts, established in 1754, counted agricultural concerns among the interests to which it offered premiums for improvement and inventions 'as shall tend to the employing of the poor and the increase of trade'. Arthur Young noted the number of such premiums on offer in 1766 for agricultural improvements, as well as the annual medal for an account of experiments with different grains. The society's first president was Viscount Folkestone, and among the vice-presidents was Lord Romney.[26] Similar societies were also founded locally. A Society for the Promotion of Industry was established in the Lindsey division of Lincolnshire during the 1780s, primarily to promote the use of locally produced wool. Its benefactors included Lady Willoughby, the dowager Duchess of Ancaster, Lady Bertie and Sir Joseph Banks.[27]

A national initiative specifically concerned with farming came in

[25] Parker, *Coke of Norfolk*, pp. 115–18; Duke of Bedford, *A Great Agricultural Estate*, pp. 29–30; H. A. Wyndham, *A Family History, 1688–1837* (1950), p. 250; Ernle, *English Farming Past and Present*, p. 221; A. S. Turberville, *A History of Welbeck Abbey and its Owners* (1939), vol. II, p. 351; Macdonald, 'Model farms', p. 214.

[26] *The Plan of the Society for the Encouragement of Arts, Manufactures and Commerce* (1755); Arthur Young, *The Farmer's Letters to the People of England* (1767), pp. 114–32. Even before this time, the Royal Society of Arts had been involved in the dissemination of ideas: J. Thirsk and J. P. Cooper (eds), *Seventeenth-Century Economic Documents* (Oxford, 1972), pp. 150–5.

[27] *A Second Account of the Origin, Proceedings and Intentions of the Society for the Promotion of Industry in the Southern District of the Parts of Lindsey in the County of Lincoln* (Louth, *c.* 1786). Some of its work is mentioned in J. A. Perkins, *Sheep Farming in Eighteenth and Nineteenth Century Lincolnshire* (Sleaford, 1977), p. 14.

1793 with the formation of the Board of Agriculture under the chairmanship of a noted Scottish innovator, Sir John Sinclair. All thirty places for ordinary members were filled by aristocrats, including three dukes and a marquess, seven earls and three barons. Moreover, these were no mere sinecures, since members regularly attended the frequent board meetings.[28] During the three decades that it existed, the board helped to promote enthusiasm for improved farming and the exchange of ideas. Although its achievements are now regarded as limited, members of the board were regarded as men of initiative, as is clear from the surviving correspondence of the Earl of Sheffield, who became president in 1803.[29] The Board of Agriculture collapsed in 1820–1, leaving a gap which was only filled in 1838 with the formation of the Royal Agricultural Society, the outcome of a suggestion made the previous year by Earl Spencer. Again its governing body was heavily aristocratic. By 1864 nearly half of the 160 governors were titled members of the aristocracy, including two members of the royal family, five dukes and six marquesses, twenty-three earls and five viscounts, seventeen barons and eighteen baronets.[30] A journal was started in 1840 under the editorship of Philip Pusey to encourage

improvement of agricultural implements, the construction of farm buildings and cottages, the application of chemistry to the general purposes of agriculture, the destruction of insects injurious to vegetable life, and the eradication of weeds.[31]

An annual show was also introduced, on a peripatetic basis, with prizes awarded to encourage agricultural advance, and by the end of the 1880s membership of the society had risen to more than 10,000.

These national institutions were supplemented by similar local organizations which sprang up in the second half of the eighteenth century. The Brecknockshire society, founded in 1755, was the earliest, but more than ninety had been founded by 1835, and a remarkable expansion thereafter brought the number to over 700 two decades later. Primarily, these provincial societies were concerned with

[28] R. Mitchison, 'The Old Board of Agriculture (1793–1822)', *English Historical Review*, 74 (1959), pp. 41–69; *Agricultural Sir John* (1962).

[29] Clements Library, Sheffield Papers. Among a variety of letters on agricultural topics was one from Charles Abbot, who wrote as 'a Sussex neighbour . . . with a farmer's question', 29 March 1803.

[30] A list of governors and members was published in *JRASE*, 25 (1864), pp. i–lii.

[31] *JRASE*, 1 (1840), pp. clxx, 1–21; Nicholas Goddard, 'Agricultural societies', in *The Victorian Countryside*, ed. Mingay, pp. 246–51.

the spread of information, and the encouragement of innovation, through annual shows. Possibly the best known was the Bath and West, founded in 1777, which sponsored an annual show at a variety of centres throughout southern England. Others operated on a smaller scale with regular discussion meetings and well-stocked agricultural libraries.[32] Almost all depended on aristocratic support in one guise or another; indeed, some were regarded as clubs for 'gentlemen who are in the habit of agricultural experiment', even restricting membership predominantly to owners.[33] Some aristocrats were founders or founder members. Thomas Johnes took a leading role in promoting the Cardiganshire society (1784), and the Earl of Egremont was partly responsible for the Sussex society (1798). The Duke of Rutland's patronage helped in setting up the Waltham society in Lincolnshire, while East Riding landowners were largely responsible for the Yorkshire society (1807).[34] The Cumberland and Carlisle was founded in 1817 by a group of landowners who had already been responsible for establishing a fortnightly cattle market at Carlisle, while John Christian Curwen founded the Workington society in 1806 to stimulate rivalry among his tenants and neighbours. In mid-nineteenth-century Lancashire, agricultural societies were seen as 'proof of the vitality of the spirit of improvement'. Every town in the northern part of the county had a society, and some had joined together under Lord Stanley's chairmanship as the Royal North Lancashire Agricultural Society. The area also had private farming clubs, including those founded by the Duke of Hamilton and the Earl of Burlington.[35]

A few aristocrats took a prominent role in society activities, but the

---

[32] Goddard, 'Agricultural Societies', pp. 246–57. Societies were proposed as early as 1704: Joan Thirsk (ed.), *The Agrarian History of England and Wales*, vol. V: *1640–1750* (1985), pt I, pp. 402–3. The societies were concerned to overcome the inbuilt prejudice of farmers against book learning. Shows were regarded as an effective means of disseminating information, hence John Farey's comment on the biannual Derbyshire Agricultural Society's shows, which were 'esteemed to have done much good in promoting the improvement of the chief domestic animals': *View of the Agriculture of the County of Derby* (1811), vol. III, p. 649.

[33] Quoted in K. Hudson, *Patriotism with Profit* (1972), p. 3.

[34] R. J. Colyer, 'The Haford estate under Thomas Johnes and Henry Pelham, fourth Duke of Newcastle', *Welsh Histoory Review*, 8 (1977), p. 260; Wyndham, *A Family History*, p. 250; J. T. Ward, *East Yorkshire Landed Estates in the Nineteenth Century* (York, 1967), p. 68; R. J. Olney, *Lincolnshire Politics, 1832–85* (Oxford, 1973), p. 17.

[35] *Carlisle Patriot*, 28 June 1817, quoted in Charles Searle, '"The odd corner of England": a study of a rural social formation in transition, Cumbria, *c.* 1700–*c.* 1914' (University of Essex, Ph.D. thesis, 1983), p. 297; W. J. Garnett, 'The farming of Lancashire', *JRASE*, 10 (1849), pp. 47–8.

majority retreated to a paternalistic back seat. Sir Thomas Dyke Acland delivered lectures to local audiences in Devon during the 1850s on the chemistry of practical farming, but more often than not substantial landowners preferred the relative anonymity of honorific roles such as the presidency. In addition, lists of vice-presidents and donors tended to read like an assembly of peers and baronets, joined during the nineteenth century by a sprinkling of brewers, bankers and industrialists. Thus the Earl of Moira was president of the Leicestershire Agricultural Society in the later eighteenth century; the president and four of the vice-presidents of the Yorkshire society in 1838 were dukes and earls; and the Earl of Yarborough was president of the Lincolnshire society from its inception in 1869.[36] The societies were undoubtedly beneficial to landowners. Not only did they need aristocratic support if they were to survive and prosper – the North Cardiganshire society failed in 1885 for lack of landed help – but they also offered a means of promoting agricultural improvement while at the same time enforcing rural paternalism. The latter was achieved through the cash prize, and the certificate denoting success in the various competitions. In this way not only were the aristocracy necessary for the societies, but the societies were important to their patrons and presidents.[37]

ARISTOCRATS AS FARMERS: PARLIAMENTARY LEGISLATION

The aristocracy could go one stage further in encouraging agriculture, by utilizing the legislative powers of Parliament.[38] The great majority of members were considerable landowners, and as such they had a firsthand interest in protecting agriculture. Essentially they were able to undertake two roles, one concerned with overall policy, and the other with promoting private legislation such as enclosure bills. The

[36] Hudson, *Patriotism with Profit*, pp. 46, 95–7; Marshall, *The Review and Abstract*, vol. IV, p. 187; J. G. Ruddock, *The Lincolnshire Agricultural Society* (Lincoln, 1983). Ruddock's centenary booklet contains a forward by the president, the Earl of Ancaster.

[37] Howell, *Land and People in Nineteenth-Century Wales*, p. 36; James Obelkevich, *Religion and Rural Society: South Lindsey, 1825–1875* (Oxford, 1976), p. 37.

[38] The aristocratic control of Parliament is examined in chapters twelve and thirteen. What follows here only touches the surface of parliamentary interest in agricultural matters. For a detailed account of government policy and the role of the legislature for the period 1640–1750, see Joan Thirsk, 'Agricultural policy: public debate and legislation', in *The Agrarian History of England and Wales*, vol. V, pt II, pp. 298–388.

first of these hats is most clearly demonstrated in regard to the Corn Laws, although landowners were also intimately involved with drainage and estate entail legislation. The Corn Bounty Acts of 1672 and 1688 introduced a sliding scale of duties designed to limit imports and to expand exports. The aim was to keep the price of grain at or above 48 shillings a quarter, thereby affording some protection to farmers by diverting excess supplies abroad, and, coincidentally, to ensure that rents could be paid, and that landowners were in a position to carry their tax burden. Even so, it seems clear that the landowners in their role as legislators were identifying their own economic interests with those of the nation, by intervening in the market in order to protect their own position. Whether they succeeded is more debatable. Given the price stability of the years 1650–1750 the real impact of the legislation is hard to determine, although the quantities sent abroad suggest that farmers saw advantages in the legislation.[39]

Although the Corn Laws were adjusted in the 1770s, no radical change took place until after the Napoleonic wars. When prices slumped in 1813, a new bill was introduced which looked suspiciously like an attempt to maintain the landed interest in its state of wartime opulence. Petitioning against the proposed legislation came from a variety of manufacturing and industrial areas, but this merely served to stiffen the parliamentary resolve. However, the worst aspects of the legislation were softened when it was amended in 1828 and a sliding scale replaced the earlier single, fixed price level. During the 1830s and 1840s agitation mounted to permit free trade in grain, but the Tory party leaders made it their business to win farmers' votes by pledging to retain protection. Strong support came from the Marquess of Chandos, who sat in the Commons until he succeeded his father in 1839 as Duke of Buckingham. Chandos was regarded as the farmers' friend, especially in Buckinghamshire, where he helped to form an agricultural association in 1833 which combined ploughing matches with speeches favouring protection. Similar Tory-based organizations sprang up in other counties. As repeal agitation rose to a crescendo in the early 1840s, and the issue became a major political battleground, the protectionists formed themselves into the Agricultural Protection Society under the presidency of the Duke of Richmond and the vice-presidency of the Duke of Buckingham.

With this aristocratic backing it is perhaps surprising that when the

---

[39] T. S. Ashton, *An Economic History of England: the eighteenth century* (1972 edn), pp. 48–50; David Ormrod, *English Grain Exports and the Structure of Agrarian Capitalism, 1700–1760* (Hull, 1985).

Corn Laws were eventually repealed in 1846 a Tory ministry was responsible. Admittedly it was the Irish potato famine which finally precipitated action, but it is clear that the landowners were split on the issue. Well-known pro-repealers included the fifth Earl Fitzwilliam, who had been converted long before 1846,[40] and Earl Spencer, while the prime minister, Sir Robert Peel, argued that the prosperity of farming depended less on artificial props such as tariffs, and much more on greater productivity derived from modern methods. Moreover, the dominance of landowners in Parliament ensured that many of them would have to vote for repeal if it was to stand any chance of success, and it is clear that the socio-economic background of MPs bore little relationship to their voting on the issue. The country gentlemen seem not to have been distinctively associated with either side,[41] which suggests that they did not vote on sectional agricultural lines when it could be shown that a national or even private interest was involved.

The second landlord 'hat' in Parliament related to private legislation, particularly enclosure bills. Something in the region of 5000 of these were passed over the period 1730–1870, and each one had to be introduced into Parliament and nurtured through its various readings, by one or more interested members. The evidence suggests that proposed bills were carefully scrutinized, and where amendments were proposed every effort was made to find an acceptable compromise. A body of good practice developed to ensure that certain clauses appeared in all enclosure bills, and some of these were reproduced in the 1801 General Enclosure Act, which was passed in order to reduce the costs of drafting, printing and engrossing bills. The procedure provided a method of investigation, and allowed minority interests to voice objections. These provisions were lost in 1845 when the General Enclosure Act appointed a board of commissioners to replace the haphazardly formed local groups.[42] However, for a bill to get into

[40] David Spring, 'Earl Fitzwilliam and the Corn Laws', *American Historical Review*, 59 (1954), pp. 287–304; 'Lord Chandos and the farmers', *Huntington Library Quarterly*, 33 (1970), pp. 257–81.

[41] W. O. Aydelotte, 'The country gentlemen and the repeal of the Corn Laws', *English Historical Review*, 82 (1967), pp. 47–60. For a fuller account, see Robert Stewart, *The Politics of Protection: Lord Derby and the protectionist party, 1841–1852* (Cambridge, 1971).

[42] Sheila Lambert, *Bills and Acts: legislative procedure in eighteenth-century England* (Cambridge, 1971), ch. 7; Michael W. McCahill, *Order and Equipoise: the peerage and the House of Lords, 1783–1806* (1978), pp. 92 ff; Spring, *The English Landed Estate*, pp. 136 ff.

Parliament in the first place, it required the sympathy and support of one or more peers and MPs. Of fifty-eight enclosure bills presented from Nottinghamshire between 1787 and 1806, peers were the principal petitioners in fifteen cases. Often landowners took a decisive part in shaping the contents of bills introduced by others. The first Duke of Northumberland's agent informed supporters of the Tynemouth enclosure that without certain resolutions his lordship's support could not be expected in Parliament. Similarly Earl Fitzwilliam refused to accept the enclosure of Hemsworth commons until provisions were inserted in the bill to compensate him for loss of manorial rights.[43] Undoubtedly landowners on occasion used their parliamentary position to push through enclosure legislation which would otherwise have been opposed by their lesser neighbours, but in general the safeguards were sufficient to ensure that they usually acted reasonably.

ARISTOCRATS AS IMPROVERS: ENCLOSURE, DRAINAGE AND BUILDING

The aristocratic role in terms of home farms and agricultural societies can be regarded as a negative rather than a positive contribution to progress, but, while it is difficult to attribute quite the fulsome praise of Lord Ernle to the agricultural activities of greater landowners, this is no reason to belittle their achievements. Even Arthur Young, so often a fierce critic of incompetence, acknowledged that his generation had witnessed a considerable upsurge of interest among the peerage and gentry.[44] If the home farm was a dubious means of leading by example, the organization of the farms and the willingness to risk capital in expensive improvements was a more reliable indication of commitment. In 1775 Nathaniel Kent informed landowners that they should assume responsibility for improvements 'out of the common way', and during the days of high farming in the mid-nineteenth century none was more vociferous than J. L. Morton in calling for liberal landlord spending on permanent improvements.[45] The demands on landlord capital ranged from enclosure and drainage costs to the erection of new farm buildings, and willingness to invest in such activi-

---

[43] McCahill, *Order and Equipoise*, pp. 90–1.

[44] Pamela Horn, 'The contribution of the propagandist to eighteenth-century agricultural improvement', *Historical Journal*, 25 (1982), pp. 316–17.

[45] Nathaniel Kent, *Hints to Gentlemen of Landed Property* (1775), p. 93; J. L. Morton, *The Resources of Estates* (1858), p. 20.

ties spoke volumes for landlord involvement in agricultural improvement.

The efficiency and productivity of an estate depended in part on having well-organized farms. Open-field strip farming was widely recognized as being inimical to maximizing output and profit. Reorganization in the form of enclosure offered potential benefits to owners through the adoption of more efficient production methods, full cultivation of common pastures which had formerly been overstocked and poorly maintained, and an increase in output per acre. Although tenure restrictions virtually gave freehold rights to tenants in parts of the north and west, and inevitably hampered landlords hoping to bring about change, where this was not the case, owners were lured towards enclosure by the carrot of rising values. In 1744 the Earl of Huntingdon was encouraged to consider enclosure at Loughborough because

it would be the most advantageous scheme towards increasing the value of your Lordship's estate there . . . when enclosed one man of substance can with the same number of servants manage a farm of three, four, or six times the value. . . . Where there is so much commoning as at Loughborough, there ever will be an outward show of great poverty, as such commons are the real cause of idleness.[46]

After analysing the various arguments, an anonymous country gentleman concluded in 1772 that enclosure benefited all parties: 'the land owner will increase the value of his lands, the farmer his profits, labour will be at least as plentiful, and provisions much more so.'[47]

As a result of these advantages, enclosure spread slowly across the country according to the dictates of local conditions. Extensive reorganization of the agrarian structure took place in the north-east between 1640 and 1750, during which time the number of farms on the Alnwick estate declined from 286 to 256. In the Midlands, enclosure was a response to economic conditions in the century or so after 1650. As grain prices declined towards the depression of 1730–50, landlords on the clays looked to convert their unprofitable arable into pasture. By 1760 or thereabouts most parts of the country had experienced some enclosure, as, for example, in South Lincolnshire, from where the open fields had already disappeared in many areas.[48]

[46] HMC, *Hastings MSS*, vol. III, p. 47.

[47] Anon., *The Advantages and Disadvantages of Inclosing Waste Lands and Open Fields* (1772), p. 73.

[48] P. W. Brassley, 'The agricultural economy of Northumberland and Durham in the period 1640–1750' (University of Oxford, B. Litt. thesis, 1974), pp. 106–34;

Since by then the limits to enclosure by agreement had been reached, landlords turned to legislation, and about 6.5 million acres were enclosed by Act of Parliament between 1760 and 1914, leaving only 5 per cent of the country untouched in 1914.[49] Enclosure by legislation had several advantages. The whole of the open fields, with any suitable common and waste, could be enclosed simultaneously, powerful proprietors were able to overcome obstinate neighbours, greater legal certainty was given to agreements, and the possibilities were opened up for tithe commutation and parish road building.[50]

Little is known of the cost of enclosure, or the anticipated returns, prior to the parliamentary movement of the second half of the eighteenth century. Agreement enclosure could take place over many years, financed out of income, and without any necessity to maintain formal records. By contrast, the use of commissioners to control the operation of enclosure by legislation ensured the keeping of records and considerable owner concern about costs and returns. Landowners had a number of variables to consider, including their ability to pay for the proposed changes, the capacity of the tenants to pay higher rents, and the level of anticipated post-enclosure rents, since this would govern the profitability of the investment. Rising prices and changing land use acted as stimulants after about 1760, while interest rates may also have influenced landowners' thinking.[51] Perhaps most importantly, landlords were persuaded to act by what they heard from neighbouring estates. From Cambridgeshire in 1794 the Board of Agriculture reporter noted that the average rent for enclosed land was 18s., as opposed to 10s. for unenclosed, while Lord Scarbrough's rent roll at Winteringham rose – partly through enclosure – from £809 in 1765 to £1887 in 1789. However, variations were considerable, even within relatively small areas. Enclosure yields on the Duke of Rutland's Belvoir estate in the 1790s varied from 10 per cent at Bisbrooke to 33 per cent at Bagworth, with an overall return on all eighteen enclosures

R. A. Butlin, 'The enclosure of open fields and extinction of common rights in England, *c*. 1600–1750: a review', in *Change in the Countryside*, ed. H. S. A. Fox and R. A. Butlin (1979), pp. 65–82; Michael Turner, *English Parliamentary Enclosure* (Folkestone, 1980); Grigg, *The Agricultural Revolution in South Lincolnshire*, pp. 49–50.

[49] J. R. Wordie, 'The chronology of English enclosure, 1500–1914', *Economic History Review*, 2nd ser., 36 (1983), pp. 483–505; Turner, *English Parliamentary Enclosure*, for the most authoritative calculations as to the impact of parliamentary enclosure.

[50] Lambert, *Bills and Acts*, p. 133.

[51] For a discussion of the signficance of interest rates, see Michael Turner, *Enclosures in Britain, 1750–1830* (1984), pp. 46–52.

of 19 per cent. The Fitzwilliam estates recorded a 16 per cent return on original outlay after enclosure.[52] Such figures were quite sufficient to convince landowners that the investment was worthwhile, since they were better than could be anticipated from paper securities or even further land investment. Even where new roads were needed, enclosure remained an attractive investment.[53] Overall, a doubling of rents after enclosure was probably about average, with some exceptional cases yielding a three- or even fourfold increase.

The investment needed to achieve such returns varied regionally and increased through time. Costs fluctuated according to the different tasks which had to be performed. Early enclosures were probably cheap because they involved relatively little reorganization, or were simply confirming earlier enclosures by agreement. When hedging and ditching, road building and drainage were also required, costs inevitably rose. In Buckinghamshire they ranged between 11*s.* and £7 an acre across the county, and through time they increased by 140 per cent over the period 1760–1800. A similar pattern can also be found elsewhere.[54] Although a proportion of the finance was provided by smaller landowners, the aristocracy still had to supply the lion's share of what may have been as much as £29 million which was invested in parliamentary enclosure.[55]

On its own, enclosure was insufficient to extract the best returns from the land, and possibly the most important investment in the fixed capital of agriculture came in the form of drainage improvements. Down to the eighteenth century ridge-and-furrow was the standard form of drainage, but experimentation and change followed in the wake of awareness about the agricultural impact of draining. Nathaniel Kent advised landed gentlemen in 1775 that 'draining is the first improvement that wet lands can receive', and others backing this advice included William Marshall.[56] Practical schemes were pioneered

[52] Marshall, *The Review and Abstract*, vol. IV, p. 617; T. W. Beastall, *A North Country Estate: the Lumleys and Saudersons as landowners, 1600–1900* (1975), p. 90; F. M. L. Thompson, *English Landed Society in the Nineteenth Century* (1963), pp. 224–5.

[53] Chambers and Mingay, *The Agricultural Revolution*, p. 84.

[54] Turner, *Enclosures in Britain*, pp. 57–8. Costs could sometimes be reduced by land sales, especially when common and waste was involved: B. J. Buchanan, 'The financing of parliamentary waste land enclosure: some evidence from North Somerset, 1770–1830', *Agricultural History Review*, 30 (1982), pp. 112–26.

[55] B. A. Holderness, 'Capital formation in agriculture', in *Aspects of Capital Investment in Great Britain, 1750–1850*, ed. J. P. P. Higgins and Sidney Pollard (1971), pp. 166–7.

[56] Kent, *Hints to Gentlemen of Landed Property*, p. 17; Marshall, *On the Landed Property of England*, pp. 38–109.

in Lincolnshire to contain flooding by the sea, and thereby provide suitable conditions for the agricultural revolution in the Fens. Individual landowners took up the challenge. Richard Arkwright began draining his Herefordshire estate in 1811. Although he cut the project during the post-war agricultural depression, for other owners this proved to be the provocation that they needed.[57] Most found themselves meeting the full cost: as a Wiltshire witness told the 1833 Select Committee on Agriculture, 'I find tenants will not do it, unless they are allowed a part of the expense or the whole of it.'[58] With tile drainage from the later eighteenth century, the convention developed whereby the owner supplied the tiles and tenants laid them. James Caird complained that the work needed more expertise than most tenant farmers could provide, but this was the practice in Cheshire and on the Earl of Scarbrough's Durham and Lincolnshire estates.[59] Once pipe drainage became common in the 1840s, landlords took full responsibility for the work, in recognition of the need for proper expertise.

Drainage improvements automatically demanded the accompaniment of better farm buildings. If animals were left in the fields, they were likely to damage the soil and make it impossible to feed the roots in the field. Furthermore, increasing farm sizes, whether by enclosure or engrossment, demanded rationalization of buildings. Fewer farmhouses were required, but men of capital, and particularly the gentlemen farmers who began to appear in the later eighteenth century, expected to be provided with a house in which they could live the life of a gentleman. In addition, more labourers' cottages were required, together with outbuildings such as cow and poultry houses, barns and dairies. As a result, building improvements began in parallel with drainage schemes and in the wake of enclosure. New farmsteads were built to a regular pattern, the norm being the quadrangle with a fixed arrangement of individual buildings. The ultimate codification was found in the fifth edition of J. C. Loudon's *Encyclopaedia of*

[57] T. W. Beastall, *The Agricultural Revolution in Lincolnshire* (Lincoln, 1978), pp. 63–70; Jones, 'Industrial capital and landed investment', p. 172.

[58] Quoted in Thompson, *English Landed Society*, p. 237.

[59] Davies, *The Agricultural History of Cheshire*, p. 109; Caird, *English Agriculture*, pp. 215, 217; A. D. M. Phillips, 'The landlord and agricultural improvements: under draining on the Lincolnshire estate of the Earls of Scarbrough in the first half of the nineteenth century', *East Midlands Geographer*, 7 (1979), pp. 168–77; 'Agricultural improvement on a Durham estate in the nineteenth century: the Lumley estate of the Earls of Scarbrough', *Durham University Journal*, new ser., 42 (1981), pp. 161–8.

Agriculture (1844). It was recognized that buildings ought to be erected cheaply to make them dispensable when agricultural methods changed, and the most obvious example of the need for flexibility was the gradual reduction of the size of barns from about 1780 in conjunction with the mechanization of threshing.[60] Landowner response to these demands varied. Between 1790 and 1820 Coke of Norfolk embarked on some thirty major building projects at Holkham, while the Marquess of Stafford included farm buildings and new offices among his estate improvements in the West Midlands in the early nineteenth century. However, although a major transformation in buildings came between the 1820s and 1870s, many landowners opted out.[61] It was reported from Devon in 1848 that 'the farm buildings are in the majority of cases very irregularly and badly constructed, and a good homestead is rarely met with in any part of Devonshire.'[62] James Caird, writing in the 1850s, was scathing about farm buildings, both because they were 'generally defective', and also because there had been 'heavy expenditure without a proportionate result . . . money squandered on expensive and ill-contrived buildings, from which the tenant reaped little advantage'.[63]

The different demands of drainage and farm building hit landowners simultaneously in the nineteenth century, and by the 1840s concern was being expressed that insufficient capital was available to promote the full range of improvements. Philip Pusey, president of the Royal Agricultural Society and editor of its transactions, pushed for government intervention to allow life tenants to borrow on the security of their estates for agricultural improvement purposes. In 1845 Pusey told a Select Committee of the House of Lords which examined the question whether possessors of entailed estates should be permitted to borrow for drainage purposes, that 'when I look at the extent of land requiring drainage and the limited means of the owners of it . . . I am perfectly convinced that unless landlords are enabled to charge their estates for this purpose, it will be imperfectly done if done at all.'[64] A year later the Public Money Drainage Act, although seen at the time as a sop to the landed interest for the repeal of the Corn Laws,

[60] J. M. Robinson, *Georgian Model Farms* (Oxford, 1983).

[61] S. Wade Martins, 'The farm buildings of the agricultural revolution', *The Local Historian*, 12 (1977), pp. 407–22; E. Richards, '"Leviathan of wealth": West Midlands agriculture, 1800–50', *Agricultural History Review*, 22 (1974), p. 111.

[62] H. Tanner, 'The farming of Devonshire', *JRASE*, 9 (1848), p. 488.

[63] Caird, *English Agriculture*, pp. 77, 89, 135, 222, 490–1.

[64] Parl. Papers, *Report of the Select Committee of the House of Lords on Entailed Estates* (1845), 490, vol. XII, p. 111.

brought to a head the activities of the improvers. Advances of up to £2 million were authorized in Great Britain, but only £360,000 was taken up in England and Wales. Consequently a second Act of 1850 earmarked a further £2 million for equal distribution around the two countries. Buildings, however, remained the responsibility of landowners.[65]

State provision was insufficient, and from the early 1840s land improvement companies began to borrow from insurance companies to lend to landowners. The General Land Drainage and Improvement Company (1853) was the first to have the additional powers of financing farm building improvements, and the private companies became popular because they were willing to sponsor a variety of improvements over longer time periods. Legislative changes gradually permitted landowners holding their estates as life tenants to borrow in order to finance improvements, and, from 1882, to apply money derived from land sales to improving the remainder of the estate.[66]

The availability of investment capital, and the ability of life tenants to finance improvements by borrowing, had a considerable impact on estate management. Expenditure sanctioned between 1846 and 1881 amounted to £13.6 million, of which two-thirds went on drainage, £3.4 million on farm buildings, and nearly £1 million on cottages.[67] Altogether between 1846 and the agricultural slump of the 1870s around £24 million was invested in drainage and related projects, of which £4 million came from the government, £8 million from private companies, and the rest from owners' own resources.[68] The Earls of Scarbrough were among those owners whose investment in drainage peaked during the 1860s and 1870s, partly because they were able to borrow from a land improvement company.[69]

What is not so clear is the return on these investments, and it seems likely that many of them did not pay. In the 1830s and 1840s landowners anticipated high returns on drainage. James Caird made much of a Northumberland farm on which pipe drainage pushed wheat production up by 20 per cent, but this was not typical, and many

[65] James Caird, *The Landed Interest and the Supply of Food* (1878), 5th edn (1967), p. 80; Spring, *The English Landed Estate*, pp. 135–54.

[66] Spring, *The English Landed Estate*, pp. 154–61, 175–6.

[67] Ibid., pp. 176–7. Caird, *The Landed Interest and the Supply of Food*, p. 83, calculated that £12 million had been charged on land over the years 1848–78.

[68] G. E Mingay, *The Agricultural Revolution* (1977), p. 46; J. H. Clapham, *An Economic History of Modern Britain* (1939), vol. II, pp. 271–2.

[69] Phillips, 'The landlord and agricultural improvements' and 'Agricultural improvement on a Durham estate'.

owners had to accept that returns were insubstantial.[70] Capital outlay fluctuated between £4 and £8 an acre. Nathaniel Kent put it at £5 in 1775, and Caird at £4.10s. for clay lands in Northamptonshire. On the Manvers estate in Nottinghamshire the cost was just under £4 an acre between 1840 and 1870, and drainage was costing the Earl of Scarbrough around £5 an acre in the 1840s.[71] The expected rate of return was seldom over 3 per cent. On eight of the largest English estates, covering 5 per cent of the land area, between 1847 and 1878 it amounted to 2.36 per cent in the form of improved rent. The return was no more than 1 per cent on the total improvement and repairs on the Earl of Scarbrough's Durham estate, or 4 per cent on drainage outlay. In Lincolnshire between 1831 and 1856 drainage failed to bring any return in the form of increased rents, although it may have prevented a more serious fall than actually took place.[72] Less is known about building, but between 1820 and 1870 five years' rent was usually considered as equivalent to the capital investment in new buildings for farms of 150–400 acres.[73]

ARISTOCRATS AS IMPROVERS: INVESTMENT

It seems clear that the level of landlord investment increased through time. Spending on some estates seems to have been minimal in the eighteenth century. Only between 1 and 5 per cent of gross rents were returned to the Nottinghamshire estates of the Duke of Kingston, and the Earl of Darlington's repair outlay during the 1780s was less than 1 per cent. Outlay is also known to have been low in Cumbria and Oxfordshire. By contrast, the light Norfolk soils required marling,

---

[70] Caird, *English Agriculture*, p. 374. As late as 1878 he was still claiming that land drainage was one of the most remunerative improvements: *The Landed Interest and the Supply of Food*, p. 87.

[71] Kent, *Hints to Gentlemen*, p. 22; Caird, *English Agriculture*, pp. 421–2: Pickersgill, 'The agricultural revolution in Bassetlaw', p. 583; Phillips, 'The landlord and agricultural improvements', p. 172.

[72] A. D. M. Phillips, 'Underdraining and agricultural investment in the Midlands in the mid-nineteenth century', in *Environment, Man and Economic Change*, ed. A. D. M. Phillips and B. J. Turton (1975), p. 254; 'The landlord and agricultural improvements', p. 176; 'Agricultural improvement on a Durham estate', p. 167.

[73] Holderness, 'Capital formation in agriculture', p. 174. Dr Holderness has also undertaken other work on this subject which has yet to be published. According to A. D. M. Phillips, 'Farm building provision in England, 1850–1900' (unpublished paper read to the Agricultural History Society, 11 April 1984), between £5.2 and

which, together with farm building, explains why Coke returned 18 per cent of gross rents into the estate during the 1790s.[74] These regional disparities were paralleled by variations through time. In the 1730s and 1740s landowners were renovating farmyards in an attempt to attract new tenants in the midst of an agricultural depression, whereas later in the eighteenth century and during the Napoleonic war years favourable conditions allowed them to leave the burden to their tenants. When depression returned after 1815, owners were again forced to rescue their tenants. On one group of East Anglian estates, landlord expenditure on repairs and improvements peaked between 1776 and 1785, and again between 1806 and 1830, although the light-soiled areas were not as badly hit after 1815 as other regions. Overall, it seems unlikely that spending on enclosure and other improvements between 1760 and 1815 represented a drain on the nation's capital resources during the war.[75]

In the post-1815 period landlords found their responsibilities increasing. Tenants were badly affected by the depression, and it was widely believed that substantial farmers could only be attracted by high levels of investment by owners. In addition, the remnants of enclosure, the responsibility for drainage and buildings, and for the introduction of new scientific methods and mechanical aids, all tended to fall squarely on the landlord's shoulders, particularly in the period of high farming in mid-century. On the Manvers estate in North Nottinghamshire repairs and improvements amounted to 17 per cent of gross rental between 1827 and 1839, and 20–26 per cent between 1850 and 1859. New works and permanent improvements on the Duke of Bedford's Bedfordshire and Buckinghamshire estates increased

---

£5.3 million was spent on farm buildings in England through government improvement loans in the period from 1852 to the early 1870s. On fixed capital formation in agriculture, see C. H. Feinstein, 'Capital formation in Great Britain', in *Cambridge Economic History of Europe*, ed. P. Mathias and M. M. Postan, vol 7, pt 1 (Cambridge, 1978), p. 49.

[74] Mingay, *English Landed Society*, p. 178; Beckett, thesis, p. 117; J. R. Walton, 'Aspects of agrarian change in Oxfordshire, 1750–1880' (University of Oxford, D.Phil. thesis, 1976), ch. 2; S. Wade Martins, *A Great Estate at Work: the Holkham estate and its inhabitants in the nineteenth century* (Cambridge, 1980), appendix 3. Figures for eighteenth-century investment need to be treated with caution, since landowners did not necessarily distinguish between capital and recurrent expenditure, and since the amounts invested almost certainly fluctuated from year to year: C. Clay, 'Landlords and estate management in England', in *The Agrarian History of England and Wales*, ed. Thirsk, vol. V, pt II, pp. 245–51.

[75] B. A. Holderness, 'Landlords' capital formation in East Anglia, 1750–1870', *Economic History Review*, 2nd ser., 25 (1972), pp. 440–7; Jones, *Agriculture and the Industrial Revolution*, pp. 108–9.

from 5 per cent in the 1820s, to 7 per cent in the 1830s, 30 per cent in the 1840s and 40 per cent in the 1850s. On the Ailesbury trust estates in Yorkshire and Wiltshire the investment cost retarded debt repayment. An estimate for Wiltshire in 1845 suggested that £5500 would be needed annually for improvements, but in 1849 £7332 was laid out, and between 1846 and 1856 the average expended on repairs, drainage and roads was £8062 a year.[76] Against this evidence should be set the picture of East Anglia, the only region to be subjected to detailed study. Here the level of investment per acre was probably no greater in the mid-nineteenth century than it had been a century earlier, and the period 1820–80 was one of consolidation during which the nature of capital investment in fixed equipment made the region increasingly unique.[77]

During the second half of the nineteenth century, repairs and improvements may have represented as much as a quarter of gross rents.[78] This reflected the twin pressures on landlords, first to invest in high farming during the 1850s and 1860s in order to maximize their returns, and then to carry on investing from the 1870s when depression threatened to rob them of good tenants. Landlords responded positively to high farming, partly because of the legal changes which allowed them to borrow, and partly because of the availability of loans. By the early 1870s high farming had certainly not been inhibited by lack of capital; indeed, the poor returns on investment may point to overcapitalization in these decades.[79] This merely served to expose landowners when a series of wet seasons in the 1870s, and falling cereal prices during the 1880s, brought a prolonged period of depression. Back in 1849 James Caird had predicted improved vegetable and livestock prices together with a relative fall in cereal prices, but such was the attachment to corn growing that landlords and farmers alike had ignored the warning. The results soon became apparent, particularly in the arable south-east, since livestock producers were not as badly hit. Landowners who had borrowed in the

[76] Pickersgill, 'The agricultural revolution in Bassetlaw', p. 553; Duke of Bedford, *A Great Agricultural Estate*, pp. 218–23; F. M. L. Thompson, 'English landownership: the Ailesbury Trust, 1832–56', *Economic History Review*, 2nd ser., 11 (1958), pp. 130–1.

[77] Holderness, 'Landlords' capital formation in East Anglia', pp. 440–7.

[78] R. J. Thompson, 'An inquiry into the rent of agricultural land in England and Wales during the nineteenth century', *Journal of the Royal Statistical Society*, 70 (1907), pp. 587–616.

[79] P. J. Perry, 'High farming in Victorian Britain: the financial foundations', *Agricultural History*, 52 (1978), pp. 370–1.

heady years of high farming to finance improvements found themselves in dire straits. On the one hand, their interest payments were fixed, and had often been calculated on the basis of significant rent increases, so that owners were squeezed as their disposable income declined. On the other hand, the capital value of their estates also fell in line with the reduction in rents.[80]

To escape this syndrome, landlords were faced with various alternatives. They could sit tight and hope to ride out the storm. This seldom proved successful; three landowners in the Lower Ouse Valley (Sussex) who adopted this tactic had all sold up by 1920. A second policy was to encourage the tenants to adopt new farming systems. At Glynde in Sussex H. B. W. Brand built a central dairy to service his farms as a means of exploiting the London and Eastbourne milk markets. Thirdly, a landowner could take vacant farms in hand and run them under vigorous management to try to extract a profit. There were obvious drawbacks to this policy, since the farms vacated were likely to be on the poorer soils and to have been run down by impoverished tenants prior to vacation. However, in the mid-1890s Lord Wantage farmed 13,000 acres in Berkshire, and as a result of economies of scale and effective management he made a commercial success of the enterprise.[81] A final course of action was grassing down. In many places such an adaptation was vital if tenants were to be attracted, and in some cases it was a success. Lord Leconfield's outlay amounted to £12. 10*s.* an acre, but his rents rose from 13*s.* to 30*s.* an acre.[82] All too often, however, grassing down took place in areas where climate, soil types and estate management might have made the second and third options more successful. It cost the Duke of Bedford between £1. 9*s.* and £10 an acre between 1878 and 1889, but in almost every instance his rents fell; indeed, on a 64-acre farm grassed down in 1881–2 at a cost of £10 an acre, the rent declined from 27*s.* 6*d.* in 1878 to only 5*s.* in 1895, a result he described as 'disastrous'.[83] In part, failure reflected the disadvantageous conditions in which the operation took place. While loans were still available for drainage, no equivalent grants could

---

[80] Duke of Bedford, *A Great Agricultural Estate*, painted a picture of ruin, but at least one reviewer read the text closely enough to point out the omissions, including the absence of reference to some of his more lucrative enterprises: David Spring, 'Land and politics in Edwardian England', *Agricultural History*, 58 (1984), pp. 18–20.

[81] S. Farrant, 'The management of four estates in the lower Ouse valley, Sussex, and agricultural change, 1840–1920', *Southern History*, 1 (1979), pp. 155–70; P. J. Perry, *British Farming in the Great Depression, 1870–1914* (1974), pp. 85–6.

[82] Perry, *British Farming in the Great Depression*, p. 86.

[83] Duke of Bedford, *A Great Agricultural Estate*, pp. 198, 204.

be raised to fund grassing down. Consequently expensive investment had to take place amidst falling rents.

Undoubtedly investment reached an all-time record in the closing decades of the nineteenth century. The Earl of Derby invested £200,000 over twelve years (7s. 8d per acre annually): Lord Sefton £286,000 in twenty-two years (14s.); and the Earl of Ancaster £689,197 between 1872 and 1893 (11s. 7d.). At Holkham, between 1872 and 1892, £153,234 was invested from a gross income of £1,109,314 (13.7 per cent), while at Chatsworth £56,084 was ploughed back into the estate from £159,309, or 35 per cent, and this at a time when the family was heavily involved in shoring up Barrow-in-Furness (see chapter nine). Between 1847 and 1894, drainage and improvement expenditure under the various Acts of Parliament amounted to £16.5 million.[84] Overall, during these decades investment was hardly related to subsequent rent changes; in fact, it is possible that landlords were overinvesting – 'throwing good money after bad' – in such a way as to channel into agriculture funds which might have been better employed in other sectors of the economy. Since part of the return on their investment accrued to tenants, this policy may also have helped to reduce the flight of farmers from the land.[85]

The aristocratic contribution to agricultural development through improvement investment was undoubtedly impressive. If they shared enclosure costs with freeholders, the majority of the outgoings still fell on their shoulders without recourse to the benefit of loans. Drainage and farm building costs were theirs alone, and if – as Caird suggested – some opted out, much of the credit for these improvements must go to the group as a whole. Admittedly loan capital became available and borrowing restrictions were eased, but the demands on landlord investment increased considerably during the nineteenth century without yielding commensurately high rewards. The returns on drainage were not as good as might have been anticipated from government funds or railway investment. Yet what is impressive is the willingness of landowners to take financial risks, often involving borrowing large sums of money, to try to improve their farms. By the end of the century some of them were even transferring funds into agriculture from other concerns, taking the profits of mines, docks, railways and urban ground rents out into the countryside. For those

[84] F. A. Channing, *The Truth about the Agricultural Depression* (1897), pp. 120–7.

[85] C. O'Grada, 'Agricultural decline, 1860–1914', in *The Economic History of Britain since 1700*, ed. R. Floud and D. McCloskey (Cambridge, 1981), vol. II, pp. 186–8.

lacking such resources, and forced to borrow, the consequence was often to hasten final sale of the estate early in the twentieth century.[86]

ARISTOCRATS AS LANDLORDS

The relationship between a landowner and his tenants was invariably complicated. Owners were anxious to ensure that tenants looked after their farms properly and made sufficient profit to pay an economic rent. Tenants looked for the best possible deal from a landlord, including capital investment and flexible lease covenants. The ideal, encouraged by agricultural writers, was for a landowner to be in a position where he could lease out his estate in large farms to well-informed tenants with plentiful capital. However, this raised questions about the size of unit to be let to a particular individual, and the type of agreement which could feasibly be entered into so as to protect the best interests of both owner and tenant. Although the landlord was dependent on his manager for advice on these problems, he could not avoid taking the final decisions about farm sizes and leases. In addition, he had to set the tone for relationships in the countryside. Landlord and tenant were joined in a business agreement tempered by a strong element of feudal connection. Owners expected tenants to farm according to their agreements and to pay their rents with reasonable regularity, as well as to receive 'guidance' on electoral issues, and to accept the landlord's right to hunt over the land. In return they could expect a reasonable bargain with a modest rent and *de facto* security. Much of the decision-making in this rather grey area inevitably lay with the landlord.

Once landowners opted out of demesne farming, they were faced with the need to let their property to tenants. In some areas of the country, traditional agricultural tenure embraced copyhold, customary-hold, and long or life leasehold tenures, which gave considerable powers over the land and were only slowly eradicated from the sixteenth century onwards. Copy and customary tenures had fixed rents, and landlords' only means of compensation for inflation was to increase the levels of fines. However, their efforts in this direction were not guaranteed success. Two-thirds of eighteenth-century Cumbria was held in customary tenure, and so numerous were the tenants that

---

[86] R. Perren, 'The landlord and agricultural transformation, 1870–1900', *Agricultural History Review*, 18 (1970), pp. 36–51; Perry, *British Farming in the Great Depression*, pp. 69–71.

they could finance resistance to legal cases brought by owners trying to raise fines.[87] Life leasehold was widespread in the west of England during the eighteenth century. Here again individuals paid only a nominal rent, although in this case the fine was paid when purchasing the tenancy. Some leases were guaranteed for the lives of three named individuals, and others for terms of ninety-nine (or occasionally sixty) years terminable on three lives.[88]

As landlords concentrated on maximizing income these forms of tenure gave way to the rack rent, which was already commonly found in the Midlands and southern England by the seventeenth century. Landlords granted fixed-term tenancies at the full annual value of the land, and most counties had between one-fifth and one-half of their land farmed under such a system in Victorian England. According to Professor David Low, writing in the 1840s, the system was advantageous because the landlord offered security of possession and beneficial terms of management in return for an equitable rent and an adequate capital outlay.[89] Moreover it was the advantages of rack-rent tenure which persuaded landlords in the north and west to try to convert the customary and copyhold alternatives. Originally such tenures had been regarded as a means of ensuring that tenants looked after the property, and financed building and improvement, spurred on through a long and perpetually renewable lease. The landlord took his share of the profit by increasing the level of fines. Over time, however, the imperfections of the tenure became apparent. The tenant spent all his capital acquiring the property, and was therefore short of resources. Restrictions on tenants were minimal and only weakly supervised – hence the accusation that Cumbrian customary tenants seemed 'to inherit with the estates of their ancestors their notions of cultivating them'[90] – and landlords knew little about the men who worked their land. On the other hand, owners contemplating ending such arrangements had to take into account the problems of overcropping and abuse which were likely to occur in the closing years of the lease.[91] This consideration encouraged owners to keep their life

---

[87] Beckett, thesis, pp. 265–6; Searle, '"The odd corner of England"', pp. 71–83.

[88] Christopher Clay, 'Lifeleasehold in the western counties of England, 1650–1750', *Agricultural History Review*, 29 (1981), pp. 83–96; 'Landlords and estate management in England', pp. 198–230. The latter essay provides a full account of the different types of tenancy found in England between 1640 and 1750.

[89] David Low, *Landed Property and the Economy of Estates* (1844), pp. 8–27.

[90] J. Bailey and G. Culley, *General View of the Agriculture of the County of Cumberland* (1797), p. 181.

[91] Clay, 'Lifeleasehold in the western counties of England', pp. 94–5; W. Marshall, *Rural Economy of the West of England* (1796), vol. I, pp. 43–8.

leaseholds going. They were still being granted at the end of the eighteenth century in Lancashire, and they remained widespread in the south-west and Wales early in the nineteenth. However, the process of conversion was inexorable. In the Vale of Porlock (Somerset) tenants were converted to rack rents during the 1830s, and by the 1870s and 1880s the majority of life leaseholds had disappeared. Almost certainly, however, copyhold and life leasehold tenures facilitated the longer-term survival of the small farmer in the north and west.[92]

The conversion to rack rent and leasehold confronted owners with some tricky questions on farm sizes and tenancy agreements if they were to get the best out of their land. With fixed-rent tenure the lord depended on fines and other casualties, but once rents were revisable he could consider reducing the tenants to a minimum by leasing large plots to a few wealthy individuals. But this was not a simple process, since the critical consideration was to find a competent farmer. It was, of course, possible merely to lay out the farms at whatever size was preferred, and let them to the highest bidder, but this was a risky business method. Public letting in Devon during the 1840s attracted men with little to lose, who overcropped, made improvement impossible, and forced up the general level of rents so that even honest farmers were compelled to bid higher than they knew a particular farm to be worth.[93] Consequently it was regarded as good practice to set farm sizes, rents and tenancy agreements in advance. A landowner had to consider whether he could hope to attract tenants at the advertised rent. If the farms were too large he could have trouble finding competent men, but on the other hand most commentators were agreed – and the Holkham case seemed to confirm the fact – that the most productive farms were the largest. If an owner set his farms too small, therefore, he might not get the best from his land. The balance was a fine one, and as a result changes in sizes took place relatively slowly through the eighteenth and nineteenth centuries.

Generally owners attempted to increase farm sizes in so far as they were justified by terrain and culture, proximity to markets and regional characteristics. If enclosure and improved farming were

---

[92] P. J. Ashford, 'The structure of landownership and occupation in the Vale of Porlock (Somerset), 1760–1850' (Open University, B.Phil. thesis, 1985); Marshall, *The Review and Abstract*, vol. I, p. 274; vol. II, pp. 12, 232; vol. V, pp. 524, 553; J. V. Beckett, 'The decline of the small landowner in eighteenth- and nineteenth-century England: some regional considerations', *Agricultural History Review*, 30 (1982), pp. 97–111.

[93] Marshall, *The Review and Abstract*, vol. V, p. 535; Tanner, 'The farming of Devonshire', p. 487; Marshall, *On the Landed Property of England*, p. 358.

widely expected to transform farm sizes, the situation in practice was not so simple. In some parts of England the most rapid changes took place prior to parliamentary enclosure. This was the case in Nottinghamshire, where amalgamation often dated from the 1730s and 1740s and was intended to weed out inefficient tenants who were squeezed by adverse economic circumstances; few of the later enclosures there resulted in a reduction of farm numbers. From Northamptonshire it was reported in the 1790s that land was often parcelled out to former tenants after enclosure, and the largest farms were to be found in the older enclosed parishes.[94] Something of what could be achieved is clear from Cumbria, a region of small farms and relatively little enclosure. Some of the largest farms were to be found on the earls of Carlisle's estate, where piecemeal enclosure took place between 1690 and 1740, while similar efforts were made to increase sizes by enclosure on Viscount Lonsdale's property. On the other hand, on the west coast the Lowthers deliberately maintained small farms in order to attract miners to the area – a policy also found in the coal districts of South Wales.[95]

Through the country as a whole, between 1720 and 1830 a general increase in mean farm sizes was insufficient to disturb the numerical dominance of smaller farms, although marked progress was made on some individual estates. On the Leveson-Gower estates in the West Midlands, between 1714 and 1832 the average size of farms over 20 acres increased from 83 to 147 acres, while the number of farms exceeding 200 acres increased from 19 to 59 per cent of the total.[96] Nor did the pace of engrossment greatly increase in the nineteenth century. On the Manvers estate in Nottinghamshire, between 1810–12 and 1862 the proportion of land in farms of 100 acres increased marginally, but the strength of the small farmer remained, and in the mid-1880s 71 per cent of English holdings were under 50 acres and barely one in 100 exceeded 500 acres.[97] The only clear trend

[94] G. E. Mingay, 'The size of farms in the eighteenth century', *Economic History Review*, 2nd ser., 14 (1961–2), pp. 480–1, 487; Marshall, *The Review and Abstract*, vol. IV, p. 348.
[95] Beckett, thesis, pp. 82, 184, 231; Martin, 'The landed estate in Glamorgan', pp. 127–8.
[96] J. R. Wordie, 'Social change on the Leveson-Gower estates, 1714–1832', *Economic History Review*, 2nd ser., 27 (1974), pp. 596–98; A. D. M. Phillips, 'A note on farm size and efficiency on the North Staffordshire estate of the Leveson-Gowers, 1714–1809', *North Staffordshire Journal of Field Studies*, 19 (1979), pp. 30–8.
[97] Pickersgill, 'The agricultural revolution in Bassetlaw', pp. 492 ff; Caird, *The Landed Interest and the Supply of Food*, p. 58; P. G. Craigie, 'The size and distribution

was for larger farms to predominate in the south and East Anglia, with much smaller sizes still widely found in the north and west.[98]

Similar considerations lay behind the type of agreement entered into by landlord and tenant. Most eighteenth-century agricultural writers favoured long leases of up to twenty-one years to give tenants security and allow scope for improved farming.[99] Landlords tended to agree when they could find good tenants who might make lasting improvements, or when economic conditions were favourable and the lease could be used to transfer to the tenant financial responsibiliy for which the owner would otherwise have remained liable, such as for alterations and extensions to farm buildings. On the other hand, long leases could also bring considerable disadvantages. An owner might be saddled with a bad tenant, and it took only a few years of negligence to ruin several decades of hard work building up a farm; while in periods of rising prices they were unable to raise rents. This was particularly true of the Napoleonic war period. Tenants with long leases commencing early in the 1790s did well, but their landlords were reluctant to grant similar terms when renewal became due. Thus Lord Darnley of Cobham converted his Kentish tenants from leases to tenancies at will between 1795 and 1812, and the Marquess of Stafford turned to annual tenancies for his West Midlands farms during the early years of the nineteenth century.[100] Landlords also stood to lose if they granted long leases when prices were falling. Farmers could not pay their rents, and owners had little option but to make abatements. Consequently the fluctuations of the war years made owners wary of granting leases, and the falling prices of the 1820s made tenants unwilling to take on long-term commitments. The Agricultural Distress Committee heard from a stream of witnesses in 1833 that tenants simply did not want long leases, and the ground lost by then to annual tenancies was never recovered. By 1870 in Wiltshire written annual agreements were found across the county, while life leasehold was replaced by annual tenancy throughout South Wales in the early

---

of agricultural holdings in England and abroad', *Journal of the Royal Statistical Society*, 50 (1887), p. 91.

[98] D. B. Grigg, 'Small and large farms in England and Wales', *Geography*, 47 (1963), pp. 268–79.

[99] For example, John Mordaunt, *The Complete Steward* (1761), vol. II, p. 328; Kent, *Hints to Gentlemen*, p. 95; Marshall, *On the Landed Property of England*, pp. 301–2.

[100] H. G. Hunt, 'Agricultural rent in South-East England, 1788–1825', *Agricultural History Review*, 7 (1959), pp. 102–3; Richards, '"Leviathan of wealth": West Midlands agriculture', p. 112.

nineteenth century.[101] Paradoxically, the long lease went out of favour at a time of landlord weakness rather than as a symbol of landowner supremacy over the tenantry.

Leases also went out of favour both because they were not necessarily beneficial in promoting agricultural improvement, and because annual tenancies turned out to be advantageous to owners and farmers alike. Agricultural experts stressed the importance of covenants designed to encourage better husbandry among tenants. Edward Laurence in 1726 and John Mordaunt in 1761 detailed more than twenty separate covenants, but the surviving evidence suggests a gap between theory and practice. Few eighteenth-century covenants appear to have included definitely progressive clauses, the majority going no further than to leave out the old injunctions about following traditional practices. On all three of the Lowther estates in Cumbria during the 1730s, for example, clauses were introduced into leases stipulating the number of acres which might be ploughed, penalties for exceeding the allocation, and the length of fallows. Reports to the Board of Agriculture at the end of the century suggested that landlords were still mainly interested in protecting their property against the mal-practices of tenants, and safeguarding soil fertility.[102] On the other hand, it would be wrong to suggest an entirely gloomy situation. In Cumberland during the 1730s the Earl of Carlisle's tenants were informed of the number of acres that might be kept in tillage, as well as the use of lime, and the planting of turnips and rye. The Earls of Dudley introduced increasingly progressive leases into their West Midlands leases during the century, and new clauses appeared in Cheshire leases towards 1800. Probably the most widely reputed leases were those at Holkham. Between the 1760s and 1780s these permitted a four-course rotation, but by the 1790s they specifically called for a six-course. Thereafter the four-course returned, but with flexibility.[103]

These changes partially reflected altered ideas as it became clear that over-restrictive covenants could prove harmful. William Marshall stressed the importance of covenants being geared to the needs of a

[101] VCH, *Wiltshire*, vol. IV (1959), pp. 74–5; Howell, *Land and People in Nineteenth-Century Wales*, pp. 58–9.

[102] H. J. Habakkuk, 'Economic functions of English landowners in the seventeenth and eighteenth centuries', *Explorations in Entrepreneurial History*, 6 (1953), p. 93; Beckett, thesis, pp. 184, 230, 281; Marshall, *The Review and Abstract*, vol. I, p. 144; vol. V, pp. 125, 376.

[103] Beckett, thesis, p. 83; T. J. Raybould, *The Economic Emergence of the Black Country* (Newton Abbot, 1973), p. 89; Davies, *The Agricultural History of Cheshire*, p. 51; Parker, *Coke of Norfolk*, pp. 68, 105, 158 ff.

particular farm, and this view prevailed in the nineteenth century. Writing of Devonshire in 1848, Henry Tanner pointed out that lease covenants often forced farmers to act against their better judgement. By the 1860s it was accepted that most covenants were primarily to prevent tenants from violating the decencies of farming.[104] Moreover, enforcing covenants was also a problem. In Coke's time husbandry covenants at Holkham were apparently taken seriously by the tenants, and, at least from 1816, they were enforced. However, evidence from Nottinghamshire suggests that leasehold estates were no more improved than those held on annual tenancies; indeed, it is clear that change was just as likely on farms held on a year-to-year basis, since covenants were usually inserted in agreements and enforced.[105]

The advantages of annual tenancies became increasingly apparent over time. Landowners could raise rents and rid themselves of poor farmers, while tenants could react to low profits by quitting before losing their capital. The system fitted a situation in which landlords needed good tenants, just as farmers required good landlords; indeed, according to James Caird, tenants were ready to invest their capital 'with no other security than their landlord's character, and the confidence which subsists between the two classes in England generally, is in the highest degree honourable to both.'[106] Moreover, as an investment incentive to tenants, a system of 'tenant right' was developed, in which compensation was paid to an outgoing farmer for his unexhausted improvements. For the tenant this offered security for his investment, and for the landlord it saved him the need to prosecute a tenant who defaulted on his rent and left early. He could deduct some or all of the arrears from the sum to be paid by the new occupier to the outgoing tenant, and thereby recover the arrears without resorting to unpopular and harsh measures which might end with a tenant being imprisoned.[107] Tenant right originated in Lincolnshire in

---

[104] Marshall, *On the Landed Property of England*, pp. 370–1; Caird, *English Agriculture*, pp. 500–1; Morton, *The Resources of Estates*, p. 155; Tanner, 'The farming of Devonshire', pp. 486–7; Spring, *The English Landed Estate*, p. 112.

[105] Parker, *Coke of Norfolk*, pp. 145, 199; D. V. Fowkes, 'The progress of agrarian change in Nottinghamshire, *c*. 1720–1830' (University of Liverpool, Ph.D. thesis, 1971), pp. 519–20; Clay, 'Landlords and estate management in England', pp. 228–30.

[106] Caird, *English Agriculture*, p. 150.

[107] T. W. Beastall, 'Landlords and tenants', in *The Victorian Countryside*, ed. Mingay, p. 432. Perry, 'High farming in Victorian Britain', pp. 372–3, outlines some of the drawbacks to tenant right.

the 1740s, and had spread into Nottinghamshire by the 1770s.[108] Despite almost universal disapproval by agricultural experts,[109] the system reached various parts of the country by 1850,[110] and it became the basis of the Agricultural Holdings Acts of 1875 and 1883. The latter gave legal recognition to 'the custom of the country'.[111]

Laying out farms and deciding on agreements was largely a managerial function, but the relationship between a tenant and his landlord was too delicate to be left entirely to stewards and agents. There is plenty of evidence that owners went out of their way to establish a rapport with their tenants. Lincolnshire was reputedly the best county for landlords, a relationship fostered by rent day dinners and even Sunday afternoon visiting. In Derbyshire the Duke of Devonshire was regarded as a good landlord despite granting no leases. According to James Caird, 'in no country, perhaps in the world, does the character of any class of men for fair and generous dealing stand higher than that of the great body of English landlords.'[112] William Marshall maintained that the qualities of a good tenant were capital, skill, industry and character, and finding tenants with all these attributes was difficult enough to ensure that landowners did not easily turn qualified men away.[113] Landlords were generally reluctant to disturb tenants who kept the land well and paid the rent regularly. They rarely turned tenants out, except for misbehaviour, and even when it was necessary to remove a man he might be granted a pension or offered some other gift in recognition of service.[114] In addition, it was generally accepted that no radical revision should take place

[108] J. A. Perkins, 'The prosperity of farming in the Lindsey uplands, 1813–37', *Agricultural History Review*, 24 (1976), pp. 126–43; Beastall, *A North Country Estate*, pp. 95–6; Fowkes, 'The progress of agrarian change in Nottinghamshire', p. 519; Pickersgill, 'The agricultural revolution in Bassetlaw', pp. 523–9.

[109] L. Kennedy and T. B. Grainger, *The Present State of the Tenancy of Land in Great Britain* (1828), p. 17; Caird, *English Agriculture*, p. 508.

[110] Caird, *English Agriculture*, pp. 119–20, 132–3, 328–9; VCH, *Wiltshire*, vol. IV, p. 75; M. M. Milburn, 'Farming of the North Riding of Yorkshire', *JRASE*, 9 (1848), p. 520.

[111] Caird, *The Landed Interest and the Supply of Food*, p. 73, attributed the passing of this legislation to the strength of the farming community after the extension of the franchise and the introduction of the secret ballot.

[112] Caird, *English Agriculture*, pp. 196, 504; Obelkevich, *Religion in Rural Society*, p. 33; H. A. Fuller, 'Landownership in Lindsey, c. 1800–1860' (University of Hull, MA thesis, 1974), p. 138.

[113] Marshall, *On the Landed Property of England*, p. 391.

[114] Spring, *The English Landed Estate*, p. 112; Brian Short, 'The turnover of tenants on the Ashburnham estate, 1830–1850', *Sussex Archaeological Collections*, 113 (1976), pp. 157–74.

during the lifetime of an established tenant, especially if the tenant's family had a long connection with the estate. Inevitably this made for some inefficiency, especially on larger estates where political conditions might dictate diplomacy in handling tenants, and some old and inefficient tenants were undoubtedly retained out of loyalty rather than for any other good reason.[115]

To encourage good relationships landlords were reluctant to screw up rents to the highest possible levels. This was despite complaints from agricultural experts. Arthur Young was of opinion that 'landlords should be prepared to sacrifice popularity for the sake of five shillings per annum per acre', and James Caird blamed under-renting on 'the character of the landlord or his agent, and the custom of the neighbourhood . . . there is not a county in England where this is not exemplified.'[116] In effect landlords were interpreting the idea of a 'rack' rent liberally. Even Coke of Norfolk let his farms at a moderate rent, while James Loch, agent of the Sutherland estate, wrote in 1830 that

Lord Stafford's rents . . . have always been fixed at rather under the general average of the district. . . . I mean that the tenants should feel that they hold their lands on rather easier terms than their neighbours. It is fit and proper that those who hold of a great man should do so.[117]

Such magnanimity often had ulterior motives. Low rents could be a useful means of swaying voting intentions, and they could also serve as compensation for foxhunting depredations. On the other hand, it is arguable that under-renting became less common in the nineteenth century, owing to a combination of the new breed of agents and the demands on owner investment. Thus, despite Loch's claims, the post-1813 policy of charging economic rents on the Leveson-Gower estate led to the Trentham interest in Staffordshire politics collapsing by about 1820. Heavy investment in improved agriculture, in which the Marquess of Stafford was 'far from being a passive *rentier*', proved incompatible with a political interest, and after 1820 the family preferred social prestige to their old electoral role.[118] High levels of

[115] When longstanding tenants were removed, they often received a form of compensation: Spring, *The English Landed Estate*, pp. 108–12.

[116] Young is quoted in Mingay, *English Landed Society*, pp. 53–4; Caird, *English Agriculture*, p. 477.

[117] E. Richards, *The Leviathan of Wealth* (1973), p. 29.

[118] J. R. Wordie, 'Rent movements and the English tenant farmer', in *Research in Economic History*, ed. P. Uselding, vol. 6 (1981), pp. 224–5, 209; Richards,

investment and high rents went together in the nineteenth century, but inevitably this tended to weaken the old landlord–tenant relations.

Landlords also had to be flexible about tenants' capital investment. The ideal, according to David Low, was that 'the landlord so regulate his demands on the tenant, as not to exact as rent any part of that fund which is necessary to the farmer as capital'.[119] The problem was to ensure that the tenant had sufficient finance to operate the farm he agreed to lease. In the 1720s Edward Laurence suggested that a farm of £100 a year rent required £300 stock, while in William Marshall's view a farm of £100–£500 rent required capital of £500–£1000 for each £100 rent, by the early nineteenth century. Philip Pusey believed £6 an acre was sufficient, but in the 1850s J. L. Morton suggested that without £8–£10 an acre no farmer could do full justice to the land, and £10–£12 was preferable.[120] Since such sums were not readily available, large farms could be difficult to let, while economic conditions could upset even the most careful calculations.

In general terms, financial responsibility for an estate was clearly divided. The owner was responsible for the fixed capital, and the tenant provided his own working capital. It was the landlord's responsibility to put the property into repair, and to finance improvements likely to add value to the estate beyond the term of the current lease. In practice the situation was seldom so clear-cut. During years of prosperity, tenants were ready to turn a blind eye to the minutiae of the landlord's responsibility, while owners might take the opportunity of transferring the tax burden and some of the fixed capital costs. When conditions altered, the owner might have to accept rather different terms. To attract tenants he might need to invest more heavily in improvements, while financial help sometimes had to be offered in the form of rent reductions and remissions. During the post-war depression in 1816 Lord Sheffield was told that

neither capital improved and good husbandry nor the most rigid economy at the present price of produce will enable the tenant of land to pay the rent and other payments which are now imposed thereon, and he rather chooses if

---

'"Leviathan of wealth": West Midlands agriculture', pp. 111–13. For a more detailed study of the interaction of landlord and tenant for the period 1640–1750, see Clay, 'Landlords and estate management in England', pp. 230–45.

[119] David Low, *Observations on the Present State of Landed Property* (1823), p. 9.

[120] E. Laurence, *The Duty of a Steward to his Lord* (1726), p. 83; Marshall, *On the Landed Property of England*, p. 391; Perry, 'High farming in Victorian Britain', p. 372; Morton, *The Resources of Estates*, pp. 19–20.

possible to save his remaining capital than longer to continue in the road to ruin.[121]

In other words, the landlord had to take second place as the rent money was turned into working capital. After all, demanding the rent from a hard-pressed tenant could simply force him to quit, leaving a farm untenanted, and saddling the landlord with an unsavoury reputation which could make finding a new tenant difficult.[122]

The lengths to which a landowner might go can be illustrated from the case of Ralph Hall, tenant of Matthew Montagu's Eryholme farm near Darlington. Early in 1789 he was reported as delinquent by the steward, William Thomas, but 'his small and numerous family as well as his being an old tenant are circumstances which render him an object of every possible indulgence.' Hall's situation continued to deteriorate, and in June he committed suicide, leaving a widow and five small children. The widow, Ann Hall, appealed to Thomas to be allowed an opportunity of farming the property herself, and this was granted; indeed, Thomas suggested a rent abatement to help her put the property back into good condition, even though, as he told Montagu,

I am aware of the great caution necessary even in the recommendation of indulgences of those kinds, yet where the future prospect of support to a widow and five small orphans are dependent on it, I consider it an act of injustice in an agent to withhold it from his employer.

Montagu accepted the representation, and by October 1789 Mrs Hall was reported to be doing well, but this proved to be a false dawn and she eventually left at the end of 1790, with an allowance for the value of seeds and in lieu of other permanent improvements.[123]

[121] Clements Library, Sheffield Papers, Samuel Tuesday (?) to Lord Sheffield, 13 March 1816.

[122] Each region of the country had its own customs in landlord–tenant relations. Sometimes the landlord left to the tenant the full liability for providing the capital for soil improvements, as at Holkham, where farmers had to find the outlay on marling and draining: Parker, *Coke of Norfolk*, p. 155. Elsewhere the owner bore the full cost of farmhouse repairs, or sometimes he might share them with the tenant, perhaps by providing the materials and leaving labour to the tenant. In other instances the tenant undertook full responsibility and was compensated by a rent reduction or a payment by the landlord: Mingay, *English Landed Society*, pp. 177–8; Thompson, *English Landed Society*, pp. 235, 252.

[123] Northumberland RO, ZAN M. 17/60a, William Thomas to Matthew Montagu, 18 April, 27 June, 5 July, 22 October 1789, 22 April, 25 December 1790, 9 March 1791; Ann Hall to William Black, 12 June 1789; William Black to Matthew Montagu, 28 June 1789. Matthew Montagu's decision was required at each stage of the process.

Sensitivity of this nature was most clearly required in the late nineteenth-century agricultural depression. Landlords had to accept rent reductions and increase capital input, especially where dairy farming was being introduced. Dutch barns were erected for storing winter fodder, and covered fold-yards were built to help winter fattening of cattle. Complaints had to be dealt with promptly, and enterprising tenants encouraged. Even so, because tenants were scarce, unsatisfactory farmers tended to be retained when they might have been evicted, and there was an increased risk of letting a farm to a man lacking the necessary capital and enterprise. In fact, at no time was it easy to discover whether a tenant had the capital that he claimed.[124] However, in the depression years the problems of finding and keeping good tenants certainly increased, and owners were forced to re-examine their policies on rents and agreements.[125] Furthermore, this period witnessed a growth in tenants' independence from landlords. They sought additional security through the 'tenant right' system, while the clearest sign of a breakdown in relationships was the formation early in the twentieth century of the National Farmers' Union, which excluded both landlords and their agents. The old cohesion of the countryside was breaking down amidst the ravages of depression.[126]

THE FINANCIAL REWARD

The incentive for aristocrats to improve their estates was the prospect of financial reward. However, any assessment of income reflects rack rents, since copyhold and life leasehold rents were fixed, and the level of fines is almost impossible to calculate on a yearly basis with any accuracy. Even rack rents varied according to agricultural conditions. In eighteenth-century Nottinghamshire, for example, rent per acre on sandy soils was half that of the clays, and while all mean rents increased, this disparity began to lessen only after about 1830.

[124] Coke seems to have been exceptional, since the farms on his estate had no shortage of tenants with sufficient capital: Parker, *Coke of Norfolk*, pp. 155–6. Elsewhere the problems were sufficient for some commentators to argue that farms were too large: Marshall, *The Review and Abstract*, vol. I, pp. 470–1; Morton, *The Resources of Estates*, p. 19. On the whole question of farm sizes, see J. V. Beckett, 'The debate over farm sizes in eighteenth- and nineteenth-century England', *Agricultural History*, 58 (1983), pp. 308–25.

[125] Mingay (ed.), *The Victorian Countryside*, pp. 434–6; Perry, *British Farming in the Great Depression*, pp. 78–85. Countryside relations are also discussed in chapter ten below.

[126] Mingay (ed.), *The Victorian Countryside*, pp. 15–16.

Furthermore, rent levels were subject to the vagaries of the agricultural depressions of the 1730s and 1740s, the 1820s and the final decades of the nineteenth century. Even when a landlord had collected his rents he could not look upon gross and net income as being the same thing. Certain outgoings were unavoidable. Many landlords rented land in addition to the property that they owned. In order to consolidate his coal-bearing lands in Cumbria, Sir James Lowther acquired leases for which he found himself paying £364 annually by the 1750s, while from their East Riding estate at Warter the Pennington family had to find a fee-farm rent of £121.[127] Renting additional land was optional, but taxation fell upon everyone. The eighteenth-century land tax, and local assessments of parish and county rates, had to be paid out of rental income, or else allowed to tenants, and tithes also had to be accounted for. In addition the long-term profitability of the estate demanded ongoing investment in farm building and repairs.[128] Taken together, these costs could be considerable, either in terms of the difference between gross and net income, or, where the burden was passed on to the tenant, as a reduction in the overall receipts below the rack-rent ceiling.

From the middle of the seventeenth century, population increase began to slacken, and as a result prices eased and rents remained stationary or even declined. On eight estates scattered through Buckinghamshire, Oxfordshire, Northamptonshire and Warwickshire, substantial rent-roll declines were experienced during the 1660s by seven of the group, and by four or five of them during the following decade. Rentals declined both because of abatements to hard-pressed farmers, and because of vacancies caused by a shortage of tenants.[129] Elsewhere rents continued upwards until the 1690s in some areas, but few further increases took place before the mid-eighteenth century. The 1730s and 1740s were decades of agricultural depression, when landlords complained of unpaid rents and bankrupt tenants from areas as far apart as Cheshire and Staffordshire, Yorkshire, the East Midlands and East Anglia, the Home Counties, Buckinghamshire and Hampshire. Not all areas were as badly hit, since the pastoral areas usually suffered less severely than their neighbouring arable territories during depressions. Cumbria, the Leveson-Gower estates in the West Midlands, Northumberland and Durham, and parts of Wales, largely

[127] Beckett, thesis, pp. 232, 340.

[128] Benjamin Disraeli, *Sybil* (1845; Oxford, 1981), p. 69, has Lord Marney complaining of being ruined by buildings.

[129] Margaret Gay Davies, 'Country gentry and falling rents in the 1660s and 1670s', *Midland History*, 4 (1977), pp. 86–96.

escaped the worse effects of depression.[130] The second half of the century witnessed a marked increase in rental incomes. Between 1750 and 1770 rents trebled in Wiltshire, while in Essex they were 67 per cent higher than over the first half of the century, and they also rose rapidly in Nottinghamshire.[131] The most significant influences affecting rents were rising prices and enclosure. With enclosure a return of 15–20 per cent could be expected, as was the case on Earl Fitzwilliam's estates in Northamptonshire and Huntingdonshire. Even after taking into account the expense of new roads, fencing and hedging, the overall return in the seven cases for which acreages can be accurately calculated on the Fitzwilliam estate was 16 per cent.[132]

Much more spectacular were the rental increases which took place during the Napoleonic war period, which were often between 80 and 100 per cent. Rents more than doubled between 1750–80 and 1780–1820 in Cheshire, and on Coke's settled estates in Norfolk between 1776 and 1816. On Lord Darnley's estate in Kent, the rents of farms held throughout the period 1788–1820 increased by 100 per cent. In a few cases even more spectacular increases were recorded.[133] However, not everyone was enjoying such prize pickings. In Essex, between 1791 and 1815 rents were just 52 per cent more than those for the period 1750–90, while on the Alnwick estates in Northumberland, rents on a constant acreage went up by just 64 per cent over the period 1790–1820.[134] On the earls of Carlisle's North Cumberland estates rents per acre rose from 1*s*. 4*d*. in 1770 to 4*s*. 2*d*. in 1805; while the Warwickshire rents moved up from 18*s*. to 29*s*. between 1794 and 1813.[135]

[130] J. V. Beckett, 'Regional variation and the agricultural depression, 1730–50', *Economic History Review*, 2nd ser., 35 (1982), pp. 35–51; Wordie, 'Rent movements and the English tenant farmer', pp. 202–7.

[131] VCH, *Wiltshire*, vol. IV, p. 62; Colin Shrimpton, 'The landed society and the farming community of Essex in the late eighteenth and early nineteenth centuries' (University of Cambridge, Ph.D. thesis, 1965), pp. 17–18, 249; G. E. Mingay, 'Landownership and agrarian trends in the eighteenth century' (University of Nottingham, Ph.D. thesis, 1958), p. 48.

[132] Thompson, *English Landed Society*, pp. 221–4; Mingay, *English Landed Society*, p. 183.

[133] Thompson, *English Landed Society*, pp. 217–20; Thomas Tooke, *History of Prices*, vol. I (1838), p. 326; Davies, *The Agricultural History of Cheshire*, pp. 44–5; Parker, *Coke of Norfolk*, pp. 77, 95–6; Hunt, 'Agricultural rent in South-East England', p. 100; Beastall, *A North Country Estate*, p. 121; Wordie, 'Rent movements and the English tenant farmer', p. 223.

[134] Shrimpton, 'The landed society and the farming community of Essex', p. 249; Thompson, *English Landed Society*, p. 218.

[135] Searle, '"The odd corner of England"', p. 300; Marshall, *The Review and Abstract*, vol. IV, pp. 30, 293, 313.

These increases closely paralleled grain prices over the war period, and the effect on rents was considerable when they stopped rising in 1812. On Lord Darnley's estate, rent increases correlated with corn prices over the years 1805–11, only to be succeeded by nil growth in 1812–15 after a sharp price fall.[136] Although rents rose in some areas for a few years after the war, most areas suffered difficulties by the 1820s which led to reductions and abatements without base levels returning to the figures current in 1793. On the Leveson-Gowers' West Midlands estates the average level of rent demanded fell by 23 per cent at Trentham and 31 per cent at Lilleshall. Rents on the Earl of Lonsdale's Westmorland estates, which had risen sharply from £15,414 in 1802–3 to £28,525 by 1812–13, fell back to £23,382 in the 1820s, and similar reductions took place for a group of estates scattered through Lincolnshire, Herefordshire, Buckinghamshire, Bedfordshire, Cambridgeshire, Essex and North Wales.[137] Many owners found themselves forced to make abatements and to wipe off arrears. On the Earl of Scarbrough's Lincolnshire estates hardly any arrears were recorded for the war years, but between 1816 and 1822 up to £3000 was outstanding, and every parish showed some arrears. Reductions had to be allowed on the Manvers estate in North Nottinghamshire, where recovery set in after 1832, and the figure achieved at Holkham in 1820 was not repeated until 1833.[138]

From the 1830s until the 1870s rents were again on the increase, and this time they moved from a higher base. In Nottinghamshire, for example, all mean rents had increased at least twice by 1830 from the level of 1750.[139] Writing in the mid-nineteenth century, James Caird found a rough doubling of rents per acre of cultivated land from 13s. 4d. in Arthur Young's day to 26s. 10d. in his own. On the Manvers estate in Nottinghamshire, rents rose from 9s. 6d. in 1780 to 27s. 6d. in 1873, and contemporary estimates for the total rental of England and Wales suggest a rise from £20.8 million in 1770–1 to £42.3 million in 1848–9. Some allowance needs to be made in these figures

---

[136] Hunt, 'Agricultural rent in South-East England', pp. 103 ff.

[137] Searle, "'The odd corner of England'", p. 300; Wordie, 'Rent movements and the English tenant farmer', p. 210; Thompson, 'An inquiry into the rent of agricultural land'. Thompson's study was one of the first systematic attempts to calculate levels of nineteenth-century rents. It was based on sixteen estates countrywide, with acreages varying between 70,000 and 400,000 for different dates.

[138] Beastall, *A North Country Estate*, p. 113; Pickersgill, 'The agricultural revolution in Bassetlaw', pp. 556 ff.; Parker, *Coke of Norfolk*, pp. 148–53.

[139] Fowkes, 'The progress of agrarian change in Nottinghamshire', pp. 475, 492; Wyndham, *A Family History*, p. 301; J. T. Ward, *East Riding Landed Estates in the Nineteenth Century* (York, 1967), p. 23.

for changes in the acreage under cultivation.[140] Figures for a wide scatter of estates indicate a gradual rise in average rent per acre from the early 1830s (18*s*. 5*d*.) to the later 1860s (24*s*. 8*d*.).[141]

After the mid-1870s, depression brought falling rents. From a peak in 1875–7 they gradually fell back until by 1892 they were at only three-quarters of the levels achieved in the late 1860s and early 1870s. The decline continued down to 1900, producing an overall fall from the early 1870s to the turn of the century of around 30 per cent. There are plenty of examples from this period of rising arrears, remissions and falling rents. Some farms in the west of England were already two years in arrears early in the 1880s. At Thorney the Duke of Bedford made remissions in every year between 1879 and 1895 except 1883 and 1884, ranging from 10 per cent of the annual rental in 1888, to an entire half-year's rent in 1885.[142] By the 1890s substantial reductions had been made in many areas, including 40 per cent on the South Downs. However, local variation was considerable, and the Earl of Derby actually enjoyed a 10 per cent increase in rents from his Bowland and Fylde estates in Lancashire between 1884 and 1904.[143]

To calculate the difference between gross and net income, it was first necessary to subtract taxation and tithe payments, and then outgoings on repairs. The land tax (1693–1798) was essentially a tax on rents, and when it was levied at four shillings in the pound it represented a 20 per cent levy. However, its incidence fell unequally across the country. In counties near to London it really did represent 20 per cent. At Holkham in Norfolk taxation took a disproportionately large share of gross income during the early years of the eighteenth century – greater than at any future time down to 1842. Between 1708 and 1710 the land tax accounted for 17.3 per cent of gross rents, a burden unequalled even in the Napoleonic war years.[144] Further from the capital the situation was easier, although on one East Riding estate land tax accounted for 16 per cent of rental income in 1695; but in the first decades of the eighteenth century, assessments do not appear to

[140] Caird, *English Agriculture*, p. 474; Pickersgill, 'The agricultural revolution in Bassetlaw', p. 552; Chambers and Mingay, *The Agricultural Revolution*, p. 167.

[141] Thompson, 'An inquiry into the rent of agricultural land', pp. 591–5.

[142] Duke of Bedford, *A Great Agricultural Estate*, pp. 113–27.

[143] Perry, *British Farming in the Great Depression*, pp. 69–76; T. W. Fletcher, 'The great depression of English agriculture, 1873–96', *Economic History Review*, 2nd ser., 13 (1961), pp. 417–32.

[144] H. J. Habakkuk, 'English landownership, 1680–1740', *Economic History Review*, 10 (1939–40), p. 9; Parker, *Coke of Norfolk*, pp. 2–3; Thirsk (ed.), *The Agrarian History of England and Wales*, vol. V, pt II, pp. 72–3.

have represented more than 1*s*. 6*d*. in the pound in the Midlands, while in Cumbria the figure was nearer to 9*d*. The Hudlestons of Millom in Cumberland, were paying just 3 per cent of their income in land tax in 1705.[145] This regional difference became less apparent over time because the tax was never revalued, and its overall impact gradually lessened. By the 1740s a four-shilling rate accounted for only 2*s*. 10*d*. on the Cowper's Kent estate, less than 10 per cent in the East Riding, and only 1.27 per cent on Sir James Lowther's Cumberland estate. Humphrey Senhouse of Netherhall was paying just 0.5 per cent in 1749.[146] By contrast some Roman Catholic families suffered considerably, since they were double-rated. This provision was not always enforced, and if the original assessment was less than 20 per cent the effect could be mitigated. However, in 1693 Sir Philip Constable of Everingham in Yorkshire paid £495 from his rental of £1704, a total of 29 per cent.[147]

In the second half of the eighteenth century, landowners were relatively lightly taxed, but towards 1800 they were affected by two developments: the rapid rise in county and poor rates, and the introduction of income, or property, tax. The twin squeeze helped to push up the cost of cultivating the land; figures given before a Select Committee in 1814–15 suggested that the expense of cultivating 100 acres of arable rose from £412 in 1790 to £772 in 1813.[148] On Coke's estate, between 1807 and 1816, £53,824 was paid in land and property tax, 13.2 per cent of gross rents. Assessed taxes amounted to a further £564. The dukes of Bedford paid over half a million pounds in taxation between 1816 and 1895 for their Bedfordshire and Buckinghamshire estates, 18.6 per cent of the total rental. The bill jumped noticeably with the introduction of a permanent income tax in 1842, from £5576 in 1841 to £7270. On the Thorney estate, tax

[145] Hull University Library, DDWA/14/10; Carlisle RO, D/Pen/109, bundle 16/7, 30/47; O. R. F. Davies, 'The Dukes of Devonshire, Newcastle and Rutland, 1688–1714' (University of Oxford, D.Phil. thesis, 1971), p. 183; Kendal RO, D/Ry, 4692, Sir Christopher Musgrave to Sir Daniel Fleming, 29 January 1694; Carlisle RO, D/Sen, 'Bridget Hudleston's cash book, 1703–8'.

[146] C. G. A. Clay, 'Two families and their estates: the Grimstons and Cowpers, 1650–1815' (University of Cambridge, Ph.D. thesis, 1966), pp. 188–9; Beckett, *Coal and Tobacco*, pp. 36–7; Carlisle RO, D/Sen, cash book, 1749–52'.

[147] Peter Roebuck, *Yorkshire Baronets, 1640–1760* (Oxford, 1980), pp. 172–3. The land tax became redeemable in 1798, but many families did not take up the option immediately, and some can even be found paying it into the twentieth century. It was abolished only in 1963.

[148] L. P. Adams, *Agricultural Depression and Farm Relief in England, 1813–1852* (1932), p. 34.

payments over the same period amounted to 27.4 per cent of rents received. Finally, it was reported from Buckinghamshire in 1855 that landowners faced tax burdens of £875,350 for the property tax, £46,551 for the land tax, and a poor rate or 2*s.* 4½*d.* in the pound.[149]

Although tenants normally paid local taxes, the division of responsibility was by no means uniform. For national assessments tenants might be required to pay the tax themselves, or to pay the tax and then deduct an equivalent sum from their rent. Alternatively responsibility might rest entirely with the landlord, or, as on Sir Charles Hotham's Yorkshire estates, it might be shared between landlord and tenant.[150] Owners attempted to transfer the burden to their tenants during prosperous times, but accepted that they might need to reassume the responsibility when conditions altered. The result was a great variety. In Cumbria, tenants were allowed the land tax by the Fletchers in 1710, but not by the Musgraves in 1720. On Lord Lonsdale's estate the tenant of Burgh demesne covenanted to pay all taxes in 1723, but such a clause did not regularly appear in leases until about 1732, and even in 1747 Lonsdale accepted tax responsibility for Hilton Mill. Most of Lonsdale's Yorkshire tenants had accepted responsibility for the tax by 1716, but Humphrey Senhouse disputed the issue with his tenants in the county in 1726 in what turned out to be an unsuccessful attempt to pass on the burden.[151]

Experts urged landowners to accept the tax burden on leasehold property. Caird believed that it was in their interest to let their land free of all charges except the poor rate.[152] Taxation also affected estate investment. Between 1803 and 1805, property owners were entitled to a repairs allowance of 5 per cent on house property and 2 per cent on farm property (under Schedule A), but this was discontinued in 1806 because of fraudulent returns by landlords demanding abatements for repairs actually done by tenants. In effect, this amounted to an additional charge on owners, and it may not be entirely coincidental that, as the burden of taxation was reduced after 1815, the level of investment increased. On the Raby estate taxation fell from 11 per cent of gross rents in 1815 to only 2 per cent in 1830, while repairs and taxes together accounted for 15 and 11 per cent respectively.[153]

---

[149] Parker, *Coke of Norfolk*, pp. 127–8; Duke of Bedford, *A Great Agricultural Estate*, pp. 218 ff.; P. V. Denham, 'The Duke of Bedford's Tavistock estate, 1820–38', *Devonshire Association Transactions*, 110 (1978), p. 25; C. S. Read, 'Report on the farming of Buckinghamshire', *JRASE*, 16 (1855), p. 311.

[150] Roebuck, *Yorkshire Baronets*, p. 90.

[151] Beckett, thesis, pp. 116–17, 188; Roebuck, *Yorkshire Baronets*, p. 322.

[152] Caird, *English Agriculture*, p. 481.

[153] Thompson, *English Landed Society*, p. 236.

Tithes were a further unavoidable outgoing, which also seems to have had an impact on land improvement, particularly on poorer lands which required heavy capital investment. Around 70 per cent of enclosure acts passed between 1757 and 1835 included commutation provisions, either for a cash sum or, more frequently, for a land allocation to the owner. Tithe owners did rather well out of commutation, obtaining more than one-tenth of the land in return for exonerating the rest in perpetuity. Commutation at enclosure also established a precedent for the legislation to interfere with property rights, thereby opening the way for the Tithe Commutation Act of 1836. In the wake of this legislation, commutation proceeded apace, with agricultural benefits. Caird, writing of Salisbury Plain, noted that extensive tracts of land had been brought under cultivation since the legislation passed, and 'it appears that the increased produce derived from the land is almost wholly the result of the tenant's exertions. The commutation of tithes was, therefore, a great boon to the landlords.'[154]

Landlords generally had a repair bill to add to their list of necessary outgoings, and this represented another fluctuating drain on their resources. In general, accounting procedures were such that it is seldom possible to distinguish repair costs as a separate item in accounts. Sometimes they were included under an umbrella heading which included expenditure on the manor house, hence the earls of Carlisle's outlay in Cumberland between 1732 and 1757 of £918 a year on average, when in Westmorland the earls of Thanet were paying only £41. 15s. They were often part of improvements, and landlords did not see reason to distinguish them as such.[155] Where they have been separately accounted, the evidence suggests that some landlords spent heavily on repairs, at least in the nineteenth century. This is clear from surviving figures for the Duke of Bedford's estates in Bedfordshire and Buckinghamshire (table 5.1), while on the family's Thorney estate between 1816 and 1895 repairs averaged 17.5 per cent of rent receipts.[156]

Calculating net income after deducting necessary outgoings for rents, taxes and repairs is by no means easy. If a landowner succeeded in passing tax payments on to his tenants, and keeping repairs to a minimum, the total could be small. In Cumbria, during the first half of the eighteenth century, it was probably less than 1 per cent on the

---

[154] E. J. Evans, *The Contentious Tithe, 1750–1850* (1976), pp. 74–6, 95. Caird, *English Agriculture*, p. 80.
[155] Beckett, thesis, pp. 73–4.
[156] Duke of Bedford, *A Great Agricultural Estate*, p. 238–9.

Table 5.1 Average annual income and expenditure on the Bed-fordshire and Buckinghamshire estates of the Dukes of Bedford

	(1)	(2)	(3)	(4)		
Years	Rent (£)	Total Income (£)	Repairs (£)	Taxes, repairs etc. (£)	Repairs as a % of rent	Taxes and repairs as a % of income
1816–25	31,238	41,387	7,509	12,506	24	30
1826–35	28,822	39,301	11,378	16,467	39	42
1836–45	31,087	42,739	8,780	14,891	28	35
1846–55	35,367	48,349	6,088	13,606	17	28
1856–65	41,423	51,106	6,405	14,211	15	28
1866–75	45,850	51,656	10,652	17,637	23	34
1876–85	40,449	51,804	6,759	14,327	17	28
1886–95	28,317	35,899	4,613	10,953	16	31

Source: Duke of Bedford, *A Great Agricultural Estate* (1897), pp. 218–25.

dukes of Somerset's estate, 4 per cent on the earls of Thanet's lands, 6–8 per cent and a maximum of 15 per cent on the Lonsdales', 8 per cent on the forfeited estates of the Earl of Derwentwater, and 23 per cent on the Carlisles' estates. On gentry estates in the same area, annually recurrent expenditure probably did not exceed 10 per cent of gross income. [157] It is more difficult to be certain just what such figures represented. Where the tax burden was transferred to the tenant, or where an agreement was in operation passing repair costs to the tenant for a similar allowance, the overall expenditure cost might appear remarkably small. This would not automatically reveal any hidden costs such as a reduced rent to compensate the tenant for paying the tax. Elsewhere in the country figures also fluctuated. In the East Riding the Pennington family found that rents and taxes consumed 39 per cent of their gross income during the 1690s, and it was still 17 per cent in 1755 when the effect of taxation had worn off. [158] On the Sheffield estates of the dukes of Norfolk, outgoings were around 10–12

[157] Beckett, thesis, pp. 74, 117.
[158] Ibid., p. 340.

per cent for much of the eighteenth century but 20 per cent in 1786. The net income of Sir John Griffin Griffin's Audley End estate was equivalent to 88 per cent of gross in 1761 and 90 per cent in 1791. Figures for Coke's estate show outgoings of 7 per cent in 1776, but 22 per cent in 1806.[159]

Unavoidable costs of this nature appear to have been considerably greater in the nineteenth century. So much is clear by comparing the earlier figures with outgoings on the dukes of Bedford's Bedfordshire and Buckinghamshire estates (see table 5.1), which show an overall average for taxes and repairs as a proportion of outgoings of 32 per cent. Since outgoings were proportional to income whatever the financial situation, repairs must have been regarded as the most flexible expense. This is clear on the family's Thorney estate, where a rising tax burden was matched by falling outlay on repairs. Such a situation was probably widespread. On the Leveson-Gower estates between 1817 and 1822 landlord expenditure was pushed up to help tenants pay their racked rents. Over those years it equalled 55 per cent of net rent receipts at Trentham and 48 per cent at Lilleshall. Higher investment was preferable to rent reductions, although these were not ultimately prevented.[160]

Owner investment increased to match falling rents in adverse economic conditions, and this was never more so than during the late nineteenth-century depression. The Royal Commission on Agriculture, which investigated the depression during the 1890s, produced figures from thirty estates covering more than half a million acres in twenty-five counties. In this sample, total expenditure as a proportion of rent had increased almost everywhere, in many cases to exceed 50 per cent during the depressed years. In 1892, overall expenditure on these estates was 43.7 per cent of rent received, while additional expenditure and permanent improvements accounted for a further 23 per cent.[161] However, an independent estimate by R. J. Thompson suggested that this was an exaggeration. Between 1872 and 1886 repairs and permanent improvements on estates scattered across the country took 27 per cent of rental income, a figure which fell to 22 per

[159] P. Nunn, 'Aristocratic estates and employment in South Yorkshire, 1700–1800', in *Essays in the Economic and Social History of South Yorkshire*, ed. S. Pollard and C. Holmes (Sheffield, 1976), pp. 32–3; Parker, *Coke of Norfolk*, p. 127; Shrimpton, 'The landed society and the farming community of Essex', p. 29.

[160] Duke of Bedford, *A Great Agricultural Estate*, pp. 238–9; Wordie, 'Rent movements and the English tenant farmer', p. 209.

[161] Parl. Papers, Royal Commission on Agricultural Depression, *Final Report* (1897), C. 8540, vol. XV, pt 1, pp. 27, 686–90.

cent between 1887 and 1891. Allowing for all other outgoings, owners were receiving a net income equivalent to between 53 and 57 per cent of gross between 1872 and 1886, but 60 per cent over the years 1887–91. In money terms, net income was the same as before, but by reducing repair costs landowners increased it as a proportion of gross. Thompson concluded that a fair average figure for the cost of repairs and improvements was 25 per cent.[162] Taking the categories of tax, repairs and permanent improvements together, their impact on estate income for the two Bedford estates is shown in table 5.2. In their own accounts the dukes also included outgoings on management and woodlands, which pushed up the total proportion of gross income spent for the whole period 1816–95 on these estates to 62 and 70 per cent respectively.

Table 5.2: Taxes, Repairs and permanent improvements as a percentage of total income on the dukes of Bedfords' estates

Years	Bedfordshire/ Buckinghamshire	Thorney
1816–35	39.8	46.6
1836–55	52.7	46.0
1856–75	50.1	61.0
1876–95	41.7	60.9

Source: Duke of Bedford, *A Great Agricultural Estate* (1897), pp. 223–39

If some aristocrats neglected their farms and estates, and if the agricultural revolution was primarily pioneered by lesser landowners and tenant farmers, the aristocratic contribution to change was much more positive than their image as *rentiers* would suggest. After all, many of the changes took place on their estates, and in accordance with terms that they helped to lay down, even if their actual role needs to be kept in perspective. Home farms failed perhaps to set the example for which experts looked, since, while a few were leading centres of experimentation and improvement, too many either did not promote better farming or were distrusted because they failed to make a profit. On the other hand sheep-shearings and agricultural shows – the latter

[162] Thompson, 'An inquiry into the rent of agricultural land', pp. 603–4.

with cash prize incentives — may have been more influential in spreading information to the working farmers. Patronizing local societies was important both for promoting agricultural change and for enforcing rural paternalism, while defending the country interest in Parliament was indispensable to the prosperity of farming.

Such roles were vital, but they are fundamentally unquantifiable. The same cannot be said of the financial commitment to enclosure, drainage and building investment, on which the outlay was considerable. When family resources ran short, government and private loan schemes enabled work to go on, and landlords showed a willingness to borrow for investment purposes. In the end this may have brought overcapitalization, and it almost certainly never paid. It was an impressive contribution, particularly since owners continued to invest even when — as will be seen — they could have expected better returns from railway and other speculative ventures.

Beyond promoting agricultural practice, aristocrats also needed to take an interest in how farms were run. This meant ensuring sensible size selection and adequate letting covenants. They also acted as a buffer between their tenants and managers. Although they often allowed an element of inefficiency, they generally ensured good relations in the countryside (at least prior to the agricultural depression late in the nineteenth century). The constant warfare of lord and tenant, which some agricultural experts described in lurid detail to emphasize their arguments, was probably not the norm, since it was only after 1870 that cracks became evident.[163] By then the agricultural revolution was complete.

[163] Kent, *Hints to Gentlemen*, p. 95.

Chapter Six

Aristocratic Entrepreneurs in Industry

In the later eighteenth and early nineteenth centuries, Britain passed through an industrial revolution which brought a fundamental and irreversible change to the structure of its economy. Resources were deployed away from agriculture into manufacturing and distributive industries, and sustained economic growth began on a scale which was altogether new. Industrialization was spontaneous, but it was hardly an accident. Already by about 1750 significant economic developments had taken place which laid the groundwork for what came later, including revolutionary agricultural changes which eventually facilitated the provisioning of a larger population and improvements in communications and finance. By 1820 the country's economic supremacy was well established. With the coming of the railway during the following decade, Britain in the 1860s stood pre-eminent as the world's first and leading industrial economy. Only from the 1870s did it encounter serious competition.

So much, and indeed much more, is well known,[1] but the aristocratic role in this process has generally been viewed with some scepticism.[2] Historians have portrayed aristocrats as debt-driven developers frantically investing in new projects and concerns in the hope of tapping a profitable vein which would help to offset their financial difficulties,[3] while a recent study of the early period of

[1] Phyllis Deane, *The First Industrial Revolution* (Cambridge, 1965); Peter Mathias, *The First Industrial Nation: an economic history of Britain, 1700–1914* (1969); Roderick Floud and Donald McCloskey (eds), *The Economic History of Britain since 1700* (2 vols, Cambridge, 1981).

[2] Harold Perkin, *The Origins of Modern English Society, 1780–1880* (1969), p. 74.

[3] F. M. L. Thompson, 'English great estates in the nineteenth century (1790–1914)', in *Contributions to the First International Conference of Economic History* (Paris, 1960), pp. 390–1. The argument has largely been associated with the writings of Professor David Spring, and a full discussion of the issue is to be found in David

industrialization has concluded that 'they "fell into the background" and were rather passive lessors and investors than active business leaders.'[4] Such arguments overlook a crucial entrepreneurial role played by the aristocracy in certain parts of the economy. After all, since an estate was held in trust to be passed on improved and developed, the minimum obligation of a life tenant was to develop his family's resources. Landed estates represented an important cog in the machinery of manufacturing and commerce. Wool, malting barley, hides and tallow formed the vital raw materials of early modern industry, and it is hardly surprising that aristocrats viewed their estates as part of the wider economy beyond the park walls.

With this background, they naturally took an interest in the commercial possibilities of their resources, of which the most obvious was their woodlands. Aristocrats planted trees for a variety of reasons. These included social assertiveness, where trees symbolized the continuity of the generations; aesthetic sensibility, largely bound up with the laying out of parks and gardens; patriotism, through such movements as the post-1660 emphasis on planting as a way of affirming a gentleman's loyalty to the restored monarchy, or the need to supply the navy with timber in the early nineteenth century; and long-term profit. To encourage planting the Royal Society for the Encouragement of Arts gave gold and silver medals between 1757 and 1835, and between 1760 and 1835 private landowners may have planted at least 50 million timber trees.[5] Once planted, timber offered a saleable resource which could be used either as an annual supplement to income, or as a short-term means of relieving pressing debts. Often sales were geared to a particular enterprise. In 1720 the second Baron Gower signed a contract with charcoal burners in the West Midlands to supply them with oaks, ash and elms over the following five-years, for which he was to receive almost £5000; while in the mid-nineteenth century James Caird reported that Sir James Graham of Netherby in Cumberland 'is at present in treaty with a thread manufacturer in Manchester for the erection of a steam-power mill at Longtown, at which the small wood of the estate is to be put into bobbins'.[6]

Cannadine's article, 'Aristocratic indebtedness in the nineteenth century: the case re-opened', *Economic History Review*, 2nd ser., 30 (1977), pp. 624–50, and the subsequent debate in the *Economic History Review*, 2nd ser., 33 (1980), pp. 564–73.

[4] François Crouzet, *The First Industrialists* (Cambridge, 1985), p. 68.

[5] Oliver Rackham, *Ancient Woodland: its history, vegetation and uses in England* (1980), pp. 147–70; Keith Thomas, *Man and the Natural World* (Harmondsworth, 1984 edn), pp. 200–11, 218.

[6] J. R. Wordie, *Estate Management in Eighteenth-Century England* (1982), pp. 133–4; James Caird, *English Agriculture in 1850–51* (1852), p. 354.

From this practice it was only a small step to exploiting the less accessible resources of an estate. In essence, the aristocratic entrepreneurial role involved working with the materials available on a landed estate, and promoting schemes in which landowners believed themselves to have a peculiar interest. They were to be found mining coal and ironstone, improving the road network, and laying down plans for urban development on their land. By contrast, manufacturing industry, canal building and town construction they left largely to merchant-manufacturers and industrialists. This was a well-established pattern even in 1660. Among the early modern European nobilities, periodic attempts by government and vested economic interests to prevent their participation in handicraft manufacture, retailing and domestic trade did not extend to exploiting and processing the non-edible products of the soil. Consequently, aristocrats were to be found at their most active in mining and heavy industry, either taking a positive lead themselves, or leasing the resources to entrepreneurs.[7] Nowhere was this clearer than in England, where the aristocracy were arguably most influential on economic growth in the period 1540–1640. Among Elizabethan aristocratic families 22 per cent owned ironworks during this century, and, according to Lawrence Stone, peers underwrote the risks of most of the great pioneering ventures of the age.[8]

By 1660 a tradition had been established, but it has generally been argued that thereafter landowners gradually faded from the scene into passive *rentier* status. This view has to be treated carefully. The pace and extent of opting out can easily be exaggerated, and, if many of those who reverted to *rentier* status lacked the financial resources for direct working, that is no reason either to belittle their initial contribution or to underplay the role of those who stayed involved and provided considerable amounts of capital, often well beyond the call of either duty or financial prudence. The tendency to downgrade the central role of coal and iron in the process of industrialization further distorts the aristocratic contribution. When these industries are viewed as central to the whole movement, the aristocracy can be seen to have played a vital and sustained part in industrialization.

[7] Barry Supple, 'The nature of enterprise', in *The Cambridge Economic History of Europe*, vol. V: *The Economic Organization of Early Modern Europe*, ed. E. E. Rich and C. H. Wilson (Cambridge, 1977), pp. 448–51.

[8] Lawrence Stone, *The Crisis of the Aristocracy, 1588–1641* (Oxford, 1965), ch. 7; J. D. Chambers, 'The Vale of Trent, 1670–1800', *Economic History Review*, supplement, 3 (1957), pp. 6–7; Philip Jenkins, *The Making of a Ruling Class: the Glamorgan gentry, 1640–1790* (Cambridge, 1983), ch. 3.

ARISTOCRATS AND MINERAL RESOURCES

Once a landowner turned from exploiting his resources above ground to searching for what might lay hidden beneath, whole new vistas began to open up. If trial borings drew positive results, he was immediately faced with a variety of options. Obviously he could sell the land at an inflated price, but this was seldom seriously contemplated, and instead owners usually selected one of two alternatives: they could employ managers and workmen to raise the minerals on their behalf; or they could lease the resources to contractors.[9] Those opting for direct management quickly found that their entanglement spread. In addition to providing capital to start the operation, more often than not they were forced to develop ancillary interests if the minerals were to be successfully exploited. Coal owners became road builders and dock constructors, and copper owners built smelting works. Within a generation or two an initial decision to undertake trial borings could blossom into a full-scale industrial enterprise involving considerable investment and, hopefully, commensurate profits.

To some extent the process can be seen as an endurance test. While many landowners sought mineral resources in the later seventeenth and early eighteenth centuries, relatively few stayed the course by the beginning of the twentieth. Some dropped out at an early stage, preferring to lease their resources to groups of adventurers, and thereby perhaps to ease the potential strain on their capital resources and give themselves peaceful nights. Others opted out along the way, forced from the track by the escalating scale of their enterprises, and the problems of raising capital. As to which owners pursued which course, a whole variety of factors intervened, not the least of which was the willingness of individual proprietors to take the necessary risks. For those who endured, the rewards were considerable, especially by the end of the nineteenth century, and even for those who retreated behind leases a role had to be performed as providors of capital and custodians of the health of the workforce. Leasing the minerals did not absolve a landowner from improving the transport facilities. As a result, in the mineral areas, few landowners were able to avoid playing a role of some proportion in the extraction of resources and the building of the industrial base.

---

[9] There was no essential difference from the policy in regard to their agricultural interests. Just as most of their land was let to farmers, perhaps with a small amount retained in hand under the direction of the steward, so their mineral resources were usually leased to tenants. In both instances leasing was a sensible safeguard for men who were away from their estates for many months of the year.

For geological reasons, mineral resources are found in relatively compact areas and large parts of the country have no economically workable deposits. Such was the state of geological ignorance before the nineteenth century that almost any landowner could imagine himself becoming a mineral magnate, and trial borings were reported from all sorts of strange places, with predictably negative results. In the north-west, unsuccessful borings took place throughout the 1730s on the Westmorland estates of the Viscounts Lonsdale (at a cost of £100 in 1729 and £140 in 1730), and of their relations the Lowthers of Maulds Meaburn. No coal appears to have been found here or on the property of the Lowthers of Holker in Furness. Although there are references in the latter family's accounts to coal being cut and carried, no extensive deposits have ever been found in Furness.[10] On the west coast of Cumberland, Sir John Pennington of Muncaster financed trials in the 1740s, unaware that his estate was just off the southern end of the established coalfield. He employed a Workington collier to search for coal at Drigg in 1748, but after initially optimistic reports the work was abandoned after nine months when the man was found to be 'a most bad character'. Later trials found 'no symptoms or the least kind of probability of finding coal'.[11]

Despite such setbacks, the dream of a wholly new source of income was encouragement for any landowner, and particularly those with pressing financial difficulties, to instigate a few trials. This was a motive which inspired the first Duke of Chandos. He became interested in minerals in 1718, but it was only in 1725 that he began to take positive measures to find coal and copper on his estate at Bishop's Castle in Shropshire. Chandos declared himself 'determined to fling away a little money in the search of it', and he hired a Mr Salter of Flint to make a five-week trial at around 50 shillings a week. For his part, Chandos started making enquiries about local markets and customary methods of working, and he encouraged his steward, Samuel Oakley, to give Salter every help. In May 1726 Salter reported finding coal, but by September the works had been shifted to a new venue. Chandos was now less optimistic: 'I confess I have been so long fooled by him [Salter] that a little more will not increase my uneasiness, and I am willing that he should have his full swing that he may not say his miscarriage proceeded from my not having allowed him time enough for a trial.'[12] In October Chandos called a halt to the

---

[10] Beckett, thesis, pp. 184–5, 261, 282.

[11] Ibid., p. 338.

[12] Huntington Library, ST57, vol. 26, fol. 273, Chandos to Captain Oakley, 28 August 1725, and subsequent letters; vol. 27, fol. 90, 8 November 1725; fol. 327, 5

coal trials, although he wanted a possible copper vein searching further. A month later even this seemed fruitless, and in January 1727 Salter's work was discontinued. However, Chandos was not discouraged, since the following month he was hoping to find coal on his Hampshire estate. When these trials were abandoned in June the collier, Mr Broderick, was dispatched to Radnorshire to conduct yet more fruitless tests. Even in December 1732 Chandos remained optimistic, informing his agent that he was expecting news of an immensely rich vein of copper ore being opened up: 'it will be a very great providence and singular blessing if I succeed.'[13]

ARISTOCRATS AND MINERAL RESOURCES: COAL

The major industrial concern of English landowners was with coalmining. Demand for coal was relatively limited in the seventeenth century. It was mainly used for domestic heating purposes, although by the end of the century some non-ferrous metals could be smelted with coal. In addition, many of the easily accessible seams had been exhausted. Between 1700 and 1830 output grew tenfold, and technological innovation ensured that this was achieved without price inflation. Growth was even faster thereafter.[14] Coal was used in a string of new enterprises, most importantly the production of iron and steel, and the industrial use of steam power; in fact, the three key technological foundations of industrial progress – steam power, canals and the steam railway – were intimately connected with coal production. Coal was at the heart of the industrial revolution, and the fact that the great majority of it came from underneath the estates of private landowners suggests a prima facie case for their playing a vitally important role. What has to be established is how far they were responsible for providing the capital and enterprise which helped to break through the technological bottlenecks without which output could never have grown so spectacularly.

Perhaps more than any other industry, coalmining is epitomized by

March 1726; fol. 334, 8 March 1726; fol. 344, 12 March 1726; vol. 28, fol. 94, 5 May 1726; fol. 327, 12 September 1726.

[13] Ibid., vol. 29, fol. 53, 29 October 1726; fol. 63, 15 November 1726; fol. 157, 19 January 1727; and letters to Mr Pescod, vol. 29, fol. 347, 8 May 1727; vol. 30, fol. 81, 22 June 1727; and Mr Price, vol. 30, fol. 119, 16 July 1727.

[14] Authoritative recent accounts of the coal industry are M. W. Flinn, *The History of the British Coal Industry*, vol. 2: *1700–1830* (Oxford, 1984), and B. R. Mitchell, *Economic Development of the British Coal Industry, 1800–1914* (Cambridge, 1984).

a handful of successful families. Prominent names on the north-east coalfield included the dukes of Northumberland and earls of Scarbrough, and the Lambton, Bowes, Liddell, Wortley, Clavering, Vane-Tempest and Brandling families; in West Cumberland it was the Lowthers, Curwens and Senhouses; in Yorkshire the Fitzwilliams and the dukes of Norfolk; in Lancashire the earls of Crawford and Balcarres and the third Duke of Bridgewater; in Leicestershire the earls of Moira; and in the West Midlands the earls of Dudley and the dukes of Sutherland. This roll-call of the famous tends to obscure the much greater numbers who were involved at one stage or another. At the end of the seventeenth century, when collieries were small and mining did not require a great deal of capital, considerable numbers of men were ready to try their fortune. In addition, the fragmentation of land-holdings prevented mining on all but the smallest of scales in some areas. At least fourteen landowners were operating pits in Nottinghamshire in 1739. Twenty landowners were working mines in South-West Lancashire in the 1740s, and on one plan of the coalfield in 1760 no less than twenty-eight shafts were shown in three fields with a total area of less than 29 acres.[15] Even on Tyneside, fragmentation was such that the Grand Allies could command less than 60 per cent of the vend during the 1720s. In these circumstances smaller landowners were able to play a significant role in the industry, among them the lesser landlords of Glamorgan and, as late as the 1790s, the smaller owners in Somerset.[16]

Over time, the capital investment requirements became too great for lesser landowners, while those able and willing to make the commitment wanted to ensure that they controlled sufficient

---

[15] Sheila Aley, 'The Nottinghamshire landowners and their estates, *c.* 1660–*c.* 1840' (University of Nottingham Ph.D. thesis, 1985), p. 47; John Langton, *Geographical Change and Industrial Revolution: coalmining in South-West Lancashire, 1590–1799* (Cambridge, 1979), p. 217; Flinn, *The History of the British Coal Industry*, p. 81. Such division caused immense jurisdiction troubles. In 1736, for example, the Duke of Bridgewater was approached by Egerton Bagot for compensation in respect of 269 square yards of coal mined by his workmen in Lancashire from land actually in Bagot's possession. He claimed that the dispute had been in progress for three years and was still nowhere near a settlement: Huntington Library, Ellesmere MSS, 10,074, letter of 21 July 1736.

[16] David Spring, 'The Earls of Durham and the great northern coalfield, 1830–80', *Canadian Historical Review*, 33 (1952), p. 240; Joanna O. Martin, 'The landed estate in Glamorgan, *c.* 1660–*c.* 1760' (University of Cambridge, Ph.D. thesis, 1978), p. 135; M. W. Doughty, 'Samborne Palmer's diary: technological innovation by a Somerset coal-mine owner', *Industrial Archaeology Review*, 3 (1978), p. 17; Crouzet, *The First Industrialists*, p. 73.

resources. What could happen in these circumstances is clear from Cumberland, where Sir James Lowther deliberately attempted during the 1720s and 1730s to create a monopoly of the coalfield. He bought out small owners anxious to reap a profit from their higher-value coal-bearing land, and even lent money to some of the more obstinate in the hope that they would overreach themselves and permit him to foreclose the mortgage. In these ways he created almost a monopoly of trade on the southern part of the coalfield, and failed by only a whisker to secure control of the rest.[17] In South-West Lancashire most of the twenty families operating in the 1740s either pulled out altogether or leased their interests, leaving only the more substantial owners – the Leghs, the Gerards, and the earls of Derby and of Balcarres – still active by the end of the century.[18] By the early years of the nineteenth century in the Erewash Valley most collieries were let, and only the more substantial owners remained active, including the Duke of Devonshire, Lord Middleton, Earl Manvers, Edward Miller Mundy and William Drury Lowe.[19] Even the north-eastern coalfield was affected. John Buddle claimed that in 1829 only five of the forty-one owners worked their own Tyneside collieries, and just three out of eighteen on the Wear, although this may underestimate the real situation, since some north-eastern owners leased mines from others or entered into lease partnerships. Buddle's figures can be recast to show that at least sixteen of the Tyneside collieries, and eleven of those on Wearside, were worked by landowners, and these calculations take no account of the thirty or forty smaller owners who still worked their collieries for land sale.[20]

This shaking-out process began to affect some of the larger concerns by the nineteenth century. In Staffordshire the Marquess of Stafford switched to renting in 1825, and the earls of Dudley also withdrew

[17] J. V. Beckett, *Coal and Tobacco: the Lowthers and the economic development of West Cumberland, 1660–1760* (Cambridge, 1981), pp. 44–5, 56.

[18] Langton, *Geographical Change and Industrial Revolution*, p. 219.

[19] John Farey, *View of the Agriculture of the County of Derby* (1811), vol. I, p. 182. In eighteenth-century Derbyshire it was still possible for freeholders to prospect for coal and iron successfully: F. J. Stephens, 'The Barnes of Ashgate: a study of a family of the lesser gentry in North-East Derbyshire' (University of Nottingham, M.Phil. thesis, 1980).

[20] David Spring, 'English landowners and nineteenth-century industrialism', in *Land and Industry*, ed. J. T. Ward and R. G. Wilson (Newton Abbot, 1971), p. 33; Flinn, *The History of the British Coal Industry*, pp. 38–9. On the East Durham coalfield by 1840 very few landowners were taking a direct part in running their collieries: M. Sill, 'Landownership and industry: the East Durham coalfield in the nineteenth century', *Northern History*, 20 (1984), p. 151.

from direct working, while in Cumbria the Curwens and Senhouses were among the producers who had let their concerns by the 1840s. By 1869 it was estimated that only 5 per cent of output was still worked by proprietors.[21] However, it would be misleading to imply that this was all one-way traffic. On the Leveson-Gower estates, industrial development was entirely in the hands of private entrepreneurs in 1748, but the pattern changed as Earl Gower started to assume a more active role, and in the 1760s the second earl established a new company – in which he held a 50 per cent share – to promote mining ventures on the estate. A similar pattern occurred in South Yorkshire. The Duke of Norfolk's Sheffield collieries were leased from the early seventeenth century, but in 1758 the Sheffield Park and Manor Collieries were taken into direct management. In this case, however, Norfolk was a reluctant entrepreneur, who took over only when no lessee was available. The collieries were relet in 1765, but when the lessees surrendered the lease in 1781 direct exploitation began again, this time under the auspices of the ninth duke's trustees. Investment and technological improvement were vital if future lessees were to be attracted, but when the eleventh duke inherited in 1786 he continued with direct management, in conjunction with his land agent Vincent Eyre. Considerable capital was invested in sinking new collieries, and local competitors were bought out, but with profits failing to come up to expectation it was decided in 1805 to abandon direct management in favour of leasing to a consortium of Sheffield businessmen.[22]

Other families either took up the cause or remained involved much further into the nineteenth century. On the Rockingham-Fitzwilliam estates in South Yorkshire, collieries were directly managed from time to time during the eighteenth century when suitable lessees could not be found. When Earl Fitzwilliam inherited in 1782 he decided to

[21] I. R. Medlicott, 'The landed interest and the development of the South Yorkshire coalfield, 1750–1830' (Open University, M.Phil. thesis, 1981), pp. 7–9; J. T. Ward, 'Some West Cumberland landowners and industry', *Industrial Archaeology*, 9 (1972), pp. 351–3; 'West Riding landowners and mining in the nineteenth century', *Yorkshire Bulletin of Economic and Social Research*, 15 (1963); R. W. Sturgess, 'Landowners, mining and urban development in nineteenth-century Staffordshire', in *Land and Industry*, ed. Ward and Wilson, p. 178; C. P. Griffin, 'The economic and social development of the Leicestershire and South Derbyshire coalfield, 1550–1914' (University of Nottingham, Ph.D. thesis, 1969), pp. 26–7; 'The end of aristocratic enterprise in the South Derbyshire coalfield', in *The Aristocratic Estate: the Hastings in Leicestershire and South Derbyshire*, ed. M. Palmer (Loughborough, 1982), pp. 95–117.
[22] Wordie, *Estate Management in Eighteenth-Century England*, pp. 111–13; I. R. Medlicott, 'John Curr and the development of the Sheffield collieries, 1781–1805', *Transactions of the Hunter Archaeological Society*, 12 (1983), pp. 51–60.

continue with direct management, despite his ignorance of the coal industry, and in the 1790s he backed his own judgement by deciding to open a new colliery at Elsecar. He bought out freeholders' coal and competitors' mines in order to establish a large area of mining, and the profitability of the enterprise encouraged the family to continue with direct working. Between 1801 and 1824 the number of collieries was increased from three to six, and production rose from 55,000 tons in 1818 to 142,000 in 1826. As late as 1890 it was claimed that one-eighth of Yorkshire coal output was still worked by proprietors, and elsewhere in the country a number of aristocrats gave up direct working only in the closing years of the century. Even in 1914 familiar names were still to be found active in the industry, including the Duke of Bridgewater's trustees in Lancashire, Earl Granville in North Staffordshire, the Earl of Dudley in the Black Country and the Marquess of Londonderry in Durham.[23]

The decision to stay put or to opt out was taken for a variety of different reasons. In the 1820s the second Marquess of Stafford withdrew from direct participation in Staffordshire mining because he found it impossible to reconcile the roles of aristocrat and captain of industry. By contrast, the Fitzwilliams regarded the role of *rentier* as a denial of their social responsibility, and both the fourth and fifth earls developed a considerable knowledge of their colliery interests and the practical problems of running them. Lord Londonderry explained his outlay on colliery development in terms of his contribution to the life of County Durham.[24] More frequent was the complaint that owners could not find adequate managers. The Dudleys withdrew into *rentier* status because, in the words of James Loch, 'a too extended management never can be carried on as economically as one which is more concentrated – least of all in the hands of a landlord.'[25] Losses at the Fitzwilliams' Elsecar ironworks and at their associated coal-tar works have been attributed to inefficient managers. Those who stayed the course usually had a manager they could trust. The Fitzwilliams gave

[23] Medlicott, 'The landed interest and the development of the South Yorkshire coalfield', pp. 79–102; Ward, 'West Riding landowners and mining', p. 63; Mitchell, *Economic Development of the British Coal Industry*, p. 54.

[24] Eric Richards, 'The industrial face of a great estate: Trentham and Lilleshall, 1780–1860', *Economic History Review*, 2nd ser., 27 (1974), p. 426; Graham Mee, *Aristocratic Enterprise: the Fitzwilliam industrial undertakings, 1795–1857* (1975), pp. 80, 83, 87; R. W. Sturgess, 'Landowners and coal in County Durham', in *Landownership and Power in the Regions*, ed. M. D. G. Wanklyn (Wolverhampton, 1978), p. 99.

[25] T. J. Raybould, *The Economic Emergence of the Black Country* (Newton Abbot, 1973), p. 199.

their unreserved backing to Benjamin Biram, and the Earl of Durham
was able to rely on Henry Morton. A financial involvement on the part
of the agent acted as a spur to efficiency, hence the equal shares of Earl
Gower and Thomas Gilbert in the 1760s, and the similar arrangement
between the eleventh Duke of Norfolk and his agent Vincent Eyre.[26]

Local and personal reasons could also dictate the policy of an
individual landowner. Londonderry and Durham were spurred on by
rivalry in north-east coal affairs and national party politics, while men
like the earls of Lonsdale and dukes of Devonshire saw coal as merely
one aspect of a complex industrial framework. Some opted out because
they were just not interested. Elizabeth Montagu, best known as a
London bluestocking, but also a Tyneside coalowner in her own right
after the death of her husband in 1775, wrote in 1786 of the differing
attitudes she found among her fellow coalowners. The Duke of
Northumberland was 'very able', and Lord Ravensworth 'very attent-
ive'. By contrast, Ravensworth's heir was 'of a very different character',
and Lord Carlisle never came near his interests but left everything to
agents. Small wonder at her relief when her own heir showed an active
interest in the collieries.[27]

Above all, the decisions were taken on financial grounds. In its early
stages, with coal outcropping near the surface, mining was relatively
inexpensive, but, as pits went deeper and technology grew more
sophisticated, costs spiralled upwards. Again the impact varied,
although the trend was undeniable. On the Erewash coalfield in
Derbyshire, landowners stayed involved until the early nineteenth
century, partly because the coal was found near the surface – which
helped to keep down costs and to protect the smaller man.[28] To live
with rising costs, owners resorted to various expedients. One was to
raise the necessary capital by borrowing. In 1777 Sir Roger Newdigate
borrowed the £20,000 he needed to reconstruct Griff collieries in
Warwickshire, while in the north-east during the 1820s John Lambton
and the Marquess of Londonderry both borrowed heavily from
bankers.[29] A second technique was partnership. Somerset's less
substantial coalowners worked in this way in the later eighteenth

[26] Mee, *Aristocratic Enterprise*, pp. 62, 75, 93; Spring, 'The Earls of Durham and
the great northern coalfield', p. 247; Wordie, *Estate Management in Eighteenth-Century
England*, p. 113; Medlicott, 'John Curr and the development of the Sheffield
collieries', p. 54.

[27] BL Add. MSS, 40,663, fols 146v–147, Elizabeth Montagu to Mary Robinson,
22 September 1786.

[28] A. R. Griffin, *Mining in the East Midlands, 1550–1947* (1971), pp. 32–3.

[29] Flinn, *The History of the British Coal Industry*, p. 207.

century in order to fund deep mining. The six-man consortium headed by Samborne Palmer and Jacob Mogg owned five mines in the Timsbury area of the county during the 1790s, and the partners were also individually concerned in other undertakings.[30] Similarly in South Wales the Aberdare Coal Company was formed in 1827 with seven coalowning partners putting in £700 each. Much larger sums could also be raised in this way, as in the case of the four partners in Partridge, Jones and Company, who put together £44,000 between 1863 and 1872.[31] Finally, the formally constituted joint-stock company became increasingly popular after the restrictions of the Bubble Act were lifted in 1825. One of the earliest was the Hetton Coal Company in the north-east, but as these developed they moved further away from the idea of the landed proprietor as chief investor.[32]

Whatever the method of funding, the sums required were considerable. Sir James Lowther invested £500,000 in his collieries during the first half of the eighteenth century, while Lord Londonderry put something over £1 million into pit improvement and expansion between 1819 and 1854. The Earl of Durham's six collieries had absorbed around £400,000 of his fortune by the 1830s. John Buddle estimated in the 1820s that it cost between £15,000 and £150,000 to open a new pit in North-East England, and the Curwens spent £160,000 on a single enterprise in Cumberland in the 1830s.[33] Annual fixed capital formation at current prices has been calculated at £44,000 between 1730 and 1789, rising to £232,000 by the 1820s. In 1788 it was estimated that the fixed capital of twenty-five Tyne collieries was about £250,000; by 1808 the figure for all Tyne collieries was nearly £900,000; and in 1828 it was £1.5 million. The five landed families to survive in County Durham owned pits and equipment valued at £1½ million in the 1830s, and this will have grossly underestimated the amount of money invested.[34]

[30] Doughty, 'Samborne Palmer's diary', p. 17.

[31] R. Walters, 'Capital formation in the South Wales coal industry, 1840–1914', *Welsh History Review*, 10 (1980), pp. 71–2.

[32] Flinn, *The History of the British Coal Industry*, pp. 208–11; Sill, 'Landownership and industry', pp. 152–4.

[33] Beckett, *Coal and Tobacco*, p. 77; R. W. Sturgess, *Aristocrat in Business: the third Marquis of Londonderry as coalowner and portbuilder* (Durham, 1975), p. 2; Ward, 'Some West Cumberland landowners and industry', p. 358. Such figures are slightly misleading in that the modern accounting concept of depreciation and saving for future investment was not employed in the eighteenth century, making it difficult to distinguish capital expenditure from day-to-day running costs.

[34] Flinn, *The History of the British Coal Industry*, pp. 201–6; Spring, 'The Earls of Durham and the great northern coalfield', p. 240.

Under the circumstances it is hardly surprising that many landowners sought refuge in leasing their interests, but even this transition
was not straightforward. The owner had to consider the loss that might
be sustained by leaving the industry, the return to be expected from
alternative capital investments, and the problems of attracting reliable
tenants. Finding good lessees was particularly difficult in the eighteenth century, hence the fact that it was sometimes necessary to take a
direct interest in management. Even when the problem eased by the
nineteenth century, however, leasing was certainly not a means of
avoiding responsibility. Lack of technical knowledge could easily lead
to an owner being fooled, either by his tenants or by his managers.
Some men showed a high level of interest, including Sir James
Lowther, who acted as London agent for his own colliery interests, and
the Somerset owners Samborne Palmer and Jacob Mogg. When they
were preparing to introduce modern technology into their pits in
1791, Palmer and Mogg journeyed to Coalbrookdale to inspect steam
winding engines and to estimate prices.[35] Naturally others left such
responsibilities to agents, but, even when opting for a leasing
agreement, responsibility could not be avoided.

Although mining leases varied considerably, they were primarily
designed to prevent the tenants from working out the seams in such a
way that the landowners' interests were not protected. In the eighteenth century a twenty-one-year term was the most common period,
although some were longer, to take account of the time required for a
colliery to be opened up. Initially an annual fixed rent was charged,
sometimes at a flat rate, and at other times according to the number of
employees and the acreage worked. To prevent premature exhaustion,
fixed rents were usually accompanied by restrictions on the number of
shafts and on care of the site. Over time, landlords grew more
experienced, and adjusted their lease clauses accordingly. When the
Duke of Norfolk let his collieries in 1805, the terms were loose enough
to allow the lessees to run down capital equipment in order to reduce
costs and maximize short-term profits. As a result, by 1820 the mines
were nearly worked out, endangering future rents and profits, so that
stricter clauses had to be introduced into leases.[36]

---

[35] Beckett, *Coal and Tobacco*, p. 69; Doughty, 'Samborne Palmer's diary', pp.
17–28.

[36] Medlicott, 'The landed interest and the development of the South Yorkshire
coalfield', p. 79. It was also possible for some owners to restrict the market.
Manufacturers who leased land in Sheffield from the dukes of Norfolk were usually
required to purchase their coal. As a result, in 1803, 81 per cent of the coal used by
Sheffield manufacturers came from Norfolk pits, and the monopoly was only broken
with the opening of the Sheffield Canal in 1821: ibid., pp. 151–8.

Landlords recognized the need to extract their income carefully, often by charging a rent proportional to the quantity of coal mined or the value of the pithead coal sold. In the north-east the common form was a fixed rent plus a tentale rent (or a royalty on each ton of coal mined). In addition when leases came up for renewal landlords might levy a fine that reflected what was seen as the probable long-term profitability. With experience, owners built into the initial lease provision for renewal every seven years, which offered them the opportunity of levying a fine. Leases also restricted tenants in the disposal of the coal. In South Wales the second Marquess of Bute bound his tenants to ship part or all of their produce at his docks.[37] All of these developments reflected the capacity of landlords to tie down tenants, and in turn this suggests that they had little difficulty attracting qualified partnerships ready to comply with the leasing terms.

On the other hand, leasing certainly did not absolve landowners of responsibility. In order to let a colliery in the first place, an owner had to venture considerable sums in exploratory trials. In the West Midlands the Bradford estate provided investment capital to prove mines at James Bridge in the nineteenth century before leasing them to entrepreneurs, and a similar policy was pursued on the Dartmouth estate to prove a seam at West Bromwich.[38] Many landowners continued to provide financial help during the course of a lease, usually in connection with fixed capital. The Duke of Northumberland began leasing collieries in the 1790s, but he continued to share the risks with his tenants by owning part of the working stock, and the Marquess of Bute also provided financial assistance for his tenants. Several Yorkshire landowners helped out their tenants, either by remitting payments or by lending money during depressions.[39] In effect, lease or no lease, landlords often had to meet the cost of new workings and new machines, and the provision of workmen's cottages, as well as bearing the financial brunt of economic fluctuations. But the task was obviously not too onerous, since major landowners from all over the north of England were to be found investing in the East Durham mining ventures during the nineteenth century.[40]

[37] Sill, 'Landownership and industry', pp. 149 ff.; Flinn, *The History of the British Coal Industry*, pp. 43–9; John Davies, *Cardiff and the Marquesses of Bute* (Cardiff, 1981), pp. 233–5.

[38] Trevor Raybould, 'Aristocratic landowners and the industrial revolution: the Black Country experience, 1760–1840', *Midland History*, 9 (1984), p. 82.

[39] Spring, 'English landowners and nineteenth-century industrialism', p. 33; Davies, *Cardiff and the Marquesses of Bute*, p. 222.

[40] Sill, 'Landownership and industry', p. 155.

Landowners could also influence the locational pattern of the colliery landscape. This can be demonstrated from what happened as the concealed coalfield in East Durham was opened up between 1820 and 1850. Through their lease covenants, landlords restricted the siting of mines. John Lyon, lord of the manor of Hetton, expressly forbade the sinking of a shaft within 300 yards of his house and pleasure grounds. Other owners were equally careful to lay down ground-rules of this nature, and even those without resources could bargain for good wayleave rents, and ensure that a wagonway remained out of their view. Consequently, leases or not, the local landowners were far from being passive agents of the process of mining colonization.[41]

Finally, owners were expected to support efforts which were made to encourage the industry, such as the North of England Institute of Mining and Mechanical Engineering, which was established in 1852. Initial patrons included the Duke of Northumberland, the Marquess of Londonderry, the earls of Lonsdale and Durham, Earl Grey, Lord Wharncliffe and Lord Ravensworth, although there is little evidence from the institute's *Transactions* to suggest that these men did more than lend their names to the enterprise. However, when a mining college was proposed in 1859, the Duke of Northumberland offered an endowment. Unfortunately his 'munificent proposition' was not matched by anyone else. The committee established to consider the feasibility of the scheme appealed

to the noblemen and gentlemen individually connected with, and interested, both locally and generally in such trade, and also to those noblemen and gentlemen who were otherwise connected with the two counties of Northumberland and Durham, and they had likewise appealed to the manufacturing and commercial interests of the district; but they regretted that they were obliged to arrive at the conclusion, that it was hopeless to expect to be able to raise the necessary funds to establish, endow, and support a college of an entirely independent character, and unconnected with any other institution.[42]

---

[41] Ibid., pp. 164–6. Wayleaves were the rights to carry coal across another person's land, and on the congested north-eastern coalfield they were a source of considerable contention: Flinn, *The History of the British Coal Industry*, pp. 159–62.

[42] North of England Institute of Mining Engineers, *Proposed College of Mining, Engineering and Manufacturing Science, in the North of England* (Newcastle, 1859), p. 3; *North of England Institute of Mining Engineers Transactions*, 1 (1852–3). Northumberland had become patron of the proposed college in 1856 when he offered to add one-third to any subscription: J. T. Ward, 'Landowners and mining', in *Land and Industry*, ed. Ward and Wilson, p. 85.

Despite this setback, landlords did participate in a number of activities to promote the industry. T. R. Beaumont was vice-patron of a society for preventing mining accidents at Sunderland in 1813, and in 1847 the third Earl Fitzwilliam supported demands for efficient inspection to improve ventilation and prevent explosions. Four years later he exhibited Barnsley coal at the Great Exhibition.[43]

ARISTOCRATS AND MINERAL RESOURCES: OTHER MINING INTERESTS

What happened in coalmining was largely mirrored in the other extractive industries, with the essential difference that the raw materials usually required processing. The extra cost of establishing smelting and finishing works was a deterrent to aristocratic entrepreneurs, with the result that there was a tendency to lease from an earlier stage. On both the Dudley estate in the Black Country and the Fitzwilliams' property in Yorkshire, coal was exploited on a mixed entrepreneurial-*rentier* basis, but iron interests were generally leased out except for a brief and unsuccessful foray into ironmaking by the fourth and fifth earls Fitzwilliam in the 1820s and 1830s. In Derbyshire, much of the relatively small amount of capital required in the leadmining industry before 1700 came from landowners, but, as the eighteenth century progressed, a wider range of sources was tapped for finance, with landowners becoming less significant after about 1750.

This picture must, however, be carefully tempered, since aristocratic enterprise was by no means negligible, and because the geological conditions whereby several different resources were often found in the same area tended to encourage a landowner to take a broad view of his interests. The iron industry provided a particular interest to landowners whose estates were blessed with resources of ore. George Sitwell was a pioneer iron producer in seventeenth-century Derbyshire, and in the 1720s Sir Thomas Lyttelton of Halesowen in Worcestershire was the most important partner in a group which ran Hales Furnace. He withdrew in 1736, but his reasons are obscure.[44] When Sir Thomas Webster moved his interests from Essex to Sussex during the 1720s, he also entered the iron industry. With Lord Ashburnham he leased Beach furnace in 1724, and three years later he acquired Robertsbridge

---

[43] Ward, 'West Riding landowners and mining', pp. 65–6.
[44] Chambers, 'The Vale of Trent', p. 7; R. L. Downes, 'The Stour partnership, 1726–36: a note on landed capital in the iron industry', *Economic History Review*, 2nd ser., 3 (1950), pp. 90–6.

furnace. Both began to blow in 1728, and in 1733 Webster also leased Echingham ironworks. However, by the 1720s the Sussex iron industry was in decline, and Webster could not make his interests pay. Robertsbridge was leased in 1734, and his other concerns were run down until they came to a halt in 1738.[45] Local landowners controlled almost all the ironworks in South Wales down to the 1740s, but they disappeared from the ranks of entrepreneurs from about 1760, even though the industry was growing rapidly.

Other landowners enjoyed more success. Thomas Lewis, from a Glamorgan landed family, was a partner in the Dowlais ironworks in 1759, and his family retained an interest in the concern until 1850, although only as sleeping partners. In Lancashire, the sixth Earl of Balcarres formed a partnership in 1788 with James Corbett, a Wigan ironfounder, and his own brother Robert Lindsay, who had made money in India, to form the Haigh ironworks, with two blast furnaces. The enterprise had mixed results, because of poor management according to Balcarres, although the unsuitability of local coal resources was also a problem. The furnaces were blown out before 1815 and demolished by 1828, but the company continued in operation as a foundry and engineering works producing paddle shafts for steamboats and wrought-ironwork for churches and locomotives. The seventh earl, who succeeded in 1825, finally withdrew in 1835.[46] The second Earl Gower's industrial company bought Donnington ironworks in 1792. A decade later it was reconstituted as the Lilleshall Company, and by 1805 it possessed five furnaces and two foundries. The company was turning out in the region of 100,000 tons of coal, 6000 tons of slack, and 30,000 tons of ironstone, with a similar amount of limestone. Gower, by now first Marquess of Stafford, died in 1803, when part of his interest passed to his second son, the first Earl Granville. He took an active interest in the works, and by 1832 also had a large, if unprofitable ironworks in North Staffordshire.[47] In Leicestershire the Earl of Moira built a large iron furnace and foundry on the banks of the Ashby canal early in the nineteenth century, in order to use ironstone found among his coal measures. The furnace was in production in 1806, and further trials took place in 1810 and 1811, although he made no further progress after 1812.[48] Finally it was not unknown for

---

[45] Huntington Library, Battle Abbey MSS, 70/11, 18, 63/13, 4/2, 61/18, 72/Seals box. Additional material on the works is to be found in the estate accounts.

[46] Crouzet, *The First Industrialists*, p. 73; A. Birch, 'The Haigh ironworks, 1789–1856', *Bulletin of the John Rylands Library*, 35 (1952–3), pp. 316–33.

[47] Wordie, *Estate Management in Eighteenth-Century England*, pp. 122–3.

[48] Palmer (ed.), *The Aristocratic Estate*, p. 61.

owners to take works back into direct management if tenants either let them down or, in depressed times, could not be found. These reasons lay behind the Fitzwilliams' direct management of Elsecar ironworks between 1827 and 1849, and the change of direction on the Dudley estate in the Black Country in 1839. In the latter case, tenants were believed not to have secured the best interests of the landlord, and the mineral agent preferred to take over the whole business, from mining the ironstone to producing the finished goods.[49]

Aristocrats blessed with extensive leadmining interests included the dukes of Devonshire in Derbyshire, the Blackett-Beaumonts in County Durham, and the earls Grosvenor in Flintshire. The dukes of Rutland and Devonshire, and Lord Scarsdale, all had royalties in the High Peak. The influence of local landowners declined as the lead industry peaked in the later eighteenth century, and the Devonshires preferred to let their interests. However, in the first half of the nineteenth century, lead mines in the county were being jointly worked on behalf of the Marquess of Buckingham, the Earl of Thanet and Lord George Henry Cavendish.[50] The Devonshires were more positively involved with the lead mines on their Grassington Moor estate in Yorkshire, but were still no match for the Blackett-Beaumonts in the north-east. The Blacketts began working lead in Allendale during the 1690s, and they also leased the Bishop of Durham's Weardale rights. By 1729 the family had established a sophisticated organization with several smelting mills, and they did not flinch when costs rose amidst fluctuating sales and profits, which ensured that their smelting mills were rarely at work throughout the year. On the other hand a major by-product of leadmining was silver refining, and the family lead mines were yielding around 5000 ounces in the 1730s and nearly 21,000 by the 1790s. The produce was sold to a London dealer. The property passed through Sir Thomas Wentworth to Colonel T. R. Beaumont by the beginning of the nineteenth century, and his family benefited considerably from the interest before leadmining faltered towards the end of the century.[51]

---

[49] Mee, *Aristocratic Enterprise*, ch. 3; Raybould, *The Economic Emergence of the Black Country*, pp. 146–7; 'Aristocratic landowners and the industrial revolution', pp. 67–8.

[50] K. Honeyman, *Origins of Enterprise: business leadership in the industrial revolution* (Manchester, 1982), pp. 22–3, 27; Huntington Library, STBF 12, Derbyshire Accounts (Mines), 1746–1813.

[51] Ward, 'Landowners and mining', pp. 88–91; W. M. Hughes, 'Lead, land and coal as sources of landlords' income in Northumberland between 1700 and 1850' (University of Newcastle, Ph.D. thesis, 1963), vol. I, pp. 40–116; vol. II, p. 31.

Several landed families were involved in promoting the Cornish copper and tin industries towards the end of the seventeenth century. The Bassett and Eyns families played an important role in the expansion of mining, and in developing ancillary services, such as the stamping mills set up by the Bassetts on their estate between 1735 and 1760. Most important, however, was their financial contribution, particularly the funding of Pool Mine for the ten years which were needed to prepare it and reach the tin and copper veins. Landowner investment was sufficient for the industry's needs, although copper works were virtually the sole province of Bristol and South Wales smelters. The growth of copper works in South Wales during the first half of the eighteenth century was largely a result of encouragement from three landowning families, the Mansels, Mackworths and Beauforts. Sir Humphrey Mackworth was a pioneer. He set up a smelting house in 1698, and helped to establish the Company of Mines Adventurers.[52] In Derbyshire the fourth Duke of Devonshire decided to work a copper mine at Ecton Hill on his own account in 1760, and between then and 1817 66,000 tons of high-grade copper ore was raised, worth £852,000. Ecton's produce amounted to the equivalent of 12 per cent of the total output of all the Cornish copper mines, and by 1786 4000 tons a year were being raised. 400 men were employed both at the mine and at Devonshire's smelting plant at Whiston, ten miles to the south. The rich vein ran out by 1800, and the sixth duke ceased operations in 1825, although the mine was leased to private adventurers until it closed in 1891. Many of the finished copper ingots were sold for brass production, but the fifth duke also had a contract with the navy to provide copper sheathing for the hulls of wooden ships, and for this purpose copper was sent to Evans's rolling mill in Derby.[53]

Beyond these examples, landowners were to be found participating, to a greater or lesser extent, in a variety of industrial concerns, arising from their mining interests. In South Wales, early in the eighteenth century, a few had scattered interests in alum and salt panning, while in Cumberland the local landowners took an interest in salt panning, and in copperas and glass manufacture, although they shied away from promoting the iron industry or the smelting of non-ferrous metals.[54]

---

[52] V. M. Chesher, 'A social and economic study of some West Cornwall landed families, 1690–1760' (University of Oxford, B.Litt. thesis, 1956); Martin, 'The landed estate in Glamorgan', pp. 194–8.

[53] Brian Cooper, *Transformation of a Valley* (1983), pp. 122–3.

[54] Martin, 'The landed estate in Glamorgan', p. 198; Beckett, *Coal and Tobacco*, pp. 125–42.

In the Black Country during the nineteenth century limestone – used for building, converting into lime for agricultural purposes, and as flux in blast furnaces – was worked on Lord Bradford's Walsall properties from 1813, and also on Lord Dudley's estate. Since coal and limestone often came out of the same shaft, this was an obvious arrangement, and development capital was supplied by both lessor and lessee.[55]

Finally, it is perhaps not surprising that, just as aristocrats exploited their estate resources for profit, some of those to whom they leased their interests succeeded in climbing into the ranks of landownership. In later seventeenth-century Cornwall, the Carlyon family established itself in land on the basis of tin and copper works. Joseph Charlesworth, who owned seven pits in South Yorkshire by 1809, bought Chapelthorpe Hall from Colonel Thomas Beaumont in 1814, while William Russell bought estates in County Durham between 1787 and 1810 for nearly £750,000 on the basis of his income from Wallsend colliery.[56] In Shropshire, lesser gentry acted as agents for larger owners, and also leased and operated industrial undertakings on their employers' estates, while in the course of the nineteenth century a group of professional coalowners emerged, whose main family income was derived from working coal mines. These people came from a variety of backgrounds, both industrial and agricultural, with mining engineers and colliery managers being most prominent.[57]

ARISTOCRATS AND MANUFACTURING INDUSTRY

In keeping with their preference for exploiting the resources found on or under their estates, aristocrats played only a limited role in promoting manufacturing industry.[58] Colonel James Grahme of Levens Hall had an interest in a workshop in Kendal. He was told in 1702 that 'several persons making of serges, stuffs and camlets &c within this Corporation meets with great encouragement from the country in your manufactory and has in great measure stripped us of our trades or at least reduced it to a very low ebb.'[59] The first Viscount

---

[55] Raybould, 'Aristocratic landowners and the industrial revolution', pp. 68–70.

[56] Chesher, 'A social and economic study of some West Cornwall landed families', pp. 18–19; Medlicott, 'The landed interest and the development of the South Yorkshire coalfield', p. 9; Hughes, 'Lead, land and coal', vol. I, p. 413.

[57] Barrie Trinder, *The Industrial Revolution in Shropshire* (1973), pp. 72–3, 208; Mitchell, *Economic Development of the British Coal Industry*, pp. 55–7.

[58] Edward Laurence, *The Duty of a Steward to his Lord* (1727), p. 49 reminded stewards of the need to encourage their employers to promote industrial concerns.

[59] Beckett, thesis, p. 308.

Lonsdale wrote in 1697 that he had hoped to have established manufactures for the benefit of the poor, but his tentative efforts at introducing textile production had fallen foul of inadequate managers. At almost the same time, his relation Sir John Lowther of Whitehaven helped a establish a woollen cloth manufacture in the town, although the scheme was quickly abandoned in 1699 when the ban on Irish woollen imports was reimposed. His son, Sir James, proved rather more adept at pious recommendations, which would have involved other people in starting such enterprises, than in taking positive action himself.[60] In 1740 the third Viscount Lonsdale re-established his father's woollen manufactory, but again bad management hampered the scheme, and it was ended within a couple of years. However, Lonsdale was less deterred than his father, and reopened the factory for linen manufacture in September 1742, to take advantage of export bounties and to exploit the American market by sending cargoes in outgoing tobacco vessels from Whitehaven. This scheme lasted for eleven years, but in the end transport costs proved too much, and when the accounts were finally closed in 1757 they revealed a deficit of over £900. Sir James Lowther, Lonsdale's cousin, predicted the failure in 1745, but not from the point of view of costs; in his rather pessimistic view

such undertakings will not answer either to lords or gentlemen that put forward such matters and therefore 'tis best for 'em to encourage tradesmen that are masters of the business to follow it themselves, by giving them a bounty for the goods they make.[61]

Lowther himself proved singularly unable to achieve such an aim.

Management was obviously a considerable problem, just as it was in relation to estates and mineral interests. The Earl of Derby built 'Lord's Factory' in Preston in 1794, but suffered at the hands of untrustworthy business associates, including Thomas Leeming, who was nearly arrested for debt. Such experiences were not necessarily offputting to other would-be entrepreneurs. In Leicestershire at the end of the eighteenth century Joseph Wilkes, a landowner from Measham, had interests in coal mines and cotton spinning. By some mysterious process his mill apparently spun cotton by day and ground corn by night.[62] In the West Riding of Yorkshire a significant number

[60] Beckett, *Coal and Tobacco*, p. 144–5.

[61] J. V. Beckett, 'The eighteenth-century origins of the factory system: a case study from the 1740s', *Business History*, 19 (1977), pp. 55–67.

[62] G. E. Mingay, *English Landed Society in the Eighteenth Century* (1963), p. 199.

of carding, scribbling and spinning mills were built and owned by landowners, but direct involvement decreased from the 1790s, and less than 6 per cent of pre-1850 textile mills in the area belonged to landowners. However, in 1805 Lord Dartmouth owned and leased out nineteen textile mills, for which he had put up much of the finance, and Sir James Graham had three large mills in the Aire Valley.[63] Relatively few of the owners who built textile mills actually operated them. In the Midlands several gentlemen became cotton mill owners, but usually they purchased existing concerns or entered as sleeping partners rather than taking the initiative themselves. Some took a more positive role in Lancashire; in Oldham, for example, at the end of the eighteenth century most of the 16,000 population was employed by no more than fifty families, and among these the four which predominated were long-established landowners. Of these the Cleggs had helped to revive the local hat trade in the early eighteenth century, and in the 1790s were the first to apply steam power to cotton production. The families had originally expanded their interests from agricultural pursuits to mineral exploitation, and from that base they were able to move into the cotton industry.[64]

Few systematic attempts have been made to examine aristocratic business interests, but a survey of gentry in the Parliament of 1841–7 is revealing. Out of 658 MPs with peerage or gentry connections, 66 (10 per cent) could be described as businessmen, a group which included bankers, merchants, manufacturers and an eminent railway entrepreneur, William Ormsby Gore. The proportion rises when men with incidental business interests are included. When railway directors, insurance company directors, directors of joint-stock banks and other similar organizations are added, the total comes to 223, or 34 per cent of MPs. However, since two-thirds of MPs lacked any business interests, these figures suggest that in general terms land and industry had not been convincingly brought together during the period of industrialization.[65]

[63] Crouzet, *The First Industrialists*, ch. 5.

[64] Stanley D. Chapman, *The Early Factory Masters* (Newton Abbot, 1967), pp. 95–6; Honeyman, *Origins of Enterprise*, pp. 89–90. It is, of course, possible that the role played by landowners in establishing new industrial projects has simply not been fully appreciated through lack of research. The evidence of advertisements for mill sales appearing in the *Manchester Mercury* suggests an ongoing involvement (information provided by Dr Stanley Chapman).

[65] W. O. Aydelotte, 'The business interests of the gentry in the Parliament of 1841–7', appendix to G. R. Kitson Clark, *The Making of Victorian England* (1962), pp. 290–305.

ARISTOCRATS AND INDUSTRY: PARLIAMENTARY LEGISLATION

If they were not particularly prominent as industrial promoters outside the mineral extractive concerns, aristocrats still had a significant role to play through Parliament. Although most enterprises did not require legislative backing, wider general issues often required support. Sir James Lowther, knight of the shire for Cumberland for much of the period 1708–55, took his constituency industrial interests seriously. In 1738 he attempted to interest William Bowles, MP for Bridport, in taking a lease of the Whitehaven glassworks; and over a number of years he held talks in the House of Commons with Charles Pelham, MP for Beverley, regarding a coal-bearing estate to the north of Workington that he hoped to acquire. He spoke in debates on the coal and tobacco trade, and presented petitions to the Commons from the Whitehaven merchants. In addition, he was one of the MPs who came from industrial regions, and were expected to give an opinion on potential projects. The most celebrated case in which he participated came at the end of the 1720s, when William Wood petitioned for an incorporation on the grounds that he was able to produce good iron using coal in the smelt. Such a process is impossible, but this was not appreciated at the time, and a Privy Council committee of inspection was appointed to adjudicate his claims. Lowther was one of several MPs from principal ironmaking regions who were included on the committee.[66] William Wood had originally negotiated to establish his ironworks at Frizington in West Cumberland, using coal from Lowther's collieries. With such direct interests, Lowther was an obvious person to include on investigatory committees. He believed Wood's claim to be 'impudent and monstrous', and in January 1730 claimed that 'I have within this week set all the chief nobility and greatest commoners of the kingdom against him.' He had told at least twenty Privy Councillors that it was a fraud. A year later he was consulted by Sir Robert Walpole on the matter, and in May 1731 he was present at the second trial of the process, when it was conclusively exposed as a fraud.[67]

As industrialization progressed, the need for parliamentary support became increasingly necessary for industrialists, but relatively few managed to find their way into the lower house until well into the

[66] J. V. Beckett, 'A back-bench MP in the eighteenth century: Sir James Lowther of Whitehaven', *Parliamentary History*, 1 (1982), pp. 90–1; J. M. Treadwell, 'William Wood and the Company of Ironmasters of Great Britain', *Business History*, 16 (1974), pp. 110–11.

[67] Carlisle RO, D/Lons/W, Sir James Lowther to John Spedding, 29 and 31 January, 7 February 1730, 16 February, 11 and 13 May 1731.

nineteenth century. Some cultivated the art of parliamentary lobbying, and many turned to the peerage for support in the upper house. There were sound reasons for such a move. Peers with coalmining interests were used to establishing contacts in neighbouring manufacturing or commercial communities in order to promote their joint interests by sponsoring relevant legislation and intervening when constituency interests were threatened. These industrial interests inevitably ensured that they were sympathetic to men outside Parliament with similar business concerns. The Earl of Derby presented many of the petitions opposing the younger Pitt's scheme for expanding commerce between England and Ireland, while the Yorkshire woollen manufacturers took Earl Fitzwilliam's advice on how best to prevent their case. Both earls vigorously attacked the resolutions when they were debated in the Lords. In the 1770s Matthew Boulton received valuable advice from the Earl of Dartmouth, and claimed to have approached a total of forty peers, in helping to secure the establishment of assay offices at Sheffield and Birmingham, while Josiah Wedgwood and his fellow Staffordshire potters relied on Lord Gower and the Marquess of Rockingham in contentious patent issues. At the end of the eighteenth century it seems likely that the balance of peerage interest was used to advance rather than to retard the goals of industrialists, and they may even have helped to protect the unreformed political system through their vitality as industrial patrons.[68]

On the other hand, it is clear both that industrialists could run into formidable parliamentary opposition to their schemes, and also that the aristocracy sometimes used its position at Westminster in order to protect its own interests at the expense of industrialists. Matthew Boulton ran into considerable Commons opposition from Edmund Burke when he sought an extension to the patent of Watt's steam-engine. Burke was supporting a rival invention, and Boulton found it necessary to approach a considerable number of MPs for their support.[69] The Alkali Act of 1863 provides an example of an aristocratic parliament defending its sectional landed interests. It was argued that the air pollution caused by alkali manufacture reduced

---

[68] Michael W. McCahill, *Order and Equipoise: the peerage and the House of Lords, 1783–1806* (1978), ch. 9; 'Peers, patronage and the industrial revolution, 1760–1800', *Journal of British Studies*, 16 (1976), pp. 84–107.

[69] E. Robinson, 'Matthew Boulton and the art of parliamentary lobbying', *Historical Journal*, 7 (1964), pp. 216–24, gives a detailed description of Boulton's lobbying techniques over both the Assay Bill and the extension of Watt's patent. Boulton found that county families were willing to help because they saw themselves as the patrons of local trade: ibid., p. 211.

rental income and land values and damaged trees. Although local Acts offered a means of proceeding against chemical manufacturers through the lawcourts, these were increasingly difficult to enforce as industrial plant became more concentrated. Early in the 1860s a select committee of the House of Lords, prompted into existence by the fourteenth Earl of Derby, recommended changes in the law, including a specific Alkali Act. The legislation, which came into force in 1864, placed the property of manufacturers under state supervision in the interests of landowners' property, although it proved to be too narrowly conceived to be of lasting benefit. However, its passing demonstrates how, even in the mid-nineteenth century, landed aristocrats could use their parliamentary position to secure what they regarded as their legitimate interests.[70]

THE FINANCIAL REWARD

How much non-agricultural revenue did landowners derive from their estates, and where did it rank in relation to their overall income? Timber was sold from estates, either as a regular income supplement, or as a means of dealing with a financial crisis. In the north-west, timber sales averaged £307 annually between 1699 and 1723 on the earls of Thanet's Westmorland estate. In Cumberland the earls of Carlisle sold an average of £179 annually between 1726 and 1751, and in the 1770s such sales represented 5 per cent of annual estate income. In Essex, the Petre family used their timber resources to supplement annual income with sales representing up to two-fifths of gross income over the period 1791–1830. Coke of Norfolk also sold timber regularly. The net income from such disposals exceeded £1000 a year between 1816 and 1831, and, although it declined in subsequent years, by the 1850s sales from the estate exceeded £2000 annually. The dukes of Bedford also regarded timber sales as part of their annual income. From their Buckinghamshire and Bedfordshire estates, sales amounted to £650,000 between 1816 and 1895, an overall annual average of 18 per cent of total income.[71] Among families using timber

---

[70] A. E. Dingle, '"The monster nuisance of all": landowners, alkali manu-facturers, and air pollution, 1828–64', *Economic History Review*, 2nd ser., 35 (1982), pp. 529–48.

[71] Beckett, thesis, p. 69; Charles E. Searle, '"The odd corner of England" a study of a rural social formation in transition, Cumbria, *c.* 1700–*c.* 1914' (University of Essex, Ph.D. thesis, 1983), p. 85; Colin Shrimpton, 'The landed society and the farming community of Essex in the late eighteenth and early nineteenth centuries'

sales for debt payments were the Lowthers of Holker and the dukes of Buckingham. Sir Thomas Lowther realized £700 from timber sales in 1738 in order to offset part of his debt to a steward, while one of the emergency measures designed to try to shore up the Buckingham finances in the 1840s was an agreement to use all timber cut on the estate for the reduction of debts.[72]

The incentive to mineral exploitation which originally attracted many families was the high level of profit in relation to outlay. In the first half of the eighteenth century, profits of 30 per cent were not unusual, and the Lowthers sometimes received in excess of 40 per cent in Cumberland. In Cornwall, the proportion of the Eyns's family income from copper mining was 44 per cent for the years 1727–31, and 40 per cent for 1738–42, but their outlay amounted to only 8 and 23 per cent (of total income) respectively for the two periods.[73] In these years, some families derived a considerable proportion of their income from mining ventures. This was the case among the coalowning landowners of West Glamorgan, while for the Bassett family in Cornwall copper-mining profits were between two and three times more lucrative than their estate rental. For many landowners, however, mineral income was negligible in regard to overall income, and this was one reason why so many opted out of direct working when costs began to rise and profit margins to fall in the course of the eighteenth century. Certainly both in South-West Lancashire and in West Glamorgan it was the combination of these two factors which produced a move into leasing.[74]

For those families that stayed the course, mineral income became an increasingly important part of their revenue over time. In the 1770s,

(University of Cambridge, Ph.D. thesis, 1965), p. 18; Susannah Wade Martins, *A Great Estate at Work* (Cambridge, 1980), p. 83; Duke of Bedford, *A Great Agricultural Estate*, 3rd edn (1897), pp. 218–26.

[72] J. V. Beckett, 'The Lowthers at Holker: marriage, inheritance and debt in the fortunes of an eighteenth-century landowning family', *Transactions of the Historic Society of Lancashire and Cheshire*, 127 (1978), p. 51; D. and E. Spring, 'The fall of the Grenvilles, 1844–1848', *Huntington Library Quarterly*, 19 (1956), p. 172.

[73] Beckett, *Coal and Tobacco*, p. 78; Chesher, 'A social and economic study of some West Cornwall landed families', p. 187. High levels of profit continued in some areas: Flinn, *The History of the British Coal Industry*, pp. 324–5. On the question of profit rates by the nineteenth century, see Mitchell, *Economic Development of the British Coal Industry*, pp. 304–5.

[74] Martin, 'The landed estate in Glamorgan', p. 173; Chesher, 'A social and economic history of some West Cornwall landed families', p. 214; John Langton, 'Landowners and the development of coal mining in south-west Lancashire, 1590–1799', in *Change in the Countryside*, ed. H. S. A. Fox and R. A. Butlin (1979), p. 141.

on the Fitzwilliams' estate in South Yorkshire, profits from coalmining and leases were slightly less than 20 per cent of a total income of £9600, but by the second decade of the nineteenth century the proportion had risen to 24 per cent of an overall income of nearly £34,000. Although profitability increased on the nearby Norfolk estate when direct management was introduced in 1781, mineral revenue was still a relatively minor part of income. In 1787–8 it amounted to 8.6 per cent, and in 1791–2 it reached 19 per cent. By 1808, when all the collieries were leased at a fixed rent of £1286, they contributed only 2.5 per cent to the total revenue. The situation on the Fitzwilliam estate, however, was more typical, and was paralleled elsewhere. In the West Midlands, gross return from industrial ventures on the Leveson-Gower estate represented only 8 per cent of the total income in 1730, but rose steadily to 28 per cent by 1833.[75]

In the course of the nineteenth century, those who persisted with direct working received their reward, but such was the demand, particularly for coal, that even those dependent on leases and royalties enjoyed a worthwhile income supplement. Some of the best returns were on the north-east coalfield. In the early years of the nineteenth century the Londonderry collieries were yielding a profit of £30,000 annually, while those of the earls of Durham averaged £17,500 a year between 1824 and 1828. The first six months of 1835 yielded Durham a profit of £24,000, and his coal income rose to £84,000 in 1856. Royalties, wayleaves and railway rents produced £59,000 in 1913. The dukes of Northumberland's mineral income was £20,000 in the 1820s, but over £82,000 in 1918.[76] But none did so well as William Russell, the Sunderland merchant who leased Wallsend colliery from the Dean and Chapter of Durham in 1787. Profits by the early nineteenth century were more than 100 per cent of costs; in 1809, for example, when costs were just over £50,000, gross revenue amounted to £110,000, and this single colliery enabled Russell to establish himself as a substantial country gentleman in Durham.[77]

Elsewhere in the country the story was much the same. In Cumberland, profits from the Lowthers' coalfield interests increased from only £200–£300 in the 1660s to about £9000 at the time of Sir

[75]Medlicott, 'The landed interest and the development of the South Yorkshire coalfield', pp. 67–9, 308; Wordie, *Estate Management in Eighteenth-Century England*, pp. 133–54.

[76] Spring, 'The Earls of Durham and the great northern coalfield', pp. 242, 251–3; Ward, 'Landowners and mining', p. 67; Flinn, *The History of the British Coal Industry*, p. 326.

[77] Hughes, 'Lead, land and coal', vol. I, p. 413.

James Lowther's death in 1755, and to around £30,000 by the beginning of the nineteenth century. Over the period 1812–43 they averaged £36,000 annually.[78] In Yorkshire the Fitzwilliams' mineral income rose from 14 to 40 per cent of their ever-increasing overall income during the nineteenth century (table 6.1), while the Beaumont family of Bretton Hall, near Wakefield, had a similar experience.

Table 6.1   The Fitzwilliams' income in the nineteenth century

Year	Rents (£)	Minerals (£)	Total (£)	Minerals as % of total
1801	26,135	4,214	30,349	13.9
1831	32,396	2,576	34,972	7.4
1841	43,489	11,082	54,571	20.3
1850	44,356	8,991	53,347	16.9
1871	71,281	37,210	108,491	34.3
1901	130,585	87,743	218,328	40.2

Source: J. T. Ward, 'West Riding landowners and mining in the nineteenth century', *Yorkshire Bulletin of Economic and Social Research*, XV (1963), p. 65

Their mineral income rose from 10 to 26 per cent of total income over the years 1829–66; in 1866 it represented £6727 out of £25,723. However, this was not the whole story, since these figures did not include income from the lucrative north-east lead mines.[79] Also in Yorkshire the Duke of Norfolk's mineral income reached £14,286 in 1866, while a series of other landowners were also reaping a rich reward from their mineral holdings.[80] In the Black Country the Dudleys derived a considerable income from their minerals, especially those directly worked by the family (table 6.2), but it fell away

[78] Beckett, *Coal and Tobacco*, pp. 227–37; Flinn, *The History of the British Coal Industry*, p. 326; Ward, 'Some West Cumberland landowners and industry', pp. 342, 349.

[79] Ward, 'West Riding landowners and mining', pp. 65–6; Hughes, 'Lead, land and coal', vol. I, pp. 86 ff.

[80] Ward, 'Landowners and mining', p. 71; 'West Riding landowners and mining', pp 61–74.

Table 6.2 Net income from minerals on the Dudley estate

Year	Pits worked by the estate (£)	Royalties (£)	Total income from direct working and royalties (£)
1704	–	–	1,941
1804	–	–	17,684
1834	28,123	4,765	32,888
1836	11,382	13,623	25,005
1847	67,045	74,955	142,000
1854	98,554	70,543	169,097
1871	141,681	26,146	167,827
1872	394,750	22,507	417,257
1890	52,141		
1896	37,087		
1899	49,461		
1908	36,696		

Source: T. J. Raybould, *The Economic Emergence of the Black Country* (Newton Abbot, 1973), p. 223

towards the end of the century as productive coal seams neared exhaustion. Finally, in South Wales the marquesses of Bute found their collieries increasingly lucrative in the course of the nineteenth century. In the second half of 1826 their mineral receipts amounted to only £872, most of which came from the Bute and Aberdare iron companies and the Crayshaw ironworks. Net income rose to £10.756 in 1848–9, and during the second half of the century the estate became increasingly dependent on mineral royalties. These averaged £32,000 during the 1850s, £38,000 in the 1860s and £56,000 in the 1870s. Between 1913 and 1918 the average was £115,742. In the 1850s the majority of this income was derived from the estate's ironworking interests, but by the 1870s coal royalties were becoming increasingly significant.[81]

[81] Davies, *Cardiff and the Marquesses of Bute*, pp. 239–41.

The aristocratic contribution to industrial development spanned a wide range. Naturally there were a few who saw themselves as pioneers. The first Duke of Chandos was an inveterate speculator, dabbling in a vast number of activities which mostly yielded disappointing results.[82] For some heart ruled head: the ninth Earl of Dundonald might have been more successful if he had found a market for the coal tar and ammonia produced at his Shropshire factory. As it was, the enterprise failed for lack of customers.[83] A few were swashbuckling tycoons, among them George Bowes, one of the original Grand Allies on Tyneside, who constantly broke agreements in order to improve his coal returns.[84] Others either ignored their industrial interests or paid them only passing concern. Earl Temple's steward wrote to him in the 1760s:

when you was at Dodrington [Somerset] you expressed a desire of being informed from time to time of any success that should attend the working of the mines there. I have now the pleasure to acquaint your Lordship that the works still continue to go on prosperously.[85]

Similarly, the second Earl Granville complained from Stoke-on-Trent in 1859 that 'I am here looking after my ironworks, a necessary but tiresome operation', and Ralph Sneyd was sufficiently unimpressed by the growing urban and industrial character of his Keele estate that he left its development to his agent.[86] Finally, a few aristocrats refused to sanction any form of industrial enterprise. One Lincolnshire squire told his Yorkshire steward in 1758 that he intended to have nothing more to do with coalmining. He did not, however, entirely forbid future ventures, unlike the seventh Duke of Bedford, who refused to allow deposits of iron ore found on his Midlands estates in 1858 to be worked, since this would spoil the countryside.[87] Similarly, Nottinghamshire villages in which one landowner was dominant did not usually develop as centres of the framework knitting industry. Bradmore, for example, had thirty-four frames in 1848, but its

[82] C. H. C. and M. I. Baker, *The Life and Circumstances of James Brydges, First Duke of Chandos* (Oxford, 1949), ch. 14.

[83] A. D. Harvey, *Britain in the Early Nineteenth Century* (1978), p. 33.

[84] Ward, 'Landowners and mining', p. 104.

[85] Huntington Library, STG box 423/50, John Roy to Lord Temple, 4 May 1763. His successor, the first Marquess of Buckingham, seems to have taken greater interest, since his steward sent him a detailed three-page letter about the mines in 1786: box 367/20 Richard Camplin to Buckingham, 17 September 1786.

[86] Crouzet, *The First Industrialists*, p. 80.

[87] Ward, 'Landowners and mining, p. 105; Crouzet, *The First Industrialists*, p. 80.

landlord lived in nearby Bunny, which had none. A similar pattern has also been established for Leicestershire.[88]

Between the extremes lay a body of men with a firm but limited commitment to industrial development. For some it was a question of funding the initial trials in the hope of leasing the resources when heavy capital outlay was required. Consequently such people were to be found withdrawing from direct involvement when the costs began to rise. In South Wales most of the landowners pulled out of their industrial interests from about 1760 onwards, but to suggest a straightforward trend would be misleading. Aristocrats may have preferred to lease, but this did not absolve them from all responsibility, and when tenants could not be found they often showed a willingness to undertake a further period of direct management. In any case, the crucial role was sometimes played in the pioneer days. Sir James Lowther, for example, was one of the earliest users of Newcomen engines. This was a costly piece of technology, still unproved when it was installed at Howgill colliery in 1716, but it was the willingness of landlords to invest in such risky ventures in order to overcome mine drainage problems which helped to break through technical bottlenecks.[89]

The importance of the aristocratic contribution to industry has to be judged by its quality rather than its quantity. Aristocrats were primarily concerned with their own estates, and the industrial activities that they chose to support or promote were usually estate-based; hence their role in mining, and small manufacturing activities such as Viscount Lonsdale's proto-factory in Westmorland. By contrast, they did not view themselves as entrepreneurs on a wider plane, and these attitudes had much in common with those of their European counterparts.[90] Their estates were their forte, and here they were prepared to work, and to invest, in order to promote industrial activities. Their crucial role was in getting things moving through pioneering technology, and encouraging entrepreneurs. If they later withdrew into *rentier* status, this was often for sound financial reasons,

---

[88] Alan Rogers, 'Rural industrial and social structure: the framework knitting industry of South Nottinghamshire, 1670–1840', *Textile History*, 12 (1981), pp. 19–20; Dennis R. Mills, 'Rural industries and social structure: framework knitters in Leicestershire, 1670–1851', *Textile History*, 13 (1982), pp. 185–7; *Lord and Peasant in Nineteenth Century Britain* (1980), pp. 80–3.

[89] Martin, 'The landed estate in Glamorgan', pp. 200–1; Beckett, *Coal and Tobacco*, pp. 68–70; Flinn, *The History of the British Coal Industry*, pp. 115–28.

[90] The similarities with the pre-Revolution French nobility can be seen from Guy Chaussinand-Nogaret, *The French Nobility in the Eighteenth Century*, tr. William Doyle (Cambridge, 1985), pp. 90, 102, 108.

and leasing did not mean opting out: some still provided financial and other help for lessees, while others took over direct working of resources when tenants could not be attracted. In addition, they used their parliamentary role to promote industrial interests, and to sponsor any necessary legislation. If industrialization is seen purely in terms of the cotton industry, then it is true that the English aristocracy played a relatively limited – although not entirely inactive – role, but, if the central importance of coalmining and iron production is recognized, the significance of the landowning contribution is inevitably enhanced.[91] In quantitative terms the role may have been limited, but taken altogether it was far from negligible.

---

[91] Flinn, *The History of the British Coal Industry*, has attempted to restore the industry to what he considers was its rightful place at the heart of the industrial revolution.

Chapter Seven

The Aristocracy and Communications Improvements

Communications in seventeenth-century England were far from ideal. Even if the exchange of goods seems to have taken place on a scale which belies some of the more vivid contemporary descriptions of road surfaces, there is little doubt that maintenance provisions were derisory. Under legislation dating from 1563, each parish had to spend six days a year on the upkeep of its roads. Since this did little more than maintain an inadequate system, particularly in the areas of heavy, poorly draining soils, the practice developed of moving bulky commodities by water. Goods were moved by river, and sometimes travelled considerable distances by a combination of river and coastal transport. Even so, the agricultural and industrial revolutions could never have taken place in such conditions, given that a primary consideration was to widen the market and increase competition.

The first indication that real change was on the way came in the later seventeenth century, as river improvement schemes and the first Turnpike Road Acts (1663 and 1695) together pointed the way ahead. The momentum of improvement increased during the eighteenth century. Turnpike Acts averaged around eight per decade down to 1750, but in the 1750s and 1760s nearly 300 were passed, and during the final phase of the movement down to 1836 another 400 went through Parliament. Also by 1750 most of what was possible in regard to river improvements had been accomplished, and, to supplement the existing waterways, canals were constructed. Between 1758 and 1802 165 Canal Acts were passed, of which nearly one-third went through Parliament in the so-called mania of 1792–5. This phase of the communications revolution largely came to an end in the 1830s, when numerous experiments with rails, and with the deployment of steam power for a moving engine, finally came to fruition in the railway age. The 1830s and 1840s saw the construction of the major lines, and the second half of the century witnessed infilling in the system. Road and water transport were largely outcompeted in this period, the latter permanently, and the former until the coming of the motor car at the end of the nineteenth century.

Aristocrats were affected from the outset by these changes, but their attitudes towards them varied. Some historians have depicted them as playing a vital role. Harold Perkin, for example, has written that

most of the early canals and 'navigations' . . . were backed if not initiated by local landowners. . . . Without the active support and, in many cases, the initiative of the landowners individually and in Parliament the transport revolution could scarcely have occurred.[1]

Certainly their backing was important, but the level of commitment varied. In general the aristocracy took a prominent part in road transport improvements, a reflection of their concern for the King's Highway. The roads were a common service, part of public administration for which the responsibility lay with all citizens. Moreover, as justices of the peace sitting in quarter sessions, aristocrats had the power to levy fines on parishes which failed to maintain their roads, and as landowners in those selfsame parishes they had a duty to give a lead in ensuring that adequate facilities existed for the movement of people and goods. The moral imperative did not operate in the same way with canals and railways, both because they were perceived as private promotions for private ends, and because land-owners were slow to grasp the advantages to be gained from such innovations. Their investments make it clear that they regarded the chief responsibility as falling upon the shoulders of the mercantile and manufacturing interests, and on the whole they limited their role to supporting schemes that had a bearing on their own concerns. In practice, this often meant backing short canal and railway lines which permitted access to the main system for their agricultural and mineral goods. This policy was despite the fact that many of the incorporating Acts passed during the 1790s to permit canal development included a share reservation for owners over whose land the waterway would pass. Since this was optional, it was often not fully subscribed, especially where prospects were doubtful. Overall, while the transport revolution could not have come about without landowner support, whether it would have taken a similar course if it had depended entirely on their initiative and investment must remain an open question.

[1] Harold Perkin, *The Origins of Modern English Society, 1780–1880* (1969), pp. 76–7.

ARISTOCRATIC ATTITUDES TO COMMUNICATIONS IMPROVEMENTS

The ambivalence of the aristocratic position largely arose from differing perceptions of what could be achieved. On the positive side the benefits to be expected from improved transportation were considerable. Faster and more comfortable travel conditions were a distinct advantage; indeed, the railway transformed the aristocratic lifestyle, permitting shorter but more frequent visits to estates, opening up new opportunities for foxhunting, and virtually inventing the country-house weekend. Economic advantages could also be expected, particularly with the movement of goods which were bulky relative to their weight. William Drake, a Lincolnshire landowner, put up £500 for the Boston–Wainfleet and Partney turnpikes in 1766, partly because it would allow his wool to be moved at any time of the year and not merely during the summer months.[2] But the most clear-cut advantages lay with the movement of coal, which could not be taken far before transport costs became prohibitive. Efficiency could be improved if the traditional packhorse was replaced by a horsedrawn cart, but this in turn required better road surfaces, and a number of turnpike schemes were deliberately geared towards the movement of coal. This was the principal motive behind the Liverpool–Prescot turnpike in 1725, and both the Somerset and Warwickshire coalfields benefited from turnpiking in the 1750s and 1760s. Coalowners were enthusiastic promoters of similar schemes in Derbyshire and South Wales, while the significance of coal movement was sometimes reflected in specially negotiated low tolls.[3]

Waterborne transport facilities were improved in various ways, with the movement of coal usually providing the impetus. Initially existing rivers were made navigable. Some rivers could be used for moving coal in their natural state, the most obvious examples being the lower reaches of the Tyne and Wear, although even in the latter case complaints were voiced that collieries downriver could not be properly exploited because owners with coal near the river took pains to prevent competition by refusing wayleaves.[4] Elsewhere, virtually any river which reached to within ten miles of a coalfield was pressed into useful service, including the Douglas in Lancashire, the Soar in

---

[2] T. W. Beastall, *The Agricultural Revolution in Lincolnshire* (Lincoln, 1978), pp. 103–4.

[3] M. W. Flinn, *The History of the British Coal Industry*, vol. 2: *1700–1830* (Oxford, 1984), pp. 147–8.

[4] Clements Library, Charles Townshend Papers, 298/7, Short state of the Durham Navigation, n.d.

Leicestershire, the Weaver in Cheshire and the Don in Yorkshire.[5] Once the possibility of improving existing waterways had been exhausted, a network of canals was constructed. The Sankey Brook navigation of 1757 opened up the St Helens area of the Lancashire coalfield to domestic and industrial consumers on Merseyside. It was quickly followed by perhaps the most famous of all canal projects, the third Duke of Bridgewater's Worsley canal, which connected his collieries to the Manchester market (see below). Over the following decades these examples were followed on all the coalfields with the exception of the north-east and Cumberland, where existing coastal and river navigations made them unnecessary. The most extensive developments were on the inland Midland coalfields, and some of the most heavily used served mines in Nottinghamshire and Derbyshire. Nor could coalowners afford to ignore the new developments, since canals tended to affect the whole market structure. The improved waterways of the East Midlands during the 1760s and 1770s were largely a response to the opening of the Don navigation, which enabled Yorkshire coalowners to undersell their rivals in the Trent Valley.[6]

Aristocrats also took a prominent role in the construction of ports and harbour facilities, and again the motive was usually provided by the coal trade. Normally they avoided responsibility for shipping, although West Cumberland coalowners purchased shares in several vessels during the 1730s and 1740s when the number of colliers on the Dublin run fell below acceptable levels.[7] Instead, owners tried to ensure that harbours had a draft of water which was sufficient to allow vessels to dock regularly, and they helped to build quays and to provide shelter for shipping. For the coal trade, storage and loading places had to be provided, and the coal ports usually built staithes, large covered warehouses with spouts which projected into the holds of colliers.

Finally, the demands of the coal industry also produced the two major developments behind the coming of the railways, although aristocrats played a relatively small part in their promotion. Rails were

[5] Flinn, *The History of the British Coal Industry*, pp. 164–6.

[6] Ibid., pp. 180–8. Canals reduced the cost of transporting coal by up to 50 per cent: Roderick Floud and Donald McCloskey (eds), *The Economic History of Britain since 1700* (Cambridge, 1981), vol. I, p. 234. Improved transportation was vital for expansion on the South Yorkshire coalfield: I. R. Medlicott, 'The landed interest and the development of the South Yorkshire coalfield, 1750–1830' (Open University, M.Phil. thesis, 1981), pp. 202–10.

[7] J. V. Beckett, *Coal and Tobacco: the Lowthers and the economic development of West Cumberland, 1660–1760* (Cambridge, 1981), pp. 89–91.

used for the carriage of coal, using horsedrawn carts, on various coalfields by the early eighteenth century. Known as wagonways, the rails were laid along gradients in order to transport coal from the pithead to the nearest water transport, at either the river or the harbour quayside. The second development was the steam-engine. Once James Watt had adapted steam power to rotary motion in 1781, it was only a matter of time before a means would be found of replacing the horse on the wagonway. In the years around 1815 the experimenters began to enjoy more success, and locomotives started to replace horses for wagonway haulage on most of the coalfields.[8] The replacement of inadequate road surfaces by wagonways, and the introduction of engines to pull the carts, paved the way for the railway age.

Aristocrats benefited financially from these developments through increased land and rent values. Road improvements were sometimes viewed as a vital complement to enclosure. The great majority of parliamentary enclosures in Leicestershire during the 1760s and 1770s took place within three miles of an existing turnpike.[9] It was alleged that subscribers to the Montgomery Canal were

noblemen and gentlemen either possessed of estates in this county, or resident therein, who had for their object the extension of agriculture, the reduction of horses . . . the increase of horned cattle, and the preservation of the roads; with the consequent advantage to the public.[10]

The landowners and farmers who provided the bulk of capital for the Grimsby Haven Company in the 1790s wanted a new dock to complement revolutionary developments in agricultural practice on the Lincolnshire Wolds.[11] Estates for sale were advertised in terms of their local communications, as in the case of a 1120-acre Lincolnshire property put on the market in February 1797:

On the north, this estate is bounded by the river Witham, opening navigable communications with the Lincoln, the Trent and the Yorkshire rivers: on the south and south-west, it is bounded by the North-forty-foot drain, opening a navigable communication with Bourne and Boston. On private canals

---

[8] Flinn, *The History of the British Coal Industry*, pp. 148–56.

[9] William Albert, *The Turnpike Road System in England, 1663–1840* (Cambridge, 1972), pp. 103–4, 115.

[10] Quoted in J. R. Ward, *The Finance of Canal Building in Eighteenth-Century England* (Oxford, 1974), pp. 137–8.

[11] G. Jackson, *Grimsby and the Haven Company, 1796–1846* (1971), p. 29.

belonging to the estate, the produce is shipped at the barn door, and the estate is intersected by a turnpike road.[12]

Railways probably did more than the other developments to raise land values. Almost invariably land alongside a line increased in value, with the result that a railway company wanting to buy land adjacent to an earlier purchase had to pay a higher price. By the 1860s, land agents in Lincolnshire were reckoning that the letting value of a farm increased by between 5 and 20 per cent depending on the proximity of a station, and by 1865 the county was England's leading wheat-producing area, largely as a result of the railway.[13] In the suburbs of a town, land values could increase by ten- or twentyfold. Captain Thomas Ross subscribed £1000 to the South London Railway in 1857 'because I lose tenants repeatedly by not being able to say positively that there will be a railway'. Some landowners were even accused of promoting railway projects to enhance the price of land they would be able to sell to the company.[14]

In general terms these advantages were only slowly perceived by landowners, although a few saw the light relatively quickly. The Earl of Derby, for example, having opposed the Liverpool and Manchester Railway Company's bills of 1825 and 1826, was among the first to offer his congratulations when the line opened in 1830.[15] Initially, however, the majority of landlords were distinctly cool and even actively hostile to improvement schemes. Their grounds for taking up such positions varied. With canals it was claimed that water would be drained from the land to service the waterway, leaving too little residue to water the meadows adequately; that they would run through low-lying areas and eat into valuable fertile land; and that the people working on them would be the rougher kind of men likely to commit property depradations. With railways, landlords feared the intrusion of black monsters which would devalue their land, split their farms, damage their foxhunting prospects, and scar the landscape much as collieries would have done without careful control.[16] Underlying these excuses was an initial fear that increased competition in the local

[12] *The Times*, 22 February 1797. The estate belonged to John Cartwright, Esq., of Brothertoft Farm near Boston. It included the manor, the manor house, and what was described as a rich freehold within a ring fence. The asking price was £52,000.

[13] Beastall, *The Agricultural Revolution in Lincolnshire*, pp. 146–7.

[14] J. R. Kellett, *The Impact of Railways on Victorian Cities* (1969), p. 401: J. T. Ward, 'West Riding landowners and the railways', *Journal of Transport History*, 4 (1960), p. 245.

[15] E. Richards, *The Leviathan of Wealth* (1973), pp. 74, 102.

[16] W. T. Jackman, *The Development of Transport* (1916), pp. 396, 497–9.

market would lead to falling prices and rents. This may have occurred in isolated cases during the early stages of change, and landlords were largely unimpressed by the counter-arguments of promoters. The Earl of Kent opposed the Wye navigation because of the threat to his ironworks monopoly, and various canal schemes were opposed on similar grounds.[17] Attitudes began to change only when the advantages of competition started to appear.

Landowners were perpetually on the lookout for what they thought might be threats to their privacy. George and Robert Stephenson placed the need to avoid parks and pleasures grounds among their three guiding principles in planning a railway line. The Basingstoke Canal Company went to considerable expense changing a line to avoid Tylney Hall, while in the original Newcastle and Carlisle Railway Act of 1829 even stationary engines were banned from coming within view of the Howards' castles at Corby and Naworth.[18] Lady Elizabeth Grosvenor, wife of the second Marquess of Westminster, greeted one proposal in a fashion which was probably not untypical when she wrote:

we are in a state of approaching frenzy from receiving by last night's post a prospectus of a railway from London to Exeter by Salisbury cutting our Motcombe property right through and going within sight of the house, which, of course, if carried into effect would force us to give up the place. Such aggressions are, I believe, common in this enlightened age. Is it really not enough to drive one mad? It is really outrageous and [my husband] is writing to try and protect ourselves against it and to say that the line should go south of Shaftesbury.

Ultimately the route was changed, and the railway passed a mile north of the house.[19] The Hampshire and Berkshire Junction Canal promoters lost their original bill because of landowner opposition, so that in advance of a second bill they altered the route to try to cut down on objectors. The Liverpool and Manchester Railway Company promoters followed a roughly similar course prior to introducing their second bill in 1826. The landed interest was appeased, even at the expense of the line's following a disadvantageous route.[20]

The types of pressure that landlords could bring to bear against the

---

[17] T. S. Willan, *River Navigation in England, 1600–1750* (1936), p. 36.

[18] Frank A. Sharman, 'The influence of landowners on route selection', *Journal of the Railway and Canal History Society*, 26 (1980), pp. 49–50; Ward, 'West Riding landowners and the railways', p. 242.

[19] Lady Elizabeth Grosvenor to the Countess of Sutherland, 1836, quoted in G. Huxley, *Lady Elizabeth and the Grosvenors* (Oxford, 1965), p. 129.

[20] Sharman, 'The influence of landowners on route selection', p. 50.

companies varied. According to a correspondent of the *Gentleman's Magazine*, writing in 1754, land was withheld from turnpike trusts to obstruct improvement:

if there be a necessity of a small strip of land to make a road more commodious, sometimes it is peremptorily refused, and if you would obtain it legally, it would cost twenty times as much as it is worth. If to obtain a short cut or avoid a morass, you want to pass through a field, you are generally refused, and put to three times as much expense as the thing is worth.[21]

Compulsory purchase was available to canal and railway companies, but they were loath to use these powers, and in any case landowners found other means of obstruction. One was to present counter-petitions to Parliament. During discussion of the Duke of Bridgewater's first bill for the Worsley-Manchester canal in 1759, a petition was presented asserting that the proposed waterway would be 'very prejudical to the respective lands and properties of the petitioners'. Bridgewater again ran into landowning opposition on his return to Parliament in 1762 for legislation permitting an extension of the navigation.[22] Devious parliament tactics became more difficult as standing orders were introduced to deal with local bills. Such rules were introduced for highway and turnpike bills in 1773, and they were designed to prevent abuses, to ensure that all interests were satisfied, and to help to provide a smooth passage for the bills.[23] Legal action was a second means of obstruction. When the Great Western Railway was announced, meetings were held in November and December 1833 at which local landowners agreed to take legal action to stop the scheme.[24] Even when a scheme was under way, legal niceties were invoked to hamper progress. One of Bridgewater's main protagonists was Sir Richard Brooke of Norton Priory. He tried to enforce a regulation in the Trent and Mersey Act of 1766 restraining Bridgewater from taking his canal within 360 yards of the house. Engineering difficulties made this stricture particularly irksome, and

[21] *Gentleman's Magazine*, 24 (1754), pp. 395–6.

[22] H. Malet, *Bridgewater: the Canal Duke* (Manchester, 1977), pp. 47, 68–77.

[23] Sheila Lambert, *Bills and Acts: legislative procedure in eighteenth-century England* (Cambridge, 1971), p. 170; Michael W. McCahill, *Order and Equipoise: the peerage and the House of Lords, 1783–1806* (1978), p. 108.

[24] Jackman, *The Development of Transport*, pp. 558–9.

Bridgewater had to seek parliamentary approval for a change in the regulations.[25]

Would-be promoters had to run the gauntlet of landowning opposition. When the London and Birmingham line was announced in 1830, objections were raised by owners anxious to defend their privacy, by others fearing for the coaching inns run by their tenants, and by yet others defending tenant-farming and canal investments.[26] However, the most damaging accusation was that the root cause of landowner opposition was financial.[27] The question of compensation was a sensitive one, and there seems little doubt that some landowners did ask for excessive payments. The Duke of Bridgewater paid Sir Richard Brooke £315 in 1772 for a parcel of land valued by Brooke's own assessors at £268, and four years later the two men agreed the route of the canal only after payment of £2000 in settlement. It was a sum Bridgwater regarded as 'considerable', and according to Thomas Gilbert, his land steward, it was a matter 'likely to be retained in his Grace's memory'. Nor was Brooke his only problem: an acre of land purchased for the Liverpool dock, in order to bring seagoing traffic on to the canal, reputedly cost £40,000.[28] Similarly notorious were a number of railway cases. The Eastern Counties Railway was reputed to have paid Lord Petre £120,000 for land worth only £5000, and other examples were reported to a select committee investigating compensation claims in 1845. Robert Stephenson complained, with reference to the Liverpool and Manchester line, that 'the charge for land was greatly augmented by the enormous and unreasonable compensation required by some proprietors beyond the correct value of the land.'[29]

Although it is difficult to distinguish large sums paid to obstreperous landowners from legitimate sums paid to compensate for

---

[25] R. B. Schofield, 'Bagshawe *v.* the Leeds and Liverpool Canal Company: a study in engineering history, 1790–99', *Bulletin of the John Rylands Library*, 59 (1976), pp. 188–225; Huntington Library, Ellesmere MSS, 10,318–10,328: Malet, *Bridgewater*, pp. 124–5.

[26] David Spring, 'English landowners and nineteenth-century industrialism', in *Land and Industry*, ed. J. T. Ward and R. G. Wilson (1971), p. 21.

[27] A fictional example was given in Benjamin Disraeli's *Sybil* (1845; Oxford, 1981), p. 101, where Lord Marney's wife claimed her husband opposed railways only until his terms were accepted by the companies involved.

[28] Malet, *Bridgewater*, pp. 80, 128–9; Huntington Library, Ellesmere MSS, 10,267, 10,268.

[29] Spring, 'English landowners and nineteenth-century industrialism', pp. 23–4; Jackman, *The Development of Transport*, p. 499; Kellett, *The Impact of Railways on Victorian Cities*, pp. 144–5.

a threatened interest, in general the evidence suggests that owners asked only for reasonable compensation and that the impression of widespread hostility may have arisen from a few well-publicized cases. Some owners certainly expected reasonable payment when their existing interests were threatened. The Milnes family of Fryston Hall in the West Riding demanded adequate compensation from the Great Northern because of the loss of business in their Great North Road coaching inns. In the same area the Ramsdens expected the Huddersfield and Manchester Railway Company to compensate them for the damage likely to be done to their wholly owned and profitable canal running between Hull, Huddersfield, Manchester and Liverpool.[30] Evidence given to the select committee which enquired into railway compensation in 1845 did not suggest a clear pattern. The solicitor for the South-East Counties Railway argued that large sums had been paid to overcome the opposition of some landowners, and on occasion considerable sums had been promised even before the legislation was passed. On the other hand, a land valuer from Kent knew of no cases where exorbitant sums had been given for land.[31] It seems likely that some smaller owners, often faced with the loss of a substantial proportion of their land, may have held out for anything up to twenty times the value, but that landowner extortion did not substantially increase the cost of railway construction. It was recognized in 1845 that

the price of land purchased, and the compensation for that which is injured, form together but a small proportion of the sum required for the construction of a railway, so that no apprehension need be entertained of discouraging their formation by calling upon the speculators to pay largely for the rights which they acquire over the property of others.[32]

In fact, during the first twenty-five years of construction from 1825 to 1850, when opposition was most apparent, land accounted for less than one-quarter of construction costs, which was surprising given the unfavourable terms on which the companies entered the market. With both canals and railways, high demands seem to have been a feature of

---

[30] Ward, 'West Riding landowners and the railways', p. 244; D. Wholmsley, 'A landed estate and the railway: Huddersfield, 1844–54', *Journal of Transport History*, 2 (1974), pp. 189–213.

[31] Parl. Papers, *Report of the Select Committee of the House of Lords on Compensation for Lands taken by Railways* (1845), vol. X, pp. 445, 460.

[32] Ibid., p. 420; Kellett, *The Impact of Railways on Victorian Cities*, pp. 156–8.

the early years of the movements, and exceptions rather than general rules.[33]

ACTIVE ARISTOCRATIC PARTICIPATION IN IMPROVEMENTS

By contrast with estate management and with efforts to develop industrial potential, aristocrats' involvement in communications did not usually face them with direct managerial decisions. Some sought to wield influence by having their own nominees appointed to the boards of commissioners established to oversee the scheme. The Leveson-Gowers and their agents were frequently named as trustees in Staffordshire Turnpike Acts, and in 1726 the Duke of Chandos sent his steward a list of twenty-one people he wanted to see made trustees of the Edgware turnpike. The steward was urged 'to use your endeavours to prevail with my friends'.[34] A few individuals played a formative role in improvements, particularly in regard to canals. The third Duke of Bridgewater, whose name is virtually snonymous with canal building in the eighteenth century, may well have set an example imitated much more widely. Despite problems with Parliament, with finance and with engineering, by 1763 Bridgewater was selling coal in Manchester transported via his canal. Flushed with this success, he proceeded to extend his navigation westwards into central Lancashire and south of the Mersey to the navigable Runcorn estuary. By then the Trent and Mersey Canal Company, which was largely financed by other landowners, some of whom were his relations, had followed Bridgewater's example to establish beyond doubt the profitability of canal construction. Others soon followed these pioneers. In the 1770s Sir Nigel Greasley cut a canal to carry coal from Apedale in Staffordshire to Newcastle under Lyme, and the Earl of Thanet built the Skipton Castle canal for moving lime and limestone to the Leeds and Liverpool Canal. Richard Bethell cut a small canal at Leven in the East Riding in 1802, and the Marquess of Stafford bore half the cost of an eight-mile canal across his property. The earls Fitzwilliam took an active interest in Yorkshire canal promotion, and the earls of Dudley similarly in the Black Country. The latter family were the moving force behind the Stourbridge Navigation, as well as being intimately connected with the

---

[33] Harold Pollins, 'A note on railway construction costs, 1825–50', *Economica*, 19 (1952), pp. 395–406; Kellett, *The Impact of Railways on Victorian Cities*, pp. 427–31.
[34] J. R. Wordie, *Estate Management in Eighteenth-Century England* (1982), p. 41; Huntington Library, ST 57, 28/126, Duke of Chandos to Mr Peters, 30 May 1726.

Dudley Castle canal and the Dudley Castle canal tunnel.[35]

Prominent coalowners who played a positive role in providing harbour facilities included the Lowthers at Whitehaven, the third Marquess of Londonderry at Seaham and the Butes in Cardiff. During the seventeenth century, the Lowthers monopolized the Whitehaven harbour developments, but in 1709 Sir James allowed control to pass to a board of trustees established under an Act of Parliament. Lowther nominated seven of the trustees (one-third), and also had a power of veto over their decisions. By underwriting the finances of harbour development he effectively protected himself from being outmanoeuvred by a combination of the coalmasters and tobacco merchants. When, in the 1740s, he clashed with the merchants, who wanted a deeper harbour for their larger vessels, Lowther successfully forced his rivals off the board. Seaham harbour was the Marquess of Londonderry's pet project during the 1820s and 1830s. He bought the estate in 1821 and founded the harbour seven years later as a new outlet for the increasing production of the Durham coalfield. John Buddle, his viewer and agent, believed the scheme would give Londonderry ascendancy over the other coalmasters because of Seaham's locational advantages over Sunderland. Plans were drawn by William Chapman, and after several false dawns the port was finally inaugurated in July 1831 when coal was loaded on to a new collier, the *Lord Seaham*. However, the new town on a grand scale which had also been envisaged failed to materialize, and profit forecasts also proved over-optimistic. The marquesses of Bute built the West Bute Dock in Cardiff during the 1820s and 1830s to encourage the burgeoning coal trade. Initially the leading ironmasters were reluctant to use the new facility; this threatened its viability, but the situation improved by the end of the 1840s and in the following decade it was even possible to construct a new dock. Although the scheme was a financial disappointment for the family, in the longer term the second marquess's initiative was crucial for developing Cardiff and the South Wales coal trade in relation to its major rivals, Newport and Swansea.[36]

---

[35] Malet, *Bridgewater*; G. E. Mingay, *English Landed Society in the Eighteenth Century* (1963), p. 198; J. T. Ward, *East Yorkshire Landed Estates in the Nineteenth Century* (York, 1967), p. 39; B. F. Buckham, 'The Fitzwilliams and the navigation of the Yorkshire Derwent', *Northern History*, 2 (1967), pp. 45–61; T. J. Raybould, *The Economic Emergence of the Black Country* (Newton Abbot, 1973), pp. 55–62.

[36] Beckett, *Coal and Tobacco*, pp. 158–71; R. W. Sturgess, *Aristocrat in Business: the third Marquis of Londonderry as coalowner and portbuilder* (Durham, 1975); John Davies, *Cardiff and the Marquesses of Bute* (Cardiff, 1981), ch. 7; M. J. Daunton, 'Aristocrats and traders: the Bute Docks, 1839–1914', *Journal of Transport History*, 3 (1975), pp. 65–85.

With railways, landowners were primarily active in promoting interests in which they had a specific concern. In Yorkshire, the fifth Earl Fitzwilliam was prepared to oppose any railway project he feared would interfere with his privacy or with the foxhunting at Milton House. By contrast, he was active in supporting local lines, particularly those which involved the movement of coal. When the prospectus for the South Yorkshire Coal Railway was published in 1845, Fitzwilliam added his support because the shareholders were locally connected, and the aim of the railway was stated in its title. Other West Riding landowners also helped to promote 'coal' branch lines, while the Dudley estate trustees were keen promoters of West Midlands railway developments in the 1840s for the same reason, and the Maryport–Carlisle line in Cumbria was run almost entirely by landed gentry and coalowners.[37]

One of the most obvious ways of indicating an interest in railway promotion was for a landowner to become a director. The desire to have an aristocrat at the head of a project was reflected in both canal and railway promotions, and among company chairmen in 1850 were the Earl of Burlington (Furness), the Earl of Carlisle (Malton and Driffield), the Earl of Yarborough (Manchester, Sheffield and Lincolnshire), the Earl of Lonsdale (Whitehaven Junction), the Earl of Powis (Shropshire Union Canal and Railway) and Lord Dacre (Roysten and Hitchen). Another forty peers, baronets and peers' sons also served on boards. It was not necessary for an aristocrat to be titled in order to become involved. Among the eight direcctors of the East Lincolnshire Railway Company were Charles Chaplin of Blankney, Sleaford, and George Heneage of Hainton Hall, Wragby. The chairman and deputy chairman of the Lancaster and Carlisle were both Cumbrian gentry, E. W. Hassell of Dalemain and Henry Howard of Greystoke Castle. Some aristocrats also ensured that their personal representatives were prominently placed on boards. It is noticeable, for example, that Joseph Paxton served on three company boards, all of them affecting the Duke of Devonshire's interests.[38]

Lending one's name was not the same as taking an active interest. Bagehot wrote scathingly of non-practical railway management, and Anthony Trollope levelled his biting sarcasm at aristocrats who sat on

---

[37] P. S. Bagwell, *The Transport Revolution from 1770* (1974), p. 96; Ward, 'West Riding landowners and the railways', p. 247; Graham Mee, *Aristocratic Enterprise: the Fitzwilliam industrial undertakings, 1795–1857* (1975), pp. 39–41; Raybould, *The Economic Emergence of the Black Country*, ch. 3.

[38] *Bradshaw's General Railway Directory* (1850), pp. 171–228.

boards without knowing anything of the business.[39] Although some men lent their name but did little else, equally clearly many aristocrats took a much more positive role. The third Duke of Buckingham became chairman of the London and North-Western Railway Company in 1853, the largest single railway system in Britain. His appointment was undoubtedly influenced by the company's desire for a 'name', but he played an active role in business, and also helped to promote local lines in Buckinghamshire.[40] Earl Fitzwilliam was a director of the South Yorkshire, Doncaster and Goole Railway for many years and chairman of the board in 1852, 1854 and 1857, and the third Marquess of Salisbury was an active chairman of the Great Eastern between 1868 and 1872. Salisbury took over an insolvent company determined to nurse it back to economic health, and he was quickly immersed in the details of the job. His correspondence and his speeches to shareholders' meetings make it clear that he had grasped the fundamentals of railway operation, and whatever the aim of the company in placing him in the chair he was much more than a dignified personage brought in to restore confidence.[41]

Financial provision was among the more important aristocratic roles in communications improvements. No shares were issued for road improvements, unlike canals and railways, on the grounds that turnpike trusts were supposedly temporary devices to maintain existing services. Consequently fixed capital was usually raised by interest-bearing mortgages secured on the proceeds of the gates. Also unlike canals and railways, the turnpikes did not usually require large capital sums. Prior to 1750 most of the lenders put in substantial sums of money and were trustees, but thereafter the division of loans into small sums brought in a greater proportion of money from shopkeepers and artisans. In general the contribution of landowners was rarely overshadowed by other groups; indeed, such was their sense of duty for maintaining the King's Highway that they continued to invest, even though few trusts offered a good return on capital.[42]

---

[39] Anthony Trollope, *The Way We Live Now* (1875; Oxford, 1982), vol. I, pp. 358 ff.

[40] F. B. Heath, 'Richard Grenville, third Duke of Buckingham and Chandos: a case study' (University of Southern California, Ph.D. thesis, 1959), ch. 3.

[41] Mee, *Aristocratic Enterprise*, p. 41; T. C. Barker, 'Lord Salisbury, chairman of the Great Eastern Railway, 1868–72', in *Business and Business Men: studies in business, economic and accounting history*, ed. S. Marriner (Liverpool, 1978), pp. 81–103; Ward, 'West Riding landowners and the railways', pp. 247–9.

[42] Albert, *The Turnpike Road System*, p. 103; G. G. Hopkinson, 'Road development in South Yorkshire and North Derbyshire, 1700–1850', *Transactions of the Hunter Archaeological Society*, 10 (1979), pp. 26–9.

Individuals took a financial stake in turnpike schemes for both industrial and personal reasons. Prominent coalowners included Sir Roger Newdigate, who invested in the Coventry–Hinckley turnpike, and Lord Dudley and Lord Gower, both of whom invested in West Midlands trusts during the 1770s and 1780s. Around Sheffield the Duke of Devonshire had shares in six different roads, the Duke of Norfolk in five, the Duke of Portland in three, the Duke of Leeds in two, the Earl of Holderness in two, and a number of other prominent local landowners in one. Sometimes landowners put up the majority of the finance. A trust established in 1809 to improve the road from the north end of Rotherham to Swinton was largely financed by Earl Fitzwilliam and his heir Lord Milton, while the Duke of Devonshire put up £6000 when the Sparrow Pit Trust was empowered to construct a new road west of Sheffield in 1812. Peerage support for a scheme could be sufficient to raise the money. Thus when the dukes of Devonshire and Norfolk gave their personal security that interest due on the Glossop turnpike would be met, investors who had been reluctant to finance the scheme came forward to provide the necessary capital.[43]

Although it is possible to find examples of landowner initiative and drive in establishing canal companies, at a general level their financial commitment was limited. River improvements were almost entirely financed by mercantile interests, and if landowners took a more positive role in canal construction the figures are likely to be distorted by the exceptional contributions of a few pioneers, including Bridgewater. J. R. Ward, in a study of fifty projects between 1755 and 1815, found that peers and gentry contributed 23 per cent of capital investment. The figure was higher than this down to 1780 (41 per cent), but lower at only 21.7 per cent for the later period. In this sample, landowner investment was hardly distinctive, particularly as it was mainly in short agricultural and mineral lines. Moreover, by contrast with roads, they seem to have been careful to assess likely profitability before investing. As a result, most canal companies drew their finance from a wide variety of sources, of which landowners were just one.[44]

The pattern was similar with harbour and railway developments. A few pioneers invested large sums of money, while a great many other

[43] Flinn, *The History of the British Coal Industry*, p. 148; Raybould, *The Economic Emergence of the Black Country*, ch. 3; Wordie, *Estate Management in Eighteenth-Century England*, p. 145; Hopkinson, 'Road development in South Yorkshire and North Derbyshire', pp. 25–6.

[44] Ward, *The Finance of Canal Building*; Malet, *Bridgewater*.

landowners had small but none the less significant financial interests. Londonderry invested £180,000 in Seaham during the 1820s and 1830s, while at the same time the Butes were pouring £350,000 into building Cardiff docks. Both families found themselves in deep financial difficulties. The dukes of Devonshire and Buccleuch were major investors at Barrow-in-Furness, and the fourth Duke of Northumberland put £10,000 into the Northumberland docks during the 1850s.[45] In other cases the risks were more carefully distributed. Sir James Lowther contributed only 18 per cent of the capital raised under the terms of the Whitehaven Harbour Acts of 1709 and 1712, but, by advancing working capital from time to time to ensure that wages were paid and materials purchased, he effectively underwrote developments.[46] The ill-fated Grimsby Haven Company, which built an unsuccessful new dock in the port around 1800, was largely a speculation of landowners and rich farmers. Whereas merchants contributed only 5.6 per cent of the subscribed capital, thirty-two known landowners and farmers put up £39,207, or 65.4 per cent. Many of these men, including the Earl of Yarborough, who made the largest single investment of £3215, were owners of land on the North Lincolnshire Wolds, and they saw Grimsby as a point of trade for the produce of their estates, which were being rapidly transformed by the techniques of the agricultural revolution. As it transpired, the lack of back-carriage turned out to be critical, and Grimsby was not destined for growth until the later 1840s, when once again the earls of Yarborough were in the forefront of change.[47] During the 1790s, the 120 shares in the Hull Dock Company were held by a total of seventy-nine individuals, of whom forty were designated esquires. By 1813, when the number of shares had risen to 180, 132 individuals held shares or parts of shares, including seventy-six designated as esquires, Sir Christopher Sykes of Sledmere and Lord William Beauclerk of Redburn. The chairman that year was Thomas Thompson, Esq., MP for Hull. By 1830 shares had been split to the extent that there were now 229 holders, out of whom 105 were esquires. Shares were also held in the names of Sir M. M. Sykes of

---

[45] Sturgess, *Aristocrat in Business*, p. 76, and 'The Londonderry Trust, 1819–54', *Archaeologia Aeliana*, 5th ser., 10 (1982), pp. 179–92; Davies, *Cardiff and the Marquesses of Bute*, ch. 7; Spring, 'English landowners and nineteenth-century industrialism', pp. 44–5. Northumberland only escaped the fate of a Bute on the advice of his agent: F. M. L. Thompson, 'English landed society in the nineteenth century', in *The Power of the Past*, ed. P. Thane *et al.* (Cambridge, 1984), pp. 204–5.

[46] Beckett, *Coal and Tobacco*, p. 162.

[47] Jackson, *Grimsby and the Haven Company*, pp. 28–33.

Sledmere, the 'Countess of St Antonio', and Lords Amelius and Frederick Beauclerk.[48]

Pioneer aristocratic railway investors included the dukes of Buccleuch and Devonshire, who jointly advanced £30,000 of the initial share capital for the Furness Railway in 1844. Among West Riding landowners signing subscription contracts in 1845 were the Marquess and Marchioness of Ailesbury (£59,333) and the Wickham family (£33,635); while the following year they were joined by – among others – E. B. Beaumont of Finningley Park (£10,750) and Ralph Creyke (£19,375). Many subscriptions were far smaller than these examples, and in any case the sums were not necessarily a reliable guide to actual investment. However, Joseph Dent of Ribston invested around £31,380 between 1843 and 1852 in eleven companies, and the Ferrand family held shares in the Great Western, ten other railway companies and eight canal companies.[49] Elsewhere peers and gentry held 40 per cent of the nominal capital in the Liverpool and Manchester line in 1826, and 43 per cent by 1845, although this figure was inflated because the Marquess of Stafford alone held one-fifth of the shares. Mineral lines were particularly attractive to landowning capital. Investment in these lines almost certainly outstripped land-lords' concern for trunk lines during the 1830s and 1840s. From 1830 onwards, peers and gentry were the largest investors in the Leicester and Swannington line – the first in the East Midlands – with 41 per cent of the nominal capital. More generally, most companies soon developed a widely distributed shareholders' register, reflecting the overwhelming importance of capital from the manufacturing and commercial sector. The most comprehensive study of investment has shown that over the period 1820–44 peers and gentry contributed about 28 per cent of the nominal capital, with a general tendency for their contribution to increase through time. They provided 20 per cent of the nominal capital for the Grand Junction Railway in 1833, the figure rising to 34 per cent by 1845; 16 per cent for the London and Birmingham in 1833, rising to 31 per cent in 1837; and 27 per cent in the London and Southampton in 1834, rising to 40 per cent in 1839. Just occasionally their interest declined. In the Great North of England, for example, peers and gentry held 24 per cent of the nominal capital in 1836, but only 9 per cent in 1845.[50] Overall, it

---

[48] Information taken from printed shareholders' lists for the Hull Dock Company. No Countess of St Antonio can be traced in the *Complete Peerage*. I should like to thank Dr Joyce Bellamy for supplying me with copies of these lists.

[49] Ward, 'West Riding landowners and the railways', pp. 245–6.

[50] Floud and McCloskey (eds), *The Economic History of Britain*, vol. I, p. 233; M. C. Reed, *Investment in Railways in Britain, 1820–1844* (Oxford, 1975); S. A.

seems that the majority of capital came from trade and industrial interests, with a much smaller proportion from land. However, the aristocratic role increased through time, particularly in the post-1850 infilling period, when branch lines were carried into predominantly agricultural areas.

In these activities many aristocrats found themselves with overlapping and sometimes conflicting interests. The Dudleys were involved with roads, canals and railways in the West Midlands; Lord Londonderry built both a harbour and a railway; and the dukes of Devonshire were concerned in both railway and port development in Furness. In Yorkshire, William Aldam was a railway company chairman and frequent investor who used his position as MP for Leeds between 1841 and 1847 to help push through legislation, and to sit on many railway committees. In Yorkshire he attended board meetings, examined tunnels, planned stations and analysed accounts.[51] Conflicting interests were a problem for the Leveson-Gowers. They began to be concerned in turnpike road and canal building schemes around 1750, and in 1803 the family benefited from inheriting the third Duke of Bridgewater's estates. The property came to the second Marquess of Stafford for his lifetime, with descent to his second son Francis (later Earl of Ellesmere). In the 1820s Stafford found himself called upon to take some delicate decisions. The Liverpool and Manchester Railway Company was established in 1824, and represented a clear challenge to water transportation. The canal companies closed ranks and attempted to extend their facilities in order to appease public opinion. When the first Railway Bill was defeated in 1826, Stafford invested £58,000 in improving the Duke of Bridgewater's canal, and he also took 200 shares in the proposed Birmingham–Liverpool Junction Canal. Later that year, however, he decided on a policy change. Only three weeks after being called upon to support local canal owners in opposing the proposed Birmingham and Liverpool Railway, he bought a thousand shares in the Liverpool and Manchester. This was an investment of £100,000 which gave him one-fifth of the total shares, and helped to push up their purchase price by 50 per cent. It was a crucial breakthrough for the railways, since it virtually guaranteed their parliamentary success, and the result was the legislation of 1826. During 1827 both the railway and the Birmingham–Liverpool Canal were started, and the success of the Rainhill trials in 1829 helped to

---

Broadbridge, 'The sources of railway share capital', in *Railways in the Victorian Economy* ed. M. C. Reed (Newton Abbot, 1969), pp. 184–211.

[51] J. T. Ward, 'The squire as businessman: William Aldam of Frickley Hall (1813–1890)', *Transactions of the Hunter Archaeological Society*, 8 (1962), pp. 196–217.

ensure the importance of rail transport and to threaten canals. Stafford's own interests appeared almost to be competing with one another, although his own view was that by influencing railway development he could prevent the canal interests from being neglected. At his death shortly after being raised to the dukedom of Sutherland in 1833 the estate was divided. His railway interests descended to the second duke, while under the terms of the Bridgewater will the canal passed to his second son. Potentially the brothers' interests appeared likely to clash, but they found it possible to work in unison to facilitate the continued profitability of canals. Collusion survived until 1840, when a rift was opened by the apparent success of the canal in restraining railway profits. However, the canal continued to be profitable for much of the nineteenth century.[52]

ARISTOCRATS AND COMMUNICATIONS: PARLIAMENTARY LEGISLATION

Conflicting interests could also occur in the parliamentary roles that landowners played in regard to communications improvements. The trusts and joint-stock companies established to run turnpike roads and canal, railway and dock schemes all required legislation, and to this end promoters needed to ensure the support of local MPs and peers if their petitions and bills were to have a reasonable chance of success. MPs usually regarded it as their duty to promote and support local bills, and there was electoral mileage to be made from steering the necessary enabling legislation through Parliament. During the 1750s the struggle for political control of Northampton was linked with a scheme to make the river Nene navigable to coal vessels, and the candidates gave lock gates rather than financial bribes. This pattern was set at the 1759 by-election by Frederic Montagu, and continued at the 1768 general election when Lord Halifax claimed the credit for passing the 1756 River Bill. In the end seven locks downstream from the town were built with money provided either by local grandees or their protégés.[53]

The need for support from local MPs and peers was imperative if a bill was to have a smooth passage through both houses. Sir James Lowther, who became a veteran campaigner for such bills, cut his teeth

[52] Wordie, *Estate Management in Eighteenth-Century England*, pp. 142 ff.; Richards, *The Leviathan of Wealth*, pp. 43–146.

[53] V. A. Hatley, 'Locks, lords and coal: a study in eighteenth-century Northamptonshire history', *Northamptonshire Past and Present*, 6 (1980), pp. 207–18.

on the 1705 Parton Harbour Bill. His father, Sir John Lowther, opposed the setting up of a pier for coal sales, only two miles to the north of Whitehaven, but neither father nor son was in Parliament when an attempt was made to secure legislation in 1705. Throughout the autumn James Lowther was busy canvassing parliamentary support, and on 8 November he told his father he had spoken to 100 MPs. Clearly, however, he was at a disadvantage, since the bill's proposer, Thomas Lamplugh, was the sitting MP for Cockermouth. When the petition for a bill was presented in December, Lowther was in the gallery, but by early January he was desperate, telling his father's steward he was forced to make 'use of anything that had a colour'. His father's untimely death later that month forced him to travel north to Whitehaven, but only after informing the Bishop of Carlisle that he would 'leave the cause of the new haven at Parton to the mercy of the Parliament'.[54] The bill passed, and it was this chastening experience which persuaded Lowther to stand for the county seat in 1708. Later he was to tell his steward that he sat in Parliament 'to make my affairs easier at Whitehaven', and it was certainly the springboard for piloting through Whitehaven Harbour Bills in 1709, 1712 and 1740, and two more for Parton – to which he became reconciled – in 1725 and 1732. On each occasion he strove to ensure sympathetic committees, and spoke in favour of the projects. Private bills of this kind were a time-consuming exercise. In 1753, at the age of eighty and in poor health, Lowther was busy steering through half a dozen turnpike bills. Nor was he alone. Lord Folkestone's diary for March and April 1774 makes no reference to the important American debates, concentrating instead on two private bills he was sponsoring, while in 1813 Samuel Whitbread actively promoted the proposed Bedford canal, because as the local MP he believed it was his duty to act as requested by his constituents.[55]

Preliminary negotiations were vital if bills were not to be emasculated or even blocked. Turnpike schemes in South Yorkshire almost invariably required the Marquess of Rockingham's support, while as projects multiplied different landowners' interests were affected. In 1801 Earl Fitzwilliam was canvassed by the Greenhill

---

[54] Carlisle RO, D/Lons/W, James Lowther to Sir John Lowther, 8 November, 6 December 1705, to William Gilpin, 1 January 1706; Clyve Jones and Geoffrey Holmes (eds), *The London Diaries of William Nicolson, Bishop of Carlisle, 1702–1718* (Oxford, 1985), p. 354.

[55] J. V. Beckett, 'A back-bench MP in the eighteenth century: Sir James Lowther of Whitehaven', *Parliamentary History*, 1 (1982), pp. 91–3; Lambert, *Bills and Acts*, p. 167n.; Roger Fulford, *Samuel Whitbread, 1764–1815* (1967), pp. 215–16.

Moor Trust to support the turnpiking of a road into Sheffield. Unfortunately the trustees had fallen foul of the Duke of Norfolk, whose own interests were threatened, and an acceptable compromise had to be found between the different interests. A scheme to turnpike the road from Sheffield to Budby, on the main Worksop–Kelham road in Nottinghamshire, was opposed in the 1780s by the Duke of Portland, and his interest was such that the bill was defeated. The Berkshire and Hampshire Junction Canal Bill failed in Parliament as a result of objections from local landowners, and a similar fate befell the first bill presented by the London and Birmingham Railway Company.[56]

To prevent such problems from occurring, it was in the interests of promoters to nip potential trouble in the bud at an early stage. Various techniques were used. The agent for the Kennet and Avon Canal Bill utilized a house from which he could 'waylay members on the way to the House', and when he suspected concerted opposition he tipped off Lords Ailesbury and Moira to assemble peerage votes, thereby to ensure a safe passage through the upper house.[57] Some promoters preferred the more direct approach, hence the reservation in 1792 of £15,000 of shares in the Ashby Canal, 'to be distributed or disposed of as occasion may require during the progress of the bill in Parliament'.[58] Above all, however, it was the preparatory work which was vital, and this can be demonstrated in regard to the Trent and Mersey Canal promotion of 1766. A major aim of the scheme was to provide transport facilities for West Midlands industrialists, none more so than Josiah Wedgwood, whose pottery fortune depended on its successful promotion. Among the initiators was Samuel Garbett, a leading Birmingham industrialist who accumulated considerable experience of parliament lobbying. He wrote to the Earl of Huntingdon in the following terms:

I have the pleasure to acquaint your Lordship that . . . the principal potters of Staffordshire and the Mayor and Corporation of Newcastle under Lyme have applied to Lord Gower who hath warmly promised them his assistance as well as good wishes, and if by this means the Duke of Bridgewater should be engaged in our favour we should hope no frightful opposition would be given

---

[56] Hopkinson, 'Road development in South Yorkshire and North Derbyshire', pp. 23–4; Sharman, 'The influence of landowners on route selection', p. 48.

[57] McCahill, *Order and Equipoise*, p. 102.

[58] Sharman, 'The influence of landowners on route selection', p. 50; Ward, *The Finance of Canal Building*, p. 160. The length and complexity of parliamentary debates is demonstrated in regard to the River Weaver navigation (1699–1727) in Lambert, *Bills and Acts*, pp. 153–66.

to us, provided we could obtain his Majesty's recommendation, but without hopes of that it requires more of the spirit of enterprise than even I have.[59]

Later that year James Brindley informed the Duke of Bridgewater that he had dined with Wedgwood and Lord Crewe. Wedgwood had come 'to solicit Lord Crewe in favour of the Staffordshire canal . . . and on Friday set out to wait on Mr Egerton to solicit him'. He also canvassed Bridgewater.[60] Earl Gower allowed Trentham Hall to be used for meetings of industrialists and landowners discussing the scheme, and when he attended such a gathering in person at the end of December 1765 he was asked to put himself at the head of the scheme as the application for legislation went to Parliament. Samuel Garbett's argument that the scheme arose from the Duke of Bridgewater's sucess implies that the promoters thought having an aristocrat in the lead would help them to acquire an Act. This groundwork certainly bore fruit. Not only was the legislation obtained, but subscribers included Bridgewater and Gower with £2000 apiece, and Samuel Egerton of Tatton Park with £3000. By 1782 Egerton, the selfsame man canvassed by Wedgwood, and both cousin and guardian to Bridgewater, had invested £42,750.[61]

THE FINANCIAL REWARD

The financial return on communications investments varied considerably and involved both the capital sum landlords acquired from selling land to the companies, and the dividends on investments. Some landowners did well. The care taken by the Ramsden family trustees in Huddersfield enabled them to pocket a total of around £87,000 from the sale of their canal and adjacent land to the Huddersfield and Manchester Railway and Canal Company. Part of this was used to buy further property, and part to promote improvements in the town.[62] By contrast, worry over the success of his dock scheme in Cardiff may have contributed to the heart disease

---

[59] Huntington Library, Hastings MSS, HA 3350, Samuel Garbett to the Earl of Huntingdon, 17 April 1765.

[60] Huntington Library, Ellesmere MSS, 10,261, James Brindley to the Duke of Bridgewater, 21 December 1765(?); Malet, *Bridgewater*, p. 110.

[61] Wordie, *Estate Management in Eighteenth-Century England*, pp. 143–4; Ward, *The Finance of Canal Building*, pp. 28–9. It is possible that Wedgwood and Garbett were preaching to the converted and that Earl Gower had already decided to support such a scheme: Malet, *Bridgewater*, p. 107.

[62] Whomsley, 'A landed estate and the railway'.

which killed the second Marquess of Bute at the age of fifty-four, and the Duke of Bridgewater also had to incur enormous debts before his canal became a paying proposition. From the commencement of his activities in 1759 the debt grew remorselessly to peak in 1787 at £346,806. From then onwards it began to decline, and by January 1801 it stood at £253,732. Thereafter it fell rapidly, and the first profits were recorded in 1806 – three years after the duke died, with £160,000 still outstanding.[63]

Anyone depending on the profits of communications investments found that their returns fluctuated. The Ramsdens were making around £5000 yearly from their canal by 1841, while on the Derwent in Yorkshire the Fitzwilliams leased out the navigation for £1300 in 1782, rising to £3000 by the early nineteenth century. This system was abandoned in 1807, and over the period 1811–34 profits were in the range of £3000–£5000. For canals generally, it was calculated in 1825 that £13,205,117 capital yielded dividends averaging 5.75 per cent, and that £3,734,910 was paying nothing at all.[64] Railways may have been more reliable. The Marquess of Stafford invested a total of £328,125 in the Liverpool and Manchester line, and although the family later sold some of this the second Duke of Sutherland held £205,000 railway stock (at par) in 1846. At the prevailing market price this was worth £526,593, and by the later 1840s railway dividends represented about 12 per cent of his total annual income.[65]

The aristocratic contribution to communications improvements was far from consistent. For every Bridgewater, Stafford, Londonderry and Bute, there was a score of hostile landlords more anxious to protect their private interests than to promote the common good. On the other hand, while a few were not to be convinced, and a number sought to feather their own nests through the sums they demanded from canal and railway promoters, the majority came to appreciate the advantages they stood to reap from improved communications. Coalowners quickly recognized which way the wind blew, but landlords without

---

[63] John Davies, 'Aristocratic town makers and the coal metropolis: the Marquesses of Bute and Cardiff, 1776–1947', in *Patricians, power and politics in nineteenth-century towns*, ed. David Cannadine (Leicester, 1982), p. 32; Malet, *Bridgewater*, pp. 178–80. The canal remained profitable for much of the nineteenth century: Richards, *The Leviathan of Wealth*, p. 143.

[64] Whomsley, 'A landed estate and the railway', p. 190; Duckham, 'The Fitzwilliams and the navigation of the Yorkshire Derwent', pp. 49–51; Ward, *The Finance of Canal Building*, p. 176.

[65] Wordie, *Estate Management in Eighteenth-Century England*, p. 154; Richards, *The Leviathan of Wealth*, pp. 145–6.

mineral resources were slower to grasp the potential benefits to agriculture, and into whichever category they fell aristocrats tended to have a clear sense of priorities. They accepted that the King's Highway was the responsibility of those who governed, hence the high profile they adopted in regard to turnpike schemes. Canals, railways and docks were artificial creations, and since they were designed largely for commercial reasons landlords left the financing of these projects to the commercial classes. Their own interest was primarily in developing links into the main systems, although when they began to appreciate the financial returns the level of investment grew.

To measure the aristocratic contribution purely in financial terms is misleading. Peers and gentry assembled in Parliament played a vital role in seeing that the necessary legislation was passed. If some had to be encouraged – perhaps by a directorship, or a line rerouting – without their support, schemes were unlikely to pass the first hurdle. Consequently, emphasis on landlord hostility, or on extortion from the companies, or on the relative lack of investment and the holding of nominal directorships, tends to obscure the fact that some invested heavily, took their board responsibilities seriously, and used their parliamentary weight to bring putative schemes to fruition. Overall it is an exaggeration to suggest that aristocratic initiative was vital for bringing about the transport revolution. More accurately, the role was to facilitate the revolution; aristocrats were willing to promote legislation, to accept reasonable compensation, and to give their support to proposals without being bribed. The few exceptions to these rules have tended to distort the whole picture; in general terms the English aristocracy accepted the need for change, and played an important role in bringing it about.

Chapter Eight

The Aristocracy and the Towns

A major concomitant of industrialization was urban growth. London, the Great Wen, expanded remorselessly throughout the period, and in size and influence was a case apart. During the second half of the eighteenth century a string of provincial towns began to experience marked growth, and this trend continued throughout the nineteenth century. At the end of the seventeenth century no more than 16 per cent of the population lived in settlements of 5000 or more. London, already in a class of its own, had a population of around half a million, while the next largest towns were probably Norwich with 30,000 people and Bristol with 20,000. Possibly only four other towns had populations exceeding 10,000. From about 1750, growth began to accelerate rapidly. London reached nearly one million by 1800; Birmingham doubled its population between 1760 and 1800; Manchester's size trebled in the last three decades of the century; and Liverpool's population grew from about 22,000 in 1750 to nearer 80,000 in 1800. But these developments proved to be only a beginning. In 1800 only fifteen towns (apart from London) had populations exceeding 20,000, but a century later this figure had risen to 185. During the 1820s, Sheffield, Birmingham, Manchester, Leeds and Liverpool all grew by 40 per cent. Bradford's population growth did not fall below 50 per cent in any of the decades 1811–51, and over the period 1801–1901 its numbers rose from 13,000 to 280,000. Spectacular growth rates were also recorded in Birmingham (71,000 to 760,000 over the century), Manchester (75,000 to 645,000), Sheffield (46,000 to 381,000) and Liverpool (80,000 to 685,000).[1]

[1] Peter Clark and Paul Slack, *English Towns in Transition, 1500–1700* (Oxford, 1976), p. 83; P. J. Corfield, *The Impact of English Towns, 1700–1800* (Oxford, 1982), pp. 8–11; C. M. Law, 'Some notes on the urban population of England and Wales in the eighteenth century', *Local Historian*, 10 (1972), pp. 13–26; E. A. Wrigley, 'A

Behind these stark figures lay a complex interplay of forces. London apart, the significant towns of the seventeenth century were not always the fastest growing of the nineteenth. Norwich and York, two of the largest seventeenth-century towns, were left far behind, not merely by the great industrial centres but even by new towns such as Middlesbrough. Moreover, it was not merely industry and trade which prospered, since a collection of new resort towns burgeoned in the nineteenth century. Although it was not always possible to be certain where growth would take place, those who owned land in the vicinity of an expanding town clearly had an important role to play. A circular sent to 261 provincial towns in England and Wales in the 1880s revealed that in 69 cases greater landowners were mentioned as considerable ground landlords (with many appearing more than once), and gentry in 34 instances. What was meant by considerable must have varied. At one extreme were a small number of towns which had a single landlord owning all or most of the site, including Whitehaven, Huddersfield, Eastbourne, Skegness and Bexhill. Grading down from these were towns where one or more owners held large blocks of land, such as the dukes of Norfolk in Sheffield, and the Calthorpes in Birmingham. Finally, at the other extreme were towns in which property was divided. More than half the towns responding to the 1886 survey had no substantial ground landlord, and among places developed on small sites belonging to a myriad of freeholders were Bath, Leeds and Bradford.[2]

The landowners were the vital pivot on which the course of urban development turned. An obstreperous owner could delay or even prevent improvement. The slow growth of Stamford in the nineteenth century reflected the Cecil family's desire to control all the land prior to enclosure, which came only in the 1870s.[3] By contrast, an enthusiast could take a leading role in development. This was not a particularly popular option, with the exception of a few outstanding cases such as the Lowthers in Whitehaven, the Ramsdens in Huddersfield and the Devonshires in Eastbourne. In between these poles lay two options. The first was to sell the freehold of the land to a developer or builder. Approximately half the building land in

---

simple model of London's importance in changing English society and economy, 1650– 1750', *Past and Present*, 37 (1967), pp. 44–70; David Cannadine, *Lords and Landlords: the aristocracy and the towns, 1770–1967* (Leicester, 1980), p. 26.

[2] Parl. Papers, *Report of the Royal Commission on Town Holdings* (1887), vol. XIII, pp. 677–812.

[3] Stuart Elliott, 'The Cecil family and the development of 19th century Stamford', *Lincolnshire History and Archaeology*, 4 (1969), pp. 23–31.

Nottingham, Hull, Portsmouth, Leeds, Leicester and Brighton was sold outright to builders in this way. The second, and by far the most popular, option was to grant ground-rent leases to builders and developers. In London, · ninety-nine-year leases were commonly granted, and time leases were also used in Bath and Sheffield. In Manchester and Bristol, and also to some extent in Bath, sales in perpetuity for a fee-farm rent were common; these gave the builder indefinite use of the land while he continued to pay the rent. Three-life leases were granted in Liverpool and Plymouth.[4]

The motives for ground-rent leasing were complex. Apart from the lucrative financial spin-offs, owners saw these leases as a means of fulfilling their duty both to the community – by taking an interest in the course of development – and to the family. The leasehold system maintained the idea that the ground landlord should pass on the value of his property to future generations at least unimpaired if not enhanced, whereas a grant in freehold devalued the actual estate and surrendered decision-making about its future use. Against these advantages were two drawbacks. First, the lease system acquired the reputation of having produced tyrannical landlord control over urban development. The great urban landowners were seen as dictatorial barons, particularly in the way that they had developed London's West End to their own advantage.[5] Second, estate settlements often precluded owners from taking this course of action. Entails normally restricted leases to no more than twenty-one years, and such a short term was unattractive to builders. Private legislation was a way of surmounting such difficulties. The Duke of Bedford obtained a private Act to begin developing Bedford Square in 1776. Similar legislation to release land for development in Birmingham between the 1740s and 1780s was largely responsible for the town's growth in that period. The fourth Duke of Newcastle needed private legislation in 1808 to permit the development of his Nottingham estates, and Lady Windsor obtained an Estate Act in 1857 to allow her to sell land and raise

---

[4] C. W. Chalklin, *The Provincial Towns of Georgian England, 1740–1820* (1974), pp. 60–1, 65; David Spring, *The English Landed Estate in the Nineteenth Century: its administration* (1963), p. 13. Contemporary figures suggest that at the end of the nineteenth century rather more than half the urban population of England and Wales lived under ordinary freehold tenure, a further 5 per cent (mainly in Lancashire and Cheshire) lived under freehold subject to chief rents, and about 40 per cent of the population were affected by leasehold tenures. Of the latter, about 10 per cent were on short leases (ninety-nine years or less), and the rest on longer leases: Dennis R. Mills, *Lord and Peasant in Nineteenth-Century Britain* (1980), p. 195.

[5] Frank Banfield, *The Great Landlords of London* (1890), pp. 111–12.

money to develop the Grangetown district of Cardiff. However, some land was deliberately kept from development. In 1801 the second Earl of Dartmouth left a restrictive will preventing any of his Sandwell Park estate near West Bromwich from being let on building leases exceeding sixty years. The agent's view was that no one could be found to take the land on these terms, and vigorous urban speculation began only after 1861. Similarly, by his will of 1821 Sir Thomas Maryon Wilson effectively halted the profitable development of his Hampstead estate by preventing freehold land from entering the building market for fifty years.[6]

Great landowners were heavily involved in London's development between the seventeenth and nineteenth centuries, and elsewhere they were particularly prominent in the period 1770–1870. Possibly their most important contribution to major provincial towns was completed by about 1820, and in some cases 1840, after which they began to withdraw. Thereafter it was only in the seaside resorts that they remained dominant, largely because this phase of town growth was characterized by single-owner initiative and because it was dependent on the railway. However, the critical question concerns how much real influence they wielded in town development. The older view of the landowners as feudal barons and moguls has increasingly been tempered by emphasis on the limitations imposed through topography and market forces. Landowners who controlled part or all of a site usually took an active interest in laying down rules and conditions governing its planning and development. Moreover, it is also clear that, in places which had a fragmented land pattern, overall planning was almost impossible. This was the case, for example, in Leeds and Bradford, where street layouts were uncoordinated, and house and plot shapes

[6] Ken Brand, 'The Park estate, Nottingham: the development of a nineteenth-century fashionable suburb', *Transactions of the Thoroton Society*, 88 (1984), p. 58; M. J. Daunton, 'Suburban development in Cardiff: Grangetown and the Windsor Estate, 1857–75', *Morgannwg*, 16 (1972), p. 55; Chalklin, *The Provincial Towns of Georgian England*, pp. 70, 91 ff.; R. W. Sturgess, 'Landownership, mining and urban development in nineteenth-century Staffordshire', in *Land and Industry*, ed. J. T. Ward and R. G. Wilson (1971), pp. 175–6; F. M. L. Thompson, *Hampstead: building a borough, 1650–1964* (1974), p. 130; Trevor Raybould, 'Aristocratic landowners and the industrial revolution: the Black Country experience, c. 1760–1840', *Midland History*, 9 (1984), p. 79. Disentangling motives is always a problem, and some landowners may have used their settlements as an excuse when in practice they had no intention of building. This could have been what happened at Sandwell: Sir John Habakkuk, 'The contribution of landowners to economic and social change', Ford Lecture, University of Oxford, 22 February 1985.

were made to fit within existing boundaries.[7] Yet considerable doubt remains about how successfully landowners were able to enforce their schemes.

The problem for the landowner did not lie in drawing up the ground-rules. Indeed, the preference for ground-rent leasing is indicative of a desire to control site development by laying out streets, providing amenities and imposing building restrictions. Sir John Lowther commissioned plans in the 1680s whereby his new town of Whitehaven was laid out to a gridiron pattern of streets; and the second Marquess of Bute used his landed control to plan the growth of Cardiff.[8] Laying down the rules was one thing; enforcing them was an entirely different exercise. Although Sir John Lowther's gridiron plan at Whitehaven is still visible on the ground today – suggesting a lasting influence – many of his building regulations were tacitly ignored from within a few years of his death in 1706. Overcrowding led to infilling in gardens, and the lack of a suitable form of town government ensured that efforts to enforce the rules met with only limited success. Although the Ramsdens never enjoyed absolute control of the land at Huddersfield, they owned enough to expect the dominant say in development. Rapid growth in the later eighteenth century under the influence of the third Sir John Ramsden was followed by several decades during which the family failed to exercise their powers in regard to building control. When they did reassert themselves after 1840, the terms were such that builders looked to acquire their land from any other owner than the Ramsdens. For thirty years they effectively priced working-class families out of the new homes market,

---

[7] M. J. Mortimore, 'Landownership and economic growth in Bradford and its environs in the West Riding conurbation, 1850–1900', *Transactions of the Institute of British Geographers*, 46 (March 1969), pp. 105–19; D. Ward, 'The pre-urban cadaster and the urban pattern of Leeds', *Annals of the Association of American Geographers*, 52 (1962), pp. 151–65. Landowner control has been much debated: see David Cannadine, 'Victorian cities: how different?', *Social History*, 4 (1977), pp. 457–82; M. J. Daunton, 'The building cycle and the urban fringe in Victorian cities: a comment', *Journal of Historical Geography*, 4 (1978), pp. 175–81; J. W. R. Whitehand, 'The building cycle and the urban fringe in Victorian cities: a reply', *Journal of Historical Geography*, 4 (1978), pp. 181–91; R. G. Rodger, 'The building cycle and the urban fringe in Victorian cities: another comment', *Journal of Historical Geography*, 5 (1979), pp. 72–8; Jane Springett, 'Landowners and urban development: the Ramsden Estate and nineteenth-century Huddersfield', *Journal of Historical Geography*, 8 (1982), pp. 129–44.

[8] J. V. Beckett, *Coal and Tobacco: the Lowthers and the economic development of West Cumberland, 1660–1760* (Cambridge, 1981), ch. 7; John Davies, *Cardiff and the Marquesses of Bute* (Cardiff, 1981), pp. 199–203.

and it was only in 1885 that they allowed smaller houses to be built on their land – at which point they had to accept the developers' terms.[9]

When landowners controlled a single site within a growing town, problems arose because they inclined towards promoting middle-class residential areas. Given the opportunity of helping to mould the new urban environment, landed magnates had two main considerations. Their personal predilection was to provide housing for the most important, wealthy and influential townspeople. In addition, their financial instincts favoured middle-class housing because it was likely to be maintained in good order, and to have a higher long-term value. Consequently the aristocracy were predominantly to be found associated with 'west ends', from the achievement *par excellence* in London, to a series of lesser provincial imitations. The Duke of Newcastle's Park estate in Nottingham was arguably the most successful of these because it was a small development. Elsewhere topography and market forces tended to ensure that on larger and less well situated sites 'west end' schemes did not always prosper. In Sheffield, for example, the location of the Duke of Norfolk's Brightside property worked against its becoming a middle-class areaa. No one could prevent the landowner from laying out the site, but the social tone tended to reflect market forces rather than aristocratic desire.[10]

LONDON

In order to examine the aristocratic role in more detail, these trends can be looked at in relation to urban developments in London, in some of the growing provincial cities, and in the resorts. Aristocratic influence can be seen in its clearest form in London. The East End, where many of the landholdings were fragmented, became predominantly a lower-class housing area, but on the larger aristocratic holdings of the West End high-quality housing was erected. Clearly this was what the aristocrats wanted, but they were also fortunate in the location of their property. The use of coal for domestic purposes brought smog conditions for many months of the year, and encouraged London's wealthier inhabitants to move westwards, since for three-quarters of the year this was the direction of the prevailing winds. In addition, the majority of their land lay ideally situated between Westminster and the City, permitting easy access to both, although in

[9] Springett, 'Landowners and urban development'.
[10] Cannadine, *Lords and Landlords*, pp. 395–416; 'Victorian cities', pp. 457–82.

the longer run the middle classes moved even further westward. Consequently market forces favoured the aristocrats, and it seems likely that London evolved as much for topographical and fashionable reasons as for the successful implementation of an aristocratic masterplan.[11]

The demand for high-quality housing began in the seventeenth century, much of it emanating from semi-resident aristocrats who preferred to spend their time in London living in the West End rather than in the merchant-dominated City. Initially the great aristocrats lived in palaces along the Strand, with courtiers, gentry and professionals in Lincoln's Inn Fields, Covent Garden and St Martin's Lane. Covent Garden, laid out by Inigo Jones for the Earl of Bedford in the 1630s, was one of the first planned schemes for high-class housing development. After 1660 the aristocracy began the first of a series of movements westwards and northwards away from the ever-encroaching City. New developments included the Earl of Southampton's Bloomsbury Square and the Earl of St Albans's St James's Square, as well as Southampton Square, Golden Square, King (later Soho) Square and Leicester Square. By 1700 the heaviest concentration of aristocratic names was in Soho Square, south of Oxford Street, and Golden Square, north of Piccadilly. Residents of the latter in 1707 included six present and future peers, a bishop and a duchess. By around 1714 another step westwards had begun, as the aristocracy moved into Hanover Square (1717–19), Cavendish Square and Grosvenor Square. In the 1720s thirteen of the twenty-five residents of Hanover Square were aristocrats, and twenty out of twenty-three in St James's Square. Simultaneously their numbers in Golden Square fell from six in 1720 to two in 1730 and only one in 1740, while in Soho Square by 1748 only three out of the six peers lived in the houses they owned in the Square. The others let their property. It was symbolic of the westward move that the old palaces in the Strand were largely demolished between 1674 and 1718.[12]

From the 1720s until the 1760s, building in London was spasmodic. Development took place in the streets and squares off Piccadilly, and on the Grosvenors' Mayfair estate. There was rapid growth on the latter between 1720 and 1740, but nine builders failed

[11] Cannadine, *Lords and Landlords*, pp. 398–401.
[12] G. Rudé, *Hanoverian London 1714–1808* (1971), pp. 41–2; Nottingham University Library, Portland MSS, Ea 8, list of the inhabitants of Soho Square, 1748; Lawrence Stone, 'The residential development of the West End of London in the seventeenth century', in *After the Reformation*, ed. B. C. Malament (Philadelphia, 1980), pp. 194–5.

between 1740 and 1742, resulting in more spasmodic development. When the Seven Years War ended in 1763 the momentum increased, with housing construction particularly noticeable in the fields north of Oxford Street. According to Sir John Summerson, 1774 'stands out as a key year in the history of London building'. The passing of the London Building Act – which was to govern metropolitan building for seventy years – was accompanied by the commencement of several great schemes, including Portman, Manchester and Bedford Squares, and Portland Place. Development began on Charles Cadogan's Chelsea estate in 1771, and during the same decade the Duke of Manchester leased a site from the Portman estate for building Manchester House, and Manchester Square to help meet the cost. In 1791 the first Baron Southampton began building Fitzroy Square. Grosvenor Square, however, remained the height of fashion, with thirty-one titled householders out of forty-seven. By the 1790s the Grosvenor estate numbered among its residents thirty-seven peers, eighteen baronets, fifteen 'honourables' and thirty-nine ladies.[13]

The period of the French Revolution was marked by the expansion of Bloomsbury and, from 1811, the development of Regent's Park under the auspices of the Prince Regent. During the 1820s the Grosvenors began to develop their Belgravia and Pimlico estates which became fashionable when George IV moved into Buckingham Palace. But by now the aristocratic estates, particularly in the West End, were complete, and landowning influence began to be felt elsewhere in the capital. A number of park-like suburban middle-class areas were laid out, including St John's Wood, Primrose Hill, Clapham Park and Highbury New Park. This last was laid out during the 1850s by Henry Rydon on a 100-acre site. Rydon both owned and developed the property as well as living on it, and originally it was designed for prosperous professional and business families. Elsewhere, the twenty-three chief proprietors in Islington owned 72 per cent of the tithable land in the 1830s, while in 1838 five owners shared 70 per cent of Hampstead and seven owned two-thirds of Camberwell. The Maryon Wilsons in Hampstead and the de Crespignys in Camberwell were among the more notable, while Lord Southampton was largely responsible for the development of St Pancras.[14]

[13] F. H. W. Sheppard (ed.), *The Survey of London*, vol. XXXIX: *The Grosvenor Estate in Mayfair*, pt I: *General History* (1977), p. 30; Sir John Summerson, *Georgian London*, 3rd edn (1978), pp. 164–5; G. Weightman and S. Humphries, *The Making of Modern London, 1815–1914* (1983), pp. 44–6.

[14] T. F. M. Hinchcliffe, 'Highbury New Park: a nineteenth-century middle-class suburb', *London Journal*, 7 (1981), pp. 29–44; Weightman and Humphries, *The*

The aristocratic landlords undoubtedly played an important role in laying out the West End of London, and some other areas of the capital – none more so that the dukes of Bedford, Portland and Westminster. But how far were these families able to determine what went on, and how far were they at the mercy of market forces? The Bedfords owned 119 acres, of which 80 were in Bloomsbury and the rest in Bedford New Town and Covent Garden. Prior to 1776, building took place south of Great Russell Street, the central feature being Bloomsbury (later Bedford) House, which stood on the north side of Bloomsbury Square. On Great Russell Street itself two mansions, Montague House (now the British Museum) and Thanet House were built, along with a number of lesser residences. Until about 1750, however, building was haphazard and was largely left to prospective inhabitants or speculative building contractors. From that point, the large aristocratic developers began to adopt a more clearly planned scheme, usually focusing on a large square with wide streets leading into it in order to form a tidy rectangular block of houses. This greater element of planning is clear from building on the estate north of Great Russell Street after 1776. Bedford Square and its adjacent streets were developed as a restricted upper-middle-class area, as part of a scheme which involved uniformity of occupation and façade. Building leases for Bedford Square specified dimensions, materials and quality, and, although it took eighty-five years to complete northern Bloomsbury, the result was an essential unity which owed much to the constant efforts of the Bedford estate office.[15]

The way in which individual squares were developed can be illustrated most clearly from the dukes of Portland's manor of St Marylebone. In December 1717 Lords Dartmouth, Chandos, Harcourt, Bingley, Bathurst and Castleton – all of them leading Tories, by contrast with the Whig clientele prominent in the opening up of Hanover Square earlier that year – proposed to Edward Harley, later second Earl of Oxford, the idea of developing Cavendish Square as a residential area north of Oxford Street. A plan was drawn up in 1719, as a result of which a market house was started in 1720 and a church in

---

Making of Modern London, pp. 49–51; Simon Jenkins, *Landlords to London* (1975), pp. 57–61; Donald Olsen, *The Growth of Victorian London* (1976), ch. 4; H. J. Dyos, *Victorian Suburb: a study of the growth of Camberwell* (Leicester, 1961), pp. 40–1; Thompson, *Hampstead*, p. 76; Francis Sheppard, *London, 1808–1870: the infernal Wen* (1971), p. 89.

[15] Donald J. Olsen, *Town Planning in London: the eighteenth and nineteenth centuries* (New Haven, Conn., 1964), pp. 39–63; F. H. W. Sheppard, *Local Government in St Marylebone, 1688–1835* (1958), pp. 16–17.

1724. James Gibb was put in charge of architecture in the square, and Charles Bridgeman was employed to lay out the garden. The Duke of Chandos leased the whole of the north side of the square, and considered several uses for the land – including a large new house for himself – before finally settling on two smaller houses on the east and west corners of his site. He settled in the square during the 1730s. However, the square filled up only slowly, and the plan was altered in 1753 when the second Baron Foley was given permission to build a large, free-standing house in the centre of the plot. By 1758 he had spent £30,000 on a magnificent house, and when the manor passed to Portland that year he granted Foley a ninety-nine-year lease of a 37-acre plot at only £800 a year from 1771. By a series of oversights, Foley gained the right to develop the area, and it took a legal dispute and private legislation for the Duke of Portland to regain his rights.[16]

A further development in building control came in the early nineteenth century with the introduction of developers. Among these the best known was Thomas Cubitt. Between 1821 and 1824 Cubitt took a series of leases from the Bedfords for Tavistock Square and other projects, in which he agreed to pay a certain sum for an area of building land on which he was to erect a specified number of houses. The ground rent for these was not to exceed a set proportion of the rack rent. Bedford took a small fixed sum as part of the profit, while acquiring an increasing interest in the joint capital as the lease drew towards an end. He was able to alter Cubitt's plans.[17] Cubitt is best known for his work on the Grosvenor estates. The dukes of Westminster acquired 500 acres of London property by a fortuitous marriage in 1677. Most of this was in modern Belgravia and Pimlico, with 100 acres in Mayfair and a slice of Millbank. The family began building in Mayfair around 1720, but from the 1820s they started to develop the larger portion of the property in Belgravia and Pimlico, to take advantage of the popularity of these areas arising from their proximity to John Nash's Buckingham Palace. Cubitt was involved from the beginning. In 1825 he leased 19 acres of what was to become Belgrave Square, and he also leased Pimlico to develop it as a mini-Belgravia.[18]

The Bedford and Westminster estates provide particularly good examples of the way in which the larger the estate the more likely it

[16] Sheppard, *Local Government in St Marylebone*, pp. 17, 103–16; C. H. C. and M. I. Baker, *The Life and Circumstances of James Brydges, First Duke of Chandos* (Oxford, 1949), pp. 265–78, 283.

[17] Olsen, *Town Planning in London*, pp. 59–63.

[18] Jenkins, *Landlords to London*, pp. 78–85.

was to be comprehensively planned from the outset. Moreover, the development could be maintained by rigorous enforcement of covenants. When their ninety-nine-year leases fell in, both landlords enforced systematic rebuilding to strengthen the residential character of their properties. They ensured that substandard mews and working-class dwellings were replaced with model block-dwellings and new open spaces, and they also encouraged the refacing of houses to bring them into line with architectural fashion.[19] In this way, the long lease was shown to have a flexibility which ensured that outmoded buildings could be demolished and replaced by better ones more suited to the times. From the maps prepared by Charles Booth for his work on the condition of the people of London, published in 1892, it is apparent that the greater owners had managed their estates in such a way as to keep them in better condition than might have been expected if the land had been freehold. This was not always the case; slums appeared on the marquesses of Northampton's Clerkenwell estate, but in most cases energetic landlords had been able to practise town planning within certain limits.[20]

Not everybody saw it in this way, and critics argued that the aristocratic landlords had outlawed working-class housing in favour of middle-class homes. By enforcing change when the leases fell in, the Duke of Westminster was said to have impoverished his tenants by compelling them to build houses that they could not afford, under threat of being thrown out of their livelihood.[21] This line of argument also lay behind several bills presented to Parliament in the 1880s to introduce compulsory leasehold enfranchisement. In practice, as the most comprehensive modern study of the subject has concluded, landlords were as subject to market forces as their tenants. The landlord was only one of several agents whose varied and conflicting actions combined to make modern London. On the Bedford estate, for example, it became impossible to maintain standards in Bloomsbury by the early nineteenth century when the competing pull of Belgravia caused demand to slacken. Such experiences reflected the economic forces from which landlords could not escape.[22]

[19] Olsen, *The Growth of Victorian London*, pp. 146, 154–5.
[20] Banfield, *The Great Landlords of London*, p. 93.
[21] Ibid., p. 34. Banfield found few complaints on the Portland estate, many on the Portman estate, and most on the Grosvenor estates.
[22] Olsen, *The Growth of Victorian London*, pp. 199–215.

THE PROVINCES

Urban development in the provinces benefited from the examples set in London. Although towns were growing prior to 1750, the really significant changes got under way only in the second half of the eighteenth century. Consequently landlords could observe what had happened in London, and weigh up the advantages of ground-rent leases, developers, and the alternative methods of building and control. None the less, much depended on the amount of land that they owned and on their willingness to become developers, since several of the expanding towns of later Georgian England were able to grow only because large blocks of land were made available.

Between the 1740s and the 1780s Birmingham was able to expand because two estates comprising around 250 acres were let on ninety-nine and 120-year leases for development. Little attempt was made to control the nature of the buildings erected. On the Colmore estate, from 1746 leases merely stated the minimum sum to be spent, and that buildings were to be three storeys high and in a straight line. In the 1790s restrictions became more specific. The hundred acres or so of land belonging to the Holte family of Aston Hall was released to builders between 1788 and 1820. From the later 1780s the property passed to Heneage Legge, a son of the Earl of Dartmouth, who inserted much more thorough covenants in his leases. Urban growth in Manchester was facilitated by the availability for building of five substantial properties in the 1770s and 1780s. Two of these, the Mynshull family's Chorlton Hall estate and Sir Ashton Lever's Alkrington property, were sold direct to developers, but on the Byron, Legh and Mosley estates the owners staked out the roads and building plots. The Mosleys even made themselves responsible for paving the streets and for the drainage, while charging the developer or builder for his share. In Liverpool, development was largely sponsored by the corporation from the time it acquired 1000 acres on a lease for 1000 years from Lord Molyneux in 1672. The land was granted outright in 1776. Even so, the Earl of Sefton, Molyneux's successor, was still able to build on other land south of the corporation estate, while the Earl of Derby developed land north of the town.[23] Across the Pennines in Sheffield, the dukes of Norfolk owned 12,000 acres on the north and east sides of the town, which the twelfth duke developed in the early nineteenth century with ninety-nine-year leases. Finally, among these examples, the growth of Exeter in the early nineteenth century was

[23] Chalklin, *The Provincial Towns of Georgian England*, pp. 81–112; Cannadine, *Lords and Landlords*, pp. 42–3.

partly dependent on the break-up of large estates, which helped to bring land on to the building market.[24]

Between 1740 and 1820 building promotion almost invariably revolved around the larger estates. Blocks of land of 20 or 30 acres facilitated planned promotions employing gridiron patterns, which provide a stark contrast with those places where the division of land prevented homogeneous planning. Developers in Bath found themselves dealing with only a few acres at a time; this gave rise to internally coherent schemes unlinked to existing developments. Only one large area was subject to a single plan, the Bathwick estate east of the Avon. Similar problems were found in towns such as Hull and Portsea, while Nottingham provides perhaps the clearest example of overbuilding through landlords' refusal to make ground available. In the confined central area of the town, high prices could be obtained by anyone with a small plot to sell. Vendors in the last two decades of the eighteenth century included a barrister, a potmaker, the trustees of a hosier and a local banker's widow. Overcrowding turned a garden town into a slum, and planned development became possible only when enclosure finally took place in 1845 and land came on to the market.[25]

As the nineteenth century progressed, landowners showed an increasing interest in developing miniature west ends, but some continued to take a leading role in a wider range of improvements. From 1857, the Grangetown suburb of Cardiff was developed by Lady Windsor initially as an industrial suburb, although it actually turned into a commuting area with respectable working-class houses and a few lower-middle-class properties.[26] In the Black Country considerable development took place before Lord Hatherton and the Earl of Bradford started to take an active interest in Walsall during the 1850s and 1860s. The Earl of Bradford's entail restrictions prevented him from playing a positive role in the development of West Bromwich before the 1860s, while in Wolverhampton the Duke of Cleveland was reluctant to develop his 447-acre estate. At least down to the 1840s, exploitation was left to middle men, and in the area as a whole over the

---

[24] David Spring, 'English landowners and nineteenth-century industrialism', in *Land and Industry*, ed. Ward and Wilson, p. 43; R. Newton, *Victorian Exeter, 1830–1910* (1968), p. 144. It is not intended to suggest that land was the only variable affecting urban growth. Although the availability of building land was of vital importance, other determinants of growth included fluctuations in the prosperity of local industries.

[25] Chalklin, *The Provincial Towns of Georgian England*, pp. 74–80, 113, 129, 135–6; R. A. Church, *Economic and Social Change in a Midland Town, 1815–1900* (1966), pp. 162–4, 184.

[26] Daunton, 'Suburban development in Cardiff', pp. 53–66.

period 1760–1840 the landed aristocrats made no real attempt directly to exploit the potential demand for working-class housing.[27]

The common factor linking nineteenth-century urban landowners was their interest in the middle-class 'park', the exclusive suburban estate characterized by villas standing in their own large gardens. Demand for such property was a natural development from the trend towards acquiring a villa and a few acres of land rather than a large-scale estate. Coinciding as it did with the middle-class desire to move out of overcrowded town centres, and the preference among landowners for erecting high-quality housing, the result was predictable – park-like, miniature west ends. Among such developments were Calverley Park in Tunbridge Wells, Papworth in Cheltenham, Sefton Park in Liverpool and Rock Park across the Mersey, the Park in Nottingham, Sandwell Park in West Bromwich, and Egbaston in Birmingham. The fifth Duke of Newcastle's Park estate lay on land due west of Nottingham's town centre, and it was developed as an exclusive residential area for industrialists and professional men, including lawyers and architects, clergymen and bank managers. The Duke of Newcastle employed T. C. Hine, a prominent local architect, to design the ground-plan, which took the form of a geometrical shape based on two tree-lined circuses. After several earlier abortive attempts, work really began in 1854, and around 600 houses had been erected by 1887, when the original plan was more or less complete. Apart from a bowling green and tennis courts, the scheme involved no facilities. Even a planned church was never built.[28]

Newcastle's Park was successful because it was constructed on a compact site, and because Nottingham had a middle class capable of occupying all the houses without any need to lower the social tone by allowing in the less wealthy. Without these conditions parks were not necessarily so successful. Edgbaston may have raised the Calthorpes from minor to major aristocrats, but the scheme did not work out entirely to plan. The family bought the 1700-acre Edgbaston estate in 1717 for £20,400. A series of consolidatory purchases, including the 88-acre Curzon estate which cost £18,500 in 1819, raised their total holding to 2064 acres by 1827. Further outlay of £47,000 pushed this

[27] Raybould, 'Aristocratic landowners and the industrial revolution', pp. 78–81.

[28] K. C. Edwards, 'The Park estate, Nottingham', in *Middle-Class Housing in Britain*, ed. M. A. Simpson and T. H. Lloyd (Newton Abbot, 1977), ch. 5; Brand, 'The Park estate, Nottingham', pp. 54–75; Anne Bosworth', 'Aspects of middle class life: the Park estate, Nottingham, 1841–1881', *Journal of Regional and Local Studies* 5 (1985), pp. 28–42.

up to nearly 2500 acres by the 1850s. The family left Edgbaston Hall and moved to Suffolk in 1783, three years before the first building lease was granted on the estate. By 1796 nine such leases, all for ninety-nine years, had been granted, but systematic development began only in 1810, under the third baron's supervision. From that point onwards a concerted effort was made to turn Edgbaston into a middle-class suburb, moulded according to the carefully controlled dictates of the family. Great care was taken in letting the plots, which had strict lease terms, and in the early stages any application for land was rejected unless it was a private housing development. But Birmingham did not have enough well-to-do people to populate Edgbaston with villas, and over time tradesmen were permitted to build smaller houses on the outskirts of the main property. Even speculative builders were tolerated. The result was an unprecedented building boom in the middle and later 1870s in a development described by its historian as 'one of the most outstanding examples of collaboration between an aristocrat who owned the land and those city dwellers who came to live on it'.[29]

THE RESORTS

Landowners' preference for middle-class suburbs in provincial town development was reflected in their attitude to resorts. Bath and Tunbridge Wells were eighteenth-century developments which came about because of the fashion for drinking the waters, but from around 1750 seawater bathing, and even drinking started to become popular. At first it was only the wealthy who could afford to patronize the few existing coastal resorts, but the nineteenth century witnessed a rapid expansion of such places in the wake of railway development. Many landowners found themselves with valuable property which could usefully be exploited, and usually they looked to encourage housing for the same clientele they were accommodating in inland towns. Unified landownership might therefore have been expected to produce the highest social tone, while poorer-quality development could be anticipated where property was fragmented. In fact, this may over simplify the situation. Eastbourne was undoubtedly a successful high-class development because of the careful overall planning of the seventh Duke of Devonshire, but there is an obvious danger in

---

[29] Cannadine, *Lords and Landlords*, chs 4–7.

generalizing from the experience of a few high-profile aristocrats in a number of prominent cases.[30]

Landowners took up the cudgels of resort development during the 1840s and 1850s, at a time when they were laying them down in many of the inland towns, but their influence was to last for only a couple of decades. Thereafter, with a few exceptions, they began to opt out in preference for development companies, and their control gave way to the influence of local government. Prior to the 1840s landowners had little need to intervene when the cost of travel ensured that most visitors were people of some financial standing. Consequently accommodation for them was developed along middle-class lines of which landowners could be expected to approve. Little large-scale speculation took place. As with eighteenth-century Bath, development tended to be on small sites and aimed at the higher classes. This was the case, for example, in Brighton. Where landowners did have substantial landed property, they tended not to interfere. The Earls of Radnor were the dominant owners in Folkestone throughout the eighteenth century, but it was only in 1807 that they took the first tentative steps towards town development. Private legislation secured in 1825 enabled the family to grant building leases, although even then the next fifteen years saw only slow progress. In Torquay the Palk family, later Lords Haldon, became interested in development early in the nineteenth century and acquired legislation in 1825 to enable them to grant building leases. However, no effective control was exercised over development before 1833, and it was only in the second half of the century that things really began to move.[31] Other early developers simply could not bring their plans to fruition. Such was the fate of Sir Richard Hotham's schemes for Bognor, where from the 1790s onwards the scale and pace of development nearly always fell short of what was planned.[32]

The signs of more active involvement by aristocrats began to appear during the 1830s, but their achievements need to be kept in perspective. In a few cases, unified landownership permitted exclusive

---

[30] The aristocratic role in resort development has recently become a source of controversy. Cannadine, *Lords and Landlords*, has suggested that the part they played was crucial, but John K. Walton, *The English Seaside Resort: a social history, 1750–1914* (Leicester, 1983), ch. 5, has pointed to the fact that, while aristocrats were clearly important in a few cases, the number of resorts in which they played an active and positive role in bringing about change was actually rather limited.

[31] Cannadine, *Lords and Landlords*, pp. 64–5; Walton, *The English Seaside Resort*, pp. 112–13.

[32] Gerald Young, *A History of Bognor Regis* (Chichester, 1983), pp. 11–38.

planning, as, for example, in Torquay, where the Palks' estate steward was chairman of the Improvement Commission from 1835 until 1860. Similarly in Bournemouth Sir George William Tapps-Gervis commissioned Benjamin Ferrey in 1836 to plan out a holiday town. During the following five years, roads were laid, gardens created and villas erected, while after Sir George's death in 1846 the trustees acquired private legislation to borrow £5000 so that a phase of more rapid development could be instituted. Estates of large detached villas in generous plots were constructed, producing an exclusive town for upper-class visitors down to the 1870s.[33] At Folkestone, Sydney Smirke drew up plans for developing the town to take advantage of the arrival of the South-Eastern Railway in 1843, and when the Devonshires decided to develop Eastbourne their first priority was a branch line into the town. This arrived in 1849, providing the opportunity – which was grasped – to develop a high-class resort. The Devonshires took upon themselves the responsibility for the promenades and sea defences, and from time to time they even rescued companies that ran into problems. By 1914 Eastbourne had become one of the most exclusive and at the same time successful resorts. At Southport, Charles Hesketh and Charles Scarisbrick, both of them local gentry, set out the town for high-class development, partly by imposing high minimum values and plot sizes, as well as an array of restrictive covenants.[34] However, in their case, road making and drainage were left to the lessees.

Despite these examples, unified landownership was not necessarily the key to high-class resort development everywhere. Some places emerged as exclusive resorts despite having no dominant landowner, including Brighton, Hastings, Worthing, Clacton and Grange-over-Sands. Coversely, although popular resorts tended to appear where landownership was fragmented, as in the cases of Blackpool and Southend, they could also be created by the policy of a single owner. A case in point was Skegness, admittedly a relatively late development, where the Earl of Scarbrough laid out the first building plots in 1873: a gridiron plan surviving from 1878 reveals his intention to build 787

---

[33] Walton, *The English Seaside Resort*, p. 116; Cannadine, *Lords and Landlords*, p. 65; Richard Roberts, 'Leasehold estates and municipal enterprise: landowners, local government and the development of Bournemouth, *c.* 1850–1914', in *Patricians, Power and Politics in Nineteenth-Century Towns*, ed. David Cannadine (Leicester, 1982), p. 179.

[34] Cannadine, *Lords and Landlords*, pp. 63–4; John Liddle, 'Estate management and land reform politics: the Hesketh and Scarisbrick families and the making of Southport, 1842–1914', in *Patricians, Power and Politics*, ed. Cannadine, pp. 134–66.

houses in the town. This proved to be over-ambitious, and only the southern half of the plan ever came into existence. He also provided many of the facilities.[35] Other owners who planned exclusive resorts were unable to deliver the goods. Among them were the Lancashire family of Fleetwood, who failed in their plans for the town of that name, and the Cliftons, similarly unsuccessful with their estate in Blackpool. Some families even preferred to suppress development in order to preserve their residential amenity and political power. This was why Pensarn in North Wales failed to grow in the later nineteenth century, while its rivals at Rhyl and Colwyn Bay were pushing ahead.[36]

With a few exceptions, by the end of the 1870s landowner initiative had begun to wane. While the Earl of Scarbrough was a late starter in Skegness, and the Duke of Devonshire remained vigorous in Eastbourne, the momentum was lost elsewhere. In part this was because maintaining a town as a high-class exclusive resort became difficult. At Torquay the second Lord Haldon found at his accession in 1883 that the cost of developing the town, particularly the harbour and railway improvements, had left his family in considerable debt. Between 1885 and 1914 the family sold most of its town property. The last three decades of the century saw a new clientele arriving in Bournemouth, and, although villa construction continued in some areas, more important was the promotion of moderately substantial semidetached houses, many of which became boarding accommodation. By the 1890s the increasing influx of excursionists and ordinary middle-class holidaymakers was met with appropriate housing, and the conversion of many of the original villas into hotel accommodation.[37] Landowners took less personal interest in these changes, tending to allow them to be conducted by commercial developers. However, the important point is that, whatever the role of topography and consumer taste in relation to landownership, aristocrats undoubtedly made a positive contribution to the early stages of resort development.

[35] Walton, *The English Seaside Resort*, pp. 122–4; R. Gurnham, 'The creation of Skegness as a resort town by the 9th Earl of Scarbrough', *Lincolnshire History and Archaeology*, 7 (1972), pp. 63–76.

[36] F. M. L. Thompson, 'English landed society in the nineteenth century', in *The Power of the Past*, ed. P. Thane *et al.* (Cambridge, 1984), p. 206; Walton, *The English Seaside Resort*, p. 120.

[37] Walton, *The English Seaside Resort*, p. 123; Roberts, 'Leasehold estates and municipal enterprise', pp. 181–2.

THE FINANCIAL REWARD

Finally, aristocratic involvement in urban development had financial implications. On the one hand, there was the expected income. A landowner selling to a developer took a once-and-for-all profit, but the financial advantages of granting long-term ground-rent leases helped to make such arrangements particularly popular. Long leases increased the value of the property in two ways. First, they affected capital values. In 1746 witnesses for the Colmore Estate Bill, Birmingham, told a House of Lords committee that land on the estate would increase in value from 30*s.* to £15 an acre if developed, and this proved to be roughly accurate, since developers paid between £12 and £16 an acre in the years 1747–50. At Portsea in 1813 land used for market gardening fetched £3–£4 an acre, suggesting a capital value of £60–£120, but sums received from builders for sites were nearer to £600 or £1800, with a median of £1200. In Mayfair, ground rents were approximately £31 an acre in 1768, compared to £3 or £4 an acre when the land was still farmed half a century earlier.[38] Second, and more pertinently for the owner who held on to his land, rental income increased substantially through time.

These advantages were gained after an initial outlay on planning costs, and possibly also on the development of roads and drains, although some owners even managed to transfer these burdens on to lessees. As a rule, the best returns were made on London property, the next best in the provincial towns, and the highest outlay and poorest returns in the resorts. London ground landlords could not avoid financial outlay, although they probably kept it to a minimum. By the end of 1782 the Bedford estate had lent £22,500 for building in Bedford Square, and other large sums had been borrowed by the paving commissioners of St George's Bloomsbury. Similar loans were also made on later projects. Between 1856 and 1865, for example, investment in Covent Garden included £15,000 on the construction of the Metropolitan Board of Works. The Westministers also made improvement loans, including interest-free sums of £11,800 for sewer construction between 1726 and 1729.[39] In the provinces it proved less easy to avoid outlay on roads and drainage. The technique of passing on such burdens to developers never seems to have caught on. Consequently the Calthorpes spent £47,000 on roads and sewers

[38] Chalklin, *The Provincial Towns of Georgian England*, p. 145; Sheppard, *The Survey of London*, vol. XXXIX, pt I, p. 33.

[39] Olsen, *The Growth of Victorian London*, p. 37; Sheppard, *The Survey of London*, vol. XXXIX, pt I, p. 8.

between 1810 and 1888, as well as giving land and money for churches. The Ramsdens spent more than £125,000 on Huddersfield by the 1880s, and Lady Windsor raised loans of over £36,000 for developing Grangetown between 1858 and 1867. By 1865 over £30,000 of this had been laid out on drains and sewers, and more outlay followed during the subsequent decade. The Duke of Newcastle planned an Improvement Act in 1854 which would have allowed him to borrow £10,000 to finance his Park in Nottingham. This failed, but he laid out £3000 between 1854 and 1855 on building a tunnel and on road construction, although it is not clear how much he spent on the project thereafter.[40] Most costly of all were the resorts. Sir Richard Hotham spent £120,000 on Bognor 1788–99; the dukes of Devonshire invested £711,000 over the period 1850–93 in Eastbourne; the Earl of Scarbrough put £53,000 into Skegness between 1878 and 1890; the Haldons laid out £100,000 on Torquay; and the Tapps-Gervises invested £40,000 in Bournemouth between 1834 and 1850.[41]

The returns on these investments varied considerably. London property produced the best, particularly for a number of aristocratic landlords. In the 1660s the Bedfords' Covent Garden property brought in ground rents of £1500 a year, and Bloomsbury – which they inherited in 1669 – about £1200. In addition, they received £340 for Bloomsbury market, and £400 rents from lands still let for farming. By 1732 the total rental of Bloomsbury and Covent Garden was nearer to £10,000, and it climbed towards £18,000 by the 1750s, and to over £20,000 in 1775. The opening up of more of the Bloomsbury estate produced a rapid increase. Bloomsbury rents rose from £13,800 in 1805 to nearly £25,000 by 1816, and by 1830 the total rental was in the region of £66,000. Once the Bedford Square leases began to fall in during the 1870s, the total rental rose again, reaching £104,880 in 1880. Under the old leases the Bedford Square rental was £2191, but the new ones raised it to £18,848. In addition, Covent Garden market was yielding £32,000 annually.[42]

Even more spectacular was the investment return on the dukes of Westminster's London property. From the Mayfair estate the family received £1133 in ground rents and £312 in improved rents in 1768.

[40] Cannadine, *Lords and Landlords*, p. 414; Daunton, 'Suburban development in Cardiff', pp. 55–6; Brand, 'The Park estate, Nottingham', p. 69.
[41] Cannadine, *Lords and Landlords*, pp. 414–15; Young, *History of Bognor Regis*, p. 32.
[42] Spring, 'English landowners and nineteenth-century industrialism', pp. 41–2; Olsen, *Town Planning in London*, pp. 47, 56, 220–3.

This was supplemented by renewal fines, which averaged £7268 over the years 1789–92. Between 1768 and 1782 the Mayfair rental was about £3450 annually, but it increased to £5550 by 1802 and to £8000 by 1820. At this point the ninety-nine-year leases granted in 1721 began to fall in, and as they were renewed the estate income shot up by leaps and bounds. In 1821 it was £20,000; five years later it had doubled, and by 1835 it reached £60,000. Gross income from all the family's London estates was about £88,000 that year, and this increased to £96,000 in 1865 and to £179,000 by 1894. In addition, fines on the Mayfair estate brought in a total of £108,538 between 1845 and 1864, and £650,000 between 1874 and 1899. Such was their impact that in two extraordinary years, 1893 and 1894, the Westminsters' gross income from London was £491,135 and £427,533 respectively.[43]

The dukes of Portland were receiving ground and improvement rents from their Soho estates of around £3000 in the mid-1730s, and just over £4000 in the 1740s and 1750s. By the 1790s the figure had risen to £4200. Disposal started in 1798, when the property was valued at £359,656, and by the 1820s much of it had been sold into freehold. However, in 1758 the family had acquired the manor of Marylebone, which was to prove a far more lucrative source in the nineteenth century. When ground rents fell in and were replaced by improved rents, the Marylebone rental increased from £43,316 in 1828 to £52,894 in 1837, and to £56,876 in 1845. No rental records survive for 1844, but in that year the fourth duke told his son that the property was yielding £50,000 annually, and that 'there can be little doubt [it] will receive additions.' His optimism was well founded; by 1850 the gross rental was £60,116, and in 1872 – the last year for which an account is available – £100,000. Renewal fines totalled £20,953 in 1872 and £14,052 in 1877.[44] Finally, the Portmans were reckoned to have received £1¼ million in March 1888 when their long leases fell in.[45]

These examples were almost certainly not typical. Even some

---

[43] Sheppard, *The Survey of London*, vol. XXXIX, pt I, pp. 30–48; M. J. Hazelton-Swales, 'Urban aristocrats: the Grosvenors and the development of Belgravia and Pimlico in the nineteenth century' (University of London, Ph.D. thesis, 1981), pp. 143, 145.

[44] Nottingham University Library, Portland Papers, box 42, Soho rentals and accounts; Pwk 503a, Duke of Portland to Marquess of Titchfield, 19 May 1844; Nottinghamshire RO, DD4P/57/21–31; F. H. W. Sheppard, *The Survey of London*, vol. XXXIII: *Parish of St Anne, Soho* (1966), pp. 40–1.

[45] Banfield, *The Great Landlords of London*, pp. 36–40.

London property owners do not appear to have done particularly well, including Falk Grenville Howard. The financial arrangements into which he entered after purchasing property in Hampstead in 1819 suggest that, while he provided fat pickings for the developer, his own reward was rather lean.[46] Certainly such sums were not to be made in the provinces. The Calthorpes did well in Birmingham, where gross income from their Edgbaston estate rose from £5024 in 1810 to £12,917 by 1850, and to over £30,000 by the early 1890s. Over the same period, as a proportion of their total gross income, receipts from Edgbaston increased from 32.4 to 72.3 per cent. The Ramsdens' income from Huddersfield was £3654 in 1769, but £42,331 a century later, and nearly £64,000 in 1919, while between 1850 and 1894 the Butes' income from Cardiff rose from £3487 to £28,348. Between 1800 and 1860 the Duke of Norfolk's ground rents in Sheffield more than doubled, and by the 1880s his net return on the town's markets amounted to £10,000 annually.[47] The poorest returns were in the resorts. Lord Radnor's income from Folkestone increased from £838 in 1851 to £8222 in 1886, and to £14,739 by 1900. Income from new building leases granted on the Scarisbrick trust estate in Southport rose from £1052 in 1861 to £22,270 by 1901. By 1885 the dukes of Devonshire were deriving £10,000 from their Eastbourne development and the Haldons were receiving £16,000 from Torquay. Devonshire also received a considerable income from his investments in town facilities including the water and gasworks, amounting to over £100,000 between 1850 and 1893. However, as late as 1896 Scarbrough's income from Skegness was only £2961.[48] Broadly speaking, there was an inverse relationship between effort and profit, with the least effort and the most profit coming from London property, and the most effort and least profit from resort development.

It is not easy to distinguish gross and net incomes in urban development, but figures have survived for Lady Windsor's Grangetown project. The aim, based on ground-rental rates, appears to have been a 17 per cent return, but what was achieved was rather different. By 1865 the return on expenditure incurred up to 1860 was 2.7 per cent,

[46] Thompson, *Hampstead*, pp. 83–90.

[47] Cannadine, *Lords and Landlords*, pp. 415, 432; Dennis Wholmsley, 'A landed estate and the railway: Huddersfield, 1844–54', *Journal of Transport History*, 2 (1974), pp. 189–213; Davies, *Cardiff and the Marquesses of Bute*, p. 433; Spring, 'English landowners and nineteenth-century industrialism', p. 43.

[48] Spring, 'English landowners and nineteenth-century industrialism', p. 44; Liddle, 'Estate management and land reform politics', p. 143; Cannadine, *Lords and Landlords*, p. 289; Gurnham, 'The creation of Skegness as a resort town', pp. 63–76.

and a decade later the return on outlay to 1873 was 4.7 per cent. To that point, eighteen years after the Estate Act permitting borrowing to finance the scheme, the gross return was just about enough to cover the cost of mortgages and maintenance. It may have reached 17 per cent by the end of the century when the estate was more fully developed, and when large outlay was complete, but it took a long time to reach this happy state of affairs.[49] Such figures demonstrate the extent to which landowners' investments yielded long-term gains, just as the ninety-nine-year leases suggest a willingness to postpone profit to the third or fourth generation. Both cases argue that the interest of landowners was in the long-term benefit accruing to the family.

Population growth and industrialization brought urbanization, but it could take place only when land was available for development. If owners refused to release their property, urban growth could be choked, and some put themselves to considerable trouble obtaining legislation to permit development. In theory, therefore, landlords with a substantial estate were strongly placed to dictate the terms of development, and their properties were the most likely to be comprehensively planned. Large owners with estates held on leases were also the best placed to control architectural standards.[50] Where land was fragmented, small-scale development often took place with no overall planning. The ground lease enabled aristocrats to fulfil their duty to the community, because it allowed them to plan layouts and to set standards, and at the same time ensured that the increased value of their property would pass to their descendants. Consequently they were to be found approving street plans, inserting detailed clauses in building leases, and attempting to enforce covenant restrictions. Generally they preferred middle-class housing development, particularly in London's West End, and the park-like imitations which sprang up both in parts of the capital itself and on the outskirts of provincial towns such as Birmingham and Nottingham.

The significance of aristocratic control must, however, be kept in perspective. Landlords could play a critical role – for good or ill. In Huddersfield, for example, Sir John Ramsden, the third baronet, encouraged the building of new roads and maintained a close control which was to the benefit of the town. By contrast, his successor, the fourth baronet, failed to build on this landlord-inspired start. Traffic was driven away from the canal, while commercial and industrial

---

[49] Daunton, 'Suburban development in Cardiff', pp. 56–7.
[50] Olsen, *The Growth of Victorian London*, p. 145.

building came to a halt. Similarly, in Cardiff, the Butes' leasing
policy was blamed for stultifying growth, and, although it is now clear
that such an explanation oversimplifies a far more complex situation, it
caused landlords' control to be resented in the later nineteenth and
early twentieth centuries.[51] Conversely, urban growth could take place
in areas were landlords made no attempt to shape the urban landscape,
as was the case with the Black Country owners. Moreover, what
happened in the resorts shows that unified ownership alone did not
produce high-class development. In the case of Skegness, unified
ownership actually produced a working-class resort.

Landlords were also subject to market forces. Lady Windsor's
Grangetown turned out rather differently from her plans, while
exclusive areas tended to appear on the west sides of provincial towns,
whether or not landowners held large tracts of land in the appropriate
area, since it was here that the well-to-do moved to escape the worst
fumes and smoke. By contrast, an owner with considerable land
elsewhere in a town might be unable to influence development in the
direction he preferred. Arguably this was the case in Sheffield, where
the Duke of Norfolk's unified holding did not become the town's
exclusive area, and middle-class suburbs developed instead on land
west of the town which had previously been held in relatively small
plots. Aristocrats were therefore faced with two important constraints
on their activities: the physical location of their land, and the size of
the middle class. If they could not attract the middle class to live in
their planned parks, or if the middle class was not sufficiently large for
the planned area, the chances of achieving successful suburban
development on their preferred lines were poor.

Despite these reservations, there is little doubt that aristocrats
played a major role in urban development, in London from the
seventeenth century, in the provinces from the later eighteenth to the
third quarter of the nineteenth centuries, and in the resorts during the
Victorian period. A few used their influence to great financial effect,
but recent scholarship has defused some of the older views of landlords
as inflicting 'a sort of white slavery' on their tenants,[52] to point to the
limitations imposed by market forces and topography. Even so, it is
clear that, without a sympathetic landlord group, urban development
would have been retarded, and would possibly even have taken

---

[51] Dennis Wholmsley, 'Market forces and urban growth: the influence of the
Ramsden family on the growth of Huddersfield, 1716–1853', *Journal of Regional and
Local Studies*, 4, (1984), pp. 27–56; Davies, *Cardiff and the Marquesses of Bute*,
pp. 211–12.

[52] Banfield, *The Great Landlords of London*, p. 112.

different directions. Ultimately the owners were almost certainly swayed by two crucial considerations: the ability to hold on to their land as it was developed, and therefore the prospects of increased values and rising rents as ground rents fell in; and the financial pickings. Beyond this was their desire to take a hand in controlling development, a role that they played until local government began to remove it from their hands in the later nineteenth century.

Chapter Nine

The Aristocratic Contribution

At the end of the nineteenth century the English aristocracy still constituted the largest group of wealth holders. In the 1880s more than half of Britain's wealthiest men were landowners. Although this was partly because only a handful of nineteenth-century businessmen bought land on a substantial scale, it also reflected the fact that some existing owners had done extraordinarily well from industrial and urban development. Between 1809 and 1858 three of the twelve millionaires were aristocratic landowners (the dukes of Buccleuch, Sutherland and Cleveland), and a quarter of half-millionaires had made their money primarily from land. However, the relative position was already beginning to slide. Although the first Duke of Sutherland may have been 'the richest man that ever died' in 1833, bankers and brewers, iron masters, armaments makers and machine manufacturers were all beginning to outstrip the landowners by the second half of the nineteenth century.[1] This loss of position took place as debts mounted, until it was possible to claim that the landowners were largely being underwritten by savings accumulated in the commercial sector of the economy. The question which has to be asked is whether this decline in their position reflected a long-term failure to contribute to economic development. Earlier chapters have looked at their contribution to a variety of activities, but it remains to place these within an overall perspective. In particular, some attempt must be made to tackle the question whether the aristocracy helped or hindered development in the crucial decades of industrialization, or whether they were merely passive political manipulators of an economic machine to which their

[1] W. D. Rubinstein, 'British millionaires, 1809–1949', *Bulletin of the Institute of Historical Research*, 47 (1974), pp. 202–23; 'The Victorian middle classes: wealth, occupation and geography', *Economic History Review*, 2nd ser., 30 (1977), pp. 605–6, 614.

contribution was minimal. There are no simple answers to such questions, particularly in view of the indebtedness amongst aristocrats during the nineteenth century. What will become clear, however, is that if debt became an endemic feature of the aristocratic way of life it did not prevent a valuable and possibly critical contribution to economic development. Moreover, this was a contribution which enabled the economy to continue to grow, even when the aristocracy ran into financial trouble after about 1880.

ARISTOCRATIC INCOMES

In the 1690s Gregory King produced figures in which he suggested that the income of peers averaged £2800 a year, baronets £880, knights £650, esquires £450 and gentlemen £280. The origin of these figures is obscure. They reflect King's efforts to calculate the wealth of England and Wales on the eve of the 1688 revolution, but they are rather too neat for comfort. The rounded-downward steps suggest a harmonious relationship between wealth and status for which there is little evidence. The peerage figure looks suspiciously low. Lawrence Stone's calculation of the mean gross income for the 121 peers of 1641 came to £6030, while it is clear that even when King was at work some families were receiving considerably more than this. In 1683 rental receipts on the Earl of Rutland's estate totalled £14,482, while at about the same time the Earl of Devonshire's annual average income exceeded £17,000. The Duke of Newcastle's various estates netted about £25,000 annually in the 1690s.[2] By the early years of the eighteenth century, King's figures were beginning to look even more unrealistic. The dukes of Newcastle, Bedford and Beaufort all had incomes in excess of £30,000, while four other magnates (the dukes of Ormonde, Somerset and Devonshire, and Lord Brooke) could boast between £20,000 and £30,000. Incomes in excess of £10,000 had become commonplace for peers above the rank of baron by 1710. King's figures for baronets also appear to be over-conservative. His contemporary social commentator, Edward Chamberlayne, suggested an average income of about £1200 a year. Even that may be too low, since figures for Yorkshire and Kent in the 1630s show mean incomes of £1500. Even Glamorgan in the later seventeenth century could boast

---

[2] Lawrence Stone, *The Crisis of the Aristocracy, 1558–1641* (Oxford, 1965), p. 762; O. F. R. Davies, 'The Dukes of Devonshire, Newcastle and Rutland, 1688–1714: a study in wealth and political influence' (University of Oxford, D.Phil. thesis, 1971), pp. 140–9.

two gentry families with incomes over £3000 annually, and another ten with between £1000 and £3000.[3]

A further set of figures prepared for 1760 by Joseph Massie suggest greater circumspection than those produced by King. Rather than calculate an average income for each social rank, Massie drew up a series of income categories for the aristocracy, ranging from ten families with incomes of £20,000 a year or more, down to 6400 families with £200 annually. Altogether he counted 18,070 families with an aggregate income of £8,720,000. Familiar names would still have been at the top of the list, including the dukes of Bedford – with a gross rental of £31,000 in 1732 – and Devonshire (£35,000 in 1764), as well as the earls of Warwick and Derby.[4] By the 1790s, according to G. E. Mingay's modern figures, 400 English landowners had incomes ranging between £5000 and £50,000, and averaging £10,000. High on this list would have been the earls of Derby, who were drawing £47,366 from thirty-two different estates by 1797. Below this elite, between 700 and 800 wealthy gentry had incomes of £3000 to £5000 annually, and 10,000 to 20,000 gentlemen were in receipt of between £300 and £1000.[5] Inevitably many of these figures are little more than informed guesswork, but the rising values accord with what is known of estate incomes in the eighteenth century. The Leveson-Gowers' gross income, for example, rose from £3917 in 1691 to £8677 in 1730, and then doubled again by 1787. Inflation during the Napoleonic war years pushed up incomes even more speedily. The Leveson-Gowers' income grew to nearly £50,000 by 1813, while the rental of Lord Lonsdale's Westmorland estate increased from £15,414 in 1802–3 to £28,525 by 1812–13.[6]

The most comprehensive set of figures was produced by John

[3] G. S. Holmes, 'Gregory King and the social structure of pre-industrial England', *Transactions of the Royal Historical Society*, 5th ser., 27 (1977), pp. 54–5; Joanna O. Martin, 'The landed estate in Glamorgan, *c.* 1660–*c.* 1760' (University of Cambridge, Ph.D. thesis, 1978), p. 205.

[4] Joseph Massie, *A Computation of the Money that hath been Exorbitantly Raised upon the People of Great Britain by the Sugar Planters* (1760). Some of Massie's findings have been analysed by Peter Mathias, 'The social structure in the eighteenth century: a calculation by Joseph Massie', *Economic History Review*, 2nd ser., 10 (1956), pp. 30–45; Harold Perkin, *The Origins of Modern English Society, 1780–1880* (1969), p. 19.

[5] G. E. Mingay, *English Landed Society in the Eighteenth Century* (1963), pp. 22–4.

[6] J. R. Wordie, *Estate Management in Eighteenth-Century England* (1982), pp. 135–50; C. E. Searle, '"The odd corner of England": a study of a rural social formation in transition, Cumbria, *c.* 1700–*c.* 1914' (University of Essex, Ph.D. thesis, 1983), p. 300.

Bateman who, in the 1880s,[7] listed 3820 owners of land with incomes of £2000 a year or more. At the peak was a small elite of fifteen families with incomes in excess of £100,000 a year (table 9.1), and a total of seventy-six with £50,000 or more. However, the accuracy of many of Bateman's figures must be questionable. Lords Calthorpe and Haldon were incorrectly attributed the whole rental of Edgbaston and Torquay – rather than just the ground rent – while London property was omitted. Although this made relatively little difference in terms of overall acreages, it was vital for incomes. The distortion of Bateman's findings is considerable. The Duke of Bedford appears here as seventh in the list, while the dukes of Portland and Westminster are completely omitted. W. D. Rubinstein has attempted to make allowance for these distortions, and his revised list (table 9.2) looks rather different from Bateman's. In come Westminister, Hamilton, Ancaster, Hertford and Portland, to take account of their London incomes and more recently available information about their nineteenth-century wealth; while out go Haldon, Calthorpe, Ramsden and Cleveland. Even these figures are open to further refinement. Bedford's income has been estimated variously at £273,000 in 1865, and at £235,000 in 1873. More seriously, Portland received nearly £105,000 net from his London estates in 1872, which, when added to the £88,350 recorded by Bateman, would put him at fourth place in the list.[8]

These figures are for only the very wealthiest families, but the link with rank is none the less clear. According to Rubinstein's calculations, all those with £75,000 or more annually were members of the titled peerage. He also found that between 1809 and 1899 landowning millionaires included eight dukes, three earls, one younger son of a peer, three baronets and six commoners. Among the half-millionaires for the same period were nine dukes, four marquesses, ten earls, five barons, two sons of peers, two baronets and ten

---

[7] Income tax returns might also have been expected to yield valuable material, but these have proved difficult to manipulate. P. K. O'Brien, 'British incomes and property in the early nineteenth century', *Economic History Review*, 2nd ser., 12 (1959), p. 262, has shown that schedule A returns for income from land, houses, tithes and real property suggest income figures for tax purposes rising from £36,669,000 in 1803 to £59,744,000 by 1814.

8 Donald J. Olsen, *Town Planning in London: the eighteenth and nineteenth centuries* (New Haven, Conn., 1964), p. 222; David Spring, 'Land and politics in Edwardian England', *Agricultural History*, 58 (1984), p. 20; Nottinghamshire RO, DD4P/57/30. The recently available death duty registers may eventually supplant the probate inventories used by W. D. Rubinstein as a research source: Barbara English, 'Probate valuations and the death duty registers', *Bulletin of the Institute of Historical Research*, 57 (1984), pp. 80–91.

Table 9.1   Landowners with a gross annual income exceeding
£100,000 in 1883

Landowner	Income (£)	England only (£)
Duke of Buccleuch	217,163	44,334
Sir John Ramsden	181,294	169,820
Duke of Devonshire	180,750	146,420
Duke of Northumberland	176,048	176,048
Earl of Derby	163,273	163,195[a]
Marquess of Bute	151,135	5,680
Duke of Bedford	141,793	141,793
Duke of Sutherland	141,667	72,728
Earl Fitzwilliam	138,801	90,947
Earl of Dudley	123,176	117,237
Lord Calthorpe	122,628	122,628
Marquess of Anglesey	110,598	100,814
Lord Haldon	109,275	109,275
Duke of Cleveland	100,485[b]	100,485
Marquess of Londonderry	100,118	56,825

Source: J. Bateman, *The Great Landowners of Great Britain and Ireland* (1883;
Leicester, 1971 edn)

[a]   Income from Derby's 2350 acres in Kent and Surrey is unstated.
[b]   Bateman claimed that fifteen landowners had incomes from land in excess of
£100,000, but only fourteen appear in his lists. Cleveland is attributed £97,398,
but it is possible that he is the fifteenth because of a reference to 'a rental of
£3,087' as being omitted.

commoners. Given the discrepancies in numbers between the different
ranks, such figures suggest a rough correlation similar to that found for
acreage.[9] At the same time these figures suggest that differences across
the range had increased through time. While it was always the case that
even some dukedoms carried relatively small acreages, and that the
neat divisions achieved by Gregory King in 1688 were probably an
invention, the gap between the very richest landowners and their lesser
brethren does appear to have widened through time. Doubtless this

---

[9]   W. D. Rubinstein, *Men of Property: the very wealthy in Britain since the industrial
revolution* (1981), pp. 209–12. See chapter two, above, for the correlation with
acreage.

Table 9.2   Gross landed incomes, 1883, revised figures

Landowner	Income (£s)
Duke of Westminster	c. 290,000–325,000
Duke of Buccleuch	232,000
Duke of Bedford	225,000–250,000
Duke of Devonshire	181,000
Duke of Northumberland	176,000
Earl of Derby	163,000
Marquess of Bute	153,000
Duke of Sutherland	142,000
Duke of Hamilton	141,000
Earl Fitzwilliam	139,000
Earl of Dudley	123,000
Earl of Ancaster	121,000
Marquess of Anglesey	111,000
Marquess of Londonderry	110,000
Duke of Portland	108,000
Marquess of Hertford	104,000
Viscount Portman	c. 100,000

Source: W. D. Rubinstein, *Men of Property* (1981), p. 194

had been fuelled not merely by the diversity among agricultural rents, but also by the unequal blessings of minerals, urban land and other vital resources.[10]

The central question arising from these figures concerns just what they represented. Bateman gave gross annual values, but he was aware that net income was likely to have been rather different. In the preface to his work he cited a fictitious example of a £5000-a-year squire with 3500 acres, whose income after unavoidable outgoings amounted to just over £1000 annually.[11] As was demonstrated in chapter five, the financial commitment of landlords to their estates increased through the period. Even in the first half of the eighteenth century the Lowthers of Holker were laying out 35 per cent of their gross income

[10] Ibid., p. 196; Perkin, *The Origins of Modern English Society*, pp. 416–17.
[11] J. Bateman, *The Great Landowners of Great Britain and Ireland* (1883; Leicester, 1971), pp. xxxiv–xxv.

in necessary and unavoidable expenditure, which included jointure and legacy payments. This figure could rise in some years to as much as 50 per cent.[12] As the level of estate investment increased, the net income receipts inevitably fell. The Duke of Bedford claimed in the 1890s that his family had received a net income of only 27 per cent from the Bedfordshire and Buckinghamshire estates, and 30.5 per cent from Thorney, over the course of the nineteenth century. He calculated expenditure as the sums spent on taxation and repairs, new works and permanent improvements, management costs and other charitable and semi-charitable outgoings.[13] With outgoings at an all-time high level towards the end of the nineteenth century, many owners must have found that net income represented half or even less of gross.[14]

In these circumstances, alternative forms of income could represent an important addition to real income. The return on industrial ventures was usually stated as profit, and on estates heavily involved in such enterprises the sums involved could be an important part of overall income. On the Leveson-Gowers' estate, for example, the industrial return increased from 8 per cent of the overall total at the end of the seventeenth century, to reach more than one-quarter by the early nineteenth.[15] Urban ground-rent returns could also represent a sizeable addition to net income returns. In the case of the dukes of Bedford, Bloomsbury and Covent Garden contributed one-third of the family's total income in 1732, but London rents rose to one-half by 1819 and to 61 per cent (£162,187 out of £264,257) by 1895. Finally, alternative investments could provide a much-needed boost. In the mid-eighteenth century Sir James Lowther's income of £12,495 from interest on his personal estate represented roughly half of his total earnings from land, collieries and investments. Similarly the first Duke of Sutherland's overall income of £120,000 in 1833 included stock dividends of £34,000, and in the 1870s Sir Tatton Sykes's investments in railway shares and mortgages gave him a personal income of £9820, or 20 per cent of his overall income. Between 1809 and 1899

---

[12] J. V. Beckett, 'The Lowthers at Holker: marriage, inheritance and debt in the fortunes of an eighteenth-century landowning family;, *Transactions of the Historic Society of Lancashire and Cheshire*, 127 (1978), pp. 54–5.

[13] Duke of Bedford, *A Great Agricultural Estate*, 3rd edn (1897), pp. 227, 239.

[14] On the Nottinghamshire estates of Earl Manvers during the 1890s income averaged £18,459 a year, but after deducting outgoings "clear money" averaged just £4,304, a mere 23 per cent of the total: Nottingham University Manuscripts Department, Manvers papers (unlisted accounts).

[15] Wordie, *estate Management in Eighteenth-Century England*, pp. 135–50.

twenty-six landowners left personal estates of £500,000 or more.[16]

Distinguishing between gross and net income is a particularly hazardous process involving calculations about the return from a number of different sources. However, what does not seem to have been in doubt is that, for all the accumulated wealth of the aristocracy, a great many families could not make ends meet. Once their unavoidable outgoings were paid, they were left with a variety of spending opportunities, many of which involved considerable outlay. These ranged from household expenditure through political costs (see chapter thirteen), housebuilding, gambling, legal battles, sport, philanthropy and self-indulgence. Even the upkeep of a large house could prove expensive; between 1801 and 1834 Wentworth Woodhouse, for example, cost approximately £1000 a year simply to maintain.[17] Gardens also consumed resources. At Stowe in the 1740s about forty people were employed in the garden and the costs were considerable (table 9.3). Gambling consumed a number of fortunes. The legendary Squire Osbaldeston sold up in 1848 to pay debts of £20,000 amassed during forty-five years of gambling. Many similar examples could also be given: the point is that families discovered that the demands of the lifestyle pushed unavoidable expenditure to ever higher levels of extravagance, the not unexpected result being a condition of indebtedness. Indeed, the overriding feature of the English aristocracy from the later seventeenth century was the growing problem of making ends meet. Thus Sir Thomas Lowther, a wealthy North Lancashire landowner, played for time when Holker Hall needed reslating in 1729:

as to slating the house I would not have too many things done at once that may be done another year, except that part of the dining room next the court, it being the most seen, would have that done before we come down, with handsome slate, because its much in view and will not cost a great deal.[18]

[16] J. V. Beckett, *Coal and Tobacco: the Lowthers and the economic development of West Cumberland, 1660–1760* (Cambridge, 1981), p. 218; Eric Richards, 'An anatomy of the Sutherland fortune: income, consumption, investments and returns, 1780–1880' *Business History*, 21 (1979), pp. 46, 50; Barbare English, 'On the eve of the great depression: the economy of the Sledmere estate, 1869–18778', *Business History*, 24 (1982), p. 39; Rubinstein, *Men of Property*, p. 199; Spring, 'Land and politics in Edwardian England', p. 20; Olsen, *Town Planning in London*, pp. 47, 56, 220–3.

[17] Paul Nunn, 'Aristocratic estates and employment in South Yorkshire, 1700–1800', in *Essays in the Economic and Social History of South Yorkshire*, ed. Sidney Pollard and Colin Holmes (Sheffield, 1976), p. 39.

[18] Lancashire RO, DDCa/22/2, Sir Thomas Lowther to John Fletcher, 14 June 1729; Pamela Horn, *The Rural World, 1780–1850* (1980), p. 229.

Table 9.3   **Expenditure on the gardens at Stowe, 1750–71**

Year	Cost (£)	Year	Cost (£)
1750	916	1761	932
1751	613	1762	605
1753	826	1763	902
1754	1004	1764	820
1755	1071	1765	1136
1756	526	1766	1676
1757	484	1767	1025
1758	1791	1768	879
1759	660	1769	816
1760	987	1770	1097
		1771	1985

*Source:*Huntington Library, Stowe MSS, ST252, 253

The situation arose in which a group of people who were enormously wealthy – on paper – had difficulty paying their way in life. Thus, according to the probate act books, Sir Mark Sykes of Sledmere in the East Riding left under £70,000 in York province, and under £45,000 in Canterbury. His gross estate was at least £100,000, and yet the Death Duty Registers record the cautionary note that all his assets had been exhausted in paying his debts.[19]

ARISTOCRATIC INDEBTEDNESS: MORTGAGES AND TRUSTS

From the second half of the seventeenth century, the condition of indebtedness among the English aristocracy became increasingly endemic. Borrowing was no new phenomenon. The Elizabethan and early Stuart aristocracy had shown considerable alacrity in borrowing to tide themselves over in difficult times, and Stone has argued that the

[19] English, 'Probate valuations and the death duty registers', p. 87.

demands they made on the credit market were sufficient to ensure high interest rates and to put a permanent brake on the speed of economic growth. Even so, apart from those individuals who in any age were likely to run the most prosperous estate into financial disaster, most borrowing was short-term, and took place in an atmosphere where contemporaries regarded it as a desperate and dangerous expedient. What changed after 1660 was the scale, permanence and attitude towards debt, and responsibility for this lay with the development of the mortgage into a long-term instrument of credit. Prior to 1660 the mortgage came near the bottom of a list of facilities available to hard-pressed landowners. Bonds, recognizances and statutes were mostly preferred, largely because estates were normally undervalued for mortgage purposes. As a result, if the debtor failed to repay the capital on time – which was usually six months or one year – he stood to forfeit the whole estate for failing to pay a sum well below its market value. In practice, the threat of such disasters usually turned out to be more serious than the actual practice, and in any case by the early seventeenth century the courts usually assured defaulters of protection from sudden confiscation, at least while they paid the interest regularly. This did not produce any immediate increase in the use of mortgages, at least prior to 1640, but the situation changed considerably after 1660.[20]

If one factor did more than any other to bring about this change, it was the evolution of the strict family settlement. As it became customary to make provision for younger sons and daughters, as first charges upon the estate, the level of funding increased. Since settled land could not easily be sold, but it could be used as security for borrowing money to pay portions, credit financing became an accepted way of meeting the cost. The problem should not be exaggerated, since some families were able to meet the demands without recourse to borrowing. The first Viscount Lonsdale charged his estate with portions totalling £35,000, of which £10,000 had been found for the portions of his eldest daughters prior to his death in 1700. His successor had to find two further sums of £5000 each for the third and fourth daughters, who married in 1706 and 1707 respectively, and £10,000 for the youngest son, Anthony. Both of his first two sons inherited the estate, while his other daughter died unmarried in 1752 after receiving £300 per annum interest on her portion. All of these costs were met without recourse to sale or mortgage.[21] However, the

---

[20] Stone, *The Crisis of the Aristocracy*, pp. 524–46.
[21] Beckett, thesis, pp. 190–1.

search for status was such that landowners had a tendency to profligacy where daughters were concerned, in their desire for a good match. The second Earl of Nottingham spent £37,000 on portions for his five daughters, and £15,000 was still outstanding when he died in 1729, making a grand total of £52,000. His eldest daughter had a portion of £20,000. Two portions in quick succession could undermine even the best-laid plans. When one of his daughters married in 1709, James Grahme of Levens Hall in Westmorland financed the £3,000 portion by means of a mortgage, but when his other daughter married the following year the portion remained unpaid. The couple separated within a year, and in 1712 the estranged son-in-law demanded payment of the portion, which Grahme could manage only by resort to land sales.[22]

Perhaps the most invidious aspect of borrowing to pay portions was the way in which it inflated the cost. If it was necessary to part with precious acres in order to pay a portion, landowners were likely to look very closely at the sums agreed to. When a man could simply borrow the money, the likelihood increased that he would overstretch himself to attract a particularly good match. In this case it was not always possible to recoup losses by reducing payments to the other children, since the sums were often dictated by his own marriage settlement. In these circumstances the temptation was for an unmarried heir to seek the highest-portioned wife he could attract, but this meant offering a commensurate jointure, and an early death could leave an estate with widow payments for many years. Sir Wilfrid Lawson of Isel in Cumberland died in 1704 leaving a widow, Elizabeth, who received her £300 jointure until 1733. His son, also Sir Wilfrid, died in 1737, and his widow's jointure of £600 a year was still being paid in 1753. In the space of half a century, over £18,000 was paid in jointure money from what was a modest gentry estate of about £1300 a year.[23]

Over time, the burden of family payments may have increased. The demographic crisis among landowners from the mid-seventeenth to the mid-eighteenth centuries meant that families had relatively few offspring to launch into the world. From the late eighteenth century the restoration of more normal fertility levels helped to increase the burden. Coke's overspending between 1776 and 1822 amounted to

---

[22] H. J. Habakkuk, 'Daniel Finch, 2nd Earl of Nottingham: his house and estate', in *Studies in Social History*, ed. J. H. Plumb (1955), pp. 139–78; Beckett, thesis, pp. 310–11.

[23] Carlisle RO, D/Law/1, Particulars of Sir Wilfrid Lawson's estate in Cumberland, April 1718; 26/4, 'Miss Lawson's case'; D/Lons/W, Sir James Lowther to John Spedding, 13 August 1743.

£188,000, of which about half was the result of finding portions for his three daughters. For some families portion payments became a permanent feature of ongoing debt. Portions totalling £80,000 which resulted from the third Earl of Radnor's two marriages in 1801 and 1814 were only discharged after his death in 1869. Portions were an almost permanent outgoing on the earls of Scarbrough's estate.[24]

Family payments were not the only cause of aristocratic indebtedness, but contemporaries usually regarded them as playing a crucial role. A correspondent of the *Gentleman's Magazine* complained in 1752 that 'high taxes and provisions necessary to be made for a family' were the major causes of indebtedness, while by the nineteenth century it became commonplace to argue that debts incurred by family payments were critical for preventing modernization. As late as 1897, even after various legal changes to reduce the financial impact of estate settlements, F. A. Channing was able to argue that

much of the inability of landlords to reduce rents to a level at which profits again become possible, or to provide the improvements and repairs on which profitable working must to some extent depend, is clearly due to the heavy charges on land, either in the form of mortgages, or under settlements for the benefit of members of the owner's family.[25]

However, it is clear that housebuilding and land buying, expenditure on agricultural improvements, and borrowing to finance urban improvement or mining, all helped to push up the level of indebtedness. The important point was the change of expectations. While the annual interest was paid, the principal was not normally demanded, and the practice of borrowing became sufficiently socially acceptable that few aristocrats felt much need to pay their debts.[26]

It would, however, be unfair to tar all landowners with the same brush. Some spent heavily without resort to borrowing. Between 1749 and 1792 Sir John Griffin Griffin of Audley End spent nearly £100,000 on buildings, slightly more on household expenditure, and £118,000 on his estate. His annual income was less than £8000, but he contrived to

---

[24] R. A. C. Parker, *Coke of Norfolk* (Oxford, 1975), p. 130; David Cannadine, 'Aristocratic indebtedness in the nineteenth century: the case re-opened', *Economic History Review*, 2nd ser., 30 (1977), p. 639; T. W. Beastall, *A North Country Estate: the Lumleys and Saundersons as landowners, 1600–1900* (1975), p. 109.

[25] *Gentleman's Magazine*, 22 (1752), pp. 365–6; F. A. Channing, *The Truth about the Agricultural Depression* (1897), p. 140.

[26] In Benjamin Disraeli's *Sybil*, Lord Marney regarded mortgage debts with disdain: 'they are nothing; you find them, you get used to them, and you calculate accordingly': (1845; Oxford, 1981), p. 69.

die solvent – although, in fairness, portions were not a serious drain on his resources. The Duke of Northumberland spent £320,000 rebuilding Alnwick Castle in the 1850s without recourse to loans. Yet others used loans carefully, largely for short-term bridging purposes. The Dudley estate trustees decided to buy the Witley Court estate in Herefordshire, Worcestershire and Shropshire in 1839 largely by mortgage, with agreed payments over a period of years. Even the wealthiest of them all, the dukes of Westminster, were prepared to resort to loans under such circumstances. Despite an income well in excess of £100,000 a year, in the final decades of the nineteenth century a total of nearly half a million pounds was borrowed between 1871 and 1899, mainly for land improvement, the payment of marriage portions and the rebuilding of Eaton Hall in Cheshire.[27] As the Westminster case demonstrates, by the later nineteenth century, landowners did not necessarily borrow merely to finance indebtedness. In 1863 Sir Tatton Sykes laid out a mortgage of his East Riding estate of £100,000 for the benefit of his younger children, with the interest being paid to them from estate income. His son, also Sir Tatton, found himself paying 4 per cent to the mortgagees, but receiving only 3 per cent on his investments in consols. He decided to repay the mortgage, and had redeemed nearly £42,000 by the end of 1867, when he changed his mind. As a result, the estate paid interest to him annually on the £42,000 as the mortgagee of his own land. On the face of it he might have appeared to be in considerable trouble with a mortgage of £100,000, but in practice in 1874 he had a total disposable income of £52,000, reduced by only £2291 as a result of interest payments.[28]

The extent of aristocratic indebtedness is almost impossible to calculate. Few landowners were ready to boast of their debts, or to lay them out clearly in their account books. Moreover, there was an inherent tendency for those with the greatest debts to be the least steadfast in keeping track of them all, since abundant extravagance

---

[27] J. D. Williams, 'The finances of an eighteenth-century Essex nobleman', *Essex Archaeology and History*, 9 (1977), pp. 116–17, 121; T. J. Raybould, *The Economic Emergence of the Black Country* (Newton Abbot, 1973), p. 120; Cannadine, 'Aristocratic indebteness in the nineteenth century', pp. 628–9; M. J. Hazelton-Swales, 'Urban aristocrats: the Grosvenors and the development of Belgravia and Pimlico in the nineteenth century' (University of London, Ph.D. thesis, 1981), p. 174. Portion raising in the nineteenth century has been much debated: see, for the two sides of the argument, F. M. L. Thompson, 'The end of a great estate', *Economic History Review*, 2nd ser., 8 (1955), p. 50, and David Spring, 'English landownership in the nineteenth century: a critical note', *Economic History Review*, 2nd ser., 9 (1956–7), pp. 472–6.

[28] English, 'On the eve of the great depression', p. 39.

seldom went hand in hand with copious attention to business. Many a steward found himself with the unenviable task of unravelling his employer's debts, recorded and unrecorded. Prior to 1640 landowners generally kept the level of debt within manageable proportions, doubtless reflecting the continuing stigma attached to such a situation. During the 1630s, for example, only about one-fifth of the peerage were in debt to individual creditors (the Crown and family apart) for more than two years' income. Of the 121 peers in 1642, 57 had debts of one sort or another. The total amount outstanding was approximately £1½ million, secured on a gross income of £730,000, and against a capital value (at twenty years' purchase) of £13 million.[29] After 1660 the evidence points to a growing level of debt among landowners of every rank, with much of the money borrowed remaining outstanding for long periods of time. The decision to switch from redeeming debts through land sales to maintaining them via mortgages is well illustrated by the activities of the second Earl of Bridgewater. In 1649 he inherited his father's estates and with them debts totalling nearly £52,000, much of it as a result of the first earl's unfortunate decision to back a disastrous voyage to the East Indies by his son-in-law William Couteen. Payment of the debts began in the 1650s through land sales totalling £13,470, but the second earl began to finance repayment through mortgages. By 1662 these totalled £16,000. Over the following two decades he was able to continue relying on mortgages, and the success of his efforts at deriving the largest possible yield from the property enabled him to pay off some of the principal sums during the 1670s. Such was his recovery of the situation that a list of land purchases by the second earl 'in several places' shows an outlay of over £10,000.[30]

Indebtedness mounted after 1660, until by the mid-eighteenth century many families already had an accumulation several generations old. The speed with which financial problems could grow is clear from the case of the second Duke of Kingston. Between 1722 and 1732 his widely scattered estate was in the hands of trustees, since he was still a minor. In these years financial problems were ironed out and rents raised. The second duke came of age in 1733 when he inherited a largely debt-free property, with a net revenue of just under £19,000. By 1736 he had borrowed £16,000 and had also promised a further £20,000 to Philip Meadows, who married his sister Frances. Land sales in 1737 enabled him to pay the portion and £6000 of the £16,000,

[29] Stone, *The Crisis of the Aristocracy*, p. 543.
[30] Huntington Library, Ellesmere MSS, 8141; Charles Hamilton, 'The Bridgewater debts', *Huntington Library Quarterly*, 42 (1978–9), pp. 217–29.

but in 1740 he found it necessary to borrow another £19,000 and to sell more land, in order to buy a London house. Two years later he borrowed a further £16,000 and by 1745 his total debts amounted to £66,000. Despite more land sales it had grown to £70,000 a decade later, largely in funding his new house at Thoresby.[31] A similar case was the great Duke of Newcastle, who inherited his estates debt-free in 1714, and thereafter never had a day of his life in which he was not in financial difficulties. A temporary trust was appointed between 1721 and 1723 to pay some of his debts, and similar arrangement was made after 1738. During these years his large debts were consolidated and some redeemed, but only by reducing his overall landed base. Between 1738 and 1768 the trust paid off over £200,000 of debts, and £79,350 was outstanding at his death. By 1786 the Earl of Scarbrough's debts totalled £77,000. In this instance the situation was considered to be critical, and property in Lincolnshire was sold, reducing his rent roll in the county from £8600 to £6653.[32]

Such problems occurred because creditors were confident about the security of land and therefore allowed unwise owners to swim well out of their depth. The usual means of rescuing a profligate from the consequences of his own indiscretions was to establish a trust, which provided a pause for retrenchment and reorganization. Trusts could be appointed during a minority – as on the Kingston estate – or, as with the Duke of Newcastle, they could be set up to deal with a particular crisis. The minority trusts on the estate of the Lowthers of Holker in North Lancashire between 1705–20 and 1745–8 acted to restore financial equilibrium, while among others established when an estate was *in extremis* were those set up for the marquesses of Ailesbury and Londonderry. Overspending on Tottenham House forced the first Marquess of Ailesbury to sell two houses and put his property into the hands of trustees in 1832. However, this was not one of the more successful trusts, since it proved possible to save only £60,000 out of income during the following twenty-four years, of which £34,000 was applied to debt payment.[33] The third Marquess of Londonderry married in 1819, and trustees were appointed to protect the set-

[31] Peter Mathias, *The First Industrial Nation: an economic history of Britain, 1700–1914* (1969), p. 56; G. E. Mingay, 'The Duke of Kingston and his estates' (University of Nottingham, BA dissertation, 1952), pp. 127–40.

[32] Ray A. Kelch, *Newcastle: a duke without money* (1974), pp. 108, 200–3; Beastall, *A North Country Estate*, pp. 108–10.

[33] Beckett, 'The Lowthers at Holker: marriage, inheritance and debt', p. 59; F. M. L. Thompson, 'English landowners: the Ailesbury Trust, 1832–56', *Economic History Review*, 2nd ser., 11 (1958), pp. 121–32.

tlement. Owing to the circumstances in which it was drawn up, the restrictive clauses it included, and Londonderry's impatience to develop his County Durham coal interests during the 1820s, a family debt of £123,000 in 1819 had risen to at least £286,000 in 1833. Two years later the trustees took control of the estate and its financial management, although they had made little impression on the wall of debt by the time a new settlement was drawn in 1842. Thereafter Londonderry's cavalier management was brought under control, and the marriage settlement trustees proved adequate to the task of preserving a great aristocratic business enterprise.[34]

ARISTOCRATIC INDEBTEDNESS: MEANS OF FINANCIAL RESCUE

Whether or not a trust was used, a family's fortunes were almost invariably rescued before permanent damage could be inflicted. The swings of fortune are particularly apparent in the case of the dukes of Devonshire. By 1790 their incumbrances totalled over £310,000, but the high living of the fifth duke, his wife and mistresses, quickly exacerbated the problem. By 1806 Duchess Georgiana was indebted to the tune of £109,135, and by 1814 the aggregate sum secured on the estates was £593,000. Interest payments alone accounted for £29,000 a year, while annuities and jointures claimed a further £15,000. At his succession in 1811 the sixth duke found that over 60 per cent of his income was not available for personal use. Since the entail had not been barred, scope still existed for borrowing, and he was not disposed to reverse the ways of his forebears. Extensions at Chatsworth, Devonshire House, Bolton Abbey and Lismore Castle, travel, collecting and display, all helped to run up the bills. He spent £147,681 on Chatsworth, and over £300,000 altogether on building. By 1830 his encumbrances topped £700,000, and this would have been higher but for the sale of his Nottingham estates, Burlington House and the Wetherby estate between 1813 and 1824 for nearly half a million pounds. Still the spending went on, and by 1844 the debt reached nearly £1 million. Yorkshire estates were sold for £575,000, and fixed payments reduced from 55 to 30 per cent of annual income by the 1850s. Even so the seventh duke inherited a mortgage debt of just under £1 million in 1858. Although he contemplated land sales, and insisted on retrenchment, by 1864 only £60,000 of debt had been

[34] R. W. Sturgess, 'The Londonderry Trust, 1819–54', *Archaeologia Aeliana*, 5th ser., 10 (1982), pp. 179–92.

cleared. However, his position was transformed by the rise of Barrow-in-Furness, as a result of which his current income shot up from £120,000 in the later 1850s to £310,000 in 1874, and the proportion of income required to service debts fell from 40 per cent in 1861 to just under 16 per cent in 1874. Sustaining this development also required considerable investment, and the duke's indebtedness had risen to a new peak of £1.2 million in 1874. At this point the Barrow boom came to an end, and the duke found himself investing ever-increasing sums for ever-diminishing returns. By the mid-1880s his investments in the town topped £2 million, and by 1888 his indebtedness reached almost that level. The income surplus in 1887 was only £12,067. It was this situation which confronted the eighth duke when he inherited in 1891. Debts were consolidated into two mortgages totalling £950,000, and then reduced by land sales in Ireland and Derbyshire which realized £790,000. At his death in 1908 the eighth duke left £1,165,000, and the family history in the nineteenth century shows quite clearly how unexampled splendour could be combined with severe indebtedness without its proving fatal.[35]

The Devonshires did on a grand scale what others achieved more modestly, but for all the apparent waste few families went bankrupt, which argues that their greatest strength was in knowing when to call a halt. Survival could depend on a number of circumstances: an astute accountant, an efficient trust, a complaisant set of creditors or a lucrative marriage – to name only some of the more obvious paths. But two routes out of the debt impasse were probably more important than any others. The first was the ability of most families to throw up every few generations an heir who took his responsibilities seriously. Among those who helped to rescue their depleted family resources was the seventh Duke of Bedford, a man who saw it as his mission to preserve the family finances: 'it must be my part therefore to repair the breaches that have been made, or the family importance and influence in this country will sink into ruin.'[36] For the Devonshires it was the eighth duke who did most to rescue a deteriorating situation, while the third Duke of Sutherland proved to be his family's saviour, after the second

[35] David Cannadine, 'The landowner as millionaire: the finances of the Dukes of Devonshire', *Agricultural History Review*, 25 (1977), pp. 77–97, 26 (1978), p. 47; Rubinstein, *Men of Property*, p. 205.

[36] Quoted in David Spring, *The English Landed Estate in the Nineteenth Century: its administration* (Baltimore, 1963), p. 26. Bedford inherited debts of £552,000 in 1839, and despite still having a clear yearly income of only £27,000 or £28,000. he paid them over the following two decades.

duke had squandered the wealth bequeathed to him. Between 1833 and 1850, holdings of government stock were cut by half, and in the 1850s it was even necessary to sell land. Vast sums were poured into Trentham, Dunrobin, Cliveden and Stafford House, while expenditure within the household hovered at between £30,000 and £40,000 a year during the 1840s. When the third duke inherited in 1861, he immediately began to diversify the family portfolio by pushing up investments in a wide variety of interests spread around the world. None the less, his multifarious interests continued to be great devourers of money, and few believed that he had spent his fortune wisely.[37]

The second route to survival, for the lucky few, was built upon the profits to be made from urban land, particularly in the capital. W. D. Rubinstein has traced a string of ostensibly landed millionaires who actually held little agricultural property but made their fortunes from urban ground rents in London.[38] For two families in particular, however, London property offered an important way out of financial difficulties: the dukes of Westminster and Portland. Sir Richard Grosvenor, seventh baronet, succeeded to his family estates in 1755. He was created Baron Grosvenor in 1761 and Earl Grosvenor in 1784. He made a disastrous marriage, and nearly ruined himself on the race-course. Continuous borrowing began in the late 1760s, and by 1779 his debts totalled £150,000. Six years later the estates were turned over to trustees because of the serious nature of the financial difficulties. Grosvenor agreed to give up racing – his Newmarket stables cost over £7000 a year to maintain – and he made over most of his rents to the trustees, leaving himself with just £4000 annually. However, he continued to borrow heavily, and he put off selling the stables until 1796. A second trust was formed in 1785, and the debt was reduced to £105,000 by 1791, but when he died in 1802 indebtedness had again risen to over £150,000. At this point the family enjoyed the dual good fortune of rising London rents and fines, and an heir anxious to restore the family's glory. Robert, the second earl and first Marquess of Westminster, was thirty-five when he inherited, and by 1809 he had more or less cleared the debts. His task was facilitated by Mayfair fines totalling £114,553 between 1801 and 1807, and lead-mine income from North Wales of £139,460 between 1801 and 1804. He spent £30,000 on land in Cheshire, and two years later started rebuilding work on the family home at Eaton. By 1819 Earl Grosvenor was considered to be one of the four richest men in

---

[37] Richards, 'An anatomy of the Sutherland fortune', pp. 45–78.
[38] Rubinstein. *Men of Property*, p. 201.

England, with an annual income – according to the Chancellor of the Exchequer – 'beyond one hundred thousand pounds clear of everything'. From that point the family never looked back, although they still contracted mortgages from time to time – £130,000 in the 1820s and 1830s in addition to nearly half a million pounds in the 1870s – and the third marquess and first duke was assessed at his death in 1899 for £600,000 in death duties.[39]

London property also had a spectacular impact on the Portland family finances. In the 1770s the third duke was in sufficiently dire straits to be having difficulty paying tradesmen's bills. He sold estates in Hampshire and Northumberland, mortgaged his Soho property in 1777 for £80,000, and parted with his hounds to the Worksop hunt. This did not prevent a crisis from arising at the end of 1780, by which time borrowing even a few hundred pounds was difficult, servants' wages were unpaid, and domestic bills were outstanding. Portland proved incapable of containing household costs, and by 1795 he was contemplating the sale either of Bulstrode in Buckinghamshire or of his Soho property. Neither had been disposed of when the fourth duke inherited in 1809 to find himself with an estate encumbered to the tune of £512,000. He sold Bulstrode to the Duke of Somerset in 1810, and he also disposed of his property at Ogle and in Cumbria. These, plus timber sales, and the income from renewal fines in Marylebone, cleared off £350,000 of his debts by 1815, when he was still owed £87,000 on the Ogle transaction. Such was the significance of his London property that by 1844 his annual income of £104,000 was clear of encumbrances.[40]

Inevitably some families pushed their luck further than it would naturally go. During the 1840s both the Duke of Beaufort and the Earl of Mornington were in deep financial trouble, and in 1870 the Duke of Newcastle, the Earl of Winchilsea and Lord De Marley were all before bankruptcy courts. The Newcastle debts stood at £158,000 in 1839, and land sales were necessary during the 1840s.[41] But most spectacular

[39] F. H. W. Sheppard, *The Survey of London*, vol. XXXIX: *The Grosvenor Estate in Mayfair*, pt I: *General History* (1977), pp. 1–48; Hazelton-Swales, 'Urban aristocrats', pp. 78–179.

[40] A. S. Turberville, *A History of Welbeck Abbey and its Owners*, vol. II (1939), pp. 154, 156, 307, 317; Nottingham University Library, Pwk 503a, Duke of Portland to Marquess of Titchfield, 19 May 1844.

[41] F. M. L. Thompson, *English Landed Society in the Nineteenth Century* (1963), p. 286; Ken Brand, 'The Park estate, Nottingham: the development of a nineteenth-century fashionable suburb', *Transactions of the Thoroton Society*, 88 (1984), pp. 61–8. According to *The Times*, Newcastle's bankruptcy 'has appreciably shaken popular confidence in the character of our nobility . . . character is to the aristocracy what credit is to a mercantile community': 13 February 1871, p. 9.

of all was the one outright – or nearly outright – disaster, the failure of
the second Duke of Buckingham in 1844 on a scale which turned the
case into a *cause célèbre*. The rise of the Grenvilles was a classic example
of what could be achieved by careful husbanding of limited resources.
When Richard Grenville succeeded his father in 1697, his annual
income was just under £2000, while fixed outgoings rendered him
relatively impecunious. In 1737 the family debts were calculated at
£25,000, but this unpromising situation was transformed via a series
of lucrative marriages. Richard Grenville's (d. 1727) alliance with
Hester Temple in 1710 eventually brought into the family Viscount
Cobham's estates, at Stowe in Buckinghamshire, and in Warwickshire,
in 1749. These had a rental value of slightly under £4000 a year.
Hester Temple, created Countess Temple in her own right in 1749,
was succeeded three years later by her son Richard, the second earl,
who proved assiduous in his attention to developing the family
fortune. His son, the third earl, was created Marquess of Buckingham
in 1784, and further enhanced the family fortunes when he married
Mary Elizabeth Nugent in 1775, as a result of which the family
inherited estates in Ireland, Cornwall and Essex. Finally, in 1796 the
second marquess married Anna Elizabeth Brydges, heiress of the third
Duke of Chandos, who brought with her estates in Hampshire,
Middlesex and Somerset. By 1831 the family property consisted of
40,000 acres in England, yielding around £50,000 annually, plus a
further £10,000 from their Irish property. In addition, a considerable
fortune was held in stocks, and recognition of this enhanced position
came with the creation of a dukedom in 1822. By 1829 the family
income stood at £69,000.[42]

In restrospect, this turned out to be the highpoint from which the
first Duke of Buckingham's extravagance brought the family to grief.
Exactly how he was running the family into debt is not clear, but in
1827 he went abroad to try to stop the spending. This move did not
succeed. Letters written in August and September 1829 to the
Marquess of Chandos, the duke's eldest son, reported the arrival in
London of thirty cases of sculpture from Rome during July and
August, and in September another eleven cases, this time carrying
books, prints, marbles, bronzes, cabinets, paintings, Etruscan vases,

---

[42] Huntington Library, STG Manorial box 41/5, Annual value of the estate,
1829. In addition, there appears to have been a Jamaican estate not included in these
accounts: F. B. Heath, 'Richard Grenville: third Duke of Buckingham and Chandos:
a case study' (University of Southern California, Ph.D. thesis, 1959), p. 14; D. and
E. Spring, 'The fall of the Grenvilles, 1844–48', *Huntington Library Quarterly*, 19
(1956), pp. 165–90.

cameos, and a variety of other artefacts. Chandos was asked what value ought to be given for payable duty.[43] By the end of the year the duke, now back in England, was proposing a trust to help him out of his difficulties, but on terms distinctly favourable to himself:

I propose that a schedule of the state of affairs of mortgage and bond debts and of encumbrances of all kinds be laid before Mr Campbell that he should endeavour to induce a set of capitalists to take mortgages on my land, taking upon themselves all existing mortgages and new ones to cover the bond debts and others and such other additional securities as I and my son can give at 3 per cent or as near that interest as possible. The estates to be put into the hands of trustees to be arranged by my stewards and a certain sum to be assigned for the payment of my family annuities to which I am bound by settlement. A further sum, for my income, the balance of the proceeds of the estates to go to pay the interest of the mortgages and to form a sinking fund for the gradual reduction at compound interest of the debt.[44]

The trust was not forthcoming, but the outlay continued to mount, and by 1835 the true extent of the duke's problems was becoming apparent. His stewards were badgered to forward money to London before they knew the extent of unavoidable commitments; second mortgages were being arranged on a series of properties; and artefacts were being taken from Stowe for sale in London. Sir John Soane was offered some cups, which he turned down 'because he cannot find an appropriate place for them in his house', but the trustees of the British Museum accepted one offer, and those of the National Gallery considered another.[45]

The full extent of Buckingham's troubles is clear from an account drawn in 1837. The duke's property amounted in total to nearly 57,000 acres, including the Irish estates, yielding a gross rental of nearly £56,000. This was even after the sale of property in Oxfordshire and Northamptonshire. Mortgage and bond debts stood at £276,000. Interest on these debts, together with annual annuity payments of

[43] F. M. L. Thompson, 'The end of a great estate', *Economic History Review*, 2nd ser., 8 (1955), p. 45; Huntington Library, STG Correspondence, 368/50, 51, Bingham, Richards and Company to the Marquess of Chandos, 15 August and (?) September 1829.

[44] Ibid., 377/71, Duke of Buckingham to Archibald Campbell, 12 December 1829.

[45] Ibid., 368/18, A. O. Baker to Duke of Buckingham, 26 June 1835, 377/8, Thomas Tindall to Duke of Buckingham, 28 August 1835; 376/28, 32, 33, 34, 37, 38, letters of William James Smith to the Duke of Buckingham, 18 June, 1, 4, 6, 14 and 17 July 1835.

nearly £11,000, and charges of £1800 on unpaid family portions and insurance payments, totalled £25,176. These, plus estate outgoings, reduced his actual income to just under £26,000 a year. However, the estates had been neglected; property in Hampshire, instead of yielding an income, was actually costing money to run. In order to put it into credit, Buckingham was told 'to let the farm, and do away with the stock of game, retaining merely sufficient keepers to protect the property from trespassers, and to dispark the Park, letting the same for sheep pasture.'[46]

It was in this unpromising situation that the first duke died in 1839. The situation called for a steady-headed heir who would attempt to relieve what was a considerable, but not yet ruinous burden of debt. Unfortunately the second duke turned out to be more profligate than his father. His debts had been mounting since his days at Eton, and in five years of glorious extravagance he amassed a deficit of about £1 million in 1844. This was secured on his life interest and personal property; and the annual premium on his life insurance of nearly £300,000, plus the interest on his debts, put his income and outgoings more or less into a straight balance. To alleviate the situation, Buckingham aimed to use his son's coming of age in 1844 to unscramble the family settlement and allow him to sell land in order to pay his debts. Chandos refused, and, after a struggle, in 1847 the estates were made over from father to son, the former becoming a pensioner of the latter. Although the family now had the thrifty son that it had needed in the previous generation, the situation was beyond redemption. In May 1847 the annual charge on the estates exceeded annual income by about £20,000, and by 1848 it was clear that everything would have to go, even down to the contents of Stowe House. The duke was declared a bankrupt dependent on his son's charity, and the family's fate was a warning to other would-be overspenders: as *The Times* conceived of it, this was not only personal ruin but public treason, a blow struck at the confidence of the aristocratic order. Cold shivers must have run down the spine of every indebted landowner, but the tenacity of the aristocratic order was reflected in the capacity of the third duke to rescue a good deal from the ruins. Despite a reduction in his life estates of over £1 million, he was still left with his two Buckinghamshire houses – Wotton, and a rather emasculated Stowe – and Chandos House in London. Through

---

[46] Ibid., Accounts box 180, rental of estates, one year to 1837; Correspondence, SY 27, 1st Duke's letter-books, George Parrott and Co. to Duke of Buckingham, 18 May 1838.

judicious investment, particularly in railway enterprise, he was able to live a respectable life, and to be recognized as a figure of major importance in his native county. Bankruptcy was by no means the end of the road.[47]

ARISTOCRATIC INDEBTEDNESS: SOURCES OF CREDIT

For aristocrats to run up debts of this magnitude, someone had to be ready to make them a loan, and the majority of money was borrowed privately. Interest rates charged on mortgages fell during the course of the eighteenth century, and money could often be borrowed for as little as 4 per cent. This encouraged landowners to increase their indebtedness, and also suggested a pool of available finance. Occasionally this ran dry, as in the immediate aftermath of the Napoleonic wars, when it was claimed that money was not to be had except through private friendship or by paying excessive brokerage.[48] The most obvious source of credit was found within the family. Only one of the outstanding loans on the second Earl of Nottingham's estate in 1729 was to someone to whom he was not related. Two of the third Viscount Lonsdale's loans prior to the South Sea Bubble in 1720 were from cousins: it took him twenty-six years to pay off one, and he failed to recompense the other despite considerable holdings in the funds at his death in 1751. Christopher Haedy was pleased to be able to tell the Duke of Bedford in 1844 that his estate was free of loans from strangers.[49]

After family, in the eighteenth century, private sources and personal contacts were probably the most significant sources of loans, while institutional lenders became increasingly important in the course of the nineteenth century. The Duke of Chandos had about £80,000 lent on three mortgages in 1720, including Bucklebury, Viscount Bolingbroke's estate, and Charles Pye's property at The Mynd, Herefordshire. In the 1730s he had £25,000 lent to Lord Powis.[50] From about 1720 Sir James Lowther began lending substantial sums to

[47] The collapse is detailed by D. and E. Spring, 'The fall of the Grenvilles', and the recovery by Heath, 'Richard Grenville'.

[48] Anon., *Thoughts on the Effects of Peace on Landed Property* (1815), pp. 13–14.

[49] Habakkuk, 'Daniel Finch', pp. 167–8; Beckett, thesis, p. 194; Spring, *The English Landed Estate in the Nineteenth Century*, p. 39.

[50] Huntington Library, STB Correspondence, box 20/62, Duke of Chandos to James Farquharson, 3 January 1738.

fellow aristocrats, including £11,000 to the Earl of Sussex in 1728, £10,000 to Lady Carew the following year, £13,000 to the Duke of Kingston in 1742–3, £24,000 to the Duke of Bedford in 1745 and, most remarkably of all, £60,000 to the fourth Earl of Carlisle. By the time he died in 1755 Lowther had £125,000 outstanding on mortgage loans.[51] The second Marquess of Stafford, after withdrawing from the heat of industrial development during the 1820s, sought a judicious combination of mortgages and government stock, and in 1826 lent £60,000 to the Duke of York and £100,000 to Lord Reay.[52]

At the local level, neighbours were probably the next best bet after family. Of the first Earl of Durham's £635,000 debts at his death in 1841, a considerable slice came from his fellow countrymen, including £30,000 from Sir John Swinburn.[53] Sir James Lowther claimed to prefer lending locally, although he found it troublesome: 'one does not know who to trust, if one be not also on the spot.' But local gentry disliked approaching both Lowther and the former East Indian Company administrator Edward Stephenson, fearing that their real design in offering a loan was to secure the property through default. This was a hazardous course of action, although Lowther did scotch the Earl of Carlisle's attempt to influence the second parliamentary seat at Carlisle in 1752 by threatening to call in the £60,000 mortgage.[54] In 1724 the Duke of Chandos complained:

My cousin Byrdges is very desirous I should lend Mr Hasken £4000 on a mortgage of his estate. I must confess I am much against that way of coming into an estate, for it generally begets a great deal of clamour, and not one mortgagee in ten ever becomes master of the estate he lends upon.[55]

Lord Temple was informed in 1771 of an estate likely to come on the market in a year or two, which he could hope to secure in advance if he was ready to lend the purchase money on mortgage.[56] However, arrangements of this nature were seldom satisfactory. Four years later

---

[51] Beckett, *Coal and Tobacco*, pp. 216–17.

[52] Eric Richards, *The Leviathan of Wealth* (1973), p. 289.

[53] David Spring, 'The Earls of Durham and the great northern coalfield, 1830–80', *Canadian Historical Review*, 33 (1952), p. 250.

[54] Carlisle RO, D/Lons/W, Sir James Lowther to John Spedding, 28 December 1725; J. V. Beckett, 'A back-bench MP in the eighteenth century: Sir James Lowther of Whitehaven', *Parliamentary History*, 1 (1982), p. 83.

[55] Huntington Library, ST 57 Correspondence, 23/272, Duke of Chandos to Mr Pescod, 4 February 1724.

[56] Huntington Library, STG Correspondence, box 418/23 Thomas Astle to Lord Temple, 31 October 1771.

Temple agreed to purchase the Northamptonshire estate of Lord Ferrers. A price of £40,000 was agreed, part of which was to be used for paying encumbrances on the estate. Over the following months, however, it became clear that Ferrers had not revealed all his debts, and the purchase price was insufficient to meet all the encumbraces, leaving Temple to foot the bill for the rest, amounting to £8000. According to Temple's steward, the situation came about because

it is impossible to ascertain what incumbrances affect this or any other estate but from what appears upon the face of the title or judgements and from the accounts that are given in (except in registered counties) for if a seller is unprincipled enough to deceive you it is impossible to avoid it.[57]

This transaction was eventually concluded successfully, but it illustrates the problems faced by landowners and suggests why many of them preferred the greater security of the funds.

The lack of trust when neighbours or friends were involved in lending money meant that many landowners preferred more impersonal sources. Attornies often acted as local brokers. In eighteenth-century Lancashire, for example, attornies dominated the county's mortgage market as a result of their knowledge of local society, and their ability to tap reservoirs of savings. Such facilities also enabled landlords to lend anonymously, and in the nineteenth century the appearance of provincial stock exchanges encouraged this process.[58] However, it was the growth of banking, and later of insurance companies, that provided the major boost to impersonal lending. Country banks may have been reluctant to bestow their resources on needy landowners, although more than half of Lord Londonderry's debts in 1825 were to bankers, which included local firms in County Durham. More substantial were loans from London banks. In 1820 the Bank of England had £1.5 million lent to landowners, but it was the West End banks founded in the eighteenth century which were the most active in this field. The second Duke of Kingston's trustees borrowed £2500 from Hoare's in the 1720s, setting a precedent much employed by their charge after he came of age. Kingston borrowed £10,000 from Hoares' in 1733, and £6000 in

[57] Ibid., box 420/52, William Froggatt to Lord Temple, 20 January 1776. The registered counties were Middlesex and the West and East Ridings of Yorkshire.

[58] B. L. Anderson, 'The attorney and the early capital market in Lancashire', in *Capital Formation in the Industrial Revolution*, ed. F. Crouzet (1972), p. 228; J. R. Killick and W. A. Thomas, 'The provincial stock exchanges, 1830–1870', *Economic History Review*, 2nd ser., 23 (1970), p. 100.

1736. He repaid the latter sum in 1737, but four years later borrowed a further £19,000. His overall debt to the bank was down to £15,000 by 1742 (partly because of the loan from Sir James Lowther), but it rose to £30,000 by 1745, when it represented slightly less than half of his total indebtedness.[59] Hoares also lent extensively to the Duke of Newcastle. Between 1738 and 1754, Newcastle, or his trust, borrowed nearly £100,000, although the whole sum was paid by 1759. Loans of this nature continued in the nineteenth century, including bridging loans (£24,000 to the Duke of Beaufort in 1842) and longer-terms mortgages, such as the £104,000 borrowed by the Ailesbury trustees in 1832. Coutts and Company had £158,000 lent to the fourth Duke of Newcastle in 1839, while the wealthy Duke of Westminster tapped his bankers, Drummond's, for no less than £200,000 in 1871.[60]

A even faster-flowing stream of loan finance was provided from the mid-eighteenth century by insurance company money. The Sun Fire Office had £98,000 lent to aristocrats by 1750, and a total of £345,000 by 1780, at which level it remained down to the 1870s. Its clients included a string of peers (table 9.4). The Equitable had £115,000 lent to landowners by 1780, and nearly half a million pounds a decade later.[61] By 1800 the two companies had £776,000 lent on mortgages, and one historian has concluded that 'half the counties in England and Wales contained some land mortgaged to one or other of the two companies.'[62] This flow increased as the companies came to see mortgages as a vital means of stabilizing their investment income. In 1825 the Royal Exchange Assurance petitioned Parliament to permit it to lend in this manner, and its mortgage loans rose to nearly half a million pounds in 1842, and to £1 million in 1850, at which point they represented almost half of the corporation's assets. The figure was just under £1 million in 1870, nearly £1½ million in

[59] R. W. Sturgess, *Aristocrat in Business: the third Marquis of Londonderry as coalowner and portbuilder* (Durham, 1975), p. 83; Sir John Clapham, *The Bank of England* (Cambridge, 1944), vol. II, pp. 82–4; Mingay, 'The Duke of Kingston and his estates', pp. 138–40; L. Pressnell, *Country Banking in the Industrial Revolution* (Oxford, 1956), pp. 344 ff.; D. M. Joslin, 'London private bankers, 1720–1785', *Economic History Review*, 2nd ser., 7 (1954), pp. 176–9.

[60] Kelch, *Newcastle*, p. 106; Cannadine, 'Aristocratic indebtedness in the nineteenth century', pp. 635–6; Brand, 'The Park estate, Nottingham', pp. 61–3; Hazelton-Swales, 'Urban aristocrats', p. 158.

[61] B. E. Supple, *The Royal Exchange Assurance: a history of British insurance, 1720–1970* (Cambridge, 1970), p. 75.

[62] A. H. John, 'Insurance investment and the London money market in the 18th century', *Economica*, new ser., 20 (1953), p. 157.

Table 9.4 Aristocratic Loans by the Sun Fire Office

Aristocrat	Date	Sum (£)
Earl of Pomfret	1760	20,000
Earl of Northumberland	1760	30,000
Earl of Lincoln	1761	40,000
Duke of Newcastle	1764	20,000
Duke of Bridgewater	1770	25,000
Duke of Leeds	1780	50,000
Lord Rivers	1780	20,000
Lord Delaval	1793	43,000
Lord Penrhyn	1800	40,000
Duke of Devonshire	1810	20,000
Duke of Bedford	1820	40,000
Lord Cowper	1850	20,500

Source: P. G. M. Dickson, *The Sun Insurance Office, 1710–1960* (Oxford, 1960), pp. 249–50.

1890, and again slightly under £1 million in 1900.[63] The desire to borrow certainly did not decrease. The Grahams of Netherby borrowed £30,000 from the Equitable in 1815, £25,000 in 1818 and £45,000 in 1825. By 1838 the family debts totalled £200,000. The London Life Assurance had £115,000 lent to the Earl of Durham in 1841, while in the mid-1860s Royal Exchange loans included £130,000 to the Earl of Strathmore and £138,000 to the Earl of Charlemont. Most spectacular of all was the Norwich Union's decision to lend the second Duke of Buckingham £1.1 million in the 1840s.[64] Clients did not necessarily have to be titled. Among those indebted to the Equitable Assurance was Thomas Johnes, a Cardiganshire landowner who borrowed £34,000 at the end of the eighteenth century, and Ralph Sneyd (£130,000 in the 1840s), while a Northamptonshire family

[63] Supple, *The Royal Exchange Assurance*, p. 332.
[64] Ibid., pp. 312–19; Spring, 'The Earls of Durham and the great northern coalfield', p. 250; David Spring, 'A great agricultural estate: Netherby under Sir James Graham, 1820–1845', *Agricultural History*, 29 (1955), p. 76; P. G. M. Dickson, *The Sun Insurance Office, 1710–1960* (Oxford, 1960), p. 250; Spring and Spring, 'The fall of the Grenvilles', p. 173.

which ran into trouble during the nineteenth century, the Cartwrights, borrowed from the Norwich Union. The Cartwright family's mortgage reached £88,000 by 1896.[65]

In these various ways the aristocracy managed to fund its growing indebtedness. Often families used a variety of different sources. The Duke of Buckingham's debts in 1837 were spread between his bankers Coutts (£84,000), the Equitable Insurance Company (£50,000) and private individuals (sums ranging from £240 to £15,000). Similarly, the first Earl of Durham divided his £635,000 of debts between mortgages to neighbours and a loan from the London Life Assurance Company. Increasingly, however, borrowing appears to have become institutionalized during the nineteenth century, a change reflected in the fact that when the eighth Duke of Devonshire consolidated the family debts in the 1890s he turned exclusively to insurance companies, borrowing £550,000 from the Equitable in 1894, and £400,000 from the Scottish Widows three years later.[66]

Despite the size of some of these sums, the weight of evidence suggests that, while indebtedness was on the increase from the seventeenth century onwards, it was by no means ruinous. Naturally this was not necessarily how contemporaries viewed the situation. James Caird was particularly gloomy in the mid-nineteenth century, concluding in 1851 that the proportion of land encumbered was 'much greater than is generally supposed'. Similarly in 1878 he wrote that 'there are few landowners who have not either inherited, or found it necessary themselves to create mortgages on their estates.'[67] But Caird was keen to emphasize the high level of debt because he regarded it as of critical importance in explaining the lack of agricultural improvement. Another jeremiah with an axe to grind was the Duke of Bedford. His gloomy book on the forlorn condition of his own estates during the agricultural depression failed to notice the prosperity of his West Country estates. The Royal Commission on the Agricultural Depression was told that the total mortgage debt on English land

[65] R. J. Colyer, 'The Halford estate under Thomas Johnes and Henry Pelham, fourth Duke of Newcastle', *Welsh History Review*, 8 (1977), p. 272; David Spring, 'Ralph Sneyd: Tory country gentleman', *Bulletin of the John Rylands Library*, 38 (1956), p. 553; Nicholas Cooper, *Aynho: a Northamptonshire village* (Banbury, 1984), pp. 218, 245–54.

[66] Huntington Library, ST 180, Rental of the estates, 1837: Spring, 'The Earls of Durham and the great northern coalfield', p. 250; Cannadine, 'The landowner as millionaire', p. 90.

[67] James Caird, *English Agriculture in 1850–51* (1852), p. 495; *The Landed Interest and the Supply of Food* (1878), 5th edn (1967), p. 106.

amounted to around £400 million, but this was the estimate of Sir Arthur Arnold, a leading land reformer with every reason to exaggerate the scale of debt.[68] In reality it is known that loans on real property made by United Kingdom Life Assurance Offices increased from £51.6 million in 1870 to £85.2 million by 1900, while the president of the Country Bankers' Association suggested in 1895 that £100–£150 million of short-term bank credit was secured in this way.[69]

These figures did not necessarily imply serious difficulty throughout the aristocracy. Although Evelyn Denison, writing in 1847, claimed that between half and two-thirds of English land was encumbered, a *Times* leader in 1873 argued that, despite an increase in landed estates sold and registered on the estate exchange, 'we apprehend it will be found on close examination that the burdens on land do not yet mount up to such a figure as to assist in accounting for the increase of sales.'[70] Only eight aristocrats went bankrupt between 1900 and 1914, and these were in the lower-income range, while the Inland Revenue accounts based on the death duty returns for the years 1904–14 also suggest that indebtedness was not crippling. On all United Kingdom agricultural property it stood at 27.4 per cent of the value of tenure, with smaller proprietors being more heavily in debt than their larger neighbours. Debt as a proportion of tenure was as low as 5 per cent on some of the largest estates.[71] Although these figures imply that more than one-third of land and house property was mortgaged, taken together with other evidence they suggest that the landlord class had adopted a form of professional pessimism. This was perhaps explicable in the later nineteenth century in view of the impact of agricultural depression on rent rolls and land values. Death duties simply heightened the gloom. The evidence of landowners diversifying their interests into shares and government bonds, and of a decline in their personal wealth during the nineteenth century, suggests that their pessimism was not entirely unfounded.[72] On the other hand, the fact that extensive land sales did not begin until after the First World War suggests that some of the complaints were not based on solid foundations.

[68] Parl. Papers, *Report of the Royal Commission on the Agricultural Depression* (1895), C. 7400, vol. III, p. 21.

[69] Supple, *The Royal Exchange Assurance*, p. 332; Avner Offer, *Property and Politics, 1870–1914* (Cambridge, 1981), pp. 142–3.

[70] *The Times*, 6 January 1873.

[71] Offer, *Property and Politics*, pp. 138–40; Spring, 'Land and politics in Edwardian England', pp. 28–9.

[72] Cannadine, 'Aristocratic indebtedness in the nineteenth century', pp. 645–9; Rubinstein, *Men of Property*, p. 207.

ARISTOCRATIC BORROWING AND ECONOMIC GROWTH

Perhaps more significant than the level of debt was the use made of the
money borrowed by aristocrats. Sometimes the reason for borrowing is
clear. It might be to finance building operations or to fund a mass of
unpaid bills. More often, debts crept up without any obvious reason.
The detailed accounts of Samuel Whitbread's estate for the years
1796–1813 reveal a regular pattern of expenditure exceeding income,
with the predictable result that interest and annuity payments were by
far the most significant single outgoing. Even banks could not control
this creeping form of debt, as Coutts found when the Duke of
Newcastle's loans reached nearly £160,000 in 1839, forcing them to
go 'much out of our usual course'. Despite their complaints, the fourth
duke made little effort to alter the situation.[73] In general, all too little
is known about the origin of debts, partly because insurance company
records do not usually state the purpose of a loan. However, some
attempt is necessary to distinguish between debts incurred as a result
of capital investment for economic development, and those which
originated merely in conspicuous consumption. Only in this way is it
possible to ask searching questions about the significance of aristocratic
debt for productive investment.

On the face of it, a social group which was extremely wealthy in
terms of capital and recurrent income hardly looks to have been an
asset when it was so heavily in debt. Rents and royalties were
apparently being sucked into conspicuous consumption and frittered
away in spiralling marriage settlements; and the gap between getting
and spending was filled not by offloading assets such as land, but by
borrowing from – in effect – the commercial, industrial and
shopkeeping members of the populace. The aristocracy might therefore
have been expected to act as a positive check on progress rather than
contributing to the expansion of the economy, although their spending
on housebuilding and other forms of consumption inevitably provided
employment and generated activity. However, it would be simplistic
to dismiss their contribution on these grounds alone, since it is
apparent that in many instances they took financial risks with their
own and other people's capital which ultimately helped to boost the
economy. The point must not be pressed too far. Risks they may have
taken, but few aristocrats were businesslike through and through, and
any assessment of their role has to take account of the fact that they

[73] Roger Fulford, *Samuel Whitbread, 1764–1815* (1967), pp. 309–16; Brand 'The
Park estate, Nottingham', pp. 61–3.

often acted in contradictory ways. Progressive agriculturalists such as the sixth Duke of Bedford and second Duke of Buckingham also turned out to be notorious spendthrifts. Even the Leveson-Gowers more than balanced their massive industrial and communications investments with conspicuous consumption on servants, houses, art, and other unproductive forms of outlay. Hence the conclusion drawn by the family's chronicler that 'the Sutherland fortune was not well used in the Victorian economy. Ostentatious consumption and eccentric investment, on most criteria, imply a misallocation of scarce capital resources.'[74]

Since estates were trusts to be maintained and developed, aristocrats had a family and public duty to take a direct lead in both conserving and improving their interests. Obviously the interpretation of this duty varied. Few were as active as Joseph Wilkes at Measham in Leicestershire in the late eighteenth century. His industrial interests lay in coal mines, cotton spinning and cheese manufacture, his communications concerns included the Ashby de la Zouch Canal and local turnpike roads, and he also held a partnership in a London bank.[75] Contributors like Wilkes played a vitally important role in stimulating economic development. It was their willingness to invest nearly half a million pounds in West Cumberland that enabled the Lowther family to dominate the coal trade. Small owners could not compete with a wealthy family prepared to risk capital on Newcomen engines and on pioneering mining developments. One pit, Saltom, stretched out beneath the sea, and cost Sir James Lowther nearly £2000 to open up between 1729 and 1732 before any coal was raised. No other West Cumberland family was in a position to take such risks, at least before 1750.[76] The Duke of Bridgewater's canal was vital to the prosperity of Manchester, but it was only possible because he was ready to underwrite an expensive, untried development. In this sense his property assets were critical for securing the finance to promote an important communications breakthrough previously untried in the English industrial environment. Similarly visionary was the third Marquess of Londonderry, whose creation at Seaham between 1821 and 1835 looked foolhardy in the extreme, but succeeded because of his willingness to promote a grandiose scheme where more sober financial counsellors would have advised caution.

Much the same can be said of the marquesses of Bute. When the

---

[74] Richards, 'An anatomy of the Sutherland fortune', p. 70.
[75] Mingay, *English Landed Society in the Eighteenth Century*, p. 199.
[76] Beckett, *Coal and Tobacco*, p. 76.

second Marquess drew up plans to build a dock at Cardiff during the 1820s, the scheme was as speculative as Seaham. Bute's only hope of success was to provide the necessary capital himself. To this end he mortgaged the whole of his Glamorgan estate to the Pelican Life Assurance Office for £100,000, and he followed this with a series of further loans from the Equitable Life amounting to £185,000 by 1846. The Equitable started to press for payment in 1843, and Bute was forced to sell property in order to relieve his position. By 1868 when the third marquess came of age, much of the outstanding debt had been consolidated into a single mortgage to the company of £190,000. By such risky means Cardiff was turned into a large town and the leading British coal-trading port, but as far as the family was concerned the advantages of the dock-building scheme was ambiguous. The enterprise may have hastened the second marquess's death, and it proved a severe financial embarrassment to the third and fourth marquesses. The return on capital was meagre, and the only measurable advantages were the more rapid increase in mineral royalties because of good dock facilities and the rise in land values in the town. Only when it became possible to float the docks as a private company in the 1880s was relief afforded to the hard-pressed family finances.[77]

Aristocrats were often prepared to invest and to go on investing in schemes which carried prestige and status, beyond the point at which more commercially minded entrepreneurs would have been expected to drop out. While this could lead to unprofitable investment in housebuilding and land purchase, it could also produce Seaham, Cardiff and, of course, Barrow-in-Furness. The activities of the seventh and eighth dukes of Devonshire in Barrow provide a pertinent example of this process. The rapid increase in the seventh duke's income between the 1850s and 1870s was a result of his Barrow investments. Largely through the discovery of iron ore, and the determination of the then Lord Burlington to develop the town, it grew from a village of 150 people in 1846 to a thriving urban centre of more than 40,000 in 1874. The duke was an active investor in the Furness Railway, in housing and in harbour and industrial development, but this was only possible by putting up vast amounts of capital, which increased his indebtedness. When the venture began to turn sour and the town was hit by falling demand for its iron, and also by falling prices, the only source of continuing investment was the Duke of Devonshire. Between 1874 and 1876 he poured no less than £300,000 into the ailing

---

[77] John Davies, *Cardiff and the Marquesses of Bute* (Cardiff, 1981), pp. 65, 67, 72, 299–300, and ch. 7.

shipbuilding company, and in 1878 he had to find a further £270,000. He was also obliged to put £150,000 into the Flax and Jute Company in 1876, and a further £87,000 in 1882. Hence Sidney Pollard's conclusion that 'in the fifteen years following 1874 the resources of the great estates of the house of Devonshire were diverted to shoring up Barrow's crumbling industrial enterprises.' And this was completely separate from his other great undertaking at Eastbourne.[78]

The dukes of Devonshire may have been unusual, but they were not alone in taking the lead in innovatory and often risky concerns. The Dudleys, Dartmouths and Leveson-Gowers in the Black Country, the earls Fitzwilliam and dukes of Norfolk in the West Riding of Yorkshire, the Lonsdales and Curwens in Cumberland, and the earls of Durham and marquesses of Londonderry in the north-east were all men of similar outlook. If it was agents who were responsible for the everyday management of an estate, it was the owners who put in the money, and to this extent some of the more gloomy pronouncements about their financial position in the nineteenth century were obviously exaggerated. James Caird was in no doubt that landlord indebtedness was detrimental to agricultural progress:

But there is one great barrier to improvement, which the present state of agriculture must force on the attention of the legislature, the great extent to which landed property is encumbered. In every county where we found an estate more than usually neglected, the reason assigned was the inability of the proprietor to make improvements, on account of his encumbrances.

Landlords were short of capital, and their settlements prevented them from disposing of their property to enterprising capitalists who would improve the land for the general benefit of society: 'a neglected estate would then become a matter of choice to men of capital, and the progress of improvement would be rapid beyond precedent.'[79] In fact it was easy to exaggerate the problems caused by indebtedness. Agriculture may have been overcapitalized in the mid-nineteenth century, and in the fifty years 1847–97 £16.5 million was spent on improvements. Although it was acknowledged that changes in settlement law would help to relieve some unwanted encumbrances, it was not clear that economic progress was positively hindered by the strict settlement. Borrowing was easiest when an owner had absolute control, but it was not prevented when this was not the case. Land

[78] Sidney Pollard, 'Barrow-in-Furness and the seventh Duke of Devonshire', *Economic History Review*, 2nd ser., 8 (1955), p. 217.
[79] Caird, *English Agriculture*, p. 495.

might be left out of settlement, or alternatively settlements might include powers allowing a family to engage in productive enterprise. Even a restricted owner such as the third Marquess of Londonderry raised considerable sums of money. Furthermore, these families were ready to borrow in order to finance industrial and other ventures, even in the mid-nineteenth century, when the return on consols offered them a better investment. In other words, their investments were not necessarily geared to the concept of an immediate return.[80]

It is easy to critize the aristocracy for not doing enough. In their own time they were alternately lauded and reviled. Consumption was inherently good for the economy according to Bernard Mandeville and Malthus, but after the publication of Adam Smith's *Wealth of Nations* contemporaries were less favourable towards the group. Aristocrats were accused of keeping tenants in subjection by means of annual leases and through their failure to compensate for unexhausted improvements. Nor have historians found it more difficult to find fault. Sir James Lowther siphoned off West Cumberland coal trade profits to finance his stockmarket dealings, and failed to promote diversification within the regional economy, while at least from the 1770s the Leveson-Gowers took more out of industry than they put in, with the result that they have been accused of misspending their fortune. But this, surely, is to miss the point. Lowther's role was still critical for building up the West Cumberland coal industry, while Black Country landowners both served the trading interests of their locality, and took 'a number of initiatives which directly influenced the timing, location, scale and prospect of economic activities within the Black Country'.[81] Aristocratic risk-taking produced Seaham and Barrow, as well as similar projects which required a man to use his landed estate in order to offer borrowing security and often to pay the interest from other income sources. It was this willingness to borrow, and to go on borrowing, as well as to back innovatory projects with their own prestige, which was distinctive. Moreover, reducing the argument to simple economic terms ignores the much broader contribution in disseminating ideas and promoting legislation. Through government they provided a favourable climate for economic development. Finally, aristocrats were not simply businessmen. The maintenance of their social position depended on conspicuous consumption and ostentatious display, so that none could be entirely rational in their spending.

[80] Channing, *The Truth about the Agricultural Depression*, p. 126.
[81] Trevor Raybould, 'Aristocratic landowners and the industrial revolution: the Black Country experience, *c.* 1760–1840', *Midland History*, 9 (1984), p. 83.

In the circumstances, the aristocratic contribution to economic development should not be underplayed. If it cannot be measured with any real accuracy in aggregative terms, it was none the less crucial, particularly in stimulating new ventures. The English aristocracy may not all have been thrusting entrepreneurs, but the desire to conserve and develop their estates gave them a vital role to play in economic development which ensured that they were active leaders rather than passive spectators.[82]

[82] The positive view of aristocratic involvement in economic development is widely accepted: H. J. Habakkuk, 'Economic functions of English landowners in the seventeenth and eighteenth centuries', *Explorations in Entrepreneurial History*, 6 (1953), pp. 92–102; G. E. Mingay, 'The large estate in eighteenth-century England', *First International Conference of Economic History* (Stockholm, 1960), p. 383; E. L. Jones, *Agriculture and the Industrial Revolution* (1974), p. 109; Cannadine, 'Aristocratic indebtedness in the nineteenth century', p. 644; Wordie, *Estate Management in Eighteenth-Century England*, pp. 272–8; F. M. L. Thompson, 'English landed society in the nineteenth century', in *The Power of the Past*, ed. P. Thane *et al.* (Cambridge, 1984), pp. 195–214.

Part III

The Aristocracy in Society and Government

Chapter Ten

The Aristocracy at Home: Social Leadership

The landowner . . . is necessarily concerned in the general prosperity and good management of his estate, and in the welfare of those who live upon it, with which his own is so closely involved. He takes a lead in the business of his parish, and from his class·the magistrates who administer the criminal affairs of the county, and superintend its roads, its public buildings, and charitable institutions, are selected. Nor do his duties end here, for the landowner, from his position, is expected to be at the head of all objects of public utility, to subscribe to, and, if so inclined, to ride with the hounds, showing at once an example to the farmers and tradesmen, and meeting them on terms of neighbourly friendship and acquaintance. The same example is carried out in his intercourse with the clergy and the schoolmaster, and his influence, where wisely exercised, is felt in the church, the school, the farm, and the cottage.

James Caird, *The Landed Interest and the Supply of Food* (1878), 5th edn (1967), pp. 56–7

The aristocratic contribution to the economy between 1660 and 1914 ensured that the group did not become an anachronism, but of itself this does not explain its continued leadership of society and politics almost into the twentieth century, particularly in view of the experiences of its Continental counterparts from 1789 onwards. This survival, when European nobilities were being challenged, was remarkable, and stemmed from the acceptance of aristocratic social mores and assumptions about English society and politics, which persisted through the upheavals of Georgian and Victorian England. Since leadership was a duty, it is hardly surprising that aristocrats continued to set social standards, and to control the reins of government unless they were challenged. More difficult to explain is why the rest of society accepted the status quo, and why, even in the 1890s, aristocrats loomed large in government. In the search for answers to these questions, attention must be turned to the formal and informal control that the aristocracy exercised in rural England, and the means that they employed to influence political life. By the end of the nineteenth century their position was slipping: in the countryside they were increasingly under challenge; in the towns they had been unable to maintain their place in the light of massive urbanization; and, in local and national political life, institutional reform was gradually undermining their entrenched position. What is most remarkable is that their control continued for so long, and that when it slipped it did so peacefully, and by agreement with the rest of society, rather than through the upheavals of revolution.

THE COUNTRY HOUSE: BUILDING AND LANDSCAPE GARDENING

The basis of aristocratic power lay in the countryside, and this was something which was never forgotten – even if constant reminders were necessary – by the governing elite.[1] James I and Charles I tried to drive those gentry too enamoured of London life back into the countryside, issuing proclamations against spending legal-term holidays in London, and even prosecuting those who failed to conform.[2] After 1660, however, the aristocracy flocked back to the capital. Solemn warnings continued to be issued, and care was taken to avoid measures which might discourage them from staying in the countryside. Thus, in the course of a parliamentary debate during the 1790s, various speakers pointed out that any attempt to repeal the game laws was not to be interpreted as an interference with gentlemen's sport. John Christian Curwen, the motion's sponsor, was 'sensible that the residence of gentlemen in the country is a most desirable object, and tends much to the happiness of the bulk of the people', while similar sentiments were expressed by another member:

the reason why he was particularly desirous of the preservation of the game was, that while the capital presented so many attractions as it did at present to country gentlemen, and that while it was of so much consequence to the country that they should reside for some time on their estates, he was anxious

---

[1] Although it has often been argued to the contrary, the importance of rural residence was widely recognized among European nobilities: William Doyle, *The Old European Order, 1660–1800* (Oxford, 1978), pp. 86–7.

[2] Lawrence Stone, *The Crisis of the Aristocracy, 1558–1641* (Oxford, 1965), pp. 393, 397–8.

that the country should present as many temptations as possible to invite them to their rural retreats.[3]

Prolonged absence had both economic consequences – as we have seen – and also social repercussions, but most aristocrats appreciated the problems and conscientiously paid regular visits, even if these were of varying duration. The coming of the railway proved to be a particular godsend to them. As Hippolyte Taine noted in the 1870s:

during the season, the Saturday evening train transports from London a number of landed proprietors who proceed to a distance of forty, eighty, one hundred miles to deliver a lecture, hold a meeting, fill the unpaid office of magistrate or overseer of the parish or the church.[4]

For most landowners this journey took them to the axis of their rural position, the country house.

If the prestige of an aristocratic family largely depended on the extent of its acreage, the size and extent of its houses and parks was of considerable significance. Furthermore, a new or rebuilt house stood as a permanent memorial to the builder, singling him out from the essential continuity of estate management. Not surprisingly, building, rebuilding and remodelling of country houses was a favoured if expensive aristocratic hobby. In the course of the eighteenth century, new houses tended to be smaller than in the past, but simultaneously the movement for improving the parkland and gardens surrounding country houses reflected a further attempt to boost prestige.

Between 1660 and 1914 the two major building periods were from 1660 until 1730, and again from the 1790s until well into the nineteenth century. Blenheim, Castle Howard, Holkham, Houghton, Moor Park and Eastbury – the six largest houses of the eighteenth century – were all begun during the years 1700–25, while no less than one-third of the 150 houses started in the period 1710–40 were begun between 1720 and 1724. Among the Cumbrian gentry who built or extended their houses in this early period were Sir John Lowther at Whitehaven, Daniel Wilson at Dallam Tower, Thomas Howard at Corby Castle and Edward Hasell at Dalemain, while even some of the lesser local families were in a position to build new houses.[5] Heather

---

[3] *Parliamentary Register*, 44 (1796), pp. 232, 240.

[4] Hippolyte Taine, *Notes on England* (1872), pp. 167, 171.

[5] M. W. Barley, 'Rural building in England', in Joan Thirsk (ed.), *The Agrarian History of England and Wales*, vol. V: *1640–1750* (1985), pt II, p. 600; Beckett, thesis, pp. 117–18.

Clemenson's sample of 500 estates indicates a rise in building activity towards the end of the seventeenth century, lasting into the eighteenth. This trend seems to have come to a halt during the 1730s and 1740s, which were decades of agricultural depression, but to have picked up again some time after mid-century. Thus, in Nottinghamshire, thirty gentry families built houses for themselves between 1760 and 1800, while more aristocratic building took place in South Yorkshire between 1750 and 1790 than either before or after.[6] However, general patterns hide a multitude of differences. Northamptonshire had seventy or eighty seats around 1640, but losses over the following century slightly exceeded newcomers, and the country had about seventy houses from 1740. Hertfordshire had about the same number in 1640, but its stock continued to increase thereafter, reaching about ninety-five in 1780, at which level it remained until a final influx pushed the total past 105 in the 1860s. Northumberland's stock grew steadily between 1660 and 1840 to reach more than sixty at the latter date.[7]

The level of building activity in the later eighteenth and nineteenth centuries has been a matter for debate. David Spring has suggested that aristocratic building activity, on English estates of 10,000 acres or more, remained buoyant in both new construction and extensive alteration down to about 1830, but fell away thereafter. Support for this argument is to be found in Clemenson's survey, since she found that 'investment in alternations, adaptations, and extensions rose to unprecedented heights from the late 1790s reaching a peak around the 1830s.'[8] The early nineteenth century was a great period for the building and rebuilding of stately homes by north-eastern coal magnates, and the period 1790–1845 witnessed the peak of building activity in Lincolnshire.[9] Spring has also argued that building activity

[6] Heather Clemenson, *English Country Houses and Landed Estates* (1982); J. D. Chambers, 'The Vale of Trent, 1670–1800', *Economic History Review*, supplement (1957), p. 49; Paul Nunn, 'Aristocratic estates and employment in South Yorkshire, 1700–1800', in *Essays in the Economic and Social History of South Yorkshire*, ed. S.Pollard and C. Holmes (Sheffield, 1976), p. 43, n. 35.

[7] Lawrence Stone and Jeanne C. Fawtier Stone, *An Open Elite? England, 1540–1880* (Oxford, 1984), pp. 359–63, 388.

[8] David Spring, 'Aristocratic indebtedness in the nineteenth century: a comment', *Economic History Review*, 2nd ser., 33 (1980), p. 566n.; Clemenson, *English Country Houses and Landed Estates*, p. 50. Spring has been accused of being unsystematic: David Cannadine, 'Aristocratic indebtedness in the nineteenth century: a restatement', *Economic History Review*, 2nd ser., 33 (1980), p. 570n.

[9] M. W. Flinn, *The History of the British Coal Industry*, vol. 2: *1700–1830* (Oxford, 1984), p. 327; R. J. Olney, *Rural Society and County Government in Nineteenth-Century Lincolnshire* (Lincoln, 1979), p. 31.

fell away after 1830. Against this, however, Clemenson has concluded that the whole period down to 1880 saw remodelling, rebuilding and extending of country houses; Girouard has argued that building activity steadily increased from 1835, only falling away in the 1870s when the agricultural depression began to bite; and Franklin has pointed to the significance of the middle decades of the nineteenth century for building.[10] Casual surveys such as those of Girouard and Franklin are not necessarily systematic, and the argument needs to be handled carefully in view of aristocratic indebtedness, and the growing preference among the newly rich for a house in the country rather than the full trappings of a country house.

Simply counting the number of houses at any one time gives a misleading impression of the level of building activity. It reveals, for example, little about the rate of replacement on the same site, or the regularity of extensions to the existing house. Nor can the disappearance of houses be taken to reflect a contraction in the number of landlords, since owners with more than one house often preferred to save on costs by dispensing with redundant properties. The sixth Earl of Thanet inherited four restored castles in Westmorland in the 1680s, but within a few years he pulled down three and used the surplus materials to alter the one he retained, at Appleby.[11] Furthermore, once abandoned, some houses deteriorated very rapidly, while others, especially those built of stone, could still be rescued after some years. Thus Elizabeth Montagu was able to revive Denton Hall in Northumberland during the 1750s, even though it had been neglected for thirty years.[12]

Much depended on style, and the recognized peak in house destruction between the 1780s and 1830s may have been a result of the move from the classical style to the Gothic revival. In the 1760s Alnwick Castle was given an 'air of Gothic grandeur', its face being 'restored to nearly the same appearance it had 300 years ago'. The first Earl of Sheffield was responsible for another of the early Gothic creations with his new Wealden house in 1779, and two decades later Sir Bysshe Shelley straddled the tastes at Castle Goring with a Gothic

---

[10] Clemenson, *English Country Houses and Landed Estates*, p. 46; Mark Girouard, *The Victorian Country House* (1979), p. 9; Jill Franklin, *The Gentleman's Country House and its Plan, 1835–1914* (1981), pp. 24–5.

[11] Beckett, thesis, p. 74.

[12] Emily J. Climenson, *Elizabeth Montagu: the queen of the Bluestockings* (1906), vol. I, pp. 289–90, vol. II, p. 136; M. Montagu (ed.), *Letters of Elizabeth Montagu* (1809), vol. IV, p. 111; N. Pevsner, *The Buildings of England: Northumberland* (1957), p. 137.

north face and a strict classical south.[13] The change in taste took place only slowly; in Girouard's sample of 500 country houses built between 1835 and 1889, 41 per cent of those dating from the years 1840–4 were still in the classical tradition, but this had fallen to only 16 per cent two decades later. By the 1830s a growing interest in the past extended the range of fashionable taste to embrace earlier styles, and with this came a preference for preservation rather than replacement.[14]

The survival of a particular house was often a matter of good fortune. The chief seat of a long-established landowner was the most likely to endure through time, but, however desirous the owners may have been to retain the place, the vicissitudes of natural disaster could often force their hand. Fire was a particular hazard. In Hertfordshire, about 10 per cent of all houses were partially destroyed by fire every hundred years. Some landowners took the opportunity thus provided to build afresh. After the destruction of Henderskelfe Castle in 1693, only a decade after it had been rebuilt, the earls of Carlisle concentrated their attention and money on the building of Castle Howard in Yorkshire. This was completed between 1699 and 1737.[15] Others were less willing to take such initiatives. The first Viscount Lonsdale rebuilt his ancestral home of Lowther Hall on a new site in the later 1690s, and his son intended further embellishments in 1714. But in 1718 the hall was partially destroyed in a fire, and the third viscount – a bachelor who spent little time in the north – did not complete repairs until the 1740s. Eventually the house was replaced between 1806 and 1811 with Smirke's Lowther Castle, a vast edifice which was gutted in the 1950s when it became too expensive to keep up.[16]

The cost of building was such that the most common practice was extension and improvement. Few country houses seem to have remained entirely in the form that they were built, as successive generations of owners attempted to imprint their own stamp on the property. Wroxton Abbey, in North Oxfordshire, was built in the early

---

[13] HMC, *Hastings MSS*, vol. III, p. 149; Howard Colvin and John Harris (eds), *The Country Seat: studies in the history of the British country house* (1976), pp. 205–7. For a lengthier discussion of taste, see Michael Reed, *The Georgian Triumph, 1700–1830* (1984 edn), pp. 114–28.

[14] Girouard, *The Victorian Country House*, p. 52; Stone and Stone, *An Open Elite?*, p. 365.

[15] Stone and Stone, *An Open Elite?*, pp. 368–9; N. Pevsner, *The Buildings of England: the North Riding* (1966), pp. 106–9.

[16] Beckett, thesis, p. 190; N. Pevsner, *The Buildings of England: Cumberland and Westmorland* (1967), p. 272.

seventeenth century on the foundations of a former priory. Later in the century a north wing and stable block were constructed, while a library and chapel were added in the 1740s, another library in the 1820s, and finally a south wing in 1859 to match the north wing thrown up in the 1670s.[17] The present house is much larger than the seventeenth-century original, and in these circumstances it is not surprising that existing houses tended to grow through time. The bulk of all building in Northamptonshire and Hertfordshire took the form of remodelling or additions. A county such as Northamptonshire had little scope for new houses after the early eighteenth century, with the result that from about 1680 country houses were tending to increase in size rather than numbers.[18]

How much did the aristocracy spend on building? Obviously it was more expensive to build from scratch than to add to the existing structure, but even some of the latter changes were costly and could outrun the best-prepared estimates. A correspondent of the *Gentleman's Magazine* wrote scornfully in 1767 of a friend in the country who had made such improvements to his house that he had 'beggared himself, and spent the fortunes of three or four children in what he called improvements, though it appeared to me that all the money had been thrown away, without either taste or common sense'[19] It is always difficult to determine exactly what was included in building accounts. The overall cost might be inflated by including the land and the interior decorations and furnishings; it might also be artificially deflated if the builder used materials such as stone already on the site from a previous house. Again, some of the highest figures were little more than contemporary guesses, such as the £150,000 quoted for Moor Park in Hertfordshire, and £140,000 for Eastbury in Dorset, although Blenheim really does seem to have cost about £300,000. An indication of the cost of some of the larger houses is given in table 10.1, although few of these sums represented the total expenditure. Some families had several homes to maintain. The second Duke of Sutherland, for example, laid out £72,000 on Trentham Hall in the 1830s, £10,000 to £15,000 annually during the 1840s on Dunrobin; £59,000 on Cliveden in 1849; and a total of £277,000 on Stafford House (including the purchase price of £92,000) by 1841. Others built and rebuilt on the same site. Examples include Thoresby (table

[17] Carol D. Frost and Blythe W. Marston, 'Wroxton: an abbey, a history', *Cake and Cockhorse*, 7 (1978), pp. 137–46. For a similar example, see Joan Wake, *The Brudenells of Deene* (1953), for Deene Hall.
[18] Stone and Stone, *An Open Elite?*, pp. 377–8.
[19] *Gentleman's Magazine*, 37 (1767), p. 287.

10.1), and the dukes of Westminster's Eaton Hall. Lord Grosvenor spent £100,000 remodelling the house between 1804 and 1812, while the first duke rebuilt it at a cost of £564,000 between 1870 and 1883.[20] At the other end of the scale a modest country house could still be built for around £3,000 late in the seventeenth century – the main expense at Earl Cowper's Cole Green Park was the internal fittings since construction cost only £1,720 – and the lesser gentry built for hundreds rather than thousands of pounds.[21]

Nor was the outlay completed when the building work was finished, since in many instances the cost of decorating and furnishing new rooms was separately accounted. Viscount Lonsdale's costs at Lowther Hall in the later seventeenth century included £195 for marble from London and £430 paid to the Italian artist Antonio Verrio for painting the hallway. The Duke of Chandos laid out considerable sums fitting up Cannons, while in the second half of the eighteenth century Sir John Griffin Griffin spent £13,424 on furniture at Audley End; more than £900 was spent on the drawing-room at Mersham le Hatch in Kent; and furnishings for Newby Hall cost over £6000. At Thoresby in the 1870s the cost of stables, a woodyard and new kennels totalled over £37,000, which was in addition to the cost of the mansion house.[22]

Few aristocrats had an income which enabled them to provide this level of finance without some inconvenience. Only the very rich could hope to build a new house from scratch, or to raze an old one and start again. It was incomers who were the most likely to build, including, for example, the London financiers who put up conspicuous houses in Hertfordshire.[23] Usually outlay could be spread over a period of time.

---

[20] Barley, 'Rural building in England', pp. 601–2; E. Richards, 'An anatomy of the Sutherland fortune: income, consumption, investments and returns, 1780–1880', *Business History*, 21 (1979), p. 55; M. J. Hazelton-Swales, 'Urban aristocrats: the Grosvenors and the development of Belgravia and Pimlico in the nineteenth century' (University of London, Ph.D. thesis, 1981), pp. 134, 173; Jill Franklin, 'The Victorian country house', in *The Victorian Countryside*, ed. G. E. Mingay (1981), pp. 399–413.

[21] Colvin and Harris, *The Country Seat*, pp. 75–9; Barley, 'Rural building in England', p. 621.

[22] Beckett, thesis, p. 190; C. H. C. and M. I. Baker, *The Life and Circumstances of James Brydges, First Duke of Chandos* (Oxford, 1949), pp. 148, 162 ff.; J. D. Williams, 'The finances of an eighteenth-century Essex nobleman', *Essex Archaeology and History*, 9 (1979 for 1977), pp. 116–17; Christopher Hussey, *English Country Houses: Mid Georgian, 1760–1800* (1956), pp. 100–1, 144; Nunn, 'Aristocratic estates and employment', p. 39; Nottingham University Manuscripts Department, Ma 2a 208.

[23] Stone and Stone, *An Open Elite?*, p. 390.

Table 10.1   Examples of spending on country houses

Owner	House	Dates	Cost (£)
Earl of Nottingham	Burley	1694–	31,000
Earl of Carlisle	Castle Howard	1699–1737	78,000
Marquess of Rockingham	Wentworth Woodhouse	1723–50	80,000
Earl of Leicester	Holkham	1732–66	92,000
Sir James Dashwood	Kirtlington Park	1742–59	32,000
Duke of Kingston	Thoresby	1745–	30,000
Sir John Griffin Griffin	Audley End	1762–97	73,000
Duke of Northumberland	Alnwick Castle	1768	10,000
Lord Clive	Claremont	1770s	16,000
Earl Spencer	Althorp	1790s	20,000
Samuel Whitbread	Southill	1795–1803	54,000
Sir Francis Baring	Stratton Park	1803–6	25,000
Marquess of Ailesbury	Tottenham House	1820s	250,000
Earl Manvers	Thoresby	1820s	8,533
Gregory Gregory	Harlaxton	1832–42	200,000
Lord Tollemache	Peckforton Castle	1840s	68,000
Earl Manvers	Thoresby	1864–75	171,000
John Walker	Bear wood	1865–75	120,000

Sources: M. W. Barley, 'Rural building in England', in Joan Thirsk, ed., *The Agrarian History of England and Wales*, vol. V: *1640–1750* (Cambridge, 1985), pt II, p. 602; R. A. C. Parker, *Coke of Norfolk* (Oxford, 1975), p. 24; G. E. Mingay, *English Landed Society in the Eighteenth Century* (1963), p. 160; J. D. Williams, 'The finances of an eighteenth-century Essex nobleman', *Essex Archaeology and History*, 9 (1979 for 1977), pp. 116–17; Paul Nunn, 'Aristocratic estates and employment in South Yorkshire, 1700–1800', in *Essays in the Economic and Social History of South Yorkshire*, ed. S. Pollard and C. Holmes (Sheffield, 1976), p. 36; HMC *Hastings MSS*, vol. III, p. 149; C. Hussey, *English Country Houses: mid-Georgian, 1760–1800* (1956), pp. 135, 203, 211, and *English Country Houses: late Georgian, 1800–40* (1958), pp. 27 and 29; Mark Girouard, *The Victorian Country House* (1979 edn), pp. 93, 156, 272; H. A. Clemenson, *English Country Houses and Landed Estates* (1982), p. 47; Nottingham University Manuscripts Department, Ma 2a 208, fols. 1–31; BL Egerton MSS 3527, fol. 144.

Expenditure during the thirty-three years of building at Holkham averaged £2700 annually, but 25 per cent of the overall sum was spent on the main block of the house between 1754 and 1757.[24] Some owners planned in advance, and others altered their plans as they proceeded. Gregory Gregory began preparing to build Harlaxton in the early 1820s, although building commenced only in 1832. By contrast, work at Doddington Park, Gloucestershire, built by James Wyatt for Christopher Codrington between 1797 and 1817, was painfully slow in order to allow Codrington to use his estate labourers and to build from income.[25] Even so, building was regarded as a major cause of financial difficulties for those unwise enough to indulge their fancy. Lord Leicester was heavily in debt by 1759 partly as a result of his building works at Holkham. The Earl of Scarbrough began rebuilding his houses at Sandbeck and Glentworth during the 1760s, and despite selling timber and raising a mortgage to meet the required outlay he still ran into considerable financial difficulty. It cost John Inglett Fortescue £40,000 to rebuild Buckland Filleigh, Devon, after 1809, as a result of which he had to sell the house and estate in 1834. The Marquess of Ailesbury was nearly ruined by building Tottenham Park in Wiltshire, and many other owners found themselves building with money that they would find difficult to repay.[26] Even the wealthy Grosvenors had to borrow in order to finance the rebuilding of Eaton Hall. However, building seldom completely ruined a family; indeed, those who foundered on the rocks of building in the three counties of Northamptonshire, Northumberland and Hertfordshire seem to have been over-ambitious new men who tried to do too much in too short a time.[27]

Ideally the country house was set in its own grounds, and the layout of the surrounding park demanded just as much attention as the house, since it emphasized the owner's power and prestige. Emparkment had been a feature of the English countryside for centuries, usually to

[24] R. A. C. Parker, *Coke of Norfolk* (Oxford, 1975), pp. 24–5.

[25] Girouard, *The Victorian Country House*, p. 93; C. F. C. Greville, *The Greville Memoirs*, ed. H. Reeve (1888 edn), vol. IV, pp. 43–4; Christopher Hussey, *English Country Houses: late Georgian, 1800–40* (1958), pp. 41–2.

[26] Parker, *Coke of Norfolk*, pp. 25–6; T. W. Beastall, *A North Country Estate: the Lumleys and Saundersons as landowners, 1600–1900* (1975), p. 54; Colvin and Harris (eds), *The Country Seat*, pp. 229–32; F. M. L. Thompson, 'English landownership: the Ailesbury Trust, 1832–56', *Economic History Review*, 2nd ser., 11 (1958), p. 121.

[27] Hazelton-Swales, 'Urban aristocrats', p. 174; David Cannadine, 'Aristocratic indebtedness in the nineteenth century: the case re-opened', *Economic History Review*, 2nd ser., 30 (1977) pp. 639–40; Stone and Stone, *An Open Elite?*, p. 393.

preserve deer (for hunting) and woodland, but in the post-1660 period greater emphasis came to be placed on the significance of landscape, and this altered the role of parks. Pleasure gardens, as opposed to the kitchen gardens where produce was cultivated for consumption in the house, were predominantly formal in Tudor and Stuart England, combining French, Italian and Dutch tastes. The formal layout, found, for example, at Boughton, was often modelled on the elaborate example of Versailles. By the early years of the eighteenth century, the idealization of nature, and the retreat from all things French, combined to outlaw the clipped symmetry of the formal garden, and in the process parks and woodlands were redesigned to produce the landscape garden. William Kent and Charles Bridgeman, the dominant landscape gardeners of the early eighteenth century, introduced walks and streams, classical or Gothic temples and follies to join the ha-ha as the essence of the early English landscape garden. Bridgeman worked at more than thirty venues, mostly in the south-east, and Kent at twenty-nine. Both worked at Stowe, which was the most magnificent and admired garden of the period.[28]

In the second half of the century, Lancelot 'Capability' Brown and Humphry Repton were the dominant figures. Brown, head gardener at Stowe when only in his mid-twenties, worked at 188 separate places between the 1750s and his death in 1783; while Repton began work in the 1780s, and was responsible for 220 gardens before his death in 1818. In many instances Repton was called upon to improve Brown's work, although his major individual contribution was to push back the park in order to reintroduce terraces, raised flowerbeds and conservatories. He thereby relaxed the rules of landscaping, and by bringing back the flower garden provided landowners with a new hobby. Repton had no apparent successor. The man who dominated the early Victorian scene was John Claudius Loudon, whose 'gardenesque' style was appropriate for the horticultural tastes of the villa rather than the country house.[29]

[28] John Dixon Hunt and Peter Willis, *The Genius of the Place: the English landscape garden, 1620–1820* (1975), pp. 1–8; Wake, *The Brudenells*, pp. 207–8; Hugh Prince, *Parks in England* (Isle of Wight, 1967), pp. 29–34. The ideal which emerged by mid-century was embodied in Henry Fielding's fictitious description of the property of Squire Allworthy, who had a Gothic house, a garden notably natural, and a park which owed more to nature than to art: *Tom Jones* (1749; Harmondsworth, 1966), pp. 58–9.

[29] Hunt and Willis, *The Genius of the Place*, pp. 30–3; Prince, *Parks in England*, pp. 35–43, 46–56; Stephen Daniels, 'Landscaping for a manufacturer: Humphry Repton's commission for Benjamin Gott at Arnley', *Journal of Historical Geography*, 7 (1981), p. 394.

The passion for landscaping reached its height between about 1760 and 1820, and stretched across the country. Of the 500 estates in Clemenson's sample, one-fifth had garden designs by Bridgeman, Kent, Brown or Repton, and more than one was employed in fourteen instances. Only Repton did not work at Stowe.[30] On the other hand, many parks were altered without the help of any of these giants. By the later eighteenth century, Nottinghamshire had fifty parks covering 23,000 acres (4 per cent of the county), but only Repton of the famous four worked in the county, and then only at three venues. The number of parks in the East and West Ridings of Yorkshire increased from sixty-three in 1772 to eighty-five in 1817, and out of the twenty-three new ones in the West Riding Repton was responsible for six. Some owners did the job themselves, including Henry Hoare at Stourhead, and Sir Francis Dashwood at West Wycombe, while lesser-known designers such as Sanderson Miller and a host of gifted amateurs filled the gaps left by the famous names. Even so, it was Brown and Repton who were fêted in contemporary society. Brown was the royal gardener, he dined with dukes and shared the confidences of statesmen.[31]

Aristocrats displayed their grandeur by increasing the size of their landscaped gardens. Walpole's garden at Houghton in the early eighteenth century was regarded as 'a considerable portion' at 23 acres, but in 1765 Luton Hoo Park ran to 900 acres. When Coke inherited Holkham in 1776, contemporary opinion held that the garden failed to match the grandeur of the newly completed house. It had been laid out by William Kent, and was now considered too formal and old-fashioned. In the 1780s Coke set about making improvements, largely to his own design, which had the effect of doubling the size of the park, and by 1800 it stretched for some 3000 acres. At Greystoke in Cumberland during the 1780s the eleventh Duke of Norfolk laid out a 5000-acre park, the largest in England, as a deliberate challenge to Lord Lonsdale's 4000-acre Lowther Park. By 1817 three of the West Riding parks exceeded 1000 acres, and ten others were of 500–1000 acres in extent.[32] The park was in fact, coming to reflect the wealth,

[30] Clemenson, *English Country Houses and Landed Estates*, pp. 67–8.

[31] D. V. Fowkes, 'Nottinghamshire parks in the eighteenth and nineteenth centuries', *Transactions of the Thoroton Society*, 71 (1967), p. 75; B. E. Coates, 'Park landscapes of the East and West Ridings in the time of Humphry Repton', *Yorkshire Archaeological Journal*, 41 (1965), pp. 467, 473; Prince, *Parks in England*, p. 8; Stephen Daniels, 'The political landscape', in *Humphry Repton: landscape gardener, 1752–1818*, ed. G. Carter *et al.* (Norwich, 1982), p. 111.

[32] Joan Bassin, 'The English landscape garden in the eighteenth century: the cultural importance of an English institution', *Albion*, 11 (1979), p. 24; S. Wade

influence and self-confidence of the families involved, as well as being a place where aristocrats could retreat from the world around. Moreover, the emphasis on trees suggested the solidity of the landowning families in the countryside. Edmund Burke referred to the greater families with their hereditary trust in the land as the 'great oaks that shade a country, and perpetuate . . . benefits from generation to generation', and since trees were essentially planted for later generations – indeed, Brown's landscapes were seen in their prime only after his death – landscaping can be regarded as an affirmation of the solidity of landed society and its principle of preserving and improving for the future glory of the family.[33]

Landscaping was by no means cheap. Landowners had to take into account both the cost of the enterprise and the loss of revenue from land taken into the park. Hiring the best designers meant paying the highest rates. Capability Brown received more than £21,500 for his work at Blenheim; his first contract at Petworth was for £11,753 (and he received three more); while he was paid over £10,000 for work at Luton Hoo, £5500 for Harewood in the West Riding and £4300 for Bowood. Some of his income came from much smaller enterprises for which he seems merely to have drawn the plans. As a result, his Drummond's bank account records payments for ninety separate landscapes between 1753 and 1782 ranging from only £20 – for Doddington Hall in Cheshire – to the £12,875 he received between 1768 and 1782 for Fisherwick in Staffordshire, and totalling alto-gether £102,000.[34] Since Brown was primarily a contractor, much of this money went into the actual business of laying out the estate. Repton charged five guineas a day plus expenses during the 1790s, and two guineas a day for his time at home drawing up plans. For some clients, where his work took a number of years, he was employed on a salaried basis, and on occasion he also tried to charge a percentage on work carried out. His charges rose in the early years of the nineteenth

Martins, *A Great Estate at Work: the Holkham estate and its inhabitants in the nineteenth century* (Cambridge, 1980), pp. 251–4; John Martin Robinson, *The Duke of Norfolk: a quincentennial history* (Oxford, 1983), p. 177; Coates, 'Park landscapes of the East and West Ridings', p. 467.

[33] Quoted in W. L. Guttsman (ed.), *The English Ruling Class* (1969), p. 21.

[34] Bassin, 'The English landscape garden', p. 24; Clemenson, *English Country Houses and Landed Estates*, p. 69; Edward Hyams, *Capability Brown and Humphry Repton* (1971), p. 42; Peter Willis, 'Capability Brown in Northumberland', *Garden History*, 9 (1981), pp. 175–6; 'Capability Brown's account with Drummond's Bank, 1753–1783', *Architectural History*, 27 (1984), pp. 382–91.

century, and by 1805 his annual income had doubled since 1790 to reach £400.[35]

The loss of annual rental income when a park was expanded was potentially more serious, although it has to be kept in perspective. Few parks were entirely ornamental, and some were situated on former waste land. They might provide grazing for deer, cattle and sheep, while trees were often exploited commercially. Home farms were sometimes located within the park walls, and between 1760 and the 1880s the profit to be made from well-managed woodland was frequently greater than the rent of an equivalent acreage of farmland. Among parks enclosed from the waste was the 4000-acre Clumber Park in Nottinghamshire.[36]

THE COUNTRY HOUSE AND THE COMMUNITY: CONSUMPTION AND EMPLOYMENT

The country house reflected the power and grandeur of the family. It served as a reminder of their longevity on the land, and in many cases it also became a museum in which aristocratic families displayed the art collections they accumulated over many generations, particularly between the French Revolution and *c.* 1840. But it was much more than this. In fact it was the centre of a considerable complex of social and business responsibilities. James I and Charles I sent the landowners home during the summer because by failing to provide employment and hospitality, and by their absence from the commission of the peace, they were not only facilitating social dislocation in the countryside, but were also threatening the idea of social deference.[37] Most aristocrats accepted that they should stand at the head of the local community, but this could be achieved in a number of ways: in particular, through the activities which took place in and around the country house, and which can be regarded as serving to enforce the ties of social deference within the community; and through the actions and events beyond the house which helped to portray the landlord as the cohesive pillar upon which local society necessarily leant for support. The landlord was there to bind the community together in order to preserve the spirit of social deference.

[35] Kedrun Laurie, 'Humphry Repton', in *Humphry Repton,* ed. Carter *et al.,* pp. 17–19.
[36] Fowkes, 'Nottinghamshire parks', p. 74; Prince, *Parks in England,* pp. 12–15.
[37] Stone, *The Crisis of the Aristocracy,* pp. 397–8.

The country house was important to the community as a centre of consumption and employment. Sir William Coventry argued in the 1670s that absence in London meant that landowners were not spending money on hospitality, and that their servants were not purchasing their clothes in market towns and drinking local ale. Spending power in the local community was thereby reduced. The same point was made rather more acidly by a correspondent of the *Gentleman's Magazine* in 1737:

the poverty of the country proceeds, in a very great measure, from the residence of the chief nobility and gentry in [London]: where they live in the utmost extravagance, and but rarely go into the country with any other design than to squeeze a supply of money out of their tenants.[38]

Clearly these were impressionistic comments, and measuring them in terms of hard cash is almost impossible. Household expenditure benefited local tradesmen, in terms of demand both for food to be consumed in the house, and for specialist skills for work on the property, as well as offering employment to numerous house servants, grooms, gamekeepers, and the like. Household costs could be considerable. In only twelve weeks at Thoresby in 1736 the Duke of Kingston ran up expenses of £1477, of which £307 was spent on meat. Wage payments also generated spending power in the local community. On Earl Fitzwilliam's estate these amounted to about £1800 in 1790, £2300 in 1815 and £3000 in 1825. From the 1830s, however, the expansion of households came to a halt. Numbers of servants fell, and the coming of the railway enabled aristocrats to take their servants with them to London.[39]

Housebuilding and park layout also generated employment. Vanbrugh had nearly 200 men at work at Castle Howard in 1703, and at one time more than 1500 were employed at Blenheim. In 1770 the Duke of Northumberland was said to have between 100 and 200 men employed widening the river, building a new chapel and undertaking other construction work at Alnwick Castle.[40] The building of larger

---

[38] *Gentleman's Magazine*, 7 (1737), pp. 104–6; Joan Thirsk and J.P. Cooper (eds), *Seventeenth-Century Economic Documents* (Oxford, 1972), pp. 81–2.

[39] G. E. Mingay, 'The Duke of Kingston and his estates: a study of landownership in the 18th century' (University of Nottingham, BA dissertation, 1952), p. 134; F. M. L. Thompson, *English Landed Society in the Nineteenth Century* (1963), pp. 188–95; Jessica A. Gerard, 'Invisible servants: the country house and the local community', *Bulletin of the Institute of Historical Research*, 57 (1984), pp. 178–88.

[40] Barley, 'Rural building in England', p. 610; HMC, *Hastings MSS*, vol. III, p. 150.

country houses in the South Yorkshire area between 1756 and 1774 provided employment for as many as 190 skilled and 115 unskilled men, together with many more subsidiary jobs. At Wentworth Woodhouse alone, in 1772 forty-four skilled workers and seventy labourers were employed on the house, home farm and landscaping works. Possibly some 6 per cent of men in rural parishes were involved in such work. Most remarkable of all were the activities of the fifth Duke of Portland at Welbeck in the 1860s and 1870s. Construction work included greenhouses and hothouses, a riding house, tunnels and a great underground ballroom. Portland operated from a desire to provide work in the area, and the many thousands of men employed knew him as 'the workman's friend'.[41] Park layout could also provide employment. Walpole had twenty-nine men and fifty women laying out and planting the gardens at Houghton in 1721. More often, however, the work took place in slack periods of the agricultural year, particularly during the winter months, in order to use current labour rather than to hire additional men. This was the policy of Elizabeth Montagu at Sandleford in Berkshire, which was one of Capability Brown's last commissions. She brought his plans to fruition after his death, using labour originally hired for agricultural work.[42]

Employment prospects increased considerably on estates with mineral and other interests. As early as 1705 over 400 men were employed in the Lowthers' Whitehaven collieries, while by the early nineteenth century more than 1200 pitmen and colliery workers were employed on the Earl of Durham's estate. In the West Midlands in 1804 the permanent staff of officials and agents in the Earl of Dudley's Mines Department numbered thirty-three. The number of colliers employed by the Fitzwilliams increased from forty-five to seventy-nine in the course of 1795, and continued upwards over the next half-century to 587 in 1845. By that time the total number of employees on the whole estate had reached 1100, while colliery workers alone totalled 869 in 1856.[43]

On the whole, landowners appear to have been good employers.

[41] Nunn, 'Aristocratic estates and employment', p. 43n.; A. S. Turberville, *A History of Welbeck Abbey and its Owners* vol. II (1939), pp. 437–42.

[42] Barley, 'Rural building in England', p. 610; BL Add. MSS, 40,663, fol. 121, Elizabeth Montagu to Mrs Robinson, 16 June 1783.

[43] J. V. Beckett, *Coal and Tobacco: the Lowthers and the economic development of West Cumberland, 1660–1760* (Cambridge, 1981), p. 65; T. J. Raybould, *The Economic Emergence of the Black Country* (Newton Abbot, 1973), p. 227; Graham Mee, *Aristocratic Enterprise: the Fitzwilliam industrial undertakings, 1795–1857* (1975), pp. 23–4.

Miners were frequently injured or even killed in accidents, and provision was needed not just for medical and funeral expenses, but also for surviving relatives. Sir James Lowther built almshouses for men who retired from the pits and provided a pension, although it is perhaps a chilling comment on this venture that the places were mainly taken by widows of men killed in accidents. In Leicestershire the Earl of Moira financed the erection of fifty houses for coal miners in 1811, and he and his descendents regarded themselves as responsible employers providing the workforce with a decent living in return for which they expected appropriate deference. The Earls Fitzwilliam provided a generous and comprehensive set of benefits for their employees in the nineteenth century, and the general impression is that wages and conditions tended to be best in those collieries worked by the landlord himself rather than being leased.[44] Naturally there were rogues. Controversy has surrounded the activities of the third Marquess of Londonderry. He has been charged with resisting efforts to improve the lot of his miners, and of taking a particularly adverse view of them in the disputes of 1831 and 1844. The accusation is that he was indifferent to their claims, and continued to seek profit at the expense of the workforce. However, apologists have pointed to the free housing and education that he offered, as well as the 'above average care', and the fact that he was by no means the greatest villain in 1844. Londonderry regarded his spending on pits, harbours and railways as important not only for personal profit, but also for the development of the county and the welfare of the inhabitants. Although he evicted pitmen after the 1844 strike – as did other coalowners – he also provided two doctors to attend his workers, and employment for the dependants of injured or killed pitmen.[45]

Landlords took pride in benefits offered to their employees and they

[44] Beckett, *Coal and Tobacco*, p. 66; C. P. Griffin, 'Three generations of miners housing at Moira, Leicestershire, 1811–34', *Industrial Archaeology Review*, 1 (1977); Graham Mee, 'Employer–employee relationships in the industrial revolution: the Fitzwilliam collieries', in *Essays in the Economic and Social History of South Yorkshire*, ed. Pollard and Holmes, pp. 46–58; J. T. Ward, 'Landowners and mining', in *Land and Industry*, ed. J. T. Ward and R. G. Wilson (1971), p. 104; B. R. Mitchell, *Economic Development of the British Coal Industry, 1800–1914* (Cambridge, 1984), p. 365, n. 23.

[45] A. J. Heesom, 'Entrepreneurial paternalism: the third Lord Londonderry (1778–1854) and the coal trade', *Durham University Journal*, new ser., 35 (1974), pp. 238–57; Roy Sturgess, 'Landowners and coal in County Durham', in *Landownership and Power in the Regions*, ed. M. D. G. Wanklyn (Wolverhampton, 1979), pp. 93–100; Christine E. Hiskey, 'The third Marquess of Londonderry and the regulation of the coal trade: the case re-opened', *Durham University Journal*, new ser., 44 (1983), pp. 1–9.

were not generally well disposed towards union organizations. Sir James Lowther took the view that trouble should be countered in advance, but when disputes did break out he used every possible means to break them rather than giving in to pressure. The fifth Earl Fitzwilliam's attitude was not dissimilar. Since he believed he knew what was best for his employees, and offered them favourable working conditions he was also uncompromisingly anti-union and dismissed workers who defied him on this matter.[46] Similarly, many landlords were hostile to the agricultural trade union movement of the 1870s, although some adopted a conciliatory position. Lord Leicester, for example, refused to join a combination of employers on the grounds that the men had a right to form unions. Even those who refused to re-engage men until they had severed their links with the union – a common reaction – often accepted that a real grievance existed, and responded by raising wages and improving working conditions.[47]

THE COUNTRY HOUSE AND THE COMMUNITY: SOCIAL MIXING

As the centre of a community, the country house also played two important but totally different roles: for the local gentry it was a socially exclusive entertainment venue; but for the community out of doors it was the centre of an organization designed to protect the integrity of the locality. The house was, first and foremost, the home of the family, and it was here that they entertained their friends and social equals. Dinner parties and balls were occasions for convivial mixing, although self-consciousness about rank also ensured that such events took on overtones concerning social acceptance. Such events also had implications for standing in the local community. Men who were often absent took the opportunity to discover from their resident neighbours what had been happening in their absence. Sir James Lowther always entertained local merchants and traders to dinner during his annual visits to West Cumberland, and, in order to be sure he did not offend, he kept lists of all those invited and when they had dined.[48]

---

[46] Beckett, *Coal and Tobacco*, pp. 65–6; Mee, 'Employer–employee relationships in the industrial revolution', p. 57.

[47] Pamela Horn, 'Landowners and the agricultural trade union movement of the 1870s', *Local Historian*, 11, 3 (1974), pp. 134–41.

[48] Wake, *The Brudenells*, pp. 226–32; Carlisle RO, D/Lons/W, box 'Housekeeping accounts, 1705–53', 'An Account of those that dine with me at Whitehaven which I keep to avoid giving offence least I should omit those that are proper to dine with me.

The clearest evidence of the way aristocrats utilized their estates for social mixing with their peer group could be found in relation to the game laws. Pursuing and killing wild animals for sporting purposes has a long history, and it has remained an obsessive preoccupation of the English aristocracy down to the present day. From the later fourteenth century, the right to hunt game, and particularly the edible game of deer, pheasants, hares, rabbits and partridges, was restricted by law to those members of society with an income of £40 a year. Such laws could be seen as buttressing a sport which was itself an assertion of social superiority. In Tudor times it was even thought impossible for anyone to be a gentleman who did not love hawking and hunting.[49] The laws were strengthened in 1671 to prevent more or less anyone from hunting hares, pheasants, partridges and moor fowl unless they had freeholds of £100 a year, or long leaseholds worth £150. Sons and heirs of esquires and other persons 'of higher degree' were also permitted to participate, while all lords of manors 'not under the degree of an esquire' were authorized to appoint gamekeepers with the right to seize guns and dogs. In contrast to the earlier legislation, the 1671 Act excluded non-landed wealth from the ranks of sportsmen, since income from trade, stocks or office was no longer sufficient to qualify a man to course a hare or shoot a partridge. Just why the legislation was passed is unclear. One suggestion is that 'it was the desire of country gentlemen to redefine and enhance their own social position *vis-à-vis* the urban bourgeoisie, rather than to punish the activities of "disorderly persons", which lay behind its enactment.'[50] However, since the Act hit hardest at country people rather than townsmen – in order to keep lesser freeholders and tenant farmers away from the game – the laws are perhaps best seen as class legislation within a rural context, even if they had the added effect of strengthening the rural–urban divide.[51]

I keep this account because if I should omit to invite any people of note in the town they would take it ill'; 'Other papers', Whitehaven 78. Lowther's cousin, Sir Thomas Lowther of Holker, understood Sir James's problem: 'it's a misfortune in the Country that one can't choose the company that's most agreeable, but be in a great measure obliged to receive all sorts': D/Lons/W, Miscellaneous correspondence, bundle 30, letter of 14 July 1726.

[49] Keith Thomas, *Man and the Natural World: changing attitudes in England, 1500–1800* (Harmondsworth, 1984 edn), pp. 145, 183.

[50] P. B. Munsche, *Gentlemen and Poachers: the English games laws, 1671–1831* (Cambridge, 1981), p. 19.

[51] F. M. L. Thompson, reviewing Munsche, *Gentlemen and Poachers*, *Agricultural History Review*, 30 (1982), pp. 162–3. Wild duck, deer and rabbits were not included in the 1671 legislation because they had a higher legal status as private property of the

Whatever the motive, the 1671 Act was clearly designed to make the hunting of game into the pastime of a minority. To enforce the legislation, illegal bagging and shooting had to be prevented, which caused friction in the countryside. Sometimes potential trouble was defused by allowing freeholders and tenant farmers to shoot 'with proper leave', and estate stewards recognized that by taking a generous approach to sporting privileges a gentleman could acquire 'not only the esteem of his tenant or tenants at home, but [also] a popular name for affability and good nature' in the rural community at large.[52] Through their liberality over the game, the gentry were thought to be maintaining the bonds of social deference. However, over time the situation became more complicated. In the 1670s it was possible to defend the new law on the grounds that hares, pheasants and partridges were all wild, and therefore Parliament sought to ensure their preservation, which could be threatened if general permission to hunt or shoot existed. Once intensive breeding began to take place within guarded coverts, game started to look like private property. Questions were asked about the continued monopoly, and these grew more pressing as investment in coverts made the gentry less willing to share the privilege of shooting with the technically unqualified.[53] Respectable but unqualified members of society who found themselves either denied sport altogether, or dependent on an occasional indulgence, naturally resented their loss of status and sought some explanation for the situation. To farmers and freeholders alike, it seemed absurd that 'a free man should be prohibited by law from killing the produce of his own lands, whatever the income of them.'[54] Efforts in 1772 and in the 1790s to repeal the laws came to nothing. They were blocked by arguments to the effect that, since the laws had been introduced to preserve the social order of the countryside as much as to protect the game, their repeal would upset the delicate social balance. In 1816 a new campaign was launched, which finally reached a successful conclusion in 1831. During the 1820s the absurdity of the law became apparent when game was protected by mantraps and spring-guns which maimed and even killed innocent people, and which were forbidden only in 1827. However, the change in the law did not concede the right of tenant farmers to kill hares on their land without landlords' permission. Poaching remained an offence, with the

landowner. Their unpermitted capture was therefore theft, and could be dealt with under existing legislation.

[52] *Gentleman's Magazine*, 5 (1735), p. 195.
[53] Munsche, *Gentlemen and Poachers*, pp. 28–51.
[54] Ibid. pp. 115–16.

effect that an undeclared state of war continued in the countryside during the nineteenth century, which was mollified but not brought to an end by the Ground Game Act of 1881. Shooting remained a socially exclusive minority interest.[55]

The country house was also important in maintaining the social cohesion of the community. This could be achieved in a number of ways, primarily through involving local people in affairs emanating from the house, and by providing facilities and services within the community. What happened within the family was the concern of everyone, whether it was birth, marriage or death. Births and marriages were often celebrated with dinners for the tenants, while birthdays could be the occasion for a ball. The coming of age of the eldest son was the opportunity for the most elaborate ritual. In 1799 the Duke of Rutland's coming of age was celebrated with three days of festivity and display, all of which was locally held to have cost £60,000, although one-sixth of that sum seems a more reasonable assessment. Earl Manvers spent over £4000 on Lord Newark's coming of age in the 1870s, including no less than £235 on fireworks.[56]

Death provided an even more critical public spectacle, since this involved not merely the household and village but the community of local landowners. When the Duke of Newcastle died in 1768, the procession from London to his final resting place in Sussex was headed by two porters on milk-white horses followed by eight domestics on grey horses, a gentleman carrying the ducal coronet, the hearse pulled by six horses, four mourning coaches each pulled by four horses, and a gentleman and six livery servants – all mounted – bringing up the rear. The funeral itself offered the landed community an opportunity of displaying its solidarity. When George Bowes, one of the Tyneside Grand Allies, died in 1760, the pall was supported by Lord Ravensworth and seven members of the House of Commons with about forty carriages following. In the words of Elizabeth Montagu, the funeral

according to the custom of this country is to be magnificent. There is to be more pomp at their funerals than weddings, as if they were of Solomon's opinion that the end of a feast is better than the beginning of a fray. All the

---

[55] Ibid., pp. 106–58; Roger Longrigg, *The English Squire and his Sport* (1977), pp. 260–1; Raymond Carr, 'Country sports', in *The Victorian Countryside*, ed. Mingay, p. 482–5. Much of the resentment of the law was directed at gamekeepers: F. M. L. Thompson, 'Landowners and the rural community', in ibid., pp. 460–1.

[56] Thompson, *English Landed Society*, pp. 77–8; Nottingham University Manuscripts Department, Ma 2a 208, fol. 90.

nobility and gentry of the counties of Durham and Northumberland are to attend this poor man to the grave.[57]

Such displays of stylized ritual helped to emphasize the position of the deceased, and expense was seldom spared. The Duke of Newcastle's last journey cost £622, while funeral and mourning expenses for the second Duke of Kingston in 1726 amounted to £1475. In 1807 the procession from London to Raby, and the subsequent burial, of the Countess of Darlington cost £1400.[58] With the coming of the railway, the slow-moving mourning train became the public demonstration of deceased·grandeur. Shops were closed in Newcastle for the funeral of the third Duke of Northumberland in 1847. His coffin was taken by road from Alnwick to Gateshead station in a procession which took over seven hours to complete, and it then went by train to London for burial in Westminster Abbey. When the fourth duke died in 1865, 7000 people filed past his coffin at Alnwick, and his special train to London passed through crowded stations at Newcastle, Durham and Darlington, while the minster bells tolled at York. Nearly 2000 people filed past Lord Cardigan's coffin in 1868, before a similarly elaborate – although local – funeral.[59]

Although events within the family were the most obvious opportunities for celebration, plenty of other occasions could be used for the purpose. These included public events such as coronations, or the recovery of George III from illness in 1789. To celebrate the accession of George I in 1714, the Whig Sir James Lowther provided his colliery workers with a barrel of beer, which proved a sufficiently alluring enticement to prevent several of them from working the following day.[60] Annual ritual events, such as harvest festivals, could also be organized from the great house, while even the visit of the owner could be an opportunity for celebration, especially if this did not occur frequently. Elizabeth Montagu regularly offered hospitality on visits to her Yorkshire and Northumberland estates, both with her husband until his death in 1775, and then on her own account. In June 1775 she spent only two days at Allerthorpe Hall in North Yorkshire, but this was long enough for her to throw a dinner for the tenants. Then she galloped on to her other Yorkshire property near Darlington,

---

[57] Ray A. Kelch, *Newcastle: a duke without money* (1974), p. 187; W. W. Tomlinson, *Denton Hall and its Associations* (1894), p. 53.

[58] Kelch, *Newcastle*, p. 188; BL, Egerton MSS, 3527, fol. 1; Thompson, *English Landed Society*, p. 79.

[59] Thompson, *English Landed Society*, pp. 80–1; Wake, *The Brudenells*, pp. 441–4.

[60] Carlisle RO, D/Lons/W, John Spedding to James Lowther, 24 September 1714.

and 'ordered every eatable that could be got from the neighbouring markets to be dressed at the house the next day, and invited all my tenants and their wives to dinner therein'. When she finally reached Denton Hall, just west of Newcastle, she invited all her colliery workers to dine on as much rice pudding and boiled beef 'as they could cram'. In September 1786 she invited 500 of them (including wives) to dine 'before the Hall door', and wining and dining was to be followed by jigs and reels which she expected to go forward 'till late in the night'.[61] Such occasions were not necessarily given for pleasure. In 1838 the Duke of Rutland invited 400 people to dinner at Belvoir:

The Duke of Rutland is as selfish a man as any of his class – that is, he never does what he does not like, and spends his whole life in a round of such pleasures as suit his taste, but he is neither a foolish nor a bad man, and partly from a sense of duty, partly from inclination, he devotes time and labour to the interest and welfare of the people who live and labour on his estate.[62]

Similarly significant for promoting social mixing while maintaining social deference were sporting events. Cricket, for example, was originally a village folk game, until it was taken up and organized by the aristocracy in the course of the eighteenth century. The Duke of Richmond is credited with being the game's first aristocratic patron, in 1725, but his example was soon followed by others, largely because the game was an ideal meeting point. It brought aristocrats into contact with a wide cross-section of the people living on their estates, and helped to increase their influence over tenants. Many of the early matches were played at the seats of interested magnates. Often they themselves were major participants, and this type of contest helped to encourage higher standards in the game as a whole. The cricket field also proved useful in breaking down the gap which existed between rural and urban interests. The eighteenth-century equivalent of the Marylebone Cricket Club (MCC) was the Hambledon Club, formed largely through the efforts of a son of the Duke of Bolton, and including among its 157 members eighteen titled aristocrats, two MPs and two knights. A further advantage of the game's aristocratic patronage was that individual landowners strengthened their teams by

---

[61] Huntington Library, Montagu Box 80, Mo 3364, Elizabeth Montagu to Elizabeth Carter, 1 July 1775; box 101, Mo 6612, same to Elizabeth Handcock, 22 September 1786; BL Add. MSS, 40,663, fol. 50, same to Mary Robinson, 10 July 1775.
[62] *The Greville Memoirs*, vol. IV, p. 45.

employing gifted players on their estates. The Duke of Richmond employed Thomas Waymark as a groom for this purpose, and Sir Horatio Mann even retained 'a poor bailiff' because of his batting prowess. Overall, aristocratic interest was a means of bringing together different social elements within the countryside, but not on an egalitarian basis, since the position of patron and squire was clearly recognized.

In the course of the nineteenth century, cricket moved away from the country house to private parks and village greens, and county and club grounds. While at the local level the landowner might continue to put out a team largely consisting of his workmen, and he himself might still open the batting, aristocrats became less significant for the game. Even so, the sport retained its patrician image throughout the nineteenth century. The MCC, despite its highly aristocratic ethos, was not displaced from governing cricket, partly because many of its most vociferous opponents could not resist the opportunity of membership. Aristocrats were recognized as patrons of the county game, while the MCC became a meeting place for landowners and the middle class. Of a total membership of 2291 in 1877, 337 were titled aristocrats. By 1886 membership had grown to 5091, but the number of aristocrats had fallen to 327. If the rapid late nineteenth-century growth of the club was at the expense of its traditional landed character, like the public schools it provided an important link between landed and middle-class society. Cricket, after all, was upheld by the proponents of muscular Christianity for its inculcation of gentlemanly values, including the discipline of supporting the team rather than playing for oneself, and of accepting the umpire's decision.[63]

The sport which came to be regarded as critical for social cohesion was foxhunting. In the seventeenth century, hunting foxes was associated with country squires and yeomen; indeed, the term 'foxhunter' was a synonym for hick, West Country, Tory bumpkin imagery. This was largely the invention of Whig writers, who after 1688 became the chief literary purveyors of the country gentleman image, and perhaps the most notable parodies were in Joseph Addison's *Freeholder* for 1716, and Henry Fielding's classic character

[63] Christopher Brookes, *English Cricket: the game and its players through the ages* (1978); K. A. P. Sandiford, 'Cricket in Victorian society', *Journal of Social History*, 17 (1983), pp. 303–17. The third Duke of Dorset was an important eighteenth-century patron of the game: V. Sackville-West, *Knole and the Sackvilles* (1958), pp. 176–7.

Squire Western.[64] Part of this image was derived from the nature of the sport, which, because of the slowness of the harriers, often began before dawn and finished as dusk fell. In 1753 Hugo Meynell rented Quorndon Hall in Leicestershire and began to hunt foxes. He revolutionized the sport by breeding hounds fast enough to keep up with the fox, while Leicestershire – much of which was grassland – proved ideal for turning foxhunting into a much more exciting sport. By the time Meynell retired in 1800, he had helped to transform it from the rather tepid amusement of elderly backwoods squires in the Squire Western mould, into an amusement for hard-riding young gentlemen. By the early nineteenth century it had become a national rural sport. Moreover, the whole community was involved. Unlike shooting, foxhunting included no legal barriers to participation, because the fox was vermin, and it was not until 1869 that a serious attack was launched on the grounds of cruelty.[65] Since the hunt had to cross the land of various owners and farmers, every reason existed to involve them, even if certain constraints were observed in regard to the extent of social mixing. Members of the community could participate even if they did not own a horse, since hundreds might follow the hunt on foot. Apologists argued that hunting was good for social relations because landowners needed to be civil to their tenants, as they intended to ride over their land, while tenants accepted this in return for being allowed to join the chase.

The dominance of the aristocracy in all but a few of the main packs helped to reinforce the social order. Great landowners saw the maintenance of a pack as a duty to their locality, and as part of the web of influence. Rising families sought social acceptance by taking over the local pack, putting on the red coat, and providing the food and drink for a meet. Since it cost £4000 or £5000 annually to maintain a Midlands pack by the 1830s, social exclusivity was guaranteed. What appeared to threaten this situation was the railway. Contemporaries

[64] Joseph Addison, *The Freeholder*, 22, 5 March 1716; 44, 21 May 1716; 47, 1 June 1716. Western appeared in Henry Fielding's *Tom Jones* (1749). Although the imagery was politically inspired, Lord Macaulay drew heavily on these sources for his depiction of the post-Restoration squire – 'his chief pleasures were commonly derived from field sports and an unrefined sensuality': *History of England*, ed. C. H. Firth (1913 edn), vol. I, p. 310. Macaulay's overdrawn picture continued to appear in textbooks until recently: Rosamond Bayne-Powell, *English Country Life in the Eighteenth Century* (1935), pp. ix, 37–8; E. Wingfield-Stratford, *The Squire and his Relations* (1956), pp. 227–8.

[65] Professor E. A. Freeman launched the first major attack in the *Fortnightly Review*, in 1869: D. C. Itzkowitz, *Peculiar Privilege: a social history of English foxhunting, 1753–1885* (Hassocks, 1977), pp. 143 ff.; Raymond Carr, *A History of Foxhunting* (1976), pp. 204–8.

feared that it would take the aristocracy out of the countryside, but in practice it encouraged Londoners to participate in the sport further afield; indeed, the years before the agricultural depression of the later nineteenth century were its heyday, with the number of packs increasing from 99 in 1850 to 137 in 1877. Paradoxically, as contributions and subscriptions were introduced, new urban wealth appeared to be propping up the old hunts, and the field became a suitable arena for social climbing. Albert Brassey, son of the railway contractor, was responsible for maintaining the Heythrop on the magnificent lines of earlier years down to 1914.[66]

During the last quarter of the century, foxhunting came under increasing attack as a cruel sport, and it also grew to be disliked by farmers. The damage done to property was resented in the difficult years of the agricultural depression. Moreover, the financial security of the sport was increasingly underpinned by infusions of new wealth, and by 1908 it was estimated that two-thirds of those in the field were businessmen. Controversy raged over the use of barbed wire, and landlords hit by the financial pressures of the late nineteenth century were unable to keep up their hounds.[67] None the less, many apologists were prepared to argue that it had served a useful purpose – both socially, in binding the rural community together, and practically, in offering cavalry training to members of the upper classes which might prove useful in wartime.[68] It was thought to have kept landowners on their estates when they might otherwise have been in London – although this was difficult to justify in the early nineteenth century when the ideal was to hunt out of Melton Mowbray – and to have helped to generate economic activity. The balls and dinners associated with the sport stimulated social life and injected finance into the local economy, while, as with cricket, it could be justified as instilling qualities of hardiness, coolness and clearheadedness into young men. Above all, however, its significance lay in the social mixing within the community, both between landlords and tenants, and between rural and urban interests. By attracting business and other new wealth to participate, and then to take over financing foxhunting, the aristocracy both conditioned them to its own interests, and ensured the survival of the sport into the twentieth century.

[66] Itzkowitz, *Peculiar Privilege*, p. 53; Carr, *A History of Foxhunting*, p. 237.
[67] Carr, *A History of Foxhunting*, pp. 152–4.
[68] The cavalry argument appeared at various intervals down to the First World War, although no evidence was produced to suggest whether or not it was well founded: Itzkowitz, *Peculiar Privilege*, pp. 20–1, 99–112.

ARISTOCRATS AND THE LOCAL COMMUNITY

To help to maintain social cohesion, the duties of land had to be respected. The country house was the centre of a community in which it fell to the landlord to undertake to protect the rights of the less well off, partly by providing financial or equivalent help. It was a duty that they could not ignore. In the 1720s the Duke of Chandos declared his intention – should the search for copper ore on his estate yield a rich vein – 'after I have discharged my debts, to devote one fourth part of the remainder to charitable uses'.[69] The copper did not materialize, but this did not relieve him of responsibility, and nor would it have done in the late nineteenth century. Hippolyte Taine noted that landed proprietors 'are bound to be first in opening their purses, as the feudal baron was bound to go first into the fight'.[70] What did these duties involve? In 1838 Lord Sidney Godolphin Osborne suggested that they included Poor Law chores, the formation and supervision of penny clothing funds, and the building of good cottages and schools. In the course of the nineteenth century, others added the task of granting allotments.[71] What happened in practice obviously varied, from landlords who merely underrented cottages to sustain poor tenants, through the vast numbers who headed – or at least appeared on – subscription lists, to those few who almost single-handedly provided the facilities of a new town. Among the latter, in the later nineteenth century, the Earl of Scarborough provided £5000 for roads, most of the finance for St Matthew's church, £450 for a school, £2000 for a cattle market, £2000 for a cricket ground and £2000 towards the town's water supply.[72] Clearly the provision of such facilities suggested an element of social control, but it was also part of the duty which went with being an aristocrat.

The different roles can be examined in a number of ways. An obvious means of supporting the local community was through the financing of a school building and of a schoolteacher to offer basic reading and writing instruction for the local community. Alternatively a landlord could support particularly bright children through existing educational channels. Offering such incentives to the children of stewards was an obvious means of ensuring loyalty; hence Sir James

[69] Huntington Library, STB Correspondence, box 16/27, Chandos to J. Farquharson, 24 December 1732.

[70] Taine, *Notes on England*, p. 71.

[71] David Roberts, *Paternalism in Early Victorian England* (1979), p. 131.

[72] R. Gurnham, 'The creation of Skegness as a resort town by the 9th Earl of Scarbrough', *Lincolnshire History and Archaeology*, 7 (1972), pp. 64–76.

Lowther's sponsorship of his colliery steward's son through Trinity College, Dublin.[73] The question of landlord support for educational provision has been much debated for the eighteenth century. Some historians have argued that schooling provision improved during the course of the century,[74] but a more persuasive view has dated any changes only from the 1780s.[75] However, in the course of the nineteenth century the standard of literacy among the labouring classes undoubtedly improved, and one of the most typical activities of the Victorian landowner was to support the village school. On the north-east coalfield the first Earl of Durham led the way in opening schools for his workforce in 1841. Others providing such schools within a year or so including the Lambtons, the Peases, the Brandlings and Lord Ravensworth. The only notable exception was Lord Londonderry, and he came into line within a couple of years.[76] However, it was the Anglican National Society and the Nonconformist British and Foreign Schools Society which were in the forefront of improving facilities. Landowners favoured the Anglican establishment, and supported National Schools on their estates, although the Duke of Bedford was president of the BFSS in the 1840s. Support for the National Society was boosted after 1870 by the threat of school boards, since few landowners relished the prospect of non-sectarian education in their villages. One consequence was that the Duke of Bedford's spending on churches and schools on the Bedfordshire and Buckinghamshire estates rose sharply in the second half of the nineteenth century from £11,875 between 1816 and 1855, to £186,761 over the years 1856–95.[77]

As with schools, the provision of churches was hardly disinterested. The ties between land and church were strong ones. Joseph Addison

---

[73] Beckett, *Coal and Tobacco*. pp. 28–9.

[74] N. Hans, *New Trends in Education in the Eighteenth Century* (1951); M. Sanderson, *Education, Economic Change and Society in England, 1780–1870* (1983), pp. 11–16.

[75] Lawrence Stone, 'Literacy and education in England, 1640–1900', *Past and Present*, 42 (1969), pp. 69–139; Roderick Floud and Donald McCloskey (eds), *The Economic History of Britain Since 1700* (Cambridge, 1981), vol. I, pp. 223–4; Rosemary O'Day, *Education and Society, 1500–1800* (1982), p. 259.

[76] The exact purpose of such institutions has been much debated: Robert Colls, '"Oh happy English children!": coal, class and education in the north-east', *Past and Present*, 73 (1976), pp. 75–99, and the subsequent debate between Brendan Duffy, A. J. Heesom and Robert Colls in *Past and Present*, 90 (1981), pp. 136–65.

[77] G. F. Bartle, 'The records of the British and Foreign Schools Society', *Local Historian*, 16, 4 (1984), p. 205; Duke of Bedford, *A Great Agricultural Estate*, 3rd edn (1897), p. 227.

expressed an idealized picture of the country gentleman at church in
the form of Sir Roger de Coverley, who had provided a prayer-book
and hassock for each of his tenants, and who 'sometimes stands up
when everybody else is upon their knees to count the congregation, or
see if any of his tenants are missing'. However, even the next village
was 'famous for the differences and contentions that arise between the
parson and the squire, who live in a perpetual state of war. The parson
is always preaching at the squire, and the squire to be revenged on the
parson never comes to church.'[78] Such landlords also existed in reality
– men who might sleep through the sermon, or otherwise divert
themselves with drinking or reading, as an obvious gesture of
contempt.[79] But the church was too important as an agent of social
control to ignore, and through its ownership of advowsons the
aristocracy was ideally placed to ensure the appointment of clerics
willing to preach the gospel of social hierarchy. In the early eighteenth
century, peers owned about 12 per cent of advowsons, and a century
later this figure had risen by a percentage point or two. Many other
advowsons were in gentry hands. The dukes of Devonshire owned
twenty-nine and a half advowsons in the early eighteenth century, and
thirty-seven a century later, while the dukes of Rutland increased their
holding from twenty-four to twenty-nine. Overall, forty-nine peerage
families held eight or more advowsons in the early eighteenth century,
and sixty-four by the early nineteenth.[80] Patronage enabled aristocrats
to offer a form of employment to their relatives and dependants. It also
enabled them to install clerics who might offer useful help at election
time. In 1728 Sir James Lowther decided 'to have a good deal of regard
to the services done me in elections' when appointing to St Nicholas's,
Whitehaven. Naturally some aristocrats took the responsibility more
seriously; in presenting to eight livings in Glamorgan, the second
Marquess of Bute's primary concern was the ability of the candidates to
speak Welsh.[81]

The importance of the church as an agent of social and political
control encouraged landlords to provide sites for new buildings, and to
take upon themselves repair costs. In the early eighteenth century the

[78] Joseph Addison and Richard Steele, *The Spectator*, 112, 9 July 1711.
[79] G. E. Mingay, *English Landed Society in the Eighteenth Century* (1963), p. 148.
[80] John Cannon, *Aristocratic Century: the peerage of eighteenth-century England*
(Cambridge, 1984), pp. 63–70
[81] Carlisle RO, D/Lons/W, Sir James Lowther to John Spedding, 26 December
1728; John Davies, 'Aristocratic town makers and the coal metropolis: the marquesses
of Bute and Cardiff, 1776–1947', in *Patricians, Power and Politics in Nineteenth-Century
Towns,* ed. David Cannadine (Leicester 1982), p. 36.

Lowthers of Whitehaven provided three sites and considerable finance for church building in the town; their cousins at Maulds Meaburn spent money on rebuilding Crosby church in Westmorland; and yet other cousins repaired the chancel at Cartmel, as a result of which they were absolved church tax.[82] In a similar vein, in the nineteenth century Sir Tatton Sykes rebuilt or restored twenty churches in and around Sledmere in the East Riding, while Earl Manvers spent £17,634 on a new church at Perlethorpe in Nottinghamshire during the 1870s, and a further £3000 on a parsonage in the 1890s.[83] It was also possible to offer financial help to the clergy. By legislation in 1704 Queen Anne's bounty was established to maintain and augment poorer benefices. By 1736 nearly 1100 had been aided in this way, with landlords often making a substantial contribution to the sum of money which had to be raised within the parish. The sixth Earl of Thanet helped to augment several Westmorland livings under this scheme, while in the 1740s the third Viscount Lonsdale contributed £70 towards augmenting the rectory at Shap.[84]

Apart from schools and churches, a variety of other openings existed for the exercise of paternal duties. Sir James Lowther went to great lengths to maintain the food supply in newly expanding Whitehaven, bringing in grain by sea from the south-west and Wales. In 1849 the seventh Duke of Bedford erected over 500 cottages at uneconomic rents in Devonshire and Bedfordshire, while others who acquired a reputation for building model cottages included the Earl of Leicester, the Duke of Northumberland and Lord Dartmouth, although it remained a minority pursuit.[85] The Duke of Newcastle granted over 2000 allotments in Nottinghamshire, and the Duke of Richmond 1500 in Sussex. A paternal eye could also be kept on the poor. In 1838 fifty-one peers and twenty baronets were chairmen of boards of guardians.[86] None, perhaps, was more conscientious than the Duke of Rutland:

He is a guardian of a very large Union, and he not only attends regularly the meetings of the Poor Law Guardians every week or fortnight, and takes an

---

[82] Beckett, thesis, pp. 192, 266, 285.

[83] Thompson, 'Landowners and the rural community', p. 469; Nottingham University Manuscripts Department, Ma 2a 208.

[84] Beckett, thesis, pp. 76, 192.

[85] Beckett, *Coal and Tobacco*, pp. 196–9; David Spring, *The English Landed Estate in the Nineteenth Century: its administration* (Baltimore, 1963), p. 52; Thompson, 'Landowners and the rural community', p. 470.

[86] Roberts, *Paternalism in Early Victorian England*, pp. 133, 145.

active part in their proceedings, but he visits those paupers who receive out-of-door relief, sits and converses with them, invites them to complain to him if they have anything to complain of, and tells them that he is not only their friend but their representative at the assembly of Guardians, and it is his duty to see that they are nourished and protected.[87]

Yet others used their parliamentary position to good effect. Peers sought to promote the wellbeing of their neighbours and dependants. The Duke of Bridgewater saw his famous canal in terms of the advantages it offered to the poor, and made his support for the Trent and Mersey scheme conditional upon its being shown to be publicly beneficial. Bridgewater's strictures explain why one of the leading promoters of the Trent and Mersey, a Birmingham industrialist, could solicit the support of the Earl of Huntingdon by stressing that the scheme was not based on 'selfish views that are not truly social'.[88] Lord Spencer agreed to serve on the committee of the Grand Junction Canal because of the project's obvious 'General Utility', while among MPs Samuel Whitbread attempted in 1795 to overcome some of the problems he perceived in dealing with the poor by introducing a minimum wage bill.[89] All too often, however, such public-spiritedness conflicted with self-interest. Efforts to increase allotments foundered on landlord apathy in the Lords, and the House proved capable during the 1840s of vetoing a bill which would have granted tenants compensation for improvements.[90]

What all this amounted to in financial terms is almost impossible to calculate. Some families gave money on a random basis, simply responding to need as it arose. Others were more formal, setting aside specific annual sums and even designating how they were to be laid out. The sixth Earl of Thanet spent £100 a year in Westmorland, distributing clothes and money to poorer tenants within strict guidelines. The steward who administered the scheme was instructed in 1702 'to give no clothes for the future but to such as are now tenants and not to any that shall purchase houses or small parcels of land the better to entitle them to expect my charity'. Clothing was not to be

[87] *The Greville Memoirs*, vol. IV, pp. 45–6.

[88] H. Malet, *Bridgewater: the canal duke* (Manchester, 1977), pp. 49–50; Huntington Library, Hastings MSS, Correspondence box 93, HA 3350, Samuel Garbett to the Earl of Huntingdon, 17 April 1765.

[89] Michael W. McCahill, *Order and Equipoise: the peerage and the House of Lords, 1783–1806* (1982), p. 198; Roger Fulford, *Samuel Whitbread, 1764–1815* (1967), p. 51.

[90] McCahill, *Order and Equipoise*, p. 200; Roberts, *Paternalism in Early Victorian England*, pp. 147, 266–7.

given to the same person more than 'every third year'. Similarly, in bad winters Sir James Lowther often instructed his steward to make charitable payments, but the people who stood to benefit were almost always members of his own workforce. Other families gave charity at fixed points in the year. Christmas was an obvious opportunity for distributing largesse, and in the early eighteenth century £5 a year was normally distributed to the poor of the village of Lowther in Westmorland on behalf of Viscount Lonsdale just prior to the festivities. It was also customary for the Lonsdales to distribute £5 at the gate when the family departed from the hall.[91]

For a few individuals it is possible to calculate how much they were spending on charitable giving. Sir John Bridger set aside £35 of his gross income of around £2500 in 1806 for charitable purposes, which was a mere 1.4 per cent of the total, and considerably less than he laid out on gambling and alcohol. Around the beginning of the nineteenth century Samuel Whitbread was distributing about £2000 a year in gifts and presents, which was usually less than 10 per cent of his income. Between 1821 and 1848 the second Marquess of Bute gave £25,000 in Cardiff (7–8 per cent of his gross income), predominantly to societies like the Cardiff Dorcas Society or the Glamorgan Prisoners' Charity Fund. Other donations to such organizations tended to be governed by Bute's contribution. On the dukes of Bedford's Bedfordshire and Buckinghamshire estates 'pensions, compassionate allowances, charities and other general payments' rose from £44,396 between 1816 and 1855, to £147,843 between 1856 and 1895. In the 1860s the future fifteenth Earl of Derby set aside one-third of his income for charities and deserving causes, while between 1863 and 1882 on average one-third of Lord Overstone's expenditure was given away. Sizeable donations included £5000 for a new church at Overstone in 1873 and £1000 to Wantage grammer school two years later.[92]

---

[91] Beckett, thesis, pp. 76, 192. Lowther told his steward that 'the poor people being sufferers by my not living in the country, besides the five pounds which I have directed to be distributed among poor and sick families before Christmas . . . I would also have forty shillings worth of bread in sixpenny loaves to be given the day before Christmas': Carlisle RO, D/Lons/W, James Lowther to William Gilpin, 6 November 1707. Unfortunately the largesse proved too little: 'the great number of poor people that are not employed about the works made the quantity somewhat insufficient. I made bold to add six shillings more to what you ordered, but there was still a good many left out which were needful enough': ibid., John Spedding to Lowther, 28 December 1707.

[92] G. E. Mingay. *The Gentry* (1976), p. 140; Fulford, *Samuel Whitbread*, p. 51; Davies, 'Aristocratic town makers and the coal metropolis', pp. 35–6; Duke of Bedford, *A Great Agricultural Estate*, p. 227; J. J. Bagley, *The Earls of Derby*

Hippolyte Taine suggested that 10 per cent of annual income was given over to charitable purposes, but a more recent estimate has put the figure at perhaps 4–7 per cent for the leading families and 1–2 per cent among the gentry. However, such figures can be little more than guesses, given the nature of the subject. Sir John Griffin Griffin, who otherwise kept meticulous accounts, had no separate list of charitable giving.[93] Moreover, through time, voluntary benevolence was often secured as permanent trusts, and by the 1830s nearly 450,000 acres belonged to charities, totalling £874,000 in rents. A total of 29,000 charities were listed by the Select Committee on Public Charities, although nearly half of these handled less than £5 a year.[94]

The most obvious problem in assessing charitable giving concerns such factors as providing land for churches and setting up schools. Where, on the financial scale, for example, is it possible to place the Duke of Ancaster's leading role in building Lincoln Assembly Rooms in 1742, or the Earl of Lonsdale's provision of a subscription library at Whitehaven in 1797?[95] For this leads into yet another aspect of the landlord's role in the countryside – the need to be seen. Paternalism was, as much as anything, an opportunity to grasp opportunities which would enhance the standing of the landlord within the community, and they seldom chose projects in a disinterested fashion. It was this concept of public display which lay behind so many of their actions. It was not merely sufficient for Sir James Lowther to visit Whitehaven every couple of years; he had to be seen to be visiting. The local gentry met him at Distington, on the road from Cockermouth, and accompanied him to the town, where it was traditional for the guns on the harbour fortifications to be fired. Prior to an election the procedure was even more elaborate. In 1734 Lowther was

met on the road by the High Sheriff, chief Gentlemen, clergymen, and principal freeholders living for above 30 miles in length in that part of the Country, who accompanied him to this town, where he was received by thousands in the high streets, the bells ringing, the great guns firing, and the

---

1485–1985 (1985), p. 190; R. C. Michie, 'Income, expenditure and investment of a Victorian millionaire: Lord Overstone, 1823–83', *Bulletin of the Institute of Historical Research*, 58 (1985), p. 63.

[93] Taine, *Notes on England*, pp. 141–2; Thompson, *English Landed Society*, p. 210; Williams, 'The finances of an eighteenth-century Essex nobleman', pp. 113–27; Mingay, *English Landed Society*, p. 128.

[94] Mingay, *The Gentry*, p. 141.

[95] C. Chalklin, 'Capital expenditure on building for cultural purposes in provincial England, 1730–1830', *Business History*, 22 (1980), pp. 64–5.

ships putting out their colours and the next Wednesday the election comes on at Cockermouth for this county.[96]

Such events were, of course, in the same tradition as family birthdays and mourning trains, but perhaps the best example of the way in which an activity was cultivated by the aristocracy for its own social ends is the case of horseracing.

The significance of the horse as a symbol of social standing in English society aroused considerable interest in the relative abilities of individual animals, particularly in the form of racing. Originally horseracing was an aristocratic preserve, but it blossomed into a mass spectator sport during the eighteenth and nineteenth centuries, although the landed elite attempted to maintain its control of the reins of authority. Newmarket, the home of racing, was an exclusive aristocratic preserve. In the 1720s Daniel Defoe noted 'a great concourse of the nobility and gentry, as well from London as from all parts of England' at Newmarket, but at the seven annual meetings crowds seldom exceeded 500. Over 400 horses were trained on the heath.[97] Ascot, where meetings began towards the end of the seventeenth century, became the most prestigious gathering outside Newmarket, with a considerable aristocratic appearance on race days. The same company also patronized Epsom, particularly on Derby Day – when half the male peerage was reputed to be visible in the saddling enclosure – and Goodwood, which was owned by the Duke of Richmond. Doncaster served much the same function in the north of England. Aristocratic patronage could also be crucial at smaller meetings. They might put up prize money or offer cups and plates. In 1703 Lord Lonsdale gave a silver candle cup, 'being a plate run for on Strickland Head on Midsummer day', and in 1712 six silver cups 'run for in Cumberland and Westmorland'.[98] By 1722, 112 cities and towns in England were holding meetings. The government attempted to control betting by outlawing stakes above £10 in 1710, and to

[96] Society for the Promotion of Christian Knowledge, Holy Trinity Church, Marylebone Road, London, CR1/17/12655, Sir James Lowther to Henry Newman, 9 May 1734; Carlisle RO, D/Lons/W, John Spedding to Lowther, 2 July 1732, Lowther to Spedding, 21 July 1752.

[97] Daniel Defoe, *A Tour through the Whole Island of Great Britain* (1724–6; Harmondsworth, 1971), pp. 98–9; J. H. Plumb, *The Commercialization of Leisure in Eighteenth-Century England* (University of Reading, 1972), pp. 16–17.

[98] Carlisle RO, D/Lons/L, AM2/20, fol. 12, AM2/18, fol. 10, AM2/56, fol. 18, AM2/57, fol. 30, AM2/59, fol. 34, AM2/67, fol. 4. Elsewhere, Monmouth Races began under the direct patronage of the Duke of Beaufort in 1717, and the Philipps family patronized meetings at Haverfordwest from the 1720s: Philip Jenkins *The Making of a Ruling Class: the Glamorgan gentry, 1640–1790* (Cambridge, 1983), p. 267.

regulate meetings involving small stakes, making it illegal in 1740 for a race to be run if the prize was less than £50. Even so, the sport flourished to become big business by the end of the eighteenth century. Some of the more distinguished meetings drew enormous crowds, and various historic races date from this period, including the St Leger (1776) and two races associated with the twelfth Earl of Derby, the Oaks (1778) and the Derby (1780).[99]

Aristocratic investment in horseracing was considerable. Many were interested in breeding. At Lowther the Lonsdales had an established stud in the 1690s. Like many others they imported Arabian stock. Lord Lonsdale was selling horses to William III almost certainly for racing purposes, and in 1696 Lord Massereene wrote that 'I have heard so much of your Lordship's breed of horses, that I am ambitious to have one of them.' Lonsdale informed his son that he had been 'much delighted with breeding of horses and accordingly had as good as anybody, and do intend to reserve the best race of them called the Royal king for you.'[100] Such business was an expensive pursuit. The Duke of Kingston spent £506 on his stables and racehorses in 1770, and in the later eighteenth century Lord Grosvenor was lavishing around £7000 a year on racing. Early in the nineteenth century Earl Fitzwilliam's racing stables at Wentworth were costing £1500–£3000 annually. Given such outlay, it is hardly surprising that the aristocracy expected to control the sport, particularly the Jockey Club, which was formed in the 1750s, partly to be an arbiter in disputes. Down to the twentieth century its internal election procedure was such as to ensure that the governing body of racing was an association of the peerage and gentry.[101]

The railway did two things for racing: it enabled horses to be taken to meetings far from their stables, at which they could compete with the best in their class, and it enabled people to be brought to racecourses from miles around. Although the prestige events retained a certain significance of their own, in general terms the sport moved from its local, landowner-orientated base to a national arena. It was widely accepted that racing transcended class barriers; indeed, a select

[99] Plumb, *The Commercialization of Leisure*, p. 17; Wray Vamplew, *The Turf: a social and economic history of horse racing* (1976), pp. 20, 199–200; Bagley, *The Earls of Derby*, pp. 147–8.

[100] Public RO, E351/1762, Declared accounts; Hertfordshire RO, D/ENa 07, accounts of the King's Master of Horse, 1692–1700 (reference courtesy of Dr P. R. Edwards); Carlisle RO, D/Lons/L, survey list 2, bundle 19, Lord Massereene to Lord Lonsdale, 22 August 1696; Memoranda Book, letter to his son, 1696, fol. 105.

[101] Mingay, *English Landed Society*, p. 151; Thompson, *English Landed Society*, p. 97.

committee report of 1884 declared this to be the case, although there is little evidence that the social intermingling of the course continued beyond its bounds.

The bulk of the crowd at race meetings tended to be from the lower classes, but attendance by the aristocracy reminded the community who was at its head. Leicester Races represented the highpoint of the county's social calendar. The most important aristocratic supporters were the dukes of Rutland, particularly the fifth duke (1787–1857), who won the Derby in 1828 and the Oaks in 1811 and 1814. When he was absent in 1850 and 1852, country gentlemen who normally attended merely for the social display stayed at home. Some of the social éclat attached to racing may have fallen away during the nineteenth century – although aristocratic sponsorship was responsible for reviving Leicester Races in the third quarter of the century – but social standing still had to be confirmed by attendance at the important meetings, with entry into the Royal Enclosure at Ascot representing the true measure of achievement. The sport also survived a scandal in the mid-nineteenth-century when two runners in the 1844 Derby were found to be over age, another mount lost its chance of victory because of foul riding, and yet another was pulled up because its jockey had backed another horse. The fight against improbity was led by Lord George Bentinck, son of the fourth Duke of Portland, who had himself lost £27,000 on the 1826 St Leger. However, it was under his leadership that corruption was rooted out, that the Jockey Club finally established itself as the sport's accepted governing body, and ultimately that this permitted the club to retain its aristocratic bias at the expense of industrialists and businessmen into the twentieth century.[102]

ARISTOCRATS AND THE LOCAL COMMUNITY: THE LIMITS OF DEFERENCE

The strength of social deference needs to be kept in perspective since it is all too easy to gloss over differences in order to depict rural society as revolving almost entirely around the country house. According to Habakkuk, 'from some eighteenth-century memoirs one might suppose that England was a federation of country houses', and this

---

[102] Jeremy Crump, '"The great carnival of the year": Leicester Races in the 19th century', *Leicestershire History and Archaeology*, 58 (1982–3), pp. 58–74; Vamplew, *The Turf*, pp. 88–107.

view has been endorsed by several other historians. Perkin, for example, has pointed to the network of patronage which bound society together.[103] But how accurate is such a picture of rural society? Even when a family was in residence, outlying parts of the estate might still not receive a visit. Some events, such as balls, and appearances at horse race meetings, were clearly designed to expose the aristocrat to as wide a cross-section of the community as possible. Some sought to monopolize local patronage as a means of displaying their influence, hence Sir James Lowther's outbursts when his nominees were not appointed to custom-house places in West Cumberland.[104] However, in many other areas it is apparent that influence was restricted, and that this was recognized by the landowning community.

Virtually every aspect of paternalism in rural life took place within circumscribed limits. The social divisiveness of the game varied with the incidence of shooting, and in 1861 individual counties ranged 50 per cent below and above the national mean of keepers per 10,000 acres. This discrepancy had increased by 1911. Foxhunting flourished in counties of large estates, and was less common where land was extensively divided.[105] The provision of paternal aid to the community also varied, constituting 'a patchy affair' overall, according to F. M. L. Thompson. Education provision, for example, varied widely, although those areas which enjoyed the friendliness and comparative absence of social friction in the hunting districts seem to have been well looked after by the landowning community, while in shooting areas a certain hostility towards helping local people may have developed. Interestingly, one of the assistant commissioners for the mid-nineteenth-century Newcastle Commission on Popular Education was of opinion that, 'where landowners are resident and study the welfare of their tenants and labourers, they usually take an interest in the schools and contribute liberally.'[106] Even more telling in this respect was the attitude of landowners towards parliamentary boroughs. At general elections during the nineteenth century the Fitzwilliams provided £200 towards public improvements at Malton in Yorkshire, in addition to the £100–£120 they gave annually to the town's charities.

---

[103] H. J. Habakkuk, 'England's nobility', in *Aristocratic Government and Society in Eighteenth-Century England*, ed. Daniel A. Baugh (1975), p. 100; Harold Perkin, *The Origins of Modern English Society, 1780–1880* (1969), pp. 42, 49.

[104] J. V. Beckett, 'A back-bench MP in the eighteenth century: Sir James Lowther of Whitehaven', *Parliamentary History*, 1 (1982), pp. 87–8.

[105] Thompson, 'Landowners and the rural community', p. 462; Carr, *A History of Foxhunting*, p. 49.

[106] Thompson, *English Landed Society*, p. 210; 'Landowners and the rural community', pp. 466–9.

When Higham, another of the family's borough interests, was disfranchised in 1832, annual benefactions to the town were sharply reduced. The second Marquess of Bute's philanthropic activities also had political ends. In 1825 he gave out blankets to the poor, and especially to the freemen's wives in Cardiff. Donations to individuals ceased if their political loyalty strayed, while even his contributions to those trying to avoid the Poor Law were not disinterested, since those in receipt of relief had no vote, and he wanted to keep his dependants on the register.[107]

Perhaps the clearest indication of the limits of country-house rural influence is to be found in the difference between open and closed villages. Closed villages normally had one or two dominant landowners who sought to control the number of families living within the boundaries by restricting the number of cottages. Since each parish was responsible for its own poor under the seventeenth-century Poor Law legislation, this helped to prevent undesirables from gaining a settlement, and to keep down the rate. Beyond this, some landlords appear to have been motivated by a simple desire to avoid the nuisance of too many families. Although this model oversimplifies the situation which existed in practice, the distinction holds for many areas of the country. In Leicestershire, for example, 174 villages were open in the nineteenth century and 134 closed, although 70 per cent of the latter had absentee landlords.[108]

Landlord control could be exercised with ruthless efficiency. To improve the parklands around a house, some villages were relocated. Eighteenth- and nineteenth-century examples of this process included Sudbury, Houghton, Lowther, Milton Abbas, Nuneham Courtenay, Harewood, Blanchland, Coneysthorpe and Tremadoc, although these were different in concept from the more typical Victorian model villages which were usually the work of a paternalist landlord.[109] Closed villages usually grew more slowly – if they grew at all – than open villages, while the leadership of the landlord in village affairs was

---

[107] Thompson, *English Landed Society*, pp. 206–8; Davies, 'Aristocratic town makers and the coal metropolis', p. 38.

[108] B. A. Holderness, '"Open" and "close" parishes in England in the eighteenth and nineteenth centuries', *Agricultural History Review*, 20 (1972), pp. 126–39; Roberts, *Paternalism in Early Victorian England*, p. 140; Dennis R. Mills, *Lord and Peasant in Nineteenth-Century Britain* (1980), pp. 76–7.

[109] Barley, 'Rural building in England', pp. 610–19, 643–5; M. A. Havinden, 'Estate villages', in *The Victorian Countryside*, ed. Mingay, pp. 414–27; H. C. Prince, 'Georgian landscapes', in *Man Made the Land*, ed. A. R. H. Baker and J. B. Harley (Newton Abbot, 1973), p. 162; W. G. Hoskins, *The Making of the English Landscape* (Harmondsworth, 1970), pp. 170–2.

seldom challenged. At Helmingham in Oxfordshire the Tollemache family expected each family to attend the parish church at least once on a Sunday, to cultivate their allotment land by spade rather than by hiring a plough, and to send unmarried pregnant daughters out of the village. Schoolboys were expected to touch their forelock and girls to curtsey in the presence of the family.[110] The scandal of closed villages was sufficiently clear by the early nineteenth century for the new Poor Law of 1834 to be partially designed to deal with the problem, but predictably it had little impact until the Union Chargeability Act of 1865 shifted financial responsibility for the poor from the parish to the union. Even then cottage building was slow to recommence, and a village such as Helmingham still had the effective appearance of being closed in 1871. By contrast, landlords could exercise relatively little influence in open villages, where land was divided, and where the majority of the rural labour force lived. Evidence presented to nineteenth-century investigative committees suggests that in these villages landlords were remote, and took little interest in either the housing or the welfare of the inhabitants.[111]

ARISTOCRATS AND THE LOCAL COMMUNITY: THE DIVERSION OF URBAN LIFE

The ties of social deference were further weakened by the aristocratic preference for town life, which kept them away from their estates for all but two or three months of the summer. During his tenure of his family's Whitehaven estates Sir James Lowther visited West Cumberland in all but eleven of the years 1706–54, usually staying for between three and five months. In the early nineteenth century, the dukes of Devonshire were seldom in Derbyshire for above three months of the year. This was probably not untypical, particularly for aristocrats with a variety of scattered estates, even if a conscientious administrator such as the second Marquess of Bute could – 'like a Medieval monarch perambulating his kingdom' – move slowly around the country visiting each of his properties in turn.[112]

---

[110] Pamela Horn, 'Victorian villages from census returns', *Local Historian* 15, 1 (1982), p. 30. Thomas Hardy's novel *The Woodlanders* describes the impact of property being restricted, and the continuance of deferential attitudes, in a closed village.

[111] Roberts, *Paternalism in Early Victorian England*, p. 140. Poor law unions, incorporating a number of parishes, were formed in 1834, but collective financial responsibility was accepted only in 1865. Between 1834 and 1865 each parish in the union was responsible for financing its own poor.

[112] Mark Girouard, *Life in the English Country House* (New Haven, Conn., 1978), p. 6; John Davies, *Cardiff and the Marquesses of Bute* (1981), p. 17.

Although town life was generally reckoned to be detrimental to relations between aristocrats and their tenants and workforce in the countryside, apologists could be found, naturally enough. In 1756 Joseph Massie wrote against the prevailing notion that London residence impoverished the countryside. He suggested that the purchasing power utilized in the capital was channelled back into the countryside through the acquisition of goods: consequently London life 'hath been a great advantage to the country in particular, and to the nation in general.[113] Later, London life came to be seen as having beneficial social effects. According to William Howitt, writing in the 1830s:

much has been said of the evil of this aristocratic habit of spending so much time in the metropolis; of the vast sums there spent in ostentatious rivalry, in equipage and establishments; in the dissipations of theatres, operas, routes and gaming-houses; and unquestionably there is much truth in it. On the other hand, it cannot be denied that this annual assembling together has some advantages. A great degree of knowledge and refinement results from it, amid all the attendant folly and extravagance. The wealthy are brought into contact with vast numbers of their equals and superiors, and that sullen and haughty habit of reserve is worn off, which is always contracted by those who live in solitary seclusion in the midst of vast estates, with none but tenants and dependents around them.

Aristocrats, he continued, mixed with men of talent and intelligence; they moved among books and works of art, and apart from buying such items they also became patrons of their makers. Consequently artists came to London to seek sponsorship, and portrait painters rose or fell by work they could acquire in the capital. Some aristocrats even had private galleries that they opened for public enjoyment.[114]

London in 1660 already offered a number of attractions which induced the aristocracy to spend part of their lives in the capital. First, it was the seat of the court. The emergence during the sixteenth and seventeenth centuries of increasingly centralized nation-states throughout Europe had particularly significant consequences for the life of the chosen capital. Local potentates came increasingly to look like state pensioners drawn to the capital and to dependence on the Crown. If this divorce was neither as necessary nor as permanent in

---

[113] Joseph Massie, *Observations upon Mr Fauquier's Essay . . . . to which is added an Account of several National Advantages derived from the Nobility and Gentry of the present Age living in London a greater part of the year than their Ancestors used to do* (1756), pp. 35–52.

[114] William Howitt, *The Rural Life of England* (1838), vol. I, pp. 25–6.

England as it proved to be elsewhere in Europe, it was still significant. Second, London was the centre of business. Landowners went to town in order to arrange their legal business at the Inns of Court, to search out large loans, sort out marriage settlements and oversee conveyances. Third, it was the home of Parliament. Even in the sixteenth and seventeenth centuries, when sessions were rare and brief, it still drew to the capital all the peers, and 500 or so of the gentry. Finally, it was the centre of pleasure, as the London 'Season' took off towards the end of the sixteenth century. Lawrence Stone has calculated that by 1632 about one in four of the peerage, one in six of the baronets and knights, and slightly less than one in 100 of the lesser gentry were residing in the capital.[115]

After 1660 the attractions increased considerably. The travelling coach enabled gentlemen to carry their families with them to the capital, while the hackney cab and the public oil-lamp made travel within the city both easier and safer. An improved postal service speeded up the dissemination of gossip, news and .fashions, which stimulated the desire to travel to London in order to experience changes at first hand. London became the location for specialist services; Sir John Lowther's daughter Jane hurried back to the capital from Whitehaven in January 1700 when she needed urgent medical attention, rather than entrust herself to Cumbrian doctors.[116] The growth of the finance market also attracted newcomers to the capital. Daniel Defoe lamented in the 1720s that the transfer of stocks and shares 'is given as one of the principal causes of the prodigious conflux of the nobility and gentry from all parts of England to London, more than ever was known in former years'. As early as Queen Anne's reign the majority of investors were part of a recognizable London plutocracy, and only three of the seventy-four holders of £5000 bank stock lived outside the capital.[117]

The post-1689 developments in the finance market, the expansion of government during the wars against Louis XIV's France, annual sessions of Parliament lasting from Christmas or earlier to July, and the development of the London Season from April to July collectively turned attendance in the capital from a pleasurable diversion from the

---

[115] Stone, *The Crisis of the Aristocracy*, pp. 385–92.

[116] Carlisle RO, D/Lons/W, Miscellaneous letter-books, Sir John Lowther to Sir William Lowther, 28 January 1700. Similar views were still held in the early nineteenth century: Jane Austen, *Pride and Prejudice* (1813; Harmondsworth, 1972), p. 86.

[117] Defoe, *A Tour*, p. 307; P. G. M. Dickson, *The Financial Revolution in England, 1688–1756* (1967), ch. 11.

lonely boredom of the countryside into a social necessity. Families of rank flocked to London to maintain their social prestige which was almost bound to suffer if they stayed at home; indeed, a recurrent theme of contemporary literature was the social divide between city and country. London was regarded as the centre of civilization, and those who eschewed the Season tended to be depicted in terms of rustic simplicity and boorishness in the eighteenth century, and as representing old-fashioned values and incorruptibility in the nineteenth. Differences certainly abounded. The first Duke of Chandos seems to have been generally abstemious when in town, but rather more given to hard-drinking in the country, while the Earl of Cholmondeley walked a careful tightrope between being a Court Whig when in town, and a Tory when in Cheshire. Even so, the divergences were undoubtedly exaggerated, largely to stress the social conformity required of the landed community.[118]

The attraction of London was reflected in the number of newspapers which appeared on its streets from the 1690s, the building of new theatres and the rebuilding of older establishments, and the growth of opera and concert facilities. Around the beginning of the eighteenth century the Duke of Chandos used his London base for a series of financial transactions, but also for a varied and busy social round. He passed many hours in the company of the Royal Society, visited the theatre – infrequently, perhaps through lack of interest – went to concerts, played cards, collected books, and visited the numerous coffee houses, taverns, chocolate houses, and other places of

[118] Baker and Baker, *The Life and Circumstances of James Brydges*, p. 41; J. V. Beckett and Clyve Jones, 'Financial improvidence and political independence in the early eighteenth century: George Booth, 2nd Earl of Warrington', *Bulletin of the John Rylands Library*, 65 (1982), p. 11n. Literary stereotypes suggested that town-bred people could not relate to the dress and manners of the countryside. Samuel Johnson's Euphelia, a town-bred girl sent to visit a distant aunt, was horrified to be greeted by her relation 'in a dress so far removed from the present fashion that I could scarcely look upon her without laughter': *The Rambler*, 42, 11 August 1750. Addison and Steele's *Spectator* also emphasized the country–city differences. At a dinner party, Sir Roger de Coverley's formal greetings were so elaborate that the food went cold: *The Spectator*, 119, 17 July 1711. Elizabeth Bennet's concern for her indisposed sister was capable of being interpreted as 'a most country town indifference to decorum': Austen, *Pride and Prejudice*, p. 82. Henry Fielding also pointed to the differences in the rules of modesty between London ladies and their country counterparts: *Tom Jones*, p. 618. Into such a rustic world, those bred in the city could hardly expect to fit. Both Euphelia and another of Johnson's characters, Dick Shifter, found it impossible to stay in the country, even for a few weeks of the summer: *The Idler*, 71, 25 August 1759.

amusement.[119] However, it was wives who were the most anxious to attend. For them the round of theatres, balls and receptions, and the opportunities for buying jewels and fashionable clothes, provided welcome relief from the tedium of the countryside. They pressed upon their husbands the significance of London in providing an education for daughters, and interests for sons, although these were probably no more than excuses for their own desire to join the social whirl. Even daughters complained that their marriage prospects would be adversely affected if for one reason or another the family could not make the Season.[120]

Over time the Season became a formal social round, which, by the second quarter of the nineteenth century, had been infused with an elaborate etiquette. It became private and exclusive, with the most important protocol surrounding the court. By mid-century presentation to the queen was regarded as the passport to society. The calendar of events became increasingly restrictive, and by the 1870s it was imperative for any family accepting the rules of Society to conform. Only late in the century was the basis of membership widened to admit newcomers from outside the landed elite. Although a few families questioned the rules and opted out, the majority conformed because to be a member was regarded as being for the long-term good of 'family' in much the same way as estate preservation.[121]

Those who opted out usually did so on the grounds of finance. While visits to the pleasure gardens at Ranelagh, Chelsea and Vauxhall were relatively cheap, and allowed the prospect of meeting many people in a short space of time, the need to rent or own a separate house, to entertain and, above all, to spend on clothes and other goods which could be paraded both in town and country bumped up the cost. Sir Robert Walpole's father rarely took his wife to London, so that he could live frugally. In 1681 she spent over £100 of the total outgoings of £290 in London, and thereafter he regarded her tastes as too expensive for long trips. But it was not always the women who were responsible for heavy expenditure. Sir Walter Calverley spent £260 in 1712–13

---

[119] Plumb, *The Commercialization of Leisure*, pp. 6–15; Baker and Baker, *The Life and Circumstances of James Brydges*, pp. 33–41.

[120] It is easiest to find fictional examples of bullying wives and recalcitrant daughters pestering their husbands and fathers who were proposing not to visit town, for the simple reason that such debates were likely to take place in the privacy of the drawing-room, rather than to be discussed in letters. However, Mrs Hardcastle in Oliver Goldsmith's *She Stoops to Conquer* (1773) provides an example of the railing wife, and dissatisfied daughters appear in Anthony Trollope's *The Way We Live Now* (1875; Oxford, 1982), vol. I, p. 192.

[121] Leonore Davidoff, *The Best Circles: society, etiquette and the Season* (1973).

merely on furniture and a 'chariot', while even leaving the family at home did not obviate the need to purchase clothes and other goods for them. Just how much was spent on London life is impossible to calculate in any systematic fashion. Lawrence Stone has suggested that in the early seventeenth century, even for a man lacking an official court position, London must have added at least £1000 to his normal country expenditure, and for the greater political figures this could rise to £5000 or even £10,000 a year.[122] Clearly it was possible to survive on much less. Bishop Nicolson of Carlisle scraped by on little more than £50 a month in the early eighteenth century, and Nicholas Blundell spent only £25 in fifteen weeks.[123] But clearly this permitted no ostentation, whereas maintaining a social position required financial outlay. The first Duke of Devonshire reputedly spent £1000 on a single supper and masked ball, while the second Duke of Kingston ran through £2000 during a mere two weeks in 1752. Lord Ashburnham spent nearly £26,000 in London between 1710 and 1716, while by the 1790s Lord Verulam was getting through about £1000 a year in the capital, and Earl Fitzwilliam twice that sum. The Duke of Northumberland was spending £10,000 a year in 1808–10, and his successor the third duke had outgoings of £15,000 in the 1820s and £20,000 or even more in the 1840s. The expansion of London clubs in the early nineteenth century added to costs not only through the price of admission but also as a result of the gambling which was ubiquitous in such institutions.[124]

Furthermore, although families were willing to live in small town houses, on a scale they would never have contemplated in the countryside, this did not prevent competition to build bigger and better edifices. In the 1750s the second Baron Foley lavished £30,000 on a new house in Cavendish Square, setting a trend which others were quick to follow as the building, embellishing and furnishing of town houses took on a competitive and expensive edge. The Lambs spent £100,000 on Melbourne House in the later 1770s, while Elizabeth Montagu put £20,000 into Montagu (later Portman) House. Between 1821 and 1825 the Londonderrys spent £243,000 buying and

[122] W. Wroth, *The London Pleasure Gardens of the Eighteenth Century* (1896); J. H. Plumb, 'The Walpoles father and son', in *Studies in Social History* (1955), pp. 187–9; Mingay, *English Landed Society*, p. 157; Stone, *The Crisis of the Aristocracy*, p. 450.

[123] Clyve Jones and Geoffrey Holmes (eds), *The London Diaries of William Nicolson, Bishop of Carlisle, 1702–1718* (Oxford, 1985), pp. 56–9; Mingay, *English Landed Society*, p. 157.

[124] G. E. Mingay, *Georgian London* (1975), ch. 3; Mingay, *English Landed Society*, p. 158; Thompson, *English Landed Society*, pp. 105–6.

refurbishing Holderness House in Park Lane, while the Metropolitan Board of Works paid £497,000 compensation for Northumberland House when it was acquired from the Duke of Northumberland in 1874.[125]

Town residence was not limited to London. From the later seventeenth century, local gentry began to escape from the solitude of their country seats into country towns. Although only two gentry families owned town houses in early seventeenth-century York, Defoe found the town 'full of gentry' in the 1720s, and in 1736 the town's historian could remark that 'the chief support of the city at present is the resort to and residence of several country gentlemen with their families.'[126] Local gentry began to build town houses in Lincoln early in the eighteenth century, and by the time Daniel Defoe produced his *Tour* in the 1720s a number of places had become social centres for the local gentry. As a result of the inhospitable Peak District, 'the gentry choose to reside at Derby rather than upon their estates as they do in other places', while Bury St Edmunds was 'crowded with nobility and gentry . . . and they that live at Bury are supposed to live there for the sake of it.' Maidstone, Petworth, Westerham, Exeter and Shrewsbury were full of gentry, and at Winchester, 'abundance of gentry being in the neighbourhood, it adds to the sociableness of the place.'[127] This movement into towns, coupled with the growth of an urban-*rentier* 'gentry', led directly to assembly rooms and ballrooms, bowling greens and coffee houses in provincial towns. Circulating libraries, provincial theatres, music festivals and subscription concerts followed in their wake, and more often than not these urban activities could number peers and landed gentry among their sponsors. Even the rules of the London Season were observed in the provinces by the nineteenth century.[128]

The other towns that became significant social centres were the spas and resorts. On one or both sides of the London Season, in the spring or autumn, the customary place for the socially ambitious was in a spa, particularly Bath or Tunbridge Wells. Bath trebled in size during the

[125] F. H. W. Sheppard, *Local Government in St Marylebone, 1688–1835* (1958), pp. 103–6; Sir John Summerson, *Georgian London*, 3rd edn (1978), p. 146; Northumberland RO, ZAN M.17/79; Thompson, *English Landed Society*, pp. 104–5.

[126] Defoe, *A Tour*, p. 523; F. Drake, *Eboracum* (1736), p. 240; VCH, *City of York* (1961), pp. 208, 245–7.

[127] Defoe, *A Tour*, pp. 75, 132, 147, 165, 192, 218, 397, 411, 457.

[128] Davidoff, *The Best Circles*, pp. 65 ff.; R. P. Sturgess, 'Harmony and good company: the emergence of musical performance in eighteenth-century Derby', *Music Review*, 39 (1978), pp. 178–95.

eighteenth century to reach 33,000 by 1801, but it was the 40,000 or so visitors who were crucial for its economy. In 1765 visitors included three princes, four dukes, four duchesses, one marquess, two marchionesses, twenty-four earls, twenty-two countesses, fourteen viscounts, forty-three viscountesses, twelve barons, twelve baronesses and six bishops. Some drank the water, but the majority were primarily intent on enjoying the social life.[129] The same was true of Tunbridge, where, according to Defoe, 'some drink, more do not, and few drink physically . . . company and diversion is in short the main business of the place.'[130] For those unable to afford these delights, Harrogate, Buxton and Scarborough were more than adequate substitutes. From the late eighteenth century interest switched towards the coastal resorts – as a result of George III's patronage of Weymouth and his son's at Brighton – and in the nineteenth century towards the Continent.[131]

The view of English society as governed by a network of country houses, each of which stood in the midst of a closely knit, forelock-touching community, provides only a partial picture of the rural world between 1660 and 1914. English aristocrats were no fools. They recognized that time spent being both seen and active in the country was not wasted, however much the pull of London threatened to divert them off course. Appearance strengthened ties of deference, and helped to shore up the existing social order, for which patronage provided the adhesive – William Cobbett's 'chain of dependence running through the whole nation'.[132] But deference had its limits. Paternalism was often limited to places in which landowners had the sole interest, or a strong political hold, and even the latter could not necessarily be turned into votes (see chapter twelve). Many landowners were neither active nor responsible enough to try to influence the rural community in a systematic fashion. In wages, rents and housing they often expressed more interest in the cash nexus than in the duties of landed property, while the monopoly of shooting game was always a social sore point. The most ruthless nineteenth-century aristocrats even sought a profit from letting allotments to labourers, while many failed to promote schools, were overzealous in prosecutions under the game laws and, in general, were insufficiently active in relieving the lot of

[129] R. S. Neale, *Bath, 1680–1850: a social history* (1981), pp. 13, 38.

[130] Defoe, *A Tour*, pp. 141–2.

[131] Gervase Huxley, *Lady Elizabeth and the Grosvenors: life in a Whig family, 1822–1839* (1965), ch. 7.

[132] William Cobbett, *Weekly Political Register*, 14 (1808), col. 585.

the rural poor. Even the role of justice was neglected on occasion (see chapter eleven).

The failure to uphold the Anglican Church had serious implications. Lack of new building permitted dissent to flourish, so that by 1851 only 20 per cent of the population attended an Anglican Church, and a significant proportion of them were doing so because they resided in closed villages. The lack of aristocratic support for the Anglican Church may even have allowed religion to act as something of a catalyst in undermining traditional rural social relations. The influence of the established church fell away with the rise of Methodism and the remoteness of the clergy. Consequently, in the long run the church abandoned its aim of promoting the temporal as well as the spiritual welfare of its parishioners. In predominantly rural South Lindsey during the second and third quarters of the nineteenth century, the state of religious practices and beliefs was an important means of bringing about a transformation in social relations, and it provides an explanation for the breakdown of the traditional village order and the emergence of a class society with a distinctive outlook and religious style.[133]

In the circumstances it is hardly surprising that the aristocratic role in the community came in for increasing criticism through time. The moral right of landowners to dominate society was questioned towards the end of the eighteenth century by writers such as Thomas Spence and William Ogilvie. Spence argued that, since the land belonged to all inhabitants in equal manner, the few who had claimed it and called it their own were depriving the rest of mankind of their rights. Individuals had acquired their property by encroaching on the common rights of the community via appropriation rather than agreement. The solution was to transfer land to public institutions, since landlords, far from being benevolent, were idle men living on unearned income extracted from the land, which deprived the propertyless of the means of enjoying a full and independent life.[134] Spence

[133] Thompson, 'Landowners and the rural community', pp. 457–74; Roberts, *Paternalism in Early Victorian England*, pp. 140–8; James Obelkevich, *Religion and Rural Society: South Lindsey, 1825–1875* (Oxford, 1976). The role of religion in the emergence of class relationships in England, and the significance of the aristocratic failure to uphold the Church of England, is stressed by Perkin, *The Origins of Modern English Society*, pp. 196–208, while the importance of dissent is emphasized by E. P. Thompson, *The Making of the English Working Class* (1963), ch. 11. Ironically, as the hold on patronage was apparently on the increase, aristocratic power was actually being undermined by the failure to build enough churches, and to make the Anglican establishment appear relevant.

[134] Thomas Spence, *The End of Oppression* (1795); William Ogilvie, *An Essay on the*

and Ogilvie came too early, but in the nineteenth century their ideas became part of the land reform movement which sought to re-establish a peasant proprietorship at the expense of the great estates. The extent of deference is also questionable. E. P. Thompson has argued that for many people from all walks of life (including tradesmen, craftsmen, labourers and paupers) a consciousness of collective difference from the ruling class existed in the eighteenth century. For these people the focal point of rural life was not the country house but markets and fairs, and the antagonism they expressed through the anonymity of the crowd reflected a desire to break with the mores of deference. Only when the bourgeois industrialists and professional people began to take on a separate role from the landowners at the end of the century did a leadership emerge for this social group. The mob was the symbol of class struggle in an aristocratic society, struggling in a class-like manner before the emergence of class relations.[135]

While these arguments reflect the limitations of the deferential community, they need to be set in context, because the aristocracy showed a remarkable capacity to respond to, and even to forestall, criticism. A clear example of this can be seen in their attitude towards sporting activities. In many respects sport was a social catalyst. From the farmer to the duke, all were equal as they jumped the fence, even if strict limits existed as to who wore the red coat, and who subscribed to the pack and had a hand in its management.[136] But this could only be the case because the aristocracy had absorbed others into their sporting activities, in such a way that their authority was not questioned. The success of foxhunting depended on the ability of the Master of Foxhounds to handle damage claims sensitively if the goodwill of the countryside was to be maintained. Keeping such goodwill was also achieved by allowing tenant farmers and owner-occupiers to participate, but in any case it is arguable that the ideals of deference upon which the openness of the hunting field depended were accepted on all sides in advance. Consequently the sport represented a major

---

Right of Property in Land, with respect to its foundation in the Law of Nature (1781). During a parliamentary debate in 1796 on the possibility of introducing death duties, Lord George Cavendish opposed the measure on the grounds that 'it would tend to equalise all property, and would operate as a confiscation of all the great landed estates in the country, for the use of the government.' Legacy duty was introduced but only on personal estate. S. Lambert (ed.), *Sessional Papers of the Eighteenth Century*, vol. 97: 1795–6, pp. 411; *Parliamentary Debates*, vol. 32, pp. 1032, 1034–5, 1038, 1041; 36 Geo. III, c. 52.

[135] E. P. Thompson, 'Patrician society, plebian culture', *Journal of Social History*, 7 (1974), pp. 382–405; 'Eighteenth-century English society: class struggle without class?', *Social History*, 3 (1978), pp. 133–65.

[136] Itzkowitz, *Peculiar Privilege*, p. 35.

prop to the existing social order. Having absorbed into foxhunting other members of the rural community, the aristocracy displayed a remarkable ability to adapt to the needs of the wider financial world. By accommodating those with the money and inclination to hunt, they ensured its successful continuation. As Lord Willoughby de Broke perceptively noted, 'if it ever presents the appearance of exclusiveness, the whole fabric will dissolve.'[137] Even with shooting game, the aristocracy drew some of the sting of countryside tension by offering facilities to farmers and unqualified freeholders. When the game laws themselves appeared to be running into terminal disrepute, they changed them before disorder got out of hand, and while poaching did not end in 1831 the worse excesses were abated. Even under the laws, it is apparent that a bad landlord was poached against more often than a good one, and that such actions had approbation in the countryside. On the cricket field the aristocratic MCC absorbed middle-class energy and talent in such a way as to forestall criticism. So successful was the divide-and-rule policy that the would-be reformers were often induced to join the club.[138]

This ability to absorb potential opposition was matched by an ability to bring about change in advance of unfavourable public opinion. Eighteenth-century sporting activities were almost invariably associated with gambling, but this was not always an acceptable image. Thus the aristocracy dropped their patronage of boxing in the early nineteenth century because of its shady image, and as part of a mounting attack on brutal sports in general. Qualified respectability was only restored with the introduction of the Queensbery Rules in 1867, and the participation of the Earl of Lonsdale. The positive approach of the MCC helped to outlaw gambling before it became a serious threat to cricket, while the Jockey Club showed a willingness to put its own house in order to protect the image of horseracing.[139]

It was this adaptability which helped to keep aristocratic values to the fore down to 1914. However, amidst the apparent stability of events such as the London Season, the seeds of decay were already apparent. Rural deference was in retreat, as labourers formed trade unions, and tenant farmers set up the non-landlord National Farmers' Union. The church was no longer able to spread the gospel of passive obedience to the prevailing social order, while the game remained a

[137] Carr, *A History of Foxhunting*, p. 242.
[138] Brookes, *English Cricket*, p. 127.
[139] Longrigg, *The English Squire and his Sport*, pp. 174–5, 282–3; R. Roberts, 'Eighteenth-century boxing', *Journal of Sport History*, 4 (1977), pp. 246–59; Vramplew, *The Turf*, pp. 86–7.

divisive issue, and financial help was needed to keep up the pack. As yet little reason existed to challenge aristocratic leadership, and the middle-class willingness to accept it helped to ensure its stability. What is perhaps most remarkable is that so little had changed over the previous two and a half centuries, and to try to explain this it is necessary to turn from the informal methods of aristocratic social control to the institutional role that the landlords played in government.

Chapter Eleven

The Aristocracy at Home: Local Government

To picture English society as a collection of small communities, each dependent upon a substantial landlord who effectively controlled their political rights, is to overdraw the situation which existed in practice. Certainly the aristocracy regarded itself – and was regarded at Westminster – as a service elite which freely offered its time in administering the countryside. Government was, after all, part of its traditional duty, and in general terms it carried out the tasks assigned from London with remarkable willingness and ability. Beatrice Webb, after spending many years of her life studying the pre-reform local government system, was impressed by the distinctiveness of the period 1688–1832, during which national government abstained from intervening locally, and Parliament merely ratified local statues when it became necessary to give legislative support to local innovations.[1] Successful aristocratic control was even more remarkable, given the absence of anything approaching the territorial feudalism which existed in Scotland. Whereas several magnates owned 40 per cent or more of individual counties north of the border, the greatest empires which could be mustered in England were those of the dukes of Devonshire in Derbyshire, of Northumberland in Northumberland, and of Bedford in Bedfordshire, and none of these extended beyond 14 per cent of the landed acreage. Only as the power shifted from the country to the towns during the nineteenth century did the old elite no longer seem adequate, but even at the turn of the century many of the traditional personnel remained in positions of local responsibility, even though the form of government had changed.

POSITIONS OF RESPONSIBILITY IN LOCAL GOVERNMENT

Local control was exercised both via the informal channels discussed in

[1] Beatrice Webb, *Our Partnership* (1975 edn), p. 151.

chapter ten, and via the formal structure of county, borough and parish authorities. Remarkably, a system which emerged to deal with the relatively small population of early modern England successfully survived well into the nineteenth century. Municipal reform in 1835 swept away many of the old corporations, and eventually reduced the urban influence of the aristocracy. In the countryside, however, reform was postponed until 1888, and even then it can hardly be described as having overturned the existing system. Apart from the 200 or so towns which were permitted separate corporate status down to 1835, local responsibility was carefully divided. The county took responsibility for law and order, bridge upkeep, gaols, and the raising of revenue; while the parish looked after the church and highways and provided for the poor. Courts baron and leet also exercised authority within the manor.

At the head of each county stood the lord-lieutenant. The position itself was associated with the militia, but by the eighteenth century it was normally held in tandem with the civilian role of *custos rotulorum*. The lieutenancy was no sinecure, since, the holder had one foot in London close to central government, and the other firmly planted in the county. He was responsible for nominating deputy lieutenants, and during the eighteenth century lords-lieutenant also gained a monopoly of appointments to the bench – a role they did not finally relinquish until 1910. The lord-lieutenant also wielded immense electoral power, and it is hardly surprising that central government expected the post to be held by a substantial member of county society, which invariably meant a peer. Twenty-two of the forty-two English lieutenancies were held by a peer throughout the period 1660–1914, and another seven had their first non-peer between 1900 and 1914. Of the other thirteen, six had a single commoner, and four had either two or three. The exceptions were Cumberland, Westmorland and Monmouth. Cumberland had four non-peers, although two were raised to titles, and Westmorland eight.[2] The problem in these counties was a lack of resident peers since governments were generally unwilling to appoint commoners. In the early 1750s Sir James Lowther of Whitehaven, one of the wealthiest landed proprietors in Cumberland, was far from pleased to be passed over for the lieutenancy in favour of the non-resident – but titled – Earl of Egremont.[3] Monmouth had six

[2] J. C. Sainty, *Lists of the Lieutenants of the Counties of England and Wales, 1660–1974* (1979). Sons of peers are also counted here as peers, while the majority of non-peers were well connected.

[3] Lord Lonsdale, the lord-lieutenant for Cumberland and Westmorland, died early in March 1751. On 11 March, Lowther wrote to the Duke of Newcastle soliciting the position in succession: BL Add. MSS, 32,724, fol. 182. The following day he told his

non-peers, but its experience was not dissimilar to the general problem in Wales of a shortfall in peers.[4] A handful of individuals held more than one lieutenancy. In the eighteenth century the Duke of Newcastle held Nottinghamshire, Middlesex and Sussex, but duplication was usually permitted only when adjoining counties were involved.[5]

Lieutenants were occasionally dismissed if their performance was deemed unsatisfactory. The Duke of Bolton lost Hampshire, Dorset and Carmarthen in 1733 when he quarrelled with the government, while two successive lieutenants were dismissed in the West Riding, the Duke of Norfolk in 1798 and Earl Fitzwilliam in 1819. In 1839 the Duke of Newcastle was dismissed in Nottinghamshire after an argument with the government. Newcastle objected to the appointment of a Mr Paget as JP, on the grounds of his political opinions and his religious dissent. The Lord Chancellor replied that Newcastle was wrong on both counts, but when the duke responded in 'a violent manner' Lord John Russell removed him from office. Newcastle appealed to the Duke of Wellington, who informed him that the government could never submit to such pressure.[6]

The next position in point of status within the county was that of sheriff, but this once-powerful post had declined by the eighteenth century into a formal job which the local gentry disliked because it was time consuming and expensive. At the end of his year in office for

---

steward: 'it looks as if they would have me be lieutenant and custos rotulorum, but as it is not certain it must not be whispered': Carlisle RO, D/Lons/W, Lowther to John Spedding, 12 March 1751. Within a few days it was known locally that he was anxious to hold the post: ibid., D/Lons/L, checklist 16/45, E. Wilson to W. Tatham, 16 March 1751. On 11 April, however, he wrote to Whitehaven to announce that Cumberland had gone to the Earl of Egremont, while Westmorland – which could hardly even boast a non-resident peer of any substance – had been offered to him. He turned it down because 'I have but £200 a year there': Lowther to Spedding, 11 April 1751.

[4] South Wales had a single lieutenancy until 1714, and North Wales until 1760, in both cases filled by peers. Thereafter, with the exception of Haverfordwest and Merioneth, all the counties had one or more non-peers holding the lieutenancy: Sainty, *Lists of the Lieutenants*.

[5] Ray A. Kelch, *Newcastle: a duke without money* (1974), p. 37; A. D. Harvey, *Britain in the Early Nineteenth Century* (1978), p. 27.

[6] Esther Moir, *The Justice of the Peace* (Harmondsworth, 1969), pp. 78–9; B. Keith-Lucas, *The Unreformed Local Government System* (1980), p. 45; C. F. C. Greville, *The Greville Memoirs*, ed. H. Reeve (1888), vol. IV, p. 201. A few aristocratic families exercised enormous local influence. Perhaps the most notable were the Stanleys, earls of Derby and 'kings of Lancashire'. Between 1660 and 1914 the 8th, 9th, 10th, 11th, 12th, 13th, 16th and 17th earls held the lord-lieutenancy of the county for a total between them of over 160 years. Unfortunately their local activities receive only passing mention from the family's most recent biographer: J. J. Bagley, *The Earls of Derby, 1485–1985* (1985).

Buckinghamshire in 1748 Henry Purefoy referred to his shrievalty as a 'plague'.[7] William Pym spent £145 during his year as sheriff of Bedfordshire in 1764, while the Buckinghamshire gentry who feared appointment subscribed five guineas annually to a fund which could be spent by the incumbent. Henry Purefoy's main concern, when he was appointed to the office, was that he would not be entitled to call upon the fund because his contributions were in arrears.[8] Not surprisingly considerable energy was expended in avoiding the post. MPs played a particularly important role ensuring that their fellow countrymen were excused. Sir James Lowther told his Whitehaven steward in 1747:

you may tell Mr How all the three on the sheriffs list for Cumberland got excused so I was afraid he would be named but I took effectual care to keep him off. I know not who recommended Mr Whitefield. I got off Mr Crackenthorpe in the first list.[9]

The mantle fell on Henry Purefoy in 1748 despite 'the kind endeavours' of local MP Richard Grenville 'to rescue me from this troublesome job', and some families were remarkably successful at avoiding the post. In Shropshire, the three branches of the Corbet family, who were of the greatest importance in county society, contributed only one sheriff between 1689 and 1760.[10]

The most important position in local government was that of justice of the peace, since it was through the medium of Quarter Sessions – in effect the county parliament – that the majority of business was conducted. Originally, as the title indicates, justices were primarily responsible for keeping the peace, and determining offences, but from the sixteenth century onwards a host of new duties were added to the list.[11] Justices came to play a part in regulating prices and wages, fixing apprenticeships, licensing alehouses, overseeing bridge and

[7] L. G. Mitchell, *The Purefoy Letters, 1735–53* (New York, 1973), p. 52.

[8] Ibid., p. 48.

[9] Carlisle RO, D/Lons/W, Sir James Lowther to John Spedding, 20 January 1747.

[10] Information on the Corbets courtesy of Dr M. D. G. Wanklyn. G. E. Mingay, *English Landed Society in the Eighteenth Century* (1963), p. 118; Mitchell, *The Purefoy Letters*, pp. 42, 53–6. The one other county position requiring a man of substance was that of high constable, but even by the seventeenth century in Cheshire this was a position held by substantial freeholders rather than gentlemen of quality: M. D. G. Wanklyn, 'Landownership, political authority and social status in Shropshire and Cheshire, 1500–1700', *West Midlands Studies*, 11 (1978), p. 24.

[11] For a closely documented example of a seventeenth-century JP at work, see Alan Macfarlane, *The Justice and the Mare's Ale: law and disorder in seventeenth-century England* (Oxford, 1981).

highway repairs, administering the Poor Laws and, in order to pay for all this, collecting taxation. These duties were carried out at a number of different venues. The most important meetings of the justices were at general or Quarter Sessions, which dealt with both administrative and legal matters. Administratively, Sessions raised a rate for bridge and road upkeep, for gaols and for the prosecution of offenders. Wearing their alternative hats, the justices also tried offenders. As the justices' work increased through time, much of it was transferred to other occasions. Petty sessions were held either monthly or fortnightly in most counties, while meetings to deal with particular issues were introduced, such as the 'brewster' sessions, for licensing alehouses, in 1753. By the early nineteenth century the justices had also acquired additional time-consuming duties in regard to prisons and lunatic asylums. Much of the JPs' work was done alone or in combination with one other justice. A magistrate performed a considerable number of functions in his own home, tackling questions of poverty, settlement, the position of children, the relationship of masters and servants, criminal offences and parish accounts. Two magistrates acting together could confirm the election by the vestry of the overseers of the poor, allow (or refuse) the overseers' accounts, and undertake a number of other minor duties.

Since JPs effectively ruled the nation, it is hardly surprising that they should have been expected to be men of substance. Dissenters and Roman Catholics were excluded by law down to the nineteenth century, and until the 1690s appointees had to meet the property qualification of £20, set in 1439. Few questions were asked, either of justices or of officers of the Restoration militia, since it was merely assumed that men in these positions would be property owners of some standing.[12] From the 1690s, however, these positions became more rigidly controlled. 'Running like a red thread through all the local institutions of the eighteenth century', according to Sidney and Beatrice Webb, 'was the assumption that the ownership of property carried with it not only a necessary qualification for, but even a positive right to carry on, the work of government.'[13] This situation arose as a reaction to the excesses of Charles II and James II, but it had the effect of preserving local government in the hands of the landed gentry until well into the nineteenth century; indeed, it permitted local landowners to retain the reins of power to the exclusion of newcomers from business and commerce. In the aftermath of 1688, fear of arbitrary

---

[12] J. R. Western, *The English Militia in the Eighteenth Century* (1965), p. 60.
[13] Sidney and Beatrice Webb, *English Local Government: statutory authorities for special purposes* (1922), p. 386.

government produced a spate of bills designed to combat what was regarded as the corruption of the age, and a number of them were to increase existing property qualifications or to introduce new ones.

Among these bills were several designed to increase the qualification of a JP. The first of these was introduced into the Commons in December 1699, read twice and then lost. According to James Lowther, the proposal was to make the qualification 'two hundred pounds a Year at least, which they think is not more considerable now than £20 per annum was when the former act was made'. His impression after the second reading was that the bill would pass because of cases in the West Country where gentlemen of estates had been turned out 'and ordinary persons put in as has been publicly complained of in the House'.[14] A second bill was introduced in 1701, this time with the more extreme Tories trying to push up the qualification to £500, in order to protect their own positions. However, this, together with further bills in 1702 and 1703, failed, and despite further negotiations in 1708 and another bill in 1711 change came about only in 1732 when the qualification was raised to £100 in line with that for land tax commissioners.[15] Originally the proposal was for a £200 qualification, except in Lancashire, Cumberland and Westmorland, Rutland, the Welsh counties and the Isle of Wight, where it was to be £100, and no attorney or solicitor was to be permitted to act while he remained in business.[16] When the legislation emerged, the terms looked slightly different:

no person shall be capable of being a Justice of the Peace, or to act as a justice of the peace for any county within that part of Great Britain called England, or the principality of Wales who shall not have an estate of freehold or copyhold to and for his own use and benefit in possession for life, or for some greater estate either in law or equity, or an estate for years . . . of the clear yearly value of one hundred pounds, over and above what will satisfy and discharge all incumbrances that may affect the same.[17]

The Act was amended in 1745 to introduce a clause whereby potential justices had to testify to their £100. Even so the figure was more symbolic than practical, since it was only in the poorest counties that

[14] Carlisle RO, D/Lons/W, James Lowther to Sir John Lowther, 9 January 1700: *CJ*, 13, pp. 74, 95, 101, 140, 164, 247.

[15] L. K. J. Glassey, *Politics and the Appointment of Justices of the Peace, 1675–1720* (Oxford, 1979), pp. 145, 164; Norma Landau, *The Justices of the Peace, 1679–1760* (1984), pp. 148–54.

[16] A copy of the bill can be found in the BL under reference 357, B 12(35).

[17] 5 Geo. II, c. 18 (1732).

men of such mean estates were appointed to the bench. It was a political victory for the nascent Tories, although it seems likely that few men were appointed to the bench who could not meet the qualification. It was amended in 1875, but repealed only in 1906.[18]

Justices were almost automatically appointed to the commissions of land and window taxes, and from 1803 they were permitted to act in these roles whether or not they were named in the legislation.[19] For the land tax a £50 property qualification was introduced in 1699, and doubled two years later, although the £100 was to represent the property at which a man was taxed under the previous Act. An attempt to exclude Middlesex from the terms of the legislation was rejected.[20] Laying down the rules was one thing, enforcing them was quite another. Edward Backhouse was in the 1708 Westmorland list despite 'want of . . . ability in estate being scarse fifty pounds per annum in land'. James Lowther expected others to be removed from the list with Backhouse if proper investigation was made into their financial position.[21] From the early years of the eighteenth century, commissioners were acting who lacked the necessary qualification, and the Land Tax Acts of both 1749 and 1765 included clauses indemnifying those who fell into this category.[22] The quality of commissioners ought to have improved through time, since both the qualification and the assessments stayed the same. Lord Chancellor Hardwicke pointed out in 1756 that 'lands assessed to the land tax at the rate of £100 per annum, are of much better value than lands barely of the rent of £100.' In practice, men acted without being qualified, and in Hardwicke's view 'many, even of the acting ones, are some of the lowest people of any kind of property in this kingdom.'[23] Even lawyers were to be found in commissions, despite a clause in the Act of 1749 that no attorney was to act unless he possessed property to the value of £100 per annum.[24]

---

[18] Landau, *The Justices of the Peace*, pp. 154–69; W. L. Burn, *The Age of Equipoise* (1964), p. 333.

[19] Landau, *The Justices of the Peace*, pp. 27–8.

[20] Carlisle RO, D/Lons/W, James Lowther to Sir John Lowther, 14 March 1699, 7 June 1701; *CJ*, 13, p. 602.

[21] Carlisle RO, D/Lons/W, James Lowther to William Gilpin, 24 January, 12 February 1708; Levens Hall, Cumbria, Correspondence Box D, William Nevinson to James Grahme, 28 February 1708.

[22] M. M. Verney, *Verney Letters of the Eighteenth Century* (1930), vol. II, p. 86; W. R. Ward, *The English Land Tax in the Eighteenth Century* (Oxford, 1953), p. 88; 22 Geo. II, c. 2 (1749); 5 Geo. IIII c. 21 (1765); *CJ*, 30, p. 116.

[23] *Parliamentary History of England*, vol. XV, 1753–61 (1813), pp. 730–1.

[24] R. Robson, *The Attorney in Eighteenth-Century England* (Cambridge, 1959), p. 110n.

These drawbacks did not prevent the introduction of property qualifications for a number of other positions. The lord-lieutenant was usually responsible for appointing deputy lieutenants and other officers of the militia, and the appointees were expected to be men of substance. To this end it was proposed in 1698 that deputies and most officers should have a property qualification, but the bill failed. When a Militia Reform Bill was introduced in 1756, a scale of property qualifications for officers was included, but this was lost, and when another bill was introduced the following year, although the principle of qualifications was retained, the sums involved were greatly reduced. The qualifications were further relaxed in 1769, but some lords-lieutenant still found it impossible to keep their establishment complete, and as a result the system was partially abandoned in 1802.[25] Overseers of the poor were expected to be drawn from among the more substantial householders of the community, while for the purposes of road maintenance the General Highways Act of 1773 limited parish surveyors to owners of land worth at least £10 a year or occupiers of land worth £30 annually.[26] Even jury service was subject to a property qualification. From 1693 jurors were to have in their own name, or in trust for them, £10 of freehold or copyhold land. The figure was £6 in Wales.[27]

Similar qualifications were also introduced during the eighteenth century for a variety of local boards of trustees, commissioners of paving and lighting, turnpike roads and Poor Law administration, but on no settled basis. Usually trustees were expected to have estates yielding £100 a year or to be heir to £300 a year, but the sums could vary. For the Hesket–Cockermouth–Keswick turnpike in 1762 the qualification was that 'no person shall be deemed qualified or capable of acting as a trustee in the execution of this Act unless he shall have . . . clear yearly value of £60 or above reprizes or is possessed of or intitled to a real and personal estate together to the amount or value of £1,500.' By contrast, the Westminster Act of 1761 settled the value of land at £300, while in other examples refinements were added such as the condition that innkeepers were to have a qualification twice as high as other people.[28] Legislation in 1773 extended the turnpike qua-

---

[25] Western, *The English Militia*, pp. 100, 130–5, 304, 309, 320.

[26] Keith-Lucas, *The Unreformed Local Government System*, pp. 87–8, 114.

[27] 16 & 17 Charles II, c. 3 (1664); 4 & 5 William and Mary, c. 24, s. 15 (1692); 3 Geo. II, c. 25, ss. 19–20 (1730); 4 Geo. II, c. 7, s. 3 (1731); J. H. Langbein, '*Albion's* fatal flaws', *Past and Present*, 98 (1983), p. 107n.

[28] B. Keith-Lucas, *The English Local Government Franchise: a short history* (Oxford, 1952), p. 153; 2 Geo. III, c. 61 (1762); 55 Geo. III, c. 22 (1815).

lification to all trusts, with trustees to have estates of £40 a year or to be heir to £80 a year or to have £800 personal property. In 1822 the estate values were raised to £100 and £200 respectively and the personal qualification was no longer considered. The change was ascribed by James McAdam in 1833 to 'the circumstance of the landed interest not being sufficiently attended to at turnpike meetings and that other parties, in town particularly, possessing considerable personal wealth, frequently attend these meetings, not having that personal interest in the road which landed proprietors must naturally have.'[29]

In the nineteenth century, property qualifications continued to act as a symbol of government efforts to keep the government of town and country alike in the hands of those classes thought most competent and best entitled to exercise power. Consequently qualifications were retained in the post-1835 boroughs. Aldermen and councillors in the reformed structure were to have £1000 real or personal property, in the larger boroughs, and £500 in the smaller ones, or, alternatively, the occupation of property rated at £30 and £15 respectively. When the qualification for MPs was abolished in 1858, attempts were made to persuade Parliament to open up borough councils in the same way, but although the law was not always strictly enforced it was not easily changed. A. J. Mundella and Joseph Chamberlain sponsored a bill in 1877 to make the ownership of property unnecessary for borough council membership, but in the absence of government support it was withdrawn. Two years later a new bill was brought in, this time covering borough councils, boards of guardians, local boards of health and all other local authorities. This was defeated on second reading, and a change was only effected by the 1882 Municipal Corporations Act, which permitted anyone on the burgess roll to be elected councillor or alderman if he lived within seven miles of the borough. Those outside this limit required a property qualification down to 1918.[30]

Property was not, however, the only important factor which helped to determine who filled positions in local government. Equally significant were political considerations. The political character of the lord-lieutenancy was indisputable. By 1886, after half a century of Whig–Liberal political domination, twenty-six lieutenancies were filled by Liberals, and sixteen by Conservatives.[31] Similar pressures were

[29] W. Albert, *The Turnpike Road System in England, 1663–1840* (Cambridge, 1972), p. 58.
[30] Keith-Lucas, *The English Local Government Franchise*, pp. 158–60.
[31] Burn, *The Age of Equipoise*, p. 333.

brought to bear on the magistracy. Central government's only real hold over Quarter Sessions was by dismissal, and the years from 1680 to 1720 saw considerable interference with the personnel of county benches. Charles II initiated the process between 1680 and 1683 by dismissing many men who were known to favour the exclusion of the Duke of York from the throne. In turn, the duke, when he became James II in 1685, purged the benches in pursuit of his own politico-religious ends. In the five months from October 1686, half the justices in the country were removed from the bench, but James could not then find enough supporters, and he was forced to appoint dissenters and Roman Catholics, some of whom lacked property or standing.[32] With William III's accession, familiar names returned to the commissions, but central government was not deterred from intervention. The party strife of William III and Anne's reigns was reflected in efforts to purge the bench when the swing of the party pendulum carried the opposition into power. In 1711 the Tories dismissed 183 justices and added 919 of their own nominees. The situation was reversed after the Hanoverian succession. In 1715 twenty-two new names were added to the Cumberland commission, and nineteen – of whom six were of dead men – removed. In these changes, however, the lessons of James II were learnt. It was one thing for the Lord Chancellor to allow the government in power to enjoy a preponderance of local authority which could be achieved through a relatively discreet remodelling, but quite another to permit a wholesale monopoly. Many counties simply lacked the personnel for such a rapid turnover, while purging always upset the local gentry, and threatened their willingness to co-operate. Fortunately the long Whig ascendancy after 1720 brought respite to the counties from central interference.[33]

Political decisions handed down from central government were matched by local considerations about the balance within a county. James Lowther informed his father in 1700 that

Sir George Fletcher tells me he is desired by Mr Latus to put him and his son in for commissioners of the land tax, which may be prejudicial to your part of the country they being like to side with the commissioners who are for laying

---

[32] Moir, *The Justice of the Peace*, pp. 81–2.

[33] An extended version of the events of these years is given in Glassey, *Politics and the Appointment of Justices of the Peace*. Purges took place at different times in different counties. Thus, in Glamorgan, the most significant changes took place between 1710 and 1717: Philip Jenkins, *The Making of a Ruling Class: the Glamorgan gentry, 1640–1790* (Cambridge, 1983), p. 85.

a greater proportion upon Whitehaven. He thinks to put in one of them only, and would put in one or more for Whitehaven.[34]

Lords-lieutenant often took advice from local gentry with regard to the constitution of the commission of the peace, thereby providing another opportunity for the airing of local prejudice. Sir James Lowther complained in 1737 that, had he not been in London when the Cumberland list was drawn up, 'five of our friends would have been kept out.' Later he and Lord Lonsdale drew up the lists, with the expressed intention 'to strengthen the Lowther interest', and after Lonsdale's death Lowther made direct representations to the Lord Chancellor in regard to his own nominees.[35] Similar struggles took place elsewhere. In Gloucestershire Lord Ducie sent a list of the men he thought proper for the bench to the lord-lieutenant in 1754, and was informed that some of those he wished to exclude must be put in but the majority would be on the right side.[36] In the nineteenth century the determination of the Lancashire cotton manufacturers to achieve a political balance on the bench ensured that in the post-1830 period party affiliation was the important factor in appointment. The secession of landed magnates from the Liberal Party in the 1880s meant that by 1892 only 15 per cent of county benches were Liberal, and over the next three years the Lord Chancellor attempted to redress the balance by appointing men who had not been recommended by lords-lieutenant.[37] In the boroughs, political considerations became all-important in the course of the nineteenth century, and even urban patricians such as the Calthorpes in Birmingham and the Butes in Cardiff, who liked to regard themselves as grand figures above the sordid world of party politics, were invariably party men who tempered and moderated their benevolence out of political considerations.[38]

[34] Carlisle RO, D/Lons,/W, James Lowther to Sir John Lowther, 18 March 1699. The problem was to find men who could meet the property qualification, even at £50 per annum.

[35] Ibid., Sir James Lowther to John Spedding, 16 July 1737, 24 July 1750, 24 December 1751.

[36] Moir, *The Justice of the Peace*, p. 80.

[37] David Foster, 'Class and county government in early nineteenth-century Lancashire', *Northern History*, 9 (1974), p. 61; Burn, *The Age of Equipoise*, p. 333; J. M. Lee, 'Parliament and the appointment of magistrates', *Parliamentary Affairs*, 13 (1959–60), pp. 88, 92.

[38] David Cannadine, 'From "feudal" lords to figureheads: urban landownership and aristocratic influence in nineteenth-century towns', *Urban History Yearbook* (1978), p. 32; *Patricians, Power and Politics in Nineteenth-Century Towns* (Leicester, 1982), p. 8.

THE PRACTICE OF LOCAL GOVERNMENT

Local government was essentially paternalistic, from the dispensing of justice to the payment of poor relief. In part this was possible because it remained the preserve of unpaid gentlemen, and England did not develop a professional bureaucracy, while the fact of its survival suggests that it was relatively successful. Naturally there were complaints. A correspondent of the *Gentleman's Magazine* in 1736 argued that the country was being corrupted and debauched by alcohol, and that the reason was a failure of the justices in their licensing role to keep the number of outlets under control.[39] More to the point, however, is the evidence of a gradual decline in landed concern with controlling local government during the eighteenth century, which was finally arrested in the nineteenth but could not in the longer term prevent reform. This trend can be seen most clearly in terms of the personnel involved in government, and also in uncertainty about paternalism.

The property and political considerations determining membership of the commission of the peace were of little significance if men could not be persuaded to act. The number of justices was clearly on the increase from 1680: in England and Wales a total of 2560 in 1680 had increased to 8400 by 1761.[40] In part, this was the result of political pressures on the Lord Chancellor, but it also reflected a growing amount of work which was involved with the job. Moreover, such a trend ensured that James II's policy of packing the bench with supporters eased the path of men who might not in the past have been considered sufficiently substantial. Unfortunately the increase of numbers was not matched by a willingness to undertake the tasks which went with the job. Simply having one's name on the list became sufficient, and all too many justices preferred the pleasures of the field, London and Bath to the mundane role of country lawkeeper. As a result, the public duties of the job were neglected. Between 1712 and 1763, only 45–55 per cent of Glamorgan's justices swore out a *dedimus*; in late eighteenth-century Kent only one-quarter of those qualified were said to have become justices; and a similar trend was to be found in Northamptonshire, Hertfordshire and even Northumberland. As late as 1835 in Sussex, 99 out of 234 justices had not taken the oaths to

[39] *Gentleman's Magazine*, 6 (1736), pp. 537–8.
[40] Landau, *The Justice of the Peace*, pp. 368–72. In Glamorgan, numbers remained at around 30 until about 1720, but they then began to creep upwards, reaching 115 in 1762, and 231 by 1836: Jenkins: *The Making of a Ruling Class*, p. 84.

qualify.[41] In these circumstances it became necessary to find men who would act, and in mid-eighteenth-century England it was the clergy who became the effective local government administrators.

Clerical magistrates were not new in 1700, but they came to occupy a position of considerable strength on the bench. Clerics were appointed in Somerset in the 1620s, while in Hertfordshire they represented 2 per cent of the total over the period 1635–99.[42] From 1740 their numerical strength increased almost everywhere. The proportion rose to 25 per cent in Hertfordshire in the 1750s, and to 33 per cent by 1800; while in Oxfordshire it was 31 per cent in 1775, 28.3 per cent in 1797 and nearly 37 per cent by 1816. Ten of the fifty-eight Wiltshire justices were clerics in 1786, while around 20 per cent of Glamorgan's magistrates were clerics in the closing decades of the century.[43] The attitude of Lord Brownlow, lord-lieutenant of Lincolnshire in the 1820s, sums up their popularity; in his view a clergyman stood well above a businessman as a potential recruit because he was likely to live in a place where gentry were thin on the ground, to understand public business and to be politically loyal.[44] Above all, it was because they were active that clerics were appointed, and this applied both to the bench, and also to the increasing role that they played as turnpike commissioners.[45] On the other hand, the impact on their role as parsons was almost certainly detrimental, especially by the 1820s and 1830s, when the church appeared to symbolize the unreformed administration. No one forgot that it was a clerical magistrate who read the Riot Act at Peterloo, and that it was the episcopal votes in the Lords which were crucial in defeating the second Reform Bill in 1831. The rise of rural anti-clericalism was

---

[41] Jenkins, *The Making of a Ruling Class*, p. 88; Landau, *The Justice of the Peace*, pp. 393–4; Lawrence Stone and Jeanne C. F. Stone, *An Open Elite? England, 1540–1880* (Oxford, 1984), pp. 274–5.

[42] G. E. Mingay, *The Gentry* (1976), p. 127.

[43] Stone and Stone, *An Open Elite?*, pp. 270–1; D. McClatchey, *Oxfordshire Clergy, 1777–1869* (Oxford, 1960), pp. 179–80; VCH, *Wiltshire*, vol. V (1957), p. 177; Jenkins, *The Making of a Ruling Class*, p. 90.

[44] R. J. Olney, *Rural Society and County Government in Nineteenth-Century Lincolnshire* (Lincoln, 1979), pp. 99–100. William Cobbett was of the view that clerical magistrates appeared as a result of the decline of the lesser gentry: 'parsons are now made justices of the peace! There are few other persons left, who are at all capable of filling the office in a way to suit the system': *Rural Rides* (1830; Harmondsworth, 1967), p. 348.

[45] Keith-Lucas, *The Unreformed Local Government System*, pp. 123–4.

almost certainly linked with the identification between parson and state which arose from the admission of clerics to the bench.[46]

For the most part, justices acted impartially and took their responsibilities seriously. Although there were doubtless some who abused the powers that they were given to administer summary justice for offences concerning their own property, generally they acted honourably. What is known of their activities during the eighteenth century suggests a rather different picture from the lurid portrayals of Fielding and Smollett.[47] William Hunt, appointed to the Wiltshire bench in 1743, kept a notebook of his activities as a justice. Although he regularly attended Quarter Sessions, the bulk of his work took place at special or petty sessions – when he was often concerned with settlement cases – or on his own. From his surviving notes, Hunt appears as a conscientious and reasonable justice, anxious wherever possible to maintain the smooth running of the community.[48] Samuel Whitbread, who was active on the Bedfordshire bench between 1810 and 1814, also kept detailed notes of his tasks. Like Hunt he appears as a man of integrity, for whom personal involvement in a case, or mere convenience, was never allowed to affect the service he offered. When problems arose in respect of his own property, Whitbread usually instructed his agent to investigate, although he was not averse to making a personal examination.[49]

Criminal offences were not solely the responsibility of the justices. In a formal sense the 'county' met two or three times a year so that the gentlemen assembled in the grand jury could decide which cases ought to go to a higher court than Quarter Sessions. Usually crimes carrying the death penalty were left to the assizes, after the grand jury had heard the preliminary evidence against an offender to decide whether he should be tried by the state. Normally the foreman of the grand jury was a leading member of county society, and the other jurymen (up to twenty-three in total) were drawn from the landed gentry. The law itself, particularly as exercised in the assizes, has been seen as an instrument serving the needs and interests of the ruling class, hence

[46] E. J. Evans, 'Some reasons for the growth of English rural anti-clericalism, *c.* 1750–*c.* 1830', *Past and Present*, 66 (1975), pp. 84–109.

[47] G. Welby, 'Rulers of the countryside: the justice of the peace in Nottinghamshire, 1775–1800', *Transactions of the Thoroton Society*, 78 (1974), pp. 75–87.

[48] E. Crittall (ed.), *The Justicing Notebook of William Hunt, 1744–1749* (Wiltshire Record Society, 37, 1982).

[49] A. F. Cirket, *Samuel Whitbread's Notebooks 1810–11, 1813–14* (Bedfordshire Record Society, 50, 1971), p. 26.

the increasingly severe penalties for property crimes during the eighteenth century. At the same time, more than 40 per cent of those sentenced to hang were reprieved, and part of the explanation for this lies in the significance of the criminal law in maintaining the bonds of obedience and deference within the state. The law could be viewed as an ideological weapon of the rich, although it is possibly going too far to see it as a conspiracy against the poor. However, the severity of the criminal code gradually relaxed during the nineteenth century as a result of changes in prosecutions, and the spread of effective policing.[50]

THE BREAKDOWN OF ARISTOCRATIC LOCAL GOVERNMENT: THE COUNTRYSIDE

Paternalism had its limits, and through time it was gradually undermined. The introduction of excise taxation in the later seventeenth century meant that the poor were no longer protected from contributing to state finance; while with the Corn Bounty Acts of 1672 and 1688 the interests of the producers were given priority over previous concern with fair prices, and the state abandoned its responsibility for upholding a moral economy of fair prices.[51] Later, the impact of enclosure, higher rents and low wages, all tended to weaken the ties of deference. Sporadic outbreaks of food rioting were further evidence of this change. Such affrays were usually dealt with firmly but fairly by local magistrates, but increasing unrest in the early years of the nineteenth century, due to a combination of high bread prices, scarcities in the Napoleonic war years, and the post-1815 agricultural depression, were not always carefully handled. Some magistrates called out the military at the slightest provocation.[52]

The focal point of discontent was the magistracy, and particularly the clerical JPs. As common land was enclosed, and as landlords took measures to protect the game on their estates, the overall result was a

---

[50] E. P. Thompson, *Whigs and Hunters: the origin of the Black Act* (1975); D. Hay, 'Property, authority and the criminal law', in *Albion's Fatal Tree: crime and society in eighteenth-century England*, ed. D. Hay *et al.* (1975), pp. 17–63; Langbein, '*Albion's* fatal flaws', pp. 96–120.

[51] J. V. Beckett, 'Land tax or excise: the levying of taxation in seventeenth- and eighteenth-century England', *English Historical Review*, 100 (1985), pp. 285–308; David Ormrod, *English Grain Exports and the Structure of Agrarian Capitalism, 1700–1760* (Hull, 1985), pp. 15–17.

[52] E. P. Thompson, 'The moral economy of the English crowd in the eighteenth century', *Past and Present*, 50 (1971), pp. 76–136.

firmer attitude towards prosecutions for offences against the game. In Wiltshire the number of commitals to prison for game offences tripled during each decade of the period 1760–90; by 1790 it was six times the average of the 1760s.[53] This increase was matched by further repressive legislation, including the Night Poaching Act of 1770, and legislation in 1800 which permitted a single justice acting alone to sentence poachers to imprisonment with hard labour. As a result, rural conflict over the game laws reached its height during the early years of the nineteenth century, and this naturally reflected on the JPs. The issue was only defused when spring-guns were outlawed in 1827, poaching penalties were reduced in 1828, and game sales were legalized in 1831.[54] By then the damage had been done, especially since changes in the countryside resulting from the French wars induced the authorities to look for revolutionary activity where once they had seen only harmless crowd activity.[55]

Perhaps the most obvious place to look for evidence of paternalism breaking down was in relation to the relief of poverty. The Poor Law was established by legislation at the end of the sixteenth century, with the worthy objects of relieving the old and impotent poor, training children in a trade, and providing work for the unemployed. The practice proved less sound. Over time the apprenticeship system was easily abused, and the administration of relief on a parish basis was less than wholly satisfactory. Even so, down to the end of the eighteenth century most people regarded the law as an honest attempt to prevent poverty and to ameliorate its effects. Although by 1800 the need for social conditioning was widely appreciated, and a growing fear of the poor had introduced an element of cynicism into charitable giving, relief appeared to be the most efficient means of encouraging a popular belief in the reality of paternal benevolence. Public relief was a necessary part of life for a significant minority of the population, who were able to claim help as a right without fear of social stigma. In such an atmosphere improved methods of offering relief were tried. Speenhamland – the system developed in Berkshire in 1795, of supplementing wages according to the ruling price of bread and the number of a man's dependants – was an expression of this concern, and

[53] P. B. Munsche, 'The game laws in Wiltshire', in *Crime in England, 1550–1800*, ed. J. S. Cockburn (1977), pp. 210–28.

[54] Mingay, *The Gentry*, pp. 131–3; Moir, *The Justice of the Peace*, pp. 126–8.

[55] Thompson, 'The moral economy of the English crowd'. Note, however, the reservations about this argument drawn by Dale Edward Williams, 'Morals, markets and the English crowd in 1766', *Past and Present*, 104 (1984), pp. 56–73; and of Stone and Stone, *An Open Elite?*, pp. 274–5.

also a reflection of the considerable local autonomy enjoyed by individual parishes and by local justices in organizing relief. The magistrates were often more willing than the overseers to dispense relief, possibly reflecting an acceptance on the part of the landed community that the privilege of property conferred an obligation on landlords to look after the poor. The whole point was that while relief was sometimes inadequate the system provided a safety net which helped to defuse social tension while maintaining the spirit of paternalism.[56]

Problems arose only when poor relief started to become too expensive. From £2 million in 1784, costs rose to nearly £6 million in 1815, and the tensions of poverty were underlined by machine-breaking and arson. Despite a fall in the rates during the 1820s spending remained high, and the humanitarian concern which had characterized relief in the 1790s turned into a preoccupation with the difficulties of the ratepayer by the 1820s. Questions were asked whether poor relief could continue in view of escalating costs, and the arguments of an abolitionist campaign were actually accepted by a select committee of the House of Commons in 1817. Recognizing the potential political damage that might accrue, the government hastily convened a select committee of the Lords to reverse the recommendation. When reform was finally contemplated in the early 1830s, it was the moral weaknesses of the poor which were highlighted, rather than the role of population pressure, and agricultural and industrial change. The result was a measure which blamed the economic ills of early nineteenth-century England on the so-called evils of the old Poor Law, and rejected the flexibility of the existing system.[57]

Following a royal commission report, the existing law was replaced in 1834 by new legislation of a much more repressive character. Able-bodied paupers were now to receive relief only in workhouses, and in these institutions their lives were to be made less comfortable than anyone who stayed outside in an effort to fend for themselves could expect to enjoy. By ensuring that only those in dire need would be ready to face the workhouse, the aim of the legislators was to slash the cost of relief. The new law was designed to be markedly less generous than its predecessor, and this suggests that the paternalism

---

[56] J. D. Marshall, *The Old Poor Law, 1795–1834* (1968); Peter Dunkley, *The Crisis of the Old Poor Law in England, 1795–1834* (1982), ch. 3; I. R. Christie, *Stress and Stability in Late Eighteenth-Century Britain: reflections on the British avoidance of revolution* (Oxford, 1984), pp. 94–123.

[57] Harold Perkin, *The Origins of Modern English Society. 1780–1880* (1969), pp. 190–1.

which marked the old relief system was finally being laid to rest. However, it has been suggested that in its application to the countryside the New Poor Law was designed to shore up the existing social order. Most landlords, so the argument goes, seem to have been in broad agreement with the aims of the legislation, and aristocratic control of the new boards helped to underscore the traditional leadership of rural society. Consequently, far from being out to grind the faces of the poor, the landowners were attempting to strengthen the social fabric of the countryside and to do so cheaply. Magistrates, as ex-officio members of boards of guardians, opposed the more harshly deterrent aspects of the new legislation, and were able in practice to moderate the impact of the new union workhouses on the rural poor.[58]

While such an argument suggests a continuity between the old and the new Poor Laws in terms of landlord paternalism, and while it can be defended for counties such as Northamptonshire with a high proportion of larger proprietors and a well-defined social hierachy, it is less clearly relevant elsewhere. In general terms it seems unlikely that gains offset losses for the aristocracy, and the evidence suggests it was tenant farmers rather than landlords who played the most significant role on boards of guardians. The gentry did not necessarily exercise their plural voting rights, and they were often absent from meetings of the guardians, while contemporary commentators pointed to the loss of influence after 1834. In this context the evidence suggests that the new legislation, with its much harsher terms, was a negation of paternalism rather than an attempt to reinforce dependency in the countryside.[59]

Despite this, the new Poor Law was passed at a point where landowners were beginning to appreciate the social dangers arising from opting out of local government. From the 1830s they flocked back to the bench. Whereas in 1831 clerics constituted around one-quarter of all magistrates in England and Wales, the number fell to 13 per cent in 1842, and to just under 6 per cent by 1887. Peers and gentry constituted 86 per cent of all county magistrates in 1842. Possibly this return to their responsibilities helped to preserve local

[58] This argument is largely associated with the writing of Anthony Brundage: 'The landed interest and the new Poor Law: a reappraisal of the revolution in government', *English Historical Review*, 88 (1972), pp. 27–48; *The Making of the New Poor Law: the politics of inquiry, enactment and implementation, 1832–1839* (1978).

[59] P. Dunkley, 'The landed interest and the new Poor Law: a critical note', *English Historical Review*, 88 (1973), pp. 836–41; William Apfel and Peter Dunkley, 'English rural society and the new Poor Law: Bedfordshire, 1834–47', *Social History*, 10 (1985), pp. 37–68; K. D. M. Snell, *Annals of the Labouring Poor: social change and agrarian England, 1660–1900* (Cambridge, 1985), pp. 116–17.

government from the reforming zeal of the 1830s which embraced the electoral system, the Poor Law and the municipal corporations. The possibility of change was certainly considered; in fact, the Royal Commission on County Rates, which reported in 1836, recommended that rural local government should be reformed, but the following year an attempt to have Quarter Sessions replaced by elective county boards was decisively defeated in the Commons by 177 votes to 84. Over the years which followed, efforts to introduce reform packages met the same fate. Conservatives in particular argued that the efficiency and integrity of Quarter Sessions was much to be desired over the unknown qualities of elected authorities, and in 1875 Tory peers, while accepting a change in the residential qualification of JPs, resisted efforts to remove the £100 land regulation. So successful were these moves that reform was delayed until 1888. However, reactionary Conservatives alone could never have been so successful in resisting reform. Two further factors were significant: the continued ability of Quarter Sessions to present themselves as a viable form of government; and the capacity of the magistracy to absorb within its ranks men from other walks of life. Although the sample sizes are slightly different, the proportion of landowners declined from 86 per cent to 74 per cent of county magistrates between 1842 and 1887, and much of the shortfall was accounted for by an influx from the middle class.[60]

The duties of the rural magistracy remained fundamentally unchanged for much of the nineteenth century. Prisons and asylums, the poor, law and order, and bridges and highways had long been part of their repertoire, and even where powers were transferred to other boards — as in the case of the poor, public health and highways — magistrates were usually well represented. The main change was that elective boards gave positions to farmers and tradesmen, thus beginning the process whereby the JPs' powers were gradually eroded. Some of these changes were in any case a long time coming; provisions for the highways did not change until 1862, and prison inspectors had relatively little authority in the countryside before 1865. Possibly more significant in the process of power erosion was the professionalization of local government. County police forces gradually

---

[60] Carl Zangerl, 'The social composition of the county magistracy in England, 1831–1887' *Journal of British Studies*, 40 (1971), pp. 118, 121–3. Zangerl's figures for 1887 have been disputed: see chapter 3, note 107. The residential qualification was altered by the Justices Qualification Act, 38 & 39 Vict., c. 54 (1875). It should be stressed that not only did the proportion of landowners on the commission of the peace increase during the nineteenth century, but that the number taking the oath to qualify also rose sharply.

replaced the existing means of investigating crime in the later 1840s and 1850s, and although they were financially accountable to the Sessions this could not prevent them from exercising a degree of control over their nominal masters. Similarly with the Poor Law unions, the role of medical officers and relieving officers often became efficient enough to limit the range of power exercised by the guardians.

The force which finally served to undermine Quarter Sessions through time was the establishment of new units of authority with overlapping functions and duties as well as physical boundaries. Although individual JPs could retain their power through membership of Poor Law unions, highway boards, school boards and sanitary districts, the state of general chaos which gradually overtook rural social services as a result of these overlapping jurisdictions gradually weakened the whole structure. By the 1880s Quarter Sessions increasingly looked like a nominated county Parliament supervising a number of permanent professional officials, and a mass of overlapping jurisdictions.[61] Even the capacity to accept new JPs from outside the traditional elite could not save the Sessions from reform by the 1880s, although their fifty-year reprieve after municipal reform indicates the strength of feeling regarding their utility. Coupled with a rising county rate, which was unevenly collected, and the extension of the franchise to rural workers during the 1880s, it was inevitable that the time for change had come.

The dethronement of Quarter Sessions came with the County Councils Act of 1888, and the election of the first councils the following year. Ostensibly this marked a decisive weakening of elite power, and diehard supporters of the old system expected little good to come from such changes. Gloomy prognostications foretold the disappearance of the larger landowners, and a direct transfer of power into the hands of the middle class. In practice, the changeover proved to be far less dramatic, and when the new councils gathered in April 1889 anything up to half the newly elected councillors turned out to be magistrates – in Westmorland it was three-quarters – and slightly over half the alderman. Anti-magisterial feeling produced more profound changes in some areas. In Lancashire and the West Riding of Yorkshire this had considerable repercussions for the staffing of local government, and the same was true of the Lincolnshire division of Holland, where only two of the new councillors were magistrates.

[61] F. M. L. Thompson, *English Landed Society in the Nineteenth Century* (1963), pp. 288–9; Moir, *The Justice of the Peace*, ch. 6.

Elections in this case represented an opportunity to respond to years of rule by a small and predominantly Tory bench of magistrates. Only one of the new councillors came from the gentry, and the predominant groups were twenty-two farmers and ten shopkeepers.[62] By contrast, in Cheshire the landowning families who had traditionally run the shire did not enter the contests in any great numbers. Only thirty-four magistrates offered themselves for election, and of these twenty-eight were returned. Although elderly and Conservative, only nine of these men were strictly from the landed elite, while fifteen were manufacturers and merchants (of whom seven were from the Manchester cotton industry), and the other four were a mining engineer, a doctor, a banker and the registrar of the Manchester County Court. The twenty-nine new members of the council who were not magistrates came largely from commerce: ten were connected with heavy industry or the warehouse trade, six were working farmers, eight were tradesmen or small entrepreneurs, and only one was a country gentleman of any description. The appearance of businessmen on the Cheshire bench prior to reform was reflected in the make-up of the new council, with great merchants and industrialists being joined by farmers and small tradesmen to administer the county.[63]

Either through the ballot box or by voluntary abdication, the old elite disappeared in many areas, but others retained their pre-reform character. In East Sussex sixty-eight of the councillors owned 59,000 acres of land between them, while in Worcestershire the peers sat on a dais beside the chairman.[64] In the Lindsey and Kesteven districts of Lincolnshire the old guard remained strong. Although eight magistrates in Lindsey and four in Kesteven were defeated at the polls, the two divisions had seventeen and nineteen gentry respectively out of seventy-six and sixty-four councillors. More than half of those returned in Kesteven were gentry or farmers, giving the new council a decidedly rural flavour, but in Lindsey a significant manufacturing and trading element sat alongside twenty-nine farmers and gentry. As a result, the social balance of the areas was reflected in the council chambers. Similarly diverse was the extent to which politics dominated the elections, although the decision to introduce or exclude national considerations varied. In Leicestershire, for example, the Liberals

[62] J. P. D. Dunbabin, 'Expectations of the new county councils, and their realization', *Historical Journal*, 8 (1965), pp. 360–1; Moir, *The Justice of the Peace*, pp. 154–5; Olney, *Rural Society and County Government*, pp. 136–8.

[63] J. M. Lee, *Social Leaders and Public Persons: a study of county government in Cheshire since 1888* (Oxford, 1963), pp. 56–8, 70–80.

[64] Dunbabin, 'Expectations of the new county councils', p. 361.

decided not to intervene unless the Conservatives made the first move. The Wigston Liberals claimed that they were ready for a compromise, but decided to force a fight when the Conservatives became active.[65]

Overall, the extent of change before and after 1888 was limited, and most of the more gloomy prognostications went unfulfilled. By 1890 only nineteen English counties had chosen a fresh person to chair the new county council, while twenty-six had elected the chairman of the Quarter Sessions, and in Cornwall, Northamptonshire and Oxfordshire the post went to the lord-lieutenant. The landed interest lived on in the English countryside, and the fact that few peers were defeated in the first elections confirmed the strength of residual deference. As the Earl of Harrowby told Lord Salisbury after the elections, 'we shall all have to live in the country for the next three years, to keep things straight.' Similarly in West Sussex, the Duke of Richmond, although opposed to reform, declared his determination to put the measure into practice. Moreover, paternalism was fostered by the rapid loss of interest in the new councils, which soon came to be regarded with no more concern than Quarter Sessions had been previously. In 1892, for example, only four of the fifty-seven Oxfordshire seats and ten of the 111 Lancashire seats were contested. The changes of 1888 turned out to be more of form than of substance, and it is worth recalling that even the power of the justices was far from being swept away. They continued as ex-officio guardians of the poor, and control of the police was placed under the command of a joint standing committee of the Quarter Sessions and the county council. The land qualification disappeared only in 1906. Whatever the political and governmental significance of the events of 1888, the landed elite was not overturned, even if an erosion of its position since 1834 was confirmed.[66]

THE BREAKDOWN OF ARISTOCRATIC LOCAL GOVERNMENT: THE TOWNS

The successful perpetuation of aristocratic power in the rural community was not matched in urban England. Aristocrats had long played an important role as both patrons and governors of towns. Peers and gentry were prime movers in establishing a general dispensary at Lincoln in the 1740s, and the idea of an infirmary at Leicester was first

[65] Olney, *Rural Society and County Government*, pp. 136–8; Dunbabin, 'Expectations of the new county councils', pp. 361–3.

[66] Lee, *Social Leaders and Public Persons*, pp. 224–5; Dunbabin, 'Expectations of the new county councils', pp. 370–5.

discussed at an assize meeting of the county gentry in 1766. At Nottingham the Duke of Newcastle gave an acre of land for Nottingham General Hospital in 1781 and headed a list of benefactors which included the Duke of Devonshire, Earl Manvers, Lord Middleton, Lord Newark, the Duke of Portland and most of the local county gentry.[67] Aristocrats held significant political powers in a number of places. No opponent of the Marquess of Exeter was reputed to have any chance of being considered to the magistracy, the council or corporate office in Stamford, while in Derby the mass creation of freemen prior to early nineteenth-century elections turned out to have the blessing of the Duke of Devonshire.[68]

Although borough corporations had originally been genuinely popular organs of local government, over time they fell into disrepute. More than 200 boroughs had corporate status, but most had become private bodies whose prime responsibility was to their constituent members. Improvement commissions had been appointed in a number of places to try to update the available services, but the general findings of a royal commission appointed in 1833 to investigate the corporations made gloomy reading. Legislative action followed in the form of the 1835 Municipal Corporations Act, which dissolved the old corporations and replaced them with 178 municipal boroughs governed by elected councils. The legislation aimed to open up town government to popular participation, and to cleanse its public image, so that representative and judicial propriety became the basis of the new system.

In the aftermath of reform, landed influence in the municipal corporations gradually weakened. According to one sample, aristocrats, squires and gentlemen represented 51 per cent of the borough magistracy in 1841, but only 24 per cent in 1885.[69] In Bradford, a single gentleman was numbered among the aldermen between 1847 and 1860, and in Leicester just four out of fifty-five between 1836 and 1870. Other towns also developed with relatively little interest or control by landlords. In the post-1850 decades in

[67] E. R. Frizelle and J. D. Martin, *The Leicester Royal Infirmary, 1771–1971* (Leicester, 1971), p. 31; F. H. Jacob, *A History of the General Hospital near Nottingham* (Bristol, 1951), pp. 12–25.

[68] Parl. Papers, *Report of the Royal Commission on Municipal Corporations in England and Wales* (1835), vols XXIII–XXIV, pp. 1857, 2538. For an eighteenth-century example of aristocratic urban influence, see Philip Jenkins, 'Tory industrialism and town politics: Swansea in the eighteenth century', *Historical Journal*, 28 (1985), pp. 103–24.

[69] Zangerl, 'The social composition of the county magistracy', p. 115.

Bournemouth, for example, landowners played a relatively small part in the social, public, political and economic life of the town.[70] Such cases may be misleading, since some evidence suggests that as late as 1884 one municipal councillor in four was likely to be a country gentleman.[71] Moreover, patrician influence remained significant in a number of towns. The Butes continued to exercise power in Cardiff, and the Ramsdens in Huddersfield, at least down to the mid-1850s, while the earls of Warwick held the important position of recorder in Warwick during the nineteenth century, and the Lowther domination of Whitehaven induced one radical to coin for them the epithet of 'emperors'.[72] The difficulty is to trace the passing of real power to middle-class civic leaders in a more systematic fashion.

The reforms of 1835 were aimed at corrupt corporations rather than at aristocratic influence, and the ties between town and country were always such as to ensure that there would be no immediate change of emphasis. Peers played an important role in promoting locally important legislation. A number were responsible for pushing through improvement Acts from the late eighteenth century, and by the mid-nineteenth these became so hotly contested that they required considerable effort on the part of their sponsors.[73] Aristocrats also continued to curry favour by promoting local services and facilities. In Birmingham the Calthorpes promoted local voluntary societies including the Deaf and Dumb Asylum and the Botanical and Horticultural Society; while in Derby Joseph Strutt provided the

---

[70] Adrian Elliott, 'Municipal government in Bradford in the mid-nineteenth century', in *Municipal Reform in the Industrial City*, ed. Derek Fraser (Leicester, 1982), p. 143; K. M. Thompson, 'Power and authority in Leicester, 1820–1870' (University of Nottingham, MA thesis, 1985), pp. 51–3; Richard Roberts, 'Leasehold estates and municipal enterprise: landowners, local government and the development of Bournemouth, *c.* 1850–1914', in *Patricians, Power and Politics*, ed. Cannadine, pp. 176–211.

[71] W. L. Arnstein, 'The myth of the triumphant Victorian middle-class', *The Historian*, 37 (1975), p. 208. Arnstein's figures were derived from unpublished work by a former graduate. They are difficult to square with evidence from Bradford – where only a handful of gentlemen became councillors – or from Lancashire, where the proportion of gentlemen councillors in the textile towns was much less: A. Howe, *The Cotton Masters, 1830–1860* (Oxford, 1984), pp. 144–5.

[72] J. E. Williams, 'Paternalism in local government in the nineteenth century', *Public Administration*, 33 (1955), pp. 442, 444; C. F. O'Neill, 'The "contest for dominion": political conflict and the decline of the Lowther "interest" in Whitehaven, 1820–1900', *Northern History*, 18 (1982), pp. 133–52.

[73] Michael W. McCahill, *Order and Equipoise: the peerage and the House of Lords, 1783–1806* (1978), p. 92; Sheila Lambert, *Bills and Acts* (Cambridge, 1971), pp. 170–1.

arboretum in 1840 at a cost of £10,000 and the brewer Sir Michael Bass financed a recreation ground in 1867 and a swimming pool in 1873.[74] Almost inevitably, however, the influence of outside magnates weakened through time. After 1832 their political role often disappeared in newly represented industrial towns such as Birmingham, and the increasing desire of municipal authorities to promote their own towns also left relatively little room for aristocratic initiative. Even so, the process of disengagement was by no means straightforward.

Aristocratic urban dominance remained considerable down to the 1820s, and in some cases even into the 1840s; indeed, they held a position in these years which was not to be repeated. Cardiff, for example, continued to expand within an antiquated administrative machinery which gave the second Marquess of Bute a power base that neither parliamentary nor municipal reform could dent. In the Black Country the earls of Dudley at Dudley and the earls of Dartmouth in West Bromwich exercised scarcely less power. In all three of these towns a middle-class elite was slow to emerge, but where it grew at an early stage landlords might work in conjunction to champion interests at Westminster. This was the role played by the fifth Earl Fitzwilliam for Sheffield. On the other hand, aristocrats like the marquesses of Bute could see themselves as champions of the poor against the depredations of new industrialists.[75] But change was in the air, and during the second quarter of the nineteenth century a process of withdrawal from urban dominance was evident. Parliamentary and municipal reform, coupled with the urban-based, anti-aristocratic rhetoric of the Anti-Corn Law League, produced a hostile climate. Richard Cobden's view was that the great political issue of the day was the class struggle between the bourgeoisie and aristocracy in town and country for the soul of England, and that this cause would be served by asserting urban authority through incorporation.[76] In the West

[74] David Cannadine, 'The Calthorpe family and Birmingham, 1810–1910: a "Conservative interest" examined', *Historical Journal*, 18 (1975), pp. 725–60; J. D. Standen, 'The social, economic and political development of Derby, 1835–1888' (University of Leeds, MA thesis, 1958), pp. 213–15.

[75] Cannadine, 'From "feudal" lords to figureheads', pp. 23–35; *Patricians, Power and Politics*, pp. 11–13; John Davies, 'Aristocratic town makers and the coal metropolis: the marquesses of Bute and Cardiff, 1776–1947', in ibid., p. 35.

[76] Derek Fraser, *Urban Politics in Victorian England* (Leicester, 1976), p. 22. It can be argued that the mid-nineteenth century saw a revival of patriarchal authority and paternalist behaviour on the part of the employing classes: F. M. L. Thompson, 'Social control in Victorian Britain', *Economic History Review*, 2nd ser., 34 (1981), p. 205.

Midlands the Dartmouths suffered defeats on the church rates issue and constituency politics, and withdrew from Sandwell to Patshull, while the Dudleys clashed with the local board of health and moved from Himley Hall to Witley Court. However, a few instances do not make a closed case, and the third quarter of the century seems to have been a period of calm and friendly relations. Huddersfield and Cardiff could still celebrate the coming of age of an aristocratic heir, while aristocratic patronage was crucial for launching middle-class charitable associations and voluntary societies. These years also saw aristocratic influence in resort development at its height.

The 1870s and 1880s brought a chill wind for aristocratic influence in the towns. It blew in from a variety of different directions. The third Reform Act, the agricultural depression, and the publication of such anti-aristocratic documents as the *Return of Owners of Land*, as well as various reports from the Select Committee on Town Holdings, all helped to whip up feeling. In 1876 Huddersfield Corporation brought out the Ramsdens' market rights; in 1881 Cardiff Corporation tried to take over the docks; and in the later 1880s the South Wales coalowners effectively ended the Bute monopoly of port facilities by building Barry dock and railway. However, the 1890s saw a final flowering of good relations symbolized by the ornamental but none the less aristocratic lord mayors. Prior to 1890 no aristocrat had held this position in a major provincial town for more than a century, and even the smaller centres had been unable to boast many since 1835. During the 1890s, by contrast, eighteen aristocrats held mayoralties in English towns, and a further fourteen followed during the first decade of the twentieth century. Usually the man selected was an important local landowner or political figure, or both, and these appointees infused drab urban life with sparkle and glamour, donating maces and chains of office, and attracting royal visitors, while at the same time providing feasts, banquets and balls. In addition, the mayoralty itself was often offered and accepted as a symbol of the ending of active aristocratic involvement, as in the cases of the Marquess of Bute's appointment in Cardiff in 1891 and the Earl of Lonsdale's at Whitehaven in 1894.[77]

What was achieved during the course of the century was a shift in the balance of power within towns, from the owners of urban estates, to the people who lived on them. If, at the beginning of the nineteenth century, the great landlords remained powerful influences, by the end they were closer to being figureheads. Down to about 1870,

[77] Cannadine, 'From "feudal" lords to figureheads'.

opportunities for the landed elite remained considerable where towns had divided or only weakly established middle-class elites. Aristocrats could still initiate schemes for economic development, they could still provide amenities, and they could still dominate social life and interfere in local government. Even so, much of the unifying influence in towns was against patrician interference rather than positively in favour of coherent middle-class endeavour. The more timid the local authority, the more likely it was to be landowner-dominated, as, for example, in the case of Southport. Others proved difficult to shake off, as is clear from the contest for dominion which took place in Whitehaven after 1860. It was only in the last quarter of the century that a qualitative weakening seems to have taken place in the old landed order, as the urban middle class became more confident, united and self-conscious. Joseph Chamberlain's Birmingham increased the attractiveness of local government to important businessmen. By the closing years of the century aristocrats could still support civic and philanthropic schemes for the good of the town, but they could no longer dictate policy, or hold the reins of power in a way which had once been possible. Civic power had passed irreversibly to the town hall, and the unseating of the Lonsdales in Whitehaven during the 1890s was symptomatic of this changeover.[78]

THE TRANSFER OF POWER IN LOCAL GOVERNMENT

Seventeenth-century England was administered by a rural aristocracy acting as magistrates, and for the most part performing their tasks adequately and effectively.[79] Local government was a public service undertaken by men of property for the good of the whole community. Wealth gave them the independence both to act voluntarily and to dispense justice impartially. It also produced a system of local government which was recognizably paternal. As duties increased in the eighteenth century, the magistrates became the administrators of the nation. At the same time a more subtle change was taking place. With leading members of county society increasingly detained in London for six months or more of the year, the administration of the localities fell into the hands of lesser families who would not previously have been admitted to the commission of the peace. This became

[78] O'Neill, 'The "contest for dominion"'.
[79] Dorothy Ross, 'Class privilege in 17th century England', *History*, 28 (1943), pp. 148–55.

increasingly the case as the size of the bench increased after 1680, and as magistrates doubled as land tax commissioners and turnpike trustees. The major safeguard preventing this expansion in the numbers of local governors from devaluing the bench was to be found in the property qualifications which came to affect more or less every position in eighteenth-century local government.

Unfortunately many of the newcomers admitted to local government administration during the eighteenth century regarded the commission of the peace as a status to be obtained rather than as a practical role to be performed. In fact, the number of non-active justices suggests that there was something of a breakdown in the tradition of public service, and with it a loss of paternalism. However, the position was partially recovered in the early nineteenth century, but, although rural local government avoided the fate of the municipal corporations in the 1830s, the complexity of local government gradually undermined the old system in the decades which followed.

An example of how the effective transfer of power took place in advance of the reform of local government is provided by policing. Under the old system each wapentake or hundred of a county had a high constable, usually drawn from among the substantial farmers or smaller freeholders, and each parish a petty constable who served for a single year. The holders of these positions were responsible to the Sessions. In the event of serious trouble the lord-lieutenant could call out the militia. Although reformed after the Restoration, this particular body gradually declined in repute and effectiveness until the invasion scares of the Seven Years War persuaded the government in 1757 to create a national force of 32,000 men raised by county quotas from all men aged between eighteen and fifty. Until 1757 the militia played relatively little part in local government, and even thereafter its effectiveness was limited. For practical purposes, local security was safer in the hands of the yeomanry, a group of amateur soldiers usually raised by a particular landlord and often manned principally by his own tenants. It was the yeomanry who were the first to be called out at Peterloo in 1819, and it was only after they failed that a regular force of soldiers was summoned.[80]

Overall, parish constables, militia, yeomanry, and justices hearing cases in their front rooms did not add up to much, but an effective police force was equally feared in case central government used it to curtail political liberty. What appeared to be a rising crime rate, along

[80] Western, *The English Militia*; Keith-Lucas, *The Unreformed Local Government System*, pp. 67–9.

with middle-class fears of disorder during the 1790s and beyond, led eventually to the London police force in 1829, and thereafter to the creation of urban and rural local forces.[81] Rural resistance was, however, considerable. In 1839 legislation was passed permitting the establishment of professional county police forces, but in March the following year Lincolnshire magistrates decided not to implement the measure. The grounds for their decision included the cost, the erosion of their own control in police matters, and the fear that paid strangers would undermine the good-neighbourliness traditional in the countryside. In 1856 Lincolnshire was obliged to establish a regular police force, although high constables were not abolished until 1869, and one petty-sessional division was still appointing parish constables at the turn of the century.[82] The magistrates yielded up responsibility reluctantly, even though the process of change outmoded the older forms of local administration.

As late as 1880 Sir Arthur Arnold could write that rural government in England was 'the possession of land'. The lord-lieutenant, he continued, 'is always as a matter of course, a great landowner. If a man choose to invest £20,000 in a landed estate, and is a person of fair character, he has no difficulty in obtaining for his name a place upon the commission of the peace.'[83] Even after reform in 1888, county government did not necessarily pass into new hands. The aristocratic control of the reins of power remained largely intact, even if they were forced to accept changes in the methods of government. It was in the towns of Victorian England that their position slipped. Nineteenth-century towns were no place for a rural aristocracy, however hard they might try to maintain their power through benevolent societies and gifts. Civic assertiveness either kept them at arm's length, or produced disputes about the limits of their power, but the use of peers as figureheads by the 1890s reflected a fundamental change in outlook and attitudes. Their power remained, as it always had been, rurally based: it did not easily transfer into the new urban environment.

[81] David Phillips, '"A new engine of power and authority": the institutionalization of law-enforcement in England, 1780–1830', in *Crime and the Law*, ed. V. A. C. Gatrell *et al.* (1980), pp. 155–89; John Stevenson, 'Social control and the prevention of riots in England, 1789–1829', in *Social Control in Nineteenth-Century Britain*, ed. A. P. Donajgrodzki (1977), pp. 27–50.

[82] Olney, *Rural Society and County Government*, pp. 122–4.

[83] A. Arnold, *Free Land* (1880), p. 247.

Chapter Twelve

The Aristocracy and the State: The Consolidation of Power

In 1649 the House of Lords was abolished, and a decade later, on the eve of Charles II's restoration, the possibility of its being revived remained in the balance. Concerned commentators could argue the rights and wrongs of abolition, and the importance of restitution,[1] but such debates soon seemed remote when, within months of Charles II's return, the structure of government reverted to its pre-Civil War format. The Earl of Clarendon expected the aristocracy to recover its prestige. He told the Lords:

Your Lordships will easily recover that estimation and reverence that is due to your high condition, by the exercise and practice of that virtue from whence your honours first sprang . . . no nobility in Europe [is] so entirely loved by the People; there may be more awe, and fear, and terror of them, but no such love towards them as in England . . . the exercise of your justice and kindness towards them will make them the more abhor and abominate that parity upon which a Commonwealth must be founded, because it would extirpate, or suppress, or deprive them of their beloved nobility, which are such a support and security to their full happiness.[2]

If anything, the Restoration settlement aided the aristocracy by strengthening Parliament. Star Chamber was abolished, enabling the Lords to resume its position as the supreme court of appeal, while frequent financial needs kept the lower house in almost constant business prior to 1679. The 1688 revolution further augmented aristocratic power, and the period down to 1832 has been described as

---

[1] Anon., *The Antient Land-Mark Skreen or Bank betwixt the Prince or Supreme Magistrate* (1659).
[2] *LJ*, 11 (29 December 1660), p. 238.

an 'age of aristocracy'.[3] One man who believed this was John Hampden, who argued in 1846 that 1688 brought in 'the reign of aristocratic humbug', and that even in his own time

a mighty and wealthy and luxurious aristocracy . . . are, in truth, the possessors of all and everything in England. They possess the crown, for it is the greatest bauble and talisman of all their wealth and honours. They possess the House of Commons, by their sons, their purses, and their influence. They possess the church and the state, the army and the navy. They possess all offices at home and abroad. They possess the land at home, and the colonies to the end of the earth. And, what is more, they possess the property and the profits of every man, for they have only to stretch out their great arm in a vote of the House of Commons, and they can take it as they please.

Clearly Hampden had an axe to grind – the purpose of his work was 'to show the one great cause of all our derangements and all our distresses, the usurpation of the total powers of the constitution by an overgrown aristocracy'[4] – but modern historians have been equally impressed by the power and influence of the group. W. L. Guttsman has described the survival of aristocratic power as 'an extraordinary historical phenomenon', and W. L. Arnstein has been surprised at the extent to which 'the machinery of national and county government remained in 1900 in predominantly aristocratic and squirearchic hands.'[5] The question arises how the aristocracy recovered and then consolidated its power after 1660; and this in turn leads to a second question: how was the grip maintained almost down to 1914? In looking for answers in this and the next chapter, the emphasis will be less on political parties and political activities, except in so far as they are relevant, than on the actions of a governing class which believed in its right and duty to rule despite the changes going on all around.

   The return to a pre-1642 position in the post-Restoration world was never complete. A favourable settlement of the land and church questions, and a return to the old positions in the countryside, appeared to herald the re-establishment of an order which had merely been temporarily suspended by the rude intervention of the Civil War and Commonwealth periods. Unfortunately, neither Charles II nor James II proved happy with the settlement, and their campaign to

---

   [3] For example, William B. Willcox, *The Age of Aristocracy, 1688–1832* (Boston, Mass., 1966).
   [4] John Hampden, *The Aristocracy of England* (1846), pp. 7, 161.
   [5] W. L. Guttsman, *The British Political Elite* (1963), p. 60; W. L. Arnstein, 'The myth of the triumphant Victorian middle class', *The Historian*, 37 (1975), p. 216.

uphold royal power – and, by the later 1670s, to ensure James's succession – took the form of a struggle over the role of Parliament. A shortfall in his finances forced Charles II to consult regularly with the Commons, and he perceived the key to lower-house pliability to rest on the avoidance of electoral contests. As a result, he retained the Cavalier Parliament from 1661 until 1679, and this gave ministers the time to organize the Commons through patronage and management. In the later years of his reign, borough charters were remodelled, ostensibly to strengthen royal control over the administration of justice in the towns, where dissenters were strongest, but also in the hope of building a court interest in the lower house.[6] The exclusion crisis brought further conflict, after which Charles proceeded to rule without Parliament, thus apparently threatening a royal tyranny. James II went even further, failing to call Parliament after 1685, remodelling charters for electoral purposes, and posing a threat to the rule of law through his Declarations of Indulgence in 1687 and 1688. In the countryside he purged the traditional elite from the militia, revised the commission of the peace without consulting the lords-lieutenant, and removed eighteen lieutenants from twenty-one counties between August 1687 and March 1688. These moves threatened the position of the existing elite, and once again produced action designed to control the monarchy.

The active role of the aristocracy in the 1688 Glorious Revolution has been a subject of debate. Most of their support for William of Orange appears to have taken a passive form, and the revolution was, after all, essentially a palace coup d'état lacking the warrior element of the Civil War. Even so, the beneficiaries were precisely the traditional rulers that James II had done so much to alienate.[7] In the closing days of 1688 it was the peers who gave a lead in the state,[8] and in the aftermath the aristocracy developed a governing function. Until 1688 the existence of Parliament was testament to the aristocratic success in resisting the predatory power instincts of the Crown; indeed, the aristocracy had promoted Parliament to give itself a role in running the affairs of state. Even in Charles II's reign, however, it retained the air of an occasional body, summoned periodically by the monarch to grant

[6] The extent to which charter remodelling was deliberately geared to political motives must not be exaggerated: John Miller, 'The Crown and the borough charters in the reign of Charles II', *English Historical Review*, 100 (1985), pp. 53–84.

[7] J. P. Kenyon, *The Nobility in the Revolution of 1688* (Hull, 1963); D. Hosford, *Nottingham, Nobles and the North* (1976).

[8] John Cannon, 'The isthmus repaired: the resurgence of the English aristocracy, 1660–1760', *Proceedings of the British Academy*, 67 (1983), p. 443.

taxation or to make a necessary alteration in the law. In 1688 the aristocracy provided effective opposition to a monarch determined to strengthen royal control at the expense of traditional liberties and privileges. The long-term result was that as Continental parliaments were contracting and disappearing, the English parliament was turned into an arm of the executive. The revolution settlement, and the fiscal demands of the 1690s, turned parliament into a permanent part of the constitution and gave it an influential position in policy-making. To ensure its position, the executive – increasingly dominated by leading members of the peerage – sought to influence the Commons, partly because through its control of supply the lower house was recognized to be the more important of the two chambers. As a result, the much vaunted independence of the lower house as the seat of country gentlemen was largely usurped in the seventy years after the revolution. By 1760 England was effectively an oligarchy. Control was preserved without resort to force, and until the early nineteenth century few questions were raised about the legitimacy of aristocratic government. Moreover, although certain aspects of aristocratic power may have reduced efficiency, and tended to promote an amateur spirit, it was almost certainly not detrimental in the long term to the interests of the state.

THE ARISTOCRACY AND THE EXECUTIVE

Eighteenth-century governments knew no real distinction between their executive and legislative functions. The growth of government in order to finance and supply the military machine assembled during the French wars provided an opportunity for the peers to dominate the expanding executive. Forty-nine peers held offices of profit in 1714, and in 1726 one-quarter of the peerage was reckoned to hold government or 'court' positions, with many other places occupied by their relatives and dependants. From the Cabinet, through the armed forces, to the judiciary and the civil service, the peers made up for their disproportionately small numbers as a group by ensuring a hold on the most senior positions available.[9]

This control can be demonstrated first of all through the Cabinet. As a separate entity the Cabinet Council emerged in the 1690s, largely in the form of a ministerial forum during William III's absences abroad.[10]

---

[9] Geoffrey Holmes, *British Politics in the Age of Anne* (1967), pp. 436–8; G. E. Mingay, *English Landed Society in the Eighteenth Century* (1963), p. 71.

[10] Henry Horwitz, *Parliament, Policy and Politics in the Reign of William III* (Manchester, 1977), traces the emergence of the Cabinet in the 1690s.

Members were appointed and dismissed by the monarch, and the concept of Cabinet responsibility emerged only late in the eighteenth century. Individual ministerial positions appeared in Queen Anne's reign. The head of the Treasury held the dominant post with responsibility for domestic affairs, and the holder came to be recognized as the prime minister, although the position received formal recognition only in the twentieth century. Of the twenty-two first lords of the Treasury (the technical name for the post) in the eighteenth century, sixteen were peers, four were the sons of peers, and of the two exceptions one was the grandson of a peer and the other, Sir Robert Walpole, was raised to an earldom on his resignation. The fact that the other three great prime ministers of the century apart from Walpole sat in the lower house was a result of the prestige of the Commons, and its control of supply, since all three – Pelham, North and Pitt – were the sons of peers. Collectively the four Commons-based prime ministers held office for fifty-six of the years 1722–1800. Of the twenty men who held the post during the nineteenth century, thirteen were peers and seven were commoners, with the time in office more or less roughly divided two-thirds to one-third, although between Pitt's death in 1806 and Disraeli's accession to the post in 1868 the only commoner premierships which lasted any length of time were Spencer Perceval's three years and Sir Robert Peel's five.

Two other positions also emerged at an early date in the Cabinet, the secretaryships for the north and south. During the eighteenth century the posts, which became home and foreign secretaryships in 1782, were held by a total of forty-nine men, of whom twenty-eight were peers, five were the sons of peers, and five the grandsons of peers. Of the other eleven, six were raised to the peerage. In the nineteenth century the foreign secretaryship was almost exclusively held by a peer, the only exceptions being Charles James Fox for a few months in 1806, and George Canning in 1807–9 and 1822–7. By contrast, the home secretaryship gradually became a commoner's post, the last peer to hold it being Palmerston between 1852 and 1855.[11]

The Cabinet as a whole was also dominated by members of the peerage. In the summer of 1744 Henry Pelham's Cabinet included six dukes, and he added another in November. The Duke of Newcastle's Cabinet in 1754 included only three commoners out of twenty, and in 1760 his inner Cabinet consisted of two dukes, four earls, two barons

---

[11] Details in this and succeeding paragraphs from Cannon, 'The isthmus repaired', pp. 450–1, and John Cannon, *Aristocratic Century* (Cambridge, 1984), pp. 116–17; C. Cook and J. Stevenson, *British Historical Facts, 1760–1830* (1980); C. Cook and B. Keith, *British Historical Facts, 1830–1900* (1975).

and a single commoner. Such a collection reflected Newcastle's supposed belief that high rank and great estates excused incompetence in a minister. In the mid-1760s George Grenville presided over a Cabinet of nine in which he was the only commoner. Over the period 1782–1830 a total of sixty-five individuals held Cabinet office, of whom forty-three were peers, fourteen were the sons of peers and only six were members of the gentry. Of the latter group, three ended up in the Lords. Between 1830 and 1900 peers were seldom outnumbered in the Cabinet, and such was their domination of Peel's 1834–5 Cabinet that he was accused of the Duke of Newcastle's predilection for high birth and connections as substitutes for other qualifications.[12] Commoners first outnumbered peers in Melbourne's Whig Cabinet of 1835, although this did not happen in a Conservative Cabinet until 1858. Gradually the balance tipped against the peers until by 1892 they were outnumbered twelve to five in Gladstone's fourth Cabinet.

The influence of land remained strong. Over the period 1830–68, 66 per cent of ministers were from the landowning community, while mercantile and administrative ranks provided 20 per cent and lawyers 14 per cent. Although an increasing number of the greater offices of state came into the hands of men of lesser rank, the power of the established ruling elite remained largely unimpaired. Between 1830 and 1868 only three Cabinet ministers can be regarded as middle-class politicians representing the aspirations of their class.[13] At the same time it has to be remembered that one reason for this peerage control was the part played by the new public service and political peers from 1782. New peers and their heirs constituted 40 per cent of the membership of Cabinets between 1782 and 1830, and 32 per cent in 1831–55. As a proportion of the total peerage in the Cabinet over this period, new peers and their sons represented never less than half. As a result, one reason for the enduring nature of aristocratic Cabinets was that new recruits were continuing a political career often begun in the lower house.[14]

The position of the peerage was similarly impregnable in the armed

---

[12] O. F. Christie, *The Transition from Aristocracy, 1832–1867* (1927), pp. 103, 114–17.

[13] Guttsman, *The British Political Elite*, pp. 36–9. Other studies of later nineteenth-century Cabinets include F. M. G. Wilson, 'The routes of entry of new members of the British Cabinet, 1868–1958', *Political Studies*, 7 (1959), pp. 222–32, and James E. Alt, 'Continuity, turnover and experience in the British Cabinet, 1868–1970', in *Cabinet Studies*, ed. V. Herman (1975), pp. 33–54.

[14] M. W. McCahill, 'Peerage creations and the changing character of the British nobility, 1750–1830', *English Historical Review*, 96 (1981), pp. 276–8, 284.

forces. Purchase of officer commissions in the army dates from the Middle Ages, but it grew in volume in the post-Restoration period. By 1700 a standing professional army had emerged, undercutting the aristocratic function of providing troops for the monarch. To prevent the army from being utilized as an instrument of royal absolutism, post-Revolution Parliaments insisted on its regulation through Mutiny Acts, expenditure controls and a proprietory officership. By making ranks up to the level of lieutenant-colonel purchasable, the aristocracy ensured that they would be favourably placed to dominate the higher echelons of the army, while the Duke of Marlborough saw it as a guarantee against excessive parliamentary influence.[15] Out of 102 colonels of regiments in 1769, forty-three were peers or the sons of peers, and more than half had a direct peerage connection. Among the major-generals, 10 per cent were peers, as were 16 per cent of the lieutenant-generals and 27 per cent of the full generals.[16] In 1780, 30 per cent of officers had titles, and, although by 1800 probably fewer than 250 adult male peers and sons of peers were commissioned in an army of 12,000 officers, they dominated the upper ranks. All the four non-royal field marshals were peers, and of the fifty-six full generals seven were hereditary peers, seven were younger sons, three were newly created peers and one was a royal duke.[17] The proportion of officers with titles was 27 per cent in both 1810 and 1830, and in 1838 462 of 6173 active officers were from peerage families and another 267 were from the families of baronets. Altogether 53 per cent of officers were from landed families, with the highest proportion in the upper ranks.

Even after the introduction of competitive entrance in 1870, and the outlawing of commission purchase in 1871, half of all army officers were from the peerage and landed gentry in 1875, and the proportion was still over 40 per cent in 1912.[18] With competitive examination, the emphasis changed to a public school education. In the mid-1850s only 21 per cent of entrants at Woolwich Royal Military Academy had a public school background, but this figure rose to 75 per cent in 1890, and to 88 per cent in 1910. Sandhurst took a similar proportion from

[15] Anthony Bruce, *The Purchase System in the British Army, 1660–1871* (1980), pp. 1, 6, 13, 25, 166.

[16] Cannon, *Aristocratic Century*, pp. 119–20.

[17] P. E. Razzell, 'Social origins of officers in the Indian and British home army, 1758–1962', *British Journal of Sociology*, 14 (1963), p. 254; A. D. Harvey, *Britain in the Early Nineteenth Century* (1978), pp. 21–3.

[18] Razzell, 'Social origins of officers', pp. 253–4. In 1830, 78 per cent of generals and 89 per cent of major-generals were from the aristocracy and landed gentry.

public schools.[19] The aristocratic preponderance reflected a commitment to military service, and a determined effort to keep the highest army ranks in the group. Their cause was aided both by the high premiums and by the low pay, which made all except the most junior commissioned ranks effectively out of bounds to the non-affluent. It worked against professionalism by excluding men lacking private means, although it did not necessarily ensure the persistent and reprehensible amateurism which is often thought to have characterized the higher reaches of the army. Even in 1830, 47 per cent of officers had middle-class backgrounds, and the proportion rose to nearly 60 per cent by 1912.[20]

The officer situation was roughly similar in the navy, although purchase was never officially permitted. During the eighteenth century, the first lordship of the Admiralty was held by twenty-three men, of whom sixteen were peers, one was a prince of the royal blood, one was the son of a peer and one the son of a peeress. By 1800 the proportion of aristocratic serving officers was even higher than in the army. Perhaps one officer in twenty-seven was aristocratic in the revolutionary and Napoleonic war years, compared to one in fifty in the (admittedly rather larger) regular army. Many of these men were eldest sons of peers. The main difference from the army was that the proportion of aristocratic officers in the navy was much the same in all ranks.[21]

The civil service also provided openings for the aristocracy, largely because of the patronage system which prevailed until the later nineteenth century. Occasionally purchase was found in the later seventeenth century Ordnance Office, and, although the trade in positions was disapproved of,[22] this did not prevent aristocrats from finding places for less-well-off younger sons and other clients. The result tended to be a lack of professionalism, although it was possible for men of humble birth to reach top positions, as was clear from the career of William Lowndes in the early eighteenth century. Occasional attempts at reform were made within individual departments, and

[19] C. B. Otley, 'The educational background of British army officers', *Sociology*, 7 (1973), pp. 196–7.

[20] John Gooch, 'Army, society and politics in Britain, 1815–1914', *Social History Society Newsletter* (Spring 1984), p. 8.

[21] Harvey, *Britain in the Early Nineteenth Century*, pp. 23–24; Cannon, *Aristocratic Century*, p. 118. The upper reaches of the naval hierarchy have been less studied than those of the army.

[22] H. C. Tomlinson, *Guns and Government: the Ordnance Office under the later Stuarts* (1979), p. 71.

from time to time sinecures were abolished. This was not sufficient to produce a particularly efficient service, and by the 1830s loud complaints were being voiced to the effect that the public service ought not to suffer through the uncontrolled use of patronage. Although the consistent abolition of sinecures since the economical reforms of the 1780s had considerably reduced the number of pensions and posts, plenty of jobs were still in the gift of ministers. In 1854 the Northcote–Trevelyan report recommended a series of changes, including competitive entry, better pay and pensions, promotion on merit, and the division of the service into administrative, executive and clerical grades. Some of these reforms were brought in two years later as a result of public indignation at the incompetence revealed by the Crimean War, but it was only in 1870 that all vacancies except those in the Foreign Office were opened to competition. Even then, in practice, many posts were filled by nomination from the head of department, while the gentlemanly tradition of administration was perpetuated by gearing the examinations to the subjects taught in the public schools.[23]

Finally, the judiciary was the earliest branch of the executive to be freed from aristocratic domination, although this was by no means complete. The head of the service, the Lord Chancellor, was also Speaker of the House of Lords, and therefore inevitably a peer. Beneath him, until 1760 about half the judges came from the landowning class, but the number declined rapidly to only one-quarter in the period 1760–90, less than one-fifth between 1790 and 1850, and only 8 per cent in the third quarter of the nineteenth century. Even those who still came from the landowning sector tended to be the sons of middling and lesser gentry, although between 1727 and 1875 a total of 73 per cent of the judges owned some land. In general, however, the judiciary was increasingly drawn from the sons of upper-middle-class families with urban origins. This reflected the background they needed in law, and the political nature of appointments in the nineteenth century. Between 1832 and 1906 sixty-three of the eighty MPs appointed to the bench directly from the Commons attained the office while their own party was in power.[24] In addition, professionalism was encouraged by the reasonable rates of pay for the job in the nineteenth century. Chief justices of the Queen's Bench and Common Pleas received £8000 annually, and the twelve puisne judges of Queen's Bench, Common Pleas and the Exchequer received £5000 apiece.[25]

[23] P. G. Richards, *Patronage in British Government* (1963), pp. 19–61.
[24] Ibid., p. 123.
[25] David Duman, *The Judicial Bench in England, 1727–1875* (1982), p. 22.

THE HOUSE OF LORDS

The House of Lords was the seat of the peerage. All peers created within the English peerage prior to 1707, the British peerage between 1707 and 1800, and the United Kingdom peerage thereafter, as well as the twenty-six bishops (and the Irish bishops from 1801), were entitled to a seat in the House of Lords. Scottish and Irish peers were not eligible unless they sat as one of the sixteen Scottish or twenty-eight Irish representatives. Although its constitutional function remained more or less unimpaired until the Parliament Act of 1911, it is clear that for much of the eighteenth and nineteenth centuries the upper house was less significant as a decision-making body than the Commons. This development came about for two main reasons. First, the House of Lords was unable to establish a claim to intervene in taxation matters. The Commons supremacy in financial matters was challenged in the Lords in 1661 and 1692, and as late as 1782 Lord Shelburne was arguing that the upper house had a right to alter supply bills. In reality, the Lords finally accepted the Commons claim to financial control in 1692. Although this intrinsically weakened the upper house, it did not affect its prestige. When the electorate was extended in the nineteenth century, the position of the Lords was infrequently questioned, even though it remained unelected, and its members turned out to be decidedly conservative on major issues such as religion and the Irish question.[26]

The second reason for the loss of position by the upper house was that it became prey to party appointments and control, which reduced its effectiveness as an independent chamber. Party strife in the quarter of a century after the 1688 revolution brought in its wake alternative administrations of a Whig and Tory hue. Since the aristocracy showed a tendency to support the Whig cause, Tory ministries had difficulty managing the upper house, and the matter came to a head during Robert Harley's term of office between 1710 and 1714. Harley, himself created Earl of Oxford, and therefore able to survey the Lords at first hand, sought a compliant upper house by ranging behind him a loose coalition of peers holding government office, peers with court places or pensions (particularly the 'poor' lords whose financial needs were such that without assistance they were unable to perform a regular political function), and the sixteen Scottish representative peers, who were particularly anxious to curry court favour. Even with

[26] Cannon, *Aristocratic Century*, pp. 93–4; W. L. Arnstein, 'The survival of the Victorian aristocracy', in *The Rich, the Well Born and the Powerful*, ed. F. C. Jaher (Urbana, Ill. 1973), pp. 221–6.

exceptionally careful manipulation of this 'party of the Crown', Oxford was often in difficulty, and several times he hovered on the brink of defeat.[27] To ease his management problems, in 1711–12 he persuaded Queen Anne to shore up his position via the exceptional creation of twelve new peerages. In defence of Oxford it was argued that the ability of the Crown to make peers was a vital freedom in maintaining the equilibrium of a mixed monarchy, but against him the claim was made that the constitution was being endangered.[28]

Oxford fell from power shortly before Anne's death in 1714, but the peerage issue remained contentious and came to a head in 1719 when a Peerage Bill was introduced into Parliament with the intention of stabilizing the size of the upper house and preventing further mass creations. By its terms George I was to be permitted to create a further six British peers, and the terms of the Act of Union (1707) were to be altered to allow the Scots to send twenty-five hereditary peers to Westminster. When these moves had been completed, the monarch's prerogative was to be limited to replacing families whose line had failed.[29] Supporters of the bill argued that it would end the interminable wrangling over creations which had taken place since James I's reign, and that it would relieve the monarch of pressure to create peerages for political purposes — as was alleged to have taken place in 1711–12. In James Stanhope's words when defending the bill:

the numerous creations of late years had made more commoners think of peerage, than formerly used to do, that he did not speak without knowledge there had been great importunities of this kind, that though a king and a ministry might withstand them, yet such common virtue and steadiness was too great to be always expected in a Court that by a limitation the Crown would be eased of this burthen, and be secure against any arguments which commoners of wealth and power should bring when they pressed for peerage.[30]

---

[27] Edward Gregg and Clyve Jones, 'Hanover, pensions and the "poor lords", 1712–13', *Parliamentary History*, 1 (1982), pp. 173–80; Clyve Jones, '"The scheme lords, the necessitous lords, and the Scots lords": the Earl of Oxford's management and the "party of the crown" in the House of Lords, 1711–14', in *Parties and Management in Parliament, 1660–1784* (Leicester, 1984), pp. 123–67.

[28] Anon., *Reflections on a Paper lately Printed, Entitled, A Letter to Sir Miles Wharton concerning Occasional Peers* (1713).

[29] William Coxe, *Memoirs of the Life and Administration of Sir Robert Walpole*, new edn (1800), vol. I, pp. 201–17; E. R. Turner, 'The Peerage Bill of 1719', *English Historical Review*, 28 (1913), pp. 243–59.

[30] Brampton Bryan MSS, Bucknell, Shropshire, bundle 117x, Mr Gwynne to Edward Harley (?), 5 March 1719. I owe this reference to Clyve Jones, and I wish to thank Christopher Harley for allowing me to quote it.

A further argument was that by relieving the Crown of pressure the bill would act as a safeguard against the possibility of an extensive series of creations divesting the lower house of talent. In addition, these promotees might maintain their electoral interests when passing into the upper house – an argument which was still being used by Lord Liverpool in the early nineteenth century.[31] Finally, supporters argued that the vagaries of demography would always ensure plenty of room for future creations: 'by the vacancies that will happen, there will be always room to enable the Crown to reward the distinguished merit.'[32]

Opponents of the bill argued that it would create an imbalance in the constitution, by increasing executive influence over the Lords. Sir Robert Walpole, one of the loudest dissenters from the bill, argued that the artificial limit was likely 'to make our government aristocratical', while to others the bill seemed designed to turn the Lords into a closed elite.[33] In the end the bill was lost by 269 votes to 177, with perhaps the most telling argument being Walpole's insistence that it would deprive members of the Commons of the prospect of honour for virtuous actions. As he correctly perceived, the Commons was unlikely to agree to a measure designed to cut off its members and their posterity from the hope of future honours.[34] Yet, despite the bill's failure, it was not until the 1780s that political manipulation along party lines was attempted, and the only further threats of multiple creations in order to pass party measures came as a result of the Reform Bill in 1832, and the Parliament Act in 1911.[35]

---

[31] Anon., *Some Considerations Humbly Offered Relating to the Peerage of Great Britain* (1719), pp. 12–13; Michael W. McCahill, *Order and Equipoise: the peerage and the House of Lords, 1783–1806* (1978), p. 262; A. S. Turberville, *The House of Lords in the Age of Reform, 1784–1832* (1958), p. 47.

[32] Anon., *Some Considerations Humbly Offered relating to the Peerage of Great Britain* (1719), pp. 12–21; anon., *An Inquiry into the Manner of Creating Peers* (1719), pp. 73–4.

[33] *The Thoughts of a Member of the Lower House in relation to a Project for Restraining and Limiting the Power of the Crown in the Future Creation of Peers* (Sir Robert Walpole) (1719), p. 6; anon., *Six Questions Stated and Answered upon which the Whole Force of the Arguments for and against the PEERAGE BILL Depends* (1719), pp. 7–23.

[34] Coxe, *Memoirs of the Life and Administration of Sir Robert Walpole*, vol. I, pp. 215, 217.

[35] The events of 1711–12 were recalled by Horace Walpole when ten barons were created on a single day in 1776: *Complete Peerage*, vol. V (1926), p. 536n. Along with the Peerage Bill, these creations were again put under the microscope in 1832: for example: *The Prerogative of Creating Peers* (1832). However, Earl Grey had no intention of devaluing the peerage in 1832. His intention was to call up eldest sons in their fathers' baronies, to promote Scottish and Irish peers, and to ennoble some elderly and childless landed gentlemen: F. M. L. Thompson, *English Landed Society in the Nineteenth Century* (1963), p. 59. Events in England in 1719 were paralleled in

The failure of the Peerage Bill made little difference to the size of the peerage because of the Hanoverian monarchs' creation policy, but the absence of pressure to create more peers was essentially a consequence of the compliant nature of the post-1720 upper house. The Whiggish hue of the Lords was in tune with the political climate and the Commons majority. Walpole strengthened the party interest by appointing a predominantly Whig bench of bishops, to add to a core of support from peers in offices or positions of trust (including the dozen or so lords of the bedchamber who were particularly open to persuasion), the Scottish representatives, and a small coterie of pensioners numbering about a dozen by the 1750s.[36] Of itself this did not make the upper house into a pawn of the executive. House minorities still had the right to publish protests, and the use of proxies ensured that ministers always had to be on the lookout for trouble. The Scottish representative peers were more independent after the resolution of 1782 which overturned the 1711 order preventing Scottish peers with British titles from sitting in the House (unless elected as one of the representatives). However, the Lords continued to exercise a restraining influence on what might have been the more extravagant excesses of the Commons, and its effectiveness as a revising chamber meant that it was 'far from acting as George III's poodle'.[37] Revolts against the ministry in 1736 over the Quaker Tithes Bill,[38] in 1766 over Rockingham's American policy, and in 1783 over the India Bill, as well as peerage opposition to Addington's ministry in 1804, suggest that the Lords still had some political teeth, and this continued to be the case throughout the nineteenth century.[39]

More serious is the accusation that the upper house became a party-political football with the resurgence of political strife in the

---

Sweden the following year, and in Russia in 1730. In each instance the monarchy was temporarily weakened by a disputed inheritance: Cannon, *Aristocratic Century*, p. 4.

[36] Sir Lewis Namier, *The Structure of Politics at the Accession of George III*, 2nd edn (1957), pp. 221–5.

[37] M. W. McCahill, 'The Scottish peerage and the House of Lords in the late eighteenth century', *Scottish Historical Review*, 51 (1972), p. 176; *Order and Equipoise*, pp. 209–14; I. R. Christie, *Wars and Revolutions* (1982), p. 26.

[38] Stephen Taylor, 'Sir Robert Walpole, the Church of England and the Quakers' Tithe Bill of 1736', *Historical Journal*, 28 (1985), pp. 51–77. This bill was defeated in the House of Lords at its second reading, when the opposition included fifteen of the twenty-five bishops present, five of the nine Scottish peers present, and major Whig figures such as the dukes of Newcastle and Bedford.

[39] Cannon, *Aristocratic Century*, pp. 101–4, has argued that the rarity of government defeats in the upper house during George III's reign does not point in the direction of independence. Even the 1766 and 1783 defeats involved use of the king's name to justify opposition.

later years of the eighteenth century. Political considerations were often taken into account when a peerage was awarded. The Leveson-Gowers, for example, achieved an earldom in 1746 for their part in foiling the 1745 Jacobite uprising, a marquessate in 1786 for the second earl's part in defeating the Fox–North coalition, and finally a dukedom in 1833 for the second marquess's efforts in pushing through the Reform Act.[40] In the later eighteenth century, borough magnates also began to receive peerages, as the ministry sought to control their Commons interests. Among them were Sir James Lowther of Lowther (created Earl of Lonsdale), Thomas Pitt (Baron Camelford) and Sir Edward Eliot (Baron Eliot), all of whom were ennobled in 1784.[41] However, William Pitt was not interested merely in strengthening his own political position, because the partisanship of the later eighteenth-century Commons rarely translated to the Lords. When, on occasion, it did, opposition peers were usually no match for well-briefed ministerial supporters.[42] By contrast, the greater social range of the post-Pitt creations may have reflected the development of party considerations in the upper house, since those sent to the Lords between 1801 and 1830 as a reward for distinguished service constituted 50 per cent of all creations.[43] While ministers gave priority to the claims of victorious military commanders, successful diplomats and knowledgeable men of business, many landowners also crossed the divide. A correspondent of the *Gentleman's Magazine* believed that by promoting so many MPs to the Lords the ministers were 'taking out of the other house almost all the large landed property'.[44] The *Quarterly Review*, looking back in 1830 over fifty years of accelerated promotion, complained that 'the weight of landed gentry in the Chamber of Commons is now diminished almost to nothing.'[45]

If it had done nothing else, the promotion policy had turned the upper house into a profoundly conservative chamber. During the 1820s it established something of a reputation for defending the old constitution, first against Roman Catholic emancipation – which it

[40] J. R. Wordie, *Estate Management in Eighteenth-Century England* (1982), pp. 247, 254, 266.

[41] Sir Lewis Namier and John Brooke, *The House of Commons, 1754–1790* (1964), vol. I, p. 94.

[42] Turberville, *The House of Lords in the Age of Reform*, pp. 47–54.

[43] F. O'Gorman, *The Emergence of the British Two-Party System* (1982), pp. 65–6; McCahill, 'Peerage creations', pp. 269–72.

[44] *Gentleman's Magazine*, 84 (1814), pt I, p. 32.

[45] *Quarterly Review*, 42 (1830), p. 320. Pitt's peerages are discussed at greater length in chapter three above.

agreed to support only when the government took a lead – and later against the prospect of parliamentary reform. The decision to reject the second Reform Bill in October 1831, and subsequent attacks on members of the Lords, reflected the unpopularity of the upper house, but significantly 96 per cent of the peers with pre-1790 titles voted in *favour* of the bill, leaving it to the relative newcomers to reject the measure.[46] After 1832 many members believed that the House of Lords had been effectively castrated by its failure to prevent reform, but although weakened this did not turn out to be the case. In fact, the Lords reacted to reform by deliberately obstructing government measures, and a crisis arose over the 1835 Municipal Corporations Bill. The peers' willingness to hinder this legislation, despite warnings from Peel and Wellington about the dangers of obstruction, turned Lords reform into a major radical demand in the mid-1830s. Archibald Alison warned them in 1834 'the popular outcry which carried through the revolution of 1832 is that "the influence of the peers has increased, is increasing, and ought to be diminished"', and the following year saw the publication of a spate of anti-Lords pamphlets. Not untypical was 'Peter Jenkins', writing in 1835, who claimed that the aristocracy had ground the faces of their inferiors, and had shown no concern for the good of the country or the welfare of the people.[47] But municipal reform passed and the crisis evaporated. By the 1860s Bagehot lamented that Lords reform was no longer on the agenda: 'nobody asks that it should be so; it is quite safe against rough destruction, but it is not safe against inward decay.' The absence of antipathy towards the Lords was surprising in view both of the widening of the electorate, and of its continuing practice of obstructing government policy. In 1860, for example, the Lords refused to accept Gladstone's proposed repeal of the paper duties, and accepted the measure only when it was presented to them a year later as part of the annual budget.[48] However, the final showdown was postponed into the twentieth century, reflecting an impressive capacity for survival on the part of the Lords.

[46] Arnstein, 'The myth of the triumphant Victorian middle class', p. 216.

[47] Archibald Alison, 'Hints to the aristocracy: a retrospect of forty years', *Blackwood's Edinburgh Magazine*, 35 (1834), p. 71; Peter Jenkins, *A Letter to Isaac Tomkins Gent* (1835), pp. 3–7. Other pamphlets included Isaac Tomkins, *Thoughts upon the Aristocracy of England*, 11th edn (1835); anon., *Who Shall be our Leaders? Addressed to the People of England* (1835); anon., *The people or the Peerage?* (1835).

[48] Walter Bagehot, *The English Constitution* (1867; 1963 edn), p. 149; Norman Gash, *Aristocracy and People: Britain, 1815–1865* (1979), pp. 151–2, 171–2, 276.

THE HOUSE OF COMMONS

If the House of Lords was the natural home of the peerage in the mid-seventeenth century, the House of Commons was regarded as the debating chamber of the landed gentry. At that time the Commons consisted of representatives from forty English counties, 203 boroughs and two universities (489 members), twenty-four single-member Welsh constituencies, forty-five single-member Scottish constituencies (from 1707) and – from 1801 – 100 Irish members. Although some sons of peers, and Irish and Scottish peers, were returned at elections – totalling 8.7 per cent of the membership in 1640 – the lower house was considered to be the preserve of country gentlemen. Traditionally it was difficult for the executive to influence membership of the Commons, although James II tried to do so in 1685 and was in the middle of preparing elaborate measures in the autumn of 1688.[49] The key to management was generally for ministers to build a strong court interest once the House was elected, consisting of those MPs who for one reason or another could normally be expected to support the government in divisions. In the aftermath of the 1688 revolution, however, the importance of Parliament, and particularly of the lower house for taxation matters, strengthened the incentive for the executive – largely under peerage control – to intervene in the Commons. This could only take place at the expense of the independent country gentlemen, since government and personal patronage had to be used to build a strong court interest in the lower house. As a result, by the mid-eighteenth century an effective oligarchy had been created, although this was neither as static nor as unpopular as has sometimes been depicted.

The establishment of executive control of the Commons was brought about between 1688 and 1760 despite intense opposition from the country gentlemen. In the post-1660 period, elections were open, and the overall outcome was frequently in doubt. In recognition of this situation Charles II prolonged the compliant Cavalier Parliament in order to avoid electoral contests. During the exclusion crisis, identifiable political parties emerged for the first time, with the Tories claiming, among other things, to represent the backbone of society – the country gentlemen. However, in the 1679 and 1681 elections Tories sponsored by the majority of the gentry were repeatedly routed by Whigs with the support of only a handful of

---

[49] J. R. Jones, *Country and Court: England, 1658–1714* (1978), pp. 30–4; P. E. Murrell, 'Bury St Edmunds and the campaign to pack Parliament', *Bulletin of the Institute of Historical Research*, 54 (1981), pp. 188–206.

gentry, but with massive support from freeholders and urban voters.[50] The Tory country gentlemen resented losing their local influence to independent-minded Whig-led corporations. However, many regarded the 1688 revolution as a victory for property owners,[51] and their resentment of interloping interests (including great magnates sitting in the House of Lords) soon resurfaced in the Parliaments of the 1690s. Its inspiration was the efforts of the executive to build a strong court party. Thus the 1690–5 Parliament was known as the 'Officers' Parliament' owing to the large number of court dependants, among them army officers and civil servants. To counter this influence, the country gentlemen attempted to stem executive intervention with three separate but related campaigns over the length of Parliaments, the number of executive members in the Commons, and the qualification of MPs. On all three counts they failed, and, although this did not mean a wholly subservient lower house, by the mid-eighteenth century the Commons was more obviously under the influence of the executive. The fact that the four leading prime ministers of the eighteenth century sat in the Commons indicates the executive's need to control business, rather than its ability to dictate membership.[52]

The length of Parliaments was a key concern in the 1690s, and was largely dictated by the Triennial Act of 1694. Short Parliaments were believed to make it unprofitable for ministers to use patronage or corruption to build a court interest, but the legislation also proved to have unforeseen consequences.[53] Between the passing of the legislation, and its repeal in 1716, when seven-year Parliaments were introduced, elections were held on average every eighteen months. If this prevented the executive from obtaining a grip on the Commons, it also produced a fever-pitch of electoral activity which was intensified by the animosities over religion, the French wars, and the succession beyond Queen Anne, into what J. H. Plumb has termed the 'rage of party'. Squeezed by falling rent rolls, and by a land tax of four shillings in the pound that they voluntarily imposed upon themselves to prevent

---

[50] Jones, *Country and Court*, pp. 67–8.

[51] Angus McInnes, 'The revolution and the people', in *Britain after the Glorious Revolution*, ed. Geoffrey Holmes (1969), pp. 80–1.

[52] The 'country' interest extended beyond the issues discussed here. It is treated at greater length by Colin Brooks, 'The country persuasion and political responsibility in England: the 1690s', *Parliament, Estates and Representation*, 4, 2 (1984), pp. 135–46; and David Hayton, 'The "country" interest and the party system, 1689–1720', in *Party and Management in Parliament, 1660–1784*, ed. C. Jones (Leicester, 1984), pp. 37–85.

[53] Triennial Acts had been passed before: in 1641, to prevent a repetition of Charles I's eleven years without Parliament; and in 1664, although this was a much weaker measure which Charles II effectively ignored.

the monarch from gaining greater control of taxation, the landed gentry were in no position to contest frequent, and often expensive, elections. However, electoral compromise was less likely during the twenty-five years after the revolution than at any other time during the eighteenth century. In the seven elections between 1701 and 1715, 12–26 English counties and 67–104 boroughs went to the polls, an average of between 35 and 52 per cent of all constituencies.

Party conflict pushed up the cost of such activity. While many gentlemen might be prepared to spend £100 on a contest, especially if the polls were opened infrequently, they were reluctant to consider laying out £500 on a single contest, especially if the exercise might have to be repeated again within three years. With this increase in electoral activity, boroughs became expert in extracting large sums from potential candidates, usually in the form of entertainment, or via fees and donations. Moreover, the cost did not stop at the election, since about 75 per cent of contests were only finally adjudicated in the House of Commons itself. Presenting a petition, or mounting a defence against one, was expensive, and many lesser gentlemen were simply unable to compete. When franchises were contested in the Commons, Whig administrations almost always found in favour of the narrower alternative, thus restricting the political nation, and making influence easier to operate. Gradually, as a result, the Whigs were able to convert their strength in the boroughs into an overwhelming political control in the nation, despite the fact that in terms of votes cast the Tories would have won nearly every general election in the first half of the eighteenth century.[54]

The rising cost of electioneering worked against the landed gentry, particularly as peers considered the increased role of the Commons to be fair grounds for electoral intervention. Interference by peers in elections was not new in the 1690s; indeed, they had been prominent in the exclusion crisis elections of 1679 and 1681, and in 1701 the Commons actually resolved 'that for any Lord of Parliament, or any Lord Lieutenant of any county, to concern themselves in the elections of members to serve for the Commons in Parliament, the same is a high infringement of the liberties and privileges of the Commons of

---

[54] J. H. Plumb, *The Growth of Political Stability in England, 1675–1725* (1967), pp. 94–104; Eveline Cruikshanks, *Political Untouchables: the Tories and the '45* (1979), p. 5; Linda Colley, *In Defiance of Oligarchy: the Tory Party, 1714–1760* (Cambridge, 1982), pp. 118–45.

England.'[55] However, the evidence clearly points to increasing activity. Even while the party battles were at their height between 1694 and 1716, the independence of a small number of boroughs was being eroded, particularly in the vulnerable burgage boroughs (where the vote was linked to the property). In Yorkshire, Thirsk was brought up by Sir Thomas Frankland during William III's reign and allowed no further contest after 1695, while the Whig Party leader, the Earl of Wharton, spent £1293 on twenty-one of the 250 Richmond burgages in 1705 in order to secure an interest. Overall, electoral strife and costly contests worked against the country gentlemen who had promoted three-year Parliaments, and, even while the political system was more representative in the post-revolution period than it was to be again before 1832, the seeds of future oligarchy were being sown.[56] The passing of the Septennial Act in 1716 marked the defeat of the country gentlemen and provided a further boost to aristocratic control of the Commons.

The second country campaign of the 1690s concerned the composition of the lower house. To show their commitment to the 1688 revolution, the landed gentry in the Commons consistently voted sums of money towards the war efforts of William III on a level that they had not seriously contemplated in the past. They forswore a general excise, which would have taxed the whole nation more equitably, and instead accepted the full weight of the tax burden.[57] In such circumstances they believed it to be only right that landed gentlemen should sit in Parliament, and placemen sitting at the behest of the court represented a canker in the system, an executive curtailment of the Commons' independence. Government officials and military officers had constituted one-quarter of the membership of the Cavalier Parliament, and more than 30 per cent of James II's only Parliament, but after the revolution country gentlemen were convinced that the influence of these groups was increasing and ought to be curtailed. They were particularly incensed by MPs who took up office after election to the Commons, and legislation in 1694, 1700 and 1701 barred a number of important groups of revenue officers.

The place clause in the 1701 Act of Settlement gave a significant boost to the campaign. The Act, passed to secure the Protestant succession, was not to come into force until Queen Anne's death, but,

---

[55] *CJ*, 13 (3 January 1701), p. 648.

[56] Plumb, *The Growth of Political Stability*, pp. 79–80; Geoffrey Holmes, *The Electorate and the National Will in the First Age of Party* (Kendal, 1976), p. 6.

[57] J. V. Beckett, 'Land tax or excise: the levying of taxation in seventeenth- and eighteenth-century England', *English Historical Review*, 100 (1985), pp. 285–308.

as a result of the ambiguous wording of the clause, by the spring of 1702 almost all petitions presented to the House brought exclusion when a placeman was involved.[58] The campaign continued throughout Anne's reign, particularly during the Tory ministries, but further success came only with the Regency Act in 1706. This legislation excluded MPs from a variety of offices, many of them to do with supplying the armed forces, while the old principle was reinstated whereby members appointed to offices which were not specifically listed as disqualifying their holders from office had to vacate their seats but could seek re-election, thus giving voters the right to endorse the appointment.[59] Overall, a brake was applied to Crown influence, but little more was achieved, partly because with frequent elections the ability of the Crown to influence the Commons was in any case restricted, and partly because too little attention was paid to the Lords. Ironically, place bills in 1712 and 1714 failed by margins in the upper house which could not have occurred but for the creation of Oxford's dozen new peers in 1711–12. Although place bills were almost an annual event until 1715, the campaign lost impetus. Bills were regularly defeated in the Lords in the later 1720s, and 1730s, and further restrictive legislation was introduced in 1734 and 1752, but Crown influence was not a serious issue again until the 1770s and 1780s, when the matter was raised in the rather different context of economical and parliamentary reform.[60]

The failure of the place campaign resulted in a lower house that was increasingly influenced by executive members. About 125 MPs were placemen in Queen Anne's reign, and, with more jobs available as a result of the expansion of government during the war years, the ability of the executive to influence the Commons was enhanced. Between 1714 and 1720 the number increased to around 155–70. and under Walpole it stood at 185, or one-third of the lower house. The Duke of Argyle claimed in 1741 that 'most of [the] flag officers are in the House of Commons', and between 1715 and 1790 fifty to sixty army officers

[58] As a younger son, James Lowther decided his Ordance post was more valuable than a Commons seat, and consequently abandoned Carlisle in 1702: J. V. Beckett, 'A back-bench MP in the eighteenth century: Sir James Lowther of Whitehaven', *Parliamentary History*, 1 (1982), pp. 80–1.

[59] W. A. Speck, *Stability and Strife: England, 1714–1760* (1977), pp. 15–16; David Hayton, 'The reorientation of place legislation in England in the 1690s', *Parliaments, Estates and Representation*, 5, 2 (1985), pp. 103–8.

[60] G. S. Holmes, 'The attack on "the influence of the crown", 1702–16', *Bulletin of the Institute of Historical Research*, 39 (1966), pp. 48–68; Betty Kemp, *King and Commons, 1660–1832* (1957), pp. 51–64.

were to be found in most Parliaments.[61] By 1761 the court administration group had risen to 250. In addition, the reliability of these men in divisions appears to have increased, although they could never be taken for granted: placemen could not save Lord North's ministry in 1782, nor Lord Shelburne's the following year. On questions of principle and conscience they might also desert the ministry, as Walpole found in relation to the excise scheme of 1733, and Lord North was to discover in the 1780s.[62] Although the reduction in places from 1780 onwards diminished the numerical support of the ministry, and the importance of party undercut the significance of placemen in the nineteenth century, exclusion from the Commons was long delayed.[63]

The third country campaign which began in the 1690s was part of a concerted effort to introduce property qualifications for positions of responsibility in central and local government. As with short Parliaments and place bills, the aim was to preserve the independence of the lower house, in this case by excluding men lacking sufficient property. The logic of the argument was unimpeachable. Between 1654 and 1660 a £200 qualification had existed, and in 1656 James Harrington argued that only those who owned the land of a country had the right to make its laws. It was a tradition which reappeared in the work of most major eighteenth-century political philosophers, including Locke, Hume – who wanted to restrict political activity to those with considerable property – and Burke. In addition, it was not a divisive party issue. It was the Whig Earl of Shaftesbury who attempted to reintroduce the interregnum qualification in 1679, but in the 1690s the country mantle fell on the Tories. Thus when a qualification was finally introduced in 1710 it was the work of a Tory administration.[64] After 1688 the demand for qualifications for MPs was both part of the country attempt to preserve the institutional power of the landowners

[61] W. L. Guttsman, 'The British political elite and the class structure', in *Elites and Power in British Society*, ed. P. Stanworth and A. Giddens (Cambridge, 1974), p. 23; R. Sedgwick, *The House of Commons, 1715–1754* (1970), vol. I, p. 155; Namier and Brooke, *The House of Commons, 1754–1790*, vol. I, p. 141.

[62] L. Namier, *England in the Age of the American Revolution*, 2nd edn (1963), p. 228; Speck, *Stability and Strife*, pp. 222, 239; J. Brooke, *The House of Commons, 1754–1790* (Oxford, 1964), p. 185.

[63] The influence of place in the nineteenth century will be clearer when the relevant volumes of the *History of Parliament* are published.

[64] M. L. Bush, *The English Aristocracy* (Manchester, 1984), p. 201; A. P. Thornton, *The Habit of Authority* (1966), p. 62; R. A. Kelch, 'The dukes: a study of the English nobility in the eighteenth century' (Ohio State University, Ph.D. thesis, 1955), ch. 2.

– threatened with usurpation by the exclusion crisis and the revolution – and also an attempt to exclude placemen, officers and, in particular, the new monied men, grown rich by lending to the government in the financially pinched 1690s.

Landed gentlemen believed that political responsibility should be confined to men of property. As such they were prepared to tax themselves to support the war effort, and not surprisingly they looked askance at the appearance in the Commons of military officers and government financiers, who made no financial contribution to the war. James Lowther told his Cumberland steward in 1708 that 'there is mighty clamours against having so many officers of the army in the House', and he opined sagely that 'there never was more need for men of estates to be chosen, when officers of the army and merchants of London are jostling the landed men everywhere out of their elections.' Henry St John complained bitterly in 1709 of the problems of the landed interest: 'a new interest has been created out of their fortunes and a sort of property which was not known twenty years ago is now increased to be almost equal to the terra firma of our island.' It was the financiers who called forth Jonathan Swift's acid remark that 'the wealth of the nation, that used to be reckoned by the value of land, is now computed by the rise and fall of stocks.'[65]

The validity of these claims has to be placed in context, since landed gentry had never held the monopoly of power that such comments imply. In the Parliaments of the period 1660–90 only 53 per cent of members were mere country gentlemen. For the rest, 12 per cent were placemen, 10 per cent were army or navy officers, 14 per cent were lawyers and 9 per cent were merchants. Almost two-thirds of the merchants had no other occupation, but a quarter acquired country estates, usually before election to Parliament.[66] Even so, the country gentlemen felt threatened, and the means of protecting their position appeared to be in property qualifications. Agitation began in Parliament in 1695, and bills were introduced in each of the following

---

[65] Carlisle RO, D/Lons/W, James Lowther to William Gilpin, 12 February 1708; G. S. Holmes and W. A. Speck, *The Divided Society: parties and politics in England, 1694–1716* (1967), pp. 134–6; Jonathan Swift, *The Examiner*, 13, 2 November 1710. Country opposition to the 'monied interest' is discussed at greater length in H. T. Dickinson, *Liberty and Property* (1977), pp. 170–1.

[66] Basil Duke Henning, *The House of Commons, 1660–1690* (1983), vol. I, pp. 6–10. It is possible that landed gentlemen seemed to be firmly entrenched because of a post-Restoration reaction in their favour. This seems to have been the case in Shropshire and Cheshire: M. D. G. Wanklyn, 'Landownership, political authority and social status in Shropshire and Cheshire, 1500–1700', *West Midlands Studies*, 10 (1978), pp. 25–6.

two years. Both were defeated, the first by William III after protests from the mercantile community, and the second in the upper house.[67] The issue was revived after the Tory election victory of 1702, and a further bill passed through the Commons only to be defeated in the Lords. There the matter rested until the swing of the political pendulum again brought a Tory government to power in 1710. In December that year a private member's bill was introduced, which was quickly taken over by the government and passed to Henry St John. His main argument in favour of the bill was that 'we might see a time when the monied men might bid fair to keep out of that House all the landed men.'[68] It passed into law in the spring of 1711. A knight of the shire was required to have an income of £600 per annum from freehold or copyhold lands, and a borough member £300. The four university and forty-five Scottish seats were excluded, and the bill's terms did not extend to the eldest sons of peers or to the heirs of country gentlemen with more than £600 a year.

For most Tories the legislation was a relief, and some spoke optimistically of one-third of the current membership's being excluded from the House, with placemen, lawyers, army officers and City men all receiving marching orders. Jonathan Swift summed up the mood:

The Qualification-Bill, incapacitating all men to serve in Parliament, who have not some Estate in land, either in possession or certain reversion, is perhaps the greatest security that ever was contrived for preserving the constitution, which otherwise might in a little time, lie wholly at the mercy of the monied interest. And, since much the greatest part of the taxes is paid, either immediately from land, or from its productions, it is but common justice that those who are the proprietors should appoint what portion of it ought to go to the support of the public.[69]

Unfortunately the legislation did not have the desired effect. Although the Whigs were still out of favour at the time of the 1713 election, they managed to return a sizeable City cohort, and while the military, legal and financial groups were reduced in size the House was not purified in the manner envisaged by some country gentlemen. Even the ministry which had passed the legislation connived at some flagrant breaches of the letter or spirit of the law. Lord Treasurer Oxford put up a relation at Aldborough whose qualification was widely doubted, while a client of Henry St John was returned at Truro who lacked either personal or

[67] Horwitz, *Parliament, Policy and Politics*, pp. 168, 177, 187, 189, 216, 218.
[68] Quoted in Holmes and Speck, *The Divided Society*, pp. 135–6.
[69] Jonathan Swift, *The Examiner*, 44, 7 June 1711.

landed estate. When the Whigs bounded back into power in 1715, they did so largely by ignoring the Act, so much so that a Tory lawyer admitted: 'I never saw any like it. Between the Army and the City there's very little room left for the Country Gentlemen.'[70] Within a few years, one country Whig had come to the conclusion that the qualification was too minor an issue to warrant a petition: James Lowther believed he could have unseated Gilfrid Lawson, who defeated him in the 1722 Cumberland election, but 'to petition . . . only upon the point of the qualification is too nice a matter.'[71]

The legislation failed because it was unenforceable. Until 1760 unsuccessful candidates might harass the victor on the basis of his qualification, but the onus of proof lay with the petitioner, and this presented considerable problems. A standing order of 1717 required petitioners to lodge with the Clerk of the House a statement of their own qualifications, which was to protect members who were challenged. By 1722 the process of fictitious qualification was enabling members to circumvent the law. A candidate could take on the title to a property before an election, and retransfer it after he was safely in the House. Efforts to prevent such conveyances included a motion in 1731 to have MPs investigated to discover whether they sat 'contrary to law'. This was rejected by 83 votes to 37. Although country Tories continued to press for the enforcement of the law, these technical problems ensured that few petitions were successful. After the 1713 election Sir Roger Bradshaigh was challenged at Wigan on the grounds that he did not have £300 real property, but the first known successful unseating was in 1735 when John Boteler, who had been returned for Wendover in 1734, lost his seat to Lord Limerick.[72]

Although the law was seldom enforced, the qualification issue did not go away. In 1760 legislation was passed to enforce the provisions by requiring MPs to deliver to the House a signed schedule showing the location of the lands providing their qualification. Since this was to be done before they took their seats, and they were to swear an oath that the lands produced the necessary annual income, it was clearly designed to catch fictitious qualifications. The Duke of Newcastle objected to the 'great inconvenience' to MPs of having to produce their

---

[70] Holmes, *British Politics in the Age of Anne*, pp. 178–82.

[71] Carlisle RO, D/Lons/L, Checklist 16, James Lowther to Lord Lonsdale, 13 May 1722.

[72] Dickinson, *Liberty and Property*, p. 168; W. A. Speck, *Tory and Whig: the struggle in the constituencies, 1701–15* (1970), p. 37. For an impassioned plea on behalf of the qualification, see *Gentleman's Magazine* 10 (1740), p. 448.

rental, but in practice the legislation made little difference.[73] Elections were voided on the qualification issue at Honiton in 1781, and at Colchester three years later, but potential members continued to be provided with a qualification by a friend. Lord Verney served Edmund Burke in this way between 1761 and 1774, and Lord Temple provided John Wilkes with a qualification in Middlesex in 1768. Other notable politicians similarly helped included Pitt, Fox, Sheridan and Wilberforce. Sometimes banks provided a rent charge, but many members were simply returned with or without a qualification. When Daniel Pulteney was elected for Bramber in 1784 without a qualification, he claimed that one-third of the House was in the same position, and in 1793 Charles Grey calculated that out of 558 members 307 were returned by patrons.[74] No one contradicted Sir William Molesworth's claim in 1838 that half the members sat on fictitious qualifications. The law was amended that year to allow personal property to rank with real estate, but the £600 and £300 figures remained until 1858. Over the whole period 1711–1858 hundreds of members must have sworn to property that they did not own, even though there were probably not more than ten instances of exclusion as a result.[75]

Did property qualifications have any impact upon the system? The fact that their abolition turned up among the six points demanded by the Chartists is testimony to their psychological significance. They symbolized the view that leadership was supposed to rest with those who had a significant stake in the land and property of the nation. Moreover, a man with land in the constituency seemed somehow better qualified for membership. As Lord Shelburne told his son in 1789, to facilitate his return at Chipping Wycombe it would be helpful to solicit the support of Mr Tollemache: 'you will likewise state it to him as more particularly your interest as I have in fact given up the estate and everything there to you.'[76] At the same time, far from protecting the interests of the landed gentry against the monied men, the legislation ultimately facilitated the strengthening of executive control in the

---

[73] 33 Geo. II c. 20 (1760); *CJ*, 28 (1760), p. 741; BL Add. MSS, 32,988, fol. 418.

[74] Thornton, *The Habit of Authority*, p. 63; Brooke, *The House of Commons, 1754–1790*, p. 185.

[75] E. and A. G. Porritt, *The Unreformed House of Commons* (Cambridge, 1909), vol. I, pp. 166–79, provides the fullest account of the impact of property qualifications.

[76] Clements Library, Marquess of Lansdowne (Shelburne) Papers, bundle 'letters to his son 1780–89', letter of 26 January 1789.

Commons. The failure to exclude peers' sons and the sons of qualified members from the terms of the legislation, proved in the longer term immensely beneficial to the executive in its attempts to control the Commons.

ARISTOCRATIC CONTROL OF PARLIAMENTARY SEATS

The failure of country measures to preserve the position of landed gentlemen in Parliament against the encroachments of the executive enabled the peers to gain a firm foothold in the lower house, which they did by gathering safe seats under their wing, and then by placing members of their families in them. Boroughs with small electorates were open to electoral corruption, and several were brought under control even in the turbulent political atmosphere of the post-revolution decades. Closing a borough became increasingly practicable with the Septennial Act of 1716. Longer Parliaments pushed up the cost of contests, partly because an outlay was required only half as often as previously. To avoid expense, and the near certainty of a petition if the result was close, potential patrons looked to secure themselves in the smaller boroughs to ensure the return of their candidate with little or no outlay. If necessary this could be achieved by a once-and-for-all payment, particularly in the twenty-nine English burgage boroughs. Seventeen of these were effectively closed by 1754, and of the remainder one ceased to be a borough by 1790, eight were closed, and only three remained open to any significant extent.[77] Burgages changed hands for large sums of money. Sir William Lowther of Swillington sold 86 to George Morton Pitt in 1741 for £9600, while at Appleby in 1754 the Earl of Thanet paid £18,051 for 60, and at Bletchingly in 1779 John Kenrick acquired Sir Robert Clayton's 90 for £10,000.[78] Much greater sums were also paid on occasion. The young Sir James Lowther of Lowther spent £58,000 buying up Cockermouth in 1756; the Earl of Egremont bought Midhurst from the executors of the seventh Viscount Montagu of Cowdray for £40,000 in 1787, and sold it again in the 1790s to the first Lord Carrington for £34,000; the Duke of Bedford sold off practically all of Camelford in 1812 for £32,000; and Gatton in Surrey changed hands for £180,000 only two

---

[77] Namier and Brooke, *The House of Commons, 1754–1790*, vol. I, pp. 33–4.

[78] Sedgwick, *The House of Commons, 1715–1754*, vol. I, pp. 335, 361; Namier and Brooke, *The House of Commons, 1754–1790*, vol. I, pp. 384–5; Brian Bonsall, *Sir James Lowther and Cumberland and Westmorland Elections, 1754–1775* (Manchester, 1960), p. 34.

years before the Reform Act.[79] Other boroughs, particularly those
controlled by small corporations, also proved susceptible to patronage,
while generally, although not inevitably, the larger the electorate the
more likely it was that a borough would remain open. Even the
eternally optimistic Duke of Chandos bit off more than he could chew
at the Hereford by-election of 1717, where a constituency of
1200–1400 voters was prepared to stand and fight.[80]

Measuring the full extent of borough patronage is complicated.
Geoffrey Holmes's finding was that in 1702 peers controlled twenty
boroughs (thirty-one MPs). By 1713 the number of controlled
boroughs had risen to twenty-eight (forty-five MPs).[81] However, with
the benefit of the *History of Parliament* data, John Cannon has
calculated that in 1715 forty-eight English boroughs were under
partial or total peerage control, returning sixty-eight MPs. Peers also
controlled a number of English county seats, two Welsh seats and
twenty-three in Scotland, giving them 105 seats, or one-fifth of the
lower house. By 1747 this total had risen to 167 seats, and by the end
of 1784 to over 200. Almost all of this increase took place in English
boroughs and, to a lesser extent, counties.[82] For 1761 Sir Lewis
Namier calculated that fifty-five peers controlled 111 seats, and
fifty-six commoners another ninety-four. Together with thirty or so
under government patronage, this suggested a total of 235 under some
form of control.[83] J. A. Phillips has also included both peers and
commoners in assessing the extent of patronage. He has calculated that
in 1690 153 borough seats were influenced by patrons, of which 133
were under private patronage. The number rose to 214 in 1734, and to
270 by 1790, with the proportion under private patronage increasing
from 32.8 per cent in 1690 to 65.2 per cent a century later. The
critical rise was from 183 in 1734 to 224 in 1761, reflecting the
intense activity of the mid-century decades.[84] The peak of influence

[79] J. V. Beckett, 'The making of a pocket borough: Cockermouth, 1722–56',
Journal of British Studies, 20 (1980), pp. 140–57; Namier and Brooke, *The House of
Commons, 1754–1790*, vol. I, pp. 395–6; H. A. Wyndham, *A Family History* (1950),
pp. 241–2.

[80] Clyve Jones, 'James Brydges, Earl of Caernarvon, and the 1717 Hereford
by-election: a case study in aristocratic electoral management', *Huntington Library
Quarterly*, 46 (1983), pp. 310–20.

[81] Cannon, *Aristocratic Century*, pp. 105–6, citing G. S. Holmes, 'The influence of
the peerage on English parliamentary elections, 1702–13' (University of Oxford,
B.Litt. thesis, 1952).

[82] Ibid., pp. 106–12.

[83] Namier, *The Structure of Politics*, pp. 148–9.

[84] John A. Phillips, *Electoral Behaviour in Unreformed England* (Princeton, NJ,
1982), pp. 53–7.

seems to have come in the first decade of the nineteenth century. Peerage patronage rose from 210 in 1786 to 226 by 1802 and to 236 in 1807. It then began to slip, remaining at over 200 down to 1830, but falling to 191 in 1831.[85]

Parliamentary reform in 1832 swept away many of the pocket boroughs but it did not destroy aristocratic influence; indeed, at least fifty-nine and possibly over seventy members of the lower house continued to appear through the good offices of a patron, and over forty peers could still virtually nominate a representative in the lower house.[86] In some counties, aristocratic interests were actually stengthened. Both Lincolnshire and Derbyshire were divided for electoral purposes in 1832 with this result. Lord Yarborough had the strongest political interest in the undivided county of Lincolnshire, and after 1832 he held North Lincolnshire virtually as a pocket constituency. In Derbyshire the influence of the dukes of Devonshire was concentrated in the county's northern division after 1832, with the result that two Whigs were returned at every election until 1867, and the western division of the county – carved out in 1868 – remained a family fief down to 1914 and even later.[87] None the less, there were a few signs of change. In County Durham aristocratic patrons found it necessary to respond to the inclinations of the county, and in the northern division this entailed avoiding contests and splitting the representation between the parties.[88] In South Nottinghamshire, an area predominantly in the hands of great landowners, the smaller owner-occupiers and large tenant farmers successfully opposed the aristocrats to bring in a candidate at the 1851 by-election, and they were able to hold the seat until 1885.[89]

[85] J. J. Sack, 'The House of Lords and parliamentary patronage in Great Britain, 1802–1832', *Historical Journal*, 23 (1980), pp. 913–37. Alternatively, F. M. L. Thompson, *English Landed Society in the Nineteenth Century* (1963), p. 47, has suggested that 177 individuals (87 peers and 90 commoners) influenced the return of 355 members (213 and 137).

[86] Norman Gash, *Politics in the Age of Peel* (1953), pp. 213, 438–9.

[87] R. J. Olney, *Lincolnshire Politics, 1832–1885* (Oxford, 1973), pp. 231–30; G. E. Hogarth, 'The Derbyshire parliamentary election of 1832', *Derbyshire Archaeological Journal*, 89 (1969), pp. 68–85; 'The 1835 elections in Derbyshire', *Ante*, 94 (1974), pp. 45–59; 'Derby and Derbyshire elections, 1837–47', *Ante*, 95 (1975), pp. 45–58. The so-called 'Chandos clause' in the 1832 Act may have been responsible for notable landlord gains in the counties: Donald Southgate, *The Passing of the Whigs, 1832–1886* (1962), p. 83.

[88] T. J. Nossiter, *Influence, Opinion and Political Idioms in Reformed England* (1975), pp. 45–78.

[89] J. R. Fisher, 'The basis of parliamentary representation in a nineteenth-century rural constituency: South Nottinghamshire, 1851–1885', (paper read in the University of Nottingham, December 1984).

Proprietory boroughs survived after 1832, and radical attacks at the height of aristocratic unpopularity in 1835 included the suggestion that a Tory return to power would herald the overthrow of reform and the restitution of corrupt borough corporations.[90] Grimsby lost a seat in 1832, but Lord Yarborough retained the right to nominate to the one that remained. The Marquess of Westminster still controlled Chester, and Earl Fitzwilliam was still able to regard Malton as being in his pocket – at least until he had to fight the first post-1832 election there in 1874. In Stamford, the Marquess of Exeter's control actually increased. The replacement of the scot and lot franchise by the £10 householder clause reduced the number of voters, and by limiting the number of new houses Exeter successfully maintained family control. The situation was partially undermined in 1867 when Stamford lost one seat, and the number of voters doubled, but Exeter's candidates were returned for the single seat until the borough lost its parliamentary status in 1885. Even after that, the Marquess of Exeter returned a member for the parliamentary division of Stamford until 1906.[91] Elsewhere proprietors were not so fortunate. Buckingham, for example, appears to have remained a pocket borough after 1832 in the control of the Duke of Buckingham, but close study reveals that the family interest was in fact considerably weakened by reform.[92] In Cardiff, the second Marquess of Bute was sufficiently concerned about his post-reform prospects to start a Tory newspaper as a means of protecting his interest. He returned his nominee at the first post-reform election, and retained the family position until 1848, but during the minority which followed his death the position slipped, and even after laying out £10,000 in 1868 the third marquess was unable to stage a recovery.[93] Despite these setbacks, landed 'influence' can be traced in forty boroughs and nineteen counties in England and Wales

---

[90] Anon., *The Peers: or, the People. A Word of Advice to the Electors of the British Empire* (1835); Gash, *Politics in the Age of Peel*, p. 204; Thompson, *English Landed Society*, pp. 48–9.

[91] Olney, *Lincolnshire Politics*; J. M. Lee, 'Modern Stamford', in *The Making of Stamford*, ed. A. Rogers (Leicester, 1965), pp. 91–115; H. J. Hanham, *Elections and Party Management: politics in the time of Disraeli and Gladstone* (1959), pp. 409–10.

[92] R. W. Davis, 'Deference and aristocracy in the time of the Great Reform Act', *American Historical Review*, 81 (1976), pp. 532–9.

[93] John Davies, 'Aristocratic town makers and the coal metropolis: the marquesses of Bute and Cardiff, 1776–1947', in *Patricians, Power and Politics in Nineteenth-Century Towns*, ed. David Cannadine (Leicester, 1982), pp. 41–51. Of aristocrats on the Liberal side returned between 1832 and 1865, more than one-quarter were from boroughs which had under 300 voters in 1832: Southgate, *The Passing of the Whigs*, p. 96.

after 1868, which suggests that approximately one-eighth of the seats remained under patronage. This was possible for a combination of reasons, including the continued county–borough constituency division, the favourable balance enjoyed by rural areas, and the absence until 1872 of a secret ballot.[94]

Once they controlled the seats, the aristocracy expected to be able to fill them with their own nominees. In many cases these were sons and closely connected clients. Sons of English, Scottish and Irish peers, and Irish peers, represented little more than 10 per cent of the House in the strife-torn years at the beginning of the eighteenth century, but between the 1740s and the 1832 Reform Act their numbers seldom dropped below one-fifth. Nor are these figures the full measure of the connection. In 1754, in addition to 113 Irish peers and sons of other peers, the House included 45 grandsons of peers, 33 MPs married to daughters of peers, 22 nephews of peers, 8 brothers and 7 brothers-in-law of peers, and one foreign nobleman, or, to put it another way, 41 per cent of the House before cousins and political clients are taken into account. In the 1761 Parliament, 28 MPs were Irish peers or their sons, 81 were sons of English peers, and 10 were sons of Scottish peers, while in 1784 peers' relations and baronets together totalled 54 per cent of the House.[95] Contemporary observers must have regarded the House as something of an aristocratic family gathering. In 1715, 42 per cent of MPs had fathers who had served in the House, and this figure stood at over 50 per cent in 1754. If close relatives are added, well over 70 per cent of members in 1754 had, or had had, close relatives in the House. Over the whole period 1734–1832, 60 per cent of MPs were drawn from 922 families, and 30 per cent from a mere 247.[96]

Nor did the situation change greatly after 1832. Of 815 MPs between 1841 and 1847, 8 were Irish peers, 172 were the sons of peers, 27 were grandsons and great-grandsons of peers (25 per cent), while 82 were baronets and 53 were sons, grandsons and great-

---

[94] Hanham, *Elections and Party Management*, pp. 405–12.

[95] The fullest analysis of eighteenth-century family connections is found in Cannon, 'The isthmus repaired', p. 447, and *Aristocratic Century*, pp. 112–13. For 1761, see Namier, *The Structure of Politics*, p. 73, and *England in the Age of the American Revolution* (1930), p. 262. Other figures are given in Mary Ransome, 'Some recent studies of the composition of the House of Commons', *University of Birmingham Historical Journal*, 6 (1958), pp. 139–41.

[96] Guttsman, 'The British political elite and the class structure', p. 25; Cannon, *Aristocratic Century*, p. 115. In 1928 only 2 per cent of MPs had a father who had served in the Commons.

grandsons of baronets (16.6 per cent). Add to this 240 MPs who were in direct line of male descent to families in Burke's *Landed Gentry*, and 71 per cent of the House had close links with land, or nearly 80 per cent if descent through wives and mothers is allowed.[97] Down to the 1860s, one-third of all MPs had aristocratic connections. Bernard Cracroft, writing about electoral reform on the eve of the 1867 Act, pointed out that in August 1865 the lower house included 71 baronets, 30 sons and grandsons of baronets, and 101 sons and 15 grandsons of peers. In addition, he found another 100 members connected by marriage or descent.[98] Even in 1868, 407 MPs came from families owning 2000 acres or more, and of 111 owners of 50,000 or more acres in Great Britain and Ireland 59 held a Commons seat.[99] Thereafter numbers began to fall. In 1880, for example, just 322 MPs were owners of 2000 acres or more. But the decline should not be exaggerated; in the mid-1880s Adam Badeau noted that 'it is through the House of Commons that the aristocracy has long exercised a great portion of its sway', and he added that 'there are few noblemen today who are unable to secure the return of their eldest son to the House of Commons.'[100] Even in 1895, 60 per cent of MPs were gentlemen of leisure, country squires, retired officers and lawyers, and there were still 23 eldest sons of peers in the House.[101] Howard Evans calculated two years later that no less than 176 MPs were connected to the peerage through birth or marriage,[102] and during the same decade Lord Eversley noted that 'ever since [1832] until quite recent years, the same class has formed by far the most important section of members.'[103] However, the landowning fraternity fell to one-quarter of the House in 1910, and only 15 per cent of MPs returned in 1918 had primary interests in the land.[104]

Having sponsored a candidate, patrons expected political loyalty. The eighteenth-century image is of political 'clans' in which the heads of great families sat in the Lords from where they tended to direct the conduct of brothers, sons and even cousins in the Commons. Even so, down to 1760 or thereabouts the capacity of peers to influence their

[97] William Aydelotte, 'The House of Commons in the 1840s', *History*, 34 (1954), p. 254.

[98] Quoted in W. L. Guttsman (ed.), *The English Ruling Class* (1969), pp. 149–58.

[99] Hanham, *Elections and Party Management*, p. xv, n.2.

[100] Adam Badeau, *Aristocracy in England* (1886), pp. 222, 225.

[101] Barbara Tuchman, *The Proud Tower* (New York, 1966), p. 14.

[102] Howard Evans, *Our Old Nobility* (1897), p. 222.

[103] G. Shaw-Lefevre, *Agrarian Tenures* (1893), p. 8.

[104] Guttsman, 'The British political elite and the class structure', p. 32.

nominees may not have been as clear-cut as it was to become by the end of the century, when MPs voting against their patron's wishes were expected to resign. Such conditions were hardly surprising: MPs were often financially dependent on their patron, both for the expenses of their return, and for financial support in London; and it was only natural that patrons would normally select men with whom they were in political agreement. However, such sycophancy inevitably bolstered peerage influence in the Commons. Charles Grey – Lord Grey of the Reform Bill – wrote of 'the chicane and tyranny of corruption' which occurred when an MP could have 'no conscience, no liberty, no direction of his own, [but] is sent here by my lord this, or the duke of that, and if he does not obey the instructions he receives, he is not to be considered as a man of honour and a gentleman.'[105] However, patrons and clients did not always see eye to eye. On a series of issues between 1811 and 1831, up to 20 per cent of peers with a patronal constituency interest found themselves in conflict with their nominated MP. This suggests a paradox, whereby what looks to have been an increase in aristocratic power was mitigated by a greater element of opposition to the appointing patrons. It may also have reflected a growing issue-orientation and party division in the lower house. Nor did rebellious MPs necessarily lose their seats in the next election, although peers could still take this line of action if they felt sufficiently betrayed, as is clear from the relatively high number of dismissals at the 1831 election, after the first Reform Bill. Peers, it would seem, were not prepared to stand idly by and watch their borough interests disappear at the behest of their nominated clients in the lower house. In general, the evidence of the years before 1832 suggests that increasing patronal control did not necessarily ensure a House of Commons more open to aristocratic influence.[106]

By 1760 English government was in the hands of an aristocratic oligarchy. Members of the great landed families controlled the offices of state, positions in the executive, the House of Lords, and a considerable portion of the House of Commons. Country campaigns to preserve the position of independent gentlemen in the lower house had all foundered. Longer Parliaments had permitted aristocrats to control borough elections, and often to place their relations and clients in safe seats. Even elections were in danger of being outlawed: in the contests

[105] Quoted in Sack, 'The House of Lords and parliamentary patronage', p. 919.
[106] Ibid. I should also like to thank Eveline Cruikshanks for several helpful comments on this subject.

of 1741, 1747, 1754 and 1761, no more than 27 per cent of English constituencies went to the polls, a far cry from the early years of the century when between one-third and one-half polled in general elections from 1701 to 1734. The nadir was in 1761, when only 19 per cent of constituencies polled and the system appeared to be on the brink of seizing up completely. Yet this did not provoke overt resentment. There was to be no English revolution to match events in France in 1789, and later across much of Europe in 1848. Even the 1832 Reform Act, hailed in its day as a revolutionary measure, scarcely dented the aristocratic hold. Businessmen and other middle-class politicians continued to find it difficult to penetrate the political and social elite, and a working-class MP was not elected until 1874.[107] Only towards the end of the nineteenth century did it become apparent that the aristocratic grip was beginning to loosen, and this raised two questions which will be the subject of the next chapter: first, how was aristocratic power maintained without creating revolutionary strains in the fabric of society; and, second, why was it finally eroded?

[107] See chapter three.

Chapter Thirteen

The Aristocracy and the State: The Maintenance of Power

The survival of aristocratic government in England was a source of annoyance to radicals, and of amazement to conservatives and historians alike. During the tense 1790s Edmund Burke was the acknowledged champion of aristocracy: 'we are resolved to keep an established church, an established monarchy, an established aristocracy, and an established democracy, each in the degree it exists, and in no greater.' In his view the dominance of land in both houses of the legislature gave added strength to the constitution:

For though hereditary wealth, and the rank which goes with it, are too much idolized by creeping sycophants, and the blind, abject admirers of power, they are too rashly slighted in shallow speculations of the petulant, assuming, short-sighted coxcombs of philosophy. Some decent, regulated pre-eminence, some preference (not exclusive appropriation) given to birth, is neither unnatural nor unjust, nor impolitic.[1]

By contrast, Tom Paine could see little reason to retain the aristocracy. To him they were 'the drones, a seraglio of males, who neither collect the honey, nor form the hive, but exist only for lazy employment'.[2] During the nineteenth century, aristocratic survival was almost always attributed to the accumulation of land into large conglomerations. As a French commentator expressed it in 1829:

England is, in point of fact, only one vast, opulent, and powerful aristocracy. Immense estates united in the same hands; colossal fortunes accumulated in the same families; a body of dependants, numerous and faithful, grouped

---

[1] Edmund Burke, *Reflections on the Revolution in France*, Everyman edn (1910), pp. 49, 88.
[2] Tom Paine, *Rights of Man*, Everyman edn (1915), p. 231.

around every proprietor, and prostituting to his will those political rights which the constitution would seem to bestow on them only to be sacrificed; and, as a final result, a national representation composed of placemen and nominees of the aristocracy.[3]

Towards the close of the century Lord Eversley was arguing in much the same way. Land had been accumulated into relatively few hands, and, since political power followed land, in turn it became concentrated in a small group – the owners of large estates. Consequently men of fortune sought to buy land to enter the group, and the system was perpetuated.[4]

By contrast with those who were willing to defend aristocracy, and those who believed they had found explanations for its longevity, other contemporaries neither expected nor perceived its survival beyond 1832. J. W. Croker expected the worst: 'no King, no Lords, no inequalities; all will be levelled to the plane of the petty shopkeepers and small farmers; this perhaps not without bloodshed, but certainly by confiscation and persecution.'[5] Some believed such forebodings had come to pass. A. V. Dicey, writing in 1898, explained how the Reform Act was intended 'to diminish the power of the gentry and to transfer predominant authority to the middle classes'; while as late as 1913 J. A. R. Marriott could refer to the period 1832–67 as 'the reign of the middle classes'.[6] Few twentieth-century writers have followed this line. Even in 1912 Arthur Ponsonby perceived that if 1688–1832 had been the golden age of the aristocracy their political power was still significant; while in 1939 a German journalist Karl Heinz Abshagen, recording his personal impressions of ten years' residence in England, could hardly conceal his surprise at the way 'a fundamentally feudal nobility maintains its position of privilege almost unchallenged in a country which has become one of the greatest industrial and commercial states of the world'. Even in the 1930s he found that 'aristocratic birth or connexions are extraordinarily useful for a political career in England', largely because the aristocracy continued to see political leadership as their 'proper occupation'.[7] The strength of the

---

[3] B. Constant, *Literary and Political Miscellanies* (Paris, 1829), quoted in anon., *The Aristocracy of Britain and the Laws of Entail and Primogeniture Judged by Recent French Writers* (1844), p. 173.

[4] G. Shaw-Lefevre, *Agrarian Tenures* (1893), pp. 7–10.

[5] Quoted in W. L. Guttsman, *The British Political Elite* (1963), p. 34.

[6] Dicey and Marriott are cited by John Cannon, *Parliamentary Reform, 1640–1832* (Cambridge, 1973), p. 254 and note.

[7] Arthur Ponsonby, *The Decline of Aristocracy* (1912), p. 18; Karl Heinz Abshagen, *King, Lords and Gentlemen: influence and power of the English upper classes* (1939), p. 100.

aristocratic hold on the institutions of government down to and beyond 1832 was explained in the last chapter – which leads naturally to the question how their hold was maintained. For, despite Croker, Dicey and their sympathisers, there can be little doubt that it was sustained, at least until things began to slide in the 1880s.

THE ARISTOCRACY AND ELECTORAL DEFERENCE

No system of government is likely to survive, except by force, unless it attains a degree of acquiescence within a nation. The fact that England avoided the European path towards revolution suggests that the political system was not entirely unpopular; in fact, until the late nineteenth century it appears to have retained a flexibility which meshed well with aristocratic government to ensure a sense of representation. It may not be mere coincidence that the first regular meetings of Parliament, in the aftermath of 1688, and the growing significance of the Commons in government, coincided with a period of intense electoral strife. With frequent polling, large numbers of contested constituencies, and something in the region of 15 per cent of adult males enfranchised – a larger proportion than at any time down to, and even beyond, 1832 – politics in these years were fiercely disputed by a surprisingly volatile electorate.[8] An equally enduring picture paints the post-1722 situation in rather different colours. Politics in the age of Walpole are seen in terms of the dominance of a propertied oligarchy, the end result being a mid-century stability typified by the relative cessation of electoral activity. Whereas never less than eighty-five constituencies polled between 1701 and 1734, such figures were not attained again before reform. Only forty-six English counties and boroughs polled in the worst year, 1761, and even in 1831 a mere seventy-five constituencies had a contest. Furthermore, the fall-off in contests was apparently accompanied by a significant rise in the number of patron-controlled seats; indeed, in the 1740s and 1750s, when patronage increased substantially, the correlation was a fall in the number of contests. Such figures, taken together with the impact of the Septennial Act, and Whig support for narrow borough

---

[8] Geoffrey Holmes, *The Electorate and the National Will in the First Age of Party* (Kendal, 1976), p. 23, puts the electorate in 1722 at 330,000 or 340,000, or 'not far short of one in four of the adult males in the country'. See also W. A. Speck, *Tory and Whig: the struggle in the constituencies, 1701–15* (1970), and J. H. Plumb, 'The growth of the electorate in England from 1600 to 1715', *Past and Present*, 45 (1969), pp. 90–116.

franchises, apparently confirmed the irrelevance of the electorate and the oligarchic nature of the political system until it was partially reopened in 1832, and more fully reformed from 1867 onwards.

Political stability is not usually achieved by suppressing electoral activity in a free state, and the relative popularity of the system was maintained in a number of different ways. First, the emphasis on patron control overlooks the extent to which only the smallest boroughs succumbed, whereas the majority of voters lived in larger constituencies. In the larger boroughs Walpole suffered popular defeats in the elections of 1734 and 1741, but he secured a comfortable majority in the rotten boroughs. Although contests fell to a minimum between 1747 and 1761, between 1768 and 1831 just four English counties and thirty-four boroughs failed to register a single contest, 16 per cent of the total.[9] Since it was invariably the smaller boroughs which had been reduced to electoral ciphers, the post-1761 general elections saw an increase in activity. Only 21 per cent of boroughs were contested in 1761, but the figure rose to 31 per cent in 1768 and to 35 per cent in 1774. The return of party considerations in the later years of the century helped to maintain the increase, while the vast difference in electorate size between many of the closed boroughs and those that remained open ensured that roughly two-thirds of the borough electorate participated more often than not in the post-1761 elections. This figure was as high as 94 per cent in boroughs that frequently allowed their electors to exercise their franchises formally, and even then it takes no account of the activity which could precede an election without the polls ever being opened.[10]

Secondly, except in the smallest and most servile of boroughs, the electorate had to be carefully nurtured both during and between

[9] Cannon, *Parliamentary Reform*, pp. 278–89. The absence of contests does not necessarily imply political stability, since the years 1742–6 were among the most unstable of the century. On the other hand, it may have resulted from the proscription of the Tories: see Eveline Cruikshanks, *Political Untouchables: the Tories and the '45* (1979), and Linda Colley, *In Defiance of Oligarchy: the Tory Party, 1714–60* (Cambridge, 1982).

[10] John A. Phillips, *Electoral Behaviour in Unreformed England* (Princeton, NJ, 1982), pp. 15, 17, 71–2. For an example of pre-electoral activity, see J. V. Beckett, 'The making of a pocket borough: Cockermouth, 1722–56', *Journal of British Studies*, 20 (1980), pp. 140–57. The present book was substantially completed before the appearance late in 1985 of J. C. D. Clark's important book *English Society, 1688–1832* (Cambridge, 1985). This chapter is not the place to do full justice to some of Dr Clark's findings, but although my argument differs from his in certain respects, in general terms the case for the ongoing influence of the aristocracy down to 1832 is similar.

elections, since it was not always easy for patrons to ensure voters' loyalty. Englishmen, as Bagehot insisted, may have liked the idea of being represented by a scion of the landed classes, but deference was obtained by responsibility in government, not by force. Constituents therefore had to be appeased.[11] This could be achieved in a number of ways. The most obvious was by obtaining positions of employment in government office for constituents. Walpole's papers are littered with requests from MPs for minor positions in government, such as the following letter from Sir Thomas Lowther, MP for Lancaster, in 1739:

If I could anyways have avoided it you should not have had this trouble, but am desired to make the following request to you. Mr Wells, the surveyor of hawkers and pedlars (who resides at Lancaster) being a dying, am desired to apply to you for one Mr Lambert to succeed him.[12]

Members who sat for open constituencies were particularly susceptible to such pressure – and they were likely to find it expedient to keep in good standing with the administration – as well as those who faced re-election on appointment to office. Charles Townshend received a variety of requests from constituents when he considered applying for re-election at Great Yarmouth in 1756 after his appointment to office. One correspondent wrote,

wishing you joy of your new employment. You know that power is always exposed to solicitation and therefore you will not be surprised that I apply for your good offices in favour of my brother George, who, I have reason to believe, is like to be recalled from the station in Jamaica. . . . As he had many proofs of your friendship while you were in the Admiralty I flatter myself that you will not abandon him in his present distress.[13]

[11] The ideal of deference was not to reduce a man to imbecile servility but to treat him so that his essential independence and self-respect were acknowledged: J. G. A. Pocock, 'The classical theory of deference', *American Historical Review*, 81 (1976), pp. 516–23.

[12] Cambridge University Library, C(H) Corresp. 2921, Sir Thomas Lowther to Sir Robert Walpole, 5 September 1739. There are many similar letters, although most are written by MPs from their constituencies. Presumably personal applications were more common during a parliamentary session.

[13] Clements Library, Charles Townshend papers, 297/3. T. Townshend to Charles Townshend, 16 November 1756. Other letters in this bundle include requests from a debtor asking for financial help, and several from constituents seeking customs places. The pressure told on Townshend, who retreated to the safe government seat of Saltash, leaving Great Yarmouth to his cousin, Charles Townshend of Honington, who was elected in December: Sir Lewis Namier and John Brooke, *The House of Commons, 1754–1790* (1964), vol. I, p. 340; vol. III, p. 541.

Patrons were also approached in this way, both as a vote-bargaining counter, and as a means of persuading them to bring pressure upon the candidate, if elected. Out of forty-nine surviving letters to Earl Fitzwilliam in three months of 1809, nearly half were requests for money, jobs or other help. Obtaining positions came to be regarded as a vital test of an MP's standing, and voters recognized the leverage to be exercised in such circumstances.[14]

Under-renting, the promotion of local business and paternalism were further methods of cultivating a constituency. The Duke of Chandos complained about the level of rent arrears on his Shropshire estates in 1721, but since he expected an election he could see little alternative to accepting the situation. However, his steward was told to give the tenants 'due notice that I will not suffer that practice to continue and as soon as the elections are over I will have no forbearance shown to any of those who are above half a year in arrears.'[15] Looking after constituency interests in Parliament has been touched upon in earlier chapters, but William Dowdeswell summed up the situation when he told Edmund Burke in 1772 that 'in private matters, turnpikes, navigations, enclosures and the like, men in certain situations must attend to carry on the business of their constituents.'[16] Paternalistic measures between elections were also useful. In 1727 the Duke of Chandos considered offering money for repairing the roads around Hereford, in order to cement his political interest, although he was sceptical about whether this was an advisable course of action:

I fear men's minds are too narrow spirited to be much moved with the view of a public good. It will certainly have no influence over the many indigent freemen, and the few of the better sort with whom such a proposal would have weight will hardly be, I doubt, enough in number to compensate for such a sum of money so laid out, and I am apt to think that such a sum laid in the usual manner of elections would produce a better effect.[17]

[14] A. D. Harvey, *Britain in the Early Nineteenth Century* (1978), pp. 12–13; Frank O'Gorman, 'Electoral deference in "unreformed" England, 1760–1832', *Journal of Modern History*, 56 (1984), p. 411.

[15] Huntington Library, ST 57/20, fol. 18, Duke of Chandos to Captain Samuel Oakley, 27 November 1721.

[16] Clements Library, Dowdeswell Papers, William Dowdeswell to Edmund Burke, 8 November 1772. Earlier chapters have included material on MPs and their local political interests.

[17] Huntington Library, ST 57/30, fol. 128, Duke of Chandos to Mr Lance, 14 July 1727.

The political implications of paternalism could not be better expressed.[18]

If the foundations for election victories were laid between contests, a good deal of work was still needed once the polls opened. The traditional view of an eighteenth-century election is of a compliant electorate marching *en bloc* to vote for the landlord's candidates, cowed by threats of eviction, and softened by corrupt largesse. It is an alluring picture, but not necessarily a very accurate one. Patrons and candidates alike often found there was no substitute for a good campaign. Although detained in London on government business, the great eighteenth-century borough-monger the Duke of Newcastle still found time in 1740 to draw up plans for the forthcoming election. For Sussex he compiled lists of potentially friendly voters, and sent them to a number of local men who were to speak to the named individuals at the assizes. His stated aim was to ensure a favourable turnout for the poll at Horsham, although he was careful – as a peer – to insist that no one should suggest that the summons emanated from him.[19] Personal attendance in the constituency helped a candidate's cause, while arrangements to secure the returning officer and to entice the voters to the polls also constituted a vitally important part of campaigning.

Such measures were necessary because voters' deference was strictly circumscribed. The degree of political control enjoyed by a landlord over his tenants, or by a patron over his voters, was by no means absolute. Tenants could not regularly be browbeaten into submission by the threat of eviction in the event of a misplaced vote, while the idea of whole villages meekly turning out to vote according to their landlord's whim looks decidedly shaky as a means of deciding county elections. Dissidence was sufficiently high for unanimity rates to be only around 10 per cent. The success of a landlord in controlling voting depended on the size of the community, and the extent to which it was 'closed', but in any case up to three-quarters of voters in a county contest were likely to be retailers or craftsmen who were not in the normal landlord-tenant relationship, although this did not prevent their being susceptible to landlords' influence. Even tenants, while accepting the landlord's right to command one vote, seldom yielded up the other as directed.[20] In rural South Lincolnshire prior to the

[18] For an example of how one MP ran his constituency affairs, see J. V. Beckett, 'A back-bench MP in the eighteenth century: Sir James Lowther of Whitehaven', *Parliamentary History*, 1 (1982), pp. 79–97.

[19] E. N. Williams (ed.), *The Eighteenth-Century Constitution* (Cambridge, 1960), pp. 170–2.

[20] O'Gorman, 'Electoral deference in "unreformed" England', pp. 402, 406–9, 413–22.

1832 contest, Sir Montague Cholmeley told G. J. Heathcote that he had written to his tenants requesting a vote for Heathcote's candidature, but that he was not ready to demand it from them against their consciences, although he was sure they would vote as directed if properly canvassed. Lincolnshire landlords could not always deliver votes to candidates, before or after reform, especially if their political allegiance wavered.[21]

If deference was difficult to enforce in the countryside, the situation was even more fraught in large boroughs. The obvious weapon, eviction, was unsatisfactory, since it could only be employed retrospectively, and it did nothing for a landowner's local reputation. Although his candidate, M. T. Sadler, was returned at a by-election in Newark in 1829, the Duke of Newcastle carried out his threat to evict dissenting tenants. For his pains he was attacked in the local press, and an indignant defence of his own position merely brought on a petition to the Commons asking that his lease of local Crown lands should not be renewed. Even after this demonstration of his intentions, fifty or so of his tenants voted for the radical candidate in the 1830 general election.[22] Evictions could also be combined with other punitive action. When Earl Fitzwilliam's candidate was defeated at Malton in 1807, he responded by turning out tenants, raising rents by 25 per cent, and manipulating the River Derwent dues. The price of coal was raised from 1s. 8d. to 3s. a ton, and corn dues rose by one-third, although some of Fitzwilliam's local supporters were exempted. However, the people who were really hurt were the small tradesmen of the town who had played little or no role in the election. At least Fitzwilliam knew when to back down: after the House of Commons overturned the election result and his candidate won the ensuing by-election in 1808, he reduced the dues.[23]

The carrot rather than the stick proved to be a more reliable way of influencing elections and maintaining deference; hence the use of treating, which occasionally amounted to outright bribery. Vote trading in this manner was not entirely sinister. It could represent payment of compensation for absence from a place of work, or the settling of debts and fines in order to seal a political alliance between voter and patron. Sometimes it took on a systematic form. Earl Grosvenor paid 20 guineas to each of 300 voters at Shaftesbury, and £60 to more than 100 voters at Stockbridge. Those who voted for

[21] R. J. Olney, *Lincolnshire Politics, 1832–1885* (Oxford, 1973), ch. 4.
[22] Rolf Vernon, *Newark before Victoria, 1827–1837* (Newark, 1984), pp. 53–7.
[23] B. F. Duckham, 'The Fitzwilliams and the navigation of the Yorkshire Derwent', *Northern History*, 2 (1967), pp. 52–5.

Newcastle at Newark received half a ton of coal at Christmas, in addition to reduced rents.[24] At East Retford each of the nominated candidates paid 20 guineas apiece to the 200 or so freemen, and selection depended entirely on the man's ability to pay. Such a cosy arrangement might never have come to light but for an election dispute during the 1820s which revealed the direct – and therefore illegal – involvement of Earl Fitzwilliam, and uncovered a major scandal.[25] The extent of corruption must not be exaggerated. In the four boroughs of Norwich, Northampton, Lewes and Maidstone, examined by Professor Phillips in his study of electoral behaviour in 'unreformed' England, little treating appears to have taken place in the second half of the eighteenth century, except at Northampton in 1768, and it was not the case that contests were invalidated on appeal simply because bribery could be proved. A successful petition was brought at Norwich after the 1786 election in which 2600 voters polled. Of the 262 challenged, bribery was alleged in only thirty-three cases, and the contest was invalidated on other grounds including the ineligibility of sixty-one freemen.[26]

Borough elections should not necessarily be seen as corrupt agreements between rogues, but there is no denying the fact that on occasion large sums of money were spent. Bribery was frequently condemned, not least by the anonymous author in 1812 who, though no parliamentary reformer, wanted to see the influence of land in elections maintained without the vast financial outlay. He believed it would not be difficult to introduce order and restrictions into elections in such a way as to reduce the cost and thereby make sure they were not dominated by money.[27] Certainly it is not difficult to find examples of large sums being laid out at a single election. The notorious Oxfordshire contest in 1754 reputedly cost the Tories £20,000, and the Whigs probably as much; a by-election in Essex in 1763 may have cost each side £30,000; and in 1784 £18,000 was raised on behalf of the Pittite candidate in Yorkshire. William Thornton spent £12,000 at York in 1758; Alexander Fordyce sunk £14,000 into an unsuccessful campaign at Colchester in 1768; and the Gloucester by-election of

[24] O'Gorman, 'Electoral deference in "unreformed" England', p. 411; J. J. Sack, 'The House of Lords and parliamentary patronage in Great Britain, 1802–1832', *Historical Journal*, 23 (1980), p. 914.

[25] R. A. Preston, 'East Retford in the last days of a rotten borough', *Transactions of the Thoroton Society*, 77 (1974), pp. 94–103.

[26] Phillips, *Electoral Behaviour in Unreformed England*, pp. 77–8, 84–6.

[27] Anon., *Thoughts on County Elections* (1812). For similar sentiments, see *Gentleman's Magazine*, 4 (1734), pp. 378–9.

1789 cost over £30,000. In the north-west the dispute between Sir James Lowther and the Duke of Portland in 1767 precipitated enormous expenditure at the Cumberland and Carlisle contests, possibly amounting to over £40,000.[28] Thomas William Coke represented Norfolk from 1776 until 1832, with the exception of a short break in 1806–7. The four contests he fought probably cost more than £40,000, including the full-scale battle of 1806, in which his expenses came to nearly £30,000. Although about one-third of this was raised by subscription, Coke probably paid out more than half of the remaining £22,000.[29]

Despite such evidence, since money was needed to oil the electoral machinery whether or not a contest took place, it may have been that heavy expenditure represented an aberration in the system, a point at which the interested parties were unable to keep the contest within bounds. This seems to have been what happened at Northampton, where £160,000 was spent on the 1768 election. As a result, Lord Northampton sought permanent exile in Switzerland, and Lord Halifax withdrew from Northampton politics. Even Earl Spencer, whose finances had not been ruined, took little further part in elections.[30] Elsewhere, recognition of spiralling costs led families to opt out before such a situation could occur. This was the case with the Leveson-Gowers in the West Midlands. The second Baron Gower's move from Tory to Whig in the 1740s, for which he received an earldom in 1746, produced much stiffer resistance to the family interest in Staffordshire, where elections between 1742 and 1758 cost at least £16,000. The family was also involved in heavy outgoings in order to return Viscount Trentham for Westminster in 1747 and 1749. At a rough estimate, election expenses between 1742 and 1757 topped £50,000, and this led 'to the landlord's neglecting the care of his estates and subordinating their welfare and his own economic interests in the pursuit of political power'. In the second half of the century the family's political interests did not have the same financial

---

[28] Namier and Brooke, *The House of Commons, 1754–90*, vol. I, pp. 4–5, 14, 21; Brian Bonsall, *Sir James Lowther and Cumberland and Westmorland Elections, 1754–1775* (Manchester, 1960), pp. 15, 34, 37, 47, 103–5.

[29] R. A. C. Parker, *Coke of Norfolk* (Oxford, 1975), pp. 130–1.

[30] Phillips, *Electoral Behaviour in Unreformed England*, p. 83. The cost of electoral involvement was once thought to have been responsible for the financial plight of the Duke of Newcastle, but Ray A. Kelch, *Newcastle: a duke without money* (1974), has shown that it was the cost of maintaining a ducal lifestyle which was the real culprit. Similarly, electioneering was a major, but not a fundamental, cause of the downfall of the Myddletons of Chirk Castle: G. E. Mingay, *English Landed Society in the Eighteenth Century* (1963), pp. 126–30.

repercussions. Between 1758 and 1801 they regularly carried between six and eight of the ten Staffordshire MPs, but the death of the first marquess in 1803 marked a loosening of political interests, both because the second marquess was less interested in politics, and because there was a renewed spirit of independence, especially at Lichfield and Newcastle under Lyme. Consequently the agent was able to raise rents to an economic level during the 1820s, and the second marquess was able to support reform in 1832, for which he was created Duke of Sutherland.[31]

The high proportion of eligible voters living in open constituencies, and the need to nurture a borough both between and during electoral contests, provide two reasons for the relative popularity of the pre-reform political system, while a third lay in the ability of the unenfranchised to exert pressure on the Commons. This was achieved by lobbying and propaganda in the case of predominantly urban, bourgeois groups, and by demonstrations and riots on the part of the less well-organized sections of society. In addition, a flourishing political press was able to keep the pot boiling, with scarcely guarded attacks on the ruling oligarchy. Electors were beginning to establish their own independent political organizations in Walpole's day, and the better-organized groups – including the Bank of England, the chartered trading companies and the dissenting churches – were able to exert considerable influence on individual MPs and on the government. Nationwide campaigns were mounted over the excise scheme in 1733, and over Walpole's general political conduct between 1739 and 1742. Constituencies sent instructions to MPs, and petitions for them to present in the Commons.[32] More obviously plebeian campaigns were also mounted, including the 1710 Sacheverell riots, the anti-Hanoverian riots of 1714–16 and the gin riots of 1736. Although predominantly London-based, these were expressions of lower-class dissent from the ruling consensus, and they recurred in one form or another throughout the century. In 1768–9 the Wilkite riots were a form of popular unrest based on opposition to parliamentary interference with the rights of voters. Similarly the Gordon riots of

---

[31] J. R. Wordie, *Estate Management in Eighteenth-Century England* (1982), pp. 248, 253, 255, 266; Eric Richards, 'The social and electoral influence of the Trentham interest, 1800–1860', *Midland History*, 3 (1975), pp. 116–48, and *The Leviathan of Wealth* (1973), p. 9.

[32] G. S. Holmes and W. A. Speck, *The Divided Society: parties and politics in England, 1694–1716* (1967), pp. 125–6, reproduce 'The advice of the County of Bucks to their knights of the shire' (1701); H. T. Dickinson, 'Popular politics in the age of Walpole', in *Britain in the Age of Walpole*, ed. Jeremy Black (1984), pp. 45–68.

1780 began with an extra-parliamentary meeting to present a monster petition to Parliament calling for the repeal of the partial measures of Roman Catholic relief introduced two years earlier. Between 1779 and 1785, pressure group activity was channelled into economical and later parliamentary reform, predominantly in the form of the Rev. Christopher Wyvill's Association Movement. Much of its energy went into parliamentary petitioning.[33]

Finally, the pre-reform political system remained because it never became moribund. The most satisfactory evidence of deference voting is the absence of a contest, since lack of opposition to a patron suggests contentment with the situation.[34] This would imply that all was nearest to being well in 1761, and from this it follows that the increase in borough contests in the later decades of the eighteenth century, and possibly the increase in expenditure, suggest that the electorate was increasingly unpredictable in its behaviour, and the aristocratic control implied by patronage and by membership of the Commons was not easily translated into returns at the polls. Dissatisfaction with aristocratic pretensions helped to stimulate the parliamentary reform movement, while the emergence of new issues put back life into the two-party system, which in turn produced greater activity at the polls.

The re-emergence of party-political debate helped to give a more competitive edge to electoral activity. Although the orthodox view is that the final remnants of the Tory Party disappeared in the aftermath of the 1745 Jacobite débâcle, and that a two-party system only re-emerged after about 1815,[35] recent research has suggested that party duality should also be sought over the preceding decades. The confusion of terminology and allegiance has always made it difficult to identify 'party' activity,[36] but it is arguable that the tranquillity of mid-eighteenth-century politics facilitated the emergence of a new and more stable form of party politics. Issues such as the role of the monarchy in the 1760s, parliamentary sovereignty over the American colonies in the 1770s, parliamentary reform – in both the 1780s and the 1790s – and the French Revolution, produced rallying points for politicians. Royal power and religious toleration further prompted

[33] I. R. Christie, *Wilkes, Wyvill and Reform* (1962); G. Rudé, *Wilkes and Liberty* (Oxford, 1962); John Brewer, *Party Ideology and Popular Politics at the Accession of George III* (Cambridge, 1976).

[34] O'Gorman, 'Electoral deference in "unreformed" England', p. 401.

[35] I. R. Christie, *Wars and Revolutions: Britain, 1760–1815* (1982), pp. 29–30, 330.

[36] B. W. Hill, *British Parliamentary Parties, 1742–1832* (1985), provides the fullest recent statement of the pro-party case.

political alignments in the early years of the nineteenth century, and the fire was fuelled in the 1820s by questions relating to the religious constitution of the state, and parliamentary reform. A Whig standpoint can be traced through the activities of the Rockinghamites in the 1760s, and later in the political groupings led by Charles James Fox, while a Conservative philosophy emerged out of Burke's writings in the 1790s. From these beginnings, a stable and coherent party system gradually emerged by the end of the Napoleonic wars. It was facilitated by the waning influence of the monarch, which enhanced the executive position of the Cabinet, and the declining number of uncommitted MPs in the Commons. Whereas in the mid-eighteenth century less than one-quarter of MPs were party men, by 1832 almost all were. This trend was particularly clear in Lord Liverpool's administration between 1812 and 1827, as the majority of MPs consistently offered support to either the government or the opposition. Party struggle also returned in the constituencies.[37]

REACTIONS TO ARISTOCRATIC POWER

For these various reasons what might appear to have been an oligarchic and relatively closed political structure actually enjoyed a strong element of popular deference. It was not, however, unchallenged. Events in 1779–80, linked with Ireland, with the Yorkshire Association's ability to present parliamentary reform on a national platform, with the Gordon riots, and with Dunning's famous parliamentary resolution on the supposedly growing influence of the monarchy, produced a situation described by Butterfield as being 'quasi-revolutionary to a degree which the world has since forgotten'. Only the survival of North's ministry, he suggested, ensured that England avoided a 'French Revolution' in 1780.[38] Such a view is rather extreme, but there is no doubting the fact that a decade later aristocratic government was plunged into crisis. In the wake of events in France from July 1789 the propertied classes were happy to line up behind Edmund Burke's influential conservative text *Reflections on the Revolution in France*, published in November 1790. In Burke's view the unity of the constitution was preserved through 'an inheritable crown;

---

[37] F. O'Gorman, *The Emergence of the British Two-Party System* (1982). The party issue ought not to be overstated. Michael Bentley has recently referred to it as a 'floating presence' in Parliament, while accepting its greater relevance in the constituencies: *Politics without Democracy, 1815–1914* (1984), pp. 26–7.

[38] H. Butterfield, *George III, Lord North and the People, 1779–80* (1949).

an inheritable peerage; and a House of Commons and a people inheriting privileges, franchises and liberties, from a long line of ancestors'. By contrast, the first part of Thomas Paine's *Rights of Man*, published a year later, rebutted much of Burke's defence of custom and privilege. Aristocracy and monarchy, Paine argued, depended on the arbitrary fortune of hereditary succession, and neither had a basis in logic. While part one of his book was just about tolerable, the government took fright when part two became a best-seller during 1792. Coming as it did in the same year as the September massacres in France, the abolition of the monarchy, and the Convention's declaration that it was ready to aid unliberated people, Paine's book posed a threat which could not be ignored.[39]

Yet despite the enthusiasm for Paine's writings aristocracy, monarchy and government survived the crisis years of the 1790s. Why this was so has long puzzled historians. Christie has recently pointed to the absence of acute class or caste divisions, or of social jealousy, to the importance of the Poor Law in underpinning society, and to the significant influence of the churches. To these factors he has added favourable economic conditions, which in themselves 'provide a cogent explanation why despite occasional fears and alarms, there was no danger of revolution in Britain in the 1790s'.[40] Perhaps even more significant was the determined government response. From 1792 proclamations were issued against seditious meetings and publications. Two years later habeas corpus was suspended, and a campaign started against the corresponding societies, which had sprung up partly as agencies for selling Paine's work. Further measures were taken in 1795 to outlaw contempt for the king, the government or the constitution, and to forbid assemblies of more than fifty people without due notice. Legislation was passed in 1797 against swearing unlawful oaths, and in 1798 to regulate newspapers in order to strengthen prosecution for seditious writings. Finally, the Combination Acts of 1799 and 1800 effectively forbade meetings of working men. However, the effectiveness of this repression is in doubt. Just as important in defeating the radical threat was the extent of loyalism, and the propaganda

---

[39] Burke, *Reflections on the Revolution in France*, p. 31; Paine, *Rights of Man*, pp. 58–63, 147, 259, 264–5.

[40] I. R. Christie, *Stress and Stability in Late Eighteenth-Century Britain: reflections on the British avoidance of revolution* (Oxford, 1984), pp. 70–87, 93, 215–18; Christie's optimistic view of economic conditions does not fit well with K. D. M. Snell's recent findings that employment conditions were moving against the less well-off in society: *Annals of the Labouring Poor: social change and agrarian England, 1660–1900* (Cambridge, 1985).

victory enjoyed by the conservative reaction.[41] The radicals had little answer. They were ill-prepared for a struggle against a parliament which had shown its willingness to unite in the face of a threat to property, and by 1803 the movement had largely been driven underground.

Few lessons seem to have been learned from the events of the 1790s; indeed, the successful control of radicalism may have encouraged what amounted to the dismantling of the whole system of paternal protection for the lower orders which had been the pride of the old society, and which had served to justify its inequalities. Justices were no longer prepared to regulate wages, hence expedients such as the post-1795 bread subsidies in southern England – and they were supported by government decisions in 1813 and 1814 to repeal the wage and apprenticeship clauses of the 1563 Statute of Artificers. The 1815 Corn Law, although designed by the Cabinet to try to reconcile the landowners to unpopular post-war financial measures, appeared to be little more than a cynical attempt to protect landowners and farmers from the impact of falling prices, while in these same years the very existence of the Poor Law was questioned. Coming at a time of widespread economic depression after 1815, these measures suggested that the aristocrats were opting out of their role as guardians of society.

Matters were made worse when, in August 1819, a crowd of 60,000 which had assembled to hear Henry Hunt address a reform meeting in St Peter's Fields in Manchester was broken up by military intervention, leaving a dozen dead and hundreds injured. The government's response to 'Peterloo', first by offering the Prince Regent's gratitude to the Manchester magistracy, and then by passing the 'Six Acts', which ostensibly conferred additional coercive powers upon the executive, was distinctly heavy-handed. Finally, the cause of aristocratic government was not helped by the queen's trial in 1820. After George III's death, his son George IV attempted to divorce his estranged wife Caroline. This brought down public opprobrium upon his head, largely because it was widely believed that he had secretly married a Catholic in 1785, and also because of his known profligacy. Public opinion took Caroline's side, the Divorce Bill had to be dropped, and efforts to bar her from the coronation only caused further embarrassment to the government.[42]

Reaction to these events took a number of different forms. Paine was

[41] H. T. Dickinson, *British Radicalism and the French Revolution, 1789–1815* (Oxford, 1985).

[42] Harold Perkin, *The Origins of Modern English Society, 1780–1880* (1969), pp. 189–95.

by no means a lone voice in the 1790s. Private landownership was questioned by Thomas Spence, beginning a tradition which carried forward into the nineteenth-century land reform movement. William Godwin also picked up and developed Paine's ideas, and he was followed, with a middle-class audience in view, by David Ricardo and James Mill. The latter's *Essay on Government* (1820) depicted the aristocracy as a naturally defective ruling order, partly because its members acted in their own rather than in society's best interests.[43] From a practical point of view, however, opposition was channelled into the parliamentary reform movement.

Originally debated in the 1760s and 1770s, reform had fallen victim to the conservative reaction after 1789, but it had not disappeared as an issue. From 1792 onwards, the Whigs recognized the need to preserve aristocratic influence through the reform of parliament, but movement in this direction proceeded in fits and starts. In 1822 Lord John Russell moved in the Commons to deprive 100 of the smallest boroughs of one seat each. As with previous efforts, the measure was roundly defeated, and little was achieved for several more years. The Whigs refused to offer wholehearted support to reform, Lord Liverpool's administration bounced back in the 1820s with a series of apparently placatory measures, and renewed prosperity took the sting out of radicalism. Even the aristocracy revived its paternal responsibilities, but reform could not be forever denied, and it arrived in 1832.[44]

THE 1832 REFORM ACT

Aristocratic government survived such attacks and other accusations of irresponsibility, but this was not the expectation of some politicians when Parliament was finally reformed in 1832. Sir Robert Peel saw the legislation as 'a fatal precedent', and predicted that the monarchy would last for no more than five years, while the Duke of Wellington believed himself to be witnessing a revolution in which power was transferred from the gentlemen of England, who conformed to the Anglican establishment, to dissenting shopkeepers.[45] The Lords resisted fiercely. Their rejection of the second Reform Bill provoked

[43] For Spence and Ogilvie, see chapter ten; M. L. Bush, *The English Aristocracy* (Manchester, 1984), pp. 129–31.

[44] Perkin, *The Origins of Modern English Society*, pp. 237–52. The fullest account of the parliamentary reform movement is given in Cannon, *Parliamentary Reform*.

[45] W. L. Arnstein, 'The survival of the Victorian aristocracy', in *The Rich, the Well Born and the Powerful*, ed. F. C. Jaher (Urbana, Ill., 1973), p. 206.

widespread rioting in which the Duke of Newcastle's Nottingham castle was burned down; and when, finally, their resistance was broken by the threat of massive peerage creations many of the peers abstained rather than vote for such a measure. By contrast, Earl Grey, leader of the ministry which introduced reform, and a veteran of similar campaigns since the 1790s, took a very different view of events. His opinion of the Act was that 'the more it is considered, the less it will be found to prejudice the real interests of the aristocracy.'[46]

So why had reform taken place? The Act was a carefully planned measure designed to protect the elite, by shoring up the existing system. This, of course, was nothing new.[47] Back in 1783 the Cornish borough-monger Sir Francis Basset had argued that parliamentary reform was not needed, since representation in the Commons was, as it should be, 'of property, not of numbers'.[48] Others argued that the system catered for all needs: county and open boroughs gave it a democratic air; Treasury boroughs offered safe seats to hardworking ministers; nomination boroughs gave an opportunity to penniless men of talent; and rotten boroughs allowed merchants and manufacturers to make an entrance. Despite such views, it was impossible to deny that the Commons was far from perfect. Occasional scandals rocked the system, as when it came to light in 1768 that Oxford Corporation had attempted two years earlier to strike a bargain with its sitting members to ensure their re-election for a payment of £4000. Although much of the response to such events came in the form of demands for a reduction of Crown influence in the Commons, particularly during the American war, the finger was also pointed at aristocratic influence. This could be countered by arguing that aristocratic patronage acted as a barrier to Crown influence, but such an argument cut little ice with reformers. From the 1780s, the parliamentary reform movement was unqualified in its hostility to aristocratic influence. Thus, when in 1792 the young Charles Grey, and other Foxite Whigs, broke with the old 'aristocratic' Whigs (who defended aristocratic influence and opposed reform) to form the Society of the Friends of the People, part of the motive was to defend aristocratic influence by arguing that reform would restore its legitimate place in elections.[49]

---

[46] Michael Brock, *The Great Reform Act* (1973), is the most recent detailed study of its progress through Parliament: W. L. Guttsman, *The British Political Elite* (1963), p. 61.
[47] G. S. Veitch, *The Genesis of Parliamentary Reform* (1964 edn), examines why the parliamentary reform movement failed in the eighteenth century.
[48] John Brooke, *The House of Commons, 1754–90* (Oxford, 1964), p. 67.
[49] Cannon, *Parliamentary Reform*, p. 54; H. A. Ellis, 'Aristocratic influence and

This outlook remained in the Whig portfolio down to 1832, but whether the Reform Act was simply a matter of statesmanlike concession, or something rather more sinister, has been a matter for debate.[50] The most convincing argument points up the continuity of Whig policy from the 1790s until 1832, partly symbolized by Grey's enduring leadership. Although the Whigs did little about reform between the 1790s and their return to power in 1830, the principles had not changed in between. In the Commons reform debates, the Whigs revived their earlier vindication of legitimate aristocratic influence. Lord John Russell refuted the objection that the bill would undercut aristocratic power and privilege: wherever they resided on their estates and worked in the local community,

it is not in human nature that they should not possess a great influence upon public opinion, and have an equal weight in electing persons to serve their country in Parliament. Though such persons may not have the direct nomination of members under this Bill, I contend that they will have as much influence as they ought to have. But if by aristocracy those persons are meant who do not live among the people, who know nothing of the people, and who care nothing for them – who seek honours without merit, places without duty, and pensions without service – for such an aristocracy I have no sympathy; and I think the sooner its influence is carried away with the corruption on which it has thrived, the better for the country, in which it has suppressed for so long every wholesome and invigorating experience.[51]

Russell was distinguishing between legitimate influence and the illegitimate influence which borough patrons had wielded to such effect that the electoral system itself was ridiculed. The Whig view was that to restore the natural influence of rank and property it was necessary to purge entrenched influence in the nomination boroughs. A real and substantive increase in middle-class influence was seen as a means of restoring confidence in the institutions of government, and such a cautiously constructive attitude towards reform would be in the best interests of the aristocracy.[52]

---

electoral independence: the Whig model of parliamentary reform, 1792–1832', *Journal of Modern History*, 5 (1979), supplement, pp. D1255–61.

[50] Cannon, *Parliamentary Reform*, and Brock, *The Great Reform Act*, provide the most comprehensive surveys of the 'statesmanlike concession' viewpoint.

[51] *Parliamentary Debates*, 3rd ser., 1 March 1831, vol. II, pp. 1086–7.

[52] The argument is most clearly set out in Ellis, 'Aristocratic influence and electoral independence'; R. W. Davis, 'The Whigs and the idea of electoral deference: some further thoughts on the Great Reform Act', *Durham University Journal*, 67 (1974), pp. 79–91; 'Deference and aristocracy in the time of the Great Reform Act', *American Historical Review*, 81 (1976), pp. 532–3.

This was to be achieved by the abolition of 143 borough seats in England and Wales, and the creation in their place of 65 new county seats, and 65 borough seats, spread among 43 boroughs. The strengthening of the rural interest through an increase in county seats was a by-product of the belief dating well back into the eighteenth century that such an increase was necessary to enhance the representativeness of the system. In addition, the rural interest was strengthened by the retention of the traditional forty shilling freehold qualification for voting, the so-called 'Chandos clause', which enfranchised the £50 rural tenant, and by the continuation of open voting. At the same time the borough franchise was standardized at £10, and this actually restricted the electorate in some of the more open boroughs, such as Preston and Colchester. Such a select franchise was justified on the grounds that it would create a body of voters above corruption and primarily interested in preserving a mixed constitution.[53]

The alternative viewpoint is that the ministry acted rather more cynically, and that the Act was something of a tactical regrouping by the governing classes to survive the crisis of the demand for reform with its strength unimpaired and possibly enhanced. Having identified a system of rural deference voting in the form of village *en bloc* voting, which they thought was being undermined, Grey and his colleagues sought to uphold the system through reform. The way that they chose to bring this about was to add to the number of county seats, and to separate them out from the boroughs. This would ensure that power was not conceded to the middle class, and that no encouragement was given to democracy. Instead, the existing electoral machinery would be strengthened. Crucial to this policy was the separation of town and county electorates. Although this scheme was lost, for some years no attempt was made to marshal the town vote to influence county elections, so that a crisis was averted until the 1860s.[54] This argument has, however, met with little support. It is not accepted that the ministry was ever wholly committed to a separation between borough and county, which would have been more or less impossible anyway,

---

[53] The terms of the Act are set out in Brock, *The Great Reform Act*.

[54] This argument is predominantly associated with the writings of D. C. Moore, including 'The other face of reform', *Victorian Studies*, 5 (1961), pp. 7–34; 'Concession or cure: the sociological premises of the first Reform Act', *Historical Journal*, 9 (1966), pp. 39–59; 'Social structure, political structure and public opinion in mid-Victorian Britain', in *Ideas and Institutions of Victorian Britain*, ed. R. Robson (1967), pp. 20–57; *The Politics of Deference: a study of the mid-nineteenth century English political system* (1976).

given the number of country towns which remained part of county constituencies. The middle class lived and voted everywhere, in country and town alike, and the legitimate influence the Whigs wished to preserve operated on all independent electorates, not merely urban ones. Independent middle-class voters would, they believed, pay proper respect to the aristocracy, and it was not necessary for the administration to provide safe rural electorates for local aristocrats to dominate. Finally, even if the motives were cynical, the Act can hardly be said to have been a success, since deference voting remained at little more than pre-reform levels in the counties used as a basis for this viewpoint.[55]

The Act did not transfer power from the aristocracy to the middle class, and neither did it have much impact on the electoral system. The social composition of post-reform Parliaments was little different from the past (chapter twelve), while contests remained open to all the old abuses. W. E. Gladstone was involved in one of the most spectacular instances of post-reform corruption at Newark in 1832. At Maidstone and Norwich, corruption appears to have increased after 1832, while what interest the dukes of Buckingham were able to command in post-1832 Buckingham cost money, whereas previously a return had been obtained without expense. The buying and selling of votes seems to have continued without much interruption, and in Nottinghamshire allegations of illegal payments by both Liberals and Conservatives were made as late as 1892.[56]

Nor did reform end deferential voting. The electoral system in the countryside remained largely unchanged until 1884 (despite alterations mainly affecting the boroughs in 1867), with the result that aristocratic representation remained considerable, party organization

---

[55] Criticisms are ventured in the articles by Davis and Ellis (note 51) and J. M. Prest's review of Moore, *The Politics of Deference*, in *English Historical Review*, 93 (1978), pp. 142–4; N. Gash, *Aristocracy and People: Britain, 1815–1865* (1979), p. 148n.; O'Gorman, 'Electoral deference in "unreformed" England', p. 414. Richard Davis has concluded that the consensus of opinion regards Moore as being wrong: 'Toryism to Tamworth: the triumph of reform, 1827–1835', *Albion*, 12 (1980), p. 132. Clark, *English Society, 1688–1832*, has argued that the 1832 Reform Act must be seen in context with repeal of the Test and Corporation Acts and Roman Catholic Emancipation, measures which collectively broke down the old Anglican-aristocratic consensus.

[56] R. A. Preston, 'W. E. Gladstone and his disputed election expenses at Newark, 1832–1834', *Transactions of the Thoroton Society*, 80 (1976), pp. 73–4; Phillips, *Electoral Behaviour in Unreformed England*, pp. 77–8; R. W. Davis, 'Buckingham, 1832–1846: a study of a "pocket borough"', *Huntington Library Quarterly*, 34 (1970–1), pp. 180–1; T. J. Nossiter, *Influence, Opinion and Political Idioms in Reformed England* (1975), pp. 195–6.

was weak, and when contests took place they were expensive. Lincolnshire farmers showed a high degree of loyalty to their landlords at the polls between the 1830s and 1880s, but this was not necessarily the result of overt pressure. The almost complete unanimity of voting on some estates stemmed not from coercion or unthinking deference, because 'legitimate' landlord influence was carefully circumscribed. To evict for voting the wrong way was widely regarded as unacceptable. The landlord still had the right to command one vote but not two, and electors could prove fickle if provoked. The vigorous self-assertion by tenant farmers in defiance of their landlords in mid-nineteenth-century South Nottinghamshire suggests that this was hardly a self-contained deferential community. On the other hand, even after the introduction of the secret ballot in 1872, Conservative landlords were still apt to place an estate manager or agent outside a polling station in order to take down the names of those who had voted, as a means of gauging how many votes in a particular village had been cast for the opposition. But the value of such a move was tempered by the high proportion of voters who were not tenants of landlords. By the mid-nineteenth century no English county was purely rural or agricultural, and probably no more than one-third of adult males were directly employed in agriculture. In such circumstances aristocratic control had to be maintained by consent not force.[57] What the Act did bring about was a greater element of competition in elections, which in the longer term was to have implications for aristocratic control of voting habits.[58]

THE SURVIVAL OF ARISTOCRATIC POWER AFTER 1832

Perhaps the most significant outcome of 1832 was the prolongation of aristocratic power for a further half-century within a partially reformed

[57] Olney, *Lincolnshire Politics*, ch. 4, and 'The politics of land', in *The Victorian Countryside*, ed. G. E. Mingay (1981), pp. 58–64; David Spring, *The English Landed Estate in the Nineteenth Century: its administration* (1963), p. 178; Martin Pugh, *The Making of Modern British Politics, 1867–1939* (1982), p. 10; J. R. Fisher, 'The limits of deference: argricultural communities in a mid-nineteenth-century election campaign', *Journal of British Studies*, 21 (1981), pp. 90–105.

[58] E. J. Evans, *The Forging of the Modern State: early industrial Britain, 1783–1870* (1983), pp. 383–4; O'Gorman, *The Emergence of the British Two-Party System*, pp. 119–21; N. Gash, *Politics in the Age of Peel* (1953), p. 118. For evidence of more consistent post-1832 party voting in boroughs, see J. A. Phillips, 'The many faces of reform: the Reform Bill and the electorate', *Parliamentary History*, 1 (1982), pp. 115–35.

central and local political system. Far from handing power over to the middle class in 1832, the aristocracy survived almost intact. Both the new Poor Law of 1834, and the Municipal Corporations Act of 1835 were partially designed to correct outstanding abuses in the boroughs, without damaging landed power in the countryside. It was even possible to question the position of the Anglican establishment, not so much with reform in mind – even the Whigs realized the importance of the established church in underpinning rural stability, and in helping to provide education – but to correct some of its more obvious abuses.[59] Moreover, after 1832, government remained firmly in the hands of property owners: the haphazard collection of borough franchises was swept away and replaced by a uniform restriction vesting the vote in £10 householders; the new Poor Law was administered by boards of guardians consisting of ratepayers; and the new municipal corporations were run by councillors and aldermen elected by the ratepayers.[60] The property qualification for MPs, although amended in 1838, survived until 1858, and that for justices until 1906. To be an elector at parliamentary and local government level carried a qualification down to the twentieth century. Small wonder that John Stuart Mill was incensed in the 1860s by the 'axiom that human society exists for the sake of property in land – a grovelling superstition which is still in full force among the higher classes'.[61]

In part this reflected the inability of the radicals to undercut the position of the aristocracy in government during the 1830s and 1840s, despite the activities of the Chartists and of the Anti-Corn Law League. Chartism flourished during the 1840s, at a time when it was clear that parliamentary reform had offered nothing concrete to the majority of the population. With its new found middle-class support the government successfully resisted the agitation. Moreover, for all its radical proposals in regard to universal suffrage, annual parliaments, the secret ballot, payment of MPs, and the abolition of the property qualification, the Chartist movement's respect for some aspects of the status quo was revealed by the absence of any questions relating to the position of the House of Lords, and by Feargus O'Connor's plans to extend private landownership by means of an allotment scheme rather than to abolish it altogether.[62]

[59] Evans, *The Forging of the Modern State*, pp. 237–42, highlights the work of the Whig Ecclesiastical Revenue Commission in uncovering financial problems, and the importance of the Ecclesiastical Duties and Revenue Commission (1835) in pointing the church along the road to reform.

[60] Strictly speaking, the aldermen were elected by the councillors.

[61] Quoted in Olney, 'The politics of land', p. 59.

[62] Gash, *Aristocracy and People*, pp. 200–19.

The anti-Corn Law agitation was more obviously middle class, and was aimed at breaking the government preference for agricultural at the expense of industrial interests. John Bright regarded the Anti-Corn Law League as 'a movement of the commercial and industrious classes against the lords and great proprietors of the soil', and the Tory *Nottinghamshire Guardian* suggested that the league wished to 'diminish or destroy the influence of the proud aristocracy and to transfer the political power of the state to the hands of "the masses".'[63] The league, founded in Manchester in 1838 to agitate for repeal of the Corn Law (see chapter five), attacked the aristocracy by emphasizing how landowners rather than occupiers benefited from the existing situation.

In practice, the most serious opposition to repeal came from farmers rather than from the landed elite. Political dissension was apparent in a number of predominantly rural constituencies. In Lincolnshire, for example, local farmers put together a strong protectionist movement to defend what they perceived both as a threat to their livelihood, and as radical aggression against the social structure of the countryside. Elsewhere, protectionists helped to elect candidates opposed to government policy, while pro-repeal aristocrats such as Earl Fitzwilliam discovered that local gentry placed protection above the maintenance of party loyalties and traditions. Even so, repeal could hardly be hailed as a middle-class victory at the expense of the landed interest. Peel repealed the law in 1846 in the wake of the Irish potato famine, and the influence of the Anti-Corn Law League on this decision is debatable. The League had backed the Whigs in the 1841 general election, yet it was a Tory government which repealed the legislation, and interest in the movement was arguably not as strong in 1845–6 as it had been earlier.[64] For his part, Peel believed that efficient farmers would benefit from the move, especially when it was coupled with the government's drainage loans, and he also expected that it would spike the radicals' guns. In his view, far from being content with repeal, they would have moved on to attack other bastions of class privilege including the game laws, the land laws and the church.[65]

---

[63] Derek Fraser, 'Nottingham and the Corn Laws', *Transactions of the Thoroton Society*, 70 (1966), pp. 103–4.

[64] Norman Gash, *Sir Robert Peel* (1972), pp. 606–7.

[65] The fullest account of the Anti-Corn Law League is given in Norman McCord, *The Anti-Corn Law League* (1957). See also Olney, *Lincolnshire Politics*, p. 153; T. L. Crosby, *English Farmers and the Politics of Protection, 1815–52* (Hassocks, 1977); Fisher, 'The limits of deference'; Arnstein, 'The survival of the Victorian aristocracy', pp. 217–29. For the agricultural and parliamentary implications of repeal, see chapter five.

For all the efforts of the Chartists, and of the Anti-Corn Law League, it was by no means clear in the 1840s that aristocratic power was on the wane. John Hampden argued in 1846 that, instead of being tamed, the aristocracy had usurped 'the total powers of the constitution', and he went on to paint a vivid picture of how their iron grip on the state had placed England on the verge of following the course of other European states where overgrown aristocracies had brought final destruction.[66] But it was not to be; in the relatively prosperous 1850s the tradition of government *for* the people rather than *by* the people, and the willingness of 'the people' to accept this situation permitted aristocratic government to continue. Bagehot, writing in the 1860s, believed that the people were not yet ready for parliamentary institutions based on universal suffrage, while, since the middle class showed little inclination to take a stake in government, the system was not really questioned.[67] From 1852 a series of reform bills were introduced into the Commons. Even so, when further parliamentary reform came in 1867, it was only partly due to mass agitation after the Liberal bill of 1866 – which had been intended to enfranchise the respectable urban working class – had failed after a Tory alliance with the Liberal right wing. Disraeli's successful measure actually turned out to be more radical than its failed predecessor, but no one regarded it as an attempt to introduce democracy; even a radical like John Bright could abhor such a thought, while Bagehot believed further reform would be disastrous for the smooth running of parliamentary government, which would become impossible. Certainly the terms of the legislation did not suggest that democracy was being introduced. County seats were increased from 144 to 172, and borough seats were reduced from 323 to 286. Within three years the electorate almost doubled, but this was partly because party agents continued to improve the registration processes, and even in 1870 only two in five Englishmen had the vote.[68] Furthermore, when the aristocracy was forced to appeal to the widened electorate, it found working men just as deferential as the middle class had proved to be after 1832. In the words of *The Times*, 'the common people tolerate and even admire a social aristocracy . . . they see real merits in it which

---

[66] John Hampden, *The Aristocracy of England* (1846), p. 7.

[67] A. P. Thornton, *The Habit of Authority* (1966), pp. 230, 241, 252; W. Bagehot, *The English Constitution* (1963 edn), pp. 62–3.

[68] F. B. Smith, *The Making of the Second Reform Bill* (Cambridge, 1966); Bagehot, *The English Constitution*, pp. 161–71; Bush, *The English Aristocracy*, pp. 202–3; H. J. Hanham, *Elections and Party Management: politics in the time of Disraeli and Gladstone* (1959), pp. ix–xii.

they do not see elsewhere.' Moreover, it was the same old values that they respected, viewing aristocracy as 'a practical guarantee for more charitable, honourable, and gentleman-like conduct than can be produced by the mere play of self-interest'.[69]

ARISTOCRATIC POWER ON THE WANE

Although the surface appeared relatively unruffled, underlying trends suggested a loosening of aristocratic authority. In the 1850s considerable disquiet was expressed in regard to the aristocracy's mishandling of the Crimean War, while as the electorate was expanded aristocratic influence became more difficult to wield.[70] Landed control of borough electorates inevitably weakened in the course of the nineteenth century. Although the decline of the Butes' influence in Cardiff during the 1850s and 1860s was partly the result of a long minority, it also reflected the migration into the town of people with no obvious loyalties towards the castle interest.[71] As electorates increased, influence weakened. In Newcastle upon Tyne the electorate increased by 55 per cent between 1832 and 1859, and the Ridleys – who had represented the town in almost unbroken succession since 1741 – found the going too tough, and abdicated from town politics in 1836. Medium-sized towns took to returning the largest employer of labour, as in Norwich, Darlington and Jarrow; while industrialized parts of counties followed a similar line, hence the return of the coalowner Arthur Markham for the Mansfield district of North Nottinghamshire. Naturally landowners survived better in rural constituencies, but even here their position did not go unchallenged. County Durham enjoyed continuing rural influence in elections from 1832 until 1865, but from 1868 industrial interests began to usurp the traditional landowners, and in turn they were faced by a challenge from organized labour in 1874. If voting continued to be an act of personal service to a magnate rather than an expression of individual opinion, the magnate might well be changing from a landowner to a businessman. In a few constituencies landowners were even forced to

[69] *The Times*, 13 February 1871, p. 9.
[70] S. G. Checkland, *The Rise of Industrial Society in England, 1815–1885* (1964), pp. 284–6. The structure of constituencies, elections and parties between 1867 and 1885 is examined in detail by Hanham, *Elections and Party Management*.
[71] John Davies, 'Aristocratic town makers and the coal metropolis: the marquesses of Bute and Cardiff, 1776–1947', in *Patricians, Power and Politics in Nineteenth-Century Towns*, ed. David Cannadine (Leicester, 1982), pp. 45–8.

give way to newcomers to the political scene, as at Morpeth in 1874, when Sir George Grey was defeated by Thomas Burt, a working miner.[72]

Despite this development it was only in the 1880s that the political position of the landowners was seriously undermined, and the tide turned irrevocably. The Corrupt Practices Act (1883) outlawed some of the more obvious forms of electoral chicanery, and it was followed by a further extension of the franchise a year later, and by the introduction of equal electoral districts in 1885, which finally swept away the old constituencies dating back in some cases to the Middle Ages. Not surprisingly the aristocracy viewed such changes without enthusiasm. Gladstone's decision ahead of the 1884 session to extend the franchise in the counties was always likely to bring the Commons and Lords into conflict. The bill proposed household suffrage – thereby maintaining a property qualification for voting – and it passed the Commons. In the Lords a second reading was refused unless the bill was accompanied by redistribution, a demand stemming from the Conservative belief that an election on a wider franchise but with the old constituencies would damage its interests. The result was a government defeat in the upper house, and, since Gladstone declared his intention of reintroducing the bill in the autumn, the position of the Lords came to centre-stage in the political arena. Joseph Chamberlain led the radical attack on the Lords, but the real issue remained seat redistribution, and the Conservative fear of being swamped at the polls. The key proved to be equal electoral districts with single members, and the Tories supported this to capitalize on their strength in suburban and middle-class areas of big cities. The result was a reform which had agreement between the parties, and gave the vote to something over 60 per cent of adult males in average English constituencies of 13,000 voters. A common franchise applied to all constituencies.[73]

From 1885 the political system required an efficient organization to facilitate registration of voters and electoral activity, and for this task the old country house tradition was inadequate. The growth of political clubs, the disappearance of corruption and a decline in the number of uncontested elections revealed just how far popular party politics was replacing the personal manipulations of the past. In the East Midlands 47 per cent of seats were uncontested in 1865, but all

[72] Nossiter, *Influence, Opinion and Political Idioms*, pp. 45, 108–9, 134; Pugh, *The Making of Modern British Politics*, pp. 9–10, 12.

[73] E. J. Feuchtwanger, *Democracy and Empire: Britain, 1865–1914* (1985), pp. 171–4.

the constituencies voted in 1885, and 82 per cent polled again the following year. Half the region's county seats were contested at every general election down to 1913, and only two missed contests at three or more of the nine elections. Moreover, the landowning position was further undermined by the increasingly obvious alignment of the great houses behind the Conservative interest, which helped to weaken the standing of the aristocracy as an impartial political force. In the East Midlands, Conservative support was still very much of the old school; between 1874 and 1913, 91 per cent of all uncontested seats returned a Conservative, while in the region as a whole the Liberals held a clear majority of contested seats.[74]

Although the Lords survived radical attacks during the reform campaign, their position in the 1880s was far from secure. Gladstone's Irish policies culminating in his espousal of Home Rule helped to alienate the old Whig elite within his own party, and to propel them into the hands of the Tories, as well as undermining the position of the Lords. His majority in 1868 was won on the issues of disestablishment of the Church of Ireland and Irish land reform, but he immediately came into conflict with the Lords as the self-appointed last line of resistance on Irish matters. These measures passed by 1873, but the future utility of the upper house remained in contention. By the 1880s Lords reform was firmly established in the radical programme, and Irish issues provided the major platform for discontent. However, they also split the ministry. The Cabinet assembled in 1880 was still in the old tradition, its membership including a duke, a marquess and five earls, but Irish issues provoked the Marquess of Lansdowne and the Duke of Argyle into resignation by 1881. When in 1886 Gladstone brought forward a Home Rule Bill to establish a domestically autonomous Parliament in Ireland, the split in Liberalism was completed. A few hereditary Liberal peers remained, but the majority gradually moved over to form a dominant Conservative and Unionist front in the Lords, which proved to be lasting.[75]

In the 1890s the situation deteriorated further. Between 1892 and 1895 the Lords defeated measures concerning Irish Home Rule, Scottish local government, succession to real property and employers' liability. The second Home Rule bill was defeated in the Lords in 1893

[74] F. W. Craig, *British Parliamentary Election Results, 1832–85* (1977); *British Parliamentary Election Results, 1885–1918* (1974). In this context the East Midlands is taken to be the historic counties of Derbyshire, Nottinghamshire, Leicestershire and Lincolnshire.

[75] G. D. Phillips, 'The Whig lords and liberalism, 1886–1893', *Historical Journal*, 24 (1981), pp. 167–73.

by 419 votes to 41. Gladstone considered a 'peers versus people' election, which might have become the starting point for a further attack on entrenched privilege. However, the bill had alienated substantial sections of the middle- and lower-class electorate, and had stirred latent British nationalism and imperialism, and these considerations, coupled with the absence of a bold social policy during the 1880s and 1890s, left the Liberals unsure of the backing they might receive on such an issue at the polls. Despite considerable posturing, especially from Lord Rosebery, the moment passed, and it was not until 1908 that the Liberals again thought seriously about upper-house reform.[76]

FINAL RESISTANCE

In the closing years of the nineteenth century some of the mortar of aristocratic government began to crumble, but the castle did not collapse; indeed, an illusion of stability was maintained, a hardening of attitudes which implied that the aristocracy was far from being defeated. Historians enjoy the benefit of hindsight, and from this perspective it is not difficult to conclude that the aristocratic position began to be undermined by about 1880, and it had been severely curtailed by 1914, but this was not clear at the time.[77] Between 1868 and 1910, the proportion of landowners fell from 46 to 26 per cent of Conservative MPs, and from 26 to 7 per cent of Liberal MPs. But decline was not necessarily progressive. While only 34 per cent of new recruits in the Parliament of 1885 were from landed backgrounds, the proportion rose to nearly 37 per cent in 1886 and to 42 per cent in 1892. The overall proportion of MPs from such backgrounds was slightly higher in the Parliament of 1892 than in either of its two predecessors.[78] The loss of position was even less clear in the Cabinet. The Conservatives retained control down to 1905 with a peer as prime minister, and, if the middle class began to break through into the Cabinet after 1868, between 1874 and 1895 they failed to achieve a

[76] Arnstein, 'The survival of the Victorian Aristocracy', pp. 221–6, 250–2; Pugh, *The Making of Modern British Politics*, p. 94.

[77] Guttsman, *The British Political Elite*, p. 87.

[78] F. M. L. Thompson, 'Britain', in *European Landed Elites in the Nineteenth Century*, ed. David Spring (1977), pp. 24–5; Guttsman, *The British Political Elite*, p. 104; Ponsonby, *The Decline of Aristocracy*, p. 104; James Cornford, 'The parliamentary foundations of the Hotel Cecil', in *Ideas and Institutions of Victorian Britain*, ed. R. Robson (1967), p. 310.

majority. Of the 101 men who held office between 1886 and 1916, forty-one were landed proprietors with, on the whole, large landed estates, and two-thirds had been educated at one of the major public schools.[79] Coupled with changes in recruitment to the civil service and the army, aristocratic control of both the legislative and the executive branches of the state appeared to be slipping. This was not entirely surprising, since aristocratic government is a negation of democracy, and its survival through a period of parliamentary reform was always likely to be in doubt. The demand for democratic institutions reflected the decline in respect for the existing hierarchy, which meant in effect the decline of old-style deference.

All was not lost, however. Salisbury's administration, which took office in June 1895, has been described as the 'last government in the western world to possess all the attributes of aristocracy in working condition', even though more than half of its members were from the middle class.[80] The illusion of stability also survived because the 'service' side of English aristocratic life tended to expand in the closing decades of the century. The connection between the aristocracy and the army may have been closer in 1900 than it had been in 1870 when commission purchase was abolished, while imperial responsibilities may have drawn disproportionately on landed families, helping to hide the real facts of a changing position.[81] Above all, perhaps, the illusion was maintained in two other, related areas. The first was the adaptability of the elite. Through upbringing and education, its members continued to believe in their inborn right to govern, and so they acted with an air of confidence which might not in reality have been justified.[82] This did not prevent a rapprochement with the middle class, reflected in admissions to the peerage, the desire of peers to take on company directorships, and their willingness to become mayors in a number of towns and cities. Second, when, in the later Victorian and Edwardian years, the elite began to grow anxious about its position, it set about defending the ramparts with characteristic determination.

Although opposition became most apparent after 1900, there was plenty of earlier evidence to suggest that the aristocracy would not

[79] Thompson, 'Britain', p. 26; Guttsman, *The British Political Elite*, pp. 75–80, 91.

[80] Barbara Tuchman, *The Proud Tower* (New York, 1966), p. 3; Guttsman, *The British Political Elite*, p. 78.

[81] David Spring, 'The role of the aristocracy in the late nineteenth century', *Victorian Studies*, 4 (1960), p. 59.

[82] See chapter three.

succumb without a fight. Lord Salisbury, for example, throughout his life fought proposals for an extension of the vote. In the 1860s, while still a younger son, he declared the interest of the Conservatives to be in preserving the rights and privileges of the propertied classes. Democracy, in Salisbury's eyes, was dangerous to liberty, and his attitude remained fixed when he became prime minister in the 1890s.[83] Salisbury's views were typical of many aristocrats of his generation, and increasingly they came to be associated with the Conservative Party. In the early 1880s the Liberals could be characterized as an alliance of the old Whig aristocrats with the urban middle classes and urban workers, while the Conservatives consisted of country squires, urban businessmen and suburban white-collar workers. Since this was not really sufficient as a power base, the Conservatives also made a strong appeal to the working-class vote, via working men's clubs, the Primrose League – which turned out to be a perfect vehicle for Conservative peers, since it was clothed in archaic terminology and traditional personalities – and an outpouring of propaganda through such media as the music hall, under the inspiration of the ultimate working-class Tory hero, Lord Randolph Churchill. At the same time the party remained firmly aristocratic, not permitting any of its newly found supporters a place in the leadership.[84]

The hour of reckoning could not be indefinitely postponed, even if the débâcle over Home Rule, with its attendant overtones of nationalism and anti-Catholicism, helped to preserve the Conservative power base in the closing years of the nineteenth century. In the event it was a short-term reprieve, because the Liberals bounced back, following up their electoral landslide of 1906 with a vigorous reform programme. With the Lords' having a built-in Conservative majority, conflict was inevitable, and clashes occurred during the early years of the ministry. On the other hand, fear of antagonizing the working class led the Conservatives to accept measures such as the Trades Disputes Act without a fight. But Lloyd George's 'People's Budget' in 1909 went too far. By raising the rate of death duties and income tax, and by introducing super-tax and land taxes, Lloyd George stirred the old elite to resist what they saw as Asquith's government's attempt to legislate them into impotence. The budget was thrown out by 350 votes to 75, precipitating a constitutional crisis. The majority reflected

---

[83] Tuchman, *The Proud Tower*, pp. 10–12.

[84] Arnstein, 'The survival of the Victorian aristocracy', p. 250; Martin Pugh, *The Tories and the People* (Oxford, 1985); R. F. Foster, *Lord Randolph Churchill: a political life* (Oxford, 1981).

the Conservative dominance of the upper house; about 60 per cent of the great landed peers took the side of the Conservatives, and only 4 per cent voted for the Liberals. It was a gamble, and it failed. Reform became an issue, and although the Lords resisted, even throwing out the first Parliament Bill of October 1910 and thereby precipitating the second election of the year, the writing was on the wall. Once George V promised to create the necessary new peers, Asquith called the bluff and the bill went through. Although limited to a two-year veto on bills, the Lords were not finished – the new Irish Home Rule Bill was delayed in 1912 and 1913, along with three other measures. If the aristocracy had lost control of the lower house, this did not mean that the peers were to become a tame arm of the state.

A century after the critical electoral changes of the 1880s, the survival of aristocratic power down to 1914 still seems remarkable. Government reaction to events in France after 1789 stemmed rather than provoked a revolution; aristocratic government continued after 1815 despite abuses of power; and electoral reform took place on terms decided by the aristocracy. Thus 1832 was to preserve legitimate aristocratic influence; 1867 was largely a government measure to rectify the inbuilt Whig majority; and even the measures of 1883–5, although they threatened the aristocratic hold on the system, took place with their acquiescence. The rising business and professional classes lacked the cohesive self-confidence of the aristocracy, and they tended to defer to the establishment. Over time, however, change was inevitable. It began in the towns after 1835, and later gathered momentum in the radical demands for parliamentary, and finally House of Lords, reform. Gradually the aristocratic grip loosened. Party conflict at the polls, and each extension of the franchise, weakened deference. Efficient organizations were needed to register votes, while increasing numbers of electors made influence less easy to operate, and electoral changes finally produced a subtle alteration in the balance of political power. Even in the 1880s a few peers enjoyed influence over a seat or two, but the old system was in retreat, a retreat enhanced by the Lords' reactionary views over electoral reform and Ireland. Aristocratic government remained in the 1890s, and its service element provided an illusion of stability, but its days were numbered; the Liberal landslide of 1906 threatened the position of the Lords, and in 1909 Lloyd George delivered the *coup de grâce*. By 1911 Parliament had been reformed, and the disputed tax changes instituted.

On the eve of the First World War the political power of the old elite had been curtailed, originally through its loss of electoral power, but also through the erosion of its influence in the Commons, to a lesser extent in the Cabinet, and finally in the constitution.[85] But the old system was not dead. In the words of one recent historian, the 1914–18 war can be seen as 'an expression of the decline and fall of the old order fighting to prolong its life rather than of the explosive rise of industrial capitalism bent on imposing its primacy'.[86] It was a war of the old elite, typified not merely by the recall of Earl Kitchener as war secretary, but also by the enthusiasm of the second Duke of Westminster. He initially enrolled in the French army (not expecting the British to enter the war) and when he escaped from that predicament he turned up on the western front by November 1914 with his own private army.[87] However, the days of the old elite were numbered, even in their traditional military stronghold. As in the Crimea more than half a century earlier, aristocratic leadership was found wanting, and if the war was won it was at an unacceptable cost in human life. The First World War proved to be the straw which broke the camel's back, and from which the aristocracy emerged permanently weakened.

[85] Ponsonby, *The Decline of Aristocracy*, p. 23; A. Meija, 'The upper classes in late Victorian and Edwardian Britain: a study of the formation and perpetration of class bias' (Stanford University, Ph.D. thesis, 1968), pp. 28–43.

[86] A. J. Mayer, *The Persistence of the Old Regime* (1981), p. 4.

[87] Robert Lacey, *Aristocrats* (1983), pp. 149–52.

Chapter Fourteen

Conclusion: The Decline of the Aristocracy

Aristocratic England was an unequal society. Its rationale depended on the capacity of the few to dominate the institutions of the state in the interests of the many. Land gave credibility, and through their control of both the legislature and the executive the landowners governed the state. The absence of revolution, or of a sustained challenge to their position, reflected a capacity to adapt to changing circumstances and to govern in what was seen to be the best interests of the majority. By the 1880s, however, the image was beginning to slip. Land, so long the key to social and political status, was increasingly becoming a burden, as the agricultural depression brought down rents and values, and in the process tripped up some of those who had wandered into debt on the assumption that land would always be a firm security. The hour of sale remained postponable for many, and if there was an understandable tendency to exaggerate the severity of the position a considerable acreage certainly found its way on to the market before 1914. Survival was beginning to depend on a mineral income or the profits of urban ground rents, and those without such safeguards – and even some with them – chose to diversify into a liquid assets portfolio.

Other changes in the closing decades of the century also boded ill. The first business peers found their way into the Lords; the civil service was opened up to competitive examination, and commission purchase in the army came to an end; the franchise was expanded in a more evidently democratic direction which undercut the political influence of the country house in favour of party machinery; and county government was at long last reformed. Moreover, the aristocracy no longer seemed to have its finger on the pulse of society as the House of Lords came into conflict with Gladstone over Ireland, and later with the 1906 Liberal government over tax and welfare reforms.

Democracy as it began to emerge in late nineteenth-century England could not coexist with aristocracy, and the evident failure of the traditional establishment – as, for example, in the Crimea – undermined its position in the state. Arthur Ponsonby noted in 1912 that 'the suspicion is growing that our aristocratic model is deteriorating, that our patricians are inadequately performing the duties which fall to them'; a consequence, he believed, of democracy requiring a higher level of trained, informed and specialized personnel.[1] Although it was an aristocratic legislature which oversaw most of the substantive changes to the civil service, army and franchise, these moves effectively undermined its monopoly of state control, and eventually brought its demise. Even so, in 1914 few people could have envisaged how speedily the position would change, but there is little doubt that in the decades after 1918 centuries of expansion and consolidation counted for nothing as the aristocratic edifice came tumbling down. Effective political power passed into other hands; large estates were broken up and sold to tenants and to public institutions; country houses were pulled down; and the divorce between land and wealth disappeared. The merging of elites which had proved so elusive in the nineteenth century finally took place in the twentieth, and in this process middle-class politicians and values triumphed. None the less, the English have found it impossible to abandon their aristocracy. Many great estates remain, even if in an emasculated form; the House of Lords retains an effective role in the legislature; and peers regularly find a seat in Conservative Cabinets. Country house visiting reflects the continued interest in the group, as well as the extraordinary extent to which the national heritage remains in private hands. In the 1930s the German journalist Karl Heinz Abshagen noted that 'subconsciously, the great majority of the English people regard a lord to this day as an individual of a special type, who is tacitly allowed a special constitutional position'; while in the 1960s Roy Perrott noted that while shorn of their powers and influence the aristocracy retained an affection – most people 'accept them as men of some consequence without always knowing quite why'.[2]

SURVIVAL THROUGH DECLINE: THE TWENTIETH-CENTURY ARISTOCRACY

Physically the twentieth-century peerage has grown considerably (table 14.1). Just over 300 new peers were created between 1830 and 1895,

---

[1] Arthur Ponsonby, *The Decline of Aristocracy* (1912), p. 23.

[2] Karl Heinz Abshagen, *King, Lords and Gentlemen: influence and power of the English upper classes* (1939), p. 94; Roy Perrott, *The Aristocrats* (1968), p. xiii.

but more than 600 were added between 1895 and 1957. As a result, the modern peerage is mainly of short date. In 1956 only 144 of the 550 baronies pre-dated 1832, and the pattern was similar among viscounts and earls.[3] Since 1958, life peerages have been granted in considerable numbers, and hereditary titles have more or less ceased to be created. This innovation, which had been discussed since the mid-nineteenth century, reflected a long-term change in the nature of appointments to the peerage. For much of the present century, hereditary peerages had gone to landless men of slender means. Virtually any politician who reached ministerial rank could expect a barony, and probably a viscountcy, while dynasties were also founded by top civil servants, eminent physicians and even a Cambridge scientist. Of new peers created between 1901 and 1957, only 46 out of 556 (8 per cent) were from landowning backgrounds, and they were outnumbered by the 91 industrialists (16 per cent) and the 100 professional men (18 per cent). In effect, this was the merger of the upper social ranks which had failed to materialize in the nineteenth century, and by 1967 43 per cent of members of the House of Lords had derived their income partly or wholly from estate ownership and 46 per cent wholly or partly from business directorships. Less than one-quarter were simply landowners.[4] Although most of the business lords were from among the newer creations of the twentieth century, notable exceptions included the Earl of Verulam with ten directorships and Viscount Hampden with seven.

Nor has the process been all one way; many peers who have lost all or a substantial proportion of their land in the course of the twentieth century have turned to business in order to make a living. For many this has meant opening their country houses to visitors, and some have even developed their remaining land as wildlife and fun parks. Whichever course of action has been taken it has usually stemmed from financial necessity. For others, with no land at all, the break with the old lifestyle has been more complete; thus in the 1960s the fifth Lord Redesdale, descendant of a family which once owned 30,000 acres of Northumberland, ran a London dry-cleaning and laundry business.[5]

---

[3] L. G. Pine, *The Story of the Peerage* (1956), p. 227.

[4] W. L. Guttsman, *The British Political Elite* (1963), p. 126. Nancy Mitford, refusing to accept a decline of the old standards, argued as recently as 1956 that the conveyance of a title still turned a man, be he what he may, into an aristocrat, and that such men did not need to work because 'effort is unrelated to money': *Noblesse Oblige: an enquiry into the identifiable characteristics of the English aristocracy* (1956), pp. 45, 48–9.

[5] Perrott, *The Aristocrats*, pp. 34, 133–40; Leslie Geddes-Brown, 'Why these rush-hour trippers are a sign of the past for the stately homes of England', *Sunday*

Table 14.1 The peerage in 1900 and 1980

Rank	1900	1980
Dukes	22	26[a]
Marquesses	22	37
Earls	124	194
Viscounts	30	127
Barons (hereditary)	324	476
Barons (life)	—	346
Total	522	1206

Source: Appendix; John Scott, *The Upper Classes: property and privilege in Britain* (1982), p. 154

[a] Includes dukes of the royal blood.

Despite such falls from grace, the demand for titles remains, and some individuals are prepared to go to considerable expense in order to establish claims to long-dormant titles.[6]

Baronetcies and knighthoods have also been liberally scattered in the twentieth century. Between 1905 and 1934, 649 baronetcies were gazetted. Many such honours were sold by Lloyd George, at least one falling to a man with a criminal record.[7] The 1945 Labour government stemmed the tide by refusing to grant baronetcies (except to retiring lord mayors of London), and, although a further 106 were created by Conservative administrations between 1951 and 1964, none has been created since that date. Knighthoods were also given out in excessive numbers during Lloyd George's premiership, including 1026 between 1921 and 1925, and over the whole period 1905-54 a total of 10,503 men were dubbed. Although numbers have fallen since, 123 knights

---

Times, 26 May 1985. Country house visiting has a pedigree stretching back into the eighteenth century: Adrian Tinniswood, 'Such lofty magnificence! Popular perceptions of the country house', *Bulletin of Local History: East Midlands Region*, 19 (1984), pp. 15–22.

[6] *The Times*, 25 July 1985, for the revival of the earldom of Annandale and Hartfell for Mr Patrick Hope Johnstone.

[7] Michael De-la-Noy, *The Honours System* (1985), pp. 93,. 105–21.

were created in 1968 and 106 in 1978. In general, knighthoods of the British Empire have gone to higher civil servants and military officers, while people from business have most commonly been dubbed knight bachelor. Titular honours in recent years have in practice taken the form of non-hereditary life peerages and knighthoods. Consequently businessmen and civil and military servants receive knighthoods part-way through their careers, which may be converted into life peerages for men and women whom it is desired to have in the political arena. In addition, MPs are often moved into the upper chamber: between 1901 and 1957 about one-fifth could expect to end their careers with a peerage, with the greatest proportion from among those who had achieved ministerial office during their lower-house career.[8]

As the aristocracy merged into a broader-based elite, its distinctive role in politics and society became less clear, although birth and connection remained significant for making progress in the hierarchy. This did not mean that the aristocratic function disappeared. Despite the 1911 Parliament Act, the House of Lords retained considerable legislative authority, including the right to initiate legislation and to amend Commons bills through certain delaying tactics. In the Cabinet the aristocratic group has declined during the twentieth century, but it has not disappeared. Between 1916 and 1955, 26 out of 207 Cabinet ministers were aristocrats (22 per cent), and as late as 1979 the Conservative Party came to power with a strong contingent of peers, baronets and gentry in the Cabinet. The first non-landed prime minister was elected only in 1908, and the last peer to hold the post was the fourteenth Earl of Home in 1963. However, as the result of a dispute in the early 1960s over whether Mr Anthony Wedgwood Benn was entitled to renounce his father's title of Viscount Stansgate, the law was changed in 1963 to permit an individual to disclaim a hereditary title for life. As a result, Lord Home felt it necessary to relinquish his title in order to hold the post. Other high offices have been in peerage hands almost down to the present day. More obvious has been the decline of aristocratic influence in the Commons. Although fifty-eight sons of peers and baronets sat in the lower house in 1928, their number had dwindled to only twelve in 1955. However, the number of Conservative MPs described as farmer or landowner remained at around 10 per cent at each election between 1945 and 1974.[9] In the civil service, the proportion of landowners'

[8] Ibid., p. 93; John Scott, *The Upper Classes: property and privilege in Britain* (1982), pp. 153–6, 163–4.
[9] M. L. Bush, *The English Aristocracy* (Manchester 1984), pp. 151–2; Guttsman, *The British Political Elite*, pp. 78–9, 91–5, 109; Scott, *The Upper Classes*, p. 175;

sons decreased from 30 to 2.5 per cent in the top positions between 1880 and 1970, while their army role has also declined considerably since 1918. The aristocracy suffered many casualties in the First World War. Twenty British peers, forty-nine direct heirs and a greater number of younger sons died in action.[10] Among 5687 Old Etonians who served, about 20 per cent were killed, 25 per cent were wounded, and 1292 won either the DSO or the MC.[11] But the war finally undermined the fragile confidence in aristocratic leadership which had been declining since the Crimea.

The aristocratic role in local politics has not diminished as noticeably. In the 1960s thirty of the fifty-two county councils in England and Wales had a titled person among the leadership, and some had several. The overall total of sixty-five included four dukes, a marquess, eight earls, two viscounts, eighteen barons, five peeresses and twenty-seven baronets. Even in 1985 the forty-six lords-lieutenant in England included a duchess, two marquesses, two earls, three viscounts, five barons, six baronets and five knights, most of the rest being untitled gentry often with a military background. The peerage has also continued to be well represented on the commission of the peace. In addition, influence in the church has been maintained, with the great majority of livings which are still in private hands held by peers'and gentry. During the 1960s at least twelve peers had the right of appointment to seven or more livings.[12] At the less formal level, the aristocracy has continued to play a significant role in the local community through the same mixture of philanthropy and paternalism which served them so well in the past. The current Duke of

---

L. G. Pine, 'Peerage in history and in law', *Law Times*, 232, 13 October 1961; 'The Peerage Act, 1963', *Ante*, 234, 20 September 1963. Lord Carrington was the most recent aristocratic holder of the foreign secretaryship (1979–82). Despite loss of numbers, the patrician image survives. One of the four ambitious politicians aiming to be prime minister in the recent novel by Jeffrey Archer, *First Among Equals* (1984), is Charles Seymour, the second son of an earl with a landed estate in Somerset and a thriving merchant bank in the City of London. Archer, a former Conservative MP, and most recently deputy chairman of the Conservative Party, has another of his characters note of Seymour's ambitions that 'his patrician background still counts for something with the Tories. Sir Alec [Douglas Home], remains the best loved of our most recent Prime Ministers' (p. 408).

[10] Robert Lacey, *Aristocrats* (1983), p. 154.

[11] Harold Perkin, 'The recruitment of elites in British society since 1800', *Journal of Social History*, 12 (1978), p. 231; Perrot, *The Aristocrats*, pp. 89, 190–1.

[12] Perrott, *The Aristocrats*, pp. 188–91; *Whitaker's Almanack*, 118th edn (1986), p. 631. Nancy Mitford deplored the tendency of aristocrats to divest themselves of their powers of appointment to livings, by turning the job over to bishops: *Noblesse Oblige*, p. 60.

Westminster, for example, with property scattered between Canada, Scotland, North Wales and London attends more than 200 local functions a year in and around the family seat at Eaton Hall in Cheshire, while many of his colleagues have undertaken a variety of roles, stretching from opening garden parties to acting as churchwarden and, of course, to making financial donations.[13]

Social leadership has also remained aristocratic, although in this case the admittance of non-landed men into the peerage and baronetage has given it something of a false continuity. In the 1960s the London Season included six times as many events as thirty years earlier, while foxhunting retains its position in the winter calendar. However, since the late nineteenth century it has been business wealth which has helped to maintain the packs, and even in 1985 the clientele of a polo school turned out to be newly rich seeking a veneer of social respectability.[14] The *nouveaux riches* have not been able to paper over all the cracks. Court presentation of well-connected young ladies ended in 1958, and entry into London society is now gained through inclusion on the list of about 150 débutantes which is compiled annually by the editor of *The Tatler*. Other events in the social calendar, including Royal Ascot, Henley Regatta and Wimbledon are also pale imitations of their former glory.[15]

THE DECLINING SIGNIFICANCE OF LANDOWNERSHIP

The merging of elites in the twentieth century has partially obscured the real problem for the traditional aristocracy, the decline of its landed power base. Even in Edwardian England it was possible to make a fetish of the land, which still had a mystique of its own that set it apart from other forms of wealth. By 1914, however, impressive amounts of land had already found their way on to the market after changes in the land law, and prolonged agricultural depression, had begun to create considerable financial problems for the landed elite. If what was already a fast-flowing river by the time war broke out slowed to a trickle during the course of the conflict, it became a raging torrent for a few years after the conclusion of peace. During 1919 probably more than one million acres changed hands, and if this was a record it survived only until the following season. At the end of 1921 the *Estates*

---

[13] Lacey, *Aristocrats*, p. 212; Perrott, *The Aristocrats*, pp. 191–8.
[14] *Sunday Times Magazine*, 28 July 1985, p. 38.
[15] Scott, *The Upper Classes*, pp. 176–9.

Gazette summed up four hectic years with the conclusion that one-quarter of the land of England must have changed hands, and it seems likely that between six and eight million acres were sold. Since then, considerable quantities of land have continued to change hands without attracting quite the attention of those immediate post-war years, and there has been no return to the static conditions of the mid-nineteenth century.[16] Clearly the sanctity of landownership has been upset, and some contemporaries and historians have depicted events in the most lurid terms. In practice the situation was not so simple, and the private estate has not disappeared. But whatever the preferred reasons – agricultural depression, death duties, the campaign against landlordism – the estate system as it existed prior to 1914 did not survive the First World War.

The change must not be overplayed in the way that some contemporaries tended to do in the 1920s. Of 219 estates of 3000 acres of more in the counties of Bedfordshire, Essex, Hertfordshire, Huntingdonshire, Norfolk and Suffolk in 1873, only 118 survived in 1941. Bedfordshire had sixty-nine estates in excess of 701 acres in 1873 but only twenty-nine by 1925, and, as a proportion of the acreage of all private estates of 100 acres or more, this represented a fall from 74 per cent to 54 per cent. Private estates of 1000 acres or more in the county declined during the period from 65 per cent of the acreage in holdings of 100 acres or more to only 49 per cent.[17] Such a change in half a century was clearly of major proportions, but significantly nearly half of the county remained in estates of 1000 acres or more *after* the great break-up. This element of continuity also comes through in a recent survey of the principal estates of 500 landowners, over one-third of the largest private owners in later nineteenth-century England. Between 1880 and 1923, 106, or 21 per cent of the estates, underwent a change of ownership, but this did not necessarily mean the disposal of more than part of the whole, and sometimes it was nothing more than an outlying part. Moreover, even though the process of estate transfer has continued during the twentieth century, in 1980 52 per cent of the sample families still had a limited continuity of landownership. Admittedly this implies that in 48 per cent of cases the family no longer owned the core, and probably had no association at all with the property, but at least it suggests that some of

[16] F. M. L. Thompson, *English Landed Society in the Nineteenth Century* (1963), pp. 329–32.

[17] Guttsman, *The British Political Elite*, p. 130; H. Durant, 'The development of landownership with special reference to Bedfordshire, 1773–1925', *Sociological Review* (1936), pp. 86–7.

the gloomier comments about the great estate have not proved well founded. If there has been a transfer of unprecedented magnitude between 1880 and 1980, with a steady decline in the number and extent of privately owned historic estates, this was not completed by the middle of the 1920s, and nor had all the traditional proprietors disappeared by 1980.[18]

In this process of change it is clear that the greater owners with 10,000 acres or more of land had a better chance of survival than the more substantial gentry in the 3000–10,000-acre bracket. From the beginning the greater owners seem to have recognized the way that the wind was blowing. With their larger overall holdings, they were able to sell detached properties without upsetting the unity of the core estate, and they were also adept at manoeuvring their portfolios. Some greater owners even took advantage of the high land prices after 1918 to convert part of their acreage into paper securities. The sale of a parcel of land could be useful for paying off mortgages, and reinvesting the surplus in securities, which, at a yield of 7 or 8 per cent, brought in twice the sum to be expected of land.[19] That such a move could be contemplated, let alone undertaken, suggests a considerable change of outlook since the 1870s. However, a number of large estates were broken up, and many more have been reduced in size. Between 1873 and 1967 the Duke of Northumberland's 186,000 acres were reduced to 80,000, the Duke of Devonshire's 138,000 declined to 72,000, and the Duke of Portland's 64,000 acres decreased to only 17,000. By 1980, in the sample of 500 estates, just under 50 per cent of the former great landowners with more than 10,000 acres still owned all or a substantial proportion of the core estate in their family's possession a century earlier.[20]

The impact of change on the smaller estates is apparent from the fact that in the same sample only 16 per cent of owners with 3000–10,000 acres continued to own 3000 acres or more including the historic principal estate. In many cases where a family has been unable to maintain its position, the tendency has been to break completely the links with property rather than to decline into the ranks of the owner-occupiers. This may have brought more land on to the market as such families sold out even at a time when they might have survived, albeit at a lesser level. Among the gentry of Essex,

---

[18] Heather Clemenson, *English Country Houses and Landed Estates* (1982), pp. 111, 127.

[19] Ibid., p. 112; Thompson, *English Landed Society*, p. 335.

[20] Perrott, *The Aristocrats*, pp. 152–3; Clemenson, *English Country Houses and Landed Estates*, pp. 119–20.

Oxfordshire and Shropshire, only one-third survived in 1952 in possession of their country seats. Another quarter continued to be listed by Burke as landed gentry after having sold their seats and moved to smaller properties, while the rest had disappeared altogether. For some it was clearly preferable to sell the land in order to maintain a semblance of their former lifestyle.[21]

The financial difficulties which provoked so many sales often originated in the nineteenth century, even if at that point they were not as pressing as some families claimed. Their professional pessimism was fuelled by what seemed to many like a deliberate attack on the aristocracy by successive governments from 1906 onwards. Lloyd George's 'People's Budget' of 1909 looked like the attack long feared by the predominantly Conservative landed interest. He proposed an increment value duty and an underdeveloped land duty, as well as introducing provisions for a valuation of all the land in England. Such measures provided a political inducement to sell, especially for those already financially hard-pressed, on the grounds that future legislation was likely to be more rather than less oppressive.

With the war and its aftermath, the financial burden increased. At Wilton and Savernake the burden of all direct taxes increased between 1914 and 1919 from 9 to 30 per cent of the rental.[22] To cap these problems, in 1919 death duties on estates over £200,000 in value were raised to 40 per cent, a blow which, however grievous in itself, was made the more so by the loss of heirs during the war. In the years that followed, a merry-go-round developed in which government raised duties and landowners sought to avoid them. Private estate companies were formed until the 1940 Finance Act brought to an end many of the advantages of this type of wealth-holding. In its place came 'gifting', whereby property was transferred to the next generation three (and, later, five) years in advance of the father's death, although this course of action was fraught with many obvious difficulties. Capital gains tax was introduced in 1965, and in the 1970s estate duty was replaced by

---

[21] Clemenson, *English Country Houses and Landed Estates*, p. 120; Perrott, *The Aristocrats*, p. 156; Thompson, *English Landed Society*, p. 342. Something of this nature had happened to Guy Crouchback's father in Evelyn Waugh's 'Sword of Honour' trilogy. The family had lived at estates at Broome since the reign of Henry I, but by the 1930s the property was reduced to a house, a park and a home farm, and Mr Crouchback let it to a convent before retiring to a small hotel in a nearby watering place. Although he sold the land at a bad time, he invested wisely, thereby procuring an annual income in the region of £7000 a year: *Men at Arms* (Harmondsworth, 1964 edn), p. 18; *Unconditional Surrender* (Harmondsworth, 1964 edn), p. 70.

[22] Thompson, *English Lnded Society* pp. 321–3, 328; Bush, *The English Aristocracy*, pp. 155–6.

capital transfer tax. Since the latter is fundamentally unavoidable, it could well bring to an end more quickly than anticipated the remaining privately held estates.[23] To make matters worse for landowners, agriculture was in recession for much of the inter-war period, during which time many owners found their land was undercapitalized. With rents compulsorily frozen during the inflation of the Second World War, owners could not take advantage of the conditions, and since 1945 estates encumbered by debt and a lack of capital have again come on to the market, despite efforts both to make agriculture more profitable and to avoid government tax demands. Furthermore, it is an indication of the changing demand that since 1880 only a handful of the estates which have been sold have passed intact to a single private owner. The twentieth-century trend has been for property to pass to owner-occupiers and to institutional owners.

What has happened in the twentieth century is that while quite a number of the great estates have remained, even if in an emasculated form, the great prestige once attached to landownership has evaporated. In 1936 Henry Durant noted that one of the main reasons for the decrease of greater estates in Bedfordshire was the declining political significance of landownership: 'an estate now comes to be regarded solely as a burden and hence the willingness to dispose of it.'[24] Once social significance was removed from the ownership of land, ownership itself lost importance. The result can be seen in two ways. First, the twentieth century has witnessed the rise of a landless aristocracy. By 1937 one-third of aristocratic families were landless, and by 1956 only one-third of peers possessed estates. In part, this turnabout was a result of the opening up of the peerage to men who lacked the traditional tenanted estates. Many owned only a house in the country. Second, owner-occupiers have enjoyed a resurgence, and institutional owners have become increasingly significant.[25] In Bedfordshire between 1873 and 1925 the total number of private estates of between 100 and 400 acres increased from 237 to 320, and as a proportion of all private estates of 100 or more acres their total rose from 19 to 32 per cent of the acreage. This trend was repeated nationally so that, whereas in 1914 only 11 per cent of farm holdings were owner-occupied, by 1927 the figure reached 36 per cent, and by 1979 it was nearer to 65 per

[23] Clemenson, *English Country Houses and Landed Estates*, pp. 110–11, 115–16; Howard Newby, *Green and Pleasant Land? Social change in rural England* (1979), pp. 54–6.

[24] Durant, 'The development of landownership', p. 89.

[25] Bush, *The English Aristocracy*, pp. 157–8.

cent.[26] Whereas in the 1880s only 4 per cent of England and Wales was owned by public and institutional bodies, by the 1970s only one of the top ten landowners in Britain was a peer, the rest being a variety of public and quasi-public bodies which collectively owned 15 per cent of the total area of Britain.[27]

The decline of the landed aristocracy, although not as considerable or as rapid as was once imagined, has brought in its wake other considerations, most notably the fate of their country houses. Out of 500 estates surveyed for the period 1880–1980, only 150 houses were still owned by the same family, while more than 300 had changed hands. Since 1880, 106 have been demolished (although thirty-two were replaced), thirteen have been allowed to become ruinous, and many more have been reduced in size or altered to suit changing financial conditions. Particularly significant periods for destruction were the years 1926–40 and 1946–65, although houses were being demolished and not replaced from 1918. Much of this destruction was coincident with the break-up of estates after 1945. Some were offered for sale, or even on lease (which was attractive when sporting rights were attached), but if no takers came forward many families preferred destruction to the growing burden of repair costs, and the difficulties of maintaining their lifestyle. Between 1945 and 1955 at least thirty disappeared and many others were reduced in size.[28]

Down to 1914 it was still possible for families to maintain the grand style of the country house, and the lifestyle that went with it. Houses were still built to demonstrate something of the owner's prestige, but the purpose of a country house was already under question. The country house parties of the past often stretched over weeks rather than days, but the motor car brought with it the weekend – much shorter visits and greater informality. As a result, by the first decade of the twentieth century the disintegration of the old county society was in full swing, and these changes, coupled with financial problems, had a significant effect on the type of housing required in the countryside. The trend was towards smaller houses, a movement facilitated after the war by the simplification of the structure of houses, and by the disappearance of a ready-made pool of servants. The shortage of

[26] Durant, 'The development of landownership', p. 86; Thompson, *English Landed Society*, p. 332; Clemenson, *English Country Houses and Landed Estates*, p. 115; S. G. Sturmey, 'Owner-farming in England and Wales, 1900–50', *Manchester School of Economic and Social Studies*, 23 (1955), pp. 246–68; J. T. Ward, *Farm Rents and Tenures* (1959), pp. 14–15.

[27] Newby, *Green and Pleasant Land?*, pp. 41, 43.

[28] Clemenson, *English Country Houses and Landed Estates*, ch. 8.

domestic labour had been commented on with increasing frequency since the 1890s, but after 1918, with the loss particularly of men both in the war and to the lure of urban employment, owners were forced to think in terms of smaller properties and greater use of technical aids.[29]

The result of these changes became most clearly apparent in the inter-war years. A number of houses built, or started, in the grander days served the purpose for which they were designed for only a short time. Thus Bryanston in Dorset, built between 1889 and 1894, became a school in 1928, while Charters, erected as late as 1938, was acquired by the Vickers aircraft company in 1950.[30] Building was becoming almost a desperate last hope for keeping the old way of life going. Those who built after 1890 were not setting themselves up in the country as had been the practice in the past, but were simply creating a semblance of landed life. Consequently houses were generally smaller than in the past, and during the twentieth century some of the great edifices have been replaced by more manageable homes. Since 1945 country houses have continued to be built, many of them by old-established families, including the dukes of Westminster, who in 1972 replaced Alfred Waterhouse's Victorian masterpiece with an office-blockish new Eaton Hall. The 1980s have even witnessed a renewal of countryhouse classicism.[31]

Since 1914 the English aristocracy has experienced greater upheavals than during any commensurate period in the past. Before the First World War aristocrats had been remarkably successful. Through their positive economic leadership, and the way in which they combined duty with service in the state and in society, they had survived periods of criticism and had maintained much of their power despite the disruptive influences of industrialization and urbanization. Political power was already slipping in 1914, and the trend has proved irreversible. Moreover, as the prestige of land has declined, as electoral democracy has finally outlawed the last vestiges of country house politics, as the welfare state has taken over much of the role provided by private charity, and as the Royal family has become a national

[29] Clive Aslet, *The Last Country Houses* (1982), pp. 58–9, 85–6.
[30] Ibid., ch. 4.
[31] Ibid., pp. 4–7; J. M. Robinson, *The Latest Country Houses, 1945–1983* (1985). Sadly, many long-established houses remained at risk of destruction: Michael Imeson, 'Rescuing the stately home', *Sunday Times*, 29 December 1985, p. 41.

symbol in much the same way that aristocrats once played the role locally, the group has had to find a new function. Above all, in 1986 the aristocracy have survived as protectors of the nation's heritage. Many of their houses have become museums, and their treasures have been accepted by a grateful nation in lieu of death duties. Aristocrats can even argue that as collectors of beautiful objects over time their families were thinking not merely of self-interest but of the national heritage. By convincing the nation of their desire to act as guardians of its heritage, they are showing that their attitudes have not changed even if their position has. The sixth Duke of Westminster, one of the wealthiest of living Englishmen, told a Sunday newspaper in 1983 that 'my father had made me understand that I was a caretaker for future generations'.[32] Others may not be so wealthy but as self-appointed protectors of the heritage they are still trying to preserve their assets in order to hand them on to – however uncertain – future generations.[33] The English aristocracy, having successfully adapted to changing circumstances throughout history, remains alive and well, and does not intend to pass away without a struggle.

[32] *Sunday Times*, 20 February 1983; Lacey, *Aristocrats*, p. 79.
[33] Linda Colley, 'The cult of the country house', *Times Literary Supplement*, 15 November 1985.

Appendix

Counting the Aristocracy

To obtain some idea of the size of the aristocracy at any given point in time, it is necessary to establish numbers within its constituent parts. As explained in chapter one, it is almost impossible to count the number of esquires and gentlemen, but the higher titles (peers, baronets and knights) were awarded by royal grant and are thus easier to enumerate. The tables which follow have been compiled from the best available sources, but the whole exercise is fraught with difficulties arising from discrepancies among the figures. Contemporaries happily compiled lists, but their findings did not always coincide.

Two categories of evidence are available. First, there are contemporary listings. Many of these survive, particularly for the peerage, but the source of information is seldom clear. Some were one-off lists, compiled for a particular reason, as was the case, for example, with a number put together in advance of the 1719 Peerage Bill. Others were more regular compilations of a semi-official nature, including the *Royal Kalendar* (1767–1893) and the *British Almanack* (1827–87). Second, there are the compilations which began with the publications of Sir Bernard Burke in the nineteenth century. GEC[okayne] *The Complete Peerage* (13 volumes, 1910–59), gives a comprehensive family listing, but the companion series, *Complete Baronetage* (5 volumes, 1900–6), covers only the period 1611–1800. W. A. Shaw, *The Knights of England* (2 volumes, 1906) covers the various strands of the knighthood down to 1904. In addition, the various volumes of Burke and *Debrett* can be utilized, as well as recent publications such as Francis L. Leeson, *A Directory of British Peerages* (Society of Genealogists, 1984), and C. J. Parry, *Index of Baronetage Creations* (Institute of Heraldic and Genealogical Studies, 1967).

To discover trends, it is necessary to count numbers at various points in time, and wherever possible this has been attempted for ten-year intervals. This has often meant relying on contemporary listings of doubtful accuracy. Annual or regular publications are likely to be the most reliable, although it is seldom clear at what point they were compiled. Fortunately major listings such as *The Complete Peerage* and *Complete Baronetage* can be used to determine the point of creation and extinction of a title. Used as a cross-check on contemporary listings, these help to iron out some of the difficulties. Even so, it is not pretended that the tables which follow are entirely accurate. Allowing for minor discrepancies, they can be taken to indicate rough numbers at various dates.

THE PEERAGE

The peerage has attracted most attention and interest and is therefore the easiest to count (tables A1 and A2). Comparative figures are given for similar dates in the nineteenth century to illustrate some of the discrepancies which arise even between apparently reputable sources such as *Hansard* (which includes a roll call for each parliamentary session, but omits women) and the *British Almanack*. The major difficulty concerns the Scottish and Irish peerages. A man holding such a title might sit in the Lords, as one of the sixteen Scottish (from 1707) or twenty-eight Irish (from 1801) representatives, or he might be elected to the Commons. Viscount Palmerston, for example, the famous nineteenth-century foreign secretary, sat in the Commons because he held an Irish peerage. Many Scottish and Irish peers acquired English, British or United Kingdom titles which gave them a seat in the Lords. However, they had to sit in the Lords under the latter title, even if it was not the one by which they were best known. On the 1856 roll, seventy-three peers sat in the Lords under a title which was not the one they normally used. Thus the Duke of Buccleuch sat as the Earl of Doncaster, the Duke of Montrose as Earl Graham, and the Duke of Atholl as Earl Strange, to name but three of the instances.[1] Disentangling who was a member of which branch of the peerage is by no means easy, but the tables give a reasonably accurate account of the size of the peerage through time.

[1] *Hansard*, 3rd ser., 140 (1856). By the 1963 Peerage Act the 31 remaining Scottish peers were all permitted to take seats in the House of Lords: L. G. Pine, 'The Peerage Act, 1963', *Law Times*, 234, 20 September 1963.

THE BARONETAGE

With the highest rank of the gentry, the situation is immediately more complicated. Fewer contemporary lists were compiled, while the major modern source, *Complete Baronetage*, stops in 1800. However, a recent compilation, C. J. Parry's *Index of Baronetage Creations*, can be used (with reservations) to carry the account into the twentieth century. From these sources lists have been compiled of creations by period (table A3).[2] Converting these figures into numbers surviving at ten-yearly intervals reveals discrepancies between the sources. In his book *Aristocratic Century*, John Cannon provides figures for baronets for every tenth year during the eighteenth century. He gives no source for this information, although it seems likely that it was the *Complete Baronetage*. Table A4, which was compiled before Cannon's book appeared, used this source to produce a figure for 1760. Cannon's figure was 624,[3] and, given the difficulties of interpreting phrases such as 'became extinct about 1760', the discrepancy between this and the 638 in table A4 is not alarming.

To carry the series into the nineteenth century, it was necessary to list creations and extinctions from 1611 as recorded in Parry's *Index*. To try to ensure that the sources were compatible, the eighteenth-century figures were cross-checked while this operation was in progress, but the results were unsatisfactory. For each decadal figure in the eighteenth century, totals produced from the *Index* were between 75 (1700) and 101 (1730) *higher* than Cannon's. A third source was introduced to check the discrepancies. The *Royal Kalendar* began in 1766, and decadal figures were abstracted and compared with those derived from the other sources:

---

[2] A. Briton, *The Baronetage under Twenty-Seven Sovereigns, 1308–1910* (1910), proved too unreliable to be used for nineteenth-century calculations. Sir Bernard Burke, *A Genealogical and Heraldic History of the Extinct and Dormant Baronetcies of England, Ireland and Scotland*, 2nd edn (1841), covers the early part of the century, and later years can be examined in *Debrett's Complete Baronetage* for 1888 and 1912. Unfortunately these sources do not take into account baronetcies created after 1841 but extinct by 1888. For this reason it was decided to use the material available in C. J. Parry, *Index of Baronetage Creations* (1967), although this will have distorted the figures slightly, on account of the reservations given in the text.

[3] John Cannon, *Aristocratic Century* (Cambridge, 1984), p. 32. Presumably he was excluding the Irish and Scottish baronetages when he calculated a total of 466 in *Parliamentary Reform* (Cambridge, 1973), p. 50.

Year	Parry	Cannon	*Royal Kalendar*
1770	706	621	647
1780	725	635	724
1790	747	659	776
1800	779	699	765

The figures for 1780 and 1790 were discounted on the grounds that the *Royal Kalendar* had overestimated Scottish baronetcies,[4] producing the conclusion that Cannon's figures are too low and Parry's too high. Confirmation that the *Index*-derived figures are too high can be gained by cross-checking with *Whitaker's Almanack* for 1880 and 1890 (table A5). In fact, the *Index* turns out to have been poorly cross-checked, with the result that although Parry has picked up a number of baronetcies missed by *Complete Baronetage* he has failed to sift out double entries. For example, the *Index* includes both a Carmichael of Keirhill (Edinburgh) and a Gibson (of the same address) as created baronets on 31 December 1702. A further Gibson of the same address is listed as created in September 1831, while a Carmichael of Carmichael, Scotland (formerly Gibson), is also listed for that date. According to *Complete Baronetage*, Carmichael, created 1702, became Gibson-Carmichael after 1800. It seems possible that four baronetcies have appeared where only one existed. A check of the surnames A–C reveals a sufficient number of discrepancies to suggest that they may explain the gap between the sets of figures.[5] The general trend in table A5 is probably accurate, with the most reliable figures in column (i) of the total.

THE KNIGHTHOOD

Including knights among the aristocracy presents problems of its own, but counting them is facilitated by using W. A. Shaw's *Knights of*

[4] The numbers given were 136 for 1770, 200 for 1780, 205 for 1790 and 145 for 1800, but, since no creations were made in the Scottish baronetage, and two middle figures seem suspiciously large.

[5] The discrepancies are endless. Borrowes of Grange Mellon, Kildare (created 14 February 1646), is also listed as Burrow of the same address and creation; Bouverie of London (created 19 February 1714) is also listed as Des Bouverie of the same address and creation; and Campbell of Ardnamurchan, Argyll, is listed as a creation of 15 January 1627 and 23 December 1628, when in fact it was created on the first date and sealed on the second. Where different names have been assumed, Parry has noted the assumed name, but he has also listed another creation under the assumed name. In some instances he also omits extinction dates, which are given in *Complete Baronetage*, without explanation.

England (table A6). Moving from the number of creations to survivals at particular dates is more complicated. By working through Shaw's volumes it is possible to list creation and extinction dates for each knight, but Cannon describes the exercise as 'tedious', and the results may not justify the means.[6] Other sources do not list knights until the mid-nineteenth century: the *Royal Kalendar* from 1843 and *Whitaker's Almanack* only from 1890 (table A7). Sorting out the different orders of knighthood is also a problem. The figures given below from *Whitaker's Almanack* indicate the size of the group at the end of the nineteenth century and early in the twentieth. However, these are gross figures, lumping together all military and civilian members of the orders of the Bath, the Star of India, St Michael and St George, the Indian Empire and the Royal Victorian Order. Many of those included were foreigners, while companions – who generally seem not to have held the title 'Sir' – outnumbered everyone else by three to one.

1890	2410
1900	2827
1910	3764
1915	4265

Table A1   The English Peerage

Date	Dukes	Marquesses	Earls	Viscounts	Barons	Total	Peeresses	Total
1658	2	2	55	7	53	119		
1676	11	3	66	11	65	156		
1684	13	2	66	9	63	153	6	159
1691	13	2	71	9	66	161		
1697	19	3	75	9	71	177		
1700						173		
1709	22	2	64	9	60	157		
1710						167		
1719(a)	22	0	73	13	68	176		
1719(b)	25	2	74	17	68	186		
1720						190		
1728	24	1	71	15	64	175	7	182
1730						189		
1740						183		
1741	28	2	75	15	63	183		
1750						187		
1753	21	1	82	12	60	176	9	185
1760						181		

[6] Cannon, *Aristocratic Century*, p. 31.

Table A1 (cont)

Date	Dukes	Marquesses	Earls	Viscounts	Barons	Total	Peeresses	Total
1770(a)						197		
1770(b)	23	1	81	13	67	185	11	196
1780(a)						189		
1780(b)	21	1	78	14	65	179	7	186
1780(c)	22	1	78	14	65	180	7	187
1790(a)						220		
1790(b)	21	6	86	13	81	207	9	216
1800(a)						267		
1800(b)	19	11	87	15	125	257	10	267
1810	17	12	94	23	138	284	8	292
1820	18	17	100	22	134	291	9	300
1830(a)	18	18	92	22	160	310		
1830(b)	19	18	104	22	160	323	10	333
1840(a)	21	20	116	20	203	380		
1840(b)	21	20	113	20	209	383	10	393
1850(a)	20	21	115	22	199	377	11	388
1850(b)	20	21	116	22	220	399		
1860(a)	20	21	110	22	212	385	12	397
1860(b)	19	21	129	23	209	401		
1860(c)	20	21	109	22	212	384	12	396
1870(a)	20	18	110	23	217	388	12	400
1870(b)	20	18	110	24	227	399		
1870(c)	20	18	110	23	224	395	10	405
1880(a)	21	19	115	25	248	428	7	435
1880(b)	22	19	117	25	248	431		
1880(c)	21	19	115	25	247	427	7	434
1890(a)	21	21	119	27	290	478	5	483
1890(b)	22	21	121	27	292	483		
1890(c)	21	21	121	28	292	483	-4	487
1900(a)	22	22	123	30	318	515	9	524
1900(b)	22	22	124	30	324	522		

Alternative figures are given when different sources give different totals for the same year. Figures at intervals of less than ten years are given for the eighteenth century because Cannon (see 'Sources') does not break down the peerage by title.

Sources: A New Catalogue of the Dukes . . . Baronets (1658); Edward Chamberlayne, *Angliae Notitia* (1676); Samuel Egerton Brydges, *Reflections on the Late Augmentation of the English Peerage* (1798) (for 1728, 1780(b)); A True and Perfect Catalogue of the Nobility . . . (1684); Guy Miegé, *The New State of England* (1691); *Gentleman's Magazine*, 54 (1784), pt II, p. 896 (for 1697, 1741); J. Cannon, *Aristocratic Century* (Cambridge, 1984), p. 15 (for 1700, 1710, 1720, 1730, 1740, 1750, 1760, 1770(a), 1780(a), 1790(a),

1880(a)); *The Peerage of England* (1709); *A List of the Peers* (1719) (for 1719(a)); *The British Compendium* (1719) (for 1719(b)); D. Defoe, *A Tour through the Whole Island of Great Britain* (1753), vol. III, pp. 299–302; *Royal Kalendar* (for 1770(b), 1780(c), 1790 (b), 1800(b), 1810, 1820, 1830(b), 1840(b), 1850(c), 1860(c), 1870 (c), 1880(c), 1890(c)); A. S. Turberville, *The House of Lords in the Age of Reform 1784–1837* (1958), p. 478 (for 1830(a)); *The Gentleman's Pocket Remembrances for 1815* (1814); *British Almanack* (for 1840(a), 1850(a), 1860(a), 1870(a), 1880(a), 1890(a), 1900(a)); *Hansard*, 3rd ser., 108 (for 1850(b)), 156 (for 1860(b)), 199 (for 1870(a)), 250 (for 1880(b)), 341 (for 1890(b)), 4th ser., 78 (for 1900(b))

Table A2 The Scottish and Irish peerage

Year	Scottish titles	Number with English titles	Number Scottish only	Irish titles	Number with English titles	Number Irish only
1700			135			88
1710			134			90
1720			109			96
1730			106			103
1740			100			100
1750			86			102
1760			82			118
1770(a)			81			129
1770(b)	98	7	91	144	20	124
1780(a)			78			145
1780(b)	92	8	84	157	17	140
1790(a)			75			155
1790(b)	92	11	81	172	22	150
1800(a)			68			169
1800(b)	88	16	72	208	41	167
1810	85	23	62	221	44	177
1820	80	26	54	217	42	175
1830	87	30	57	206	62	144
1840	83	37	46	204	75	129
1850	81	38	43	201	72	129
1860	86	43	43	194	71	123
1870	86	41	45	187	78	109
1880	87	46	41	179	78	101
1890	86	48	38	177	86	91

Sources: J. Cannon, *Aristocratic Century* (Cambridge, 1984), p. 32 (for 1700, 1710, 1720, 1730, 1740, 1750, 1760, 1770(a), 1780(a), 1790(a), 1800(a)); *Royal Kalendar* (for 1770(b), 1780(b), 1790(b), 1800(b), 1810, 1820, 1830, 1840, 1850, 1860, 1870, 1880, 1890); since no new Scottish titles were granted after 1707, the discrepancies must result from the compilation procedures.

Table A3   Creation of baronets, 1660–1915

Years	England	Scotland	Ireland	Great Britain (from 1707)	United Kingdom (from 1801)
1660	136	—	6		
1661–5	168	28	17		
1666–70	28	29	4		
1671–5	29	18	5		
1676–80	39	10	5		
1681–5	31	18	9		
1686–90	22	17	7		
1691–5	8	6	—		
1696–1700	23	18	2		
1701–5	11	31	4		
1706–10	1	11	2	10	
1711–15			—	27	
1716–20			—	18	
1721–5			3	5	
1726–30			3	6	
1731–5			—	10	
1736–40			—	5	
1741–5			2	5	
1746–50			1	8	
1751–5			—	9	
1756–60			7	12	
1761–5			6	23	
1766–70			7	21	
1771–5			5	35	
1776–80			14	28	
1781–5			16	40	
1786–90			11	17	
1791–5			8	50	
1796–1800			10	30	
1801–5					70
1806–10					53
1811–15					78
1816–20					33
1821–5					43
1826–30					17
1831–5					39
1836–40					59
1841–5					22
1846–50					15
1851–5					12
1856–60					21

Table A3 (contd)

Years	England	Scotland	Ireland	Great Britain (from 1707)	United Kingdom (from 1801)
1861–5					10
1866–70					46
1871–5					30
1876–80					24
1881–5					37
1886–90					54
1891–5					65
1896–1900					61
1901–5					89
1906–10					86
1911–15					96

In view of the reservations expressed about Parry's calculations in the text, these figures must be marginally too high. However, they show the trend.

Sources: GEC Complete Baronetage (5 vols, 1900–6); C. J. Parry, *Index of Baronetage Creations* (1967)

Table A4 Baronetcies in existence, 25 October 1760

	English	Great Britain (1707)	Scottish	Irish	All
James I	61		0	8	59
Charles I	88[a]		49	8	145
Charles II	159		54	13	226
James II	8		18	3	29
William III and Mary II	14		24	0	38
Anne	7	10	26	5	48
George I		25		3	28
George II		43		12	55
Total	337	78	171	52	638

[a] Includes some not on the record but created *de novo* later.

Source: GEC *Complete Baronetage* (5 vols, 1900–6)

Table A5   Number of Baronetcies,   1660–1915

Year	England[a] (i)	(ii)	Scotland (i)	(ii)	Ireland (i)	(ii)	Nova Scotia Resident in England (i)	Total (i)	(ii)	(iii)	(iv)
1660											678
1670											891
1680											936
1690											967
1700										860	935
1710										839	924
1720										809	892
1730										735	836
1740										711	800
1750										651	738
1760										624	713
1770	431		136		71		9	647		621	706
1780	444		200		72		8	724		635	725
1790	456		205		107		8	776		659	747
1800	488		145		121		11	765		699	779
1810	572		139		101			812			852
1820	632		137		94			863			906
1830	630		141		89			860			914
1840	684		130		86			900			964
1850	689		118		79			886			958
1860	674		111		75			860			942
1870	686		108		70			864			942
1880	690	694	102	103	64	65		856	862		946
1885		700		99		67			866		
1890	732	734	97	94	65	66		894	894		999
1900		802		88		64			954		1072
1910									1060		1194
1915									1111		1259

[a]   'England includes Great Britain from 1707, and United Kingdom from 1801.

Sources: (i) *Royal Kalendar;* (ii) *Whitaker's Almanack;* (iii) J. Cannon, *Aristocratic Century* (Cambridge, 1984), p. 32; (iv) Derived from C. J. Parry, *Index of Baronetage Creations* (1967)

Table A6 Creation of knighthoods, 1660–1904

Years	KG	KT	KP	KB		GCB(Mil.)		GCB(Civ.)		KCB(Mil.)		KCB(Civ.)		KSI	GCSI	KCSI	GCMG	KCMG	KCIE	GCIE	GCH	KCH	KH	Bachelors
				T	NT	T	NT	T	NT	T	NT	T	NT											
Charles II 1649–85																									
1646–50	5(5)																								
1651–5	4(1)																								
1656–60	4																								
1661–5	6			8	60																				471
1666–70	3(1)																								100
1671–5	8																								148
1676–80	5																								123
1681–5	5																								138
James II 1685–8																									
1681–5	4																								27
1686–90	2(1)	7(1)																							71
William & 1686–90	4																								51
Mary 1691–5	2(1)																								55
1689–1702 1696–1700	5																								66
1701–5	2																								12
Anne 1701–5	4	7[1]																							49
1702–14 1706–10	3	3																							41
1711–15	6(1)	1																							33
George I 1711–15	4	3																							49
1714–27 1716–20	8	3																							33
1721–5	7	3[1]																							32
1726–30	2	1		22	13[2]																				15
George II 1726–30	3	1																							17
1727–60 1731–5	3	4		3	1																				14
1736–40	2	3[1]																							16
1741–5	6(1)	3		4	6																				40

Period												Total
1746–50	6	1		6								9
1751–5	5	4		6								21
1756–60	8		1	1								17
George III 1760–1820 1756–60												13
1761–5	6(1)	3	6	9(1)								60
1766–70	3	3[4]	4(1)	1								14
1771–5	2(1)	4	3	10								36
1776–80	(3)	1	2	6(3)								34
1781–5	4(1)	17(1)[1]	(1)	5								53
1786–90	12(1)	2	2	2(1)								53
1791–5	6	1[1]	2	6(3)								44
1796–1800	2(1)	2		6(3)								55
1801–5	8(1)	3	1	6(3)								50
1806–10	4	[1]	6	11(1)								50
1811–15	13	5	5	9		44	150					117
1816–20	4	1		19		8	12		7	4		80
George IV 1820–30 1816–20	1	2	17		3	2	5	10	14			21
1821–5	6	4	7		–	1	5	5	7	39	20	80
1826–30	7	4	4		–	3	7			4		47
William IV 1830–7 1826–30	3	1[1]	3		2			12	9	58	119	27
1831–5	7	2	30		6	42		13	1	18	29	198
1836–40	4	11	8		3	15						51
Victoria 1837–1901 1836–40	5	3	23	6	3	19	31	6	6			84
1841–5	14	4	12	8	8	5	19	7	6	6	6	68
1846–50	6	4	11	5	5	1	6	3	3	3	4	42
1851–5	8	5	22	5	5	–	8	40	5	5	4	55
1856–60	13	3[1]	24	10	10	–	3	90	10	11	11	89
1861–5	19	6[1]	29	7	7	13	67	20	1	4		36
1866–70	15	5	17	9	9	5	43	16	11	21	66	100
1871–5	4	5	29	4	4	6	57	12	6	33	26	97

Table A6 (contd)

Years	KG	KT	KP	KB NT	KB T	GCB(Mil.) NT	GCB(Mil.) T	GCB(Civ.) NT	GCB(Civ.) T	KCB(Mil.) NT	KCB(Mil.) T	KCB(Civ.) NT	KCB(Civ.) T	KSI	GCSI	KCSI	GCMG	KCMG	GCIE	KCIE	GCH	KCH	KH	Bachelors
1876–80	7	5	6			17	7	3	3	30	7	16		20	24	21	71							89
1881–5	14	3	9			15	12	1	9	50	3	26		9	17	22	74							117
1886–90	7	1	10			31	18	1	8	60	10	29		14	21	32	115	56	15					179
1891–5	13	3	5			24	16	2	10	52	6	36		9	18	22	72	35	10					174
1896–1900	6	4	8			25	18	1	10	101	15	50		13	24	38	104	28	18					229
1901–4	1	–	–			–	2	–	–	–	2	1		–	1	1	3	3	2					2
Edward VII 1901–10	15	4	6			33	15	–	8	64	11	39		4	24	31	96	33	11					254

T	=	Titled before honour granted
NT	=	Not titled before honour granted

KG   = Knights of the Garter
KT   = Knights of the Thistle (all titled before)
KP   = Knights of St Patrick
KB   = Knights of the Bath
GCB (Mil.) = Knights of the Bath Grand Cross Military Division
GCB (Civ.) = Knights of the Bath Grand Cross Civil Division
KCB (Mil.) = Knights of the Bath Commanders Military Division
KCB (Civ.) = Knights of the Bath Commanders Civil Division
KSI   = Knights of the Order of the Star of India
GCSI   = Knight Grand Commanders of the Star of India
KCSI   = Knight Commander of the Star of India
GCMG   = Knight Grand Cross of the Order of St Michael and St George
KCMG   = Knight Commanders of the Order of St Michael and St George
KCIE   = Knight Commanders of the Order of the Indian Empire
GCIE   = Knight Grand Commanders of the Order of the Indian Empire
GCH   = Knights Grand Cross of the Guelphs of Hanover
KCH   = Knights Commanders of the Guelphs of Hanover
KH   = Knights of the Order of the Guelphs of Hanover

Table A6 (contd)

Figures in rounded brackets are for knights who were never installed. These are not included in previous figures.

Figures in square brackets are for those who were created Knights of the Garter at a later date. They are included in KG figures but not in the previous figures.

The Order of the Bath was remodelled on 2 January 1815, and 47 KB were declared GCB (Mil.) and 11 KB were declared GCB (Civ.).

The Order of the Star of India was enlarged in 1866, and 24 KSI were made GCSI. These are not included in GCSI list.

KCIE figures for 1886–90 included 24 original knights on first enlargement of the order, 15 February 1887.

A second enlargement of the Order of the Indian Empire was made on 21 June 1887, and creations were then called Knight Grand Commanders of the Order of the Indian Empire.

Source: W. A. Shaw. *The Knights of England* (1906), vol. 1

Table A7   Number of knighthoods (bachelor) by decade

Year	Number	Year	Number
1700	290	1843	451
1710	180	1850	365
1720	180	1860	314
1730	150	1870	274
1740	70	1880	269
1750	70	1890(a)	379
1760	70	1890(b)	375
1770	110	1900	488
1780	90	1910	808
1790	130	1915	1017
1800	160		

Source: 1700–1800, J. Cannon, *Aristocratic Century*, (Cambridge, 1984), p. 32; 1843–1890(a), *Royal Kalendar*; 1890(b)–1915, *Whitaker's Almanak*

Index

In general, members of the peerage are indexed under the title that they finally held, and their family name is given in brackets.

P 58 - 61

settlement

p73 - 75   Small Estates
    p202-204   Expenditure
P428 - 435
  p304 - 308   Debt
  p211 - 217   Coal
  p222 · 225   Industry
  p474 - 481   Berlin